You Can Read Biblical Hebrew

Simple Lessons and a Basic Dictionary

Third Edition

James C. Bangsund

You Can Read Biblical Hebrew: Simple Lessons and a Basic Dictionary

First edition: *Biblical Hebrew: A Simplified Grammar*
Second edition: *Reading Biblical Hebrew: A Grammar and Basic Lexicon*

First two editions published for
Research Institute of Makumira University College
P.O. Box 55, Usa River - Tanzania

Cover, typesetting and illustrations by the author.

To

my wife Judy

and my parents

Clifford✠
and Leona✠
Bangsund

Forward to the First Edition

This book has developed out of years of experience of teaching Hebrew in the classroom. However, it is also designed so that it can be used by an individual student, such as a pastor in the parish. The book contains many self-tests in the lessons, and there are keys to selected exercises so that the individual student can evaluate his or her progress. In addition, although the lessons are comprehensive, care has been taken to place material of secondary importance in footnotes rather than in the main text.

Biblical Hebrew: A Basic Grammar has been used very effectively for several years in unpublished form at two theological colleges in northern Tanzania. Makumira University College is now pleased to offer it as the second volume of the new *Makumira Text Book Series*.

Ernest Mhando
Chair, Department of Biblical Studies
Makumira University College

Easter 2001

PREFACE TO THE THIRD EDITION

In a world of many available Hebrew textbooks, one might wonder why another needs to be offered. Like others, it is the result of many years of classroom teaching, and it was written because the author/teacher felt that other offerings just didn't quite meet his need.

But there are also several features which make this book different.

First, it is easy to read and understand because of having, originally, been written for students overseas for whom English was a third language. Great effort has, therefore, been taken to simplify explanations and keep to the essentials. Matters of secondary importance, which fascinate teachers but sometimes frustrate students, have been confined to "technical notes" at the bottom of the page.

Second, it is written not merely for students in a classroom (although that is where it was primarily used) but also for a student who would like to – or who is forced to – study on his or her own. The text contains many "check boxes" (see page xii) which allow the student to review and check progress immediately in the lesson; there is also a key to select exercises at the end.

Third, the last two chapters provide introductions to Hebrew poetry, which has its own very unique characteristics, and to *Biblia Hebraica Stuttgartensia*, the edition of the Hebrew Bible most commonly used in seminaries and by pastors and scholars.

Fourth, a basic but quite complete Hebrew-English dictionary (or "lexicon") of Biblical Hebrew is given at the end. All Hebrew textbooks provide short dictionaries, but few if any are as complete as this one.

It is therefore hoped that this third edition will make a useful and lasting contribution to – and be an encouragement to! – those who would make a study of this beautiful and sacred language.

James C. Bangsund
San Jose, California

March 2015

PREFACE TO THE SECOND EDITION

The first edition, titled *Biblical Hebrew: A Simplified Grammar*, was received well and is in use at several theological colleges in East Africa, as well as by individuals. The title has now been changed because, as has been observed on more than one occasion, it is the presentation, not the content, which has been simplified. Thus, the original title may have given a false impression of incompleteness.

But more than the title has been changed. Over the past six years of use, the need for a revision became apparent for several reasons. First of all, of course, a number of typographical and printing errors became apparent with use. Most were minor, but several were potentially troublesome. Second, there were several places in which the presentation needed clarification, and this meant the rewriting of complete sections of the book. Third, there were two chapter, in particular, which were overly long and have now been divided into two chapters apiece.

There is, finally, some new material which was not present in the first edition. A brief section on Hebrew poetry has been added, as well as a table for the verb הָיָה. And, in addition to the Index of Subjects, there is now also an Index of Hebrew Words which refers to places in the text where particular words receive larger discussion.

Again, I owe much to my students – primarily from Africa, but also from Europe, America and even Palestine – who always taught me much about how to teach.

PREFACE TO THE FIRST EDITION

This textbook is written first of all for my students at Makumira University College (formerly Lutheran Theological College, Makumira) in Tanzania, who have continually shown themselves to be excellent students of Biblical Hebrew. At times, however, they have had difficulty with the complex English of the standard grammars. These students are among many in the world who have learned English not as a *second* language, but rather as a third or fourth language. They are already linguists in their own right, and for this reason one of the titles considered earlier for this book referred to EFL (English as a *Foreign* Language) rather than to the more common ESL.

But I have a second audience in mind as well, and that is the individual pastor in the parish who would like to learn Hebrew. It is assumed that such a person already knows English and has probably already studied New Testament Greek (though knowing Greek is not necessary in order to use this book). For this reason, there is a brief review of grammatical terms at the beginning of the book, as well as answers for selected exercises so that the individual students may measure their progress as they move through the lessons. There has also been an attempt to explain things clearly enough in the lesson that a teacher is not absolutely necessary. (A classroom situation is certainly to be preferred, however.)

The standard grammars presented two difficulties for those who had learned English as a third or fourth language. First, as already mentioned, the vocabulary and syntax of such books are at times quite complex. Second, it is at times difficult for beginning students in Hebrew to distinguish between matters which are absolutely essential and those matters which, though interesting to the linguist, could perhaps be left for another time. I hope that those two difficulties have been kept to a minimum in this book.

I have sought to use several techniques in writing this text. Most of them are described in the following Introduction under the heading "A Note to the New Student" (to which the reader is invited to turn at this point). One technique is not mentioned there: vocabulary introduction and repetition. Approximately 12 new words are introduced in each exercise. Each new word, once it is introduced, will appear at least nine times in the exercises which follow. The spacing of this repetition is carefully measured: exercise intervals of 1, 2, 4, 8. If a word is introduced in the vocabulary before exercise 20, then it will appear twice in exercise 20, twice in 21, and at least once each in exercises 23, 27, and 35.

In addition, there is the matter of visual appearance. Some Hebrew textbooks are so typographically "dense" that they tend to intimidate. An attempt has been made in this text to keep enough "air" on the page so that the text is less psychologically oppressive. This, of course has led to the use of more paper than might seem necessary. It is hoped, however, that student response will vindicate this decision.

I am thankful to many who helped make this project possible, and mention first of all my wife Judy, without whose love and support the work might at times have proved tedious but never did. My parents, whose names appear with Judy's on the dedication page, first introduced me to the Scriptures, the love of which eventually led to a love of Hebrew. And Victor and Evelyn Stueland generously made it possible for Makumira to engage in this publishing venture.

I am also deeply indebted to Stefan Höschele, Hebrew and Old Testament instructor at the Tanzania Adventist College, who has used this material for several years and offered many corrections and helpful suggestions. *Schönen Dank!* And I am thankful to several Makumira students who poured over the details of the verb charts and vocabulary list; *Asanteni sana!* Jonathan M. Kyaruzi, in particular, has a veritable eagle's eye. Finally, I would be very grateful to any who would notify me of yet undiscovered lapses and make suggestions which might be beneficial for a second edition. E-mail may be sent to jim.bangsund@hotmail.com.

CONTENTS

INTRODUCTION

1. A Note to the New Student

Welcome to the study of Biblical Hebrew. I hope you find this book both helpful and user-friendly. You will find several useful tools as you read this text:

1.1 Definition triangles. When new words or terms are defined, you will see a small black triangle (▲). This triangle will help you quickly find new definitions in the text.

1.2 Footnotes. There are two kinds of footnotes in this book.

(a) **More information.** Sometimes additional information is given to make the lesson clearer. Other times, there is information which is interesting but less important than other material in the lesson. In general, this information may be of interest to some people but not to all, and knowing it is not necessary in order to study Biblical Hebrew. Thus, it has been put in a footnote.

(b) **Technical notes.** Sometimes there is information which is detailed and technical. It may be important for the teacher, or it may be interesting to the advanced student. However, it is not necessary for the beginning student who is just trying to learn the basics. When you see the words **Technical note** in a footnote, you do not need to read this information (unless you are interested, of course – and I hope you are!).

1.3 Check boxes. Sometimes it is good to review something immediately after you learn it, to see if you understand it well. To help you do this, there is occasionally a "check box" which contains a question. The answer will be written upside-down at the bottom of the box. For instance:

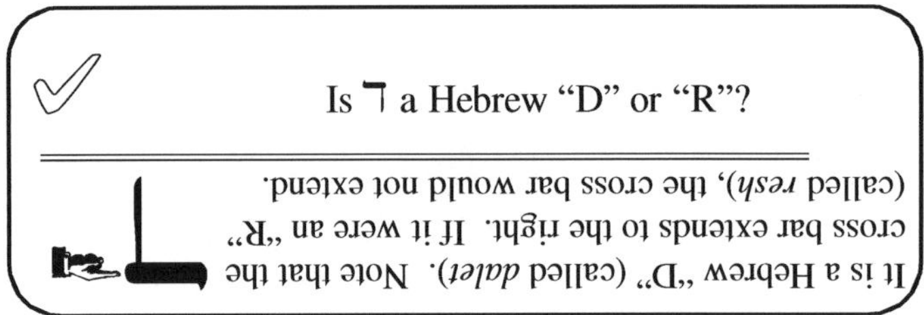
Is ד a Hebrew "D" or "R"?
It is a Hebrew "D" (called *dalet*). Note that the cross bar extends to the right. If it were an "R," (called *resh*), the cross bar would not extend.

When you see a box like this, you should first read the question and try to answer it. Then turn the page upside down and read the answer to see if you were right. If you were wrong, then go back and study the material just before the check box until you understand both the question and the answer.

1.4 Cross-references and the symbol §. Note the number "1.4" at the left of this paragraph. That number is a section number. Later, if I refer back to this paragraph; I will write, "See section 1.4." If I want to remind you about footnotes and how they work, I can say, "See section 1.2, above."

This also helps locate information in other chapters. In this case, I will use the symbol § to mean "chapter." For instance, on page 9 you will read the following sentence:

בִּי and בּוֹ are discussed in §4.3.3.

When you read this, if you want to learn more about these two words, you can turn to §4.3.3 (chapter 4, section 3.3, which is on page 10) and read about them.

1.5 Chapter Summaries. At the end of each chapter there is a summary to help you be sure you understand the material. These summaries are also very useful when you are reviewing previous chapters for a test. You do not need to read the whole chapter again; you may just read the chapter summary and it will show you if you have forgotten any material. These summaries are placed inside boxes which have the title Things You Should Know. For instance, at the end of this introductory chapter, you will find a summary which begins:

> **Things You Should Know**
>
> 1. This book contains **tools to help you in your study** of Biblical Hebrew:
>   a. **Definition triangles (▲)** will mark definitions of new words and phrases.
>   b. **Footnotes** will contain additional information to make things clearer. Information which is technical will be marked with the words **Technical note**. You do not need to read "technical notes" unless they interest you.
>   c. **Cross-references** will use the mark § to mean *chapter*. They will also use section numbers. These help you find information in earlier lessons so that you can review it.
>   d. **Check boxes** and Things You Should Know boxes help you check whether you have understood the material.
>
> . . . .

Be sure you know and understand all the material in these Things You Should Know boxes before you go to the exercises. If you do not understand something, review the chapter until you do understand it.

1.6 Exercise Keys. A set of exercises is found at the end of most chapters. In order to help the student who is studying alone, some of these exercises will have answers (a "key") in the back of the book, beginning on p. 303. You should first do the exercises, and then check the key to see if you have done them correctly. When you are successful on the "keyed" exercises, then you should do the rest of them.

2. A Short Overview of Biblical Hebrew

Hebrew is one of the Semitic[1] languages; two others are Aramaic and Arabic. All three languages are very ancient. Today, Arabic continues to be used in many countries, but Aramaic is used in only a few small areas of Syria, Turkey and Iraq.

Hebrew is the language of most of the Old Testament[2]. It was the language of Israel until Jerusalem was

---

[1] **Technical note.** The word ▲"Semitic" comes from the name "Shem" (Gen 5:32; 6:10; 7:13; etc.). According to Genesis 9, Noah's sons, Shem, Ham and Japheth, and their descendants filled the world after the flood. Genesis 10 then says that the descendants of Shem filled much of the Ancient Near East. The languages of these peoples were considered similar, and so this "family" of languages has come to be known as "Semitic."

[2] **Technical note: Old Testament vs. Hebrew Scriptures.** The debate over this terminology is sometimes heated. My sense is that "Hebrew Scriptures" is the appropriate phrase for those who work in Hebrew and whose canon concludes with 2 Chronicles. If, however, you consider the text to be part of the Christian canon, and if you are working in English (or any language other than Hebrew), and your canon ends with Malachi, then "Old Testament" is appropriate. But, again, I realize that the feelings of some are very strong on this issue, and so I

destroyed by the Babylonians around the year 600 B.C. After that time, the people of Israel began more and more to use Aramaic, which had become the major language of the Middle East.[3] By the time of Jesus, Hebrew was used only as a religious language, for instance in the Temple and synagogues. Like other people of that time in Israel, Jesus and the disciples spoke Aramaic and perhaps some Greek, but they did not use Hebrew in daily life.

Finally, in the middle of the twentieth century, Hebrew was revived as a spoken language and became the language of the modern state of Israel.[4] Thus, the Hebrew of the Old Testament, which we shall be studying, is somewhat different from modern Hebrew.

Ancient Hebrew was written with consonants but no vowels. An ancient Israelite who read a Hebrew text knew the language well enough to know the vowels even though they were not printed. For instance, look at the following sentence, written in English without any vowels:

Th prsn wh knws nglsh vr wll cn rd ths sntnc

It says, "The person who knows English very well can read this sentence." Usually this method of writing in Hebrew did not cause confusion, but sometimes it did. For instance, in English again, if I write,

Pls gv hm th cp

I could mean, "Please give him the cup" or "Please give him the cap" ... or even "Paulos gave him the cape."

Because of this type of problem, a system of *vowel points* was invented. Vowel points are small marks which are placed under and over the consonants to tell readers what the vowels are. For instance, consider our first example. We could write it in the following way:

o o o
Th prsn wh knws nglsh vr wll cn rd ths sntnc
e e E i ey e a e i e e e
a

It is now easier to read the sentence. This is what has been done in the Hebrew Bible, and therefore this is the system of Hebrew we shall be learning. If you go to Israel today, however, you will find that, once again, they write Hebrew using "nl cnsnnts nd n vwls" (that is, "only consonants and no vowels").

3. The Hebrew Alphabet

Semitic languages such as Hebrew, Arabic and Aramaic are written from the right to the left:

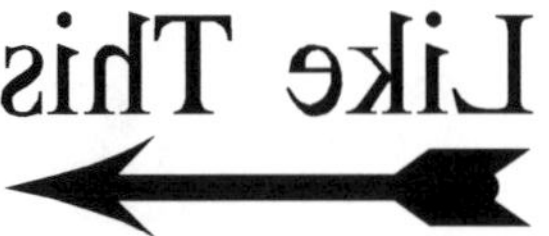

---

offer my apologies to those for whom this does not seem to be a sufficient excuse for the use of "Old Testament" in this text.

[3] **Technical note.** Aramaic was the official language of Mesopotamia (modern Iraq) from the eighth to the fourth century BC. Certain parts of the Old Testament are written in Aramaic (Gen 31:47; Ezra 4:8-6:18; 7:12-26; Jer 10:10-11; and Dan 2:4-7:28). Aramaic uses the same alphabet as Hebrew, whereas Arabic has a very different alphabet.

[4] Modern Israel is not the same nation as the Israel found in the Bible. For about 1800 years – from about 100 years after the time of Jesus until 1948 – there was no nation of Israel. The modern nation of Israel was created after World War II at the recommendation of the United Nations. Today, therefore, we call the Biblical people Israelites, but the citizens of modern Israel are called Israelis.

This is the opposite of English and many other languages. In addition, as mentioned above, Hebrew originally used only consonants. Therefore, if we use the letters שׂ (s) ר (r) and ה (h), we are able to write the name Sarah: שׂרה (s r h). The vowel points are then placed below (and sometimes above) the consonants, and are pronounced after the consonants are pronounced. For instance, a vowel point which looks like a little "T" (ָ) is used to represent the letter "a." If we write the name Sarah and add the vowel points, we get שָׂרָה (= sa + ra + h = sarah).

Originally, written Hebrew had only 22 letters (all consonants, of course). The letter ש was used to represent both "s" and "sh." Later, this letter was made into two new letters by adding a dot above either the top left corner (שׂ) or the top right corner (שׁ). Today, therefore, Biblical Hebrew has 23 consonants, with שׂ representing "s" and שׁ representing "sh."

And here is some good news: there are no capital (upper case) and small (lower case) letters in Hebrew. In English we have *R* and *r*, but Hebrew has only ר .

4. A Word of Encouragement

Biblical Hebrew is, in many ways, much less complicated than English or New Testament Greek. However, the alphabet is quite different, and there are many small rules about vowels, syllables, doubling of letters, etc.

If you have studied New Testament Greek, you were able to read some words in the very first lesson. The Greek alphabet is quite similar to the English alphabet, and this was probably very encouraging. In this book, however, you will not learn any Hebrew words until the end of chapter 11. The first chapters will simply teach you about consonants, vowels, syllables, accent, etc. This can be v-e-r-y t-i-r-e-s-o-m-e work for both student and teacher:

לַהַג הַרְבֵּה יְגִעַת בָּשָׂר׃

... much study makes the body weary.

Ecclesiastes 12:12

But there is hope!! After you finish hapter 11, you will really start to read Hebrew. Then it will become rewarding! Keep this hope in front of you, especially when you are struggling with composite *shewa*, *dagesh lene*, *dagesh forte*, and so on. Soon you will be reading Scripture as it was originally written. You will be reading the Bible of Jesus, the Bible of Peter and Paul – because it was the Old Testament that was used by Jesus and his disciples, and the earliest Christians, long before the New Testament was written.

Keep this goal in mind, and let it give you energy in the weeks ahead as you begin your study.

(Be sure to read the next page for "Things You Should Know.")

Things You Should Know

1. This book contains **tools to help you in your study** of Biblical Hebrew:

   a. **Definition triangles** (▲) will mark definitions of new words and phrases.

   b. **Footnotes** will contain additional information to make things clearer. Information which is technical will be marked with the words "**Technical note**." You do not need to read "technical notes" unless they interest you.

   c. **Cross-references** will use the mark § to mean *chapter*. They will also use section numbers. These help you find information in earlier lessons so that you can review it.

   d. **Check boxes** and **Things You Should Know** boxes will help you check whether you have understood the material.

   e. **Exercise Keys** at the end of the book will give you answers to some of the exercises so that you can check your progress.

2. The **Hebrew language** has the following characteristics:

   a. It is written from right to left.

   b. Hebrew originally had 22 letters. It now has 23 letters, since the letter ש has been made into two letters: שׁ and שׂ.

   c. Its major letters are all consonants. Vowels are small marks which are written above and below the consonants.

   d. Hebrew does not have capital (upper case) and small (lower case) letters.

3. **The first weeks of study** are going to be challenging and perhaps even tiresome. After chapter 11, however, your studies will become far more rewarding.

GRAMMAR: AN OVERVIEW

This section is for the student who may not be familiar with grammatical terms and concepts such as

consonant, vowel and syllable
sentence and clause
subject, verb and predicate
noun
object (direct and indirect)
adjective and adverb
pronoun (demonstrative, personal, possessive, relative)
article (definite and indefinite)
conjunction
participle
preposition
tense, person, gender and number of verb

If you already know these terms, you may skip this section. However, a quick review is always helpful.

1. Consonants, vowels and syllables

Vowels are the letters a, e, i, o, u.[1] All others letters are **consonants**. Vowels can be *long* or *short*, depending upon how they are pronounced. In the following sets of words, the first word contains a short vowel and the second word contains a long vowel:

Short	*Long*
at	**ate**
bet	**be**
bit	**bite**
not	**note**
cut	**cute**

A **syllable** is the smallest pronounceable piece of a word, and must contain a vowel. The word *letter* has two syllables: *let-ter*. The word *alphabet* has three syllables: *al-pha-bet*.

2. Sentences and clauses

(1) A **sentence** is a group of words which makes sense and which has a *subject* and a *predicate*. It may also have a *direct object* and/or an *indirect object*. For instance, consider the sentence:

John sings the song to us very loudly.

In this sentence:

The **subject** is: *John*. The subject is the main person, place, thing or idea in the sentence. The subject usually does the action of the sentence.
The **predicate** is: *sings the song to us very loudly*. The predicate is the rest of the sentence and tells what the subject does. The predicate has several parts:

The **verb** is *sings*. The verb is the action word in the predicate.

The **direct object** is *the song*. A direct object receives the action of the subject and verb.

[1] In English, the letter *y* is also sometimes a vowel.

The **indirect object** is *us*.[2] The indirect object is an object which *indirectly* receives the action of the subject and verb.

(2) A **clause** is a group of words which work together within a sentence. The main part of the sentence is called the **independent clause** (or *main clause*). It could stand alone and be a complete sentence. A **dependent clause** (or *subordinate clause*) depends upon the independent clause. It does not have a subject, and thus it is not a complete sentence. For instance, consider the sentence, *I saw the student who went to town.* The independent clause is *I saw the student*; it is a complete sentence by itself, because it has a subject and a verb.[3] The dependent clause is *went to town*.[4] It tells more about the student, but it has no subject and so it is not a complete sentence by itself.

3. Basic parts of speech

(1) A **noun** is a word which represents a thing (an object, person, place or idea). Some examples of nouns are *book, Abraham, Israel* and *faith.*

(2) A **pronoun** is word which is used in place of a noun. Some examples of pronouns are the words *this, that, who?, what?, I, you, he, she, his, her, who* and *which.* As you can see, there are several types of pronouns. The most important types are as follows:

(a) **Demonstrative pronouns** demonstrate or show which object is being discussed: *this, that, these, those.* Examples: *This* is the one. *These* are larger than *those.*

(b) **Interrogative pronouns** ask questions. Examples: *Who* said that? *What* is the answer? To *whom* did you speak? Note how these are different from relative pronouns (below).

(c) **Personal pronouns** represent persons. They are words such as: *I, you, they*, etc. Examples: *I* spoke to *her*. *You* went to *him*. *She* brought *us* to *them*. Personal pronouns are either

subjective (that is, used as the subject of a sentence): *I* saw her; *he* saw me; *they* saw us

or they are

objective (that is, used as the object of a sentence): I saw *her*; he saw *them*; they saw *us*

In English, the word *you* is used both as subject and as object, but Hebrew uses different words.

(d) **Possessive pronouns** show ownership: *mine, ours, yours, his, hers, theirs*. Examples: *His* shirt is red but *mine* is blue and *theirs* are yellow.

(e) **Relative pronouns** create a relationship between the main part of a sentence (the independent clause) and a smaller part (a dependent clause): *who, whom, whose, which, that.* They will refer back to an earlier noun in the sentence, which is called an **antecedent**. Consider the following two sentences:

I saw the student *who* went to town.

The word *who* is a relative pronoun which connects the dependent clause *went to town* to its antecedent *the student.*

The book on the table is the one *which* I borrowed.

The word *which* refers back to *the book.* The word *book* is the antecedent of *which.* Note that relative pronouns do not ask questions as do interrogative pronouns (above).

---

[2] The word *to* is a preposition. Prepositions are discussed below, on page xix.

[3] It also has a direct object, but this is not necessary. A sentence requires only a subject and a verb.

[4] The word *who* is a relative pronoun which connects the two clauses. It will be discussed below.

(3) A **verb** is a word which represents "being" or an action. Some examples of verbs are *be, sing, walk, carry, say*. There are several types of verbs:

Verbs can be *transitive* or *intransitive*:

A **transitive** verb has a direct object: *I carried the box. They sing the songs.*
An **intransitive** verb has no direct object: *The man runs. The grass grows.*

Verbs can be *active, passive* or *reflexive*:

An **active** verb is one in which the subject does something or acts upon something: *The children read. The dog chases the cat.*
A **passive** verb is one in which the subject *receives* the action of the verb: *The books are read* (the subject is *the books*). *The cat is chased by the dog* (the subject is *the cat*, not *the dog*).[5]
A **reflexive** verb is one in which the subject acts upon itself: *The man praised himself.*

(4) A **modifier**[6] is a word which describes a noun or a verb. There are two types of modifiers:

(a) An **adjective** is a word which "modifies" or describes a noun. Some examples of adjectives are *good, bad, large, great, red, heavy, thin, my, her*. Thus, we can speak of *good* people, *bad* fruit, *large red* books, *great* love, and so on.

An **article** is a special kind of adjective which tells whether a noun is particular or general. In English, there is

- a *definite article* – the word *the* – which refers to a particular object
- an *indefinite article* – the word *a* (or *an*) – which refers to a general object

In Hebrew, there is only a *definite article.*

(b) An **adverb** is a word which modifies a verb.[7] In English, words which end with the letters *-ly* are often adverbs. Some examples of adverbs are *very, quickly, slowly, well, smoothly.* Thus, someone might run *quickly*, speak *slowly*, or sing *well.*

(5) A **preposition** is a word such as *in, on, by, with, of.* It shows the relationship of one noun or pronoun to another. Examples: The book is *on* the table. The child is *with* her father. They are reading the book *of* Genesis.

(6) A **conjunction** joins words, sentences or clauses: *and, or, but, because, yet*. Examples: The woman *and* her husband are coming. You may study Hebrew *or* music. I like walking *but* they like swimming. I warned him, *yet* he went anyway.

4. Conjugating and Parsing

Nouns and verbs can come in different forms. These forms have **number**, **gender** and **person**.[8]

Number (singular and plural): I can have *a book* or *some books*. The word *book* is **singular** because it refers to only one book. *Books* is **plural**, because it refers to more than one book.

---

[5] Note that English must use a helping verb such as *is* or *was* in the passive. Hebrew does not.

[6] To "modify" actually means to change. A "modifier" changes the meaning of a word.

[7] **Technical note:** In English, adverbs can also modify other adverbs and even adjectives. For instance, we can run *very* quickly and sing *fairly* well (adverbs modifying other adverbs). Or we can carry a *very* big book or eat a *fairly* good meal (adverbs modifying adjectives). In Hebrew, things are much simpler.

[8] Many languages also have **case** (for instance, nominative, accusative, genitive, dative). Hebrew does not. **Technical note:** We will later learn about "absolute" and "construct" forms of nouns, and in this situation there is a genitive "relationship." But this is much simpler than what is found in, for instance, Greek or German.

Gender (masculine, feminine, etc.): In many languages, nouns, verbs and adjectives are masculine, feminine and perhaps neuter or ▲ common[9]. English has gender for pronouns (*he*, *she*, etc.), but not for nouns or verbs and adjectives. In Hebrew, verbs, nouns and adjectives are **masculine** (*m.*) or **feminine** (*f.*) and occasionally **common**[10] (*c.*); but there is no neuter.

Person: *I* and *we* are **first person**;
you(*s*)[11] and *you*(*p*) are **second person**;
he, *she*, and *they* are **third person**.

4.1 Conjugation. We conjugate verbs by putting them in their various forms. If we conjugate the verb *to sing*, we get:

	singular	*plural*
1st person	I sing	we sing
2nd person	you(*s*) sing	you(*p*) sing
3rd person	he/she sings	they sing

The verb "to be" is irregular (that is, it does not follow a normal or "regular" pattern):

	singular	*plural*
1st person	I am	we are
2nd person	you(*s*) are	you(*p*) are
3rd person	he/she is	they are

4.2 Parsing. We *parse* verbs, nouns, pronouns or adjectives by listing their gender, number and person. For instance,

"he sings" is *third person, masculine*, and *singular*, which is abbreviated **3ms**.
"she sings" is *third person, feminine*, and *singular*, which is abbreviated **3fs**.

The word "we" is "common" because it is used for both masculine or feminine. Thus,

"we sing" is *first person, common, plural* or **1cp**.[12]

---

[9] A word is "common" when it is used for either masculine or feminine. In English, the word *he* is masculine and *she* is feminine, but the words *I, we, you,* and *they* are all common because they can refer to men or women. In Hebrew, there are also words which are treated inconsistently; sometimes they are treated as masculine and sometimes as feminine. They, too, are said to be "common."

[10] As mentioned in note 9, above, words such as *I, we* and *it* are common. But Hebrew also has a few nouns which are sometimes treated as masculine and sometimes as feminine. (In other words, the language is inconsistent). These words are also called "common."

[11] **Important note:** Some textbooks will use the old English words "thou" and "thee" to represent "you (singular)." This is helpful, but the words "thou" and "thee" are no longer used in modern English. In this text, we shall use "you(*s*)" for "you" singular, and "you(*p*)" for "you" plural.

[12] **Technical note:** At this point, we have not mentioned the "tense" or the "mood" of the verb. Issues of tense (past, present, future) and "mood" (active, passive, reflexive) are handled somewhat differently in Hebrew than in English or Greek. They will be discussed later.

The Hebrew Alphabet (Consonants)

א ב ג ד ה ו ז ח ט י כך ל מם נן ס ע פף צץ ק ר שׂ שׁ ת

Hebrew letters are written from right to left. Thus the first letter of the Hebrew alphabet, א, is on the right, above. Note how the letters fit on the lines. Some letters drop below the bottom line. One goes above the top line. Two have dots above the top line. Actually, Hebrew letters are "hung" from the top line. See especially the tenth letter above (counting from the right).

Note also that in Hebrew there are no lower case (small) letters, but some letters have "final forms" (see below) when they come at the end of a word.

PRINTED FORMS Hard	Normal	Final	Hand Lettering	Letter Name	Pronunciation	Transliteration
	א		א	Aleph	*	ʾ (not "c")
בּ	ב		ב	Bet (rhymes with *fate*)	בּ = b, ב = v	בּ = b, ב = ḇ
גּ	ג		ג	Gimmel	g	גּ = g, ג = ḡ
דּ	ד		ד	Dalet	d	דּ = d, ד = ḏ
	ה		ה	He (rhymes with *day*)	h	h
	ו		ו	Vav	v	w
	ז		ז	Zayin	z	z
	ח		ח	Het (rhymes with *fate*)	hard h*	ḥ
	ט		ט	Tet (rhymes with *fate*)	t	ṭ
	י		י	Yod (rhymes with *rode*)	y	y
כּ	כ	ך	כ ך	Kaf (pronounced *cough*)	k*	כּ = k, כ = ḵ
	ל		ל	Lamed	l	l
	מ	ם	מ ם	Mem	m	m
	נ	ן	נ ן	Nun (pronounced *noon*)	n	n
	ס		ס	Samek	s	s
	ע		ע	Ayin	*	ʿ (not "c")
פּ	פ	ף	פ ף	Pe	פּ = p, פ = ph (f)	פּ = p, פ = p̄
	צ	ץ	צ ץ	Tsade	ts	ṣ
	ק		ק	Qof (rhymes with *loaf*)	q	q
	ר		ר	Resh	r	r
	שׂ		שׂ	Sin	s	ś
	שׁ		שׁ	Shin	sh	š
תּ	ת		ת	Tuv	t	תּ = t, ת = ṯ

*See lesson 2 for a discussion of the pronunciations of these letters.

Study especially those letters which are similar in appearance but different in meaning:

ך ן   צ ע   שׁ שׂ   ס ם מ ט   ת ח ה   י ר ד ך   נ ג ו ז   נ כ ב

CONSONANTS: Their Shapes

Look at the chart of *The Hebrew Alphabet* on the preceding page. There are five columns, and the first column (*Printed Forms*) has three sections: hard, normal and final:

Printed Forms:	the way the letters are printed in books
Hand Lettering:	the way you should learn to write the letters by hand
Letter Name:	the way we will refer to the letters in this book
Pronunciation:	the way the letter sounds
Transliteration:	the way the letter is represented in books which cannot print Hebrew. This will be discussed in chapter 3

1.1 How to Write Hebrew Consonants by Hand

Compare the first and second columns (Printed Forms and Hand Lettering). Often, when letters are *printed*, they are given "serifs." ▲ Serifs are small marks which are placed at the ends and corners of letters (see below). This book is printed with letters which have serifs. On the other hand, **this** sentence is printed with letters which do **not** use serifs.

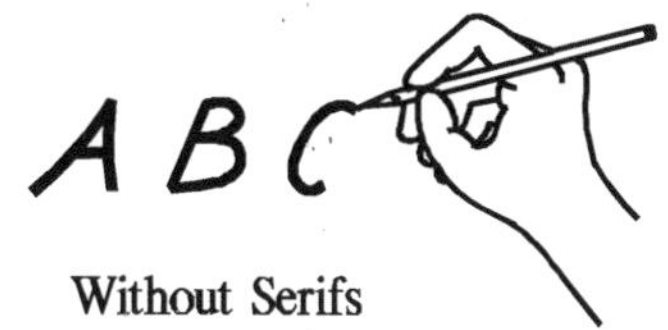

Usually, when we write by hand, we do not use serifs. Serifs are decorations. If we drew the serifs as we wrote, it would take a long time; people would wonder why we were doing it.

Printed Hebrew letters also have serifs. They also are decorations, and they are usually placed at the top of the letters. And, again, when we write by hand we do not draw them. For instance, when you write the Hebrew letters א נ ר י by hand, you will not use serifs:

If you try to put in the serifs, it will take you too long. Also, several of the letters are very similar, and when students try to put in the serifs they often get these letters confused. For instance, if you write the letter י (*yod* = *y*) with its serif — and if you write it too large — it will look like ר (*resh* = *r*).

For this reason, you should carefully study the second column of the alphabet chart (*Hand Lettering*), and you should practice writing these letters. For instance, the serifs at the top of the letters שׁ and נ should not be drawn. But the small cross bar at the top of the ז and the bottom legs of ג and נ are *not* serifs and therefore *must* be drawn.

Note also that the י (*yod*) floats *above* the line,[1] and that some other letters drop *below* the line (ך ן ף ץ). This is the only difference between the letters ד and ך.

1.2 "Hard" pronunciations of letters

Look at column 1 of the chart of *The Hebrew Alphabet*. Six letters have "hard" and "soft" forms which are sometimes pronounced differently. The hard forms have a dot in their center. For instance, the letter בּ is pronounced *b*, but the letter ב (without a dot) is pronounced *v*. This is discussed more in the next chapter.

1.3 Final Forms of Letters

Five letters have different shapes when they come at the end of a word. (This is just like in Greek, where a final σ will be ς.) For instance, the Hebrew letter מ (*m*) is written as ם when it is the last letter of a word. The other four letters have "tails" which drop down when the letter is found at the end of a word (for example, a final פ is ף).

In the chart below, the Normal Form of the letter is given first. Then the Final Form is shown. Finally, three examples are given. The first example shows the letter at the beginning of a word; the second shows the letter in the middle of a word; the last has the letter at the end of the word and thus uses the final form.

Normal Form	Final Form	Three Examples				
כ (*k*)	ך	כרת	or	נכה	but	מלך
מ (*m*)	ם	מאד	or	למד	but	שׁכם
נ (*n*)	ן	נהר	or	בנה	but	נתן
פ (*p*)	ף	פלל	or	נפל	but	שׂרף
צ (*ts*)	ץ	צרה	or	נצל	but	רוץ

1.4 Letters with Similar Shapes

Several letters are quite similar in appearance. One of the most common mistakes in reading Hebrew is to confuse the letters ד and ר. Note that the cross bar of the ד extends slightly to the right of the letter. This does not happen with the ר.

---

[1] Actually, Hebrew letters *hang from* a line, rather than rest upon a line (review the first paragraph on p. xxii). Thus the י is not floating, but is hanging at the same level as all of the other letters. The only exception is the ל, which has a head which rises above the line.

In *writing*, students sometimes have problems with the following:

- There must always be a space or opening in the letter ה so that it does not look like a ח.
- The letters צ and ע must be drawn carefully to distinguish them; also take care with ת and ח.
- The *serifs* should never be drawn (especially on ג ו נ and י).
- The cross bar on ז and the bottom legs on ג and נ are *not* serifs and so *must be drawn.*

These letters, and others which can easily be confused, are listed at the bottom of *The Hebrew Alphabet* chart (opposite p. 1). Be sure to study them closely.

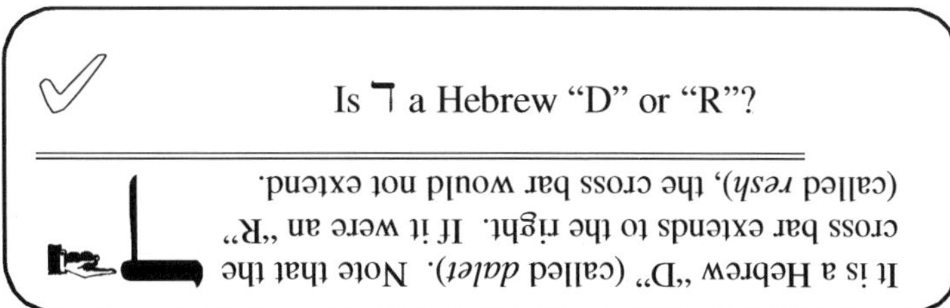

Is ד a Hebrew "D" or "R"?
It is a Hebrew "D" (called *dalet*). Note that the cross bar extends to the right. If it were an "R" (called *resh*), the cross bar would not extend.

Things You Should Know

1. **No serifs.** When you write Hebrew by hand, **do not** try to put in the serifs. Study and learn well the *Hand Lettering* column on the chart of *The Hebrew Alphabet.*
2. **Hard and soft pronunciation.** Six of the letters (ב ג ד כ פ ת) have hard and soft pronunciations. There is a dot in the middle of the letter when it has a hard pronunciation. This will be discussed in the next chapter.
3. **Final forms.** Five consonants (כ מ נ פ צ) have different forms when they come at the end of a word (ך ם ן ף ץ).
4. **Similar shapes.** Several of the letters have similar shapes and can be confused. They are listed at the bottom of *The Hebrew Alphabet* chart.

Exercise #1

1. Learn to write all the consonants of the Hebrew alphabet as they are shown in the *Hand Lettering* column of *The Hebrew Alphabet* chart. Do ***not*** use serifs.
2. Practice writing the letters shown below. Note the small differences between similar letters. Again, do not use serifs. Begin at the right with the א and work toward the left.

   א   ב כ   ג נ ו ן ז   ך ד ר י   צ ע   ה ח ת   ט מ   ס ם   ף ק

3. From memory, write those letters which have "hard" forms (that is, those which have a dot in their centers).
4. From memory, write those letters which have a different final form. Write both the normal and the final forms together as you do this.

2

CONSONANTS: Their Pronunciations

Most of the letters of the Hebrew alphabet are pronounced like the letters of the English alphabet. There are several exceptions, however.

2.1 Letters with Hard and Soft Pronunciation

As we saw in the last chapter, six consonants have "hard" and "soft" forms. The hard forms are written with a dot (which is called a ▲*dagesh*). Normally, the hard form is used when the letter is at the beginning of a word or a syllable. These six letters, בּ גּ דּ כּ פּ תּ (b g d k p t), are often called the ▲**BEGADKEPAT** letters, in order to help remember them. The "final forms" ך and ף are always soft and never have a *dagesh*[1].

In modern Hebrew, the hard and soft forms of three of the BEGADKEPAT letters are pronounced differently[2]:

Hard (with *dagesh*)			Soft (without dagesh)		
בּ	b	**B**ible	ב	v	**v**ery
כּ	k	**k**it	כ or ך	ch	(Ba**ch**)
פּ	p	**p**et	פ	f	**f**ast

2.2 Other Letters

Pronunciations of the other letters are similar to those of English. (The pronunciations of the letters א and ע will be discussed below.)

ה ח Hebrew has two types of letter *h*. ה is like the *h* of English. ח is a "hard *h*," and we will also pronounce it like the *ch* in the word *Bach*

ט This letter is pronounced *t*.

שׂ שׁ ס צ These are the four Hebrew types of letter *s*. Note:

שׂ and ס have the same pronunciation: *s*.

שׂ and שׁ were originally one letter: ש (probably pronounced *sh*[3]). Eventually, dots were placed at the upper left or upper right to get the letters שׂ s (*s*) and שׁ (*sh*).

צ has the sound of the two letters *t* and *s* together, as in the word *bits*.

ק This letter is similar to the letter *q* in English. (Unlike in English, however, it will not usually be followed by the letter *u*). It is pronounced *k*.

---

[1] **Technical note:** the letter ך will often have a raised *shewa* (ךְ) or *qamets* (ךָ), however.

[2] **Technical note:** In older "classical" Hebrew, the other three BEGADKEPAT letters also had different hard and soft pronunciations. ג (without the *dagesh*) was pronounced *gh* (almost like a guttural [throat] *r*). ד was pronounced *th* as in *th*is. And ת was pronounced *th* as in *th*ing.

[3] **Technical note:** See Judges 12:6, where the context makes this clear.

2.3 The letters א and ע

These letters are consonants, but are different from any letter in the English language.[4]

Note: The letter א (*aleph*) does *not* represent the letter "A."[5]

Perhaps the closest we come to א or ע in English is the silent letter *h* in the word *hour* or *honest*. Or compare the two ways the letter *a* is pronounced in the words *man* and *an*. In the first word (*man*), the *a* flows smoothly after the consonant which comes before it. In the second case (*an*), however, there is no consonant before the *a*. Instead, our throat gives a slight "kick" before the *a* is pronounced. The same is true when we compare the sound of the letter *e* in *mend* and *end*. This slight throat kick, or grunt, apart from the pronunciation of the *a* or the *e*, is similar to the sound of the letters א or ע[6].

In transliteration (see the right column of the chart of *The Hebrew Alphabet*, p. xxii), the marks ʾ and ʿ are used for the letters א and ע. This shows they are different from the other consonants; the other consonants are represented by regular Roman[7] letters.

Things You Should Know

1. Six consonants (ב ג ד כ פ ת), called the BEGADKEPAT letters, have hard and soft pronunciations. When they are hard, they will have a dot at the center (בּ גּ דּ כּ פּ תּ).
2. Know how to pronounce all of the consonants – especially those that are similar in sound.
3. א is not the letter *a*. The letters א and ע are consonants. They act like the *h* in the words *hour* and *honor*.

---

[4] **Technical note:** These letters are called *glottal stops* because their sound is produced by first closing up, or "stopping," the glottis (part of the throat).

[5] This is often confusing to students. The first two letters of the English alphabet are *a* and *b*. The first two letters of the Greek alphabet are α (*alpha*) and β (*beta*). Both *a* and α are vowels, and both *b* and β are consonants. But now comes the surprise. The first two letters of the Hebrew alphabet are א (*aleph*) and ב (*bet*). However, although *aleph* may sound somewhat like *alpha*, there is no relationship between the two. א is a consonant, not a vowel, and it just *happens* to come at the beginning of the Hebrew alphabet. Again, א is not an *a*, and it has no relationship to the letter *a*. (We will learn the vowels later.)

[6] **Technical note:** There is actually a slight difference in the pronunciation of these two letters, but we do not need to learn it for reading.

[7] **Technical note:** The letters used in the English language (and in many other languages) are known as "Roman" letters because they were first developed by the Romans more than 2,000 years ago.

3

CONSONANTS: Their Transliterations

Sometimes, the writer of a book will want to use Hebrew words for readers who do not know the Hebrew alphabet. It is then necessary to use Roman[1] letters and symbols to represent the Hebrew letters. This method is known as ▲"transliteration."

3.1 Transliteration

The letters and symbols which are used for transliteration are found in the right hand column of the chart of *The Hebrew Alphabet* (p. xxii). For instance,

- the letter *h* is used to represent ה
- *z* is used to represent ז
- *m* is used for מ or ם

A line below or above a letter is used to show the soft pronunciation of the BEGADKEPAT letters:

b = בּ	but	ḇ = ב
g = גּ	but	ḡ = ג
d = דּ	but	ḏ = ד
k = כּ	but	ḵ = כ
p = פּ	but	p̄ = פ
t = תּ	but	ṯ = ת

In three cases, a dot is used under the transliteration letter:

h = ה	but	ḥ = ח	(the "hard" *h*)
t = תּ	but	ṭ = ט	
s = ס	but	ṣ = צ	(the "*ts*" sound)

The transliterations of שׂ (another *s* sound) and שׁ (the *sh* sound) use special marks over the letter *s*.

š = שׁ   ś = שׂ.

If we use these letters and symbols, we can write as follows:

ʾbḏ	represents	אבד
ʿḇr	represents	עבר
mlḵ	represents	מלך
šlḥ	represents	שׁלח

[1] See page 5, note 7.

Note that **transliterations are written left to right**, while the Hebrew letters are read from right to left. Following are some more examples:

חיה	חץ	חטא	זקן	הלל	היכל	ודבר	דּבר	גּם	גמל	בּגד	אמר
ḥyh	ḥṣ	ḥṭʾ	zqn	hll	hyḵl	wḏbr	dḇr	gm	ḡml	bḡḏ	ʾmr

שׁפט	קרא	קרע	קדשׁ	עצה	משׁתּה	כּסף	כּנען	ישׂראל	ירד	חסד
šp̄ṭ	qrʾ	qrʿ	qḏš	ʿṣh	mšth	ksp̄	knʿn	yśrʾl	yrḏ	ḥsḏ

3.2 Consonants and numerical value.

Hebrew consonants sometimes represent numbers. For instance, א = 1, ב = 2, י = 10, כ = 20, ק = 100, etc. This information is not important for the beginning student. Further information is found in §58.

Things You Should Know

1. ▲ *Transliteration* is a method of using Roman letters and other symbols to represent Hebrew letters.
2. The soft pronunciation of the BEGADKEPAT letters is represented in transliteration by a letter with a line under it (that is, בּ = b, but ב = ḇ).
3. There are several letters with *h, t* and *s* sounds. Therefore, dots and other marks are used to distinguish them. For instance, ס = s ; צ = ṣ ; שׂ = ś ; and שׁ = š. Be sure also to note the transliterations of ח (ḥ) and ט (ṭ).

Exercise #2

1. Transliterate the Hebrew words below. Read the Hebrew words from right side of the page to the left (← . . . מאד נגשׁ), but write your transliterations from left side to the right (mʾḏ ngš . . .→). The first two are done for you. You may compare your anwers to the key at the back of the book.

a. מאד נגשׁ ספר רדף צוה תּחת ארבּע זבח הרג בּטח למד

mʾḏ ngš

____

b. שׂרף קבּץ עין טוב לקח סיני זקן כּאשׁר שׂים דרך פּנים

____

c. כּסא זרע שׁאול נטח נצל גּלעד גּזל נשׂא מצוה יד צעקה

____

d. בּקשׁ זהב יריחו לקראת שׂפה שׁמשׁ עץ פּסח שׁכם עבודה

____

2. Write the transliterations below in Hebrew letters. Read the transliterated words from left to right (mlḵ ʿḇḏ . . . →), but write the Hebrew words from right to left (← . . . מלך עבד). Again, the first two have been done for you.

a. mlḵ ʿḇḏ brḵ zḇḥ yʿqḇ ṣdyq nḇyʾ mlḥmh sṯr šwḇ śrh

מלך עבד

____

b. ʾmh bḏl hḇdl yṭb yryḥw śm šm swr nśʾ twḵ mwṯy

____

c. nḡš dḡn qṭl ywsp̄ ḥḵmh sws nṭʿ lḥm brḵh bḡḏ šḥṯ

____

d. dʿṯ ʾrṣ glʿḏ yrwšlym kn nws mlṭ ṣʿq qwm bzh bḵwr

____

VOWEL POINTS

Hebrew, like English, has long and short vowels.[1] In Hebrew, these vowels are represented by symbols called ▲"vowel points." These are placed below the consonants (for instance, מַ = ma), and sometimes above or between them (for instance, כֹל = kōl). The Hebrew short and long vowels are given below.

4.1 Short Vowels.

In the second column, the letter ב (b) is used as an example to show where the vowels go (for instance, בַ = ba). Actually, of course, the vowels can go under or over any consonant: אַ בַ גַ דַ הַ, etc. The last column gives English words which have vowels with similar sounds.

Vowel Class	*Vowel with* ב	*Vowel name*[2]	*Transliteration of vowel alone*	*Vowel Sound (as in)*
A	בַ	*pathah*	a	b**a**r
E	בֶ	*seghol*	e	b**e**d
I	בִ	*hireq*	i	b**i**t
O	בָ	*qamets-hatuph*	o	b**o**x
U	בֻ	*qibbuts*	u	b**u**ll

4.2 Long Vowels.

Vowel Class	*Vowel with* ב	*Vowel name*	*Transliteration of vowel alone*	*Vowel Sound (as in)*
A	בָ	*qamets*	ā	b**a**r
E	בֵ	*tsere*	ē	th**ey**
I	בִי	*hireq-yod*	î	mach**i**ne
O	בֹ	*holem*	ō	l**o**w
U	בוּ	*shureq*	û	r**u**le

Pathah (short a) and *qamets* (long a) are generally pronounced the same (though be sure to learn their names and transliterations). And, yes, unfortunately the short vowel *qamets-hatuph* and the long vowel *qamets* look the same. This is discussed below in §4.3.2. בִי and בוּ are discussed in §4.3.3.

---

[1] Compare the words "not" and "note." The *o* in the word "not" is short; this short *o* is transliterated "o". The *o* in "note" is long, and is transliterated "ō." For further examples, see "An Overview of Grammar," p. xvii.

[2] The names given here are simplified. See the next page regarding their technical pronunciations.

4.3 More Information about Vowels

4.3.1 **Pronunciation.** The pronunciations given above (*pathah*, *seghol*, *hireq*, etc.) have been simplified for use in this textbook. See the **Technical Note** below[3] for the more formal pronunciations

4.3.2 **The meaning of the vowel point** ָ . The same vowel point (ָ) is used to represent the short *o* (*qamets-hatuph*) and the long *a* (*qamets*). We shall learn how to distinguish between these two vowels in §12. Until then, every ָ will be a *qamets* (ā).

4.3.3 **The letters** י **and** ו. Two of the long vowels use a combination of a consonant and a vowel point:

> **The long *i*** is formed by placing a *hireq* under the consonant and then a *yod* after it. Thus, bî = בִּי, sî = סִי, etc.
>
> **The long *u*** is formed by a *vav*-plus-dot (וּ). (The dot is not a *dagesh*). This *vav*-dot combination is called a *shureq*. It is placed after (to the left of) the consonant. Thus, bû = בּוּ, sû = סוּ, etc. .

When ו and י are used this way, they are called ▲"vowel letters." They are from an older form of Hebrew. More will be said about them in the next chapter. For now, note that their transliterations have little "tents" (^) over them. That is, î and û represent the long vowel letters ִי (*hireq-yod*) and וּ (*shureq*). Transliterations with straight lines over them (ā, ē and ō) represent vowel points only.

4.3.4 **Two vowels cannot stand together.** In English, two vowels often are found together – such as the *o* and the *u* in the word *found*, or the *a* and the *i* in the word *mail*. In Hebrew, this never happens. Two vowels are never found together; they are always separated by consonants.

4.3.5 **Vowels under final *kaph*.** When a vowel appears under a final *kaph* (ך) it will be raised. Thus, we will see ךָ and not ךָ.

Things You Should Know

1. **Vowel points:** know the vowels they represent and whether they are long or short; know also their shapes, names, pronunciations, and transliterations.
2. **The symbol** ָ is used to represent both long *a* (*qamets*) and short *o* (*qamets-hatuph*). We shall learn later how to distinguish between these two vowels.
3. **A combination of pointing and a consonant** (י or ו) is used to represent the long vowels î and û . Thus, î = ִי and û = וּ . Note the "tents" (^) over the transliteration letters.
4. **A vowel point under a final *kaph*** will be raised. For instance, we will see ךָ and not ךָ.

---

[3] **Technical note.** The formal transliterated names of the vowel points are below. (Note the accent mark: ' .)

pā'taḥ, sᵉgōl, ḥî'req, qā'meṣ-ḥāṭûp', qibbûṣ', qā'meṣ, ṣē'rê, ḥî'req-yōḏ, ḥō'lem, šû'req.

Exercise #3

1. Transliterate the following, working from right to left. In this exercise, the vowel point ָ stands for ā. Remember that you can check your work by using the key to the exercises at the back of the book. (The key begins on page 303.)

   a. שָׁמַע מוּת מִן מִין חֶסֶד יַיִן אֹת זָקֵן הָרַג בָּטַח בֶּץ זֶרַע הוּא

   b. חֹדֶשׁ שָׁנִים שֹׁפֵט יָשִׁים לַיִל כֶּסֶף חֹק אוּלַי אָרֶץ צוּר דָּוִד

   c. עֹרֶף אָשׁוּב כַחֶרֶשׁ פָּצוּ אָחִינוּ בֵּן נָגַד סֹרֵר שָׁטִית מָתַי יָקֵם לֵךְ

   d. פָּנִים חֹצֵץ יָשִׁישׁ עֵשֶׂב כּוּמָז לֵא נָשַׁף קֹבֵץ מֵצַח עִרָם לָכַד

2. Write the following transliteration in Hebrew letters.

   a. nešek̲ ḥōrēb̲ ṭap̄ haḥay kāp̄ar yûʿam lāqaṭ bēnayim ʾōmen ʿeṣeb̲ kāt̲ût̲

   b. nōqep̄ mālēʾ yiḥar ʾeqûṭ beṣer ʿēṣ hûʾ gôren zānāb̲ naḥam ket̲er

   c. nōb̲aḥ śîr ḥûṣ gād̲îš zēk̲er susāt̲î qešeb̲ nāt̲an ʾûlām ʿāwel ḥāṭāʾnû

   d. kešep̄ kesep̄ pōśēq māḥaṣ yîʿap̄ lēb̲āb̲ ʾim tārû pet̲aḥ sig̃îm nāṭaš

5

VOWEL LETTERS

As mentioned at the end of the previous chapter, long *i* and long *u* are formed by using a vowel point with a consonant. When a consonant is used this way, it is called a *vowel letter*.

5.1 History of Vowel letters

In an earlier form of Hebrew, the letters ה י and ו were used to represent vowels

- The letter ה was used to represent long *a*
- The letter י was used to represent long *e* or long *i*
- The letter ו was used to represent long *o* or long *u*

Later, when vowel points were invented, some of these vowel letters became unnecessary. But often they were left in the words, appearing *along with* the vowel point. This is still true today. Thus, if we again use the letter מ (*m*) for our example, we find that

m-plus-long-*a*	may be written either	מָ (mā)	or	מָה (mâ)
m-plus-long-*e*	may be written either	מֵ (mē)	or	מֵי (mê)
m-plus-long-*o*	may be written either	מֹ (mō)	or	מוֹ (mô)

There is only one way of representing long *i* (ִי) and one way for long *u* (וּ).

5.2 The complete vowel table

Vowel Class	*Short Vowels* point	vowel name	transliteration	sound	*Long Vowels* point	vowel name	transliteration	sound
A	ַ	*pathah*	a	bar	ָ	*qamets*	ā	bar
					ָה	*qamets-he*	â	"
E	ֶ	*seghol*	e	bed	ֵ	*tsere*	ē	they
					ֵי	*tsere-yod*	ê	"
I	ִ	*hireq*	i	bit	ִי	*hireq-yod*	î	machine
O	ָ	*qamets-hatuph*	o	box	ֹ	*holem*	ō	low
					וֹ	*holem-vav*	ô	"
U	ֻ	*qibbuts*	u	bull	וּ	*shureq*	û	rule

Transliteration Notes:

1. Letters without any mark over them (a, e, i, o, u) represent ***short vowel points***.
2. Letters with a line over them (ā, ē, ō) represent ***long vowel points***.
3. Letters with a "tent" (^) over them (â, ê, î, ô, û) are used to represent ***vowel letters*** (and their accompanying vowel point in some cases).

5.3 How to distinguish Vowel Letters from Consonants.

There are only five cases in which the letters ה, י and ו represent vowels; at all other times they will represent consonants. If we use the symbol O to represent "any consonant," then we can say that the vowel letters are *only* the following:

הOָ = â   יOִ = î   יOֵ = ê   וֹ = ô   וּ = û

Notes:

1. הOָ is found only at the *end* of a word, never in the middle. (In the middle, ָ is used.)
2. ח is never a vowel letter. (Do not confuse ח and ה).
3. Two vowels cannot stand together (§4.3.4), and so a vowel point cannot stand next to a vowel letter. Therefore, ה י and ו are consonants and not vowel letters if:
   a. the ה י or ו has a vowel point[1] *beneath* it (or *holem* after it), or
   b. the ו has a vowel point[1] or vowel letter *before* it.

   Thus, for example, עוֹד = ʿôḏ, but עָוֹן must be ʿāwōn where the ו is a consonant, not a vowel letter. עָוֹן cannot be ʿāôn since this would place two vowels (ā and ô) together.

Vowel examples: in the following words, ה ו and י are used as *vowels*:

בָּנָה (bānâ); מִין (mîn); אֵלִי (ʾē-lî); בֵּין (bên); מוֹת (môṯ); שׁוּב (šûḇ)

Consonant examples: in the following words, ה ו and י are used as *consonants*, not as vowel letters:

פֶּה מָהֹר הֶבֶל   מָוֶת שָׁוַע עָוֹן   חַי בַּיִת

פֶּה	(peh)	ה is preceded by a vowel (e); thus it is a consonant (h). The only vowel letter which uses a ה is הָ
מָהֹר	(māhōr)	הָ is not a vowel letter since it is not at the end of the word (see Note 1, above).[2]
מָוֶת	(māweṯ)	ו is a consonant (w) since it has a vowel before it (ā) and one under it (e).
עָוֹן	(ʿāwōn)	וֹ is a consonant with a *holem*. As in the previous example, it cannot be a vowel letter since another vowel (*qamets*, ā) comes *before* it.
חַי	(ḥay)	יַ is a consonant (y) preceded by a vowel (a). The only vowel letters which use the letter י are יֵ and יִ (review the five cases above).

---

[1] "Vowel point" includes the *shewa* mark (ְ) which will be learned in §8.

[2] In addition, if the הָ were a vowel letter, then we would have רֹ + מָה (mâōr). But this would give us (1) two vowels standing together, and (2) a syllable which begins with a vowel (ōr). Both are impossible.

Things You Should Know

1. הָ ִי ֵי וֹ and וּ are vowel letters:
   - when they appear as shown, and
   - if there is no other vowel point (or *shewa*; see p. 13 footnote 1) under or before them.

   In all other cases, these letters are consonants. And the letter ח is *always* a consonant.

2. In transliteration,
   - the letters a e i o u represent *short vowel points*;
   - the letters ā ē ō represent *long vowel points*;
   - the letters â ê î ô û represent vowel *letters*.

Exercise #4

1. Transliterate the following words from Isaiah 1, working from right to left. In this exercise, the vowel point ָ stands for ā (or â if it comes before a ה at the end of a word).

   a. ישעיהו[3] בֶּן אָמוֹץ חָזָה וִירוּשָׁלָם בִּימֵי יוֹתָם אָחָז שָׁמַיִם אֶרֶץ כִּי

   b. בָּנִים יָדַע קֹנֵהוּ אֵבוּס לֹא חוֹי חֹטֵא עַם [4]עָוֹן זֶרַע נָזֹרוּ אָחוֹר

   c. עַל מֶה עוֹד תּוֹסִיפוּ סָרָה לֵבָב אֵין בּוֹ פֶּצַע עָרֵיכֶם אֵשׁ זָרִים

   d. לוּלֵי הוֹתִיר לָנוּ שָׂרִיד הָיִינוּ דָּמִינוּ תּוֹרַת לִי רֹב עֹלוֹת אֵילִים

   e. פָּרִים תָּבֹאוּ לֵרָאוֹת פָּנָי מִי הָבִיא תּוֹעֵבָה הִיא חֹדֶשׁ אוּכַל אָוֶן

2. Write the following transliteration in Hebrew letters. Start reading at the left (with hāyû). But when you write the Hebrew words, start at the right side of your paper and work to the left.

   a. ḥāyû ʿālay lāṭōraḥ ʿênay gam kî dāmîm mālēʾû hāsîrû hêṭēḇ ḥāmôṣ

   b. yāṯûm rîḇû yōʾmar ʾim tōʾḇû ṭûḇ hāʾāreṣ tōʾḵēlû ḥereḇ ʾēḵâ

   c. ṣeḏeq yālîn hāyâ māhûl śārayiḵ ʾōhēḇ šōḥaḏ yāḇôʾ lāḵēn hāʾāḏôn hôy

   d. yāḏî sîḡāyiḵ lāḵ ʿîr šeḇer yēḇōšû mēʾêlîm nōḇeleṯ ʿālehā mayim

   e. ʾên lâ heḥāsōn ḥāzâ wîrûšālayim nāḵôn har bêṯ hehārîm ʾēlāyw yōrēnû

---

[3] These are the consonants from the name Isaiah. The name contains two vowel points which you have not yet learned, and so the name is printed here with no vowel points.

[4] Does the וֹ represent wō (a consonant and a long vowel) or ô (a vowel letter)? Review §5.3 if you are unsure.

6

SYLLABLES

6.1 Syllables: a review

A *syllable* is the smallest piece of a word which can be pronounced. A syllable must also have a vowel.[5] For instance, the syllables of the first six words of the first sentence on this page are:

A syl la ble is the small est piece

One way to make the syllables easier to see is to separate them by hyphens (-) :

A syl-la-ble is the small-est piece

6.2 Hebrew syllables

In Hebrew, we must divide words into their proper syllables in order to get the proper meaning. There are several important rules which must be learned. We shall learn the first two in this chapter.

Syllable Rule 1: In Hebrew, every syllable begins with a consonant.

For instance:

גָּדַל	דָּמִים	בָּנוֹת	מוֹעֵד	גּוֹיִם	בָּבֶל	יוֹשֵׁב	לָשׂוּם
gā-ḏal	dā-mîm	bā-nôṯ	mô-ʿēḏ	gô-yim	bā-ḇel	yô-šēḇ	lā-śûm

Note how every syllable begins with a consonant. Vowels are placed beneath (or after) the consonants and are pronounced *after* them. (That is, -בָּ = bā-).

The word גָּדַל is pronounced gā-ḏal. It is not possible to pronounce it gāḏ-al, because it is not possible for a Hebrew syllable to begin with a vowel (Syllable Rule 1). Thus, it is impossible to have a syllable such as -al. This also means that

Hebrew words cannot begin with a vowel.[6]

In order to deal with this "problem," we must use the two consonants א and ע, as described below.

6.3 The use of א and ע

These letters were discussed in§2.3 (p. 5; review this section if necessary). In English, it is possible to begin words and syllables with vowels. But when we do, we close the throat and give a slight kick of air before the vowel. Compare the way you say the vowels in the following pairs of words:

---

[5] In English, the vowels are *a, e, i, o, u* and sometimes *y*.

[6] **Technical note:** There is one exception to this rule. The Hebrew word for *and* is sometimes written -וּ and is then attached to the beginning of a word. We will study this in chapter 18.

race	ace
mend	end
mill	ill
more	or
cup	up

In each case, the vowel in the first word comes after a consonant and is pronounced smoothly. But the second word *begins* with a vowel, and you must give a little kick of air or "grunt" as you say it. This little "grunt" becomes a letter in Hebrew: either א or ע.

Above, we learned that Hebrew words cannot begin with vowels. However, we can still write a sound like "im" in Hebrew if we write it as אִם (ʾim) or עִם (ʿim). Note the two transliteration characters ʾ and ʿ. They are small, but important. And the letters they represent, א and ע, are *consonants*, not vowels. Likewise, the names Adam and Eli, which begin with vowels in English and other languages, are written in (the original!) Hebrew as אָדָם (ʾā-ḏām) and עֵלִי (ʿē-lî).

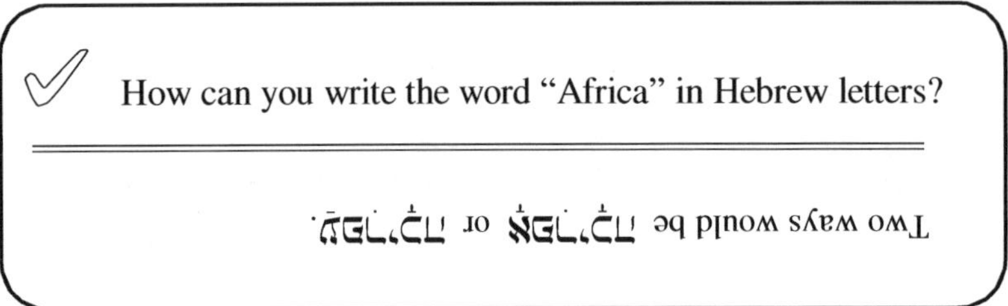

6.4 Open and closed syllables

A syllable which ends with a vowel is called an *open syllable*. A syllable which ends with a consonant is called a *closed syllable*. For instance, the word בָּבֶל has two syllables: -בָּ (bā-) and -בֶל (-ḇel). The first syllable (-בָּ = bā-) is an open syllable because it ends with a vowel. The second syllable (-בֶל = -ḇel) is a closed syllable because it ends with the consonant ל. The word is transliterated bā-ḇel.

Syllable Rule 2: A syllable which ends with a vowel is *open*; a syllable which ends with a consonant is *closed*.

And note: the word cannot be divided bāḇ-el (closed first syllable) because of Syllable Rule 1. We cannot have a syllable like -el which begins with a vowel.

Syllables which end with vowel letters are also open. Thus, בָּה בֵּי בִּי בּוֹ and בּוּ (bâ bê bî bô and bû) are all open syllables. But בֶּה (beh) is not open since ֶה is not a vowel letter.

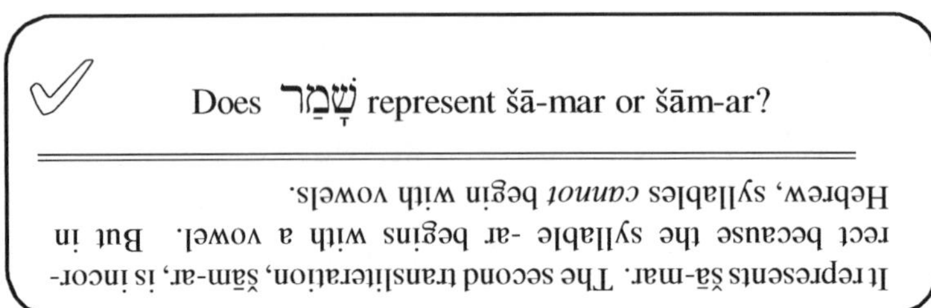

Hint: As you learn to divide syllables, start from the end of the word and work toward the right. As you work, make sure that each syllable begins with a consonant.

Understanding open and closed syllables is important in Hebrew. In the next chapter, we shall study the relationship between long and short vowels and open or closed syllables.

Things You Should Know

1. A *syllable* is the smallest piece of a word which contains a vowel and can be pronounced.
2. In Hebrew, every syllable begins with a consonant. Syllables cannot begin with vowels.
3. Words like Adam or Eli, which begin with vowels in English and other languages, will begin with the consonants א or ע in Hebrew: thus, אָדָם and עֵלִי.
4. An *open syllable* is one which ends with a vowel point (בָּ) or vowel letter (בּוֹ). A *closed syllable* is one which ends with a consonant (for instance, בַּב or בֵּה).

Exercise #5

1. What is a syllable? What are the two syllable rules which you learned in this chapter?
2. Use Hebrew letters to write the following sounds: *ah* *em* *in* *or*
3. Use Hebrew consonants and vowels to write three examples of open syllables and three examples of closed syllables.
4. Transliterate the following words from Genesis 1. Use hyphens (-) to separate the syllables. Put a check (✔) over closed syllables, as in the three following examples. Again, ָ is ā.

   שָׁמַר šā-mar✔   הָיָה hā-yâ   בֵּן ben✔

   a. בָּרָא אֵת הָאָרֶץ תֹּהוּ וָבוֹהוּ הָאוֹר הַחֹשֶׁךְ[7] עֶרֶב בֹּקֶר אֶחַד

   b. מַיִם לָמָיִם מֵעַל מָקוֹם תֵּרָאֶה תּוֹצֵא בֵּין הָיוּ קָטֹן לַילָה[8]

   c. כּוֹכָבִים אֹתָם אֶלֹהִים הָעִיר עוֹף עוֹפֵף הָרֹמֶשֶׂת כָּנָף לֵאמֹר

   d. יֵרֶב בָּאָרֶץ חַמִישִׁי נֶפֶשׁ וָרֶמֶשׂ הָאַדָמָה אֹתוֹ זָכָר שָׁמַיִם הָעֵץ

---

[7] When a *holem* appears immediately before a שׁ, the *holem* and the dot of the שׁ will sometimes combine and you will see only one dot. Thus, this word may also be written הַחשֶׁךְ . You will know there is a *holem* because the ח *must* have a vowel. Another example is the name Moses, which is sometimes written משֶׁה.

[8] **Technical note:** The Hebrew teacher will note the missing *shewa*, which has not yet been taught to the student. Its absence should not affect the transliteration at this point. Likewise, the word אֱלֹהִים has been simplified in the next line (line c.), by changing the composite *shewa* to a simple *seghol*. Composite *shewas* have been changed in a few other words, as well.

7

ACCENT

Accent means "stress" or "emphasis." The accented syllable in a word is the one which we say the most loudly. We emphasize the first syllable of the word *alphabet*: **AL**-pha-bet. Therefore, we say that the accent is on the first syllable. In the word *revision,* the accent is on the second syllable: re-**VI**-sion. In the rest of the book, we will use an accent mark (′): al′-pha-bet, re-vi′-sion

7.1 Hebrew accents in general

In Hebrew, there are only two places where the accent can be placed:

(1) on the last syllable of the word, or
(2) on the next to last (last but one) syllable.

The accent *usually* falls on the last syllable.[1]

In this book, all words are accented on their last syllable *unless* they have a < mark over the next to the last syllable. For instance:

בָּבֶל (bā-ḇel′)	but	מֶ֫לֶךְ (me′-leḵ).
accent on last syllable is not marked		accent on *next* to last syllable *is* marked with <

7.2 Accents, Syllables and Vowels

Usually, open syllables have long vowels and closed syllables have short vowels. Note the example of בָּבֶל above. The first syllable is open and has a long vowel, and the second syllable is closed and has a short vowel. There are exceptions[2] to this pattern, but one important rule never changes:

Syllable Rule 3: A closed unaccented syllable always has a short vowel

Learn this rule well. It will help you recognize the two forms of *qamets* (ָ), that is, *qamets* and *qamets-hatuph* (§4.3.2).

---

[1] **Technical notes.** Many language textbooks (Greek as well as Hebrew) will call the last syllable of a word the "ultimate" syllable, and the next to last syllable the "penultimate" syllable.

There are two other terms which are used in some Hebrew textbooks to describe the two ways of accenting words. Words which have the accent on the last (ultimate) syllable are called *Milra.* Words which have the accent on the next to the last (penultimate) syllable are called *Milel.* It is not necessary to learn these two terms, and they will not be used again in this book.

[2] If a syllable is accented, this general rule may not be followed. For instance, in the word מֶ֫לֶךְ the first syllable is open and would normally have a long vowel. Since it is also accented, however, it has taken a short vowel. But this change does not always happen, especially when the accent is on the last syllable (as it usually is). For instance, the last syllable of בָּבֶל is closed *and accented*, and yet the short vowel remains and does not change to a long vowel.

	Accented	Unaccented
Closed syllable	Usually short vowel	**ALWAYS short vowel**
Open syllable	Usually long vowel	Usually long vowel

7.3 Accents in the Hebrew Bible.

In the Hebrew Bible, *every* accented syllable of *every* word has one kind of accent mark or another under it (or occasionally over it). For instance, the first verse in the Bible (Gen 1:1) is printed as follows in *Biblia Hebraica Stuttgartensia* (the standard Hebrew Bible):

בְּרֵאשִׁ֖ית בָּרָ֣א °אֱלֹהִ֑ים ° אֵ֥ת הַשָּׁמַ֖יִם ° וְאֵ֥ת ° הָאָֽרֶץ׃

The small circles (°) are not important, and you will learn the marks ◌ְ and ◌ֱ in the next chapter. But note the other marks such as ◌֖ ◌֣ ◌֥ ◌ֽ and ◌֑ which appear next to certain vowel points. They are accent marks, and they tell you which syllable to stress when you read the word. In this case, every word is accented on the last syllable except the fifth word (הַשָּׁמַ֖יִם) and the last word (הָאָֽרֶץ׃).

These marks have various meanings[3], but only three of them are important for us (although all of them help in pronouncing the words):

7.4 *Soph Passuq* (׃), *silluq* (◌ֽ), and *athnah* (◌֑)

7.4.1 ***Soph passuq*** (׃) is actually punctuation, not an accent. It is the Hebrew full stop (or period), and it is found after the last word of a sentence. (See the example above.)

7.4.2 ***Silluq*** (◌ֽ) is placed below the *accented syllable* of the *last word* of each sentence. A *soph passuq* is then placed after this word, as described above. Thus, *soph passuq* and *silluq* are always found together with the last word of the sentence. For instance, when the words בָּבֶל or מֶ֫לֶךְ appear at the end of a sentence, they will look like this:

. . . בָּבֶֽל׃   . . . מֶֽלֶךְ׃

In the case of מֶֽלֶךְ, the *silluq* shows the accent, and so the < mark is not needed.

7.4.3 ***Athnah*** (◌֑) is the Hebrew comma (,). In Hebrew, almost every sentence is divided in two parts, and this division is indicated by the *athnah*. Since the *athnah* is also an accent mark, it will also take the placed of a < mark if there is one. Thus מֶ֫לֶךְ with *athnah* is מֶ֑לֶךְ .

Now look again at the first sentence of the Bible, this time printed with only the ***silluq***, the ***athnah***, and the ***soph passuq*** (plus the < accent mark one time):

הָאָֽרֶץ׃	וְאֵת	הַשָּׁמַ֫יִם	אֵת	אֱלֹהִ֑ים	בָּרָא	בְּרֵאשִׁית
. the-earth	*and-(-)*	*the-heavens*	*(-)*	*,God*	*created*	*In-the-beginning*

Note the *athnah* below the accented syllable of the word אֱלֹהִ֑ים (*God*). It shows that the sentence is

[3] **Technical note:** The different shapes indicate whether the accents are *conjunctive* (meaning that certain words should be read together as a phrase) or *disjunctive* (meaning that there is a certain conceptual distance between the words or phrases).

divided as follows:

In the beginning God created, *the heavens and the earth.*

This differs from English. In English, we would put the comma after the word *beginning*. It is the *athnah* that shows how the sentence should be read in Hebrew, however. Sometimes the meaning of the sentence will be greatly affected by the position of the *athnah*.

Note also the *silluq* below the accented syllable of the last word of the sentence, and the *soph passuq* at the very end of the sentence. Since the word הַשָּׁמַ֫יִם is accented on its next to last syllable, it has received a < to show this. The last word of the sentence is also accented on its next to last syllable, but since there is a *silluq* the < is unnecessary.

Study the above example well, since this is how the sentences will appear in this book.

7.5 Pause

Words which have an *athnah* or a *silluq* under them are "in pause," since readers naturally pause at this point in their reading. This is similar to the way one pauses for a comma or full stop (period) in English.

Because of this, the **vowel** of the syllable which is in pause **may lengthen**. For instance, a word like שָׁמַר will become שָׁמָֽר or שָׁמָ֑ר.[4]

Things You Should Know

1. In Hebrew, the accent is usually on the last syllable of a word. If the last syllable is not accented, then the next to last (last but one) syllable will be accented.
2. Open syllables usually have long vowels, and closed syllables usually have short vowels. But the presence of an accent may change this.
3. A closed unaccented syllable will always have a short vowel.
4. The last word of a Hebrew sentence will have a *silluq* (ֽ) under its accented syllable. It will also have a *soph passuq* (׃) after it.
5. Hebrew sentences are divided into two parts. An *athnah* (֑), which acts like a comma, shows this division. It is not placed after a word, as in English. Rather, it is placed under the accented syllable of the word.
6. Words with a *silluq* or an *athnah* under them are "in pause" because they cause the reader to pause. The vowel of the syllable which is in pause may lengthen.

---

[4] **Technical note:** Another change also sometimes occurs. Most Hebrew words have the accent on the last syllable, but on rare occasion this accent may move to the next to the last syllable in pause.

Exercise #6

1. In Hebrew words, where may the accent be?

2. Explain the relationship between the following three things: (1) open and closed syllables, (2) long and short vowels, and (3) accent. What is the one rule about these three things which never changes?

3. Use an *athnah*, a *silluq* and a *soph passuq* to punctuate the following *English* sentences:

   a. Pharaoh enslaved Israel but God had mercy on his people

   b. I am the LORD your God you shall have no other gods

   c. I shall make a new covenant not like the covenant I made with your fathers

4. What does "in pause" mean? What marks show us that a word is "in pause"? Where are they placed (that is, under which syllable)? What do these marks cause the reader to do? What sometimes happens to the accented vowel when a word is "in pause"?

5. The four lines of Hebrew below are from the Psalms.
   - Transliterate them, using hyphens (-) to divide the syllables (§6.1)
   - Write a comma for the *athnah* and a full stop (period) for the *soph passuq*.
   - Place a check mark (✔) over transliterated syllables which have *athnah* or *silluq*.

   Do not try to transliterate the colon-like mark (:) which is found under some letters. It will be explained in the next chapter.

   a. אִם לֹא יָשׁוּב חַרְבּוֹ יִלְט֑וֹשׁ קַשְׁתּוֹ דָרַךְ וַיְכוֹנְנֶֽהָ׃[5] (Ps 7:13)

   b. כִּי דֹרֵשׁ דָּמִים אוֹתָם זָכָ֑ר לֹא שָׁכַח צַעֲקַת עֲנָֽיִים׃ (Ps 9:13)

   c. עֵינַי תָּמִיד אֶל יהו֑ה[6] כִּי הוּא יוֹצִיא מֵרֶשֶׁת רַגְלָֽיו׃ (Ps 25:15)

   d. בָּרוּךְ יְהוָ֑ה כִּי שָׁמַע קוֹל תַּחֲנוּנָֽי׃ (Ps 28:4)

---

[5] **Technical note for the teacher.** For the purposes of this exercise, the *metheg* under the *vav-pathah* has been removed in this final word. This of course closes the syllable and makes the *shewa* silent. Thus, a *dagesh lene* has been added to the following כ, although in the original this *d.l.* is absent.

[6] יהוה represents God's name as he gave it to Moses. You may transliterate it YHWH. **Technical note:** Traditionally, Jews do not pronounce this name when reading the Bible, since it is considered sacred. Rather, the word אֲדֹנָי (*Adonai*) is said in its place. In the Hebrew scriptures, the vowels of יהוה have been removed, to prevent readers from trying to pronounce the name. In place of these original vowels, the vowels from אֲדֹנָי are written with the consonants יהוה, producing an almost unpronounceable word (usually יְהֹוָה or יְהוָה). This reminds readers to say "Adonai" rather than YHWH. Those who have not understood this have, in the past, tried to pronounce this "unpronounceable" and wrongly-pointed word by saying "Jehovah." But "Jehovah" is not the name of God. It is just a mispronunciation of the name YHWH.

In most English language translations, the words "the LORD" are used to represent יהוה. (Note the special printing. The letters are "the LORD" and not "the Lord.") In some places, both אֲדֹנָי and יהוה are used, giving the double name אֲדֹנָי יֱהֹוִה (for instance, Ezek 28:2,24,25). Here, the odd vowel pointing of יֱהֹוִה is supposed to make the reader think of and say אֱלֹהִים (note vowel pointing). English translations will thus translate יֱהֹוִה אדֹנָי as the Lord GOD. In this case, it is the word "GOD" that represents the divine name יהוה.

8

SHEWA

Sometimes a consonant does not have a vowel under it (for instance, בָ or בֵ) or after it (בּ, בוֹ or בוּ). Instead, a special sign known as a *shewa* (:) may be placed under it. For instance, לְבַד or מִדְבַּר. This *shewa* may be "simple" or "composite."

8.1 Simple Shewa.

The simple *shewa* is the mark shown above (:) . It can be either *silent* or *vocal.* If it is **silent**, then it is neither pronounced nor transliterated. If it is **vocal**, then it is pronounced with a very short sound like the *a* in the word *syllable* or in the word *alone.* It is transliterated as a small raised letter *e* (^{e}). Thus, we could show the sound of the word *syllable* as follows: *sil'-l^{e}-bl.* The rule for silent and vocal *shewa* is:

A simple *shewa* after a short vowel is silent. Other *shewas* are vocal.

Consider the following situations. (We shall use circles (OOOO) to represent the consonants in a Hebrew word.)

8.1.1. If the *shewa* is under the **first letter of the word** (OOOO̰), it is always **vocal**.

> *Example*: שְׁמוֹ. This word is pronounced *sh^{e}-mo.* Since vocal *shewa* is such a short and weak sound, the word is actually considered to be just **one syllable**. Thus, it is transliterated š^{e}mô with no hyphen between š^{e} and mô. But each part of the syllable (š^{e} and mô) must still begin with a consonant.

8.1.2 If the *shewa* is **under a letter within the word** (OOO̰O), then look at the vowel which comes before the *shewa*:

(a) **If the vowel before the *shewa* is long** (for instance, OOO̰Ö or OOO̰וֹO), then the *shewa* is **vocal** and the consonant over it begins a new syllable.

> *Example*: in the word שׁוֹמְרִים, a long vowel (וֹ) comes before the מְ. Thus the *shewa* will be vocal, and the מ begins a new syllable. The word is transliterated šô-m^{e}r îm and is pronounced *sho-m^{e}reem'.* And, just like š^{e}mô, the syllable m^{e}rîm is considered to be one syllable, not two.

(b) **If the vowel before the *shewa* is short** (OOO̰O), then the *shewa* is **silent**[1] and closes the syllable.

> *Example*: in יִשְׁמֹר, a short vowel (the *hireq* under the *yod*) comes before the שְׁ. Thus, the *shewa* is silent and it closes the syllable. The word is pronounced *yish-mor'* (not *yi-sh^{e}-mor'*), and is transliterated yiš-mōr.

This matter of long and short vowels is important. Be sure to study it until you understand it.

---

[1] **Technical note:** This rule will have two exceptions: (1) when a preposition is added to a word, and (2) when the short vowel before the *shewa* has a mark known as a *metheg*. Both exceptions will be discussed later.

8.1.3 **If there are two *shewas* together inside a word**[2] (○○ְ○ְ○), the first is silent and the second is vocal. The syllables then divide between them.

Example: the word יִשְׁמְרוּ is pronounced *yish-mᵉ-ru'*, and is transliterated yiš-mᵉrû.

8.1.4 **If the *shewa* is under a letter within a word and with a *dagesh* (○○⊙ְ○), both the letter and the *shewa* are doubled (○○⊙ְ○ = ○○ְ○ְ○○):**

Explanation: You already know that a *dagesh* in the middle of a BEGADKEPAT letter will harden it. In addition, we shall learn in §11 that a *dagesh* in any *other* letter will double that letter. For instance: מּ = ממ. And, if there is a *shewa* under the letter, then both the letter and the *shewa* are doubled: מְּ = מְמְ. Since there are now two *shewas* in a row, the first *shewa* will be silent, and the second one vocal (§8.1.3).

Example: The word שַׁמְּרוּ is really the same as שַׁמְמְרוּ, where the first *shewa* is silent, and the second is vocal. Thus, the word שַׁמְּרוּ is pronounced *sham-mᵉ-ru'* and is transliterated šam-mᵉrû.

8.1.5 Sometimes, there is a silent *shewa* at the end of a word: שָׁמַרְתְּ = šā-mart'. (Both *shewas* are silent in this word.) This is unusual, however.

Summary

○○○○ְ	*Shewa* under first letter is **vocal**.
○○○ֵ○ְ	*Shewa* after long vowel is **vocal**.
○○○ַ○ְ	*Shewa* after short vowel is **silent**. (It closes the syllable).
○○ְ○ְ○	Two *shewas* in a row. First *shewa* is **silent** (and closes the syllable). Second *shewa* is **vocal**.
○○⊙ְ○	*Shewa* under letter with *dagesh*. This is the same as ○○ְ○ְ○○. First *shewa* is **silent**; second is **vocal**.

Explain the two *shewas* in the word יְקֻטְּלוּ

The first *shewa* of יְקֻטְּלוּ is vocal, because it is under the first letter of the word. The second *shewa* comes after a short vowel (ֻ), and this would usually make it a silent *shewa*. However, the ט has a *dagesh*. ט is not a BEGADKEPAT letter, and so this *dagesh* doubles the ט and its *shewa*: טְּ = טְטְ. Now we have two *shewas* together, and so the first will be silent and the second vocal. The word is transliterated yᵉqut-tᵉlû.

[2] In §9.1, we shall discuss two *shewas* together at the *beginning* of a word or syllable.

8.2 Composite *Shewa*:

8.2.1 A composite *shewa* is a combination of a *shewa* plus a short-vowel point (for instance ֲ). It is actually a single vowel point, and it appears under a single letter. And, like vocal *shewa*, its transliteration is a small raised letter. But this letter will have a small mark (˘) over it:

hateph pathah (ֲ)	transliteration: ᵃ̆	*a*-vowel
hateph seghol (ֱ)	transliteration: ᵉ̆	*e*-vowel
hateph qamets (ֳ)	transliteration: ᵒ̆	*o*-vowel

Composite shewas are considered to be half-vowels in pronunciation. We shall pronounce them just like a vocal *shewa*. Also, like a vocal *shewa*, no hyphen comes after them in transliteration. (אֱמֹר is transliterated ʾᵉ̆mōr, not ʾᵉ̆-mōr). Again, both pieces of the syllable (ʾᵉ̆ and mōr) must begin with consonants.

A Note on *hateph qamets* and *qamets-hatuph*. These words are different; do not confuse them. We first saw *qamets-hatuph* in §4.1. It is the short-*o* vowel which looks just like *qamets* (both are ָ), and we will study it in §12. Thus, both *qamets-hatuph* and *hateph qamets* are short *o*-vowels, not short *a*-vowels. But *qamets-hatuph* is a regular vowel point (ָ) and *hateph qamets* is a composite *shewa* (ֳ).

8.2.2 **Gutturals:** The four letters א ה ח and ע are called ▲*gutturals,* because they are made with the throat. We shall learn several special rules for gutturals in §13. However, the first rule concerns *shewa*, and so we shall learn it now:

> **Gutturals at the beginning of a word *cannot* stand over a *simple vocal shewa*. They will stand over either a regular vowel point (ָ ַ ֶ ֵ etc.) or a *composite shewa*.**
>
> *Examples:* אֱמֹר and עֲבֹד. The first letters of these words are gutturals. Therefore, they cannot be written with simple vocal *shewa* as אְמֹר or עְבֹד. They must use composite *shewa*.

The difference is very small, but it becomes more important when there are two *shewas* together at the beginning of a word or syllable. We will study this point in the next chapter.

Things You Should Know

1. **Simple *shewa*** (ְ) is a sign which is placed under consonants which do not have vowels.
2. Simple *shewa* is **silent** when it comes after a short vowel (○○○ְ○ֶ).
3. Simple *shewa* is **vocal** (pronounced with a very short sound, like the *a* in *alone*):
   a. when it comes after
      - a long vowel (○○○ְ○ֵ)
      - another *shewa* (○○ְ○ְ○; the second shewa is vocal)

   b. when it is under
      - the first letter of a word (○○○○ְ)
      - a letter with a *dagesh* (○○◉ְ○ = ○○○ְ○ְ○; first *shewa* is silent, second vocal)
4. A **composite *shewa*** is a *shewa* plus a short-vowel point (*pathah, seghol* or *qamets-hatuph*).
   a. The three composite *shewas* are:

      ֲ = *hateph-pathah*
      ֱ = *hateph-seghol*
      ֳ = *hateph-qamets*

   b. Their transliterations are a small raised letter with a (˘) over it: ă ĕ ŏ

   c. Gutturals (א ח ה or ע) at the beginning of a word will take composite *shewa* instead of simple vocal *shewa*.

Exercise #7

1. What is the difference in *appearance* between simple *shewa* and composite *shewa*?
2. A simple *shewa* will be vocal in 4 situations. What are those 4 situations?
3. What happens when two *shewa*s appear together in the middle of a word?
4. Transliterate the following verses from Psalm 24. Use ᵉ for vocal *shewa*. Use ă ĕ or ŏ for composite *shewa*. Silent *shewa* is not transliterated. Translate יְהוָה as YHWH.

5 ... בְּרָכָה מֵאֵת יְהוָה צְדָקָה מֵאֱלֹהֵי יִשְׁעוֹ׃
6 זֶה דּוֹר דֹּרְשָׁיו מְבַקְשֵׁי פָנֶיךָ יַעֲקֹב סֶלָה׃
7 שְׂאוּ שְׁעָרִים ... פִּתְחֵי עוֹלָם וְיָבוֹא מֶלֶךְ ... ׃
8 מִי זֶה מֶלֶךְ ... מִלְחָמָה׃

9

SHEWA (Continued)

In this chapter, we shall consider three other features of *shewa*:

(1) *shewas* at the beginning of a syllable,
(2) *shewas* "in pause," and
(3) *shewa* before וֹ

Students often find the details of this chapter and the previous one to be a bit overwhelming. But *shewa* is so common in Hebrew that you will eventually get used to it and know it well. Do not get discouraged!

9.1 *Shewas* at the Beginning of a Syllable:

Two *shewas* cannot remain together at the beginning of a word or syllable. If two *shewas* are placed together at the beginning of a syllable, one of the following things will happen:

9.1.1 **If both *shewas* are *simple*,** then the first one will become a *hireq* (ִ).

Example: when the preposition -לְ (which means *to* or *for*) is added as a ▲ *prefix*[1] to the name שְׁמוּאֵל (*Samuel*), we would get the word לְשְׁמוּאֵל (*to Samuel*). But two *shewas* cannot appear at the beginning of a word. Thus, the first one becomes a *hireq* and we will see לִשְׁמוּאֵל instead.

Note on pronunciation: Normally, the remaining *shewa* will be silent, since it now comes after a short vowel (the *hireq*, see §8.1.2(b)). But when **prepositions** are added like this, the *shewa* remains vocal, as it was before the change. Thus, we transliterate לִשְׁמוּאֵל (*to Samuel*) as li-š^{e}mû-ʾēl, not liš-mû-ʾēl.[2] The same thing happens when we attach the preposition -בְּ (*in, at, with, by*) to the place name שְׁכֶם (*Shechem*):

בְּ+ שְׁכֶם → בְּשְׁכֶם → בִּשְׁכֶם.

בִּשְׁכֶם is then transliterated bi-š^{e}k̲em, not biš-k̲em, because of the preposition.

9.1.2 **If the second *shewa* is a composite *shewa*** (for instance, לְאֱדוֹם), then the first *shewa* becomes the "corresponding short vowel" (לֶאֱדוֹם). That is,

simple *shewa* before	ֲ	will become	ַ
simple *shewa* before	ֱ	will become	ֶ
simple *shewa* before	ֳ	will become	ָ (*qamets-hatuph*, not *qamets*).

Explanation: This time, the first *shewa* does not become a *hireq*. Instead, it becomes a short

---

[1] A *prefix* is a letter or a group of letters added to the beginning of a word. A *suffix* is added to the end of the word.

[2] **Technical notes.** Why is there this exception to the rule? Probably in order to leave the basic pronunciation of the original word unchanged. In li-š^{e}mû-ʾēl we can still hear the sound of š^{e}mû-ʾēl. In liš-mû-ʾēl we cannot.

In the second case (בִּשְׁכֶם), we shall learn later that the lack of a dagesh in the כ also shows us that the preceding *shewa* must be vocal. If the *shewa* were silent, the word would be בִּשְׁכֶּם.

vowel which matches, or corresponds to, the composite *shewa*. That is, if the composite *shewa* is a *hateph pathah*, then the simple *shewa* will become a *pathah*, and so on. Since this new vowel corresponds to (matches) the composite *shewa*, it is called a "corresponding short vowel."

Examples:

Like a dream:	כְ + חֲלוֹם	→	כְחֲלוֹם	→	כַחֲלוֹם
To Edom:	לְ + אֱדוֹם	→	לְאֱדוֹם	→	לֶאֱדוֹם
In the tents:	בְ + אֳהָלִים[3]	→	בְאֳהָלִים	→	בָּאֳהָלִים

In this last example, note again that the *hateph qamets* (ֳ) is a short *o* vowel, from *qamets-hatuph*. Thus the "corresponding short vowel" (the ָ under the ב) will be a *qamets-hatuph*, not a *qamets*. The word is thus transliterated bo-ʾŏhā-lîm.

9.2 *Shewas* "in pause"

At the end of §7, we saw that when a word is "in pause"[4] vowels may lengthen and accents may change. This may also affect *shewas* if they come near the end of a word.

9.2.1 **Vocal *shewa*.** If a vocal *shewa* appears near the end of a word, it will become a *seghol* in pause and will receive the accent.

Example: לְעַבְדְּךָ (*to your servant*) has vocal *shewas* under both the ל and the ד. And, as is usually the case, the accent is on the last syllable (דְּךָ-). When this word comes at the end of a sentence, however, it becomes לְעַבְדֶּֽךָ׃; and over an *athnah* it will become לְעַבְדֶּ֑ךָ. In both cases, the vocal *shewa* under the ד lengthens to *seghol* and the accent moves to -דֶּ-. This will also happen with a short word like פְּרִי (*fruit*). In pause, it will become פֶּ֑רִי or פֶּֽרִי׃.

9.2.2 **Composite *shewa*.** A composite *shewa* near the end of a word will become the corresponding *long* (not short) vowel in pause, and will again receive the accent.

Example: the word אֲנִי (*I*) will become אָֽנִי׃ or אָ֑נִי, with *qamets* instead of *hateph pathah*.

9.3 *Shewa* before וֹ

If a *shewa* (simple or composite) appears before the letter וֹ, then the וֹ represents the two letters wō (a *vav* with a *holem* over it), not the single vowel letter ô.

Example: The word מִצְוֹת is transliterated miṣ-wōṯ (not miṣ-ôṯ and not miṣ-wôṯ).

---

[3] **Technical note.** The plural of the word אֹהֶל is actually אֹהָלִים. But when this plural is combined with the preposition בְּ (*in, with, by*) it does become בָּאֳהָלִים. Thus, the first part of this illustration is not completely accurate, although it serves the purpose of showing the change of the *shewa* to the "corresponding short vowel."

[4] That is, when the word has an *athnah* (֑ the Hebrew comma) under it, or when it is at the end of a sentence.

Things You Should Know

1. If two simple *shewas* occur together at the beginning of a word, the first *shewa* will become a *hireq*. The second *shewa* will remain and will be silent. (Exception: it will remain vocal after the addition of the prefixed prepositions -בְּ -כְּ or -לְ .)
2. If a simple *shewa* is placed before a composite *shewa* at the beginning of a word, the simple *shewa* will become the corresponding short vowel. לְ+אֱדוֹם → לְאֱדוֹם → לֶאֱדוֹם
3. In pause, vocal and composite *shewas* will attract the accent. Vocal *shewa* will become *seghol* (accented); composite *shewa* will become the (accented) corresponding *long* vowel.
4. If a *shewa* (simple or composite) occurs before וֹ, the וֹ is wō and not the vowel letter ô.

Exercise #8

1. What happens when two *shewas* appear together? Consider the following cases:
   - middle of a word
   - beginning of a syllable or word
   - a simple *shewa* and a composite *shewa*.
2. Transliterate the following verses from 1 Samuel 1.

1 אִישׁ אֶחָד מִן הָרָמָתַיִם צוֹפִים מֵהַר אֶפְרָיִם שְׁמוֹ אֶלְקָנָה ... בֶּן אֱלִיהוּא ....

3 וְעָלָה הָאִישׁ הַהוּא מֵעִירוֹ...לְהִשְׁתַּחֲוֹת[6]...בְּשִׁלֹה וְשָׁם שְׁנֵי בְנֵי עֵלִי...כֹּהֲנִים לַיהוָה[5]:

6 וְכִעֲסַתָּה צָרָתָהּ גַּם כַּעַס בַּעֲבוּר הַרְּעִמָהּ כִּי סָגַר יְהוָה בְּעַד רַחְמָהּ׃

12 וְהָיָה כִּי הִרְבְּתָה לְהִתְפַּלֵּל[8] לִפְנֵי[7] יְהוָה וְעֵלִי שֹׁמֵר אֶת פִּיהָ׃

3. Transliterate the following words:

אֲבִי אָסָף אֱדוֹם אָהֳלִי בָּמָה חֲלוֹם חֳלִי הֶחֱרִיד הֶחֳרָבוֹת עֲבֹדָה אֶעֱנֶה

---

[5] See page 21, note 6.

[6] Is the וֹ ô or wō? See §9.3, above.

[7] This is a word with a preposition: פְּנֵי + לְ. See the "Note on pronunciation" in §9.1.1. It will tell you how to transliterate this word.

[8] Transliterate the last three letters of this word (-פַּלֵּל) as: pal-lēl. We shall learn about *dagesh* (dot) in a non-BEGADKEPAT letter like ל in §11.

10

MAQQEPH AND METHEG

Maqqeph and *metheg* are small marks used like a hyphen (*maqqeph*) and an accent mark (*metheg*).

10.1 *Maqqeph*

English and other languages often use a hyphen (-) to join words and syllables together. Example: the word *first-born*. Hebrew uses a similar sign (¯) called a *maqqeph* (ma-kēf' [1] – the last syllable rhymes with *safe*). For instance, Genesis 1:3 reads as follows:

וַיֹּאמֶר אֱלֹהִים יְהִי אוֹר וַיְהִי־אוֹר׃

light   *and there was*   *light*   *Let there be*   *God*   *And (he) said*

The last two words have been joined together by a *maqqeph*. (Note also the *athnah* under the fourth word, and the *silluq* under the last. Review §7.4, p.19, if you have forgotten what these marks mean.)

Usually only two words will be joined together by a *maqqeph*. But it is possible to join several words together as we see in Genesus 1:29:

וַיֹּאמֶר אֱלֹהִים הִנֵּה נָתַתִּי לָכֶם אֶת־כָּל־עֵשֶׂב . . .

plant   *every*   ( )   *to you*   *I have given*   *Behold*   *God*   *And (he) said*

In this case, the last three words have been joined together with *maqqephs*.

There is one important rule concerning *maqqeph*:

When words are joined together with *maqqeph*, only the last word keeps its accent. The accents on the other words disappear.

This will sometimes cause the vowel-points to change in closed syllables. Why? Because "closed **unaccented** syllables always have short vowels" (Syllable Rule 3, §7.2, p. 18).[2]

> *Example*: the word כֹּל means *all*. Since every word has an accent (including single syllable words) this word is a closed *accented* syllable with a long vowel (ō). But in Genesis 1:29 (above), it is joined by *maqqeph* to the word עֵשֶׂב. This means that כֹּל loses its accent. Now it has become a closed *un*accented syllable. Therefore its long ō vowel must become a short *o* vowel. Thus, the ָ in the word ־כָּל־ must be the *short* vowel *qamets-hatuph* (o), and not the long vowel *qamets* (ā) (§4.3.2, p. 10). For this reason, we know that ־כָּל־ is -kol- not -kāl-. Review this example until you understand it.

---

[1] The ' is an accent mark. See the top of p. 18 if necessary.

[2] **Technical note:** There is an exception. A word like קוֹל, with a middle long-vowel letter, will not usually take a *maqqeph*. But when it does, it keeps its vowel letter. For instance, we find ־קוֹל in 1 Sam 7:10; 15:14; 1 Kgs 18:27; etc. Vowel letters do not generally reduce.

10.2 *Metheg*

Metheg is a small vertical mark (ֽ). It looks just like a *silluq* (§7.4.2, p.19), and it acts like a half-accent. It never appears under an accented syllable (*silluq* always does). It usually occurs two syllables before the accented syllable. Example: the word הָֽאָדָם (*hā'-ʾā-ḏām'*). Note that the syllable -הָֽ is not accented, and thus the ֽ under it cannot be a *silluq*.

A *metheg* also causes the reader to pause briefly in reading. And, most important:

a *metheg* shows that the syllable is open.

Example: the word תַּֽדְשֵׁא is found in Gen 1:11 and is transliterated ta-ḏᵉšēʾ (not taḏ-šēʾ). We usually see a silent *shewa* after a short vowel; however, the *metheg* forces us to pause briefly and opens the syllable. Thus, the ד becomes the first letter of the second syllable (-דְשֵׁא), rather than the last letter of the first syllable. This also means that

a *shewa* after a *metheg* will be vocal.

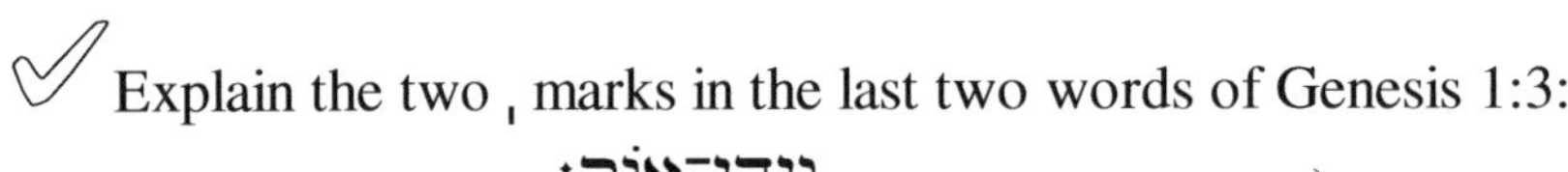

Explain the two ֽ marks in the last two words of Genesis 1:3:

וַֽיְהִי־אֽוֹר׃ ("... and there was light.")

וַֽיְהִי־אֽוֹר׃ : **The first mark** (under the וַ) is a *metheg*. It cannot be a *silluq*, because *silluq* appears only in the last word of a sentence. The *metheg* opens the syllable, and shows that the word is to be transliterated wa-yᵉhî, not way-hî. **The second mark** (under the א) is a *silluq* because it is under the accented syllable (in this case, the *only* syllable) of the last word of the sentence. It cannot be a *metheg* because *metheg* never appears under an accented syllable.

Things You Should Know

1. *Maqqeph* (־) is the Hebrew hyphen (-).
   - When words are joined by a *maqqeph*, only the last word keeps its accent.
   - All words which come before a *maqqeph* lose their accents.
   - Closed syllables which lose their accents will then take short vowels.
2. *Metheg* (ֽ) is a "half accent" mark.
   - It never appears under an accented syllable or the last syllable of a word.
   - It shows that the syllable is open.
   - A *shewa* after a *metheg* will be vocal.
3. In general, *maqqeph* steals the accent and shortens vowels. *Metheg* adds accent and causes short vowels to *act* longer. For instance, *shewas* after *methegs* will be vocal.

11

DAGESH AND MAPPIQ

We have noted the dot in the middle of certain letters (בּ, דּ, מּ, etc.). This dot is usually called a *dagesh*. However, when it is found in the letter ה it is a *mappiq*. *Mappiq* is found only in the letter ה at the end of a word. If we use OOOO to represent a four letter Hebrew word, then:

הּOOO
Mappiq may appear in a final ה only
Dagesh may appear in any of these letters[1]

11.1 Dagesh.

A dot in the middle of any letter except ה is a *dagesh* (בּ, מּ, etc.). There are two kinds of *dagesh:*

11.1.1 ***Dagesh lene*** (lē′-nē) (*d.l.*) appears only in BEGADKEPAT letters and hardens them (§2.1, p. 4). Thus, ב = ḇ but בּ = b, ג = ḡ but גּ = g, etc.

11.1.2 ***Dagesh forte*** (fōr′-tē) (*d.f.*)

- doubles a letter: מּ = ממ
- acts as a syllable divider. The first of the doubled letters gains a *shewa* and closes the previous syllable: -מַּ- = -מְמַ-. Thus שִׁמֵּר = שִׁמְמֵר = šim-mēr
- appears, therefore, **only in the middle of a word**, never at the beginning
- can appear in any letter except a guttural (א ה ח and ע) or ר
- doubles *and hardens* a BEGADKEPAT letter. Thus בּ = בב = bb if the *dagesh* is *d.f.* See the rules below, since בּ can be either *d.l.* or *d.f.*

11.1.3 **In general, the rules for letters with *dagesh*** are:

- if there is a vowel before the letter, the *dagesh* is *forte* (and doubles): לָמָּה = lām-mâ
- if there is no vowel before the letter[2], the *dagesh* is *lene* (and hardens): מִשְׁפָּט = miš-pāṭ

Here are the details:

---

[1] **Technical note:** A *dagesh* can also, on rare occasion, appear in the last letter of a word: שָׁמַרְתְּ, שָׁמַרְתְּ.

[2] A silent *shewa* before the letter means there is no vowel before the letter, as in the example מִשְׁפָּט. (Only silent *shewas* may be/ found before a letter with *dagesh*.)

11.1.3.1 ***Dagesh* in a *non*-BEGADKEPAT letter** is always *forte* and doubles the letter. לָ֫מָּה = lām-mâ.

11.1.3.2 ***Dagesh* in a BEGADKEPAT letter** is usually *lene*, but will be *forte* if a vowel precedes it.

- If the dagesh is in the **first letter of the word**, it is *dagesh lene*. It only hardens the letter. בֵּן = bēn. (Only a BEGADKEPAT letter can appear with a *dagesh* as the first letter of a word.)
- If there is a **shewa before the *dagesh***, then the *dagesh* is *d.l.* which only hardens. מִשְׁפָּט = miš-pāṭ (Note also that *shewa* before *dagesh* will always be silent.)
- if there is a **vowel before the *dagesh***, then the *dagesh* is a *d.f.* It both doubles and hardens the letter. הַבֵּן = hab-bēn.

Study the difference between the above words בֵּן (*son*) and הַבֵּן (*the son*). In the first case, the BEGADKEPAT ב is just hardened (bēn). In the second case, the ב is both doubled and hardened (hab-bēn). Study the rules until you know why.

11.1.4 Missing *dageshes*.

When a BEGADKEPAT letter is the first letter of a word, it almost always had a *dagesh lene*. However, sometimes this *d.l.* will be missing. This will happen when the previous word ends with a vowel. *D.l.* does not want a vowel or vocal *shewa* to appear before it, and thus it will usually disappear if this happens.[3] Compare the two following cases:

עָמוֹס בָּא means "*Amos* entered." בָּא has a *d.l.*, as we expect (since it is a BEGADKEPAT at the beginning of a word). The word before בָּא is עָמוֹס, and it ends with a consonant (ס).

מִיכָה בָא means "*Micah* entered." This time, the word before בָא is מִיכָה, and this word ends with a vowel. (Remember that ָה- is a single vowel letter: â .) Thus, the *d.l.* in the ב has disappeared because a vowel comes before it.[4]

This can also happen when a prefix with a vowel or vocal *shewa* is added to a word. If the word has a *dagesh* in its first letter, this *dagesh* will disappear:

- prefix with vocal *shewa*: בִּלְתִּי + -לְ becomes לְבִלְתִּי = lᵉḇil-tî
- prefix with a vowel: בָּטַח + -יִ becomes יִבְטַח = yiḇ-ṭaḥ

[3] Actually, there are two things which can happen if a vowel or vocal *shewa* appears before a *d.l.* First, the *d.l.* can disappear, as we mention here. Second, the *d.l.* can become a *d.f.* so that the letter is not only hardened but also doubled. We saw this when we compared בֵּן (*son*) and הַבֵּן (*the son*), above.

[4] **Technical note.** There is an exception to this rule, too: If a BEGADKEPAT occurs at the **beginning of a verse**, it will *alway* have a *d.l.* This is true even if the last word of the previous verse ended with a vowel. For example, Exod 5:8-9 reads: .... נִזְבְּחָה לֵאלֹהֵינוּ׃ [9] תִּכְבַּד הָעֲבֹדָה ....[8] Even though verse 8 ends with וּ-, the BEGADKEPAT at the beginning of verse 9 keeps its *d.l.*

Transliterate מִצְוֹת and מְצַוְּךָ.

---

(1) מִצְוֹת is miṣ-wōṯ. Syllables cannot begin with a vowel; thus וֹת- cannot be the syllable -ôṯ. Another reason that וֹ cannot be a vowel letter is that it has a *shewa* before it (p. 13, §5.3, Note 3.a. and footnote 1).
(2) מְצַוְּךָ is m^{e}ṣaw-w^{e}kā. The וּ cannot be a vowel letter since it has a vowel before it and a *shewa* under it. Thus, the dot is *dagesh forte* which doubles the letter. Remember also: Consonants can have only *one vowel under or after them*, and the צַ already has a *pathah* under it.

11.2 Mappiq.

Mappiq is a dot in a **final** ה (thus, הּ-). It shows that the ה is a consonant (not a vowel letter), and thus it should be pronounced as an *h*. A *mappiq* is not a *dagesh*, and it appears *only* in the letter ה at the end of a word. הּ is transliterated the same as ה (both are *h*). But it does not form a long vowel when a *qamets* comes before it. In other words, מָה = mâ; but מָהּ = māh and you should hear the *h*.

Explanation: When the letter ה stands at the end of a word, it is usually a vowel letter (ָה- = -â). The ה itself is then silent. Thus, the word מָה (mâ) sounds the same as the open syllable מָ (mā).

Sometimes, however, the final ה is still a consonant, and is supposed to be pronounced as *h*. In these cases, it will have a dot which *looks* like a *dagesh* but is called a *mappiq*. The *mappiq* does not harden or double the ה like a *dagesh*. (Remember, ה is a guttural and cannot take a *dagesh*, §11.1.2.) Rather, it simply shows that the ה is a consonant and should be pronounced.

The *mappiq* is important because it shows the difference between words which have different meanings, such as סוּסָה (sû-sâ) and סוּסָהּ (sû-sāh).[5]

How can you tell a *mappiq* from a *dagesh*?

If a dot appears in a final ה of a word it is a *mappiq*.
In all other cases the dot is a *dagesh*.

Transliterate הַֽלְלוּיָהּ.

הַֽלְלוּיָהּ is transliterated ha'-l^{e}lû-yāh' (and means *Praise the Lord!*). The *metheg* next to the *pathah* opens the first syllable and makes the *shewa* vocal. Thus the word cannot be hal-lû-yāh'. And the *mappiq* shows that the final syllable must be yāh and not yâ.

[5] **Technical note:** סוּס means *male horse*, and סוּסָה means *female horse* (or *mare*). But סוּסָהּ means *her male horse* (ָהּ- + סוּס). We will learn more about this later.

Things You Should Know

Dagesh

1. There are two kinds of *dagesh*:
   - *Dagesh lene* (*d.l.*) hardens the BEGADKEPAT letters
   - *Dagesh forte* (*d.f.*) doubles any letter except gutturals and ר and hardens BEGADKEPATs
2. A *dagesh* in a non-BEGADKEPAT letter is *d.f.* and doubles the letter.
3. A *dagesh* in a BEGADKEPAT letter is
   - *forte* if it comes after a vowel. *D.f.* doubles and hardens a BEGADKEPAT.
   - *lene* if it is in the first letter of the word, or if it comes after a *shewa*. *D.l.* hardens only.

Mappiq

4. *Mappiq* is a dot which appears in a final ה (thus, הּ).
   - It shows that the ה is a consonant, and not a vowel letter. *Mappiq* is not a *dagesh*, since *dagesh* never appears in a guttural.)
   - It causes us to pronounce the ה as *h*. Thus, מָה = mâ but מָהּ = māh.
   - The *mappiq* does not appear in transliteration (הּ and ה are both transliterated "h").

Exercise #9

1. How is *dagesh lene* different from *dagesh forte*?
2. If a BEGADKEPAT letter has a *dagesh*, how do we know if it is *d.f.* or *d.l.*?
3. Where is the only place a *mappiq* may be found? How do we know it is not a *dagesh*?
4. What is the difference in pronunciation between בָה and בָהּ?
5. What four things are wrong with this word: מְּלְהֶּשְׁטֶל ?
6. Transliterate Ruth 1:7-10 (below). When א appears without a vowel (וַתִּשֶּׂאנָה) , treat it as if it has a silent *shewa* (וַתִּשֶּׂאְנָה = wat-tiš-še'-nâ) :

[7] וַתֵּצֵא מִן־הַמָּקוֹם אֲשֶׁר הָיְתָה־שָׁמָּה שְׁתֵּי כַלֹּתֶיהָ עִמָּהּ וַתֵּלַכְנָה בַדֶּרֶךְ לָשׁוּב
אֶל־אֶרֶץ יְהוּדָה׃ [8] וַתֹּאמֶר נָעֳמִי לִשְׁתֵּי כַלֹּתֶיהָ לֵכְנָה שֹּׁבְנָה אִשָּׁה לְבֵית אִמָּהּ
יַעַשׂ יהוה עִמָּכֶם חֶסֶד כַּאֲשֶׁר עֲשִׂיתֶם עִם־הַמֵּתִים וְעִמָּדִי׃ [9] יִתֵּן יהוה לָכֶם
מְצֶאנָה מְנוּחָה אִשָּׁה בֵּית אִישָׁהּ וַתִּשַּׁק לָהֶן וַתִּשֶּׂאנָה קוֹלָן וַתִּבְכֶּינָה׃
[10] וַתֹּאמַרְנָה־לָּהּ כִּי־אִתָּךְ נָשׁוּב לְעַמֵּךְ׃

12

QAMETS HATUPH

In this chapter, we shall learn how to distinguish between *qamets* and *qamets-hatuph*. As we have learned:

qamets is a long *a*-vowel	written ָ	and transliterated ā
qamets-hatuph is a short *o*-vowel	also written ָ	but transliterated o

These are pronounced *kah-mets* and *kah-mets ha-toof*. They were first introduced in §4.3.2, where we learned that a single vowel point was used for these two different vowels. Until now, we have seen only *qamets* in the exercises. Now we shall start to work with *qamets-hatuph* also. This will now be easy, since you have learned about open and closed syllables, as well as accents. For instance, you already know that

- *qamets* is a long vowel, and *qamets-hatuph* is a short vowel, and
- closed unaccented syllables have a short vowels (Syllable Rule 3, §7.2, p. 18).

Therefore, the rule for *qamets* and *qamets-hatuph* is:

12.1 **The vowel point ָ is usually *qamets* (ā), BUT in closed unaccented syllables it is *qamets-hatuph* (o).**

Example: שָׁמַר has a *qamets* (šā-mar), since the first syllable (-שָׁ) is open; but כָּל־אִישׁ has a *qamets-hatuph* (kol-ʾîš) since the first syllable (־כָּל) is both closed and unaccented.[1]

There is one situation in which this could become unclear. A word such as חָכְמָה is ambiguous[2], since it could be either

ḥok̲-mâʹ — if we consider the first syllable to be -חָכְ. In this case, the first syllable is closed and unaccented,[3] and thus the vowel must be *qamets-hatuph*.

or

ḥā-k̲ᵉmâʹ — if we consider the first syllable to be -חָ. In this case, the first syllable is *open*. Thus, according to our rule above, the vowel would be a plain *qamets*.[4]

When this happens, then look for a *metheg*. If there is a *metheg* next to the *qamets*, you know that it is

---

[1] Remember, words which lie before (to the right of) a *maqqeph* lose their accent (§10.1, p. 29).

[2] ▲"Ambiguous" means that the information we have is confusing or unclear, and can have more than one possible meaning.

[3] The accent is on the last syllable, as usual. This is always the case in this textbook unless an accent mark appears over another syllable.

[4] Why is the *shewa* vocal in this case? Answer: Because it comes after a long vowel (*qamets*) (see §8.1.2, p. 22). However, if the word is ḥok̲-mâ, then the *shewa* comes after a short vowel (*qamets-hatuph*) and is then silent.

qamets and not *qamets-hatuph*. Thus:

12.2 If a syllable is ambiguous (that is, if it is not clear whether it is open or closed), then a *metheg* will usually appear if the syllable is open.[5]

Thus, חָכְמָה is ḥok-mâ′ but חָֽכְמָה is ḥā-kᵉmâ′.

Now study carefully four other examples given below:

כָּל־עֵשֶׂב We studied this example in §10 (p. 29). The word כָּל has lost its accent because of the *maqqeph*. It is thus a closed unaccented syllable. Our rule tells us that the ָ must therefore be a *qamets-hatuph*, and therefore כָּל־ is transliterated kol.

וַיָּ֫קָם The accent is on the next to last syllable. Thus, the syllable -יָּ֫- is neither closed nor unaccented, and so its ָ is not a *qamets-hatuph*. It is a *qamets*, and we transliterate -yā-. The second ָ is found in the syllable קָם-, which is both closed and unaccented. Thus, this second ָ is a *qamets-hatuph*, and we transliterate the syllable -qom. The word is transliterated way-yā′-qom.

חָנֵּנִי Look at the *d.f.*[6] in the first נ. This means that the נ is doubled (§11.1.2, p. 31). Therefore, what we have is the same as חָנְנֵנִי, where the *shewa* is silent.[7] Thus, the ָ is in a closed and unaccented syllable and is a *qamets-hatuph*. The word is transliterated: ḥon-nē-nî.

לָ֫מָּה This time, the *dagesh* gives us לָ֫מְמָה. Again, the first syllable is closed, but this time it is an accented syllable. Since *qamets-hatuph* appears in closed *unaccented* syllables, the vowel under the ל must be a *qamets*. The word is transliterated lām′-mâ.

Things You Should Know

1. The vowel point ָ is used to represent both long ā (*qamets*) and short o (*qamets-hatuph*).
2. *Qamets* is **much** more common than *qamets-hatuph*.
3. In a closed unaccented syllable, the vowel ָ will be *qamets-hatuph*. When ָ appears in an open syllable or in an accented syllable or with a *metheg*, it will usually be a *qamets*.

[5] **Technical note:** There are always exceptions, of course. For instance, in Gen 45:10 (*BHS*) we find בְּקָרְךָ, which should read בְּקָֽרְךָ (bᵉqā-rᵉḵā). And Ruth 1:7 should have הָֽיְתָה instead of הָיְתָה. In this second case, the lack of a *dagesh* in the ת shows that the preceding *shewa* is vocal and thus the first ָ is a long vowel. This happens most often in common words which the reader is expected to know well.

[6] How do we know that it is a *d.f.*? There are two reasons: (1) נ is not a BEGADKEPAT letter, and *d.l.* appears only in BEGADKEPAT letters (§11.1.1, p. 31), and (2) there is a vowel before the *dagesh* (§11.1.3).

[7] When a non-BEGADKEPAT letter with vowel point is doubled (for instance, מֵּ), the vowel is placed under the second (left) letter (מֵּ > מְמֵ). The first letter then takes a silent *shewa*: מֵּ = מְמֵ. (If the doubled letter is already over a *shewa* (מְּ), the result will be a double *shewa*: מְּ = מְמְ, as we saw in §8.1.4.)

Exercise #10

1. Transliterate the following words:

   a. קָטַל הָקְטַל וְאָֽמְרוּ אַבְרָהָם מְלָכִים הַפָּלִיט מִצְרַ֫יְמָה אֲכָלָֽתְהוּ לֵבָב

   b. בְּכָל־אֶ֫רֶץ בְּרָכָה יָקְטְלוּ מִגְרָשׁ מָתְנַ֫יִם הַדָּבָר אָכְלָה הַמָּקוֹם שָֽׁמְרָה

2. At the end of the next chapter, we shall begin translating. In preparation, learn the following words. (Other words will be added at the beginning of the next exercise.)

אִישׁ a man, husband	אִשָּׁה a woman, wife	אֶל to, toward	אֵל God, a god
בַּ֫יִת a house	בְּרָכָה a blessing	מֶ֫לֶךְ a king	מִן from
נָתַן he gave	נָתְנָה she gave	רָאָה he saw	שָׂרָה Sarah

Vocabulary Cards

At this point, you should start using vocabulary cards. A set of vocabulary cards has been produced which goes along with this text book. If you have this set, skip the next section ("Making the cards") and read the section "Using the Cards," below. If you do not have this set of cards, then use the following directions for making them.

Making the cards: Cut pieces of paper which are approximately 4 cm by 6 cm (or 1½ inches by 2½ inches). Put the Hebrew word on one side, and the English on the other:

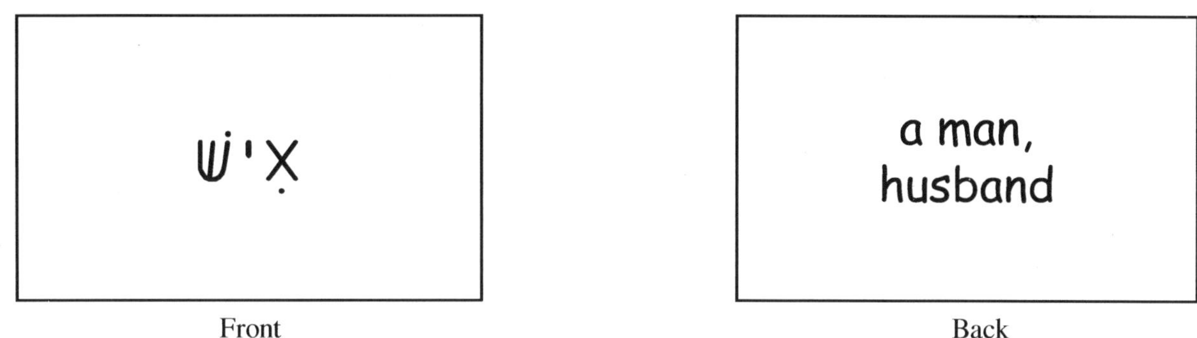

Front Back

Make a separate card for each word. Do not try to save time or paper by putting several words on a single card, because you will need to separate and sort the cards as you learn.

Using the cards: (If you are using the printed cards, ignore *Ni, Pi, Hi,* etc., at this time. They will be explained later.) Read the Hebrew side of the card, try to remember what it means, and then look at the back of the card to see if you were correct. If you were wrong, put the card in a separate pile. When you are finished, put away the large pile of cards. Put the smaller pile of cards (words which you do not know) into your pocket. Study them throughout the day when you have some free time.

Repeat this process every day. Eventually, you will have many words which you know very well. You can put those cards away and look at them only once each month.

13

THE GUTTURALS

Four letters are called ▲"gutturals," because they are made with the throat: א ה ח and ע. As we have already seen, these letters have special rules:

13.1 Composite *shewa.* Gutturals at the beginning of a word cannot stand over a *simple vocal shewa*. They must stand over either another vowel point or a composite *shewa* (§8.2.2, p. 24).

13.2 Rejection of *dagesh.* Gutturals and the letter ר cannot take a *dagesh* (§11.1.2, p. 31).

In addition, there are two other characteristics of gutturals:

13.3 Preference for pathah. Gutturals like to have *pathahs* near them. Thus, they will often "attract" them. That is, the vowel under or just before a guttural will often change to a *pathah*.

Example: The normal pattern for verbs is: three letters with a *qamets* under the first letter and a *pathah* under the second. For instance, שָׁמַר. The verb שָׁלַח is similar *except* that its last letter is a guttural. We have not yet learned the various forms of the Hebrew verb. But note the differences when these two verbs are put into the Imperfect form:

Normal verb: שָׁמַר	Normal imperfect: יִשְׁמֹר
Final guttural verb: שָׁלַח	Final guttural imperfect: יִשְׁלַח (not יִשְׁלֹח)

The Imperfect usually has a *holem* between the middle and last letter, but with יִשְׁלַח the final guttural attracts a *pathah* before it (under the ל), and the *holem* disappears.

13.4 Furtive *pathah*. Furtive means sneaky or devious, and the furtive *pathah* is indeed sneaky: it appears under a final guttural, but it is pronounced ***before*** the guttural, not after it.[1]

Example: the word רוּחַ (*spirit, wind*). It is transliterated rû-aḥ (not rû-ḥa), and is pronounced RU-aḥ (not RU-ḥa).

Things You Should Know

1. Gutturals at the beginning of a word cannot stand over a simple vocal *shewa*. They will stand over either a composite *shewa* or a vowel point other than *shewa*.
2. Gutturals (and the letter ר) cannot take *dagesh*.
3. Gutturals prefer to have *pathahs* near or under them and so may attract them.
4. Furtive *pathah* is a *pathah* which appears under a final guttural and is pronounced before it.

[1] Thus, we have what *sounds* like a syllable which starts with a vowel!

Exercise #11

אַבְרָהָם Abraham	גַּן a garden (*in pause*[2] גָּֽן, גָּ֑ן)	הָלְכָה she walked, went
-בְּ[3] in, at, with, by	-וְ[3] and, but	-לְ[3] to, for
בָּרָא he created	הָלַךְ he walked, went	עִיר a city

Be sure to make vocabulary cards for these words if you do not already have them.

Translation exercise: Use the vocabulary from this chapter and the previous one to **translate** the sentences below. You do not need to transliterate them.

Important note: In Hebrew, the subject usually comes immediately *after* the verb. Thus, the phrase רָאָה מֶ֫לֶךְ is translated: *A king saw* (not *He saw a king*).

[1] הָלְכָה אִשָּׁה׃ [2] הָלְכָה אִשָּׁה אֶל עִיר׃ [3] רָאָה אִישׁ׃ [4] רָאָה אִישׁ בַּיִת׃
[5] נָתַן מֶ֫לֶךְ בְּרָכָה׃ [6] נָתַן מֶ֫לֶךְ בְּרָכָה לְאַבְרָהָם׃ [7] הָלַךְ אִישׁ מִן בַּ֫יִת אֶל עִיר׃
[8] רָאָה אֵל מֶ֫לֶךְ וְגָן׃ [9] נָתְנָה שָׂרָה בַּ֫יִת לְאַבְרָהָם׃ [10] בָּרָא אֵל גָּן׃ [11] הָלַךְ
אֵל בְּגָן׃ [12] בָּרָא אֵל אִישׁ וְאִשָּׁה׃ [13] נָתַן אֵל בַּ֫יִת וְגַן לְאִשָּׁה׃ [14] הָלְכָה שָׂרָה
מִן בַּ֫יִת אֶל גָּן׃ [15] רָאָה מֶ֫לֶךְ בַּ֫יִת בְּעִיר׃ [16] נָתְנָה שָׂרָה בְּרָכָה לְמֶ֫לֶךְ בְּגָן׃
[17] בְּעִיר הָלַךְ אַבְרָהָם מִן גַּן אֶל בַּ֫יִת׃

[2] See p. 20 for the meaning of "in pause."

[3] The hyphen (-) shows that these single-letter words attach directly to the beginning of the next word. For instance, using the word עִיר (*city*) we can write: בְּעִיר *in a city*, וְעִיר *and a city*, לְעִיר *to a city.*

14

THE DEFINITE ARTICLE AND Hē INTERROGATIVE

The letter ה is used to represent the definite article (the word *the*). It is also used as the "question mark" (the "?" sign). In this chapter, we shall learn both of these uses, and how they differ.

14.1 The Definite Article.

Words with *the* in front of them are "definite": *the* book, *the* woman, *the* house, etc. We know that the speaker or writer means a *certain* book, woman, or house. On the other hand, words with *a* or *an* are "indefinite." If someone mentions *a* book, *a* woman, *a* house, we do not know which of these objects the speaker or writer means. Hebrew also has a definite article (*the*), but it has no indefinite article (*a* or *an*).

14.1.1 How the definite article is used in Hebrew. In Hebrew, the definite article is the letter ה, with a *pathah* under it and a *dagesh* after it (·הַ). It is attached to the beginning of a word, and the *dagesh* is then placed in the first letter of the word. For instance:

מֶ֫לֶךְ means ***a** king* (Remember, there is no indefinite article in Hebrew.)

But if we add the definite article, then:

מֶ֫לֶךְ *a king* + ·הַ → הַמֶּ֫לֶךְ ***the** king*

Note that the מ has gained a *dagesh.*

14.1.2 If the first letter of the word already has *dagesh lene*, this *dagesh lene* becomes *dagesh forte* (see p. 32, note 3) and the letter is doubled. For instance:

בַּ֫יִת = ba-yit̲ but בַּ֫יִת + ·הַ → הַבַּ֫יִת = hab-ba-yit̲

14.2 Hē Interrogative.

14.2.1 How Hē Interrogative is used. In English and many other languages, a question is formed by putting a "question mark" (the "?" sign) at the end of the sentence. In Hebrew, the letter -הֲ (no *dagesh* after it) is placed at the very *beginning* of the question, in front of the first word. Note the *hateph pathah.* This prefixed -הֲ is called *hē interrogative*, which means "*hē* question mark."

For example, using the verb יָדַע, *he knew*, we can write:

יָדַע הַמֶּ֫לֶךְ	*The king knew.*
הֲיָדַע הַמֶּ֫לֶךְ	*Did the king know?*
לֹא יָדַע הַמֶּ֫לֶךְ	*The king did not know.*
הֲלֹא יָדַע הַמֶּ֫לֶךְ	*Didn't the king know?*

14.2.2 Its form. Hē interrogative is different from the definite article because:

(1) it uses *hateph pathah* rather than *pathah*
(2) it has no *dagesh* after it, and
(3) it comes *only* as a prefix to the first word of a question.

The question is often at the beginning of a verse or sentence, but it may also be inside the verse or sentence. For instance, in Gen 43:27 Joseph is speaking to his brothers: *And he asked them . . . 'Is your father well?'*:

וַיִּשְׁאַל	לָהֶם	...	הֲשָׁלוֹם	אֲבִיכֶם...
And-he-asked	*them*	...	*(Is he) well?*	*your-father*

Here, the *hē* interrogative does not appear at the beginning of the verse. Rather, it is found before the word שָׁלוֹם which is the first word of the speaker's question (but not the first word of the sentence).

14.3 The Definite Article and Hē Interrogative before Gutturals, ר or *Shewa*.

If a definite article or a *hē* interrogative are placed before a word which begins with

- a guttural,
- a letter with a simple *shewa*, or
- the letter ר

then there may be vowel point changes:

- The definite article will become -הַ (no *dagesh*), -הָ or -הֶ.
- *Hē* interrogative will become -הַ or -הֶ.

The rules are complex, and you do not need to learn them. (The large Technical Note, which begins on the next page, explains them.) But see the examples below so you will know what to expect:

Examples with definite article:

אָדָם + הַ· → הָאָדָם   חָלָב + הַ· → הֶחָלָב   חֵלֶב + הַ· → הַחֵלֶב

Examples with hē *interrogative:*

עָבַד + הֲ- → הֶעָבַד   אֶשְׁמֹר + הֲ- → הַאֶשְׁמֹר   שְׁמוֹ + הֲ- → הַשְׁמוֹ

Yes, there will be cases in which the definite article and *hē* interrogative may look the same. The ▲context[1] will tell you how to translate. Remember: The definite article appears only on nouns; *hē* interrogative will appear only before the first word of a question.

---

[1] The **▲context** is the surrounding verses or story; it is "what is happening." We often need to know the context in order to translate properly. For instance, if I say "Bring me my glasses," you need to know whether I want to read or to drink. The context is the situation; it is what is happening around the word or text.

Technical note: Gutturals, ר and simple *shewa*

You do not need to read this section unless you are interested. From here to the end of the chapter are the detailed rules concerning the pointing of the definite article and *hē* interrogative after gutturals, ר and simple *shewa*. This material will not appear on tests, and you will be able to read Hebrew without learning it.

14.3.1 The Definite Article before Gutturals and ר. When a definite article is placed before a word like מֶ֫לֶךְ we get הַמֶּ֫לֶךְ. The *dagesh* in the מ is part of the definite article. Gutturals and ר will reject this *dagesh* (§13.2, p. 38), and this will cause some changes of vowel pointing. For instance, if the first letter of the word is א, the *pathah* under the definite article will lengthen to *qamets*:

אָדָם *a man* + הַ· → הָֽאָדָם ***the** man* (the *metheg* does not always appear)

Words which begin with gutturals will use הָ הֶ or הַ (with no *dagesh* after them) for their definite article, and will follow the pattern in the two tables below.

The tables below show what form the definite article takes in front of various gutturals. Note that ע✢ means a word beginning with the letter ע and any vowel *except qamets*. That is, ע✢ means words beginning with -עַ, -עֶ, -עֵ, etc. but not -עָ. The same is true for ה✢ and ח✢. They stand for words beginning with ה or ח over any vowel *except qamets*.

Table I

Non-guttural	א ע✢ ר	חָ	ה✢ ח✢
הַ·-	הָ-	הֶ-	הַ-

Table II

	הָ עָ
Accented	הָ-
Unaccented	הֶ-

Table I shows us that:

- A word with a non-guttural first letter such as מֶ֫לֶךְ will use הַ· for its definite article (d.a.).
- Words which start with א, ר or ע without *qamets* (such as אָדָם, עֵ֫זֶר or רֶ֫גֶל), will all use -הָ for their d.a.: הָאָדָם, הָעֵ֫זֶר, and הָרֶ֫גֶל.
- A word like חָלָב, with a *qamets* under its ח, will use -הֶ for its d.a. (הֶחָלָב)
- But חֵ֫לֶב (which does not have *qamets* under the ח) will use הַ for its d.a. (thus, הַחֵ֫לֶב).

Table II shows us that words beginning with either -עָ or -הָ will use -הָ for d.a. if the first syllable of the word (the -עָ or the -הָ) is accented. If this first syllable is *un*accented, then the word will use -הֶ.

> *Example:* עָב means *cloud.* הָעָב means ***the** cloud.* Since עָב is accented[2], it uses -הָ for a definite article. But in the plural, עָבִים *clouds,* the accent moved away from -עָ to the last syllable, בִים-. The syllable -עָ is now unaccented, and so it takes -הֶ for a definite article: הֶעָבִים.

14.3.2 *Hē* Interrogative before gutturals or simple *shewa*. *Hē interrogative* also follows certain rules

---

[2] Remember that *all* words (if they are not in construct) have accents. This includes single syllable words.

when it appears before gutturals or simple *shewa*:

Before Non-gutturals and ר	Before simple *shewa* or guttural without *qamets*	Before guttural with *qamets*
-הֲ	-הַ	-הֶ

There will be times when the *hē interrogative* will have the same vowel pointing as a definite article (especially before words beginning with ה and ח). The context will usually tell you which one it is. And remember: the *hē interrogative* appears *only* before the first word of a question. This question, and its *hē interrogative*, may be at the beginning of a verse, or it may start later in the verse.

(End of Technical Note)

Things You Should Know

1. The Hebrew definite article (the word "the") is the letter ה, with a *pathah* under it and a *dagesh* after it (·הַ). It is prefixed to the word. Example: מֶלֶךְ + ·הַ ➔ הַמֶּלֶךְ.
2. The Hebrew question mark ("?") is also a prefixed letter ה. But:
   a. it is pointed with a *hateph pathah* (-הֲ) and has no *dagesh* after it.
   b. it comes only before the first word of a question.
3. Both the definite article and *hē interrogative* are pointed differently when they come before gutturals. The definite article is also pointed differently before ר; and *hē* interrogative is pointed differently before simple *shewa*.

15

INTRODUCTION TO DEFINITE DIRECT OBJECTS

The "direct object" of a sentence is the word which receives the action. (If necessary, review "Grammar: An Overview," pp. xvii-xviii). In the sentence *the boy chased a cow,* the subject is *the boy,* the verb is *chased,* and the direct object is *a cow.*

In Hebrew, if the direct object is definite (*the cow* rather than *a cow*), it will have not only a definite article (·הַ) but also the little word אֶת־. (Sometimes it is just אֵת with a *tsere* and no *maqqeph*. But this is less common.). For instance, in Exercise 11 sentence 5, we read:

נָתַן מֶ֫לֶךְ בְּרָכָה׃ *a king gave a blessing*

The subject is *a king,* and the direct object is *a blessing.*

On the other hand, if we want to say ***the** king gave **the** blessing* there will be three changes:

נָתַן הַמֶּ֫לֶךְ אֶת־הַבְּרָכָה׃ *the king gave the blessing*

- The word מֶ֫לֶךְ is the subject, of course, and it now has a definite article.
- The word בְּרָכָה, which is the direct object, has gained a definite article, too. But:
- It has also gained the little word אֶת־.

This אֶת־ is a very helpful little word. It tells you that the next word is the direct object and that it is definite (that is, ***the** blessing,* not just ***a** blessing*). The אֶת־ is not translated, and you will learn more about this in §26.

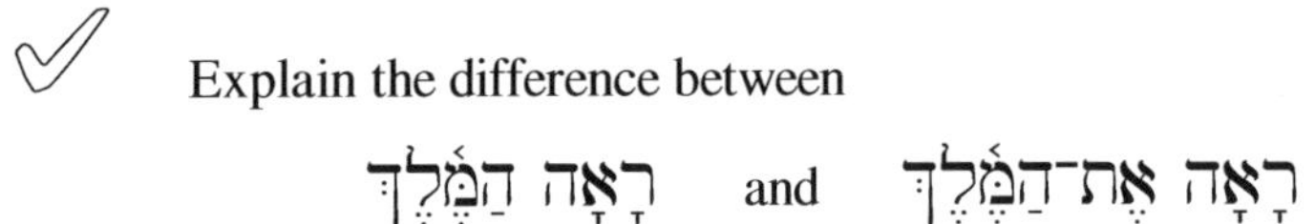

Explain the difference between

רָאָה הַמֶּ֫לֶךְ and רָאָה אֶת־הַמֶּ֫לֶךְ

רָאָה הַמֶּ֫לֶךְ means "the king saw." (Remember that the subject is usually found *after* the verb.) But in the sentence רָאָה אֶת־הַמֶּ֫לֶךְ, the word הַמֶּ֫לֶךְ is preceded by אֶת־. This אֶת־ shows us that הַמֶּ֫לֶךְ is the *definite direct object*, not the subject. It *receives* the action. Thus, we must translate "he saw the king." Who is "he"? We do not know. The sentence does not tell us. It could be any male person. But it is not the king.

With names (Sarah, Abraham, etc.) there will not be a definite article, but the אֶת־ will still appear. For instance:

רָאָה הַמֶּ֫לֶךְ אֶת־שָׂרָה *the king saw Sarah.*

Things You Should Know

1. The little word אֶת־ (or אֵת with no *maqqeph*) appears with the definite article in front of the direct object of the sentence if the direct object is definite:

   נָתַן מֶ֫לֶךְ אֶת־הַבְּרָכָה *a king gave the blessing*

2. Names of people do not take definite articles. If the name is used as a direct object, however, the אֶת־ will still be seen:

   רָאָה מֶ֫לֶךְ אֶת־שָׂרָה *a king saw Sarah*

3. More will be learned about this in §26.

Exercise #12

- אֱלֹהִים God, gods
- אָמַר he said
- אָנֹכִי, אֲנִי I
- הָיָה he/it was, became, happened
- יְהוָה the Lord (see p. 21, note 6)
- יִשְׂרָאֵל Israel
- כִּי because, that, when
- מִצְרַ֫יִם Egypt, Egyptians
- מֹשֶׁה Moses
- עֵץ tree, wood
- פְּרִי fruit
- פַּרְעֹה Pharaoh
- שָׁלַח he sent

[1] הָיָה יִשְׂרָאֵל בְּמִצְרָיִם׃ [2] נָתַן אֱלֹהִים בְּרָכָה לְמֹשֶׁה׃ [3] אָמַר אֱלֹהִים לְמֹשֶׁה
אָנֹכִי [2] יְהוָה׃ [4] רָאָה יְהוָה אֶת־יִשְׂרָאֵל[1]׃ [5] שָׁלַח אֱלֹהִים אֶת־מֹשֶׁה אֶל מִצְרָיִם׃
[6] שָׁלַח יְהוָה אֶת־מֹשֶׁה אֶל פַּרְעֹה כִּי רָאָה אֶת־יִשְׂרָאֵל בְּמִצְרָיִם׃ [7] בָּרָא אֵל עֵץ
בְּגָן׃ [8] רָאָה הָאִישׁ פְּרִי בְּעֵץ׃ [9] הֲנָתַן אִישׁ אֶת־הַפְּרִי לְאִשָּׁה׃ [10] הָלַךְ אַבְרָהָם
מִן הָעִיר אֶל הַבַּיִת כִּי נָתְנָה שָׂרָה פְּרִי לְאִשָּׁה׃ [11] הֶהָיָה פַּרְעֹה מֶלֶךְ בְּמִצְרָיִם׃
[12] הֶאָמַר מֹשֶׁה לַיהוָה[4] כִּי פַּרְעֹה [3] בְּגָן׃ [13] הֲבְמִצְרַ֫יִם נָתַן יְהוָה אֶת־יִשְׂרָאֵל
לְפַרְעֹה׃

---

[1] Names of nations and people are always definite. They therefore do not need the definite article (-ה). But when they are used as objects, they will have an אֶת־. Again, this makes it easier to tell the subject from the object.

[2] Hebrew often omits the verb "to be." We must add it in translation. (Use <brackets> for words which you add.) Here you should translate "... I <am> Yahweh," or "... I <am> the Lord."

[3] Add the word *is* or *was*.

[4] This odd vowel pointing reminds the reader say *Adonai* instead of the divine name. See p. 21, note 6.

16

PREPOSITIONS

Prepositions are words which show relationships such as *to, from, in, with, by,* etc. You have already learned several of them in earlier chapters. In Hebrew, four prepositions are different because of the way they join the word which comes after them. The first of these prepositions is the word מִן (*from*).

16.1 The Preposition מִן (*from*)

The preposition מִן can stand by itself in front of a word (מִן שָׂרָה = *from Sarah*). But it may also join the word which follows it. When it does, then certain rules are followed. These rules depend upon the first letter of the following word:

16.1.1 **Usually,** the *nun* of the מִן is "swallowed"[1] by the first letter of the following word. This "swallowed" *nun* is then represented by a *dagesh* which ▲"compensates" (pays) for the *nun.*

מִן שָׂרָה ➜ מִנְשָׂרָה ➜ מִשָּׂרָה = miś-śā-râ

Note the *dagesh* in the שּׂ. This *dagesh* represents the "swallowed" *nun.*[2] If the first letter of the word is a *begadkepat* with *d.l.* (which hardens), this *d.l.* becomes *d.f.* (which hardens and then also doubles the letter):

מִן בָּבֶל ➜ מִבָּבֶל = mib-bā-ḇel

16.1.2 **Before words starting with gutturals or ר**, such as אָדָם or רָחֵל (*Rachel*): Gutturals and ר cannot take *dagesh* (§13.2). Therefore, although the *nun* is "swallowed," the guttural rejects the *dagesh.* In "compensation" for this rejection, **the *hireq* under the מ is lengthened** and becomes a *tsere*[3]:

מִן אָדָם ➜ מִנְאָדָם ➜ מִאָּדָם ➜ מֵֽאָדָם[4] = mē-ʾā-ḏām

מִן רָחֵל ➜ מִנְרָחֵל ➜ מִרָּחֵל ➜ מֵרָחֵל = mē-rā-ḥēl

The same is true before a definite article, since the definite article is also a guttural:

---

[1] The technical word is "assimilated."

[2] **Technical note:** In general, if a נ with a *shewa* ends up in the middle of a word, the נ will be assimilated ("swallowed") by the next letter. This is often for reasons of euphony (good sound). That is, it is simply easier to say the word *wthout* the נ. Try to say *min-sepher* or *min-melek* several times quickly, and you will see how your lips and tongue want to say *mis-sepher* or *mim-melek* instead.

[3] Here is an easy way to learn this: Think of the rejected *dagesh* returning to the מ and standing beside the *hireq* and thus turning the *hireq* into a *tsere.* **Technical note:** Actually what is happening is this: when the *dagesh* is rejected, this leaves -מִ standing as an open syllable. Open syllables prefer long vowels, and so the *hireq* lengthens to a *tsere.*

[4] The *metheg* is added for pronunciation only. It is not the result of the "swallowing" of the *nun* or the lengthening of the *hireq* into *tsere.*

מִן הַמֶּלֶךְ → מִנְהַמֶּלֶךְ → מִהַמֶּלֶךְ → מֵהַמֶּלֶךְ

This leads to a general rule:

When a *dagesh* is rejected by a guttural or the letter ר,
the vowel which stands before the rejecting letter often lengthens.

16.2 The Inseparable Prepositions

Three of the Hebrew prepositions *must* be connected to the word which follows them. They are:

-בְּ = in, at, with, by

-כְּ = as, like, according to

-לְ = to, for

16.2.1 **Normally,** these prepositions, with their vocal *shewas*, simply attach to the following word:

מֶלֶךְ + בְּ → בְּמֶלֶךְ

מֶלֶךְ + כְּ → כְּמֶלֶךְ

מֶלֶךְ + לְ → לְמֶלֶךְ

16.2.2 **If the word begins with a *dagesh lene*,** the *dagesh lene* will disappear, since a vowel or a vocal *shewa* cannot appear before it (see §11.1.4, p. 32, above):

בָּבֶל + לְ → לְבָבֶל

16.2.3 **If the word begins with a *shewa*,** vowel pointing changes will occur (review §9.1, p. 26):

16.2.3.1 **If the first letter of the word is** -יְ, then the *shewa* under the preposition becomes *hireq* and the *shewa* under the י disappears:

יְהוּדָה + בְּ → בִּיהוּדָה

יְהוּדָה + כְּ → כִּיהוּדָה

יְהוּדָה + לְ → לִיהוּדָה

16.2.3.2 **If the first letter is not** י **and has a *simple shewa*,** then the *shewa* under the preposition becomes *hireq* (§9.1.1, p. 26):

שְׁכֶם + לְ → לְשְׁכֶם → לִשְׁכֶם

In this case, the *shewa* will remain vocal, even though the vowel before it is short. (This has already been mentioned in the Note in §9.1.1, p. 26.)

16.2.3.3 **If the first letter is a guttural with *composite shewa*** (example: חֲלוֹם), then the *shewa* under the preposition becomes the "corresponding short vowel" (§9.1.2, p. 26):

חֲלוֹם + כְּ → כְּחֲלוֹם → כַּחֲלוֹם

The name אֱלֹהִים with prepositions behaves in an unusual way: the א loses its vowel point completely. This will be discussed in the next chapter:

אֱלֹהִים + לְ → לֵאלֹהִים (lēʾ-lō-hîm, pronounced lē-lō-hîm)

16.2.4 **Before a definite article:** If the preposition joins a word with a definite article (for instance, הַמֶּ֫לֶךְ), then the preposition replaces the ה of the article. That is, the ה disappears but its vowel and *dagesh* remain. Study the following comparison of words with and without definite articles:

מֶ֫לֶךְ + בְּ → בְּמֶ֫לֶךְ but הַמֶּ֫לֶךְ + בְּ → בַּמֶּ֫לֶךְ

אֱלֹהִים + לְ → לֶאֱלֹהִים but הָאֱלֹהִים + לְ → לָאֱלֹהִים

In the examples on the right, the vowel which was originally under the ה remains, and is now under the inseparable preposition. Study this difference very carefully. Only the vowel point and *dagesh* mark the difference between *by **a** king* (בְּמֶ֫לֶךְ) and *by **the** king* (בַּמֶּ֫לֶךְ).

But remember that with מִן, the ה of the definite article remains (see §16.1.2, above).

16.2.5 **Before an accented syllable**, the inseparable preposition *may* take a *qamets*:

מַ֫יִם +לְ → לָמַ֫יִם

(Note that this only *may* happen. It does not happen with the word מֶ֫לֶךְ: מֶ֫לֶךְ + לְ → לְמֶ֫לֶךְ)

Things You Should Know

1. **The preposition** מִן ***(from)*** can either stand alone or be joined to the following word. When it joins the following word:
   a. The *nun* is "swallowed" by the first letter of the word, and that letter gains a *dagesh* : מִמֹּשֶׁה.
   b. If the first letter is a guttural or ר, the *dagesh* is rejected, and the *hireq* under the מ lengthens to a *tsere*: מֵרָחֵל. This is also true for the definite article: מֵהַמֶּ֫לֶךְ.

   General rule: When a *dagesh* is rejected by a guttural or the letter ר, the vowel which stands before the rejecting letter is often lengthened.

2. **The three "inseparable" prepositions** are -בְּ (*in, at, with, by*), -כְּ (*as, like, according to*) and -לְ (*to, for*). They *must* be joined to the word which follows.
   a. Normally, they attach without any changes: בְּמֶ֫לֶךְ .
   b. Before a simple *shewa*, the *shewa* under the preposition becomes *hireq*: לִשְׁכֶם .
   c. Before -יְ, however, the *shewa* under the preposition becomes *hireq* and the *shewa* under the י disappears. This creates a *hireq-yod*: לִיהוּדָה .
   d. Before composite *shewa*, the preposition takes a corresponding short vowel: כַּחֲלוֹם .
   e. Before a definite article, the preposition replaces the ה. The *pathah* from under the ה and the *dagesh* both remain: בַּמֶּ֫לֶךְ . (But with מִן the ה will remain: מֵהַמֶּ֫לֶךְ.)
   f. Before an accented syllable, the preposition *may* take a *qamets*: לָמַ֫יִם .

17

SILENT (QUIESCENT) LETTERS

"Silent letters" are letters which are written and transliterated but they are not pronounced. Other textbooks call them ▲"quiescent" letters. This happens most often with א. It is never pronounced at the end of a word: לֹא is simply pronounced lō although it is transliterated lōʾ.

> **Note**: The final א is so silent that words like לֹא are treated as if they end with a vowel. This will cause the *d.l.* in a following BEGADKEPAT word to disappear (§11.1.4, p. 32). We will therefore see לֹא תִשְׁמְעוּ (Gen 34:17) not לֹא תִּשְׁמְעוּ. And we will see לֹא תָמוּתוּ (Gen. 42.20) not לֹא תָּמוּתוּ.[1]

Sometimes א stands without a vowel in the middle of a word and is silent. For instance, consider the word יֹאמַר (*he will say*). The א has no vowel or *shewa*. It has quiesced (become silent), and the word is pronounced yō-mer. However, it is still transliterated yōʾ-mer (note the ʾ).

Sometimes, the letters י and ו can change from being consonants to vowel letters. This can happen when inseperable prepositions are added before words like יְהוּדָה (*Judah*), or תָּוֶךְ (*midst, middle*):

consonant ☟ יְהוּדָה (*Judah*) + לְ (*to*) → לְיְהוּדָה → לִיְהוּדָה → *vowel letter* ☟ לִיהוּדָה[2] (lî-hû-d̲â) (*to Judah*)

consonant ☟ תָּוֶךְ (*midst*) + בְּ (*in*) → *vowel letter* ☟ בְּתוֹךְ (bᵉ tôk̲) (*in (the) midst*)

Technically, the י and ו are then silent, and we hear only the vowel points which come before them.

Things You Should Know

1. When the letter א stands without a vowel, it is silent (quiescent) and is not pronounced. You pronounce the word as if the א were not there. It must be transliterated, however.
2. The letters י and ו may sometimes change from consonants to vowel letters. This will happen especially when prepositions are added at the beginning of words.

---

[1] **Technical note:** Ironically, the Ten Commandments transgress the "laws" of Hebrew! In both Exodus 20 and Deuteronomy 5 we find לֹא תִּרְצָח׃ לֹא תִּנְאָף׃ לֹא תִּגְנֹב׃

[2] **Review:** In this case, the י was originally above a vocal *shewa* (§5), and thus it was pronounced (yᵉ). When the לְ was added, however, we ended up with a word which began with two *shewas* (לְיְהוּדָה) which is impossible (§9.1.1, p. 26). Thus, the first *shewa* changed to a *hireq* and joined with the י to produce a long *i* vowel (*hireq-yod* = î), which gives us: lî-hû-dâ. The former consonant י has quiesced into a vowel.

Exercise #13

אַהֲרוֹן	Aaron	יְהוּדָה	Judah	לָקַח	he took
אֲרוֹן	ark[3]	יְהוֹשֻׁעַ	Joshua	לָקְחוּ	they took
אֶרֶץ[4]	land, earth (world)	-כְּ[5]	according to, as, like	עַם	a people
בָּא	he entered, came, went	כְּנַעַן	Canaan	הָעָם	the people[6]

[1] בָּרָא אֱלֹהִים עֵץ בַּגָּן וְאֶת־הַפְּרִי בָּעֵץ׃ [2] רָאָה הָאִישׁ פְּרִי בָּעֵץ׃ [3] אָמַר הָאִישׁ
כִּי הַפְּרִי [8] מֵאֱלֹהִים׃ [4] נָתַן הָאִישׁ פְּרִי לָאִשָּׁה בַּגָּן׃[7] [5] שָׁלַח יְהוָה אֶת־הָאִישׁ וְאֶת־
הָאִשָּׁה מֵהַגָּן׃ [6] נָתַן אֱלֹהִים בְּרָכָה לִיהוּדָה׃ [7] הֲלָקַח הַמֶּלֶךְ בַּיִת מִן הָאִשָּׁה׃
[8] אָמַר פַּרְעֹה אָנֹכִי הַמֶּלֶךְ בְּמִצְרָיִם׃ [9] שָׁלַח אַבְרָהָם פְּרִי מֵהָאָרֶץ לִכְנָעַן׃ [10] מֹשֶׁה
[9] כֵּאלֹהִים לְפַרְעֹה׃ [11] הֲלָקְחוּ אַבְרָהָם וְשָׂרָה אֶת־הָאָרוֹן׃ [12] בָּא עַם־מִן־מִצְרַיִם
הָאָרֶץ[10]׃ [13] שָׁלַח אַהֲרוֹן אֲרוֹן אֶל עִיר בִּיהוּדָה׃ [14] אָמַר יְהוֹשֻׁעַ אֶל יְהוָה כִּי בָא
יִשְׂרָאֵל הָאָרֶץ׃ [15] הֲלָקַח מֹשֶׁה פְּרִי מֵהָעָם בְּיִשְׂרָאֵל׃ [16] לָקְחוּ מֹשֶׁה וְאַהֲרוֹן עַם
מִן מִצְרַיִם אֶל כְּנָעַן׃ [17] אָמַר מֹשֶׁה לְשָׂרָה הֲרָאָה אַבְרָהָם אֶת־יְהוֹשֻׁעַ בָּעִיר׃

---

[3] אֲרוֹן usually refers to the ark of the covenant (אֲרוֹן־בְּרִית, אֲרוֹן־יְהוָה, אֲרוֹן בְּרִית־יְהוָה, etc.). With the definite article, the א takes a *qamets*: הָאָרוֹן.

[4] With definite article: הָאָרֶץ.

[5] See page 39, note 3.

[6] When עַם receives a definite article, the *pathah* under the ע lengthens to a *qamets* (הָעָם). This also happens with other words, for instance גַּן (הַגָּן) and אֶרֶץ (above). (If you do not know why there is a *qamets* under the ה in הָעָם and הָאָרֶץ, review §14.3, p. 41).

[7] The sentences in the exercises will not always follow the story as it is in the Bible. This is to be sure that you are actually translating Hebrew, and not just remembering the story.

[8] Add the word *is.*

[9] Add the word *was.*

[10] בָּא . . . הָאָרֶץ׃ = *entered the land.* If the people came *to* the land, we would read בָּא . . . אֶל הָאָרֶץ׃.

18

THE CONJUNCTION

Conjunctions[1] are words such as *and* and *but.* In Hebrew, these words are represented by the letter ו prefixed to the word. This letter is called ▲"*vav* conjunction," and the context[2] of the sentence will tell you whether to translate the ו as *and* or *but.*

Vowel point rules: The following rules tell us what kind of vowel goes with the ו:

18.1 Usually the *vav* conjunction follows the **rules for inseparable prepositions** (§16.2, p. 47):

18.1.1 Before most letters, it uses a vocal *shewa* (-וְ):

שָׂרָה + וְ ➜ וְשָׂרָה = *and Sarah* or *but Sarah*

18.1.2 Before *yod-shewa* (-יְ) it becomes -וִי:

יְהוּדָה + וְ ➜ וִיהוּדָה = *and/but Judah*

18.1.3 Before a composite *shewa*, the ו takes the corresponding short vowel:

אֱדוֹם + וְ ➜ וֶאֱדוֹם = *and/but Edom*

18.1.4 But before אֱלֹהִים: אֱלֹהִים + וְ ➜ וֵאלֹהִים = *and/but God*

18.1.5 And before יהוה: יהוה + וְ ➜ וַיהוָה[3] = *and/but the* LORD

18.1.6 Before an accented syllable, the conjunction is often -וָ. This is especially true when the ו connects two words which go together, such as *day and night.* Thus:

יוֹם וָלַ֫יְלָה = day and night. (Note that -לַ֫יְ is an accented syllable.)

18.2 Before simple *shewa* and labials.[4] In these cases, the *vav* conjunction does not follow the rules for inseparable preposition. Instead, the conjunction becomes -וּ (û):

---

[1] Review the Grammar lesson, section 3.(6), p. xix, if necessary.

[2] P. 41, footnote 1.

[3] **Historical note:** This strange vowel pointing is based upon the vowels in וַאדֹנָי (wa-ʾădō-nāy), which means "and/but the Lord." See the Technical Note in footnote 6, p. 21. Today, both יְהוָה and אֲדֹנָי are found in the Hebrew Bible. Therefore, because of this history, modern English translations of the Bible usually translate the name יְהוָה as "the LORD" (note the small capital letters), and the word אֲדֹנָי as "the Lord."

[4] The ▲labials are letters made with the lips: פ פּ מ ב בּ.

before simple shewa:	שְׁכֶם + ו	➜	וּשְׁכֶם[5]	= *and/but Shechem*
before labials:	בַּ֫יִת + ו	➜	וּבַ֫יִת	= *and/but a house*
	מֹשֶׁה + ו	➜	וּמֹשֶׁה	= *and/but Moses*
	פֶּה + ו	➜	וּפֶה	= *and/but a mouth*

In this case, we have an exception to the rule which says that every Hebrew syllable or word must begin with a consonant.[6] When a *vav* conjunction is added before a simple *shewa* or labial, this produces a word which begins with a vowel (û).

And again, remember that a prefixed *vav* can stand for *but* as well as *and.* Thus:

שָׁמַע הָאִישׁ וְלֹא רָאָה = *The man heard* **but** *he did not see.*

Things You Should Know

1. The Hebrew conjunction (the words *and* or *but*) is a prefixed -וְ.
2. This "*vav* conjunction" usually takes vowels in the same way as the inseparable prepositions. Before *shewa* and labials (פ מ ב), however, the conjunction is -וּ.

[5] The remaining *shewa* will still be vocal, as it was with the inseparable prepositions (§8.3.1, p. 26). One reason is that it comes after a long vowel (§18.1.2(a), p. 22). In addition, if the *shewa* was silent in this example there would be a *dagesh* in the כ of וּשְׁכֶם (§11.1.4, p. 32).

[6] See Syllable rule 1 on p. 15, and also footnote 6 on that same page.

19

THE VERB: PERFECT

The Hebrew verb has only two "tenses," the Perfect and the Imperfect.[1] In general:

the **Perfect** usually represents **completed action**
the **Imperfect** usually represents **uncompleted action**

Usually (though not always), we can think of these two tenses as follows:

Perfect:	**past** action (like a past tense), and sometimes present action
Imperfect:	**future** action (like a future tense)

The root (simplest) form of the verb is the Perfect 3ms.[2] (If you do not understand the parsing indicators 3ms, 1cp, etc., review the section on parsing in "Grammar, an Overview," p. xx.) Example: שָׁמַר is Perf 3ms and means *he guarded, he watched, he kept.* The Hebrew verb develops in the Perfect by adding ▲suffixes[3] to this basic form:

he/it kept (3ms)	שָׁמַר	they kept (3cp)	שָֽׁמְרוּ
she/it kept (3fs)	שָֽׁמְרָה		
you kept (2ms)	שָׁמַ֫רְתָּ (šā-mar-tā)[4]	you kept (2mp)	שְׁמַרְתֶּם
you kept (2fs)	שָׁמַרְתְּ (šā-mart)[5]	you kept (2fp)	שְׁמַרְתֶּן
I kept (1cs)	שָׁמַ֫רְתִּי	we kept (1cp)	שָׁמַ֫רְנוּ

Note that **3cp is used for both masculine and feminine** subjects (just as in English).

Notes:

1. **Usage.** If someone is speaking to a group which contains both men and women, 2mp is used.
2. ***Methegs.*** The *methegs* in the 3fs and 3cp show that the first vowel is *qamets* and not *qamets-hatuph*. Thus, the 3fs is šā-mᵉrâ not šom-râ, and the 3cp is šā-mᵉrû not šom-rû.
3. **Accent.** The accent usually falls on the last syllable in Hebrew. But it falls on the next to the last (last but one) syllable in the 2ms, 1cs and 1cp.

---

[1] **Technical note:** Hebrew has several *moods*, however. The Perfect and Imperfect *tenses* may be considered to make up the Hebrew *indicative* mood. We will eventually learn four other moods: the Imperative, the Participle (active and passive), and two types of Infinitive.

[2] This is the form which will be found in the dictionary. In Greek, the simplest form of the verb is Present Active Indicative 1cs, for instance, λέγω. This is what one looks for in the dictionary or lexicon. In Hebrew, however, we will look for the Perfect 3ms when we use a dictionary, since it is the simplest form of the verb.

[3] A *suffix* is a letter or group of letters added to the end of a word. A *prefix* is a letter or group of letters added to the beginning of a word.

[4] The final *qamets* is pronounced after the תּ. Only the *furtive pathah* is pronounced before the consonant.

[5] The Perf 2fs is unusual. It has a *dagesh* in a final letter, and it has two silent *shewas* together.

4. **Gutturals.** In 2mp and 2fp, a guttural first letter will have a composite *shewa*. Example: אֲמַרְתֶּן.
5. **Parsing.** When parsing on a test, use the following patterns:

   Perf 3ms < שׁמר
   Perf 1cp < אמר
   ...and so on

   Thus, if you are told to parse לְקַחְתֶּם on a test, your answer will be: Perf 2mp < לקח
   This answer means: **Perfect**, **second** person, **masculine**, **plural** from the root לקח. The < sign means "from." In other words, the verb form לְקַחְתֶּם comes from the verb root לקח.

6. **No neuter.** Hebrew has masculine and feminine, but no neuter. Thus, a word like *it* will use either masculine or feminine verbs, depending upon what the word *it* is referring to.

Things You Should Know

Memorize the verb chart well. You should be able to conjugate verbs as well as parse them (see Grammar, p. xix).

Exercise #14

אָדָם	man, Adam	חֹשֶׁךְ	darkness	קָרָא לְ-[8]	to call to, to name or call
אֲדָמָה	ground, soil	יוֹם	day	קָרָא בְּ-[8]	to read aloud (in)
אוֹר	light, brightness	לֹא	not	עָפָר	dust
אֲשֶׁר	that, which, who	לַיְלָה	*m.*[6] night	שָׁמַיִם	(the) sky, (the) heavens
הוּא	he, it	קָרָא	to call, name, read[7]	שָׁמַר	to guard, watch, keep

[1] קָרָא[10] אֱלֹהִים לָאוֹר יוֹם וְלַחֹשֶׁךְ קָרָא לָיְלָה׃ [2] בָּרָא יְהוָה אִישׁ [9] עָפָר מִן־
הָאֲדָמָה׃ [3] קָרָא יְהוָה לָאִישׁ אָדָם כִּי מִן־הָאֲדָמָה הוּא׃ [4] לֹא בָרָא הָאִישׁ אֶת־
הַגָּן׃ [5] אָמַר יְהוָה אָנֹכִי אֵל אֲשֶׁר בָּרָא יוֹם וָלָיְלָה׃ [6] אָמְרוּ אֶל־שָׂרָה הַשֹּׁמֶרֶת

[6] We will learn in the next chapter that Hebrew nouns are either masculine (*m.*) or feminine (*f.*).

[7] The Perf 3ms is the dictionary form of the verb (see note 2, above). Thus, in the vocabulary definitions, we shall use the infinitive form (the "to" form) instead of the technically correct 3ms (the "he" form).

[8] When the word after קָרָא has the preposition לְ-, we translate *call to* or *name*. But if the word after קָרָא has the preposition בְּ- then we translate "read aloud in." Thus, the phrase קָרָא לְשָׂרָה means "he called to Sarah," but קָרָא בְּסֵפֶר means "he read aloud in a scroll (book)."

[9] Add the word *from*.

[10] When the preposition לְ- comes after the verb קרא, the subject will usually come between them.

בַּ֫יִת אֲשֶׁר בָּעִיר הוּא[12]׃ [7] אָמְרָה שָׂרָה בָּאתִי[11] עִיר וְלֹא שָׁמַ֫רְתִּי בַּיִת׃ [8] הֲלֹא
לְקַחְתֶּן בְּרָכָה מֵהַמֶּלֶךְ׃ [9] נָתְנוּ עִיר וְאֶ֫רֶץ נָתַנּוּ[13]׃ [10] הֲשָׁמַ֫רְתָּ אָרוֹן בִּכְנָעַן׃
[11] הֲלַכְתֶּם[14] בָּאָרֶץ אֲשֶׁר נָתַן יְהוָה לְאַבְרָהָם׃ [12] אֲמַרְתֶּן כִּי בָאנוּ גַן בִּיהוּדָה׃
[13] בְּחֹ֫שֶׁךְ נָתְנָה אִשָּׁה בְּרָכָה׃ [14] הֶאָמַרְתָּ לְאַהֲרוֹן כִּי רָאָה יְהוֹשֻׁ֫עַ אָרוֹן׃
[15] שָׁלַ֫חְתִּי אֶת־אַהֲרוֹן אֶל־יְהוּדָה כִּי לֹא בָאתֶם כְּנָעַן׃ [16] הָאִישׁ אֲשֶׁר הָלַךְ בֶּעָפָר
לֹא רָאָה אוֹר כִּי לַ֫יְלָה וְלֹא יוֹם׃ [17] יְהוָה אֲשֶׁר בָּרָא אֶת־הַשָּׁמַיִם הוּא[15] אֵל׃
[18] קְרָאתֶן לְשָׂרָה כִּי עַם בָּא עִיר אֲשֶׁר בִּיהוּדָה׃

---

[11] Why is there no *dagesh* in the ת? Answer: because the א is silent (quiescent). The word is read *as if* the א were not there – that is, *as if* the word were בָּתִי. In other words, -בָּא = -בָּ = open syllable. Thus there is a vowel before the ת (which was originally תּ) and it has lost its *d.l.* Review §17 and §11.1.4, p. 32.

[12] Add the word *is.* The word הוּא is masculine and so it refers to בַּ֫יִת. The word עִיר is feminine.

[13] The *dagesh* shows that there are two *nuns*: נוּ + נָתַן → נָתַנְנוּ → נָתַנּוּ.

[14] The first ה on this word is not a *he*-interrogative. Rather, it is the first letter of the verb הָלַךְ. Look again at the verb chart for the Perfect verb. The 2mp and 2fp usually have a simple *shewa* under the first letter. But remember that gutturals at the beginning of a word cannot take simple *shewa* (§13.1, p. 38). They must take either a regular vowel or a *composite shewa* (§8.2.2, p. 24). In this case, the ה has taken a composite *shewa*. **Technical note:** (1) This is a long word. (2) In Hebrew the accent comes at or near the end of the word. (3) Therefore, as words become longer, the first syllable moves farther from the accent. We will later learn that as vowels move farther from the accent, they sometimes "reduce" and become shorter. That is why the Perfect 2mp and 2fp have *shewa*s under their first letter. They have reduced from *qamets*.

[15] Add the word *is.*

20

NOUNS: SINGULAR, PLURAL AND DUAL

Hebrew has only two genders: masculine and feminine. Unlike New Testament Greek, there is no neuter gender for nouns and adjectives.[1]

20.1 Singular nouns

20.1.1 **Feminine nouns** will usually end with an *accented* ָה- (note the *qamets*).

Thus, the word בְּרָכָה (*blessing*) is feminine, but מִקְנֶה (*cattle*), which has a *seghol* before the ה, is masculine. Likewise, לַיְלָה (*night*) is not feminine because the accent is not on the final ָה.

There are **exceptions**, of course. There are feminine words such as אֵם (*mother*). And parts of the body which come in pairs are also feminine: יָד (*hand*), עַיִן (*eye*), רֶגֶל (*foot*). Also, place names such as *Israel, Canaan, Jerusalem* and *Bethlehem* — and even the words *city* (עִיר) and *land* (אֶרֶץ) — are feminine. (But the word *place* itself, מָקוֹם, is masculine.)

20.1.2 **Masculine nouns** have no particular form, but they will usually not end with a ה-. (Thus, מִקְנֶה and לַיְלָה are unusual.)

20.2 Plural nouns

20.2.1 Feminine plural nouns will have an וֹת- ending. It will usually replace the ָה-.

20.2.2 Masculine plural nouns will usually add the suffix ִים - (îm, not yim).

Example: the words סוּס (*male horse*) and סוּסָה (*female horse*).[2]

	Singular	Plural
Masculine	סוּס	סוּסִים
Feminine	סוּסָה	סוּסוֹת

20.3 Dual nouns

"Dual" is similar to plural, but it usually means "exactly two," rather than "more than one."

יוֹם *a day* יוֹמַיִם *two days*

A noun can have both dual and plural forms. Be sure to study carefully the difference between the *dual*

---

[1] Some words may be "common," however, and they will be marked *c.* instead of *m.* or *f.* This simply means that in the Hebrew Bible these words are sometimes found as masculine, and sometimes as feminine. See the discussion of Gender in the Grammar section, p. xx (especially the footnotes).

[2] The word for a female animal is often just the word for a male animal plus a ָה- suffix.

ending ַ֫יִם- (-ayim, note the accent) and the *masculine plural* ending ִים- (-îm).

יוֹם *a day* יוֹמַ֫יִם *two days* (du.) יָמִים *days* (pl.)

(Be sure to learn the irregular plural of יוֹם. It is יָמִים, not יוֹמִים.)

20.4 Changes in vowel pointing.

Additing suffixes to words sometimes causes changes in vowel pointing. Syllables which were closed may become open. This can cause short vowels (usually found in closed syllables) to become long. For instance, note what happens in the case of the masculine word פַּר (par, young bull). The plural becomes פָּרִים (pā-rîm). The first syllable is now open (-פָּ), and so the vowel has lengthened.

On the other hand, the opposite can also happen. When words gets longer, vowels at the beginning may become shorter as the accent moves away from them. For instance, compare דָּבָר, to its longer plural דְּבָרִים. In the plural, the first *qamets* shortens to *shewa.*

20.5 -מ and -ת Nouns

Sometimes nouns will be formed by putting a -מ[3] or a -ת prefix on a verb root. Thus שָׁפַט means *to judge,* but מִשְׁפָּט means *judgment.* Here are some other examples:

מַחֲנֶה	a camp	from	חָנָה	to camp
מִלְחָמָה	war, battle	from	לחם[4]	to fight
מִצְוָה	commandment	from	צָוָה	to command
מִקְנֶה	cattle, possessions	from	קָנָה	to get, to buy
תּוֹרָה	direction, instruction, law	from	יָרָה	to instruct, teach
תְּפִלָּה	prayer	from	פלל[4]	to pray

Knowing this pattern can sometimes help you figure out an unfamiliar word. If the word is four or more letters in length, and begins with -מ or -ת, look for a familiar verb root after the first letter.

Things You Should Know

1. Hebrew nouns are either masculine or feminine. Masculine nouns have no particular form, but feminine nouns usually end with an accented ָה - .
2. Plural masculine nouns usually add an ִים - suffix. Plural feminine nouns usually replace the final ָה- with a final וֹת- .
3. Some nouns have "dual" forms. They end with ַ֫יִם - (not ִים). Dual means "exactly two;" thus, יָדַ֫יִם means *two hands.*
4. Nouns are sometimes formed by by prefixing a -מ or -ת to a verb root.

---

[3] **Technical note:** We will learn later that a prefixed -מ is also often the sign of a participle.

[4] **Technical note:** No vowel points are included under לחם or פלל because these verbs do not occur in this simple form. We will learn their forms later.

21

NOUNS: ABSOLUTE AND CONSTRUCT

The Hebrew noun does not have nominative, accusative, dative and genitive forms, as are found in New Testament Greek. Instead, there are just two forms: *absolute* and *construct*. The absolute is the basic form of the noun, which you have already learned.

21.1 The meaning of "Construct"

In Hebrew, a noun that is not related to another noun is said to be ▲*absolute*. But sometimes two nouns stand together, with the second noun modifying[1] the first. When this happens, the two words form a "construction" and the first noun is said to be ▲*in construct* to the second one. Consider the following three words:

son of Adam

the words *son* and *Adam* have been put together in a "construction" (usually called a phrase). If the words were in Hebrew, we would say that the word *son* was "in construct" to the word *Adam*. Because they are in this relationship, Hebrew does not need to use the word *of*.

21.2 Construct, accent and vowel-shortening

Let us now consider the above phrase in Hebrew, using the words בֵּן and אָדָם:

בֶּן־אָדָם *son (of) Adam*

The word בֵּן is "in construct" to the word אָדָם.[2] In translation, we add the word *of*: "son *of* Adam."

In addition, the vowel under the בּ shortens to *seghol* because of the *maqqeph*.[3] Note, however, that the *maqqeph* is not necessary in construct.[4] Yet, even without the *maqqeph* we will see vowel shortening: בֶּן אָדָם. Thus, the *seghol* under the בּ shows us that the word is in construct.

---

[1] To "modify" means to change. A "modifier" changes the meaning of a word. See the section "Grammar: an overview," p. xix number (4).

[2] **Technical note:** Other textbooks may say that the word אָדָם is in a "genitive relationship" to the word בֵּן. While this is true, it can also be confusing to the student, and so we do not use this terminology here. (Note that it is the *relationship* which is genitive, not the word.) Again, remember that (unlike Greek) Hebrew **does not have a genitive noun form**. There are just two noun forms: *absolute* and *construct*. In our example, the word אָדָם is absolute – although its *relationship* to בֵּן may be described as genitive.

[3] Remember that a *maqqeph* causes the word before (to the right of) the *maqqeph* to lose its accent (§10.1, p. 29). Thus, we end up with a closed, unaccented syllable which requires a short vowel (§7.2, p. 18).

[4] **Technical note:** In the Hebrew Bible, a construct word *without* a *maqqeph* will have a conjunctive accent which shows that it is connected to the word after it. For instance, note the ◌֣ mark under the accented syllable of רוּחַ in רֽוּחַ אֱלֹהִים. This shows that רוּחַ is in construct to אֱלֹהִים and that the first syllable -רוּ is accented.

21.3 The forms of Absolute and Construct

In **masculine singular** and in **feminine plural**, the absolute and construct forms are the same. In **masculine plural** and in **feminine singular**, however, the construct form will be different from the absolute. In the following example, we again use the words סוּס (horse) and סוּסָה (female horse):

		Absolute		Construct	
M	Singular	סוּס	*horse*	סוּס(־)	*horse-of*
	Plural	סוּסִים	*horses*	סוּסֵי(־)	*horses-of*
F	Singular	סוּסָה	*(female) horse*	סוּסַת(־)	*(female)-horse-of*
	Plural	סוּסוֹת	*(female) horses*	סוּסוֹת(־)	*(female)-horses-of*

Thus, we shall see construct relationships such as:

סוּס־שְׁלֹמֹה	Solomon's horse	(with or without the *maqqeph*)
סוּסֵי־שְׁלֹמֹה	Solomon's horses	(")
סוּסַת־שְׁלֹמֹה	Solomon's (female) horse	(")
סוּסוֹת־שְׁלֹמֹה	Solomon's (female) horses	(")

Some unusual plurals and constructs

Several words which you have already learned in the singular absolute have unusual plural and construct forms. You should learn them here. Note: "*cs.*=" means the *cs.* is the same as the *abs.*

Singular	**Plural**
אִישׁ *m.* man, *cs.*=	*abs.* אֲנָשִׁים, *cs.* אַנְשֵׁי
בַּ֫יִת *m.* house, *cs.* בֵּית	*abs.* בָּתִּים, *cs.* בָּתֵּי (the *methegs* are often missing in the Bible, but the *qamets* is always *qamets* not *qamets-hatuph*)
אִשָּׁה *f.* woman, *cs.* אֵשֶׁת	*abs.* נָשִׁים, *cs.* נְשֵׁי (looks like masculine, but is feminine)
עִיר *f.* city, *cs.*=	*abs.* עָרִים, *cs.* עָרֵי (looks like masculine, but is feminine)

We know the word עִיר is feminine because when it is the subject of a sentence it uses feminine verbs.

21.4 Parsing Nouns

We *parse* a word by describing its grammatical form. For example, we can describe the word סוּסַת as a noun (*N.*) which is feminine (*f.*), singular (*s.*) and construct (*cs.*). And it comes from the singular absolute noun סוּסָה (we can write "< סוּסָה" to show this). We can abbreviate this information as **Nfsc < סוּסָה**. Thus, when you are asked to parse nouns on a test, you should use the following system:

On the test, you will see:	You should write:	
סוּס =	Nmsa[5] < סוּס	*or, if it is in construct*: Nmsc < סוּס
סוּסִים =	Nmpa < סוּס	
סוּסֵי =	Nmpc < סוּס	
תּוֹרָה =	Nfsa[5] < תּוֹרָה	
תּוֹרַת =	Nfsc < תּוֹרָה	
תּוֹרוֹת =	Nfpa < תּוֹרָה	*or, if it is in construct* Nfpc < תּוֹרָה

21.5 Construct with a Definite Article or with a Proper Noun (Name)

21.5.1 Definite Articles. If a definite article (the word *the*) is needed, it will go on the second word, not the first. For instance,

אִישׁ־אֱלֹהִים means ***a** man of God*

BUT

אִישׁ־הָאֱלֹהִים means ***the** man of God* (not *a man of the God*)

Note that there is no -הָ on the first word אִישׁ. It goes *only* on the second word.

21.5.2 Proper Nouns. If the second word is a proper noun (that is, a name such as מֹשֶׁה or יְהוּדָה), then the construct combination is usually *definite* just as if it had a definite article. Thus:

דְּבַר־מֹשֶׁה usually means ***the** word of Moses* (not ***a** word of Moses*)

This is because we know *whose* word it is. It is a *definite* word. It is not just *any* word, but rather *Moses'* word. Likewise, בֶּן־אָדָם on p. 58 would usually be translated *the son of Adam* not *a son of Adam.*

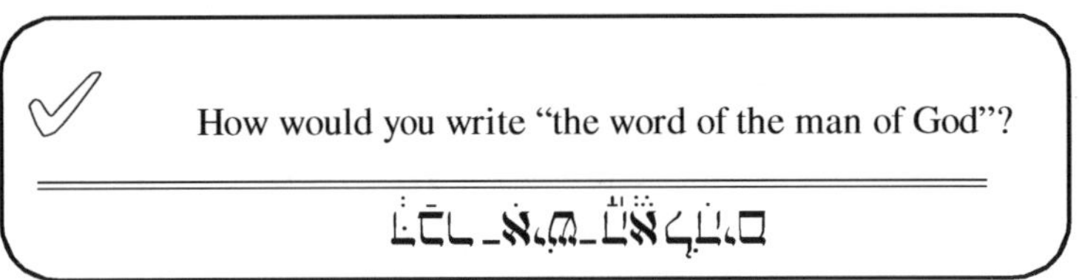

It is possible, of course, for בֶּן־אָדָם to mean *a son of Adam.* The context will tell us how to translate. In Judges 7:14, for instance, we find examples of both situations:

גִּדְעוֹן בֶּן־יוֹאָשׁ אִישׁ־יִשְׂרָאֵל

This is translated *Gideon, **the** son of Joash, **a** man of Israel.* בֶּן is in construct to the name יוֹאָשׁ (Joash), and so we translate *the son of Joash.* Likewise, אִישׁ is in construct to a proper noun (the name *Israel*). But Gideon is only one of *many* men of Israel, and so we cannot translate *Gideon ... **the** man of Israel.*[6]

---

[5] Actually, if the noun is already *s.* and *abs.*, there is no need to write < סוּס, < תּוֹרָה, etc.

[6] **Technical note.** There are other ways to handle the situation. For instance, the preposition -לְ (*to*) can be placed before the second word, and the first word is then left in the absolute: בֵּן לְיִשַׁי, *a son of Jesse* (literally, *a son **to** Jesse*), 1 Sam 16:18. And in 2 Sam 9:3, *a son of Jonathan* is בֵּן לִיהוֹנָתָן. In these cases, we do not have a construct relationship, and thus the *tsere* in בֵּן does not shorten to *seghol.*

Things You Should Know

1. When one noun modifies (describes) another, the first is "in construct" to the second. Thus, in בֶּן־אָדָם, *son of Adam*, the word בֵּן (בֶּן־) is in construct to אָדָם.
2. Vowels may shorten in the construct word (that is, the first word). Note the above example, where the *tsere* in בֵּן has shortened to *seghol*: בֶּן. The second word (אָדָם in בֶּן־אָדָם) remains in its "absolute" (original) form.
3. There will often be a *maqqeph* between the two words.
4. In the **masculine plural**, and in the **feminine singular**, the construct form will be different from the absolute. Know these forms.
5. If a definite article is required, it will go on the second word, not the first. Thus, *the man of God* is אִישׁ־הָאֱלֹהִים.
6. If the second word is a proper noun (name), then the phrase will usually be definite even though it has no definite article. Thus, דְּבַר־מֹשֶׁה, *the word of Moses*.
7. Be sure to learn the unusual plurals listed in the box on page 59.

Exercise #15

In addition to the vocabulary words below, be sure to learn the unusual plurals and constructs which are found on p. 59.

אָכַל	to eat[7]	עַל	above, over, against, near
בֵּן	son, *cs.* בֶּן; *pl.* בָּנִים, *cs.* בְּנֵי	נָשִׁים	*f.* women (*pl.* of אִשָּׁה) *cs.* נְשֵׁי
דִּבֶּר	to speak, talk	קוֹל	*m.* sound, voice; *pl. abs. & cs.* קוֹלוֹת[8]
יָצָא	to go or come out	שָׁמַע	to hear, listen
יָרֵא	to fear, be in awe	שָׁמַע לְקוֹל *or* שָׁמַע בְּקוֹל	to obey[9]
עָבַד	to work, serve, cultivate (the soil), worship (God)	אֲנָשִׁים	men (plural of אִישׁ), *cs.* אַנְשֵׁי

[7] We are now using the English infinitive form in the vocabulary definitions (see p. 54, note 7).

[8] This masculine plural looks feminine but it is not. There are several words like this in Hebrew. For instance, the plural of the masculine noun אָב, *father*, is אָבוֹת, *fathers*.

[9] *to listen to or hear (the) voice (of)* would be שָׁמַע אֶת־הַקּוֹל. Or, for instance, שָׁמַע אֶת־קוֹל־הַמֶּלֶךְ, "he heard the voice of the king."

[1] הָיָה חֹשֶׁךְ עַל הָאָרֶץ בַּלַּיְלָה[11] וְאֶת־אוֹרֵי־הַשָּׁמַיִם[10] רָאָה אָדָם׃ [2] עָבְדוּ הָאִשָּׁה
וְהָאִישׁ בֶּעָפָר וּבַיּוֹם שָׁמְרוּ אֶת־הָאֲדָמָה׃ [3] אָכְלוּ הָאִישׁ וְהָאִשָּׁה פְּרִי מִן הָעֵץ׃
[4] יָרְאוּ כִּי שָׁמְעוּ אֶת־קוֹל־יְהוָה כִּי הָלַךְ בַּגָּן׃ [5] קָרָא יְהוָה אֱלֹהִים[12] לָאָדָם וּבָעֵצִים
אָמַר הָאָדָם יָרֵאתִי[14] כִּי שָׁמַעְתִּי קוֹל בַּגָּן׃ [6] דִּבֵּר יְהוָה אֶל־הָאִישׁ לֵאמֹר[13] הֲמִן־
הָעֵץ אָכַלְתָּ אֶת־הַפֶּרִי׃ [7] אָמַר הָאִישׁ אָכַלְתִּי אֶת־הַפְּרִי כִּי בְעֵץ הוּא׃ [8] שָׁלַח
אֱלֹהִים אֶת־[16]הָאָדָם מֵהַגָּן כִּי לֹא שָׁמַע בְּקוֹל[15]־אֱלֹהִים׃ [9] יָצְאוּ הָאִישׁ וְהָאִשָּׁה מִן הַגָּן
וַיהוָה[17] נָתַן בְּרָכָה׃ [10] דִּבְּרוּ הַנָּשִׁים אֶל הָאֲנָשִׁים לֵאמֹר נָתַן יְהוָה בְּרָכָה לְיִשְׂרָאֵל׃
[11] עָבְדוּ בְנֵי־יִשְׂרָאֵל אֶת־פַּרְעֹה כִּי אָמַר אֶל הָעָם מֶלֶךְ־מִצְרַיִם אָנִי[18]׃ [12] דִּבֶּר מֹשֶׁה
אֶל־פַּרְעֹה וְלֹא שָׁמַע מֶלֶךְ־מִצְרַיִם לְקוֹל־אֱלֹהִים׃ [13] הָיָה חֹשֶׁךְ כַּלַּיְלָה עַל אֶרֶץ־
מִצְרָיִם וְאוֹר בְּבָתֵּי־עַם־יִשְׂרָאֵל׃ [14] לֹא יָרְאוּ הַנָּשִׁים אֶת־פַּרְעֹה כִּי עָבְדוּ אֶת־יְהוָה
אֲשֶׁר בָּרָא אֶת־הַשָּׁמַיִם וְאֶת־הָאָרֶץ׃ [15] יָצְאוּ בְנֵי־יִשְׂרָאֵל מֵאֶרֶץ־מִצְרָיִם׃ [16] שָׁלְחוּ
אַנְשֵׁי־פַרְעֹה אֶת־מֹשֶׁה וְאֶת־עַם־יִשְׂרָאֵל מִן מִצְרַיִם לַיְלָה[19] וּבַיּוֹם הָלְכוּ בַּעֲפַר־הָאָרֶץ׃

---

[10] Here, the אֶת־ shows us that this phrase is the definite direct object, not the subject. In this case, the subject, אָדָם is found at the end of the sentence.

[11] "by night" or "in the night." You will often see just לַיְלָה without the preposition. Likewise, "by day" may be either בַּיּוֹם or just יוֹם. See Gen 31:39-40 for examples of both usages.

[12] The second creation story (Gen 2:4-25) uses this double name יְהוָה אֱלֹהִים for God. In most English translations, this name is translated as "the LORD God" (note: not "the Lord God").

[13] לֵאמֹר is a very common word which may be translated "saying." Many times, it may be left untranslated. **Technical note:** it is actually an infinitive form of the verb אָמַר plus a -לְ prefix; we will learn this later.

[14] Perf 1cs < ירא (the silent א has caused the slight changes).

[15] שָׁמַע בְּקוֹל: *to obey* (see vocabulary). Compare this sentence to sentence 5, where the meaning is simply *heard a sound.*

[16] "The man." If הָאָדָם did not have the definite article, it would mean "Adam." See bottom of p. 44.

[17] When the subject comes before the verb, it often gives additional emphasis: the man and the women did one thing, ***but the LORD*** did something else.

[18] Pausal (in pause) form of אֲנִי. See §9.2.2, page 27. (For "pause," see page 20.)

[19] See footnote 11, above.

22

THE VERB: IMPERFECT

In §19, we briefly described the two "tenses" of the Hebrew verb: the Perfect and the Imperfect. The Perfect shows "completed action," and is usually translated as a Past Tense. In this chapter, we shall learn the Imperfect. It shows "incomplete action," and is usually translated as a Future Tense. We shall abbreviate the Perfect as Perf and the Imperfect as Impf (not "Imp"[1]).

The Perf had only suffixes, but the Impf has both prefixes and suffixes:

he will keep (3ms)	יִשְׁמֹר	they will keep (3mp)	יִשְׁמְרוּ
she will keep (3fs)	תִּשְׁמֹר	they will keep (3fp)	תִּשְׁמֹרְנָה
you will keep (2ms)	תִּשְׁמֹר	you will keep (2mp)	תִּשְׁמְרוּ
you will keep (2fs)	תִּשְׁמְרִי	you will keep (2fp)	תִּשְׁמֹרְנָה
I shall keep (1cs)	אֶשְׁמֹר	we shall keep (1cp)	נִשְׁמֹר

Notes:

1. **Prefixes:** The Perf *never* has a prefix; the Impf *always* has a prefix.
2. **Third plural:** Perf had a 3**cp**; Impf does not. Rather, Impf has both a 3**mp** and a 3**fp**.
3. **Usage:** In the Perf, we saw that 2mp is used when speaking to a mixed group of men and women (Notes, p. 53). This is also true in the Impf. In addition, the Impf uses **3**mp when talking *about* a mixed group.
4. **Parsing order:** We parse[2] in the following order:

   שָׁמַרְתִּי = Perf 1cs <[3] שמר

   יִשְׁמְרוּ = Impf 3mp < שמר

   Always put Perf or Impf first, and the person (1, 2 or 3) second. Then put the gender (m or f or c) third, and the number (s or p) last. Then write the < sign and give the verb root.
5. **Identical forms:** The **Impf 3fs and 2ms** look the same. So do the **Impf 3fp and 2fp**. The context of the sentence will tell you how you should translate. When you parse without a context (for instance, parsing verbs which stand alone on a test), then

   parse תִּשְׁמֹר as Impf 3fs **or** 2ms < שמר, and

   parse תִּשְׁמֹרְנָה as Impf 3fp **or** 2fp < שמר

---

[1] Hebrew also has an Imperative mood. It is therefore important to use "Impf" for Imperfect and "Impv" for Imperative. "Imp" could mean either, and so is not clear. On tests, "Imp" will be marked as wrong.

[2] Parsing and conjugating are discussed on page xix of "Grammar, an Overview."

[3] The < means *from* (see the note on parsing on p. 54). You do not need to put vowel points under the verb.

6. **A learning help:** Study the relationship between the singular and the plural in the second and third person. In three of the four cases, the plural simply adds a suffix (וּ or נָה) to the singular.
7. **Final וּ-:** In the Perf, the 3cp has a וּ- suffix (שָׁמְרוּ). In the Impf, there is no 3cp. Rather, there are 3mp and 3fp. Impf 3mp has the וּ- suffix (יִשְׁמְרוּ), but Impf 3fp has a נָה- suffix (תִּשְׁמֹרְנָה).

Things You Should Know

1. The Imperfect (abbreviated Impf) represents "incomplete action," and is usually translated as if it were a future tense.
2. The Impf *always* has a prefix (and often a suffix); the Perf *never* has a prefix.
3. You should be able to parse and to write the verb charts of Perf and Impf from memory.

Exercise #16

אִם	if	זֶרַע	seed, descendant (in pause: זָרַע)
בֵּין	between (do not confuse with בֵּן)	כּוֹכָב	star, *cs.* כּוֹכַב
בְּרִית	*f.* covenant	כָּרַת	to cut, cut off, cut down
הָגָר	Hagar	כָּרַת בְּרִית	to make a covenant[4]
הֵן *or* הִנֵּה	look, behold (emphasizes importance of the words which follow)	עִם	with (do not confuse with אִם)
זָכַר	to remember	שָׁאַל	to ask

[1] אָמַר אֱלֹהִים לְהָגָר הִנֵּה תִּשְׁלְחִי אֶת־אַבְרָם[5] וְאֶת־שָׂרַי אֶל־אֶרֶץ־כְּנָעַן׃ [2] דִּבֶּר
יְהוָה אֶל־אַבְרָם לֵאמֹר[7] אַבְרָם לֹא־תִּירָא[6]׃ [3] יֵצְאוּ אַבְרָם וְשָׂרַי מִבֵּית־אַבְרָם אֶל אֶרֶץ־
כְּנָעַן׃ [4] הֲדִבֶּר יְהוָה אֶל הָגָר לֵאמֹר אֶכְרֹת בְּרִית עִם אַבְרָהָם׃ [5] שָׁאֲלָה שָׂרַי
אֶת־יְהוָה לֵאמֹר הֲתִזְכֹּר אֶת־אַבְרָם כִּי בְּבֵית־אַבְרָם[10] לֹא[9] זָרַע׃ [6] יָרְאָה[8] שָׂרָה אֶת־

---

[4] In Hebrew, to "cut" a covenant means to "make" a covenant. Animals were sometimes sacrificed, or "cut," when covenants were made. See, for instance, Gen 15:7-18.

[5] אַבְרָם (Abram) and שָׂרַי (Sarai) were the original names of Abraham and Sarah (in Genesis 11-16). In Genesis 17, God changes their names to אַבְרָהָם (Abraham) and שָׂרָה (Sarah).

[6] תִּירָא = Impf 2ms < יָרֵא. Words which begin with letters such as נ or י (or end with ה or have gutturals) will not always follow the rules. We will study them later. Until then, footnotes will explain them and help you get used to them. You do not need to learn the material in these footnotes. Just read it, and you will slowly start to recognize the patterns.

[7] לֵאמֹר see page 62, note 13.

[8] Is this Perf 3fs < ירא? Or is it Impf 3ms < ראה? The vowel pointing will tell you. It is very important to learn the vowel pointing of the various verb forms at this point.

[9] The singular word זֶרַע (literally "seed") can mean "descendant" (singular) or "descendants" (plural). **Technical note:** As you can see in this sentence, the word זֶרַע and its verb are both singular in form. But it *means* "the descendants (plural) of Abraham." In Galatians 3:16, Paul does a very literal interpretation of Gen 22:17 (which is similar to this sentence you are translating) and says that the singular (זֶרַע) means only one

הָגָר כִּי אָמְרָה[12] הִנֵּה לָקַח בֶּן־הָגָר אֶת־הַבְּרִית׃ [7] אָמַר אֱלֹהִים כִּי [11]יִהְיֶה זֶרַע־אַבְרָהָם
כְּכוֹכְבֵי[14]־הַשָּׁמַיִם וְכַעֲפַר־הָאָרֶץ׃ [8] הֶאָמַר הַמֶּלֶךְ תֹּאכַל[13] פְּרִי־אֶרֶץ־יְהוּדָה אִם עָבַדְתְּ
אֶת־הָאֲדָמָה׃ [9] דִּבְּרוּ[16] אֶל הַנָּשִׁים לֵאמֹר לֹא תִכְרֹתְנָה בְּרִית בֵּין עַם־יִשְׂרָאֵל וּבֵין[15]
עַמֵּי־כְנָעַן׃ [10] אֲמַרְתֶּן אֶל־יְהוֹשֻׁעַ וְאֶל־אַנְשֵׁי־יְהוּדָה יָצָא הָעָם עִם אֲרוֹן־הַבְּרִית׃
[11] בָּאנוּ עַל הָעִיר[18] בַּלָּיְלָה׃ [12] אָמְרוּ הַנָּשִׁים [17]נִשְׁמַע לְקוֹל־יְהוֹשֻׁעַ כִּי עָבַד אֶת־
יְהוָה׃ [13] שָׁאַל אַהֲרוֹן הֲלָקַח עַם־כְּנַעַן אֶת־אֲרוֹן־הַבְּרִית כִּי לֹא זָכַרְנוּ אֶת־אֱלֹהִים׃
[14] לֹא תַעֲבֹד[20] אֶת־כּוֹכְבֵי־הַשָּׁמַיִם אֲשֶׁר בָּרָא אֱלֹהִים׃ [15] בָּאָה[19] הָאִשָּׁה אֶל־הַבַּיִת
כִּי דִבְּרוּ הָאֲנָשִׁים אֶל אַהֲרוֹן׃ [16] אָכַלְתִּי פְּרִי עִם הָעָם כִּי שָׁמַעְנוּ בְּקוֹל־הַמֶּלֶךְ אֲשֶׁר
[21] עַל הָאָרֶץ הוּא׃ [17] הָלַכְנוּ בֵּין הָעֵצִים וּבֵין הַגָּן עִם נְשֵׁי־הָעִיר׃

---

descendant, not many; that is: Jesus Christ. We who are Christians would say that Paul is right theologically, but we might argue with his Hebrew interpretation.

[10] Add the words *there is.*

[11] Impf 3ms < הָיָה. See footnote 6, above. The letters ה and י can make verbs act in unusual ways.

[12] Who is the subject of this verb? Hagar or Sarah? The context is not clear. But the later use of "son of Hagar" (בֶּן־הָגָר) instead of "my son" gives us the probable answer.

[13] Impf 3fs or 2ms < אכל. The context of the sentence will help you decide. **Technical note:** This verb has unusual vowel pointing because of the א. We would expect תֶּאֱכֹל. But the א has become silent (§17, p. 49), and this has caused vowel changes. For instance, the א has attracted a *pathah* after it, since it is a guttural (§13.3, p. 38). Again, you do not need to learn this material at this point. Just note it as you do the exercise.

[14] Nmpc + inseparable preposition prefix.

[15] בֵּין . . . בֵּין. In English, we say *between Abraham and Sarah.* Hebrew uses the preposition twice, and says *between Abraham and between Sarah.* In translation, you do not need to translate the second בֵּין.

[16] Perf 3cp < דִּבֵּר. This verb has some unusual characteristics which will be studied later.

[17] Impf 1cp < שָׁמַע. Again, the guttural has attracted a *pathah* so that the verb is נִשְׁמַע and not נִשְׁמְע.

[18] To "enter the city" is usually בָּא הָעִיר with neither a preposition nor אֶת־ before הָעִיר. To "come *to* the city" (but not yet enter it) will usually have the preposition אֶל or עַל or עַד (*until, as far as*) before the word הָעִיר.

[19] The accenting of this word is important. It is accented on the *first* syllable, although Hebrew words are usually accented on the last syllable. Learn this particular form of בָּא well, because you will later learn another form of the word, בָּאָה, which is accented on the last syllable and has a different meaning.

[20] Note the effect of the guttural (ע), as learned in §13. This Imperfect verb form usually follows the pattern תִּשְׁמֹר. But the guttural has taken a composite *shewa* under it (instead of the normal simple *shewa*) and has attracted a *pathah* before it (under the תּ).

[21] Add the word *is.*

23

NOUNS: SINGULAR WITH POSSESSIVE SUFFIXES

Many languages use a *possessive adjective* such as *my* or *your* to show who owns (or possesses) an object. If a book belongs to me, I say it is *my* book. If it belongs to you, it is *your* book.

In Hebrew, possessive *suffixes* are used instead of possessive adjectives. These suffixes are attached to the construct form of the noun. For instance, the word for *instruction, law, torah* is תּוֹרָה. The word is feminine. To say *your (mp) instruction*, we first put תּוֹרָה into its construct form (תּוֹרַת); then we add the 2mp possessive suffix, which is כֶם-. That is:

First:	תּוֹרָה (abs.) *instruction*	➜	תּוֹרַת (const.) *instruction of*
Then:	תּוֹרַת + כֶם-	➜	תּוֹרַתְכֶם = (const + 2mp) *your instruction*

23.1 Masculine Singular Nouns with Possessive Suffixes

The masculine singular noun takes possessive suffixes as follows:

Singular Absolute: סוּס *horse*

Singular Construct: סוּס *horse of*

3ms	סוּסוֹ	*his horse* [i.e., *horse-of-him*]	3mp	סוּסָם	*their* (m) *horse*
3fs	סוּסָהּ	*her horse* [note *mappiq*]	3fp	סוּסָן	*their* (f) *horse*
2ms	סוּסְךָ	*your* (ms) *horse*	2mp	סוּסְכֶם	*your* (mp) *horse*
2fs	סוּסֵךְ	*your* (fs) *horse*	2fp	סוּסְכֶן	*your* (fp) *horse*
1cs	סוּסִי	*my horse*	1cp	סוּסֵנוּ	*our horse*

Notes:

1. Although the noun סוּס (*horse*) is singular, it can take either a singular or a plural suffix:

סוּסָהּ	*her horse*	Noun is singular, suffix is singular (3fs)
סוּסֵךְ	*your(fs) horse*	Noun is singular, suffix is singular (2fs)
סוּסִי	*my horse*	Noun is singular, suffix is singular (1cs)

סוּסָם	*their(mp) horse*	Noun is singular, suffix is plural (3mp)
סוּסְכֶם	*your(mp) horse*	Noun is singular, suffix is plural (2mp)
סוּסֵנוּ	*our horse*	Noun is singular, suffix is plural (1cp)

2. As you can see above, masculine plural (*mp*) suffixes are used for mixed groups (groups that have both men and women).
3. Nouns with possessive suffixes are definite. They will *not* have a definite article, but if they are the direct object of the sentence they *will* have the sign of the definite direct object. For instance:

   רָאָה סוּסִי אֶת־סוּסָהּ = *my horse saw her horse.*

   Both סוּסִי and סוּסָהּ are definite. Neither has a definite article, but סוּסָהּ (the object) has the sign of the definite direct object.
4. There is an accent on the next to the last (last but one) syllable in the 1cp: סוּסֵ֫נוּ
5. The *shewas* are vocal, because they are preceded by long vowels (§8.1.2, p. 22).
6. There is no *dagesh* in the כ of the כֶם- and כֶן- suffixes, because they come after a vocal *shewa*.
7. There is a *mappiq* in the 3fs suffix. This *mappiq* is the only thing that makes the word סוּסָהּ (*her horse*) different from the word סוּסָה (no *mappiq*), which means *female horse.*
8. The 3ms suffix is occasionally ֵהוּ - (סוּסֵ֫הוּ).

23.2 Feminine Singular Nouns with Possessive Suffixes

Feminine singular nouns take the same suffixes. But, as we already learned, the feminine singular construct is different from the feminine singular absolute:

Absolute:	תּוֹרָה	*instruction*
Construct:	תּוֹרַת	*instruction of*

3ms	תּוֹרָתוֹ	*his instruction*	3mp	תּוֹרָתָם	*their* (m) *instruction*
3fs	תּוֹרָתָהּ	*her instruction* [note *mappiq*]	3fp	תּוֹרָתָן	*their* (f) *instruction*
2ms	תּוֹרָֽתְךָ[1]	*your* (ms) *instruction*	2mp	תּוֹרַֽתְכֶם[1]	*your* (mp) *instruction*
2fs	תּוֹרָתֵךְ	*your* (fs) *instruction*	2fp	תּוֹרַֽתְכֶן[1]	*your* (fp) *instruction*
1cs	תּוֹרָתִי	*my instruction*	1cp	תּוֹרָתֵ֫נוּ	*our instruction*

Notes:

1. The *shewas* in the second person are again vocal, *even though they come after short vowels in the plurals.* Thus: tô-rā-ṯ^{e}ḵā[2], tô-ra-ṯ^{e}ḵem, tô-ra-ṯ^{e}ḵen. (Technically, the 2mp and 2fp should be תּוֹרַֽתְכֶם and תּוֹרַֽתְכֶן).
2. Again, note the *mappiq* in the 3fs suffix.

23.3 Similarity of Noun Possessive Suffixes and Perfect Verb Suffixes.

The *noun possessive* suffixes are very similar to the *Perfect verb* suffixes (see p. 53). For instance,

---

[1] The shewa is vocal.

[2] The *metheg* in תּוֹרָֽתְךָ shows that the second syllable is -rā- and not -roṯ-.

Both the *Perf* 1cp suffix and the 1cp *possessive* suffix are נוּ- Thus:

שָׁמַ֫רְנוּ	*we kept*
סוּסֵ֫נוּ	*our horse*

The *Perf* 1cs suffix is תִּי-, and the 1cs *possessive* suffix is ִי - Thus:

שָׁמַ֫רְתִּי	*I kept*
סוּסִי	*my horse*

The *Perf* 3fs suffix is ָה -, and the 3fs *possessive* suffix is ָהּ -. Thus:

שָׁמְרָה	*she kept*
סוּסָהּ	*her horse*

Sometimes this makes it easier to learn the possessive suffixes, but other times it can be confusing. Study the differences carefully.

Students often have trouble with **second person singular and plural.** For instance, consider the verb עָבַד (*to serve*) and the noun עֶ֫בֶד (*servant*). עֲבַדְתֶּם means *you*(mp) *served* but עַבְדְּכֶם means *your*(mp) *servant*. They at first look quite similar. But the matter is simple if you note the כ and ת difference:

Nouns use כ and verbs use ת.

To remember, you might think of the relationship of the letters in the alphabet. K is near N; T is near V:

a b c d e f g h i j **K** l m **N** o p q r s **T** u **V** w x y z

כ (K) ➔ **N**oun ת (T) ➔ **V**erb

Thus, **verbs will use** ת in the second person Perfect suffixes. (Think of the *first* person שָׁמַ֫רְתִּי which also uses ת). But **nouns will use** כ (or ךָ) in their 2p suffixes:

you(ms) *served*	עָבַ֫דְתָּ	עַבְדְּךָ	*your*(ms) *servant*
you(fs) *served*	עָבַדְתְּ	עַבְדֵּךְ	*your*(fs) *servant*
you(mp) *served*	עֲבַדְתֶּם	עַבְדְּכֶם	*your*(mp) *servant*
you(fp) *served*	עֲבַדְתֶּן	עַבְדְּכֶן	*your*(fp) *servant*

And remember: the **Perf** 1cs suffix is תִּי- but the **possessive** 1cs suffix is only ִי :

I served	עָבַ֫דְתִּי	but	עַבְדִּי	*my servant*

Be sure to learn these similarities and differences well, so that you will not later confuse Perfect verbs and suffixed nouns.

For instance:

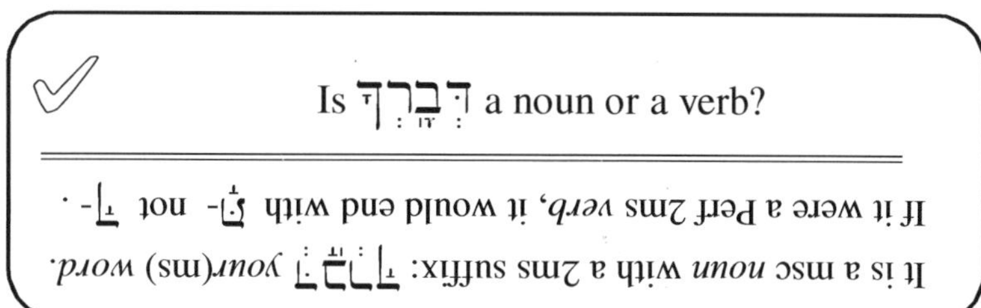

23.4 Other Noun Forms

We have looked at two simple noun forms: סוּס (*m.*) and תּוֹרָה (*f.*). Each has a strong vowel letter which never reduces to a short vowel or *shewa*. With other noun forms – especially longer ones – the vowel pointing will change when suffixes are added. This is because the accent moves farther away from the front of the word when the word gets longer.[3] Vowels at the beginning of the noun will then often reduce to shorter vowels or even to *shewa*.

Study the following examples of some other masculine nouns (columns 1-3) and feminine nouns (columns 4-5). The top line shows the singular absolute (*s.abs.*) Below that, the singular construct (*s. cs.*) and a few examples of nouns with suffixes are shown.

	1	2	3	4	5
s.abs.	נָבִיא	דָּבָר	רוּחַ	שָׁנָה	בְּרָכָה
s. cs.	נְבִיא	דְּבַר	רוּחַ	שְׁנַת	בִּרְכַּת
1cs	נְבִיאִי	דְּבָרִי	רוּחִי	שְׁנָתִי	בִּרְכָתִי
2ms	נְבִיאֲךָ	דְּבָרְךָ	רוּחֲךָ	שְׁנָתְךָ	בִּרְכָתְךָ
2fs	נְבִיאֵךְ	דְּבָרֵךְ	רוּחֵךְ	שְׁנָתֵךְ	בִּרְכָתֵךְ
2mp	נְבִיאֲכֶם	דְּבַרְכֶם	רוּחֲכֶם	שְׁנַתְכֶם	בִּרְכַּתְכֶם

In the **first column** (נָבִיא), we have a syllable with a vowel letter which does not reduce (the *hireq-yod*, similar to the וּ in סוּס on p. 66). But an open syllable with a long vowel (-נָ) comes before it. In construct, and when suffixes are added, the long vowel of the first syllable reduces to *shewa*: נְבִיא .

In the **second column** (דָּבָר), both syllables have long vowels. In construct, and when suffixes are added, the *qamets* under the ב of the second syllable reduces to *pathah* when the syllable is closed. The first *qamets* reduces all the way to a *shewa*.

In the **third column** (רוּחַ), we again have two consonants separated by a vowel letter (similar to סוּס). In this case, however, the final letter is a guttural and had attracted a furtive *pathah*. This does not cause any difference until we add a *2ms* suffix. The guttural then takes a composite *shewa* rather than a simple *shewa* (that is, רוּחֲךָ, instead of the pattern seen in סוּסְךָ).

Columns **four** and **five** are similar to the first three columns, except they are feminine nouns. Thus the ָה- endings change to ת- in construct and to -ת- when suffixes are added. The first *qamets* in שָׁנָה

[3] Remember, the accent can only appear on the last or next to last syllable (§7.1, p. 18).

reduces to *shewa* in construct and when suffixes are added.[4] In the case of בְּרָכָה, the first syllable already has a *shewa* (because the word is already long). In construct, and with suffixes, the second vowel (the *qamets*) also reduces to *shewa*. This produces two *shewas*, and so the first *shewa* becomes a *hireq* (§8.3.1):

בְּרָכָה (*abs.*) → בְּרְכַת (*cons., preliminary form*) → בִּרְכַּת (*cons., final form*)

23.5 Parsing

Singular nouns with possessive suffixes are parsed in the following way:

סוּסְכֶן = Nmsc + 2fp < סוּס

תּוֹרָתוֹ = Nfsc + 3ms < תּוֹרָה

Note: If a noun has a suffix, the noun *must* be construct. It cannot be absolute. Think of it as a "construction." A new word has been constructed by adding a suffix. Thus, the word must be *construct*.

Things You Should Know

1. In Hebrew, possession (ownership) of a noun (*your* book, *her* house, etc.) is shown by adding suffixes to the construct form of the noun.
2. Possessive suffixes are similar in appearance to Perfect verb suffixes. It is easy to confuse the two. Study both carefully. Note the כ ת difference mentioned above (p. 67).
3. Noun vowel pointing will often change when a suffix is added. The noun becomes longer, and vowels near the beginning of the word may become shorter or reduce to *shewa*.
4. Nouns with possessive suffixes are *definite*. They do not need or take definite articles, however, since the possessive suffix is enough to show you that they are definite.
5. Nouns with possessive suffixes are parsed Nmsc + 2fp <סוּס, Nfsc + 3ms <תּוֹרָה, etc.

Exercise #17

גַּם	also, even, indeed	כֹּהֵן	priest	נְבִיאָה	woman prophet, prophetess
כָּתַב	to write	כֹּל, כָּל־	all, each, every	סֵפֶר	writing, scroll, "book"[5]
הֵיכָל	*m.* temple, palace (*pl.* הֵיכָלוֹת)	דָּבָר	word, affair, thing	שְׁמוּאֵל	Samuel
יָשַׁב	to sit; to live or dwell	נָבִיא	prophet	תַּחַת	instead of, under

[4] However, in many words such as בָּמָה and רָעָה the *qamets* will remain.

[5] A scroll is a long piece of leather or other material which can be rolled up for storage. They did not have books in Old Testament times. Instead, they wrote on scrolls. Some English translations of the Old Testament will use the word "book" for סֵפֶר, however, and so this word is included in the definition.

[1] סוּסֵךְ׃ בִּרְכָתֵ֫נוּ׃ כּוֹכָבִי׃ תּוֹרַתְכֶם׃ דְּבַרְכֶן׃ סוּסָהּ׃ דְּבָרֵךְ׃ תּוֹרָתָם׃
[2] תּוֹרָתִי׃ סוּסָן׃ בִּרְכָתוֹ׃ תּוֹרָֽתְךָ׃ סוּסֵ֫נוּ׃ דְּבַרְכֶם׃ בִּרְכָתֵךְ׃ כּוֹכָבוֹ׃
[3] שָׁמַע שְׁמוּאֵל אֶל־הַכֹּהֵן וְגַם כָּתַב כֹּל דְּבָרוֹ בְּסֵפֶר׃ [4] הָֽלְכוּ הַנָּבִיא וְהַנְּבִיאָה מִן
בֵּיתָם[6] בַּלָּֽיְלָה׃ [5] אָֽמְרוּ הִנֵּה כּוֹכְבֵי־הַשָּׁמַ֫יִם כַּעֲפַר־הָֽאֲדָמָה׃ [6] יָֽצְאוּ מִבֵּיתָם
וְאֶת־הֵיכַל־הַמֶּ֫לֶךְ בָּֽאוּ׃ [7] יָשַׁב הַכֹּהֵן בְּהֵיכַל־יְהוָה בַּיּוֹם וְגַם קָרָא בְּסֵפֶר־הַבְּרִית
אֶל־הָֽעָם׃ [8] אָכַל אָדָם אֶת־הַפֶּ֫רִי[8] וְלֹא[7] אָכַל אֶת־זַרְעוֹ׃ [9] קָֽרְאָה הַגָּר לֵאלֹהִים
וְגַם שָֽׁאֲלָה [9]לֵאמֹר הֲתִשְׁמֹר בֵּין בֵּיתִי וּבֵין בֵּית־שָׂרָה׃ [10] דִּבֵּר הָאִישׁ אֶל הַגָּר לֵאמֹר
יִשְׁמַע[13] אֱלֹהִים אֶת־קוֹלֵךְ[12] וְגַם יִזְכֹּר אֶת־בֵּיתֵךְ׃ [11] [11]הַקְּרָאתֶם לִשְׁמוּאֵל אֶת־כָּל[10]־
הַדְּבָרִים אֲשֶׁר כָּֽתְבָה הַנְּבִיאָה׃ [12] שָׁאַ֫לְתִּי אֶת־הַנָּשִׁים הֲתִכְרֹ֫תְנָה בְּרִית עִם עַמָּהּ
תַּ֫חַת עַמִּי׃ [13] יָֽשְׁבוּ הַנְּבִיאִים בְּיִשְׂרָאֵל תַּ֫חַת בִּכְנַעַן וְגַם יָֽשְׁבוּ תַּ֫חַת הַכּוֹכָבִים[14]׃
[14] הִנֵּה תִּכְרְתוּ עֵצִים בַּיּוֹם וּבְחֹשֶׁךְ־הַלַּ֫יְלָה תִּשְׁמֹ֫רְנָה אֶת־הַהֵיכָל׃ [15] אָמַר יְהוָה
לְשָׂרָה לֵאמֹר[15] יִזְכֹּר אַבְרָהָם אִם אֶכְרֹת בְּרִית עִם זַרְעוֹ׃ [16] לֹא עָבַד הָאָדָם אֶת־
הָֽאֲדָמָה אֲשֶׁר [16] בֵּין הָעֵצִים׃ [17] בַּחֹ֫שֶׁךְ קָרָ֫אנוּ לֵאלֹהִים אֲשֶׁר בָּרָא אֶת־הַשָּׁמַ֫יִם
וְאֶת־הָאוֹר׃

[18] In sentence 14, above, is the speaker speaking to one group or two groups? How do you know?

---

[6] Masculine verbs and possessive suffixes will be used if the subject of the sentence is a man *and* a woman, or a group which has both men and women in it.

[7] Translate the -וְ as "but" to show contrast.

[8] Pausal form of פְּרִי. See §9.2.1, p. 27.

[9] For לֵאמֹר, see page 62, note 13.

[10] Remember: this word is pronounced *kol* not *kāl*. Because of the *maqqeph*, it is a closed unaccented syllable and must have a short vowel. The ָ is therefore a *qamets-hatuph*, not a *qamets.*

[11] What is the ה at the beginning of this word? See §14.3, p. 41. If necessary, see also §14.3.2, p. 42.

[12] Note that this is שָׁמַע אֶת־קוֹל, not שָׁמַע לְקוֹל or שָׁמַע בְּקוֹל. How does that affect the translation?

[13] The guttural ע has attracted a *pathah* under the מ. This is why you do not see the usual *holem* in the last syllable.

[14] Context often determines meaning. The words יָשַׁב and תַּ֫חַת are each used twice in this sentence. And their meaning is different each time.

[15] See page 62, note 13.

[16] Add the word *is*.

24

ADJECTIVES

Adjectives are words such as *large,* or *red,* or *great* which describe (or "modify") nouns. We may speak of a *large* house, a *red* book, a *great* king, etc. Hebrew adjectives follow certain rules, which we shall learn below. We shall also learn that *nouns* can be used as adjectives.

24.1 Adjectives: gender and number

Adjectives, like nouns, will be either masculine or feminine, singular or plural. (They do not have absolute and construct forms.) They will be masculine if they modify (describe) a masculine noun, and feminine if they modify a feminine noun. A feminine adjective is the same as a masculine adjective plus an added ָה - (or, rarely, ת-) suffix. Thus:

מֶ֫לֶךְ גָּדוֹל *a great king* and בְּרָכָה גְדוֹלָה[1] *a great blessing*

Likewise, in the plural we get:

מְלָכִים גְּדוֹלִים *great kings* and בְּרָכוֹת גְּדוֹלוֹת *great blessings*

Vowel Reduction (shortening)

As mentioned in the previous chapter, when words get longer, vowels at the beginning of the word often get "reduced" from a long vowel to a short vowel or even to a *shewa.* As an example, consider the two English words *able* and *ability.* The word *able* has a long *a* at the beginning. The word *ability* is formed from the word *able* by adding two additional syllables. When this happens, the long *a* from *able* reduces to a very short "uh" sound in the word *ability.*

The same thing often happens in Hebrew. Note what happened to the *qamets* under the ג of גָּדוֹל, above, when suffixes were added. A *shewa* appeared under the ג in all three of the longer words: גְּדוֹלָה, גְּדוֹלִים and גְּדוֹלוֹת.

This also often happens in construct nouns, since they lose their accent completely. Consider the word דָּבָר. Its singular *construct* becomes דְּבַר. The *qamets* under the ב reduces to *pathah,* and the *qamets* under the ד reduces all the way to *shewa.*

This even happens in the absolute form when it becomes plural. The plural absolute adds a suffix which lengthens the word. This again causes the first *qamets* to reduce: דְּבָרִים. When this plural absolute becomes a plural construct, even the *qamets* under the ב reduces to *shewa.* This at first leaves a double *shewa* at the beginning of a word (דְּבְרֵי). But then the first *shewa* becomes a *hireq* (§8.3.1): דִּבְרֵי .

[1] The ג has lost its dagesh because of the preceding vowel (that is, because of the ָה - at the end of בְּרָכָה).

24.2 Adjectives: the way they are used

Adjectives are usually used to modify nouns. But they can also be used like verbs.

When adjectives are used to modify nouns, the following rules apply:

24.2.1 Definite Article.

- **If the noun has a definite article**, there will also be a definite article on the adjective: הַמֶּ֫לֶךְ הַגָּדוֹל, *the great king.*
- **If the noun has a possessive suffix,** the adjective will *usually* have a definite article (סוּסִי הַגָּדוֹל *my great horse*). But sometimes it will not (סוּסִי גָּדוֹל *my great horse*).

Remember: a noun with a possessive suffix is definite, but it will not have a definite article (See Note 1 on p. 66). Thus, we will never see הַסּוּסִי הַגָּדוֹל or הַסּוּסִי גָּדוֹל.

24.2.2 Word Order. The noun usually comes first, the adjective second.

מֶ֫לֶךְ גָּדוֹל, *a great king*
הַמֶּ֫לֶךְ הַגָּדוֹל, *the great king*

When an adjective is used like a verb, the rules change as follows:

24.2.3 Definite Article. The noun has the definite article, but the adjective does not:

גָּדוֹל הַמֶּ֫לֶךְ OR הַמֶּ֫לֶךְ גָּדוֹל mean *the king (is) great*

In translating these two short sentences, the word *is* must be added, as above.

24.2.4 Word Order. Usually, the adjective will come first.[2] Compare the two short sentences above to *a great king* and *the great king* in §24.2.2.

24.3 Using Nouns as Adjectives

The Hebrew language does not have many adjectives. Therefore, nouns are sometimes used instead of adjectives. This is done by using the construct relationship which we learned in §21. For instance, in English we can say *a wooden ark* or *an ark of wood.* In the first case, we used the adjective *wooden;* in the second case we used the noun *wood* along with the word *of.* Hebrew often uses this second method.

Using the words אֲרוֹן, *ark* and עֵץ, *tree, wood* we can write *a wooden ark* in the following way:

אֲרוֹן־עֵץ = *an ark-of-wood;* that is, *a wooden ark*

Both words are nouns, but the noun עֵץ is being used like an adjective. Likewise:

אִישׁ־אֱלֹהִים = *a man-of-God;* that is, *a godly man*

Furthermore, it is not necessary that the gender of the two nouns agree. For instance, the word תּוֹרָה (*torah*) is a feminine noun and קֹ֫דֶשׁ (*holiness*) is a masculine noun. Yet they may be placed together:

תּוֹרַת־קֹ֫דֶשׁ = *a Torah-of-holiness;* that is, *a holy Torah*

In each of these cases, a noun (עֵץ, אֱלֹהִים, קֹ֫דֶשׁ) has been used where we would use an adjective in

---

[2] **Technical note:** For examples of the adjective coming second, see 1 Sam 12:17; 1 Chron 29:1.

English.

Finally, note again that these two words are in a construct relationship. This means that a definite article or a possessive suffix will be placed on the second noun, not the first (§21.5.1, p. 60). Thus we will see:

עִיר־הַקֹּדֶשׁ = *a-city-of the-holiness* . . . which means *the holy city*

עִיר־קָדְשְׁךָ = *a-city-of your-holiness* . . . which means *your holy city*

But we will *not* see הָעִיר־קֹדֶשׁ or עִירְךָ־קֹדֶשׁ.

This is just like the use of the definite article (§21, p. 60): *the man of God* = אִישׁ־הָאֱלֹהִים.

24.4 Parsing Adjectives

Adjectives are masculine or feminine, singular or plural. And they may have definite articles. When you parse, use "A" to represent "adjective." Thus, you will parse

גָּדוֹל = Ams [Adjective, masculine singular]

הַגְּדוֹלוֹת = Afp + d.a. [Adjective, feminine plural plus definite article]

Etc.

Things You Should Know

1. Adjectives are words which modify nouns. They will be masculine or feminine, and singular or plural. They do not have absolute and construct states, however.
2. Feminine adjectives are the same as masculine adjectives, with the addition of a ָה- suffix. Masculine adjectives modify masculine nouns; feminine adjectives modify feminine nouns.
3. The adjective usually comes *after* the noun.
4. If a noun has a definite article, its adjective will have a definite article: הַמֶּלֶךְ הַגָּדוֹל, *the great king*.

BUT

5. If an adjective is used to form a simple sentence, it will not have a definite article even if its noun does have one. הַמֶּלֶךְ גָּדוֹל, *the king (is) great.*
6. Nouns may be used like adjectives by putting them into a construct relationship.
   - The two nouns may have different genders.
   - Definite articles or possessive suffixes will go on the second noun.
7. Adjectives are parsed as follows: הַגְּדוֹלוֹת =Afp + d.a.

Exercise #18

גָּדוֹל *adj.* great

דַּעַת *f.* knowledge

הָיוּ they were (< הָיָה[3])

חָכָם *adj.* wise

חָכְמָה *f.* wisdom (note the *qamets-hatuph*)

טוֹב *adj.* good

יָדַע to know

מַיִם water (*pl.*[4] only), *cs.* מֵי

עַיִן *f.* eye[5], spring (of water), *cs.* עֵין, *dual* עֵינַיִם

קָדוֹשׁ *adj.* holy

קֹדֶשׁ *n.* holiness, holy place (that is, sanctuary or temple), a holy thing

רַע *adj., m.* bad, evil, inferior, *f.* רָעָה

[1] הָיוּ אַבְרָהָם וְשָׂרָה בְּאֶרֶץ־כְּנָעַן וְאֶת־אַנְשֵׁי־הָאָרֶץ יָרֵאוּ׃[6] [2] טוֹב דְּבַר־אַבְרָהָם
בְּעֵינֵי־שָׂרָה [7]וְרַע בְּעֵינֵי־אֱלֹהִים׃ [3] לָקְחוּ הָאִישׁ וְהָאִשָּׁה מַיִם מִן הָעַיִן וּבַבַּיִת נָתְנוּ
אֶת־הַמַּיִם לַנָּבִיא׃[10] [4] לֹא יָדְעוּ הָעָם אֶת־חָכְמַת[9]־הַנָּבִיא וּשְׁמוּאֵל[8] יָדַע׃ [5] הֲנָתַן יְהוָה
לְכָל־בְּנֵי־שְׁמוּאֵל אֶת־בִּרְכָתוֹ׃ [6] תִּכְתֹּב הַנְּבִיאָה אֶת־דִּבְרֵי־אֱלֹהִים בְּסֵפֶר׃ [7] בָּאוּ
הַנָּשִׁים הַחֲכָמוֹת הָעִיר[11] הַקְּדוֹשָׁה וּבַהֵיכָל דִּבְּרוּ לַמֶּלֶךְ׃ [8] טוֹבוֹת דַּעְתָּן וְחָכְמָתָן
בְּעֵינֵי־הַמֶּלֶךְ הַגָּדוֹל׃ [9] עָבְדוּ הַכֹּהֲנִים אֶת־אֵל־כְּנַעַן תַּחַת אֶת־יְהוָה׃ [10] יִשְׁמְעוּ[12]
בְּנֵי הַנְּבִיאָה אֶת־קוֹלָהּ וְגַם יִשְׁמְעוּ בְּקוֹל־אֱלֹהִים׃ [11] יָצְאוּ אַנְשֵׁי־קֹדֶשׁ מִן הַהֵיכָל
הַקָּדוֹשׁ׃ [12] רָאָה הָאִישׁ עֵין־מַיִם בַּגָּן אֲשֶׁר בָּרָא אֱלֹהִים׃ [13] הֲיָדַע הַנָּבִיא כִּי
יָשְׁבָה הָאִשָּׁה בְּבֵית־עֵץ׃ [14] חָכָם הַכֹּהֵן וּגְדוֹלָה דַעְתּוֹ׃ [15] הָיוּ כָּל הָאֲנָשִׁים בָּעִיר
וְרַע הַדָּבָר בְּעֵינֵי־הַמֶּלֶךְ׃ [16] יָשְׁבוּ הַנָּשִׁים עַל הָאֲדָמָה תַּחַת הָעֵץ וּבְסֵפֶר־קֹדֶשׁ
כָּתְבוּ׃ [17] הָלַכְנוּ בְגַנֵּךְ וּמִן עֵצֵךְ אָכַלְנוּ פֶּרִי[13]׃

---

[3] The "<" sign means "from." Here, it shows us that the word הָיוּ is from the verb הָיָה.

[4] **Technical note:** Although this word appears to be dual, it is really masculine plural. See *Gesenius' Hebrew Grammar*, edited by E. Kautzsch and revised by A. E. Cowley (Oxford: University Press, 1946), §88*d*.

[5] Parts of the body which come in pairs (eyes, ears, hands, etc.) are feminine, and will usually have duals rather than plurals. When עַיִן means "spring (of water)," it can also have a plural: עֲיָנוֹת.

[6] Who is afraid here? Abraham and Sarah? Or the men of the land? How do you know?

[7] Translate the -וְ as "but."

[8] The subject usually comes after the verb. But it may come *before* the verb in order to add emphasis: "... *Samuel* knew." The contrast is further emphasized by translating the *vav* before "Samuel" as "but" (not "and"): "... *but Samuel* knew."

[9] Note the *qamets-hatuph.*

[10] Did they give the water to *a* prophet or to *the* prophet? How do you know? See §16.2.4 on p. 48.

[11] בָּאוּ הָעִיר. See p. 65, note 18.

[12] In this sentence, note the two different ways of using שָׁמַע with קוֹל. If necessary, review the vocabulary on p. 61 and also footnote 9 on the same page.

[13] Pausal form of פְּרִי. See §9.2.1, p. 27.

25

THE VERB: IMPERATIVE

The Imperative (Impv) is used to give commands. In Hebrew, the Impv comes only in second person. (There is no first or third person Impv in Hebrew.[1]) The Impv is formed by removing the prefix from the second person Imperfect (Impf). When this leaves a double simple *shewa* at the beginning of the word, the first *shewa* becomes *hireq* (§9.1.1, p. 26). Compare the following:

	Second person Imperfect (Impf)		**Imperative (Impv)**	
ms	תִּשְׁמֹר	*you will keep*	שְׁמֹר	*Keep!*
fs	תִּשְׁמְרִי	*you will keep*	שִׁמְרִי	*Keep!*
mp	תִּשְׁמְרוּ	*you will keep*	שִׁמְרוּ	*Keep!*
fp	תִּשְׁמֹרְנָה	*you will keep*	שְׁמֹרְנָה	*Keep!*

Notes:

1 The *shewas* in the fs and mp are vocal, *even though they come after short vowels*: ši-m^{e}rî, ši-m^{e}rû.[2] These vocal *shewas* become composite under gutturals (for instance, עֲבֹד or בַּחֲרִי)

2. The abbreviation for Imperative is Impv. The abbreviation for Imperfect is Impf.

3. When you parse an Imperative verb, you do not need to mention the "person" since in Hebrew all Imperatives are second person. Thus שִׁמְרוּ is simply "Impv mp." You do not need to write "Impv 2mp" (although this would not be technically wrong).

4. Be sure not to confuse the following:
   - שִׁמְרִי (Impv fs) and שָֽׁמַרְתִּי (Perf 1cs) and also Nmsc + 1cs such as דְּבָרִי
   - שִׁמְרוּ (Impv mp) and שָֽׁמְרוּ (Perf 3cp; note the *metheg*)

THINGS YOU SHOULD KNOW

1. The Imperative is obtained by removing the prefix from the second person Imperfect.
2. The Imperative is abbreviated Impv; Imperfect is abbreviated Impf. Do not use "Imp," since this could mean *either* Impf or Impv.

---

[1] **Technical Note:** We shall learn, however, that there are indeed imperative-type moods for the first and third person. But they will have different names, and will not be called "imperative."

[2] **Technical Note:** This keeps the original sound of -m^{e}rî and -m^{e}rû, as found in the imperfect, and is similar to what we saw with the inseparable preposition (p. 26, Technical Note). It is most clearly seen in words such as כָּתְבוּ. If the *shewa* were silent, it would make a closed syllable (-כָּתְ) before the *begadkepat* ב. The ב would then be at the beginning of a syllable. It would not be after either a vowel or a vocal *shewa*; therefore, it would have a *dagesh lene*: כָּתְבּוּ. But this is not the case. There is no *dagesh* in the ב; therefore the *shewa* before it must be vocal.

26

MORE ABOUT THE SIGN OF THE DEFINITE DIRECT OBJECT (אֶת־)

The definite direct object is a form of the direct object.[1] The direct object is the word which *receives* the action in a sentence, and was introduced in §15. For instance, consider the sentence: *I hit a ball.* The subject of this sentence is *I.* The verb is *hit.* The direct object is *a ball.* If the direct object is "definite" (that is, "*the* ball," or "*her* ball," or "*John's* ball"), then we call it a "definite direct object." This is because we know *which* ball is being mentioned.

As we have already learned, it is very easy to find a definite direct object in a Hebrew sentence, because a special word or "sign" is usually placed before the object. The sign can be either אֵת or אֶת־.[2] Thus:

	The man took a horse	is	לָקַח הָאִישׁ סוּס
but			
	The man took the horse	is	לָקַח הָאִישׁ אֶת־הַסּוּס (note the אֶת־)

In the first example, סוּס has no definite article. It is thus a direct object but not a *definite* direct object. In the second example, however, סוּס does have a definite article. It is thus a definite direct object, and so it has a definite article and also has the sign of the definite direct object: אֶת־.

All names (proper nouns) are also definite: Abraham, Sarah, Samuel, etc. If they are the object, you will see אֵת or אֶת־ before them, although they will not have a definite article. For instance:

רָאָה שְׁמוּאֵל *Samuel saw.* BUT רָאָה אֶת־שְׁמוּאֵל *He saw Samuel*

In the sentence on the left, there is no object. It says *Samuel saw,* but we do not know *what* (or *whom*) he saw. In the sentence on the right, however, *Samuel* is the *object* not the subject (the אֶת־ tells us this). Samuel was *seen* – although we do not know *who* saw Samuel. The subject of רָאָה is just *he.* It could be any male – but not Samuel. The presence or absence of אֶת־ (אֵת) is therefore very important. Here is another example:

יָדְעָה הָאִשָּׁה The woman knew. BUT יָדְעָה אֶת־הָאִשָּׁה She knew the woman.

As we have seen, a direct object is definite (and will have a preceding אֶת־ or אֵת) *if*:

(1) it has a definite article, ***or***
(2) it is a proper noun (name)

In addition, an object is definite:

---

[1] If necessary, review "Sentences and clauses" in the introductory section "Grammar, an Overview," p. xvii.

[2] The vowel has shortened in the second case because of the *maqqeph* (§10.1, p. 29). Later you will learn that אֵת can also mean *with.*

(3) if it has a possessive suffix (that is, if it belongs to someone, §23):

For instance: *my* horse, *her* book, John's family. Thus, if סוּסוֹ is used as a direct object, it will be a *definite* direct object and will use the אֶת־ sign: רָאָה הָאִישׁ אֶת־סוּסוֹ

(4) if it is *in construct to* a proper noun (name):

For instance: if סוּס־שְׁמוּאֵל is used as the direct object, we will see אֶת־סוּס־שְׁמוּאֵל

(5) if it is *in construct to* a definite noun (that is, in construct to a noun which has a definite article or a possessive suffix):

For instance: if אֲרוֹן־הָעֵץ (*the ark of wood*) or הַר־קָדְשְׁךָ (*your holy mountain*) are used as objects, we will see אֶת־אֲרוֹן־הָעֵץ or אֶת־הַר־קָדְשְׁךָ.

Here are more examples, where סוּס is used as a definite direct object and then as an object which is not definite:

Definite direct object	Object, but not definite
לָקְחָה אִשָּׁה אֶת־הַסּוּס *A woman took the horse*	לָקְחָה אִשָּׁה סוּס *A woman took a horse*
לָקְחָה אִשָּׁה אֶת־סוּס־הַמֶּלֶךְ *A woman took the king's horse*	לָקְחָה אִשָּׁה סוּס־מֶלֶךְ *A woman took a king's horse*
לָקְחָה אִשָּׁה אֶת־סוּס־שְׁמוּאֵל *A woman took Samuel's horse*	לָקְחָה אִשָּׁה סוּס־נָבִיא *A woman took a prophet's horse*
לָקְחָה אִשָּׁה אֶת־סוּסִי *A woman took my horse*	לָקְחָה אִשָּׁה סוּס *A woman took a horse*

Things You Should Know

1. The direct object of a sentence is the word which receives the action. It can be definite or indefinite.

2. If a direct object is definite, it will have אֵת or אֶת־ before it.

3. A direct object is definite if
   - it has a definite article: הַסּוּס or
   - it is a proper noun (a personal name): שְׁמוּאֵל or
   - it has a possessive suffix : סוּסוֹ or
   - it is *in construct to* a proper noun, a word with a definite article, or a word with a possessive suffix: סוּס־הַמֶּלֶךְ, סוּס־שְׁמוּאֵל, etc.

Exercise #19

אֶבֶן	*f.* stone (*pl.* אֲבָנִים)	נָהָר	*m.* river, *cs.* נְהַר; *pl.* נְהָרוֹת (*rarely* נְהָרִים)
בָּקָר	cows, (herd of) cattle, oxen	עֶרֶב	evening
בֹּקֶר	morning	עֵשָׂו	Esau
הַר	mountain (with d.a.: הָהָר)	רֹאשׁ	head
זָקֵן	*adj.* old; *noun* an elder	שָׁפַט	to judge
יַעֲקֹב	Jacob		

[1] שָׁמַר: שְׁמֹר: שִׁמְרִי: שָׁמַרְתִּי: שִׁמְרוּ: שָׁמְרוּ: שְׁמֹרְנָה: שָׁמְרָה: [2] שִׁפְטוּ אֶת־
הָעָם: כְּרֹת עֵץ: כְּתֹבְנָה אֶת־הַדְּבָרִים: כִּרְתוּ בְרִית: כָּרְתוּ בְרִית: [3] רָאָה פַרְעֹה
עֵצִים גְּדוֹלִים בֵּין הַנָּהָר [3]וּבֵין הָהָר: [4] אָמַר מֹשֶׁה זִכְרִי אֶת־הַבְּרִית אֲשֶׁר כָּרַת יְהוָה
עִם יִשְׂרָאֵל: [5] בַּבֹּקֶר הָלַךְ יַעֲקֹב אֶל הָהָר עִם בְּקָרוֹ וְהִנֵּה בָּא עֵשָׂו: [6] אָמַר
פַּרְעֹה לְשָׂרָה מֶלֶךְ רֹאשׁ־עַמּוֹ הוּא וּמֶלֶךְ־מִצְרַיִם אֲנִי: [7] הֲנָתַן יַעֲקֹב אֶת־בְּקָרוֹ לְעֵשָׂו
בַּבֹּקֶר: [8] כָּרַת אֱלֹהִים מֵי־הַנָּהָר וְרַע הַדָּבָר בְּעֵינֵי־פַרְעֹה: [9] תִּשְׁלַחְנָה[4] הַנָּשִׁים
הַחֲכָמוֹת אֶת־הָאֲנָשִׁים וְגַם תִּשְׁאַלְנָה[4] אֶת־הַנְּבִיאָה: [10] רָאָה הַזָּקֵן כִּי זָקֵן הָעֵץ וְטוֹב
פִּרְיוֹ: [11] בָּעֶרֶב לָקְחוּ אֲבָנִים מִן הַנָּהָר וּלְזַרְעָם אָמְרוּ זִכְרוּ כִּי כָרַת יְהוָה אֶת־מֵי־
הַנָּהָר: [12] כִּתְבוּ אֵת הַדְּבָרִים הַקְּדוֹשִׁים עַל הָאֶבֶן וּבָעֶרֶב קִרְאוּ אֶת־הַדְּבָרִים אֶל
הָעָם: [13] יָדְעָה הָגָר כִּי טוֹבִים הַזְּקֵנִים וּגְדוֹלוֹת דַּעְתָּם וְחָכְמָתָם: [14] הֲיִשְׁפְּטוּ
בְּנֵי־שְׁמוּאֵל אֶת־עַם־יִשְׂרָאֵל: [15] רַע הַדָּבָר בְּעֵינֵי־הַכֹּהֵן הַזָּקֵן: [16] עִבְדוּ אֶת־
אֱלֹהֵי[5]־יִשְׂרָאֵל תַּחַת כּוֹכְבֵי־הַשָּׁמָיִם: [17] הִנֵּה יְהוָה עִם עַמּוֹ וְרֹאשׁ־בְּנֵי־יִשְׂרָאֵל הוּא:
[18] יָדְעוּ הַכֹּהֲנִים הַחֲכָמִים כִּי הָיוּ דַּעַת וְחָכְמָה מִן אֱלֹהֵי־הַקֹּדֶשׁ: [19] יִזְכֹּר פַּרְעֹה
אִם נִכְרֹת אֶת־עֵצוֹ:

---

[3] For בֵּין . . . בֵּין, see page 65, note 15.

[4] The guttural has attracted a *pathah*. Thus we do not see the תִּשְׁמֹרְנָה vowel pattern.

[5] Construct form of אֱלֹהִים. This sentence can be translated several ways, depending upon how you translate אֱלֹהֵי and תַּחַת.

27

VAV CONSECUTIVE

Hebrew has several characteristics which are not found in English or most other languages. One of them is called "*Vav* Consecutive." *Vav* Consecutive is a *vav* (ו) placed in front of (prefixed to) a Perfect or Imperfect verb: שָׁמַר + ו → וְשָׁמַר. It changes the meaning of the translation, as described below.

27.1 Function of *Vav* Consecutive

27.1.1 **Location:** *Vav* Consecutive may be attached to Perfect or Imperfect only. A *vav* on any other verb (such as an Imperative) is just a *vav* conjunction.

27.1.2 **Parsing:** In parsing, use "w.c." for *vav* consecutive, and "vav" for *vav* conjunction. (The "w" comes from an alternate spelling: *waw* consecutive.)

27.1.3 **Translation:** W.c. will usually be translated *and* or *but* (just like *vav* conjunction).

27.1.4 **Meaning:** W.c. will change the *meaning* of a Perfect verb to "future;" it will change the *meaning* of an Imperfect verb to "past." Note: The verbs remain Perfect or Imperfect in parsing; only their *meaning* changes. Thus:

וְשָׁמַר	is parsed Perf 3ms + w.c. < שׁמר	**but** it means	*and/but he will keep*
וַיִּשְׁמֹר	is parsed Impf 3ms + w.c. < שׁמר	**but** it means	*and/but he kept*

This fourth point (§27.1.4) is very important because it is **very** common in Hebrew. It occurs in almost every sentence. Note the following:

If you want to say *He will keep and he will judge,* you do **not** write יִשְׁמֹר וְיִשְׁפֹּט. Rather:

יִשְׁמֹר וְשָׁפַט = *He will keep and he will judge*

The *vav* consecutive has the effect of changing the meaning of the Perfect שָׁפַט from past (*he judged*) to future (*he will judge*). In the same way, note that

שָׁמַר וַיִּשְׁפֹּט = *He kept and he judged* (**not** *he kept and he will judge*).

But remember: only the *meaning* changes; the parsing does not:

- a Perfect with w.c. still remains a Perfect and is parsed as "Perf + w.c."
- an Imperfect with w.c. still remains an Imperfect, and is parsed as "Impf + w.c."
- the w.c. can mean either *and* or *but*

Thus:

וְשָׁמַרְתִּי =	Perf 1cs + w.c. < שׁמר =	*And I shall keep*	or	*But I shall keep*
וַיִּשְׁמְרוּ =	Impf 3mp + w.c. < שׁמר =	*And they kept*	or	*But they kept*

27.2 Pointing of *Vav* Consecutive

27.2.1 When w.c. is attached to **Perfect** it is pointed just like *Vav* Conjunction (§18).

27.2.2 When w.c. is attached to **Imperfect** it is pointed ·וַ (like the definite article). Thus: וַיִּשְׁמֹר. **Note the dagesh and the *pathah*.** This shows it is w.c. and not *vav* conjunction.[1]

An exception: w.c. before Impf 1cs is pointed וָ, since the א of the 1cs prefix rejects the dagesh. Thus, the Impf 1cs + w.c. of שָׁמַר is וָאֶשְׁמֹר

27.3 Parsing of verbs with *Vav* Consecutive:

וְשָׁמַר	is parsed	Perf 3ms + w.c. < שמר
וַיִּשְׁמֹר	is parsed	Impf 3ms + w.c. < שמר

27.4 Other Characteristics of *Vav* Consecutive

27.4.1 **No other word** can come between the *w.c.* and the verb. If there is another word between the *vav* and the verb, then the *vav* is *vav* conjunction, not *w.c.* Therefore

שָׁפַט וְלֹא שָׁמַר

is translated *he judged but he did not keep*[2] (not *he judged but he will not keep*).

27.4.2 ***Vav* Consecutive and Short Forms of Imperfect.** Short Imperfect forms are often found with verbs which have י or ו for their middle letter, or ה for their final letter.[3] *W.c.* will use the "short form" of the Imperfect if there is one.[4] An example is the very common verb הָיָה (*to be*). The normal form of the Impf 3ms (*he/it will be*) is יִהְיֶה[5] but there is also a short form יְהִי (y^e^hî). This short form is used with *w.c.* to give us the very common וַיְהִי,[6] *and it was/happened.*

27.4.3 **Accent:** The addition of *w.c.* will often cause the accent to move.

(a) ***W.c.* with the Perfect** tends to move the accent toward the **end** of the word. Thus,

שָׁמַ֫רְתָּ *you(ms) kept*, but וְשָׁמַרְתָּ֫ *and you(ms) will keep.*

(b) ***W.c.* with the Imperfect** sometimes causes the accent to mowe toward the **beginning** of the word (especially in the "weak verbs," which we shall study later). Thus,

---

[1] **Technical note:** Impf + w.c. is very common in Hebrew. Impf + *vav* (that is, *vav* conjunction) is not common, and never appears in this textbook. When Impf + *vav* appears in the Bible, it does not use *dagesh* or *pathah*, and it does not change the meaning of the Impf. Thus, וְתַגֵּיד לִבְנֵי יִשְׂרָאֵל *and you will declare to the sons of Israel* (Exod 19:3).

[2] Remember, w.c. is translated *and* or *but*, according to the context. Here, the word *but* is appropriate..

[3] **Technical note:** These types of verbs are called "weak verbs," and their vowel pointing often changes.

[4] There is an exception: The short form of the Impf will *not* be used for the first person singular (1cs).

[5] Not יִהְיֶה . Vowel pointing often changes in verbs with ה and י in them. We will study such verbs later.

[6] The *dagesh* is not written in the first י of this word. Thus: וַיְהִי, not וַיְּהִי. **Technical note:** This happens because י over *shewa* usually does not take *dagesh.* We will see this again when we study the Piel form of the verb.

יֹאמַר *he will say* (accent is on last syllable, as usual), but

וַיֹּ֫אמֶר *and he will say* (accent has moved forward).

(In the second case, the vowel under the מ has also changed. The point to watch here, however, is the change of accent.)

27.4.4 **More about the verb** **הָיָה**. The word וַיְהִי (mentioned above) is often found as the first word of a sentence. It can be translated *And he/it was*, but most often it is translated *And it happened* (*that*) or *And it came to pass* (*that*). Likewise, וְהָיָה at the beginning of a sentence is usually translated, *And it will happen* (*that*) or *And it will come to pass* (*that*).

Things You Should Know

1. A ו placed immediately before (prefixed to) a Perfect or Imperfect verb is called "*vav* consecutive." It is usually translated *and* or *but*, and is abbreviated w.c.
2. **Location:** A *vav* consecutive (w.c.) may be prefixed to Perfect or Imperfect only.
3. **Meaning:** A w.c. will change the *meaning* of a Perfect verb to future, and the *meaning* of an Imperfect verb to past. The verbs themselves remain Perfect and Imperfect, however.
4. **Parsing:** A Perfect verb with a w.c. is parsed "Perf + w.c." Likewise, an Imperfect verb with w.c. is parsed "Impf + w.c."
5. **Pointing:**
   a. **With Imperfect:** W.c. will be pointed (like the definite article) with *pathah* and a following *dagesh forte*: ·וַ (The א of the 1cs will reject the *dagesh*, and we will see -וָ.)
   b. **With Perfect:** W.c. will *not* have this *pathah* or *dagesh*, and will be pointed just like *vav* conjunction.
6. No word can come *between* the w.c. and its verb.
7. If a verb has a short form of the Imperfect, this short form will be used by the w.c.
8. וַיְהִי is usually translated *And it happened* (*that*) or *And it came to pass* (*that*). וְהָיָה is usually translated, *And it will happen* (*that*) or *And it will come to pass* (*that*).

Exercise #20

אֶחָד, אַחַד *m.* one; *cs.* אַחַד

אַחַת *f.* one; *cs.* אַחַת (same as *abs.*)

אַחַר, אַחֲרֵי after, behind

אֵשׁ *f.* fire

יָד *f.* hand; *dual* יָדַיִם

כֹּה so, thus, in this way

לָכַד to take, catch, capture

מְאֹד greatly, very

נַ֫עַר boy, young man

רָדַף to pursue; to persecute

שָׂרַף to burn

Note also the following word usage:

אַחַת מִן, אֶחָד מִן one of the; *example:* אַחַת מִן הַנָּשִׁים one of the women

וְהָיָה and he/it shall be, shall happen וַיְהִי and he/it was, happened

רָדַף אַחֲרֵי *and* רָדַף לְ- *both mean* "to pursue" (not "to persecute")

[1] רָדְפוּ וַיִּלְכְּדוּ׃ תִּשְׁמַע[7] וְשָׁפְטָה׃ תִּכְתֹּב סֵפֶר וַתִּכְרֹת בְּרִית׃ לָקַחְנוּ וְשָׂרַפְנוּ׃ [2] רָאָה
עֵשָׂו כִּי גָדוֹל מְאֹד בְּקַר־יַעֲקֹב [9]וַיֹּאמֶר נָתַן אֱלֹהִים בְּרָכָה אֶל יַעֲקֹב׃ [3] וַתְּהִי[8] יַד־
יַעֲקֹב עַל רֹאשׁ־עֵשָׂו וְגַם נָתַן אֶת־בִּרְכָתוֹ׃ [4] רָאָה הַנַּעַר נָהָר וְהַר גָּדוֹל מְאֹד אַחֲרֵי
הַנָּהָר׃ [5] וַיְהִי זָקֵן מְאֹד יַעֲקֹב וְהִנֵּה בָּא מִצְרָיִם׃ [6] וְקֹדֶשׁ־יְהוָה כְּאֵשׁ בְּרֹאשׁ־הָהָר
בְּעֵינֵי־זִקְנֵי־יִשְׂרָאֵל׃ [7] וְהָיָה בָּעֶרֶב [10]וְשָׁמַר אַהֲרֹן אֶת־אֲרוֹן־הַבְּרִית כִּדְבַר־מֹשֶׁה׃
[8] רָדְפוּ יְהוֹשֻׁעַ וּבְנֵי־יִשְׂרָאֵל לָעָם וַתְּהִי[11] יַד־יְהוָה עַל אֶרֶץ־כְּנָעַן׃ [9] לְכֹדְנָה אֶת־
הָעִיר בַּבֹּקֶר וּבָעֶרֶב שְׂרֹפְנָה אֶת־הֵיכָלָהּ [14]בָּאֵשׁ׃ [10] בָּאָה[13] נְבִיאָה אַחַת[12] אֲשֶׁר יָשְׁבָה
בִּיהוּדָה אֶל שְׁמוּאֵל כִּי שָׁפַט אֶת־יִשְׂרָאֵל׃ [11] וַיְהִי דְבַר־יְהוָה[16] אֶל־הַנָּבִיא וַיֹּאמֶר[15]
שִׁמְעוּ דְבַר־יְהוָה כֹּה אָמַר יְהוָה׃ [12] שָׁמַר הַזָּקֵן אֶת־בְּקָרוֹ בְּאַחַד בָּתֵּי[18]־הָאָבֶן[17]׃
[13] רָדַף אֶחָד מִן[19] הַנְּעָרִים אַחֲרֵי בְקַר־הַזָּקֵן כִּי בָּאוּ אֶל הֶהָרִים׃ [14] אָמְרָה הַנְּבִיאָה
כֹּה אָמַר יְהוָה כְּתֹבִי אֶת־כָּל־דִּבְרֵי־שְׁמוּאֵל תַּחַת אֶת־דִּבְרֵי־הַכֹּהֲנִים׃ [15] הֲיָשַׁב הַמֶּלֶךְ
בְּבֵית־אֶבֶן זָקֵן עַל[21] הַנָּהָר׃ [16] וְהָיָה בַבֹּקֶר [20]וּבָאוּ הַכֹּהֵן וְהַנָּבִיא אֶת־הַהֵיכָל וְקָרְאוּ
בִּדְבַר־יְהוָה׃

---

[7] The guttural has attracted a *pathah*. Note also how the grammar can help you in translation. This first verb can be parsed and translated two different ways (3fs or 2ms). But the verb which comes *after* it can be parsed only one way. Let the parsing of the second verb guide you in your parsing of the first verb.

[8] Note how similar this verb is to the 3ms וַיְהִי, which you often see. This time we have Impf 3fs + w.c. < הָיָה. Verbs which end with ה are weak, and often lose their final ה. We will study them in detail later.

[9] Impf 3ms + w.c. < אָמַר = "and he said." This form is very common, and you will see it often.

[10] Translate "that Aaron shall keep." This type of construction, where w.c. is translated "that" rather than "and" or "but," is often found in Hebrew.

[11] See footnote 8, above.

[12] Translate "a certain" rather than "one." In this context, the word אַחַת (or אֶחָד) is similar to the word τὶς in New Testament Greek.

[13] See p. 65 footnote 19.

[14] The בּ still has its *dagesh* because it is *not* preceded by a vowel. Remember that הָ is not a vowel letter, but is rather a *qamets* followed by a consonant: ה with *mappiq*.

[15] See footnote 9.

[16] וַיְהִי דְבַר־יְהוָה. This very common phrase is usually translated, "And the word of the LORD *came* ...."

[17] Notice how the first *seghol* of the word אֶבֶן lengthens to *qamets* "in pause."

[18] Plural construct of בַּיִת.

[19] אֶחָד מִן. See the note on usage under the vocabulary list.

[20] Review footnote 10, above, for the translation of this *vav* consecutive.

[21] Translate "near" or "next to," not "upon."

28

FURTHER IMPERATIVE-TYPE MOODS: COHORTATIVE, EMPHATIC IMPERATIVE AND JUSSIVE

In §25, we learned that the Hebrew Imperative comes only in the second person. But Hebrew has three other imperative-type (or forceful) moods which also add emphasis to sentences:

the **Cohortative** (which works like a first-person[1] Imperative),

the **Emphatic Imperative** (a stronger second person Imperative), and

the **Jussive** (which works like a third person Imperative).

28.1 The Cohortative

The Cohortative is formed by adding a ָה- suffix to the Imperfect 1cs or 1cp. Note the following comparison of first person Imperfect and Cohortative:

	First common Singular (1cs)		*First common plural (1cp)*	
Imperfect	אֶשְׁמֹר	*I shall keep*	נִשְׁמֹר	*We shall keep*
Cohortative	אֶשְׁמְרָה	*Let me keep,* or *I will keep*	נִשְׁמְרָה	*Let us keep,* or *We will keep*

Again, note that the Cohortative is found *only in the first person.*

Parsing: אֶשְׁמְרָה = Coh 1cs < שׁמר נִשְׁמְרָה = Coh 1cp < שׁמר

28.2 The Emphatic Imperative

The Emphatic Imperative occurs *only in the second person masculine singular* (2ms). Again, a ָה- suffix is added; this time it is added to the Impv ms:

Ordinary Imperative, ms: שְׁמֹר *Keep* (a command)

Emphatic Imperative (ms): שָׁמְרָה *Keep!!* (a strong command)
(Note: *Shewa* has changed to *qamets-hatuph*. The *shewa* under the מ is vocal.)

Parsing: שָׁמְרָה = Emph Impv (or Emph Impv ms) < שָׁמַר

[1] **Technical note:** The Cohortative is, on rare occasion, found outside the first person. Likewise, the Jussive is occasionally found in the second person (and even more rarely in the first person). We shall not be considering these unusual cases. We shall merely consider the Cohortative to be first person and the Jussive to be third person. For further information, see *Gesenius' Hebrew Grammar*, edited by E. Kautzsch and revised by A. E. Cowley (Oxford: University Press, 1946) §48.2.

Notes on Emphatic Imperative:

1. The Emphatic Imperative comes only in the masculine singular.
2. The first *qamets* (under the שׁ) is *qamets-hatuph* (šo-m^{e}râ[2]).
3. Do not confuse the Emphatic Imperative (שָׁמְרָה) with Perf 3fs (שָׁמְרָה). The Perf 3fs has a *qamets* with *metheg* instead of *qamets-hatuph*.

28.3 The Jussive

The Jussive comes in the third person, and usually has the same form as the Imperfect. Thus:

יִשְׁמֹר הַמֶּ֫לֶךְ can mean either *The king will keep* OR *Let the king keep.*

The context[3] will determine the meaning. But there are also two other signs which may be present.

28.3.1 **Short form of Imperfect**. The Jussive will use a shortened form of the Imperfect, if one is available. This was also true of the *vav* consecutive (§27.4.2).

28.3.2 **Prefixed *vav* conjunction.** Although Jussive usually looks just like the Imperfect, note that:

Jussive cannot take *vav* consecutive.

Thus, a *vav* attached to **Jussive** will simply be a *Vav* Conjunction, and will not have a *pathah* or a following *dagesh*. It will be translated *and* or *but,* and it will not change the translation of the Jussive itself. Note this point well, because it will help you:

Impf + w.c.: וַיִּשְׁמֹר הַמֶּ֫לֶךְ *And the king kept*

BUT

Juss + vav: וְיִשְׁמֹר הַמֶּ֫לֶךְ *And let the king keep*

↑ Note: no *dagesh* in the *yod.* and no *pathah* under the *vav*

Other examples (again note that there are no *dageshes* in the prefixes and no *pathah*s under the *vavs*):

Gen 1:9:	וְתֵרָאֶה הַיַּבָּשָׁה	*And let the dry land appear ....*
Judg 9:19:	וְיִשְׂמַח גַּם־הוּא בָּכֶם	*And let him also rejoice in you.*
Jonah 3:8:	וְיִקְרְאוּ אֶל־אֱלֹהִים	*And let them cry to God ....*
Lam 1:21:	וְיִהְיוּ כָמוֹנִי׃	*And let them become as I am.*
1 Chr 16:31:	וְיֹאמְרוּ בַגּוֹיִם יְהוָה מָלָךְ׃	*And let them say among the nations, "Yahweh rules."*

---

[2] **Technical note:** On this unusual pointing (a short vowel before a vocal *shewa*) see *Gesenius* §48(*i*).

[3] P. 41, footnote 1.

28.3.3 Parsing Jussive and Imperfect with *vav*: We have seen that Jussive cannot take w.c. Thus:

וַיִּשְׁמֹר is parsed Impf 3ms + w.c. < שָׁמַר and means *and he kept*

BUT

וְיִשְׁמֹר is parsed Juss 3ms + *vav* < שָׁמַר and means *and let him keep*

↑ Note: not w.c.

Things You Should Know

1. **Cohortative** adds a ָה - suffix to the Imperfect 1cs or 1cp, and acts like a first person imperative: אֶשְׁמְרָה "Let me keep" נִשְׁמְרָה "Let us keep"

   The Cohortative comes only in the first person.

2. **Emphatic Imperative** adds a ָה - suffix to the ms Imperative, and forms a strong imperative: שָׁמְרָה "Keep!!" (a strong command; note *qamets-hatuph* and *vocal* shewa)

   The Emphatic Imperative comes *only* in the (second) masculine singular.

3. **Jussive** usually has the same form as the Imperfect. It acts like a third person imperative.

   a. Since the Jussive has the same form as the Imperfect, יִשְׁמֹר הַמֶּלֶךְ can mean either "The king will keep" OR "Let the king keep." The context will help you decide.

   b. The Jussive will use a shortened Imperfect, if one is available.

   c. The Jussive cannot take *vav* consecutive, but may take *vav* conjunction.

4. **Parsing:** Cohortative is parsed Coh 1cs or Coh 1cp.
   Emphatic Imperative is parsed Emph Impv.
   Jussive is parsed Juss 3ms, Juss 3fs, etc.

Exercise #21

גָּנַב	to steal	מָכַר	to sell
דָּוִד	David	מָשַׁל	to rule (-מָשַׁל בְּ to rule over)
דָּם	blood	קָבַר	to bury
דָּמִים	killing, murder, bloodshed (*pl.* of דָּם)	קֶבֶר	a grave
חֲלוֹם	*m.* a dream, *pl.* חֲלוֹמוֹת	שְׁלֹמֹה	Solomon
חָלַם	to dream (Impf. יַחֲלֹם[4])	שָׁפַךְ	to pour out, spill, shed (blood)

[1] [5]וַיִּקְרָא אֱלֹהִים לָאוֹר יוֹם וְלַחֹשֶׁךְ קָרָא לָיְלָה וַיְהִי־עֶרֶב וַיְהִי בֹקֶר יוֹם אֶחָד׃
[2] לָקַח יְהוָה אֶת־הָאָדָם מֵעֲפַר־הָאֲדָמָה [7]וַיֹּאמֶר עֲבֹד וּשְׁמֹר אֶת־הַגָּן׃ [3] רָדְפָה[6] אַחֲרֵי
הָאֲנָשִׁים אֲשֶׁר גָּנְבוּ מִן הָאִשָּׁה וַיִּמְכְּרוּ אֶת־בְּקָרָהּ׃ [4] תִּשְׂרֹפְנָה אֶת־הָעִיר וּגְדוֹלָה מְאֹד[8]
הָאֵשׁ׃ [5] וַיֹּאמֶר יְהוָה אֶל אַבְרָהָם כַּעֲפַר־הָאֲדָמָה וּכְכוֹכְבֵי־הַשָּׁמַיִם כֹּה יִהְיֶה[9] זַרְעֶךָ׃
[6] הֲיָדַע עֵשָׂו כִּי הָיוּ יַעֲקֹב וְעִמּוֹ אַחֲרֵי הַבָּקָר׃ [7] אָמְרוּ אַנְשֵׁי־דָוִד לֹא נִרְדְּפָה אֶת־
הַנְּעָרִים [10]וְנִלְכְּדָה אֶת־הָעִיר׃ [8] הֲתִמְכֹּר מַיִם מִן הָעַיִן אֶל אַנְשֵׁי־דָוִד׃ [9] אִישׁ־דָּמִים
דָּוִד כִּי שָׁפַךְ דָּם וְרַע הַדָּבָר בְּעֵינֵי־אֱלֹהִים׃ [10] וַיֹּאמְרוּ[12] הָעָם יִמְשֹׁל[11] אִישׁ טוֹב
בְּיִשְׂרָאֵל׃ [11] וַיְהִי בַּלַּיְלָה וַיַּחֲלֹם[14] שְׁלֹמֹה חֲלוֹם וַיִּשְׁמַע אֶת־קוֹל־אֱלֹהֵי[13]־הַשָּׁמָיִם׃
[12] [15]וַיִּשְׁאַל שְׁלֹמֹה אֶת־אֱלֹהִים וַיֹּאמֶר אֶמְשְׁלָה בְּדַעַת וּבְחָכְמָה גְדוֹלָה׃ [13] קָבְרָנָה
אֶת־הַנָּבִיא הַקָּדוֹשׁ בְּקֶבֶר אַחַר הֵיכַל־הַמֶּלֶךְ׃ [14] שָׁלְחָה[17] אֶת־הָאֲנָשִׁים וְיִרְדְּפוּ[16]
וְיִלְכְּדוּ אֶת־הַנְּעָרִים אֲשֶׁר גָּנְבוּ אֶת־הַבָּקָר׃ [15] וַיֹּאמֶר אֶחָד מִבְּנֵי־הַנְּבִיאִים כֹּה
אָמַר יְהוָה יָדַי עִם יִשְׂרָאֵל׃ [16] שָׁפְכוּ אַנְשֵׁי־דָמִים דָּם בְּעִיר־קֹדֶשׁ־אֱלֹהִים׃

---

[4] The vowel pointing has changed because of the guttural (§13.1, §13.3, p. 38).

[5] Impf 3ms + w.c. A *qamets* has been attracted because of the guttural.

[6] Emphatic imperative; the first *qamets* is *qamets-hatuph.* (Perf 3fs would normally have a *metheg* under the ר – though, unfortunately, not always.) The word is thus pronounced ro-ḏ^{e}p̄â (see p. 85, Note 2 and footnote 2).

[7] See p. 83, note 9.

[8] Add the words *will be.*

[9] Impf 3ms < הָיָה. The verb *to be* is irregular in Hebrew, as in many languages. Here, the final ה has brought a *segohl* instead of a *holem.* And the form הָיוּ (Perf 3cp) will be found in the next sentence.

[10] Should this ו be translated "and" or "but"?

[11] Should this be translated as Imperfect or Jussive?

[12] In Biblical Hebrew, the word עַם sometimes takes a plural verb (such as וַיֹּאמְרוּ) and sometimes a singular verb (such as וַיֹּאמֶר).

[13] Construct form of אֱלֹהִים. The form is plural, but in this case translate it as a singular.

[14] In this verb (and the next one), the guttural has attracted a *pathah.* Review §13 (page 38) if necessary.

[15] See the previous footnote.

[16] This verb and the one after it cannot be Impf plus w.c. Look at the *vavs.* There is always a *pathah* under a w.c. which stands before an Imperfect. But these *vavs* have *shewa* instead of *pathah.* What does this tell you? Review §28.3.2 (p. 85) if you are not sure.

[17] The lack of a *metheg* under the שׁ shows you that this is not Perf 3fs (see note 6, above).

[17] וַיִּקְבְּרוּ אֶת־הַנָּבִיא עַל[18] קֶ֫בֶר־הַמֶּ֫לֶךְ כִּי טוֹב הוּא וּגְדוֹלוֹת מְאֹד דַּעְתּוֹ וְחָכְמָתוֹ׃
[18] נֻתְּנָה אֶת־אַחַת מִן־הֶעָרִים[20] בְּיַד־הַמֶּ֫לֶךְ וַיִּשְׂרֹף אֶת־הָעִיר בָּאֵשׁ׃ [19] תַּחֲלֹם[19]
אַחַת מִן הַנְּבִיאוֹת הַחֲכָמוֹת חֲלוֹם וְיָדְעָה דְּבַר־יְהוָה׃

---

[18] Remember that עַל means not only *over* or *upon* but also *against* and *near*.

[19] Impf 3fs. The guttural has attracted a *pathah* under the prefix, and the *shewa* has become composite.

[20] Plural of עִיר. Translate "one of the cities."

29

THE VERB: INFINITIVE CONSTRUCT AND INFINITIVE ABSOLUTE

An infinitive is a type of verb. In English, an Infinitive is the "to" form of the verb:

to sing
to run
to read

Hebrew has two kinds of Infinitives: *construct* and *absolute*. The **Infinitive Construct** (IC) is similar to the English Infinitive. The **Infinitive Absolute** (IA) is more like an adverb.

> **Note**: Infinitive Construct and Infinitive Absolute have **nothing to do with the absolute and construct form of the noun**. We could call them Infinitives Type 1 and Infinitive Type 2; in fact, it might be better to do this, to avoid confusion. But since the rest of the Hebrew-reading world speaks of IA and IC, we need to learn to do this, too.

29.1 Infinitives and Finite Verbs

"Infinite" means "unlimited." An Infinitive is an "infinite" verb form because it is not limited by tense (past, present, future) or number or gender or person (2ms, 3fp, 1cs, etc.). This is because the Infinitive *has no tense, number, gender or person*. Rather, each of the two Hebrew Infinitives has only a single form, and this form can refer to *any* tense or number or gender or person (depending upon the context). On the other hand, verbs which *do* have tense, number, gender or person are limited – they are finite – because they must be either past, present or future; masculine or feminine, etc. Thus, they are called ▲*finite verbs.*

29.2 The Infinitive Construct (IC)

The IC works like the English Infinitive, and gives the "to" form of the verb. Its is written: שְׁמֹר .

Notes:

1. The IC usually looks just like the Impv ms (both are שְׁמֹר), but the two are not related.
2. In the following two cases, however, the IC will be different from the Impv ms:

   - The IC of verbs which end with ה- will gain a וֹת- ending. Thus, the IC of רָאָה is רְאוֹת.
   - The IC of verbs which end with other gutturals will have a furtive *pathah*. Thus, the IC of שָׁמַע is שְׁמֹעַ

3. If the first ▲radical[1] is a guttural it will have composite *shewa*: עֲבֹד. This is also like the Impv ms.

4. The IC will almost always have a prefix. Thus, we will see a "construction" of IC + prefix.

   This prefix will usually be -לְ (to, for), but occasionally it will be -בְּ (when) or -כְּ (as, when). For instance: לִקְבֹּר = *to bury,* or בִּקְבֹּר *when he* (or *she, they, etc.*) *buries* (or *buried, will bury,* etc.)[2]

   We have already seen the special case of אמר + לְ → לֵאמֹר which is usually translated *saying*.

29.3 The Infinitive Absolute (IA)

The Infinitive Absolute (IA) is a long-vowel version of the IC. It has a *qamets* instead of the *shewa*, and a *holem-vav* instead of a *holem*:

שָׁמוֹר

Verbs ending with guttural will also gain a "furtive *pathah*" in their IA (שָׁמוֹעַ), but verbs which end in ה- will be fairly regular (for instance, the IA of רָאָה is רָאֹה).

The IA usually means either *indeed* or *continually.* It is most often[3] found either immediately before or immediately after a Perfect or Imperfect verb. In these cases, it acts like an adverb, and it has **two uses**:

- **before the verb: it means *indeed*.** It gives emphasis.
- **after the verb: it means *continually*.** It shows continuous action.

Study the following examples, where the IA is used with the 3fs (finite) verb:

Perfect 3fs:

normal:	שָׁמְרָה	=	she kept
emphasis:	שָׁמוֹר שָׁמְרָה	=	she **indeed** kept
duration:	שָׁמְרָה שָׁמוֹר	=	she kept **continually**

Imperfect 3fs:

normal:	תִּשְׁמֹר	=	she will keep
emphasis:	שָׁמוֹר תִּשְׁמֹר	=	she will **indeed** keep
duration:	תִּשְׁמֹר שָׁמוֹר	=	she will keep **continually**

Here are three suggestions to help you with these Infinitives.

- **First,** note that both Infinitives have a second *o* vowel (IC=שְׁמֹר, IA=שָׁמוֹר). But it is the Infinitive

---

[1] **Radical.** Since words in Hebrew take prefixes and suffixes, it is important to be able to identify and discuss the basic (root or radical) form of the word. Thus, the three letters of the simplest form of a verb are called "radicals." The first radical of שָׁמַר is thus שׁ, the second is מ, and the third radical is ר. Even if a verb has prefixes and suffixes, the word "radical" will refer to a letter of the root (most basic) form of the verb. Thus, the second radical of יִשְׁמְרוּ is still מ, even though it has a י prefix.

[2] **Technical note:** The *shewa* will be silent in this case. This differs from what we learned about adding inseparable prepositions in general (§16.2.3.2, p. 47). (If the *shewa* were vocal, it would chase away the *dagesh* in the ב and we would see לִקְבֹר; see §11.1.4, p. 32 and footnote 2 on p. 31.)

[3] **Technical note:** Most often but not always. The IA can sometimes stand alone, and, when it does, it functions in a number of ways (not all of them verbal). See *Gesenius* §113 for a complete discussion.

Absolute that has the long ***a*** vowel under the first letter (שָׁמוֹר). Think: Absolute.

- **Second,** watch for places where two forms of the *same verb* appear together, one right after the other (for instance, שָׁמוֹר תִּשְׁמֹר or תִּשְׁמֹר שָׁמוֹר). When this happens, one of them will almost always be an Infinitive Absolute.

- **Third,** learn to say the examples in the order shown: ***indeed*** *kept* and *kept* ***continually***. This is the order in which the IA and the finite verb will be found in Hebrew:

← →

שָׁמוֹר שָׁמַר = he *indeed kept*

but

← →

שָׁמַר שָׁמוֹר = he *kept continually.*

29.4 Parsing Infinitives

Infinitives are the easiest verb forms to parse. They are parsed as follows

שְׁמֹר = IC < שמר   לִשְׁמֹר = IC + ל < שמר   שָׁמוֹר = IA < שמר

Things You Should Know

1. **Two forms:** Hebrew has two Infinitive forms: the Infinitive Construct (IC) and the Infinitive Absolute (IA). These names have nothing to do with absolute and construct nouns.

2. **IC:** The form of the IC is שְׁמֹר. It usually has a prefixed -לְ (to). Sometimes it will have a prefixed -בְּ or -כְּ (both mean "when"). It seldom stands alone without a prefix.

3. **IA:** The IA works like an adverb. It usually stands before or after a finite verb.
   - Its form is שָׁמוֹר. Think: Absolute.
   - When it comes before the verb, it gives **emphasis** and may be translated "indeed."
   - When it comes after the verb, it means **continual action** and may be translated "continually."

4. **Parsing:**
   - שְׁמֹר is parsed IC < שמר
   - לִשְׁמֹר is parsed IC + ל < שמר
   - שָׁמוֹר is parsed IA < שמר

30

PERSONAL PRONOUNS

Personal pronouns are words such as *I, me, you, he, him, she, her, we, them*, etc. They have two forms: subject (*I, she, they*) and object (*me, her, them*). That is, we use words like *I, he, they* as subjects of sentences, and *me, him, them* as objects ("Grammar," p. xviii). Below are the Hebrew personal pronouns. (There is no neuter gender in Hebrew, and thus the word *it* will be the same as either *he, him, she* or *her*.)

Subject		**Object**	
he, it	הוּא	him, it	אֹתוֹ
she, it	הִיא	her, it	אֹתָהּ (note *mappiq*)
you (ms)	אַתָּה (אָתָּה in pause)	you (ms)	אֹתְךָ
you (fs)	אַתְּ	you (fs)	אֹתָךְ
I	אֲנִי, אָנֹכִי (אָנִי, אָנֹכִי, אָנֹכִי in pause)	me	אֹתִי
they (m)	הֵם, הֵמָּה	them (m)	אֹתָם, אֶתְהֶם
they (f)	הֵן, הֵנָּה	them (f)	אֹתָן, אֶתְהֶן
you (mp)	אַתֶּם	you (mp)	אֶתְכֶם
you (fp)	אַתֶּן	you (fp)	אֶתְכֶן
we	אֲנַחְנוּ	us	אֹתָנוּ

Notes:

1. **The difference** between the subject and object personal pronouns is easy to learn. The object personal pronouns are simply a combination of the sign of the definite direct object (אֶת־) and a suffix. Thus: אֹת + וֹ ← אֹתוֹ, אֹת + ךָ ← אֹתְךָ, etc. **Only the object personal pronouns have את** (with no *dagesh* in the ת) just like אֶת־. All of the others are *subject* personal pronouns. Thus, אַתֶּם and אַתֶּן are not object personal pronouns because they have a *dagesh*, and אֶת־ does not.

2. **Similar words:** (Make notes on the back of your vocabulary cards to avoid later confusion.)
   - The word אַתָּה (*you*, ms) is similar to the common word עַתָּה (*now*), in the vocabulary below.
   - The word הֵמָּה (*they*, m) is similar in appearance to two words which you may learn later (though not in this book): חֵמָה (*anger*) and הָמָה (*to murmur, roar, be boistrous*).
   - The word הֵן (*they*, f) is spelled the same as one of the word for *look, behold* (הֵן, הִנֵּה).

Things You Should Know

Learn the personal pronoun chart. Note that, in general,

- אֹת- and אֹתָ- indicate *object* pronouns,
- other forms indicate *subject* pronouns.

Exercise #22

Learn the personal pronouns from the lesson: אֲנִי ,אָנֹכִי, אַתָּה, אַתְּ . . . אֹתִי, אֹתְךָ, אֹתָךְ, אֹתוֹ, etc.

אַיֵּה, אֵי	where?[1]	פָּנִים[2]	face, presence (*cs.* פְּנֵי; פָּנָיו his face, his presence)
בְּכוֹר	first-born	צֹאן	*c.*[3] flock(s), sheep
הֶ֫בֶל	Abel (son of Adam and Eve)	צָעַק	to cry out, call for help
הָרַג	to kill, to murder	קַ֫יִן	Cain (son of Adam and Eve)
מִנְחָה	*f.* offering, gift	רֹעֶה	*m.* shepherd (*cs.* רֹעֵה; *pl.* רֹעִים, *pl. cs.* רוֹעֵי)
עַתָּה	now		

[1] וְהֶ֫בֶל רֹעֵה־צֹ֫אן וְקַ֫יִן עֹבֵד אֶת־הָאֲדָמָה׃ [2] וַיְהִי בַבֹּ֫קֶר וְקַ֫יִן נָתַן מִפְּרִי־הָאֲדָמָה
מִנְחָה לַיהוָה׃ [3] וְהֶ֫בֶל נָתַן גַּם־הוּא מִנְחָה מִבְּכוֹרוֹת־צֹאנוֹ׃ [4] וַיֹּ֫אמֶר קַ֫יִן אֶל־הֶ֫בֶל[4]
וְגַם יֵֽצְאוּ וַיַּהֲרֹג[5] קַ֫יִן אֶת־הֶ֫בֶל׃ [5] וַיֹּ֫אמֶר יְהוָה אֶל קַ֫יִן אֵי הֶ֫בֶל וַיֹּ֫אמֶר לֹא יָדַ֫עְתִּי
הֶאָנֹכִי[8] לִשְׁמֹר אֶת־הֶ֫בֶל׃ [6] וַיֹּ֫אמֶר[7] קוֹל־דְּמֵי־[6]הֶ֫בֶל צָעַק אֶל־אֲנִי מִן־הָאֲדָמָה׃
[7] וַיְשַׁלַּח יְהוָה אֶת־קַ֫יִן מִן הָאָ֫רֶץ וַיֹּ֫אמֶר[11] הֵן[10] שִׁלַּ֫חְתָּ אֹתִי הַיּוֹם[9] מֵעַל פְּנֵי־הָאֲדָמָה
וּמִפָּנֶ֫יךָ[13]׃ [8] עֵשָׂו הַבְּכוֹר הוּא וְגָנוֹב גָּנַב יַעֲקֹב אֶת־בִּרְכָתוֹ׃ [9] הוּא אֱלֹהֵ֫ינוּ[12] וַאֲנַ֫חְנוּ
עַמּוֹ וְצֹאן־יָדוֹ׃ [10] תִּזְכְּרִי זָכוֹר אֶת־דְּבַר־אֱלֹהִים לִשְׁמֹר אֹתוֹ׃ [11] וּבָעֶ֫רֶב צָעֲקוּ
הַנָּשִׁים אֶל הַזָּקֵן וְשָׁמוֹעַ שָׁמַע לְקוֹלָן׃ [12] דִּבֵּר דָּוִד אֶל שְׁלֹמֹה בַּבֹּ֫קֶר לֵאמֹר וְעַתָּה

---

[1] Note the question mark. The word is "where?" not "where." Example: "*Where* is the king?" not "The place *where* the king is." The word is found at the beginning of a question, and it occurs *instead of* a *he* interrogative. Be sure to include the question mark on vocabulary tests.

[2] This word is found only in the plural form. It is usually translated in the singular, however.

[3] *c.* means *common.* The word is sometimes treated as masculine (using masculine verbs and adjectives), and sometimes as feminine (using feminine verbs and adjectives). In other words, usage is inconsistent in the Bible. *Common* is not the same as neuter. Greek has a neuter gender, but Hebrew does not.

[4] The word אָמַר must be followed by the words which are spoken. In Gen 4:8, however, what Cain said to Abel is missing from the text in the Hebrew (though not in the Septuagint). This sentence of the exercise follows the broken pattern seen in Genesis.

[5] The guttural has attracted a *pathah* before it, and the *shewa* beneath it has become composite *shewa.*

[6] Gen. 4:10 uses the plural, as here. Thus, translate "the murder of your brother" or (with RSV, NRSV) "your brother's blood." Since the cry is "from the ground," we should probably translate "your brother's blood."

[7] Who is the subject of this verb? God? Cain? The voice? Sometimes it is not clear in the Hebrew text, and we must let the context tell us.

[8] *Hē* interrogative before guttural (§14.3.2, p. 42). Add the word *am*: "Am I ...?"

[9] Translate "today."

[10] Remember that this word has two meanings.

[11] See footnote 7, above.

[12] Construct form of אֱלֹהִים with suffix.

[13] Plural construct of פָּנִים with two prefixes and a suffix.

מֹשֵׁל בְּיִשְׂרָאֵל כִּי בְנִי אַתָּה׃ [13] [14]הַיְרֵאתֶם כִּי בַחֲלוֹמוֹ רָאָה דָוִד אֲנָשִׁים עַל הֶהָרִים׃
[14] נִקְבְּרָה בְקֶבֶר־אֶבֶן אֶת־הַזָּקֵן אֲשֶׁר חָלַם חֲלָמוֹת׃ [15] וַיְהִי זָקֵן שְׁמוּאֵל וְשָׁפוֹט
שָׁפַט אֶת־הָעָם וַיִּמְשֹׁל מָשׁוֹל אֶתְהֶם׃ [16] בָּאוּ אֲנָשִׁים לַהֲרֹג[15] אֶת־הָרֹעֶה וַיִּצְעַק לֵאמֹר
דָּמִים דָּמִים׃ וְלֹא שָׁפְכוּ אֶת־דָּמוֹ׃ [17] וַיְהִי בָעֶרֶב [16]וַיַּחֲלֹם כִּי בָאוּ הַנָּשִׁים לִמְכֹּר
צֹאן וְלֶאֱכֹל פְּרִי׃ [18] הָאִישׁ־דָּמִים אֲשֶׁר גָּנַב בָּקָר דָּמוֹ בְרֹאשׁוֹ[18] וַיִּקְבְּרוּ[17] אֹתוֹ
בְּקָבֶר[19]׃ [19] אַיֵּה הַנָּשִׁים אֲשֶׁר תִּמְכֹּרְנָה אֶת־הָאֲבָנִים הַזְּקֵנוֹת׃ [20] יֵצְאוּ אַנְשֵׁי־
שְׁלֹמֹה לִרְאוֹת[20] אֶת־הַצֹּאן וְאֶת־הַבָּקָר׃

---

[14] See §14.3.2, p. 42 for the ה. The verb is Perf 2mp, and the *sere* (instead of *pathah*) is because of the א.

[15] Why is there a *pathah* under the ל? If you do not know, then review §16.2.3.3, p. 47.

[16] Study the first three words of this sentence carefully, because this pattern is very common in Hebrew. We usually translate -ו as *and* or *but*. However, it can also mean *and when* or *then*. This often happens when the -ו appears twice in the sentence. Example: וַיִּזְכֹּר אֶת־הַדְּבָרִים וַיִּכְתֹּב אֹתָם בְּסֵפֶר "*And **when** he remembered the words, **then** he wrote them in a scroll.*" So how should you translate the first three words of this exercise?

[17] Is this Imperfect or Jussive? How do you know? See §28.3.2, p. 85.

[18] Translate "upon his (own) head." That is, his death is his own fault.

[19] Pausal form of קֶבֶר plus preposition.

[20] See Note 2 on page 89 regarding verbs ending with ה-.

31

INTERROGATIVE PRONOUNS

Interrogative Pronouns are words such as *Who ...? What ...?* and *How ...?* They are used in questions.

31.1 The word for *who?* or *whom?* is מִי. It never changes its form. *To whom?* is לְמִי and *from whom?* is מִמִּי.

31.2 The word for *what?* or *how?* or *why?* is מה. The consonants in this short word do not change, but its vowels depend upon the first letter of the word which follows it.[1] The rules are similar to those for the definite article (§14):

Before non-gutturals:	·מַה־ (note *dagesh forte*)	מַה־זֶּה[2]	*What (is) this?*
Before ה and ח:	מַה־ (no *dagesh forte* this time)	מַה־הִיא	*What (is) it?*
Before א ע and ר:	מָה־	מָה־אֵלֶּה	*What (are) these?*
Before gutturals with *qamets*	מֶה־	מֶה־אָכַל	*What did he eat?*
In combination with -לְ:	לָמָּה = *Why?*	לָמָּה גָּנַבְתָּ	*Why did you steal?*

31.3 No *He* interrogative. When an interrogative pronoun is used, there will be no *he* interrogative at the beginning of the question. We will see מֶה־עָשָׂה, but not הֲמֶה־עָשָׂה.

Things You Should Know

1. The word מִי means "who?".
2. The word מַה means "what?" or "how?" It will usually cause a *dagesh* to be placed in the first letter of the word which follows it.
3. מַה may also be pointed מָה or מֶה if it comes before a word which starts with a guttural.
4. When these interrogative pronouns are used, there will be no *he* interrogative.

---

[1] **Technical note:** The pattern is not followed rigidly. For instance, there is not always a *maqqeph*, and the rules for words beginning with ע are somewhat fluid. See *Gesenius* §37*d*.

[2] זֶה means "this," and will be learned in §30. **Technical note:** Note how the addition of ·מַה־ produces a *dagesh forte* in the first letter of a non-BEGADKEPAT word (זֶה becomes זֶּה). This is usually impossible (see §11.1.3 and §11.1.4 on p. 31).

32

THE VERB: ACTIVE PARTICIPLES

We have now learned five basic forms of the Hebrew verb: two "tenses"

Perfect
Imperfect

and three "moods":[1]

Imperative (plus Cohortative, Emphatic Imperative and Jussive)
Infinitive Absolute
Infinitive Construct

There is one more verbal mood in Hebrew: the participle.

32.1 Participles: their characteristics

A Participle is a verb form which acts like an adjective. In English, we have participles such as "the *singing* man" or "the *planted* seeds." The Hebrew participle is similar, and will be

(1) masculine or feminine
(2) singular or plural
(3) active or passive

Note that **a Participle does not have "tense"** (past, present or future) **or "person"** (first, second or third). That is, you cannot have a first person, or second person or a third person Participle. And there are no past or future forms of the participle.

32.2 Active Participles: their form

Participles are Active or Passive. The Active Participle develops as shown below. (We shall discuss Passive Participles in §40.)

	Singular	Plural
Masculine	שֹׁמֵר	שֹׁמְרִים
Feminine	שֹׁמֶרֶת (sometimes שֹׁמְרָה)	שֹׁמְרוֹת

There are also construct forms, as will be seen below.

[1] **Technical note:** We learned earlier (at the beginning of §19) that the Perfect and Imperfect tenses, taken together, form what may be considered an Indicative mood.

Notes:

1. There is a *holem* in the first syllable. This is a characteristic of the active participle.
2. The *shewas* are vocal, because they come after long vowels (*holems*). Thus, for instance, the masculine plural absolute is šō-mᵉrîm, not šōm-rîm.
3. With a final guttural (for instance, the verb שָׁמַע), there will be a furtive *pathah* in the masculine singular Active Participle (שֹׁמֵעַ), and the feminine uses *pathahs* instead of *seghols* (that is, שֹׁמַעַת , not שֹׁמֶעֶת).

32.3 Participles: their uses

A participle is like a "verbal adjective." It shows a state of **continuing activity** – past, present or future:

הָאִישׁ שֹׁמֵר = *The man* (*was/is/will be*) *keeping*

אִשְׁתּוֹ שֹׁמֶרֶת = *His wife* (*was/is/will be*) *keeping*

The context will tell us whether to translate as past, present or future. The emphasis, however, is upon activity which continues. Because of this, the Participle is used in the following three ways:

32.3.1 **To act as a "present tense."** Normally, the past is represented by the Perfect (שָׁמַר), and the future by the Imperfect (יִשְׁמֹר). The Participle, on the other hand, can give a sense of present activity. Thus, הָאִישׁ שֹׁמֵר can mean *The man is keeping.*

32.3.2 **To represent the word "who."** If the Participle has a definite article (·הַ) and comes after a noun, the definite article will act like the word "who." Thus:

הָאִישׁ הַשֹּׁמֵר = *the man* ***who*** (was/is/will be) *keeping*
(literally, *the man, the keeping* [one])

אִשְׁתּוֹ הַשֹּׁמֶרֶת = *his wife* ***who*** (was/is/will be) *keeping*
(literally, *his wife, the keeping* [one])

Again, the context will show us whether we should translate past, present or future.

32.3.3 **To represent a person who regularly does something (habitual use).** For instance,

רָעָה means *to take care of sheep*. Thus
רֹעֶה means *taking care of sheep*, **but it can also mean** *a shepherd* (a noun).

יָשַׁב means *to live or reside*. Thus,
יֹשֵׁב means *living or residing*, **but it can also mean** *a resident* (a noun).

In such cases, the participle actually becomes a noun, and can have construct states and plural forms:

	Singular	Plural
Absolute	יֹשֵׁב *resident*	יֹשְׁבִים *residents*
Construct	יֹשֵׁב *resident of*	יֹשְׁבֵי *residents of*
Construct + absolute	יֹשֵׁב־הָאָרֶץ *resident of the land*	יֹשְׁבֵי־הָעִיר *residents of the city*
Construct + suffix	יֹשְׁבָהּ *its (fs) resident*	יֹשְׁבֶיהָ[2] *its (fs) residents*

32.4 Parsing Participles

Participles are parsed as active or passive, masculine or feminine, singular or plural. If they are used as nouns, they will also be parsed according to whether they are absolute or construct. If they have suffixes, these must be noted. Here are some examples:

As verb:

שֹׁמֵר Part Act ms < שׁמר [Participle, Active, masculine, singular]

שֹׁמְרוֹת Part Act fp < שׁמר

As a noun:

יֹשְׁבִים Nmpa [Noun, masculine, plural, absolute] < ישׁב

יֹשְׁבוֹתָהּ Nfpc + 3fs < ישׁב

Sometimes only context will tell you whether to parse as a verb or a noun.

Things You Should Know

1. A participle is a verbal adjective. The Hebrew participle is masculine or feminine, singular or plural, active or passive. (This chapter is about *active* participles.)
2. The Active Participle develops as follows: שֹׁמֵר (ms) שֹׁמְרִים (mp),
   שֹׁמֶרֶת (fs) שֹׁמְרוֹת (fp).
   (sometimes שֹׁמְרָה)
3. The participle may be used:
   a. as a present tense
   b. to represent the word "who" (when used with a definite article).
   c. to represent a person who regularly does something. In this case, the participle becomes a noun, and will also have plural and construct forms.

[2] We will study plural nouns with suffixes in §34.

Exercise #23

אֹיֵב	enemy (*pl.* אֹיְבִים, *cs.* אֹיְבֵי)	מָה	what? how? why? (לָמָּה = Why?)
חֵן	favor, attractiveness (vs. הֵן)	מִי	who?
יִשַׁי	Jesse (*in pause:* יִשָׁי)	מָצָא	to find
לִפְנֵי[3]	before (time or place)	עָמַד	to stand
לְפָנַי	before me, in my presence	שָׁאוּל	Saul
מַדּוּעַ	why?	שְׁאוֹל	Sheol (place of the dead[4])

[1] מָה־אָמַר קַיִן לְהֶבֶל אַחֲרֵי נָתְנוּ מִנְחָתָם׃ [2] הֲצָעַק הֶבֶל בְּקוֹל גָּדוֹל מְאֹד בַּהֲרֹג[5]
אֹתוֹ קָיִן׃ [3] מַדּוּעַ דִּבֶּר אַבְרָם אֶל שָׂרַי אִשְׁתּוֹ[6] אִמְרִי לִפְנֵי־פַרְעֹה כִּי לֹא אִשְׁתִּי
אָתְּ׃ [4] שְׁאֵלָה אַחַת מֵהַנָּשִׁים הֲיִהְיֶה[7] זֶרַע־הָגָר כְּכוֹכְבֵי־הַשָּׁמָיִם׃ [5] כֹּה אָמַר יְהוָה
אֶזְכֹּר הַכֹּרְתוֹת[9] אֶת־הַבְּרִית עִם בְּכוֹר־הָגָר׃ [6] אַיֵּה הַבָּתִּים[8] אֲשֶׁר שָׂרְפוּ אֹיְבֵי־אַבְרָהָם
אֹתָם[13] בָּאֵשׁ׃ [7] אָמַר יַעֲקֹב הִנֵּה יִרְאֶה[12] עֵשָׂו אֶת־הַמִּנְחָה הַהֹלֶכֶת לְפָנָי[11] וְאַחֲרֵי־כֵן[10]
אֶרְאֶה[15] פָּנָיו[14]׃ [8] שָׁאוּל שָׁאַל שָׁאוּל אַיֵּה שְׁאוֹל׃ [9] וַיִּשְׁלַח שָׁאוּל אַחַד מֵאַנְשֵׁי־בֵיתוֹ
אֶל יִשָׁי וַיֹּאמֶר[16] שָׁלְכָה אֶת־דָּוִד בִּנְךָ הַשֹּׁמֵר אֶת־צֹאנֶךָ׃ [10] וַיִּשְׁאַל דָּוִד מִי אָנֹכִי
וּמָה בֵיתִי[18] כִּי אֶהְיֶה בְּבֵית־הַמֶּלֶךְ׃ [11] וּבַבֹּקֶר בָּא דָוִד אֶל־שָׁאוּל וַיַּעֲמֹד לְפָנָיו[17]׃

---

[3] **Technical note:** The word לִפְנֵי is formed by combining פְּנֵי (the construct of פָּנִים) with the preposition -לְ. Thus, it literally means "to the face of" or "before the face of."

[4] Sheol is not Hell. In the Old Testament, people believed that *all* people, both good and bad, went to Sheol when they died. Thus, Sheol is the place of all the dead, not just a place of punishment for the wicked.

[5] Infinitive construct plus preposition. The guttural has produced the composite *shewa*, and thus the preposition has taken the corresponding short vowel (§16.2.3.3, p. 47).

[6] In construct, אִשָּׁה loses its *dagesh*.

[7] This is the verb היה with a prefix. For the prefix: see p. 40, §14. For the verb: see p. 87, footnote 9.

[8] **Technical note:** The plural of בַּיִת is an unusual word because it has a *begadkepat* letter with a *dagesh* immediately after a (long) vowel. Thus, a *metheg* is added to tell us that the vowel under the ב is a *qamets* and not a *qamets-hatuph.*

[9] This participle has become a noun. It also has a definite article.

[10] The word כֵּן usually means "so, thus, therefore." But אַחֲרֵי־כֵן means "afterwards" (literally "after thus"). This sentence is based upon Gen 32:20 (Gen 32:21 in the Hebrew Bible).

[11] The *pathah* which was originally under the *nun* has lengthened to *qamets* in pause.

[12] Impf 3ms < ראה. The vowel pointing has changed because of the ה, and thus is similar to יִהְיֶה < היה.

[13] אֲשֶׁר שָׂרְפוּ ... אֹתָם, *which they burned ... them.* This is the Hebrew way of saying *which they burned.* This structure will be discussed in the next chapter.

[14] פְּנֵי + ו: "his face."

[15] This is an Impf 1cs verb. It doesn't follow the אֶשְׁמֹר pattern because of the final *he*. We will study these kinds of verbs later.

[16] Do not let the *holem* fool you. This is not a participle. You have already seen it often. See p. 83, note 9.

[17] לִפְנֵי + ו : "before him..."

[18] The expression is usually וּמִי בֵיתִי.

[12] וַיִּשְׁלַח שָׁאוּל אֶל־יִשַׁי לֵאמֹר יַעֲמֹד[19] דָּוִד לְפָנַי כִּי־מָצָא חֵן בְּעֵינָֽי׃ [13] וַיְהִי דָּוִד
רֹדֵף אַחֲרֵי־אֹיְבֵי־שָׁאוּל וְיַד־יְהוָה עִם בֶּן־יִשָֽׁי׃ [14] שָׁאַל בְּכוֹר־שָׁאוּל מַדּוּעַ יָֽדְךָ עַל
דָּוִד לִרְדֹּף אֹתוֹ׃ [15] וְעַתָּה לֹא תִכְרֹתְנָה בְּרִית בֵּין אֶת־זֶרַע־שָׂרָה וּבֵין אֶת־כֹּכְבֵי־
הַשָּׁמָֽיִם׃ [16] מִי הַנְּעָרִים הַהֹלְכִים לִרְאוֹת אֶת־הָרֹעִים׃ [17] וַיִּמְצָא אִישׁ אַחַד חֵן
בְּעֵינֵי־הַמֶּלֶךְ כִּי לָכַד צֹאן־אֹיְבֵי־הָעָֽם׃ [18] וְעַתָּה אַיֵּה הַנְּעָרִים הַבָּאִים[20] לַהֲרֹג אֶת־
הָרֹעִים וְלִשְׂרֹף אֶת־הָעִיר בָּאֵֽשׁ׃ [19] צָֽעֲקָה אַחַת מֵהַנְּבִיאוֹת בְּקוֹל גָּדוֹל מְאֹד לֵאמֹר
הִנֵּה הָֽאִשָּׁה לֹלֶדֶת אֶת־צֹאנֵֽנוּ׃ [20] זִכְרוּ אֶת־יְהוָה אֱלֹהֵיכֶם וְלֹא תִכְרְתוּ בְּרִית עִם
שְׁאוֹל׃

[19] Translate as jussive.

[20] Participial form.

33

THE RELATIVE PRONOUN אֲשֶׁר

A **relative pronoun** relates one word or phrase to another. Instead of saying, *He is the man. I saw him,* we can say *He is the man* ***whom*** *I saw.* The word *whom* is a relative pronoun, and it creates a relationship between *He is the man* and *I saw.*

In English, we have many words which create such relationships:

the place ***where*** *he lives*
the man ***whose*** *child I saw*
the city ***from which*** *I came*
etc.

In Hebrew, there is only one relative pronoun: אֲשֶׁר . It means *who, which, where*, etc. We have already been using it in the exercises, so you have seen its general use. In English, we usually connect short phrases with relative pronouns, but Hebrew often connects complete sentences:

English:	*He is the man*	***whom***	*I saw*
Hebrew:	*He is the man*	***whom***[1]	*I saw him*

Likewise with words of place:

English:	... *the place*	***where***	*she lives*
Hebrew:	... *the place*	***which***	*she lives there*
English:	... *the place*	***from where***	*you came*
Hebrew:	... *the place*	***which***	*you came from there*

In each case, Hebrew will use אֲשֶׁר. This will become more clear in the following examples:

הַמֶּלֶךְ אֲשֶׁר שָׁלַח אֶתְכֶם — *the king* ***who*** *sent you* (2 Kgs 1:6)
(literally: *the-king who he-sent you*)

הָאִישׁ אֲשֶׁר בְּנָהּ הַחַי — *the woman* ***whose*** *son was alive* (1 Kgs 3:26)
(literally: *the-woman who her-son* [*was*] *the-living-one*)

---

[1] **Technical English grammar note:** The difference between *who* and *whom* is as follows: *who* is used as a subject, and *whom* is used as an object. This is just like the words *he* (subject) and *him* (object). Thus, in the sentence *He is the man* ***who*** *went to the store*, the word *who* is the **subject** of *went to the store*. That is, ***Who*** *went to the store*. (Compare to ***He*** *went to the store.*) But in the sentence *He is the man* ***whom*** *I saw*, the word *whom* is the **object** of *I saw*: That is, *I saw* ***whom*** (compare to *I saw* ***him***). If English is your second or third language and this seems confusing, do not worry. Even many who speak English as a first language do not understand this difference!

הַכְּנַעֲנִי אֲשֶׁר אָנֹכִי יֹשֵׁב בְּאַרְצוֹ *the Canaanite(s)* ***in whose*** *land I live* (Gen 24:37)
(literally: *the-Canaanite who I [am] living in-his-land*

הַגּוֹיִם אֲשֶׁר אָנֹכִי שֹׁלֵחַ אֹתְךָ אֲלֵיהֶם *the nations* ***to whom*** *I send you* (Jer 25:15)
(literally: *the-nations which I [am] sending you to-them*)

הַמָּקוֹם אֲשֶׁר עָמַד שָׁם *the place* ***where*** *he stood* (Gen 19:27)
(literally: *the-place where he-stood there*)

הָאָרֶץ אֲשֶׁר־יָצָאתָ מִשָּׁם *the land* ***from where*** *you came*
(literally: *the-land which you-came from-there*)

הַבָּמָה אֲשֶׁר־אַתֶּם בָּאִים שָׁם *the high place* (בָּמָה) ***to which*** *you go* (Ezek 20:29)
(literally: *the-high-place which you [are] going there*)

These patterns are different from English. When you translate, first do a very literal and rough translation (like the ones on the second line of each example above). Then make a smoother translation.

Finally, do not confuse the *relative* pronoun "who" (אֲשֶׁר) with the *interrogative* pronoun "who?" (מִי). Interrogative pronouns are questions; relative pronouns are not. (See §31 to review interrogative pronouns.) The following sentence gives an example of each:

מִי הָאִישׁ אֲשֶׁר דִּבֶּר אֶל מֹשֶׁה *Who (is) the man who spoke to Moses?*

Things You Should Know

1. **Relative pronouns** are words which show a relationship between things. Hebrew has only one relative pronoun: the word אֲשֶׁר which means "who, which, where," etc.
2. In Hebrew, the word אֲשֶׁר is often used to connect (relate) complete sentences rather than phrases. (See the examples in the chapter.)
3. Be sure you know the difference between the *relative* pronoun אֲשֶׁר and the *interrogative* pronoun מִי .

34

NOUNS: PLURAL WITH POSSESSIVE SUFFIXES

In §23, we studied singular nouns with possessive suffixes. This chapter considers plural nouns. It is very similar to §23, and so you should review that chapter (especially the opening paragraphs, §23.3 and the "Things You Should Know" on p. 70).

34.1 Masculine Plural Nouns with Possessive Suffixes

Review the following:

Singular Absolute:	סוּס	*horse*
Plural Absolute:	סוּסִים	*horses*
Plural Construct:	סוּסֵי	*horses of*

The masculine plural noun adds possessive suffixes to its *plural construct* form as follows:

3ms	סוּסָיו[1]	*his horses*	3mp	סוּסֵיהֶם	*their (ms) horses*
3fs	סוּסֶיהָ	*her horses*	3fp	סוּסֵיהֶן	*their (fs) horses*
2ms	סוּסֶיךָ	*your (ms) horses*	2mp	סוּסֵיכֶם	*your (mp) horses*
2fs	סוּסַיִךְ	*your (fs) horses*	2fp	סוּסֵיכֶן	*your (fp) horses*
1cs	סוּסַי	*my horses*	1cp	סוּסֵינוּ	*our horses*

Notes:

1. **The Suffixes:** In §23, we saw that a singular noun can take either a singular or a plural possessive suffix (p. 66). The same is true for a plural noun. It can take either a singular or a plural suffix:

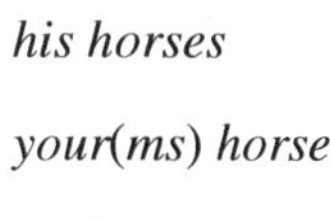
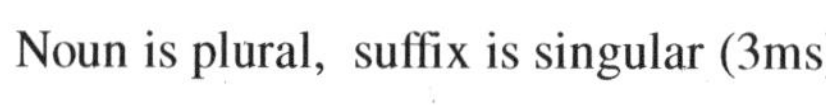
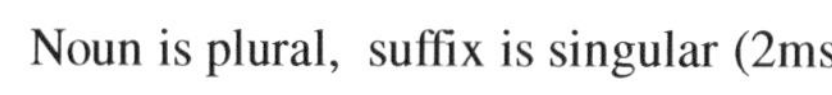
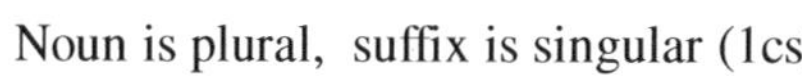

סוּסָיו	*his horses*	Noun is plural, suffix is singular (3ms)
סוּסֶיךָ	*your(ms) horses*	Noun is plural, suffix is singular (2ms)
סוּסַי	*my horses*	Noun is plural, suffix is singular (1cs)

סוּסֵיהֶן	*their(fp) horses*	Noun is plural, suffix is plural (3fp)
סוּסֵיכֶן	*your(fp) horses*	Noun is plural, suffix is plural (2fp)
סוּסֵינוּ	*our horses*	Noun is plural, suffix is plural (1cp)

2. **Characteristic *yod*:** This is the most important thing to learn in this chapter. When the noun is *plural*,

[1] The final ו is a consonant, not a vowel letter.

a י appears before the suffix: סוּסָיו, סוּסֶ֫יהָ, etc.

- This י is the major difference from the *singular* noun with suffixes (סוּסוֹ, *his horse*; but סוּסָיו, *his horses*; compare to p. 66). Thus, this י is an important sign, and you should learn to watch for it. This will also happen with feminine plural nouns, as you will see below.
- This extra י is *silent* in all cases except 1cs (סוּסַי *my horses*) and 2fs (סוּסַ֫יִךְ *your horses*).[2]

3. **Mixed groups:** Again, masculine plural (*mp*) suffixes will be used for mixed groups (groups that have both men and women). See the examples in §23 (p. 66).

4. **Third singular:** This time the masculine suffix is ו not וֹ. And there is no *mappiq* in the feminine suffix: סוּסֶ֫יהָ *her horses.* (There was one with the singular noun: סוּסָהּ *her horse.*)[3]

5. **Third plural:** The 3p suffixes are now ־הֶם and ־הֶן (not ־ָם - and ־ָן - as in the singular)[3].

6. **Small but important differences:** Only the final vowel point is different between:

   סוּסִי *my horse,*
   סוּסַי *my horses,* and
   סוּסֵי *horses of* (the plural construct)

   Study these forms carefully so that you will not confuse them.

34.2 Feminine Plural Nouns with Possessive Suffixes

Feminine plural nouns take the same suffixes. Again, an extra י appears before the suffix.

Singular Absolute:	תּוֹרָה	*instruction*
Plural Absolute:	תּוֹרוֹת	*instructions*
Plural Construct:	תּוֹרוֹת	*instructions-of*

3ms	תּוֹרוֹתָיו	*his instructions*	3mp	תּוֹרוֹתֵיהֶם	*their (mp) instructions*
3fs	תּוֹרוֹתֶ֫יהָ	*her instructions*	3fp	תּוֹרוֹתֵיהֶן	*their (fp) instructions*
2ms	תּוֹרוֹתֶ֫יךָ	*your (ms) instructions*	2mp	תּוֹרוֹתֵיכֶם	*your (mp) instructions*
2fs	תּוֹרוֹתַ֫יִךְ	*your (fp) instructions*	2fp	תּוֹרוֹתֵיכֶן	*your (fp) instructions*
1cs	תּוֹרוֹתַי	*my instructions*	1cp	תּוֹרוֹתֵ֫ינוּ	*our instructions*

Review notes 1-6 for the masculine plural, above (§34.1). There is one **exception**: the 3mp suffix on feminine plural nouns will sometimes be ־ָם rather than ־ֵיהֶם. For instance, *their lands* is found as אַרְצֹתָם (= אַרְצוֹתָם), not as אַרְצֹתֵיהֶם.

---

[2] Technically, the י is silent even where we find ־ֵי. Review §17.

[3] **Technical note:** This is actually not a matter of singular vs plural. Rather, it is a matter of open vs. closed syllables. Singular nouns usually end with consonants (though not always), and thus take suffixes which begin with vowels such as וֹ ָהּ and ָם. Thus, סוּסוֹ, סוּסָהּ, etc. Plural nouns have the extra י which open their last syllable. Thus, they take suffixes which begin with consonants: ו, הָ, הֶם, etc. Thus, סוּסָיו, סוּסֶ֫יהָ, etc.

We have been looking at the simplest types of nouns. We also need to look at more complicated nouns, as we did in §23 ("Singular nouns with possessive suffixes"). Again, vowels near the beginning of the word will become shorter as the noun becomes longer. We will consider just two examples, דָּבָר (*m.*) and בְּרָכָה (*f.*):

	דָּבָר	בְּרָכָה
pl. abs.	דְּבָרִים	בְּרָכוֹת
pl. cs.	דִּבְרֵי	בִּרְכוֹת
1cs	דְּבָרַי	בִּרְכוֹתַי
2ms	דְּבָרֶ֫יךָ	בִּרְכוֹתֶ֫יךָ
2fs	דְּבָרַ֫יִךְ	בִּרְכוֹתַ֫יִךְ

34.3 Parsing

Plural nouns with possessive suffixes are parsed in the following way:

סוּסֶ֫יהָ = Nmpc + 3fs < סוס

תּוֹרוֹתֵ֫ינוּ = Nfsc + 1cp < תּוֹרה

Reminder: If a noun has a suffix, the noun *must* be construct. It cannot be absolute. Think of it as a "construction." A new word has been constructed by adding a suffix.

Things You Should Know

1. Plural nouns take suffixes which are added to the plural construct form of the noun.
2. These suffixes are almost exactly the same as the suffixes for singular nouns. The major differences are as follows: With plural nouns:
   a. There is a silent י which appears before the suffix.
   b. The 3fs suffix on plural nouns has no *mappiq*. (There was a *mappiq* in the 3fs suffix of the singular noun.)
   c. There is an extra ה in the 3p suffixes (that is, הֶם- and הֶן-, not ָם - and ָן -).

Exercise #24

אָב	*m.* father (*cs.* אֲבִי, *pl.* אָבוֹת, *pl.+3mp* אֲבֹתָם)	מָקוֹם	*m.* place, *pl.* מְקוֹמוֹת[4]
אֶת־, אֵת	with (see Vocabulary notes, below)	עָשָׂה	to do, to make
יָרַד	to come down, to go down	קָטֹן, קָטָן	small, young, insignificant
מִדְבָּר	desert, wilderness	שָׁלוֹם	peace, wholeness
		שָׁם	there

Vocabulary notes: First, the plurals אָבוֹת and מְקוֹמוֹת are masculine, even though they appear feminine. Second, remember that the words אֵת and אֶת־ are also used as signs of the definite direct object (§26).

[1] הָלַךְ יַעֲקֹב[6] אֶת־עֵשָׂו אֶל הַמָּקוֹם אֲשֶׁר יֵשְׁבוּ שָׁם לִקְבֹּר אֶת־אֲבִיהֶם[5]׃ [2] וַיִּשְׁמַע
אֲבִי־אֵשֶׁת־מֹשֶׁה אֵת כָּל־אֲשֶׁר עָשָׂה אֱלֹהִים לְמֹשֶׁה וּלְיִשְׂרָאֵל עַמּוֹ׃ [3] מִי הַכֹּהֵן אֲשֶׁר
הָלַךְ אֶל הָעִיר וּמַה־עָשָׂה שָׁם׃ [4] בָּאוּ אֹיְבֵי־אָבִיו אֲשֶׁר יֵשְׁבוּ בַּמִּדְבָּר לִגְנֹב אֶת־
הַבָּקָר׃ [5] וַיֹּאמְרוּ נִמְכְּרָה אֶת־הַבָּקָר בְּיִשְׂרָאֵל אֲשֶׁר שָׁאוּל מֹשֵׁל שָׁם׃ [6] וַיֹּאמֶר
יְהוָה לִשְׁמוּאֵל בַּחֲלוֹם יִמְשֹׁל דָּוִד לְפָנַי תַּחַת שָׁאוּל׃ [7] מַדּוּעַ יָצָא שְׁמוּאֵל הַנָּבִיא אֶל
מָקוֹם אֲשֶׁר יָשַׁב יִשַׁי שָׁם׃ [8] וַיַּעַמְדוּ לִפְנֵי־שְׁמוּאֵל כָּל־בְּנֵי־יִשָׁי וַיִּמְצָא הַבְּכוֹר חֵן
בְּעֵינוֹ׃ [9] וַיֹּאמֶר אֱלֹהִים לִשְׁמוּאֵל הַקָּטֹן[8] מָצָא חֵן בְּעֵינַי תַּחַת הַבְּכֹר[7]׃ [10] וְאַחֲרֵי
הַדְּבָרִים הָאֵלֶּה[9] יָרְדוּ דָּוִד וַאֲנָשָׁיו אֶל הַמִּדְבָּר וַיְהִי אֱלֹהִים אֶת־דָּוִד׃ [11] וְיֵרְדוּ
לְשָׁאוּל אֹיְבֵי־הַנְּבִיאָה אֲשֶׁר חָלְמָה בַּהֵיכָל׃ [12] עָמַד הַנָּבִיא לִפְנֵי דָוִד וַיֹּאמֶר יִמְצְאוּ[10]
דִּבְרֵי חֵן בְּעֵינֶיךָ[12]׃ [13] לֹא שְׁלֹמֹה אִישׁ־דָּמִים וְגַם שָׁלוֹם בְּיָמָיו[11]׃ [14] יִכְתֹּב הַכֹּהֵן
אֵת דִּבְרֵי־שְׁלֹמֹה בְּסֵפֶר קָטָן וְיִקְבֹּר[14] אֵת הַסֵּפֶר בְּקָבֶר[13]׃ [15] גָּנְבוּ אַנְשֵׁי־הָעִיר
וַיִּשְׁפְּכוּ דָם וְלֹא שָׁלוֹם שָׁם׃ [16] מִי הַנְּבִיאָה הַחֹלֶמֶת חֲלוֹמוֹת וּמָה חָלְמָה׃

---

[4] Place names such as *Jerusalem, Canaan*, etc., are usually feminine. But the word מָקוֹם (*place*), itself, is masculine – even though its plural *looks* feminine.

[5] *Their father*, not *their fathers*. The suffix is on the singular construct (אֲבִי), not on the plural construct (אָבוֹת). Singular constructs usually end with consonants and take ָם-. Here, the singular construct is unusual and ends with a י just like a plural construct with suffix. Thus it takes ֶהם-. See technical note 3, page 104.

[6] The context determines whether the אֶת־ means *with* or whether it is the sign of the definite direct object.

[7] Many words which have a *holem-vav* (וֹ) will also be found written with only a *holem*. Thus בְּכוֹר = בְּכֹר.

[8] When the subject comes before the verb, it often gives stronger emphasis.

[9] "These." We will learn this adjective (אֵלֶּה) in §38.

[10] Should this be translated Imperfect or Jussive?

[11] The word יוֹם is irregular. Its dual is יוֹמַיִם, its plural is יָמִים, and its plural construct is יְמֵי.

[12] Dual with prefix and suffix.

[13] Why is there a *qamets* in this word? Answer: because it is in pause (§7.5, p. 20).

[14] Is this verb Jussive or Imperfect? See §28.3.2, p. 85, if you are unsure. And then what about the first verb of the sentence? Hint: the way you parse the second verb (וְיִקְבֹּר) gives the context; the context then tells you how to parse the first verb (יִכְתֹּב).

35

PREPOSITIONS WITH SUFFIXES

In §16, we studied the inseparable prepositions -בְּ, -כְּ and -לְ. They cannot stand alone and are attached as prefixes to words. We also learned that מִן may stand alone or it may attach directly to a word. In this chapter, we shall learn that these prepositions can also take personal pronoun suffixes. For instance:

ִי (1cs suffix) + -לְ ➜ לִי = *to me* or *for me* .

We shall see that this is also true for the preposition: אֵת (*with*). אֵת is spelled exactly like the sign of the definite direct object (§26), and when it takes personal pronoun suffixes it looks quite similar to the personal pronoun (§30). But we shall learn a very easy way to tell one from the other.

35.1 The Prepositions -בְּ, -לְ, אֵת and עִם with suffixes

3ms	in him/it	בּוֹ	to him/it	לוֹ	with him/it	אִתּוֹ	עִמּוֹ
3fs	in her/it	בָּהּ	to her/it	לָהּ	with her/it	אִתָּהּ	עִמָּהּ
2ms	in you	בְּךָ[1]	to you	לְךָ[1]	with you	אִתְּךָ[1]	עִמְּךָ[1]
2fs	in you	בָּךְ	to you	לָךְ	with you	אִתָּךְ	עִמָּךְ
1cs	in me	בִּי	to me	לִי	with me	אִתִּי	עִמִּי or עִמָּדִי
3mp	in them	בָּהֶם or בָּם	to them	לָהֶם	with them	אִתָּם	עִמָּם
3fp	in them	בָּהֵן	to them	לָהֵן	with them	אִתָּן	עִמָּן
2mp	in you	בָּכֶם	to you	לָכֶם	with you	אִתְּכֶם	עִמְּכֶם
2fp	in you	בָּכֶן	to you	לָכֶן	with you	אִתְּכֶן	עִמְּכֶן
1cp	in us	בָּנוּ	to us	לָנוּ	with us	אִתָּנוּ	עִמָּנוּ

How to distinguish אֵת with Suffixes from the Personal Pronoun (Object)

The preposition אֵת with suffix is very similar to the personal pronoun (§30, p. 92). The preposition with suffix (above) takes forms like אִתּוֹ, אִתְּךָ, אִתָּן, etc. The personal pronouns take very similar forms such as אֹתוֹ, אֹתְךָ, אֹתָן.

It is easy to tell one from the other if you remember that the word *w<u>i</u>th* has an *i* and that the preposition אֵת with a suffix also always has an *i* (the *hireq* under the א). That is, the preposition אֵת with suffix (in the table above) always has the form -אִתּ: אִתּוֹ, אִתָּהּ, אִתְּךָ, etc.

Personal pronouns never have this *hireq*.

---

[1] In pause, the 2ms will be בָּךְ , לָךְ, אִתָּךְ and עִמָּךְ – and will look just like the 2fs. Watch the context.

35.2 The Prepositions -כְּ and מִן with Suffixes

The prepositions -כְּ and מִן may also take suffixes, but they do this in a slightly different way.[2]

- -כְּ usually adds an extra syllable -מוֹ-
- מִן adds an extra -מִּ-[3] (though not in 2p and 3p).

In some cases an extra -נ- is also added.

3ms	like him, like it	כָּמוֹהוּ	from him, from it	*מִמֶּנּוּ
3fs	like her, like it	כָּמוֹהָ	from her, from it	מִמֶּנָּה
2ms	like you	כָּמוֹךָ	from you	מִמְּךָ
2fs	like you	כָּמוֹךְ	from you	מִמֵּךְ
1cs	like me	כָּמוֹנִי	from me	מִמֶּנִּי
3mp	like them	כָּהֵם or כְּמוֹהֶם[4]	from them	מֵהֶם
3fp	like them	כָּהֵנָּה	from them	מֵהֵנָּה or מֵהֶן
2mp	like you	כָּכֶם	from you	מִכֶּם
2fp	like you	כָּכֶן	from you	מִכֶּן
1cp	like us	כָּמוֹנוּ	from us	*מִמֶּנּוּ

*Note that *from him* and *from us* have the same form: מִמֶּנּוּ. You will need to watch the context.

Things You Should Know

1. The prepositions -בְּ, -לְ, אֵת, עִם, -כְּ and מִן can take suffixes as personal pronouns do.
2. One can tell the difference between אֵת (*with*) plus suffix and the personal pronouns by watching the vowel under the א. -אִתּ plus suffix means *with*. Other forms are personal pronouns. Let the ***i*** (*hireq*) under the א remind you of the ***i*** in the word *w**i**th*.
3. -כְּ with suffix usually adds -מוֹ-. מִן with suffix usually adds a -מִּ-.
4. -כְּ and מִן add an extra -נ- in the 1cs, and מִן adds an extra -נ- in the 3ms.

---

[2] **Technical note:** -כְּ with suffixes is usually found in poetry.

[3] The *dagesh* in the מ represents the assimilated (swallowed) נ.

[4] **Technical note:** For both -כְּ and מִן, the 3p suffixes have several forms. Only the most common are shown here. Examples of other forms: there are single occurrences of the 3mp כָּהֶם in 2 Kgs 17:15, and of כָּהֵמָּה in Jer 36:32. The 3fp כָּהֵן is found only in Ezek 18:14. The 3mp מֵהֵמָּה occurs twice, and מִנְּהֶם once. The 3fp מֵהֵנָּה occurs seven times, and so is included in the chart. For more information, see *Gesenius*, §103(h).

36

COMPARISON

English adjectives often have three forms: the simple adjective, the comparative, and the superlative:

Simple adjective:	big	great	fast	heavy
Comparative:	bigger	greater	faster	heavier
Superlative:	biggest	greatest	fastest	heaviest

Hebrew also has simple adjectives (§24), but comparatives and superlatives are done differently.

36.2 Comparative

The Hebrew comparative usually uses the word מִן. Something is "better" *from* something else:

חָכְמָה טוֹב מִן יַ֫יִן = *Wisdom is better than wine.*
Literally, *wisdom* (*is*) *good from wine*

מֹשֶׁה גָּדוֹל[1] מֵאַהֲרוֹן = *Moses* (*is*) *greater than Aaron.*
Literally, *Moses* (*is*) *great from Aaron*

36.3 Superlative

The superlative can be shown in several ways:

1. The adjective may have a definite article:

בְּנָהּ הַקָּטָן = *Her youngest son*[2]
Literally, *her son, the young* (*one*)

הוּא הַגָּדוֹל = *He* (*is*) *the greatest*

בְּנֵי־יִשַׁי הַגְּדֹלִים = *Jesse's oldest sons* (1 Sam 17:13)

This is different from the *noun* having the d.a. (§24.2.3, p. 73). And note that מִן or -בְּ may also be used:

דָּוִד הַגָּדוֹל מִמְּלָכִים (using definite article and מִן)
דָּוִד הַגָּדוֹל בִּמְלָכִים (using definite article and -בְּ)
} *David is the greatest of the kings.*

2. The adjective may be in construct to a plural noun which has a suffix:

קְטוֹן־בָּנֶ֫יהָ = *her youngest son* Literally, (*the*) *young-one of her-sons*

---

[1] **Review question:** Why is the *tsere* under the מ? **Answer:** The word started as מִן אַהֲרוֹן. When the two words joined, the ן was swallowed by the א (§16.1.1, p. 46). Usually a *dagesh* appears in a letter which swallows a ן. But א is a guttural and rejects *dagesh.* Therefore, the *hireq* under the מ lengthened to *tsere* (§16.1.2).

[2] **Technical note:** Other grammars may call this a "correlative comparative" and translate *her younger son.*

3. The word מְאֹד may be used:

רַע מְאֹד = *most wicked*

4. A noun may be doubled, with its singular in construct to its plural:

מֶלֶךְ־מְלָכִים = *the greatest king* (literally, *king of kings*)

קֹדֶשׁ־הַקֳּדָשִׁים = *the most holy place* (literally *the holy of holies*)

5. There can even be a doubling of מְאֹד:

טוֹבָה הָאָרֶץ מְאֹד מְאֹד = *the best land* (literally *good (is) the land very very*)

Things You Should Know

1. Comparatives are words like *larger, smaller.* Superlatives are words like *largest, smallest.*
2. In Hebrew, the **comparative** is usually formed using the word מִן:

   מֹשֶׁה גָּדוֹל מֵאַהֲרוֹן *Moses is greater than Aaron.*
3. The **superlative** may be formed by
   - placing a definite article on the adjective
   - placing the adjective in construct to a plural noun with suffix
   - using the word מְאֹד
   - doubling the noun, where the second is plural (or even doubling the word מְאֹד)

Exercise #25

הוֹי, אוֹי	Woe! (cry of despair)	בָּחַר	to choose
אֹזֶן	*f.* ear (*du.*: אָזְנַיִם)	גּוֹי	nation; *pl.* גּוֹיִם nations, Gentiles
אָח	brother (*cs.* אֲחִי; *pl.* אַחִים, *cs.* אֲחֵי)	דֶּרֶךְ	*c.*[5] way, path, behavior
אַחֵר	*m.* other, another, different[3]	יוֹסֵף	Joseph
אַחֶרֶת	*f.* other, another, different	יְרוּשָׁלַםִ[6]	Jerusalem; *in pause:* יְרוּשָׁלָםִ
אַיִן	there is not (*cs.* אֵין)[4]	לֵב, לֵבָב	heart

---

[3] Do not confuse this word with אַחַר, אַחֲרֵי *after, behind,* which you learned earlier.

[4] Do not confuse these words with עַיִן, *eye, spring.*

[5] *c.* means *common.* See p. 93 footnote 3.

[6] This strange spelling is the one which is usually used. The word originally had a *yod*: יְרוּשָׁלַיִם, but this spelling is found only four times in the Old Testament.

[1] הֲבָחַר הֶ֫בֶל לִשְׁמֹר צֹאן בַּמִּדְבָּֽר׃ [2] וַיִּשְׁאַל קַ֫יִן בִּלְבָבוֹ וְעַתָּה אַיֵּה אֶֽהֱרֹג[7] אָחִֽי׃
[3] וַיְהִי בִּצְעֹק הָ֫בֶל[11] וַיַּהֲרֹג[10] קַ֫יִן אֶת־אָחִיו[9]׃ [4] יָצָא קַ֫יִן מִלִּפְנֵי־יְהוָה וַיָּבֹא[8] אֶל־
אֶ֫רֶץ אַחֶֽרֶת׃ [5] יֵרְדוּ הָרֹעִים עִם צֹאנָם אֶל מָקוֹם אֲשֶׁר מַ֫יִם טוֹב שָֽׁם׃ [6] הָלַךְ
בְּכוֹר־אַבְרָהָם אֶל הָהָר וְגַם עָשָׂה מִנְחָה שָׁם וֵאלֹהִים אִתּֽוֹ׃ [7] הֶהָיָה[12] יוֹסֵף הַקָּטֹן
מֵאֶחָיו[14]׃ [8] נָתַן אֱלֹהִים חָכְמָה גְדוֹלָה לְיוֹסֵף וְדַעַת־חֲלוֹמוֹת׃ [9] וַיֹּאמְרוּ הָעָם[13]
הוֹי לָ֫נוּ כִּי אַ֫יִן עַ֫יִן בְּדֶרֶךְ־הַמִּדְבָּֽר׃ [10] וַיְהִי אַחֲרֵי נָתַן הָרֹעֶה אֶת־מִנְחָתוֹ לִפְנֵי־יְהוָה
[16]וּבְשָׁלוֹם יָרַד מִירוּשָׁלָֽםִ[15]׃ [11] יְרוּשָׁלַ֫םִ הַגְּדוֹלָה־מִכָּל־הֶעָרִים וּבֵית־קָדוֹשׁ־אֱלֹהִים בָּֽהּ׃
[12] וַיֹּ֫אמֶר לִי אָבִי יְהוָה הוּא הָאֱלֹהִים וְאֵין כָּמֽוֹהוּ׃ [13] דִּבֶּר לָ֫נוּ יְהוָה וַיֹּאמַר[17] אוֹי
לְגוֹי אֲשֶׁר עָשָׂה רַע בְּעֵינַי לַעֲבֹד אֱלֹהִים אֲחֵרִֽים׃ [14] אָמַ֫רְתִּי בְּלִבִּי הַמָּקוֹם אֲשֶׁר
הָלַ֫כְנוּ שָׁם מָקוֹם־קֹ֫דֶשׁ הֽוּא׃ [15] הֲלֹא־נָתַן יְהוָה לָכֶם לֵב לָדַ֫עַת[19] וְעֵינַ֫יִם לִרְאוֹת[18]
וְאָזְנַ֫יִם לִשְׁמֹֽעַ׃ [16] אֵי הַגּוֹיִם הַחֲכָמִים הַיֹּדְעִים־יְהוָֽה׃ יִשְׁלַח אֹתָם בַּדֶּ֫רֶךְ אֲשֶׁר יִבְחָֽר׃
[17] נָתַן אֱלֹהִים שָׁלוֹם לַאֲבוֹתֵיכֶם כִּי שָֽׁמְעוּ אָזְנֵיהֶם אֶל־דְּבָרָיו וְגַם יָֽדְעוּ לְבָבֵהֶם
אֶת־דְּרָכָֽיו׃ [18] וְעַתָּה יִהְיֶה אֱלֹהִים אִתְּכֶן כִּי אַתֵּן צֹעֲקוֹת[20] לֽוֹ׃

---

[7] This Impf 1cs verb is pointed in this way because of the guttural ה. Review §13 if necessary.

[8] Impf 3ms < בָּא. The root of this verb is actually בוא, and we will study it later.

[9] Translate "his brother." The word אָח is irregular, and we will study it in the next chapter.

[10] This is the second -ו in this sentence. Review note 16 on page 94 concerning the translation. And be sure you can parse all three verbs in this sentence.

[11] The vowel pointing of this name has changed because it is in pause.

[12] See §14.3, p. 41.

[13] Remember that the Old Testament sometimes treats the word עָם as a singular (and gives it 3ms verbs) and sometimes as a plural (giving it 3mp or 3cp verbs). And sometimes singular and plural are mixed in a single verse.

[14] Translate "of (*lit.* from) his brothers." See note 9, above.

[15] In the Old Testament, people always go "down" when they leave Jerusalem. This does not mean that Jerusalem is on a very high mountain. Rather, the point is that Jerusalem is God's holy city, and so is "above" all others.

[16] See footnote 10, above.

[17] The accent and vowel pointing have changed because the word is in pause.

[18] When verbs end with the letter ה-, their Infinitive Constructs will end with וֹת- rather than ה- (§29.2, Note 2, p. 89). This is similar to the pattern for feminine nouns which end in ה- and have plurals ending in וֹת-. This pattern will be studied in more detail §72.

[19] Infinitive construct of יָדַע (plus -לְ). Verbs which begin with a *yod* sometimes act differently. They will be discussed in §63.

[20] Feminine participle. The guttural has produced the composite *shewa*.

37

SOME IRREGULAR NOUNS

Irregular nouns are nouns which do not follow the normal rules. They may be masculine but take feminine plural endings. Or their vowel pointing may change as they are put into the plural or construct. In most languages, it is the very common words which are often irregular.[1] This is also true in Hebrew, especially with words of family relationship. Study the following common words and the way they take possessive suffixes. In the Old Testament[2], not every possible suffix is found on every word. In the chart below, forms which do not occur are either left blank or are put in [square brackets].

People and Family Relationships

Absolute	*Construct*	*+1cs*	*+2ms*	*+2fs*	*+3ms*	*+3fs*	*+1cp*	*+2mp*	*+3mp*
אִישׁ (*man*)	אִישׁ	אִישִׁי		אִישֵׁךְ	אִישׁוֹ	אִישָׁהּ			
אֲנָשִׁים (*men*)	אַנְשֵׁי	אֲנָשַׁי	אֲנָשֶׁיךָ		אֲנָשָׁיו		אֲנָשֵׁינוּ		אֲנָשֵׁיהֶם
אִשָּׁה (*woman*)	אֵשֶׁת	אִשְׁתִּי	אִשְׁתְּךָ		אִשְׁתּוֹ				
נָשִׁים (*women*)	נְשֵׁי	נָשַׁי	נָשֶׁיךָ		נָשָׁיו		נָשֵׁינוּ	נְשֵׁיכֶם	נְשֵׁיהֶם
אָב (*father*)	אֲבִי [אַב]	אָבִי	אָבִיךָ	אָבִיךְ	אָבִיו אָבִיהוּ	אָבִיהָ	אָבִינוּ	אֲבִיכֶם	אֲבִיהֶם
אָבוֹת (*fathers*)	אֲבוֹת	אֲבוֹתַי	אֲבֹתֶיךָ		אֲבֹתָיו		אֲבֹתֵינוּ	אֲבֹתֵיכֶם	אֲבֹתָם
אֵם (*mother*)	אֵם	אִמִּי	אִמְּךָ	אִמֵּךְ	אִמּוֹ	אִמָּהּ		אִמְּכֶם	אִמָּם
אִמּוֹת (*mothers*)	אִמּוֹת						אִמֹּתֵינוּ		אִמֹּתָם
אָח (*brother*)	אֲחִי	אָחִי	אָחִיךָ	אָחִיךְ	אָחִיהוּ אָחִיו	אָחִיהָ	אָחִינוּ	אֲחִיכֶם	אֲחִיהֶם
אַחִים (*brothers*)	אֲחֵי	אַחַי	אַחֶיךָ	אַחַיִךְ	אֶחָיו	אַחֶיהָ	אַחֵינוּ	אֲחֵיכֶם	אֲחֵיהֶם
אָחוֹת (*sister*)	אֲחוֹת	אֲחֹתִי[3]	אֲחוֹתְךָ	אֲחֹתֵךְ	אֲחֹתוֹ	אֲחֹתָהּ	אֲחֹתֵנוּ		אֲחֹתָם
[אֲחָיוֹת] (*sisters*)	[אֲחָיוֹת]	אֲחוֹתַי		אֲחוֹתַיִךְ[4]	אַחְיוֹתָיו			אֲחוֹתֵיכֶם	אַחְיֹתֵיהֶם
בֵּן (*son*)	בֶּן	בְּנִי	בִּנְךָ	בְּנֵךְ	בְּנוֹ	בְּנָהּ	בְּנֵינוּ		
בָּנִים (*sons*)	בְּנֵי	בָּנַי	בָּנֶיךָ	בָּנַיִךְ	בָּנָיו	בָּנֶיהָ	בָּנֵינוּ	בְּנֵיכֶם	בְּנֵיהֶם
בַּת (*daughter*)	בַּת	בִּתִּי	בִּתְּךָ		בִּתּוֹ	בִּתָּהּ	בִּתֵּנוּ	בִּתְּכֶם	
בָּנוֹת (*daughters*)	בְּנוֹת	בְּנוֹתַי	בְּנוֹתֶיךָ	בְּנוֹתַיִךְ	בְּנוֹתָיו	בְּנוֹתֶיהָ	בְּנוֹתֵינוּ	בְּנוֹתֵיכֶם	בְּנוֹתֵיהֶם

---

[1] For instance, in English, nouns like "man, men," "wife, wives;" or the verb "to be": I *am*, you *are*, she *is*.

[2] See p. xiii for the use of "Old Testament" and not "Hebrew Scriptures." [3]Also אֲחוֹתִי [4]Also אֲחוֹתֵךְ

It is not necessary to memorize the entire chart. Instead,

(1) Learn the four major forms of each noun:

singular absolute	singular construct
plural absolute	plural construct

Example:

אִשָּׁה	אֵשֶׁת
נָשִׁים	נְשֵׁי

(2) Then look at how the suffixes join the construct forms.[4] Develop an understanding of how this is done.[5] If you do this, you will usually be able to figure out what you are looking at even if you have not memorized it.

(3) Notice how similar the construct forms of אָב (*father*) and אָח (*brother*) are to the construct + 1cs:

Absolute	Construct	Construct + 1cs
אָב	אֲבִי	אָבִי
אָח	אֲחִי	אָחִי

(4) The word אָחוֹת (*sister*) needs to be studied carefully. The singular form looks like a plural, but the plural is different: אֲחָיוֹת.[6]

---

[4] Remember, suffixes always go on the *construct* form. The absolute form cannot take suffixes.

[5] Note, for instance, that the *plural* nouns with suffixes often (though not always) have an extra *yod* (י).

[6] **Technical note:** The unsuffixed plural form (אֲחָיוֹת) is not found in the Bible, but various plurals with suffixes are found, as shown in the chart.

38

DEMONSTRATIVE ADJECTIVES

Demonstrative adjectives are words which *demonstrate* which thing is being discussed. We can speak not only of *a book* or *the book* but also of *this book, that book, these books,* or *those books.* The words *this, that, these* and *those* are the demonstrative adjectives.

The demonstrative adjectives are as follows:

this (ms) זֶה	*that* (ms) הוּא
this (fs) זֹאת	*that* (fs) הִיא
these (cp) אֵ֫לֶּה	*those* (mp) הֵ֫מָּה, הֵם
	those (fp) הֵ֫נָּה, הֵן

Notes:

1. The words for *that* and *those* have the same form as those of the *personal pronoun subject* (§30, p. 92). Again, context will tell you how to translate.

2. Nouns which have demonstrative adjectives (*this* man, *that* woman) are **definite**. Thus:
   (a) These nouns will have definite articles;
   (b) The demonstrative adjectives **may or may not** have a definite article. The situation is the same as it is for the ordinary adjective (§24). Note the following comparison:

Ordinary adjectives:

הָאִישׁ הַטּוֹב	*the good man*
טוֹב הָאִישׁ	*the man (is) good*

Demonstrative adjectives:

הָאִישׁ הַזֶּה	*this man*
זֶה הָאִישׁ	*this (is) the man*

Things You Should Know

1. Demonstrative adjectives are words which mean *this, that, these,* and *those.* (Learn the Hebrew demonstrative adjectives which are given above.)

2. In Hebrew, the words for *that* and *those* are the same as the personal pronoun subject.

3. If the demonstrative adjective has no article and comes *before* the noun, we translate "This *is* the ...," "Those *are* the ...," etc.

Exercise #26

In addition to the following words, be sure to add the demonstrative adjectives to your vocabulary cards.

אָחוֹת	sister (*pl.* אֲחָיוֹת[1])	יַרְדֵּן	Jordan	עָבַר	to cross [do not confuse with the word עָבַד]
אֵם	*f.* mother (*pl.* אִמּוֹת)	לָבָן	Laban, white	רָחֵל	Rachel, ewe (female sheep)
בַּת	*f.* daughter (*pl.* בָּנוֹת)	לוֹט	Lot		

[1] לָקַח אַבְרָם אֶת־שָׂרַי אִשְׁתּוֹ וְאֶת־לוֹט בֶּן־אָחִיו וְאֶל אֶרֶץ־כְּנַעַן יָצְאוּ׃ [2] וְגַם־לְלוֹט
הַהֹלֵךְ אֶת־אַבְרָם הָיוּ[3] צֹאן־וּבָקָר׃ [3] וַיְדַבֵּר[2] אַבְרָם אֶל־שָׂרַי לֵאמֹר אִמְרִי אֲשֶׁר
אֲחוֹתִי אַתְּ וְהָיָה טוֹב לִי׃ [4] וַיֹּאמֶר אַבְרָהָם וְגַם־אֲחוֹתִי בַת־אָבִי הִיא[4] וְלֹא בַת־אִמִּי
וַתְּהִי[8]־לִי לְאִשָּׁה׃ [5] וַיְהִי בִּרְאוֹת[7] יַעֲקֹב אֶת־רָחֵל בַּת־לָבָן אֲחִי־אִמּוֹ [6]וַיֹּאמֶר אֶעֱבֹד[5]
אֹתְךָ בְּרָחֵל[9] בִּתְּךָ הַקְּטַנָּה׃ [6] וְרָחֵל מָצְאָה חֵן בְּעֵינֵי־יַעֲקֹב וְלֹא מָצְאָה חֵן בַּת־לָבָן
הַגְּדוֹלָה׃ [7] בַּבֹּקֶר רָאָה עֵשָׂו אֶת־הָאֲנָשִׁים וְאֶת־הַנָּשִׁים הָעֹבְרִים אֶת־הַנָּהָר לִפְנֵי־
יַעֲקֹב [12]וַיִּשְׁאַל מִי־אֵלֶּה לָךְ[11]׃ [8] וַיַּעֲמֹד[10] יוֹסֵף לִפְנֵי־מֶלֶךְ־מִצְרַיִם וַיֹּאמֶר נָתַן אֱלֹהֵי־
אֲבוֹתַי בְּרָכָה אֶל־אָבִי וְאֶל־אֶחָי[13]׃ [9] וַיֹּאמֶר יוֹסֵף אֵין־גָּדוֹל מִמֶּנִּי בַּבַּיִת הַזֶּה וּמָה
אֶעֱשֶׂה[15] הַדָּבָר הָרַע הַזֶּה׃ [10] וַיֹּאמֶר יְהוֹשֻׁעַ אֶל־בְּנֵי־יִשְׂרָאֵל לֵאמֹר אֲשֶׁר[14] יִשְׁאָלוּ
בְּנֵיכֶם אֶת־אֲבוֹתָם לֵאמֹר מָה הָאֲבָנִים הָאֵלֶּה׃ וַאֲמַרְתֶּם אֲשֶׁר עָבַר יִשְׂרָאֵל אֶת־הַיַּרְדֵּן
הַזֶּה׃ [11] וַיֹּאמֶר הַזָּקֵן אוֹי לָעִיר הַהִיא אֲשֶׁר לֹא מָצָא דַרְכָּהּ חֵן בְּעֵינֵי־יְהוָה וְאוֹי
לַגּוֹיִם הָהֵם אֲשֶׁר בָּחֲרוּ אֶל אַחֵר׃ [12] וַיִּשְׁאֲלוּ הַזְּקֵנִים מִי הַנָּשִׁים הַזְּקֵנוֹת הָהֵנָּה אֲשֶׁר

---

[1] The plural form is not found alone in the Bible; it always has suffixes.

[2] Impf 3ms + w.c. < דָּבַר. This vowel pattern will be explained in a later chapter. For now, just note that the verb דבר always uses it. For the missing *dagesh* in the *yod*, see the technical note in footnote 6, p. 81.

[3] "They were ... to Lot." That is, "Lot had them." **Technical note:** Normally, there is a *dagesh* in the prefix of an Impf + w.c. But *yod* over *shewa* normally rejects this *dagesh*. This was first noted on p. 81, footnote 6.

[4] Add "is." Then let the context tell you whether the next וְ should be translated "and" or "but."

[5] Why is there a composite *shewa* under the ע, instead of the normal simple *shewa* (as in אֶשְׁמֹר)?

[6] This is the second -ו in this sentence. Again, consider p. 94, note 16.

[7] If you do not recognize this form, see p. 111, note 18.

[8] Compare this verb to the 3ms וַיְהִי, which you often see. See also p. 83, note 8.

[9] Here the -בְּ means "for," that is, "in exchange for."

[10] The original form was וַיַּעְמֹד, but the guttural has attracted both a composite *shewa* beneath it as well as a *pathah* before it.

[11] Translate "with you(ms)." Remember that, in pause, לְךָ becomes לָךְ (see page 107, footnote 1).

[12] Impf 3ms + wc. The guttural has attracted a *pathah.*

[13] From אַחַי. The vowel pointing has changed because the word is in pause. Note: the word does not mean "my brother." See p. 112.

[14] Translate "that" (although in this case both לֵאמֹר and אֲשֶׁר can be left untranslated).

[15] Impf 1cs < עשׂה. The ע and the ה have changed the vowel pointing (as we shall study later).

יָרְדוּ מִן רֹאשׁ־הָהָר לִשְׁפֹּט אֶת־יְרוּשָׁלָֽםִ׃ [13] בָּרָא אֱלֹהִים אֶת־לֵב־הָאָדָם וְאֶת־אֹזֶן־
הָאָדָֽם וּמַדּוּעַ לֹא שָׁמַע הָאָדָם בְּקוֹל־אֱלֹהִים׃ [14] יְהוָה אֲשֶׁר שָׁלַח אֹתָנוּ לַעֲבֹר אֶת־
הַיַּרְדֵּן וְגַם נָתַן לָנוּ צֹאן וּבָקָֽר[16] הוּא הָאֱלֹהִים וְאֵין כָּמוֹהוּ׃ [15] וַיֹּאמֶר שָׁאוּל הַנְּבִיאָה
הַהִיא לִֽי וְהַנְּבִיאוֹת הָהֵן לְבֶן־יִשָׁי׃ [16] וַיֹּאמֶר הוֹי לָאִישׁ הַהוּא וְלָאִשָּׁה הַהִיא אֲשֶׁר
בָּחֲרוּ אֶת־דֶּרֶךְ־אֹיְבָי׃ לֹא יַעַמְדוּ[17] לְפָנָי׃ [17] בָּעֶרֶב הַהוּא שָׁאַל שָׁאוּל הֲיָרְדוּ אֹיְבֵי־
בֶן־יִשַׁי הַהֵמָּה אֶל־שְׁאוֹל׃ [18] יְרוּשָׁלַםִ כַּגּוֹיִם כִּי לִבָּהּ כְּאֶבֶן וְלֹא שֹׁמְעוֹת[18] אָזְנֶיהָ אֶת־
דְּבָרָי׃

---

[16] Translate "herds" (plural). בָּקָר is used for both the singular "herd" as well as the plural "herds." (The plural form בְּקָרִים is found only twice in the Old Testament.)

[17] Note again the effect of the guttural. The normal vowel pattern is יִשְׁמְרוּ.

[18] If you have trouble parsing this word, note the *holem* after the שׂ. If you still have trouble, see page 96.

39

SOME MORE IRREGULAR NOUNS

In §37, we saw that many common words used for family relationship are irregular. This is also true for some words used for common objects. Again, not all possible suffix patterns are shown below. Only those which are actually found in the Old Testament are listed.

Common Objects

Absolute	*Construct*	*+1cs*	*+2ms*	*+2fs*	*+3ms*	*+3fs*	*+1cp*	*+2mp*	*+3mp*
בַּ֫יִת (*house*)	בֵּית	בֵּיתִי	בֵּיתְךָ	בֵּיתֵךְ	בֵּיתוֹ	בֵּיתָהּ		בֵּיתְכֶם	בֵּיתָם
בָּתִּים (*houses*)	בָּתֵּי		בָּתֶּ֫יךָ	בָּתַּ֫יִךְ	בָּתָּיו		בָּתֵּ֫ינוּ	בָּתֵּיכֶם	בָּתֵּיהֶם
יוֹם (*day*)	יוֹם		יוֹמְךָ		יוֹמוֹ				
יָמִים[1] (*days*)	יְמֵי	יָמַי	יָמֶ֫יךָ	יָמַ֫יִךְ	יָמָיו	יָמֶ֫יהָ	יָמֵ֫ינוּ	יְמֵיכֶם	יְמֵיהֶם
כְּלִי (*thing, container*)	[כְּלִי]		כֶּלְיְךָ						
כֵּלִים (*things, containers*)	כְּלֵי	כֵּלַי	כֵּלֶ֫יךָ		כֵּלָיו	כֵּלֶ֫יהָ	כֵּלֵ֫ינוּ	כְּלֵיכֶם	כְּלֵיהֶם
עִיר (f. *city*)	עִיר	עִירִי	עִירְךָ		עִירוֹ	עִירָהּ			עִירָם
עָרִים (f. *cities*)	עָרֵי	עָרַי	עָרֶ֫יךָ	עָרַ֫יִךְ	עָרָיו	עָרֶ֫יהָ	עָרֵ֫ינוּ	עָרֵיכֶם	עָרֵיהֶם
פֶּה (m. *mouth*)	פִּי	פִּי	פִּיךָ	פִּיךְ	פִּיו[2]	פִּיהָ	פִּ֫ינוּ	פִּיכֶם	פִּיהֶם
פִּיּוֹת (m. *mouths*)	פִּיּוֹת						3	3	3
רֹאשׁ (*head*)	רֹאשׁ	רֹאשִׁי	רֹאשְׁךָ	רֹאשֵׁךְ	רֹאשׁוֹ	רֹאשָׁהּ	רֹאשֵׁ֫נוּ	רֹאשְׁכֶם	רֹאשָׁם
רָאשִׁים (*heads*)	רָאשֵׁי				רָאשָׁיו	רָאשֶׁ֫יהָ	רָאשֵׁ֫ינוּ	רָאשֵׁיכֶם	רָאשֵׁיהֶם
שֵׁם (m. *name*)	שֵׁם	שְׁמִי	שִׁמְךָ	שְׁמֵךְ	שְׁמוֹ	שְׁמָהּ	שְׁמֵ֫נוּ	שִׁמְכֶם	שְׁמָם
שֵׁמוֹת (m. *names*)	שְׁמוֹת								שְׁמוֹתָם

Again, as noted in §37, it is not necessary to memorize the entire chart. Instead, memorize the major forms (singular and plural, absolute and construct), and then study the way the suffixes are applied. You will soon develop an instinct for this, just as you have done in your own mother tongue.

---

[1] A few times in the Bible this form is יְמוֹת. The word also has a dual: יוֹמָ֫יִם. [2] Also פִּיהוּ.

[3] To say "our mouths," "your (pl) mouths," or "their mouths," Hebrew uses the *singular* construct noun with plural suffixes (as in the line above: פִּ֫ינוּ פִּיכֶם פִּיהֶם). Thus, literally, "our mouth," "your (pl) mouth," "their mouth." This also happens with words for other parts of the body, such as "ears," etc.

40

THE VERB: PASSIVE PARTICIPLE

In chapter 32, we learned about Active Participles. Review §32.1, "Participles: their characteristics," p. 96. Review also §32.3, "Participles: their uses," p. 97. A participle is a type of verb which acts like an adjective. It has gender (m or f) and number (s or p) and is active or passive. But it does not have tense (past, present, future) or person (1, 2, or 3).

▲**Active and Passive.** An **active** verb is a verb which shows that the *subject* ***does*** *something* (often to an object). A **passive** verb, on the other hand, is a verb which shows that *something* ***happens to*** *the subject.* Thus,

She *sings* the song	uses an active verb (*sings*)
The song *is sung*	uses a passive verb (*is sung*[1])

Form: The Passive Participle is as shown below. Note especially the וּ.

	Singular	Plural
Masculine	שָׁמוּר	שְׁמוּרִים
Feminine	שְׁמוּרָה	שְׁמוּרוֹת

Translation: Following is a comparison of translation of the Active and Passive Participles:

Active: הָאִישׁ הַשֹּׁמֵר, *the man who is keeping* (lit., *the man, the keeping* [*one*])

Passive: הָאִישׁ הַשָּׁמוּר, *the man who is being kept* (lit., *the man, the being-kept* [*one*])

Parsing of passive participles: Review parsing of active participles (p. 98).

As a verb: שָׁמוּר = Part Pass ms < שׁמר

As a noun: הַכְּתוּבִים = Nmpa + d.a. < כתב

Notes:

1. The Passive Participle (שָׁמוּר) and the Infinitive Absolute (שָׁמוֹר) are very similar in appearance. Do not confuse them. The Infinitive Absolute uses וֹ, but the Passive Participle uses וּ.
2. As with the *Active* Participle, if the final letter is a guttural, there will be a furtive *pathah*: שָׁמוּעַ.
3. On occasion, the *shureq* (וּ) will reduce to a *qibbuts* (ֻ). For example, we may see שְׁמֻרִים instead of שְׁמוּרִים for the Part Pass mp.

---

[1] In English, the passive voice must use a helping verb such as *is, was, will be*. In Hebrew, this is not the case. In Hebrew, the passive participle will be just a single word.

Things You Should Know

1. "Active" means the subject does the action. "Passive" means the subject receives the action.
2. The Active Participle and its forms are based upon שֹׁמֵר. The Passive Participle and its forms are based upon שָׁמוּר. Review §32 on Active Participles.
3. Be sure you do not confuse the Passive Participle (שָׁמוּר) with the IA (שָׁמוֹר).
4. Active and Passive Participles with final guttural will use furtive *pathah*: שֹׁמֵעַ, שָׁמוּעַ.
5. Occasionally, the *shureq* (וּ) of the Part Pass fp will be replaced by a *qibbuts* (ֻ). For example, we may see שְׁמֻרוֹת instead of שְׁמוּרוֹת.

Exercise #27

כַּאֲשֶׁר	just as, when	נָשָׂא	to lift up, carry, forgive
כְּלִי	thing, container, weapon	סִינַי	Sinai
לְבַד	alone (*with suffix:* לְבַדּוֹ him only, by himself)	פֶּה	mouth, *cs.* פִּי, *pl.* פִּיּוֹת
לוּחַ	*m.* flat piece of stone or wood[2] *pl.* לוּחוֹת; *du.* לוּחֹתַיִם	צִוָּה	(ṣiw-wâ[5]) to command
לְמַעַן	in order to, for the sake of	שֵׁם[6]	*m.* name, *pl.* שֵׁמוֹת
מִצְוָה[3]	*f.* commandment *pl.* מִצְוֹת (miṣ-wōṯ[4])	תּוֹרָה	instruction, law[7] (Torah)

[1] הַמִּצְוֹת הַשָּׁמוּר׃ הָעֵץ כָּרוּת[8]׃ הַפְּרִי הָאָכוּל׃ הָעִיר שָׂרוּף בָּאֵשׁ׃ [2] יָשַׁב לוֹט
בְּעִיר וּשְׁמָהּ סְדֹם[9]׃ [3] שָׁאַל אַבְרָהָם הַנֹּשֵׂא אֱלֹהִים אֶת־הָעִיר אֲשֶׁר לוֹט יֹשֵׁב שָׁם
לְמַעַן הָאֲנָשִׁים הַטּוֹבִים בָּהּ׃ [4] יָצְאוּ רָחֵל וְיַעֲקֹב מִבֵּית־אָבִיהָ וַתִּגְנֹב אֶת־אֱלֹהָיו׃

---

[2] This word is sometimes translated *plank* (of wood), *slab* (of stone) or *tablet* (of stone, clay or wood). It refers most often to the pieces of stone God gave to Moses with the Ten Commandments written on them.

[3] Compare this word to the word צִוָּה (*to command*), which is also found in this vocabulary list. It is almost the same, except it has a prefixed -מ. Review §20.5, p. 57, regarding nouns which are formed by adding a מ (or sometimes a ת) to the beginning of a verb.

[4] The ו cannot be a vowel because there is a *shewa* before it. Thus, it must be wō (§5.3, Note 3b, p. 13).

[5] The ו cannot be a vowel because it is over a *qamets*. Remember, two vowels cannot come together in Hebrew (§5.3, p. 13).

[6] This is another masculine noun with a plural that looks feminine. Also, do not confuse this word with שָׁם, *there* (Exercise 24, p. 106).

[7] *Law* is a popular translation of תּוֹרָה, but it is not a good translation. It is better to translate תּוֹרָה as *instruction*, *guidance*, or even *teaching*. In the Old Testament, it does not have exactly the same meaning as it does in the New Testament (especially for Paul).

[8] Compare this example to the previous one. The previous one has a definite article on the participle, but this one does not. How does this change the translation? (Review §32.3, p. 97, if you are not sure.)

[9] Sodom.

[5] וַיְהִי כַּאֲשֶׁר רָאָה לָבָן כִּי יָֽצְאוּ בִתּוֹ וְאִישָׁהּ וַיִּרְדֹּף[11] אַחֲרֵיהֶם לְמַ֫עַן [10]לְכֹד אֹתָֽם׃
[6] לֹא מָצָא לָבָן אֶת־אֱלֹהָיו בִּכְלֵי־יַֽעֲקֹב וְלֹא יָדַע כִּי בִתּוֹ יֹשֶׁ֫בֶת עֲלֵיהֶֽם[12]׃ [7] וַיֹּ֫אמֶר
מֹשֶׁה אֶל־פַּרְעֹה שְׁלוּחִים בְּנֵי־יִשְׂרָאֵל לַמִּדְבָּר לְמַ֫עַן עֲבֹד אֶת־הָאֱלֹהִֽים׃ [8] יָֽצְאוּ בְנֵי־
יִשְׂרָאֵל מֵאֶ֫רֶץ־מִצְרַ֫יִם וְגַם בָּ֫אוּ מִדְבַּר־סִינָֽי׃ [9] וַיֹּ֫אמֶר יְהוָה אֶל־מֹשֶׁה בֹּ֫א[13] אֵלַי
לְבַדֶּ֫ךָ עַל־הַר־סִינָֽי׃ וְשָׁם נָתַן יְהוָה אֶל־מֹשֶׁה אֶת־לוּחוֹת־הָאֶ֫בֶן אֶת[14]־הַתּוֹרָה וְאֶת־הַמִּצְוָה
אֲשֶׁר כָּתַב אֹתָם בְּיָדוֹ׃ [10] וּמִן הָהָר יָרַד מֹשֶׁה נֹשֵׂא אֶת־לוּחוֹת־הָאֶ֫בֶן הַכְּתוּבִים בְּיַד־
אֱלֹהִים׃ [11] וְאֶת־הָעָם צִוָּה מֹשֶׁה לֵאמֹר שִׁמְרוּ אֶת־הַתּוֹרָה הַזֹּאת וְאֶת־הַמִּצְוֹת הָאֵ֫לֶּה
הַנְּתוּנוֹת הַיּוֹם הַזֶּה[15] מִפִּי־יְהוָֽה׃ [12] וַיְהִי כַּאֲשֶׁר עָבַר הָעָם אֶת־הַיַּרְדֵּן וּנְעָרִים נָֽשְׂאוּ
אֲבָנִים מֵהַנָּהָר׃ [13] בַּיָּמִים הָהֵם יָֽצְאָה אַחַת מִן אַחְיוֹתָיו אֶת־אִמָּהּ אֶל־הַמָּקוֹם הַהוּא
אֲשֶׁר נְשֵׁי־הָאֱלֹהִים הָיוּ שָֽׁם׃ [14] עָשָׂה יְהוֹשֻׁ֫עַ שָׁלוֹם לְיֹשְׁבֵי־גִבְעֹ֫ן[17] וְאֶת־פִּי־יְהוָה[16] לֹא
שָׁאָֽל׃ [15] וַתֹּאמַ֫רְנָה[18] אִמֹּתֵ֫ינוּ עָֽבְרוּ אֲחִיכֶן אֶת־הַיַּרְדֵּן לְמַ֫עַן שֵׁם־יְהוָֽה׃ [16] תִּשְׁאַל
הַנְּבִיאָה כְּלִי קָטֹן מַ֫יִם וְנָתַן אָבִיהָ אֹתוֹ לָֽהּ׃ [17] רָאָה יִתְרוֹ[19] אֵת כָּל־אֲשֶׁר־עֹשֶׂה מֹשֶׁה
לָעָם וַיֹּ֫אמֶר מָה אַתָּה שֹׁפֵט לְבַדֶּ֫ךָ וְכָל־הָעָם עֹמֵד עָלֶ֫יךָ[20]׃ [18] צִוָּה אֶת־הָעָם לֵאמֹר
שִׁמְרוּ אֶת־מִצְוֹת־יְהוָה וְהָיָה שָׁלוֹם בַּמְּקוֹמוֹת אֲשֶׁר אַתֶּם יֹשְׁבִים שָֽׁם׃ [19] כֹּה אָמַר יְהוָה
יִהְיֶה שְׁמִי גָדוֹל מְאֹד בְּעֵינֵי־עַמִּי כִּי נָשָׂ֫אתִי לָהֶֽם[21]׃ [20] יָֽרְדוּ מִן יְרוּשָׁלַ֫ם אַחוֹתֵיכֶם
אֶת[23]־אֲחֵיהֶן לַעֲשׂוֹת[22] רַע בְּעֵינֵי־יְהוָֽה׃

---

[10] We have seen that the Infinitive Construct usually has an inseparable preposition attached to it (for instance, לִשְׁמֹר). In this case, however, the preposition (לְמַ֫עַן) is not inseparable, and thus it stands *before* the IC.

[11] Translate the w.c. as *then*, or leave it untranslated.

[12] When the preposition עַל takes suffixes, an extra ' appears. This will be studied in §52.

[13] Impv ms < בָּא.

[14] Note the two meanings of אֵת in this sentence.

[15] In the Bible, the phrase "this day" is often just written הַיּוֹם (without הַזֶּה).

[16] That is, "advice from (the mouth of) the LORD."

[17] Gibeon. The complete story is found in Judges 9.

[18] Impf 3fp + w.c. < אמר.

[19] Jethro, Moses' father in law.

[20] See note 12, above. Here, translate "around you."

[21] Translate "I forgave them."

[22] Reminder: the IC of a verb which ends with ה loses its final ה- and takes וֹת- instead.

[23] Is this the sign of the definite direct object or is it the word *with*?

41

SEGHOLATE NOUNS

Segholate nouns are nouns which have *seghol*s under one or more of their letters. They also usually have an accent on the first syllable. You have already seen one of these words many times: מֶ֫לֶךְ. The *seghols* are seen only when the word is singular and without suffixes. When segholate words have suffixes, or when they are plural, their vowel pointing changes and returns to an older form.

41.1 Three Types of Segholate Nouns

There were originally three different kinds of words which became segholates. That is, words like מֶ֫לֶךְ, סֵ֫פֶר, and קֹ֫דֶשׁ were originally מַלְךְ, סִפְר and קֻדְשׁ, based upon a *pathah*, a *hireq* and *u*-vowel. The *seghols* disappear, and the original vowel forms return, when the words are given suffixes (*my king* is מַלְכִּי) or when they are plural (the plural of מֶ֫לֶךְ is מְלָכִים).

The following chart shows **singular** segholate nouns. The absolute and construct forms have *seghols*, but when suffixes are added the *seghols* disappear. (In the last column, the *qamets* under the first letter (-קָ) is *qamets-hatuph*, not *qamets*.)

41.2 Singular Segholate Nouns with Singular and Plural Suffixes

	Absolute:	מֶ֫לֶךְ *(king)*	סֵ֫פֶר *(scroll)*	קֹ֫דֶשׁ *(holiness)*
	Construct:	מֶ֫לֶךְ *(king-of)*	סֵ֫פֶר *(scroll-of)*	קֹ֫דֶשׁ *(holiness-of)*
Sing.	*1cs (my)*	מַלְכִּי	סִפְרִי	קָדְשִׁי
	2ms (your)	מַלְכְּךָ	סִפְרְךָ	קָדְשְׁךָ
	2fs (your)	מַלְכֵּךְ	סִפְרֵךְ	קָדְשֵׁךְ
	3ms (his)	מַלְכּוֹ	סִפְרוֹ	קָדְשׁוֹ
	3fs (her)	מַלְכָּהּ	סִפְרָהּ	קָדְשָׁהּ
Pl.	*1cp (our)*	מַלְכֵּ֫נוּ	סִפְרֵ֫נוּ	קָדְשֵׁ֫נוּ
	2mp (your)	מַלְכְּכֶם	סִפְרְכֶם	קָדְשְׁכֶם
	2fp (your)	מַלְכְּכֶן	סִפְרְכֶן	קָדְשְׁכֶן
	3mp (their)	מַלְכָּם	סִפְרָם	קָדְשָׁם
	3fp (their)	מַלְכָּן	סִפְרָן	קָדְשָׁן

The next chart shows this same pattern for the **plural** segholate noun (where the *seghols* never appear). Again, in the last column, the *qamets* under the first letter (-קָ) is *qamets-hatuph.*

41.3 Plural Segholate Nouns with Singular and Plural Suffixes

	Absolute:	מְלָכִים *(kings)*	סְפָרִים *(scrolls)*	קֳדָשִׁים *(holinesses)*
	Construct:	מַלְכֵי *(kings-of)*	סִפְרֵי *(scrolls-of)*	קָדְשֵׁי *(holinesses-of)*
Sing.	*1cs (my)*	מְלָכַי	סְפָרַי	קֳדָשַׁי
	2ms (your)	מְלָכֶיךָ	סְפָרֶיךָ	קֳדָשֶׁיךָ
	2fs (your)	מְלָכַיִךְ	סְפָרַיִךְ	קֳדָשַׁיִךְ
	3ms (his)	מְלָכָיו	סְפָרָיו	קֳדָשָׁיו
	3fs (her)	מְלָכֶיהָ	סְפָרֶיהָ	קֳדָשֶׁיהָ
Pl.	*1cp (our)*	מְלָכֵינוּ	סְפָרֵינוּ	קֳדָשֵׁינוּ
	2mp (your)	מַלְכֵיכֶם	סִפְרֵיכֶם	קָדְשֵׁיכֶם
	2fp (your)	מַלְכֵיכֶן	סִפְרֵיכֶן	קָדְשֵׁיכֶן
	3mp (their)	מַלְכֵיהֶם	סִפְרֵיהֶם	קָדְשֵׁיהֶם
	3fp (their)	מַלְכֵיהֶן	סִפְרֵיהֶן	קָדְשֵׁיהֶן

Notes:

1. **Segholate nouns with final gutturals** will follow the rules for gutturals:
   a. Words such as זרע will take the form זֶרַע, since gutturals prefer *pathah* (§13.3, p. 38).
   b. If a suffix causes a double *shewa* (as in מַלְכְּךָ on the previous page), a word with a final guttural will use composite *shewa*:

   ךָ + זֶרַע → זַרְעְךָ → זַרְעֲךָ (§8.2.2, p. 24).

2. **Segholates in pause.**[1] In §41.1, above, we learned that segholates had older original forms, based upon *pathah, hireq* or a *u*-vowel. For some original-*pathah* segholates, the *pathah* will return in pause, and then lengthen to *qamets*. For instance, אֶרֶץ (originally אַרְץ) becomes אָרֶץ at the end of a sentence, and אָ֑רֶץ with *athnah*.

3. **Unusual cases.** Some segholates have the same form as מֶלֶךְ (that is, two *seghols*) but they follow the pattern of סֵפֶר when they take suffixes. For instance, the words בֶּגֶד (*piece of clothing*) will take suffixes as follows: בִּגְדִי, בִּגְדְךָ, בִּגְדוֹ, etc. This will also be true for the words צֶדֶק (*righteousness*) and קֶבֶר (*grave*).

4. **In parsing**, there is no need to write "segholate noun." מְלָכָיו is simply parsed Nmpc+3ms.

---

[1] Review: A word is in pause if it has an *athnah* (֑) or if it is the last word of the sentence (§7.5, p. 20).

Things You Should Know

1. **Segholate nouns** are nouns which have one or two *seghols* when they are in the singular and without suffixes.
2. **Suffixed or plural segholates:** In the singular *with* suffixes, and always in the plural, the *seghols* disappear, and the vowels from an earlier form of the word reappear.
3. **Segholates with a final gutturals:** In the singular absolute, there will be a *pathah* under the letter before the guttural: זֶ֫רַע. If a double *shewa* appears when adding suffixes, the *shewa* under the guttural becomes a composite *shewa*: זַרְעֲךָ.

42

STATIVE VERBS

Stative Verbs tell the *state* or *condition* of the subject, not its action. For instance, the sentence *he ran* is active, not stative, since it describes an *action* of the subject. But the sentences *he is old* or *he was small* are both stative, since they describe the state of the person (that is, the subject).

We have seen that the Perf 3ms of *active* verbs is built around *a*-vowels (*e.g.,* שָׁמַר uses *qamets* and *pathah*). However, the second vowel of the Perf 3ms *stative* verb is usually an *e* or an *o*. That is:

כָּבֵד *he was heavy* קָטֹן *he was small*

In the rest of the Perfect and Imperfect conjugations, however, Stative Verbs are almost identical to active *a*-vowel verbs. **Note also that statives have no *passive* form.**

	-Active-	Stative		
	a-vowel	*e*-vowel	*o*-vowel	
Perf. 3ms	שָׁמַר	כָּבֵד	קָטֹן	
3fs	שָׁמְרָה	כָּבְדָה	קָטְנָה	
2ms	שָׁמַרְתָּ	כָּבַדְתָּ	קָטֹנְתָּ	
2fs	שָׁמַרְתְּ	כָּבַדְתְּ	קָטֹנְתְּ	
1cs	שָׁמַרְתִּי	כָּבַדְתִּי	קָטֹנְתִּי	
3cp	שָׁמְרוּ	כָּבְדוּ	קָטְנוּ	(Compare to 1cp below)
2mp	שְׁמַרְתֶּם	כְּבַדְתֶּם	קְטָנְתֶּם	(Note *qamets-hatuph*)
2fp	שְׁמַרְתֶּן	כְּבַדְתֶּן	קְטָנְתֶּן	(Note *qamets-hatuph*)
1cp	שָׁמַרְנוּ	כָּבַדְנוּ	קָטֹנּוּ	(< קָטֹנְנוּ)
Impf. 3ms	יִשְׁמֹר	יִכְבַּד	יִקְטַן	
3fs	תִּשְׁמֹר	תִּכְבַּד	(These forms follow the pattern of כָּבֵד)	
2ms	תִּשְׁמֹר	תִּכְבַּד		
2fs	תִּשְׁמְרִי	תִּכְבְּדִי		
1cs	אֶשְׁמֹר	אֶכְבַּד		
3mp	יִשְׁמְרוּ	יִכְבְּדוּ		
3fp	תִּשְׁמֹרְנָה	תִּכְבַּדְנָה		
2mp	תִּשְׁמְרוּ	תִּכְבְּדוּ		
2fp	תִּשְׁמֹרְנָה	תִּכְבַּדְנָה		
1cp	נִשְׁמֹר	נִכְבַּד		

Cohort. 1s	אֶשְׁמְרָה	אֶכְבְּדָה	(These forms also follow כָּבֵד)
1p	נִשְׁמְרָה	נִכְבְּדָה	
Impv. 2ms	שְׁמֹר	כְּבַד	
2fs	שִׁמְרִי	כִּבְדִי	
2mp	שִׁמְרוּ	כִּבְדוּ	
2fp	שְׁמֹרְנָה	כְּבַדְנָה	
Jussive 3ms	------------------ Same	as Imperfect 3ms	----------------------
Act. Pt. ms	שֹׁמֵר	כָּבֵד	קָטֹן
mp	שֹׁמְרִים	כְּבֵדִים	קְטֹנִים
fs	שֹׁמֶרֶת (שֹׁמְרָה)	כְּבֵדָה	קְטֹנָה
fp	שֹׁמְרוֹת	כְּבֵדוֹת	קְטֹנוֹת
Inf. Abs.	שָׁמוֹר	כָּבוֹד	קָטוֹן
Inf. Const.	שְׁמֹר	כְּבַד	קְטַן

Notes:

1. **Perfect.**
   - ***E*-type Stative Verbs:** the *tsere* appears only in the 3ms. Otherwise, the vowel points are the same as for an active verb.
   - ***O*-type Stative Verbs:** the *holem*[1] remains in all forms of the Perfect (unless it reduces to a *shewa*, of course).

2. **Imperfect and Imperative.** There is *pathah* instead of *holem*. Note the following comparison.
   - **Active *a*-type verbs (like שָׁמַר)** use *o* vowels in the Impf and Impv (that is, יִשְׁמֹר and שְׁמֹר).
   - **Stative *e*- and *o*-type verbs**, on the other hand, use *a*-vowels in Impf and Impv. For example:
     - the Imperfects of כָּבֵד and קָטֹן are יִכְבַּד and יִקְטַן (not יִכְבֹּד and יִקְטֹן)
     - their Imperatives are כְּבַד and קְטַן (not כְּבֹד and קְטֹן).

3. **Active Participle.** The Active Participle ms (כָּבֵד and קָטֹן) looks just like the Perf 3ms. Context will show you how to translate.[2] (Again, **stative verbs have no passive forms**, and thus there is no Passive Participle.)

4. ***a*-vowel Statives**. There are verbs which are stative in *meaning,* but which have regular *a*-vowel patterns. For instance, both of the following are statives:

   שָׁכַב *he lay, slept*

   שָׁכַל *he was bereaved* (that is, a loved one died)

5. In parsing, there is no need to write "stative verb." כָּבֵד is simply parsed Perf 3ms < כבד.

---

[1] In the 2mp and 2fp, the *holem* becomes a *qamets-hatuph*, but this is still an *o*-vowel. **Technical note:** This happens because the syllable becomes closed and unaccented; it therefore requires a short vowel.

[2] The feminine singular Active Participle (כְּבֵדָה) has the same consonants as the Perf 3fs (כָּֽבְדָה), but the vowels are quite different.

Things You Should Know

1. **Stative verbs** tell the *state* or *condition* of the subject, not its action.
2. **Perfect 3ms stative verbs** usually have *e* or *o* for their second vowel, rather than *a*. The rest of the *e* vowel Perf, and much of the *o* vowel Perf, has the same form as non-stative verbs.
3. **The Imperfect, Impv and I.C. of stative verbs** use *a*-vowels rather than *o*-vowels.
4. **Stative active participles** will look just like the stative Perf 3ms.
5. Stative Verbs have **no passive forms**.
6. A few verbs are stative in meaning, but look just like regular *a*-vowel verbs.

Exercise #28

גָּדֵל	to be(come) great	כָּבֵד	to be heavy, dull, honored	צְדָקָה	*f.* righteousness
זָקֵן	to be old	מִלְחָמָה	*f.* fighting, war (*cs.* מִלְחֶמֶת)	קָטֹן	to be small[3]
יָכֹל	to be able	עֶבֶד	servant	רָעֵב	to be hungry
יָשֵׁן	to sleep	צֶדֶק	*m.* that which is just, right	שָׁכַב	to lie down, sleep

[1] הָיָה יוֹסֵף הֶחָכָם מֵאֶחָיו וַיִּמְכְּרוּ אֹתוֹ לִהְיוֹת[4] עֶבֶד בְּאֶרֶץ־מִצְרָיִם׃ [2] וַיְהִי כַּאֲשֶׁר
שָׁכַב מֶלֶךְ־מִצְרַיִם וַיַּחֲלֹם חֲלוֹם׃ [3] וַיִּגְדַּל יוֹסֵף בְּעֵינֵי־פַרְעֹה כִּי יָכֹל לֵאמֹר[5] אֶת־
דְּבַר־חֲלוֹמוֹ[7]׃ [4] צִוָּה פַרְעֹה אֶת־יוֹסֵף לֵאמֹר אַתָּה לְבַדְּךָ תִּהְיֶה עַל־בֵּיתִי וְעַל־פִּיךָ[6]
יַעֲשֶׂה כָּל־עַמִּי׃ [5] כָּתַב יְהוָה אֵת מִצְוֹתָיו עַל־לוּחוֹת־הַתּוֹרָה וּמִסִּינַי נָשָׂא מֹשֶׁה אֶתְהֶם׃
[6] צִוָּה אֱלֹהִים אֶת־מֹשֶׁה לֵאמֹר [8]לוּחוֹת־עֵץ תַּעֲשֶׂה אֶת־הָאָרוֹן׃ [7] וַיְהִי כַּאֲשֶׁר בָּאוּ
מֹשֶׁה וְאַהֲרוֹן וְהָעָם מִן סִינַי כְּמִצְוַת־יְהוָה וְאִתָּם לָקְחוּ אֲרוֹן־הַבְּרִית׃ [8] וַיֹּאמֶר יְהוֹשֻׁעַ
אֶל־הָעָם נָתַן אֱלֹהֵינוּ לָנוּ אֶת־תּוֹרָתוֹ מִפִּיו וְאֵין אֵל אַחֵר כָּמוֹהוּ׃ נִבְחֲרָה לָנוּ לַעֲבֹד

---

[3] The verb קָטֹן occurs only four times in the Old Testament. The adjective קָטֹן occurs much more often.

[4] Reminder: When a verb ends with ה, its I.C. loses the ה- and takes וֹת- instead.

[5] Translate "to say," or "to explain." In this case, we will not translate לֵאמֹר as "saying." Remember that the word לֵאמֹר is actually the IC of אמר (plus לְ-). Thus, although it is *usually* translated "saying," it is not *always* translated this way.

[6] "according to your mouth." That is, "according to what you say" or "according to your command."

[7] לֵאמֹר אֶת־דְּבַר־חֲלוֹמוֹ׃, that is, "to say the meaning of his dream" or "to interpret his dream."

[8] Add the word *of* before this construct phrase.

אֶת־יְהוָה׃ [9] וַיֹּאמְרוּ הָעָם אֶל־שְׁמוּאֵל מֶלֶךְ יִהְיֶה עָלֵינוּ׃ וְהָיִינוּ[9] גַם־אֲנַחְנוּ כְּכָל־
הַגּוֹיִם וְשָׁפַט מַלְכֵּנוּ אֹתָנוּ בְּצֶדֶק וְיָצָא לְפָנֵינוּ בְּמִלְחֲמוֹתֵינוּ׃ [10] וַיֹּאמֶר אֲחִי־
שְׁלֹמֹה־הַגָּדוֹל[12] אֶמְשְׁלָה אַחֲרֵי אָבִי כִּי אָנֹכִי בְּנוֹ הַגָּדוֹל וַיִּקְטְנוּ[11] דְּבָרָיו בְּאָזְנֵי[10]־אָבִהוּ׃
[11] [14]וַיִּזְקַן דָּוִד וַיִּשְׁכַּב עִם־אֲבֹתָיו[13] וַיִּמְשֹׁל שְׁלֹמֹה בְּנוֹ תַּחְתָּיו׃ [12] וַיְהִי שְׁלֹמֹה קָטָן
מֵאֶחָיו[16] וַיִּמְשֹׁל בִּירוּשָׁלַםִ אַחֲרֵי דָּוִד אָבִיו׃ [13] אוֹי לָכֶם עַם־יְרוּשָׁלִַם כִּי כָבְדוּ[15]
אָזְנֵיכֶם וּבִלְבַבְכֶם לֹא־בְחַרְתֶּם אֶת־דְּרָכַי׃ [14] כֹּה אָמַר יְהוָה לֹא כָבֵד שֵׁם־קָדְשִׁי כִּי
שָׁפוּךְ דָּם בִּיהוּדָה׃ [15] יָשֵׁן[17] בְּשָׁלוֹם אִישׁ־הַצְּדָקָה וְקָבוּר אִישׁ־הַדָּמִים לְבַדּוֹ בְּקִבְרוֹ׃
[16] בָּאוּ אֲנָשִׁים מִן הַמִּדְבָּר אֶל־אֶרֶץ־כְּנַעַן לְמַעַן [18]גְּנֹב וְלֹא יָכְלוּ לִגְנֹב אֶת־כְּלֵי־
מִלְחֶמֶת־הַמֶּלֶךְ׃ [17] לֹא יִרְעַב עֶבֶד־צִדְקָתִי וְגָדַל[20] שְׁמוֹ [19]בָּעָם׃ [18] זָקְנָה הַנְּבִיאָה
וַתֹּאמֶר הוֹי הָאִישׁ הַהֹלֵךְ בְּדַרְכֵי־הַגּוֹיִם וְלֹא בְּדַרְכֵי־יְהוָה׃ [19] כְּתוּבִים דִּבְרֵי־צְדָקָה
בְּסֵפֶר־צֶדֶק׃ [20] וְנָשְׂאוּ אֶת־הַסֵּפֶר בִּכְלִי־עֵץ לְמַעַן שְׁמֹר אֹתוֹ׃

---

[9] "And we shall be" < היה.

[10] Note *qamets-hatuph*.

[11] That is, they were unimportant, insignificant; they had no influence. (Should the w.c. on this word be translated "and" or "but"?)

[12] "Solomon's older brother."

[13] That is, "he died." This is a very common expression in the Old Testament, especially when a king dies. The verb שָׁכַב also often means "to have sex." Thus, the phrase שָׁכַב עִם אִשְׁתּוֹ means "he had sex with his wife."

[14] Translate the ־וְ "when." See p. 94, footnote 16.

[15] "heavy, dull;" that is, "unable or unwilling to hear."

[16] Study carefully the small but important differences between אָחִיו and אֶחָיו (p. 112).

[17] The stative Perf 3ms and the stative Active Participle ms have the same form. The context will tell you how to translate.

[18] See p. 120, note 10.

[19] Translate "among the people."

[20] גָּדַל is an alternative form of גָּדֵל.

43

THE הָ- OF "DIRECTION TOWARD"

Some nouns can take a הָ - suffix which means "movement toward" the noun.[1] For instance:

הָהָר	means *the mountain*	BUT	הָהָ֫רָה	means	***toward** the mountain*
הָעִיר	means *the city*	BUT	הָעִ֫ירָה	means	***toward** the city*
מִצְרַ֫יִם	means *Egypt*	BUT	מִצְרַ֫יְמָה	means	***toward** Egypt*

Note that the accent remains where it was originally, and does not move onto the הָ - suffix. Thus, we have הָהָ֫רָה, not הָהָרָ֫ה.

הָלַךְ הָאִישׁ הָעִ֫ירָה *the man walked toward the city*

This ה of "direction toward" may also be found on

- words with prepositional prefixes: לִשְׁא֫וֹלָה, *to Sheol*
- words in the plural: הַשָּׁמַ֫יְמָה, *toward the heavens*
- words in construct: בֵּ֫יתָה דָוִד, *toward the house of David*

But it cannot be put on the names of people. (*Toward David* would be אֶל־דָּוִד.)

Finally, not every word can take this suffix. Only some words will be found with ה of "direction toward."

Examples:

וַיָּבֹא הָאִישׁ הַבַּ֫יְתָה. . . *And the man went toward the house ....* (Gen 24:32)

בָּא שָׁאוּל אַחֲרָיו הַמִּדְבָּ֫רָה: *Saul came after him toward the wilderness.* (1 Sam 26:3)

---

[1] **Technical note:** In many Hebrew grammars, this הָ - suffix is called an "old accusative ending." While this is true as a historical statement, it is not particularly helpful or meaningful to the beginning Hebrew student. We shall, therefore, simply call it the ה of "direction toward."

44

THE DERIVED FORMS OF THE VERB

We have now learned that the Hebrew verb is based on a three-letter root, and that we get various meanings when we add prefixes, suffixes or change the vowel pointing. These changes produce Perfect or Imperfect; first, second or third person; masculine or feminine, etc.

In addition to Perfect and Imperfect, we have learned about Imperatives, Participles and Infinitives. These are all called ▲"moods." And we learned that Stative Verbs also come with all these moods.

In this chapter, and in the chapter s which follow, we are going to learn that Hebrew verbs also have six ▲"derived forms." Something which is "derived" is made from something else. We may consider these "derived forms" to be made from the form of the verb which we have already learned.

The Qal form: The verb parts we have learned so far — Perfect, Imperfect, Imperatives, Participles and Infinitives — have all been the parts of the simplest form of the Hebrew verb, called the Qal (קַל, = *light, quick*) form. The derived forms also have these same parts. These derived forms give us additional meanings such as passive, intensive, causative and reflexive. You have already learned the meaning of "passive;"[1] the other words will be explained as we go along.

The derived forms: There are seven forms of the Hebrew verb: the basic Qal form (which you have already learned) plus the six derived forms. In this chapter, we shall just introduce the six new forms. They will be studied in detail in the chapters which lie ahead. For now, do not try to memorize the Hebrew of the six new forms shown below. Rather, just learn how they work (for instance, learn that the Piᶜel form is "Intensive Active"). We will use the verb שָׁמַר for our ▲paradigm.[2]

The first four forms are as follows:

Name of Form	*Description*	*Perf 3ms*	
1. Qal (קַל)	Simple Active	שָׁמַר	*he kept*
2. Nip̄ᶜal (נִפְעַל)	Simple Passive	נִשְׁמַר	*he was kept*
3. Piᶜēl (פִּעֵל)	Intensive Active	שִׁמֵּר	*he completely kept*
4. Puᶜal (פֻּעַל)	Intensive Passive	שֻׁמַּר	*he was completely kept*

"Intensive" means stronger. For instance, שָׁבַר means *he broke* (*something*), but שִׁבֵּר means *he broke* (*something*) *completely* or *he shattered* (*something*). [3]

---

[1] Review the introduction to §40 if you do not understand "passive."

[2] "Paradigm" means "model" or "pattern." It is pronounced like the three words "pair a dime." The "g" is silent. Charts of verb and noun patterns are often called "paradigms."

[3] **Technical note:** שמר is used in the paradigm rather than שבר because the *begadkepat* ב in שבר will sometimes add a *dagesh* (such as נִשְׁבַּרin the Nip̄ᶜal). It is important for the beginning student to learn which forms have a characteristic *dagesh* (such as the Piᶜel and Puᶜal), and which forms do not (such as Qal and Nip̄ᶜal).

The fifth and sixth forms, Hip̄ʿîl and Hop̄ʿal, are "causative." That is, the action does not merely happen (*he kept, he was kept,* etc.), but rather someone *causes* it to happen: *he caused (someone) to keep.* The last form, Hiṯpaʿēl, is "reflexive," which means that the action is reflected back to the subject. That is, the subject does the action to itself: *he kept himself.*

5. Hip̄ʿîl (הִפְעִיל)	Causative Active	הִשְׁמִיר	*he caused (someone) to keep*
6. Hop̄ʿal (הָפְעַל)	Causative Passive	הָשְׁמַר	*he was caused to keep*
7. Hiṯpaʿēl (הִתְפַּעֵל)	Reflexive	הִתְשַׁמֵּר[4]	*he kept himself*

Notes:

1. **The names of the derived forms** are simply the form applied to the verb פעל. That is, the Nip̄ʿal form of פעל is נִפְעַל (nip̄-ʿal), the Hip̄ʿîl form of פעל is הִפְעִיל (hip̄-ʿîl), etc.[5] In the rest of the book, when writing the names of the forms, we shall not print the ʿ mark which represents the ע or the other transliteration characters. Rather, we shall simply write Niphal, Piel, Pual, Hiphil, Hophal and Hithpael.

2. **Active and Passive Pairs.** Notice how Qal and Niphal work together as a simple Active and Passive pair. Piel and Pual work this way also – as an Active and Passive pair. So do Hiphil and Hophal.

3. **Characteristic *dagesh forte.*** Be sure to note the characteristic *dagesh forte* in the second radical (root-letter) of Piel, Pual and Hithpael (שִׁמֵּר שֻׁמַּר הִתְשַׁמֵּר). This *dagesh forte* will always appear, unless the second radical is a guttural or the letter ר.

4. ***Qamets-hatuph.*** The first vowel in Hophal verbs is *qamets-hatuph.* Thus, הָשְׁמַר is hoš-mar.

5. **Parts.** Each of the seven forms will have all five parts: Perfect, Imperfect, Imperative, Participle and Infinitive. We shall study each form carefully in the chapters ahead; you do not need to learn all seven of them right now. (We shall begin with Niphal in the next chapter.)

6. **Learning the forms.** Most verbs come in only one, two or three of the above forms, not in all seven. For instance, although we use the verb שָׁמַר in all the paradigms, this verb is really found only in Qal and Niphal. When you learn a verb, learn which forms it has. This will make parsing much easier since you will only have to choose between two or three forms and not seven.

7. **A word of encouragement.** Do not become discouraged. There is some good news: The suffixes and prefixes which you have learned for the Qal Perfect and Qal Imperfect will be the same in the other forms. Now is a good time to go back and review them and be sure you know them well.

---

[4] **Technical note:** This particular form, using שׁמר, cannot actually occur as shown, since in the Hiṯpaʿel the ת and the שׁ will transpose (switch position): הִשְׁתַּמֵּר. This will be discussed later.

[5] **Technical Note:** Many years ago, the verb פעל was used for the paradigm. It did not work very well, however, because its middle guttural refuses to take a *dagesh,* and the *dagesh* is an important part of the Piʿēl and Puʿal. So other verbs have been used in more recent times, although we continue to use the original names Nip̄ʿal, Piʿēl, Puʿal, etc.

Things You Should Know

1. The Hebrew verb comes in **seven forms**: the Qal (which has already been learned) and six "derived forms": Niphal, Piel, Pual, Hiphil, Hophal and Hithpael.

2. Each of these forms has all the **parts** which we have learned in the Qal: Perfect, Imperfect, Imperative, Participle and Infinitives.

3. **Qal and Niphal** work together as a simple Active and Passive pair. **Piel and Pual**, which are both "intensive" forms of the verb, also work together as an Active and Passive pair. The third Active and Passive pair is "causative": **Hiphil and Hophal**. The **Hithpael** form is neither Active nor Passive, but rather Reflexive (the action returns to the subject).

4. Three of the forms (Piel, Pual and Hithpael) have a characteristic *dagesh forte* in the middle radical of the verb root (שִׁמֵּר שֻׁמַּר הִתְשַׁמֵּר).

5. Hophal has a *qamets-hatuph* under its -ה prefix.

Exercise #29

בָּטַח	to trust, be confident; -בָּטַח בְּ or בָּטַח עַל to trust in (something)
יִצְחָק	Isaac
יִרְאָה	*f.* fear, reverence
יֹשֵׁב	resident, inhabitant (√יָשַׁב)[6]
יְשׁוּעָה	*f.* help, salvation
כָּבוֹד	glory, weight, honor
נָא	please, just, now
מָוֶת	*m.* death, dying (*cs.* מוֹת)
מַלְאָךְ	messenger, angel
עַד	until, up to, near
עוֹלָם	eternity (עַד־עוֹלָם forever)
צַדִּיק	*adj.* righteous, just

[1] וַיְהִי כַּאֲשֶׁר בָּרָא אֱלֹהִים אֵת הַשָּׁמַיִם וְאֶת־הָאָרֶץ וַיִּקְרָא לָאוֹר יוֹם וְלַחֹשֶׁךְ קָרָא
לָיְלָה׃ [2] הֲנָתַן אָדָם אֶת־הַמִּנְחוֹת הָאֵלֶּה אֶל־אִמּוֹ בַּגָּן׃ [3] וַיִּקְרָא יְהוָה אֱלֹהִים אֶל־
הָאָדָם וַיֹּאמֶר לוֹ[9] אֵי אָתָּה׃ [4] וַיַּהֲרֹג[8] הֶבֶל אֶת־קַיִן[7] וַיִּצְעַק דַּם־אָחִיהוּ מִן עֲפַר־
הָאֲדָמָה׃ [5] וַיִּשְׁלַח לוֹט מַלְאָכִים אֶל־אַבְרָם לֵאמֹר לָמָּה [10]תִּהְיֶה מִלְחָמָה בֵּין רֹעֵי־
צֹאנְךָ וּבֵין רֹעָי׃ [6] עָבוֹר עָבְרוּ רֹעֵי־לוֹט אֶת־הַיַּרְדֵּן וַיִּשְׁמְרוּ שָׁמוֹר צֹאנוֹ׃ [7] וַיֹּאמֶר

---

[6] √ means *root* or *radical*. This tells you that the noun יֹשֵׁב comes from the verb יָשַׁב. We could also write יֹשֵׁב < יָשַׁב.

[7] Be sure to translate the Hebrew carefully. Do not just try to remember the story.

[8] See p. 127, note 14, above.

[9] Note: this is not the word לֹא.

[10] Qal Impf 3fs < הָיָה.

אַבְרָהָם אֵין־צֶ֫דֶק וְאֵין־יִרְאַת־יְהוָה בַּמָּקוֹם הַזֶּה וְלֹא בָטַח עַל־יְשׁוּעַת־יְהוָה׃ [8] וַיֹּ֫אמֶר
אֲבִימֶ֫לֶךְ[11] הֲלֹא הוּא אָמַר־לִי אֲחֹתִי הִוא וְגַם הִיא אָֽמְרָה אָחִי הוּא׃ צַדִּיק אֲנִי לִפְנֵי־
אֱלֹהִים׃ [9] וַיְהִי כִּי־זָקֵן יִצְחָק וַתִּכְבַּ֫דְנָה עֵינָיו[13] וְלֹא יָכֹל לִרְאוֹת[12]׃ וַיִּקְרָא אֶת־עֵשָׂו
בְּנוֹ הַבְּכוֹר וַיֹּ֫אמֶר בְּנִי וַיֹּ֫אמֶר עֵשָׂו הִנֵּנִי[14]׃ [10] וַיֹּ֫אמֶר יִצְחָק הִנֵּה־נָא זָקַנְתִּי וְלֹא
יָדַ֫עְתִּי[17] יוֹם־מוֹתִי׃ [11] וַיָּבֹא[16] יַעֲקֹב לִפְנֵי־אָבִיו וַיֹּ֫אמֶר אָנֹכִי עֵשָׂו בְּכֹרֶךָ עָשֹׂה[15]
עָשִׂ֫יתִי[20] כַּאֲשֶׁר [19]דִּבַּ֫רְתָּ אֵלָי[18]׃ [12] וַיֹּ֫אמֶר לָבָן אֶל־יַעֲקֹב הַבָּנוֹת בְּנֹתַי וְהַבָּנִים בָּנַי
וְהַצֹּאן צֹאנִי וְכֹל אֲשֶׁר אַתָּה רֹאֶה[24] לִי־הוּא[23] [22]וְלִבְנֹתַי וְלִבְנֵיהֶן מָה־אֶעֱשֶׂה[21] לָאֵ֫לֶּה הַיּוֹם׃
[13] לָ֫מָּה לֹא בָטַח לָבָן בְּרָחֵל וּבְאִשָּׁהּ׃ [14] וַיֹּ֫אמֶר יְהוֹשֻׁעַ יְשׁוּעָה מֵיְהוָה אֲשֶׁר גָּדוֹל
כְּבוֹדוֹ וּלְעוֹלָם צִדְקָתוֹ׃ [15] וַיִּרְעֲבוּ יַעֲקֹב וּבָנָיו וּמִצְרַ֫יְמָה יָֽצְאוּ וְשָׁם הָיוּ יֹשְׁבֵי־
הָאָֽרֶץ׃ וְאַחֲרֵי מוֹתוֹ הָיוּ עֲבָדִים׃ [16] וַיֹּ֫אמֶר אֱלֹהִים תִּגְדַּל וְהָֽיְתָה[26] יִרְאָֽתְךָ[25] עַל
יֹשְׁבֵי־הָאָֽרֶץ׃ וְרָאָה הָעָם אֶת־כְּבוֹדִי וְשָׁכוֹב יִשְׁכְּבוּ בְּשָׁלוֹם׃ [17] וּבַלַּ֫יְלָה שָׁכַב הָאִישׁ
אֲשֶׁר עָשָׂה צֶ֫דֶק וְלֹא יָשֵׁן עַד־בֹּ֫קֶר׃ [18] וּבַיָּמִים הָהֵם רָֽעֲבוּ רָעוֹב הָאֵם וּבְנוֹתֶיהָ
וְהָעִ֫ירָה הָֽלְכוּ וְיָכוֹל יָֽכְלוּ לֶאֱכֹל׃ [19] זָקֵן הָאִישׁ הַצַּדִּיק וַתְּהִי[27] מִלְחָמָה בֵּין מַלְאָכָיו
וּבֵין עַבְדֵי־הַמֶּ֫לֶךְ׃ [20] קָטֹן דָּוִד בְּעֵינֵי־אָבִיו וֵאלֹהִים נָתַן אֵלָיו[28] בְּרִית־עוֹלָם וַיִּכְבַּד
בְּעֵינֵי־הָעָם׃ [21] מָקוֹם־צְדָקָה הָעִיר הַזֹּאת אֲשֶׁר יָשֵׁן הָעָם בְּשָׁלוֹם שָֽׁם׃

---

[11] This is the name "Abimelek" (king of Gerar). What does his name mean?

[12] If you have trouble with this word, review page 111, footnote 18.

[13] His eyes were "heavy" or "dull;" that is, he could not see well.

[14] הִנֵּה plus suffix. Translate "I am here" or "Here I am."

[15] Infinitive Absolute < עָשָׂה.

[16] Imperfect plus w.c. from בָּא.

[17] Translate as a present tense. This is the way the verse appears in Genesis, and it is not unusual to use the Perfect in this way.

[18] "to me." We will learn about this preposition plus suffix in §52.

[19] You may have wondered why the verb דִּבֵּר has had the *seghol* and *dagesh*. It is a Piel verb. Here it is parsed Piel Perf 2ms < דבר. We will study Piel in §47.

[20] Perf 1cs < עָשָׂה. You do not need to learn this form at this time. But you can see that, again, the final ה has disappeared. This time it has been replaced by a י. Later in the book, we will study verbs with final ה.

[21] Impf 1cs. The two gutturals have produced several changes of vowel pointing.

[22] This word has two prefixes: a *vav* and a preposition.

[23] Add the word "is": "to me it (is)." In other words, "it is mine."

[24] Do not confuse this word with רָעָה.

[25] Translate "fear of you."

[26] Perf 3fs + w.c. < הָיָה. This time the final ה has been replaced by a ת.

[27] You know וַיְהִי. So then how do you parse this verb (וַתְּהִי)?

[28] "to him." (Preposition אֶל plus suffix.)

45

THE VERB: NIPHAL

We have already learned the Qal form of the Hebrew verb. We now turn to the second form, the Niphal. The Qal is active,[1] and the Niphal is passive.[2] **In parsing, we will abbreviate Niphal as Niph.**

45.1 The Niphal Verb Chart

	Perfect	*Imperfect*
3ms	נִשְׁמַר	יִשָּׁמֵר
3fs	נִשְׁמְרָה	תִּשָּׁמֵר
2ms	נִשְׁמַ֫רְתָּ	תִּשָּׁמֵר
2fs	נִשְׁמַרְתְּ	תִּשָּֽׁמְרִי
1cs	נִשְׁמַ֫רְתִּי	אֶשָּׁמֵר
3cp	נִשְׁמְרוּ	3mp יִשָּֽׁמְרוּ 3fp תִּשָּׁמַ֫רְנָה
2mp	נִשְׁמַרְתֶּם	תִּשָּֽׁמְרוּ
2fp	נִשְׁמַרְתֶּן	תִּשָּׁמַ֫רְנָה
1cp	נִשְׁמַ֫רְנָה	נִשָּׁמֵר

Participle (passive)

	Singular	Plural
m	נִשְׁמָר	נִשְׁמָרִים
f	נִשְׁמָרָה	נִשְׁמָרוֹת

	Imperative
ms	הִשָּׁמֵר
fs	הִשָּֽׁמְרִי
mp	הִשָּֽׁמְרוּ
fp	הִשָּׁמַ֫רְנָה

	Cohortative
1cs	אִשָּֽׁמְרָה
1cp	נִשָּֽׁמְרָה

Jussive	יִשָּׁמֵר
Impf + w.c.	וַיִּשָּׁמֵר
Jussive + vav	וְיִשָּׁמֵר
Inf. Abs.	הִשָּׁמֵר, הִשָּׁמֹר, נִשְׁמֹר
Inf. Const.	הִשָּׁמֵר

Notes:

1. **The Imperative and Infinitives** have an extra -ה prefixed to them. We shall learn below how to tell the difference between these and the Hiphil, which also has a prefixed -ה.
2. **Parsing:** Now that we are learning the derived forms, we must always start our parsings with "Qal," "Niph," etc. From now on, "Perf 3ms" (without Qal, Niph, etc.) will be an incomplete parsing.
3. **Similar parts.** Be sure to study the differences between those parts of the Niphal and Qal which are

---

[1] The Qal is passive only once: in its Passive Participle. The Qal is unusual in this way; it is the only one of the seven forms which has both an active and a passive participle.

[2] Sometimes it also has a reflexive meaning, like the Hithpael. This will be discussed below.

very similar to each other:

a.	נִשְׁמַר	נִשְׁמָר	נִשָּׁמֵר	נִשְׁמֹר
	(Niph Perf 3ms)	(Niph Part ms)	(Niph Impf 1cp)	(**Qal** Impf 1cp)

b.	נִשְׁמְרָה	נִשְׁמָרָה
	(Niph Perf 3fs and **Qal** Cohort 1cp)	(Niph Part fs)

45.2 Characteristics of the Niphal

45.2.1 **The meaning of Niphal.** Niphal verbs are usually passive (נִשְׁמַר, *he was kept*), but they can also be reflexive[3] (נִשְׁמַר can also mean *he kept himself*).

45.2.2 **The Niphal Perfect and Niphal Participles are formed by adding a -נִ prefix** to the verb stem. The suffixes remain the same as they were in the Qal. As mentioned above, the Niph Perf 3fs (נִשְׁמְרָה, *she was kept*) has the same pattern as the *Qal* 1cp Cohortative (*let us keep;* see §28.1, p. 84). As usual, the context will determine the meaning.

45.2.3 **Other parts "swallow" this -נִ prefix.** The Imperfect, Imperative, etc., put additional prefixes before the prefixed -נִ. When this happens, the נ is "swallowed"[4] by the first radical of the verb, and a *dagesh* (representing the "swallowed" נ) will appear in this radical. A *qamets* will then also appear under it.

Niph Impf 3ms of שׁמר: שׁמר + נ + י → יִנְשָׁמֵר → יִשָּׁמֵר

Important Note: Only the Niphal has this first radical *dagesh* and *qamets*.

If the first radical is a guttural, the *dagesh* will be rejected (§13.2, p. 38), and the *hireq* under the prefix will then lengthen to a *tsere*. Thus, the Niph Impf 3ms of אָסַף is יֵאָסֵף.

45.2.4 **Niphals with active meanings.** Some verbs are found only, or primarily, in the Niphal, and have active meanings. For instance, the verb שׁבע comes in the Niphal but not in the Qal. Thus, נִשְׁבַּע means simply *he swore* (took an oath), not *he was sworn.* Likewise, לחם is found primarily in the Niphal (נִלְחַם) and means *he fought,* not *he was fought.*

45.3 A Visual Parsing Tool

Usually, the Perfect tense is not difficult to recognize because the names of the forms (Niphal, Piel, Pual, etc.) tell us what to expect. For instance,

- Niphal Perfect will have a -נִ prefix (the Ni- of the word "Niphal"): נִשְׁמַר
- Piel Perfect will have a *hireq* under the first radical (the *i* of "P*i*el"): שִׁמֵּר
- Pual Perfect will have a *qibbuts* under the first radical (the *u* of "P*u*al"): שֻׁמַּר
- Hiphil Perfect will have a -הִ prefix (the Hi- of "Hiphil"): הִשְׁמִיר

---

[3] For a definition of "reflexive," review p. 130.

[4] The technical word is "assimilated." Why does this happen? See the technical note 2 on page 46.

The Imperfect and some of the moods can be more difficult, however, because they often have prefixes which change the vowel pointing. Therefore, it is helpful to have a system which makes parsing easier.

Let us use circles (○) to represent the radicals of the verb, a triangle (△) to represent the prefix, and a star (*) to represent a possible suffix.[5] (Not all forms will have suffixes, of course.) For instance, the Niph Impf 2/3fp is תִּשָּׁמַרְנָה. In this case, the -תִּ prefix can be represented by△, the three radicals of the verb by ○○⊙ (note the *dagesh* and *qamets*), and the -נָה suffix by the *. If we do this, then **in tenses and moods other than Perfect and participles** we shall see the following pattern in the Niphal:

Thus, you will be looking for:

- a *hireq* under the prefix, and
- a *dagesh-qamets* combination in the first radical of the verb, just after the prefix.[6]

Study the verb chart on p. 133, and note how this *dagesh-qamets* pattern is seen everywhere except in the Perfect and the Participles (where the *nun* remains as a prefix).

Important note: This is also how we shall know that the Niphal Imperative and Infinitives (which have -ה prefixes) are not Hiphil. Hiphil verbs never have the *dagesh-qamets* combination in the first radical.

And again, note that this pattern **is not seen in the Perfect.**

Things You Should Know

1. The Niphal is a passive verb form, which works like a "team" with the Qal (active). In parsing, it is abbreviated "Niph." Thus: Niph Perf 3fs, Niph Impf 1cp, etc.
2. Although the Niphal usually has passive meaning, it can also be reflexive. And sometimes verbs are found only (or primarily) in the Niphal and have active meanings.
3. The **Niphal Perfect and Participles** add a -נִ prefix.
4. In **other parts** (such as Imperfect, Imperative and Infinitive, which have additional prefixes) this -נ is "swallowed" by the first radical of the verb and appears there as a *dagesh*.
5. Therefore, in parts other than the Perfect and Participles, watch for the following pattern:

Not all parts will have a suffix (*), of course.

---

[5] I owe the basis of this idea to Dr. Mark A. Throntveit of Luther Seminary, St. Paul, Minnesota.

[6] And, as we have already noted above, if the first radical is a guttural, it will reject the *dagesh* and the vowel under the prefix will lengthen.

Exercise #30

זָהָב gold

כֶּ֫סֶף silver, money

לֶ֫חֶם *c.*[7] bread

לחם[8] ***Ni*** נִלְחַם to fight (נִלְחַם בְּ-, נִלְחַם עִם *or* נִלְחַם אֵת to fight against)

מלט ***Ni*** נִמְלַט to escape [***Pi*** to save, leave alone][9]

מְרַגֵּל a spy (√רגל)[10]

מִשְׁפָּט justice, judgement, lawsuit (√שׁפט)[10]

סתר ***Ni*** נִסְתַּר to hide oneself [***Hiph*** to hide something or someone; ***Hithp*** to hide oneself][9]

עֲבֹדָה *f.* work, service, worship (√עבד)

עֵצָה *f.* counsel, advice, plan (*do not confuse with the word* עֵץ, tree wood)

רֶ֫גֶל *f.* foot, *dual*: רַגְלַ֫יִם

[1] וַיֹּ֫אמֶר אֱלֹהִים יְדַעְתִּי[13] אֶת־אַבְרָהָם וְצִוָּה אֶת־בָּנָיו וְאֶת־בְּנוֹתָיו אַחֲרָיו[12] לְמַ֫עַן יַעֲשׂוּ[11]
עַל־פִּי[14] יְהוָה׃ [2] דִּבֶּר אֲבִי־יִצְחָק אֶל־עַבְדּוֹ הָעֹמֵד לְפָנָיו לֵאמֹר לֹא בֹטֵ֫חַתִּי[13] עַל
יֹשְׁבֵי־הָאָ֫רֶץ הַזֹּאת׃ [3] וַיֹּ֫אמֶר הָעֶ֫בֶד הַצַּדִּיק הַשָּׁלוּחַ[15] בְּאַבְרָהָם אֶל־לָבָן מִי מִן
הַנָּשִׁים הָאֵ֫לֶּה תִּמְצָא חֵן לְפָנָי׃ [4] וַיֹּ֫אמֶר אֶל־לָבָן בָּאתִי לְבַדִּי לְמַ֫עַן יִצְחָק בֶּן־
אַבְרָהָם כִּי יִרְאַת־יְהוָה בָּאָ֫רֶץ הַהִיא׃ [5] וַיֹּאכַל עִם־אַנְשֵׁי־בֵית־לָבָן בַּיּוֹם הַהוּא וְגַם
נָתַן כְּלֵי־כֶ֫סֶף וּכְלֵי־זָהָב אֶל־אֲחוֹת־לָבָן׃ [6] וַיֹּ֫אמֶר מֹשֶׁה וְהָיָה כִּי־תַעַבְדוּ אֶת־אֱלֹהִים
וְאָמְרוּ אֲלֵיכֶם[17] בְּנֵיכֶם מָה הָעֲבֹדָה הַזֹּאת לָכֶם׃ [7] וַיֹּ֫אמֶר יִתְרוֹ[16] לְמֹשֶׁה לֵאמֹר
שְׁמַֽע־נָא אֶת־דְּבָרָי[18] כְּבֵדָה מְאֹד עֲבֹדָתְךָ כִּי אַתָּה לְבַדְּךָ נֹתֵן מִשְׁפָּטִים אֶל־הָעָם׃
וְאֶל־מֹשֶׁה נָתַן עֵצָה׃ [8] נָתַן אֱלֹהִים אֶל־מֹשֶׁה אֶת־לֻחֹת[19]־הָאֶ֫בֶן עִם הַתּוֹרָה וְהַמִּצְוָה
אֲשֶׁר כָּתַב אֱלֹהִים בְּהַר־סִינָי׃ [9] שָׁלַח־מֹשֶׁה מְרַגְּלִים אַ֫רְצָה וַיֹּאמְרוּ אֶל־מֹשֶׁה

---

[7] *c.* means common. See p. 56, note 1.

[8] Sometimes a verb will appear with no vowel points in the vocabulary list, or in the lexicon (dictionary) at the end of the book. This means that it never (or *almost* never) appears in the Qal form.

[9] We have not yet studied the other forms (Piel, Hiph, etc.). But since this information will soon be important, we are putting it here in [square brackets] for future use. You do not need to learn this information until you study the other forms. However, be sure to put it on your vocabulary cards.

[10] The √ sign shows the root, or most basic form, of the word which is the source of the vocabulary word. See p. 131, note 6.

[11] Qal Imf 3mp < עָשָׂה. This time, the final ה has just disappeared. **Technical note:** Compare to p. 132, footnotes 20 and 26, where we saw the final ה being replaced by י or ת. You do not need to learn these patterns at this point. Just watch them and be aware of them. We will study them later.

[12] אַחֲרֵי plus suffix.

[13] Translate as a present tense.

[14] The phrase עַל־פִּי יְהוָה is often translated "according to the command of the LORD."

[15] Translate the -בְּ "by."

[16] *Jethro*, Moses' father-in-law.

[17] "To you" (mp). (Preposition אֶל plus suffix.)

[18] The last vowel has lengthened because the word is in pause.

[19] The word לוּחוֹת is sometimes found in this shortened form.

הִשָּׁמֵר[21]־נָא אֶת־עַם־הָאָֽרֶץ׃ לֹא אֲנַ֫חְנוּ יְכֹלִים לְהִלָּחֵם[20] בָּֽם׃ [10] שָֽׁמְעוּ הָעָם אֶת־
מִצְוֹת[22]־הָאֱלֹהִים מִפִּי־מֹשֶׁה כַּאֲשֶׁר נָשָׂא אֶת־לוּחוֹת־הַתּוֹרָה מִסִּינָֽי׃ [11] הֲשָׁמַע הָעָם
בְּקוֹל־מֹשֶׁה כִּי צִוָּה אֹתָם בְּשֵׁם־יְהוָֽה׃ [12] וַיָּבֹא[25] שְׁמוּאֵל בֵּית־לֶ֫חֶם[24] וַיִּירָא[23] בֶּן־
יִשַׁי הַקָּטֹן וַיִּסָּתֵר אֶל־הַכֵּלִֽים׃ [13] נִשְׁאֹל נִשְׁאַל שָׁאוּל אֵי שְׁאוֹל וְנִשְׁאַל נִשְׁאֹֽל׃
[14] נִרְאָה[26] דָוִד וַיִּשְׁלְחוּ הַמְרַגְּלִים מַלְאָכִים אֶל־שָׁאוּל וַיִּמָּלֵט דָּוִד בְּרֶ֫גֶל וַיִּסָּתֵֽר׃
[15] נָשָׂא דָוִד אֶת־קוֹלוֹ וַיֹּאמַר יְשׁוּעָתִי[27] בְּשֵׁם־יְהוָֽה׃ אֶבְטַח בּוֹ עַד־עוֹלָֽם׃ [16] שָֽׁאֲלוּ
יֹשְׁבֵי־הָעִיר מַדּוּעַ שָׁלַח אֱלֹהִים מָוֶת עַל־הָאָֽרֶץ׃ [17] וַיִּלָּחֲמוּ אֹיְבֵי־יְרוּשָׁלַם בָּעִיר
וְאֵין לֶ֫חֶם בָּעִֽיר׃ וּבַלַּ֫יְלָה יָצָא הָעָם וַיִּמָּלְטוּ[28] בְּרֶֽגֶל׃ [18] לֹא יִמָּצֵא כְּבוֹד־אִישׁ
בְּכֶ֫סֶף וּבְזָהָֽב׃ [19] נָתַן הַזָּקֵן הַצַּדִּיק מִשְׁפָּטִים וְעֵצָה אֶל־הָעָם עַד־מוֹתֽוֹ׃ [20] וַיֹּאמֶר
הַמַּלְאָךְ גָּדֹל כְּבוֹד־אֱלֹהִים [29]וִישׁוּעָתוֹ עַד־עוֹלָֽם׃ וְלָ֫מָּה אֵין־יִרְאַת־אֱלֹהִים בָּאָֽרֶץ׃

---

[20] This word has a ל prefix. You will find help for the rest of its parsing on p. 133.

[21] The Niphal of שָׁמַר often means "beware of" or "watch out for."

[22] Remember that the וֹ is wō and not ô in this case. See p. 119, footnote 4.

[23] Impf 3ms + w.c. < ירא. Who was afraid? Was Samuel afraid of the son of Jesse, or was the son of Jesse afraid? Hint: If the object of ירא was בֶּן־יִשַׁי, then there would be a sign of the definite object before these words.

[24] בֵּית־לֶ֫חֶם is "Bethlehem." What is the meaning of this name?

[25] Impf 3ms + w.c. < בא. Translate the two cases of w.c. as "When ... then." (See p. 94, footnote 16, for the reason why.

[26] The Niphal of רָאָה can mean "to be seen" or "to appear." **Technical note:** The word here can be parsed either as Perfect, or as Participle, since both would have a *qamets*. (The א attracts a *qamets* even in the Perfect).

[27] This is a feminine noun with possessive suffix, not a verb. Thus, the *tuv* is part of the noun. If it were a Perf 1cs suffix, there would be a *dagesh* in the *tuv*.

[28] As we have seen before, the word עַם can take either singular or plural verbs. In this sentence, the first verb is singular and the second is plural. Technically, this is incorrect; but this sometimes happens in the Old Testament when עַם is the subject. Examples may be found in Ex 1:20; 4:31; 12:27; 17:2; Lev 9:24; Num 11:32; 20:3; 25:2; Josh 6:20; Judg 20:22; 21:2; 1 Sam 4:4; 14:32; 1 Kgs 18:24,39; 2 Kgs 7:16; and many other places.

[29] For this pointing, see §18.1.2, p. 51.

46

THE HEBREW EXPRESSION "TO HAVE"

We have seen how often the verb *to be* is not present in Hebrew sentences. We have often added it in our translations. It is similar with the verb *to have.* Hebrew does not have this verb, and so it must say the idea in different ways.

46.1 "To have" in the Present

To speak about having something in the present, Hebrew uses two special words:

יֵשׁ = *there is* אַ֫יִן (*cs.* אֵין) = *there is not*
(do not confuse אַ֫יִן with עַ֫יִן)

(You have already learned אַ֫יִן in the vocabulary of Exercise #25). These words have no other forms. That is, there is no 1, 2 or 3 person, no masculine or feminine, no singular or plural. Thus, *there is a man* is יֵשׁ אִישׁ and *there are women* is יֵשׁ נָשִׁים.

To say *I have a horse* or *I do not have a horse,* we must also use the inseparable preposition לְ- plus a suffix. Consider the following:

Hebrew	Literal translation	Smooth translation and comments
יֵשׁ לָהּ סוּס	*there-is for-her a-horse* (Remember that לְ- can mean "for" as well as "to.")	*She has a horse.* **Comment**: In Hebrew, סוּס is the subject, יֵשׁ (*there-is*) is the verb, and לָהּ (*for-her*) is an indirect object. In smooth English translation, we turn this around and say "She (subject) has a horse (object)."
אֵין לִי סוּס	*there-is-not for-me a-horse*	*I do not have a horse.* **Comment:** Again, סוּס is really the subject of the Hebrew sentence. The literal translation can also be *A-horse is-not-there for-me*. But in smooth English we turn subject and object around again.

46.2 "To have" in the Past or Future

To say *I had* (past) or *I shall have* (future), we must use the verb הָיָה. This verb *does* have person (1, 2 or 3), gender (masculine or feminine) and number (singular or plural); therefore, it must be conjugated. That is, it must be put into its proper person, gender and number according to its subject ("Grammar," p. xix). We therefore need to study הָיָה in more detail. It is a weak verb, and we study weak verbs later. For now, it is enough to learn only 12 forms of הָיָה. The following occur 50 or more times in the Bible:

	Perf		Impf	Impf + w.c.
3ms	הָיָה		יִהְיֶה	וַיְהִי
3fs	הָיְתָה		תִּהְיֶה	וַתְּהִי
2ms	הָיִיתָ		—	—
1cs	הָיִיתִי		אֶהְיֶה	—
3cp	הָיוּ	3mp	יִהְיוּ	וַיִּהְיוּ

Now study the following chart. Note especially the relationship between subject, object and verb. The subject in Hebrew becomes the object in smooth English translation. To get the negative, we must add the word לֹא before the verb.

Hebrew	Literal translation	Smooth translation and comments
הָיָה לָהּ סוּס	*it-was to-her a-horse*	*She had a horse.* Remember that, in Hebrew, סוּס is the subject (not *she*). And since סוּס is a ms noun, הָיָה is conjugated as 3ms, not 3fs.
יִהְיֶה לִי סוּס	*it-will-be to-me a-horse*	*I shall have a horse.* The Impf tells us that it is "future."
הָיְתָה לוֹ בַּת	*she-was to-him a-daughter*	*He had a daughter.* In Hebrew the subject is *daughter*. Therefore הָיָה is conjugated 3fs.
לֹא יִהְיוּ לָהּ בָּנִים	*not they-will-be to-her sons*	*She will not have sons.* לֹא tells us that it is negative. The Impf 3mp of הָיָה tells us that it is future, and that the subject (בָּנִים) is masculine plural.

Things You Should Know

1. Hebrew does not have the verb *to have.* Other words are used to give this concept.
2. **In the present,** Hebrew uses יֵשׁ (*there is/are*) and אֵין or אַיִן (*there is/are not*). (Do not confuse אַיִן and עַיִן.) These words cannot be conjugated, and always remain the same. Thus, יֵשׁ לִי סוּס means *I have a horse,* and אֵין לִי סוּס means *I do not have a horse.*
3. **In the past and future,** the verb הָיָה is used. Since הָיָה is a verb, it *must* be conjugated. Thus, יִהְיֶה לִי בֵּן means *I shall have a son,* and הָיְתָה לִי בַּת means *I had a daughter.* In these sentences, the subjects are בֵּן and בַּת, and the verbs agree with them.
4. **The negative in past and future** is made by adding the word לֹא.

47

THE VERB: PIEL

Piel is an "intensive" verb form. It is active, like the Qal, but it often gives a stronger emphasis to the verb. שָׁמַר (Qal Perf 3ms) means *he kept.* שִׁמֵּר (Piel Perf 3ms) means *he completely kept.* Note the *dagesh* in the second radical. It is always found in the Piel (except when the second radical is a guttural or ר). It is therefore a primary sign of Piel. A *tsere* is often found under the second radical, too.

47.1 The Piel Verb Chart

	Perfect	***Imperfect***		***Imperative***
3ms	שִׁמֵּר	יְשַׁמֵּר	ms	שַׁמֵּר
3fs	שִׁמְּרָה	תְּשַׁמֵּר	fs	שַׁמְּרִי
2ms	שִׁמַּרְתָּ	תְּשַׁמֵּר	mp	שַׁמְּרוּ
2fs	שִׁמַּרְתְּ	תְּשַׁמְּרִי	fp	שַׁמֵּרְנָה
1cs	שִׁמַּרְתִּי	אֲשַׁמֵּר		
				Cohortative
3cp	שִׁמְּרוּ	3mp יְשַׁמְּרוּ 3fp תְּשַׁמֵּרְנָה	1cs	אֲשַׁמְּרָה
			1cp	נְשַׁמְּרָה
2mp	שִׁמַּרְתֶּם	תְּשַׁמְּרוּ		
2fp	שִׁמַּרְתֶּן	תְּשַׁמֵּרְנָה	***Jussive***	יְשַׁמֵּר
1cp	שִׁמַּרְנוּ	נְשַׁמֵּר	***Impf + w.c.***	וַיְשַׁמֵּר[1]
			Jussive + w.c.	וִישַׁמֵּר[1]

Participle (active)[2]	Singular	Plural
m	מְשַׁמֵּר	מְשַׁמְּרִים
f	מְשַׁמֶּרֶת (מְשַׁמְּרָה)	מְשַׁמְּרוֹת

Inf. Abs.	שַׁמֹּר (שַׁמֵּר)
Inf. Const.	שַׁמֵּר

47.2 Characteristics of the Piel

47.2.1 **Perfect.** There is a *dagesh* in the second radical, and a *hireq* under the first radical.[3] The suffixes are the same as in Qal and Niphal (and will be the same in all the other forms, as well).

---

[1] This time there is no *dagesh* in the י (see §27.2.2, p. 81). This happens only with Piel and Pual *yod* prefixes, and it is because we have a *yod* over a *shewa* (see the technical note in footnote 6, p. 81). In the jussive + w.c., however, we began with -וַיְ which first went to -וִיְ and then -וִי . See p. 49, footnote 2, for more detail.

[2] The Piel is an active verb form, and so it has an active participle. Only the Qal has both active and passive participles. All other forms have *either* active *or* passive participles (cf. the Niphal).

[3] In the Perf, the *tsere* under the second radical is not particularly helpful, since it appears *only* in the 3ms. In the rest of the Perf, the second radical has *pathahs* and *shewas*. And there are verbs such as גדל which sometimes have *pathah* even in the Piel Perf 3ms: גִּדַּל. In other parts of the Piel the *tsere* appears more often.

47.2.2 Imperfect, Participle, Jussive, and Cohortative. All these parts have prefixes, and in the Piel these prefixes will all have a *shewa*. Thus, in Piel Impf, Part, Juss and Coh, you will see:

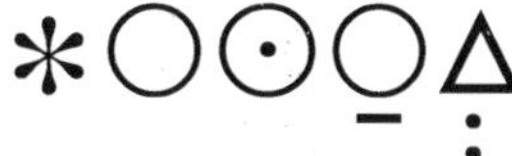

47.2.3 The Participle has a -מְ prefix. In Hebrew, all participles have a -מ prefix except the Qal Participles (שֹׁמֵר, שָׁמוּר) and the Niphal participle (נִשְׁמָר). Thus, we shall see this -מ in Piel, Pual, Hiphil, Hophal and Hithpael.

47.2.4 A helpful hint: "doubling dots." Note again the *shewa* under the prefixes of the Imperfect, Participle, Jussive and Cohortative. This prefix-*shewa* appears only in Piel and Pual.[4] Both Piel and the Pual make the verb "stronger" in meaning. To help us recognize the Piel and Pual, we might say that these forms "double" the force of the verb. Think of the "double" dots of the *shewa* as "doubling" the force of the verb. Remember also the "doubling" *dagesh* in the second radical.

47.2.5 Identical parts. The Imperative ms, the Infinitive Construct, and one type of the Infinitive Absolute are the same (all are שַׁמֵּר). Context will tell you how you should translate.

47.2.6 Non-intensive meanings. Although Piel (and Pual) usually intensify the meaning of a verb, there are some verbs which come only (or primarily) in the Piel. In these cases, the verbs will not have an "intensified" or "stronger" meaning. For instance, the verb בקשׁ (to seek, look for) does not have a Qal form; it comes only in Piel and Pual. Thus, בִּקֵּשׁ simply means *he looked for* not *he completely looked for.* Likewise, דבר (to speak) is almost always Piel; and דִּבֵּר means simply *he spoke,* not *he completely spoke* or *he strongly spoke.* Likewise, הִלֵּל means *he praised,* not *he completely praised.*

Things You Should Know

1. The Piel is an "intensive" verb form, which often (though not always) gives a stronger meaning to a verb. שִׁמֵּר = *he completely kept.* (Some verbs come only in the Piel, and will not have a stronger meaning.)
2. The primary sign of a Piel verb is a *dagesh* in the second radical. There is often a *tsere* under the second radical, too: שִׁמֵּר, יְשַׁמֵּר
3. In the **Perfect**, there is also a *hireq* under the first radical.
4. **Prefixed parts** (Imperfect, Participle, Jussive and Cohortative) have a *shewa* under their prefix. These parts will have the following pattern:

   *○⊙○̱Δ̣

5. The participle has a -מְ prefix. (All participles except Qal and Niphal will have a -מ prefix.)

[4] The Pual will be studied in §49.

EXERCISE #31

בקשׁ[5] *Piel* בִּקֵּשׁ to seek, look for

ברך *Qal* Pass. Part. ms בָּרוּךְ; *Piel* בֵּרַךְ[6] to bless

דבר *Piel* דִּבֵּר to speak

יָם sea, west[7] *pl.* יַמִּים[8]

יֵשׁ there is

סָפַר *Qal* to count; *Piel* סִפֵּר to report, tell [9] [*Pual* to be reported]

קָבַץ *Qal* to gather (*tr.*)[10]; *Niph* נִקְבַּץ to gather together (*intr.*), assemble; *Piel* קִבֵּץ to gather (*tr.*)

רוּחַ *c.*[11] wind, breath, spirit; *pl.* רוּחוֹת

שַׁעַר a gate

שָׁבַר *Qal* to break; *Niph* נִשְׁבַּר to be broken; *Piel* שִׁבֵּר to break in pieces, shatter

שֹׁפֵט a judge (= *participle of* שָׁפַט)

תָּוֶךְ middle, midst, *cs.* תּוֹךְ; בְּתוֹךְ = in the midst of

Reminder: When parsing, always give the form (Qal, Niphal, Piel, etc.) first: קִבְּצוּ = Piel Perf 3cp < קבץ

[1] וַיְדַבֵּר אֱלֹהִים אֶל־אַבְרָהָם וַיֹּאמֶר הִנֵּה הַשָּׁמַיִם וּסְפֹר אֶת־הַכּוֹכָבִים אִם תּוּכַל[12]
לִסְפֹּר אֹתָם וַיֹּאמֶר לוֹ כֹּה יִהְיֶה זַרְעֶךָ׃ וְהָיְתָה[13] לָהֶם כָּל־הָאָרֶץ אֲשֶׁר הֹלְכוֹת רַגְלֶיךָ
שָׁם׃ [2] וַיִּזְכֹּר יְהוָה אֶת־הָגָר וַיְבָרֶךְ אֶת־בְּנָהּ וַיִּכְרֹת בְּרִית עִם בֶּן־שָׂרָה׃ [3] עָשָׂה
יַעֲקֹב כָּל־אֶת־הָעֲבֹדָה אֲשֶׁר צִוָּה לָבָן אֹתוֹ׃ וַיְגַדֵּל וַיְקַבֵּץ[14] אֶת־נָשָׁיו וְאֶת־בָּנָיו וּמִבֵּית־
לָבָן יָצָא׃ [4] וַיֹּאמְרוּ הַמְרַגְּלִים יֵשׁ לְעַם־הַמָּקוֹם הַהוּא זָהָב וְכֶסֶף וַיִּרְעֲבוּ כִּי אֵין
לָהֶם לָחֶם[15]׃ [5] וַיְקַבֵּץ הָעָם וַיֹּאמְרוּ נְבַקְשָׁה שֹׁפֵט וְנָתַן לָנוּ עֵצָה וּמִשְׁפָּטִים׃ [6] קָטֹן

---

[5] If you do not understand why this verb has no vowel points, see p. 136, note 8.

[6] The ר has rejected the Piel's *dagesh*. Thus, the vowel under the ב has lengthened to *tsere*.

[7] In Israel, the sea was to the west. Therefore, the word for *sea* is often used for the direction *west*.

[8] Do not confuse יַמִּים with יָמִים (the plural of יוֹם). Memorizing Hebrew vocabulary often requires some silly mental games. For יַמִּים, *seas*, think of the מ as the *sea* and the *dagesh* in the מ as a stone thrown into the sea. Thus, the plural of יָם (*sea*) is יַמִּים, not יָמִים. It may be silly to think about throwing a stone into the sea – but you will not forget it.

[9] Many Hebrew textbooks give "recount" for the meaning of the Piel of ספר (סִפֵּר). This can be misleading, since the word "recount" has two meanings: (1) to count again, and (2) to report or tell. It is only the *second* meaning which applies to סִפֵּר. There are several places in the Old Testament where סִפֵּר means "to count" (like the *Qal*), but it never means "to count again."

[10] Transitive. For transitive (*tr.*) and intransitive (*intr.*) verbs, see the "Grammar," p. xix.

[11] For *c.*, see the discussion of "Gender" on p. xx. The word רוּחַ is usually feminine, but is also sometimes masculine. Both will be seen in the exercise.

[12] Qal Impf 2ms < יָכֹל . The י has changed to a וּ. We will discuss this type of verb later. Translate as present tense.

[13] See the verb chart of הָיָה on p. 139.

[14] Is this verb Qal or Piel? Both have *dagesh* in the ב because it is a BEGADKEPAT. Look at the vowel under the prefix (under the י) and remember the parsing guide for Piel. That will tell you whether this verb is Qal or Piel.

[15] This time the word has ח, not ה. The word is in pause, and so the first *seghol* has lengthened to *qamets*.

הַנַּעַר שְׁמוּאֵל וַיְהִי כַּאֲשֶׁר זָקֵן וַיְהִי[16] שֹׁפֵט וַיְהִי רוּחַ־אֱלֹהִים עָלָיו׃ [7] עָשָׂה הָעֶבֶד
לֶחֶם לַעֲבֹדַת־בֵּית־יְהוָה כַּעֲצַת־הַכֹּהֵן׃ [8] בָּאָה רוּחַ גְּדוֹלָה מִיָּם וַיְשַׁבֵּר אֶת־כָּל־עֵץ
אֲשֶׁר בְּתוֹךְ הָעִיר׃ [9] דִּבֶּר הַמְרַגֵּל אֶל־הַמֶּלֶךְ וַיְסַפֵּר כִּי נִמְלְטוּ הָאֲנָשִׁים בְּרֶגֶל
הַמִּדְבָּרָה׃ [10] שָׁכְבָה הַנְּבִיאָה בַּשַּׁעַר כִּי זָקְנָה וַתְּכַבֵּדְנָה עֵינֶיהָ׃ וַתִּישַׁן[17] בְּשָׁלוֹם׃
[11] סִפֵּר עֶבֶד־הַצְּדָקָה אֶת־הַכֶּסֶף וַיְסַפֵּר אֹתוֹ לַכֹּהֲנִים וְלַאֲבוֹתָם׃ [12] וַיֹּאמֶר הַמֶּלֶךְ
אִם אֱלֹהִים עִם־אֹיְבֵינוּ בַּמִּדְבָּר וְהָיְתָה[18] מִלְחָמָה וְלֹא נִמָּלֵט׃ [13] נִלְחֲמוּ הָאֲנָשִׁים
בָּעִיר וַיְשַׁבְּרוּ אֶת־שְׁעָרֶיהָ וְגַם יָכְלוּ לִגְנֹב אֶת־כָּל־הַכֶּסֶף וְהַזָּהָב׃ [14] בִּקְשָׁה בַּקֵּשׁ
הָאֵם אֶת־בָּנֶיהָ בְּתוֹךְ הָעִיר וַתִּמְצָא[19] אֶתְהֶם וַתְּקַבֵּץ אֶתְהֶם וַתְּבָרֵךְ אֶתְהֶם׃ [15] וַתְּהִי
מִלְחָמָה בֵּין יִשְׂרָאֵל וּבֵין יְהוּדָה וַיְסַתְּרוּ הָעָם וַיִּשְׁאֲלוּ לָמָּה אֵין שָׁלוֹם׃ [16] בָּא הָעָם
הַיֹּשֵׁב עַל־הַיָּם וַיִּלָּחֲמוּ מִיָּם[20] לָעִיר׃ [17] בָּהָר נִסְתַּר הַנָּבִיא כִּי יָרְדָה רוּחַ־גְּדֹלָה
מִן־אֱלֹהִים וַתְּשַׁבֵּר אֶת־הָאֲבָנִים׃ [18] כֹּה אָמַר יְהוָה מִשְׁפָּטִי עַל יְרוּשָׁלִַם כִּי אֵין
מִשְׁפָּט[21] וְצֶדֶק בָּעִיר׃ [19] גִּדֵּל עֶבֶד־הַצְּדָקָה כִּי עָשָׂה צֶדֶק וַיְכַבֵּד לִפְנֵי־הָעָם׃

---

[16] Remember that the verb הָיָה can mean "to be" or "to happen" or "to become." All three of these meanings appear in this sentence.

[17] Qal Impf 3fs + w.c. You should be able to recognize the root.

[18] Translate the -וְ as *then*. Hebrew often uses this pattern for "if ... then ..." sentences: The *if* is expressed by אִם, and the *then* is simply a *vav* consecutive (w.c.). (For הָיְתָה, see the verb chart on p. 139.)

[19] Translate the w.c. "and when." Leave the next w.c. untranslated (or translate it "then").

[20] מִיָּם לְ- That is, "on the west side of."

[21] This word appears twice in this sentence. It has a different English meaning each time.

48

PROHIBITION ("DO NOT")

In Hebrew, one prohibits, or says *Do not,* by using the word אַל or לֹא plus the Imperfect. (The Imperative is never used for prohibition.)

Normal prohibition uses אַל plus the Imperfect: אַל תִּשְׁמֹר = *Do not keep.*

Strong (emphatic) prohibition uses לֹא plus the Imperfect: לֹא תִּשְׁמֹר = *Do not **ever** keep.*

Notes:

1. **Normal prohibition** (using אַל) will use the shortened form of the Imperfect, if such a form is available.

> **Shortened form of the Imperfect: its uses**
>
> We now have learned three situations in which the shortened form of the Imperfect will be used:
>
> - with *vav* consecutive (§27.4.2, p. 81)
> - with Jussive (§28.3.1, p. 85)
> - with אַל (normal prohibition)

2. **Strong (or emphatic) prohibition** is used especially when God prohibits, for instance in the Ten Commandments:

לֹא תִּרְצָח	*Do not (ever) kill/murder*
לֹא תִּנְאָף	*Do not (ever) commit adultery*
לֹא תִּגְנֹב	*Do not (ever) steal*

3. Be sure not to confuse the word אַל with the words אֵל (*God*) and אֶל (*to, toward*).

Things You Should Know

1. Hebrew uses the word אַל plus Impf for normal prohibition, and לֹא plus Impf for strong (emphatic) prohibition. The imperative is never used for prohibition.
2. Normal prohibition (אַל) will used a shortened imperfect if one is available.

49

THE VERB: PUAL

The Pual is an "intensive" verb form, like the Piel, but it is passive. The Piel שִׁמֵּר means *he completely kept;* the Pual שֻׁמַּר means *he was completely kept.* The Pual looks almost exactly like the Piel except for a *qibbuts* (ֻ) under the first radical. This first-radical *qibbuts* is found only in the Pual, and it is your most important clue.[1]

49.1 The Pual Verb Chart

	Perfect		*Imperfect*		*Imperative*
3ms	שֻׁמַּר		יְשֻׁמַּר		(Does not occur)
3fs	שֻׁמְּרָה		תְּשֻׁמַּר		
2ms	שֻׁמַּ֫רְתָּ		תְּשֻׁמַּר		
2fs	שֻׁמַּרְתְּ		תְּשֻׁמְּרִי		
1cs	שֻׁמַּ֫רְתִּי		אֲשֻׁמַּר		
3cp	שֻׁמְּרוּ	3mp	יְשֻׁמְּרוּ		*Cohortative* (Does not occur)
		3fp	תְּשֻׁמַּ֫רְנָה		
2mp	שֻׁמַּרְתֶּם		תְּשֻׁמְּרוּ		
2fp	שֻׁמַּרְתֶּן		תְּשֻׁמַּ֫רְנָה	*Jussive*	יְשֻׁמַּר
1cp	שֻׁמַּ֫רְנוּ		נְשֻׁמַּר		
				Impf + w.c.	וַיְשֻׁמַּר[2]

Participle (passive)[3]	Singular	Plural		
m	מְשֻׁמָּר	מְשֻׁמָּרִים	*Inf. Abs.*	שֻׁמֹּר
f	מְשֻׁמֶּ֫רֶת (מְשֻׁמָּרָה)	מְשֻׁמָּרוֹת	*Inf. Const.*	(Does not occur)

Review the notes on Piel. Pual is essentially the same as Piel, except for having the *qibbuts*. In the prefixed moods (Imperfect, Jussive and Participles), you will see the following pattern:

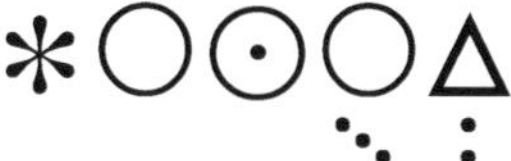

---

[1] **Important note:** *Qibbuts* may appear under other radicals in forms which are not Pual, as we shall see later. But only the Pual has it under the *first* radical.

[2] Again, there is no *dagesh* in the י. This happens only with Piel and Pual Impf *yod* prefixes (3ms and 3mp).

[3] The Pual is a passive verb form. Therefore, it has only a passive participle. See p. 140, note 2.

Things You Should Know

1. **The Pual** is an "intensive" verb form, like the Piel, but it is passive. שֻׁמַּר means *he was completely kept.*
2. **General:** In the Pual there is a *qibbuts* (ֻ) under the first radical; and, as in the Piel, there is a *dagesh* in the second radical. (Review the notes on Piel.)
3. **Prefixed parts** (Imperfect, Participle and Jussive) will have a *shewa* under their prefix. These parts will have the following pattern:

4. **When parsing,** always be sure to start with the form: Qal, Niphal, Piel, Pual, etc.

Exercise #32

אַל	not (do not)
הלל	***Piel*** הִלֵּל to praise[4]; ***Pual*** הֻלַּל to be praised
מִצְרִי	an Egyptian (pl. מִצְרַיִם[5]); *adj.* Egyptian
פזר	***Piel*** פִּזֵּר to scatter, disperse (*tr.*)
מֵת	*adj.* dead
צָרָה	*f.* trouble, *cs.* צָרַת
שָׂפָה	*f.* lip, edge, shore or bank, *cs.* שְׂפַת
קָדַשׁ	be holy; ***Niph*** נִקְדַּשׁ show oneself to be holy; ***Piel*** קִדֵּשׁ make holy, dedicate; ***Pual*** קֻדַּשׁ[6] be made holy
שבח	***Piel*** שִׁבַּח to praise
שָׁכַח	to forget
שֶׁמֶשׁ	the sun

[1] לֹא תְהַלְלוּ אֶת־הַשֶּׁמֶשׁ כְּמִצְרַיִם כִּי מְקֻדָּשַׁי[7] אַתֶּם [2] סִפְּרָה הַנְּבִיאָה אֶל־הַכֹּהֵן
לֵאמֹר מְפֻזָּרִים הָעָם וּבַחֲרוּ אֶת־דֶּרֶךְ־הַגּוֹיִם׃ [3] הָיָה יוֹסֵף הֶחָכָם מֵאֶחָיו וְלָמָּה נִשְׁלַח
מִצְרַיְמָה׃ [4] וַיֹּאמֶר הַנָּבִיא אוֹי לִירוּשָׁלַםִ כִּי אֵין יִרְאַת־אֱלֹהִים בָּהּ וַיִּשְׁכְּחוּ[8] כֹּל
יֹשְׁבֶיהָ אֶת־יְהוָה׃ [5] מֵת יִצְחָק וַיְסַפְּרוּ מַלְאָכִים אֶת־הַדָּבָר לְבָנָיו׃ [6] וַיֹּאמֶר שְׁמוּאֵל
אַל תִּכְתְּבִי אֶת־הַדָּבָר בְּסֵפֶר בַּהֵיכָל[10] וְכִתְבִי אֹתוֹ בִלְבָבֵךְ[9]׃ [7] נִקְבְּצוּ בְנֵי־יִשְׂרָאֵל עַל

---

[4] In Impf and Imv, the *dagesh* is often missing in the first ל: יְהַלֵּל (Impf 3ms), הַלְלוּ (Impv mp), etc.

[5] מִצְרַיִם also means *Egypt*.

[6] **Technical note:** In the Bible, the *Pual* of קדשׁ actually occurs only in participial forms such as מְקֻדָּשִׁים.

[7] Participle with 1cs suffix. It may be treated as a noun (§32.3.3, p. 97): *my-being-made-holy-ones*.

[8] This is Qal not Piel. Look at the vowel under the prefix (ִ). Piel would have *shewa* ("Things You Should Know" 3, above). The *dagesh* in the כ is *dagesh lene*; it is required because the letter is a BEGADKEPAT.

[9] Note both prefix and suffix.

[10] Should this *vav* be translated *and* or *but*?

יַם־ס֫וּף[11] וַיְסֻפַּר הַמִּצְרִי אֶת־הַדָּבָר לְפַרְעֹה לֵאמֹר מֻצְאָה צָרָה אֶת־עַם־יִשְׂרָאֵל כִּי שָׁכַח
אֹתָם אֱלֹהֵיהֶם׃ [8] אַל תִּירָאוּ[13]׃ בִּטְחוּ אֶת־יְהוָה כִּי צַדִּיק הוּא וִישׁוּעָתוֹ[12] עַד־עוֹלָם׃
בְּשִׂפְתֵיכֶם שַׁבְּחוּ־נָא אֹתוֹ וִיהֻלַּל[14] שְׁמוֹ׃ [9] כֻּבְּדוּ אָזְנֵי־הָעָם וְעָבוֹד עֻבְּדוּ אֱלֹהִים
אֲחֵרִים תַּחַת אֶת־יְהוָה׃ [10] יֻשְּׁבוּ בַּשַּׁעַר הַשֹּׁפְטִים וְרוּחַ־אֱלֹהִים עֲלֵיהֶם׃ [11] וַיֹּאמֶר
הַמִּצְרִי יְהִי[16] שֵׁם־יְהוָה מְבֹרָךְ[15] כִּי יֵשׁ לִי בַּת׃ [12] קַבְּצִי אֶת־הָעָם וְדַבְּרִי לָהֶם לֵאמֹר
תְּפֻזְּרוּ אִם לֹא תְקֻדְּשׁוּ׃ [13] בִּקֵּשׁ הָרֹעֶה אֶת־צֹאנוֹ בְּתוֹךְ הַמִּדְבָּר׃ [14] בָּא רוּחַ
גָּדוֹל מִן הַיָּם וַיְשַׁבֵּר אֶת־שַׁעֲרֵי־הָעִיר׃ [15] לֹא יְבֹרַךְ[17] הָעָם אִם יְשַׁבַּח אֶת־הַשֶּׁמֶשׁ׃
[16] מֵת שֹׁפְטֵנוּ וּבְצָרָה[18] גְדוֹלָה אֲנַחְנוּ [17] וַתֹּאמֶר הַנְּבִיאָה יֵשׁ אִשָּׁה בְּתוֹךְ הָעִיר אֲשֶׁר
מְבֻקֶּשֶׁת הִיא אֶת־בְּנָהּ׃ [18] וַיְהִי כַּאֲשֶׁר סֻפַּר הָאִישׁ אֶת־כַּסְפּוֹ[21] [20]וַיְשַׁבְּרוּ[19] אֹיְבָיו אֶת־
שַׁעֲרֵי־בֵיתוֹ׃

---

[11] *Sea of Reeds* (wrongly translated "Red Sea" in many English versions). Here, ־יַם has *pathah* because of the *maqqeph*, which has removed the accent. Closed unaccented syllables require short vowels (§7.2, p. 18).

[12] Feminine construct noun with prefixed *vav* and suffix. How did the beginning of the word go from -וְיְ to -וִי? See §9.1.1 on p. 26, and §17 on p. 49.

[13] Qal Impf 2mp. You should be able to recognize the verb.

[14] Jussive. How do we know? Answer: If it were Imperfect with w.c., the *vav* would have a *pathah* under it (וַיְהֻלַּל, §27.2.2, p. 81). But we do not have this. Rather, we had a *vav* conjunction (-וְ) placed before the -יְ prefix of the Pual. This gave two *shewas* at the beginning of a word (-וְיְ), which then become -וִי as in the footnote above. (See also p.140 footnote 1).

[15] The vowel point under the prefix is your most important clue for parsing this verb. The מ shows that it is a participle. The *shewa* under the מ tells you that the verb is either Piel or Pual. The other vowel pointing has changed because the ר has rejected a *dagesh*. This has caused vowel lengthening: the *qibbuts* which was under the ב has now lengthened to a *holem*.

[16] Shortened form of the Imperfect. What does this tell you about the translation? See p. 144 if you don't know.

[17] Again, the vowel point under the prefix is your most important clue for parsing this verb. The *shewa* shows that it must be either Piel or Pual. But which is it? Again, the ר has rejected a *dagesh*. This time, this has caused the *qibbuts* which was under the ב to lengthen to a *holem*.

[18] This word has two prefixes.

[19] Is this verb Qal or Piel? The *dagesh* in the second radical could come from Piel, but it could also simply be there because the letter is a BEGADKEPAT. The answer: look at the prefix. What do we expect to see under the prefix of a Piel Imperfect verb? Do we see it here?

[20] Concerning the -וַ, see p. 94, note 16.

[21] Segholate with suffix.

50

THE VERB: HIPHIL

Hiphil is a "causative" verb form. That is, the subject causes the object to do something. Example: the sentence *Samuel came near to David* is not causative. A causative sentence would be *Samuel **caused** **David** to come near*, or, more simply, *Samuel brought David near.* In Hebrew, the verb *to come near* is קָרַב. Its Hiphil is הִקְרִיב. Thus, we have:

Qal:	קָרַב שְׁמוּאֵל אֶל־דָּוִד	*Samuel came near to David*
Hiphil:	הִקְרִיב שְׁמוּאֵל אֶת־דָּוִד	*Samuel caused David to come near*, or better *Samuel brought David near*

Other examples:

Qal:	שָֽׁמְעָה שָׂרָה אֶת־הָגָר	*Sarah heard Hagar*
Hiphil:	הִשְׁמִ֫יעָה שָׂרָה אֶת־הָגָר	*Sarah caused Hagar to hear*, or better *Sarah told Hagar*
Qal:	קָֽדְשׁוּ	*They were holy*
Hiphil:	הִקְדִּ֫ישׁוּ אֹתָ֫נוּ	*They made us holy*

50.1 The Hiphil Verb Chart

	Perfect	*Imperfect*
3ms	הִשְׁמִיר	יַשְׁמִיר
3fs	הִשְׁמִ֫ירָה	תַּשְׁמִיר
2ms	הִשְׁמַ֫רְתָּ	תַּשְׁמִיר
2fs	הִשְׁמַרְתְּ	תַּשְׁמִ֫ירִי
1cs	הִשְׁמַ֫רְתִּי	אַשְׁמִיר
3cp	הִשְׁמִ֫ירוּ	3mp יַשְׁמִ֫ירוּ 3fp תַּשְׁמֵ֫רְנָה
2mp	הִשְׁמַרְתֶּם	תַּשְׁמִ֫ירוּ
2fp	הִשְׁמַרְתֶּן	תַּשְׁמֵ֫רְנָה
1cp	הִשְׁמַ֫רְנוּ	נַשְׁמִיר

	Imperative
ms	הַשְׁמֵר
fs	הַשְׁמִ֫ירִי
mp	הַשְׁמִ֫ירוּ
fp	הַשְׁמֵ֫רְנָה

	Cohortative
1cs	אַשְׁמִ֫ירָה
1cp	נַשְׁמִ֫ירָה

Jussive	יַשְׁמֵר
Impf + w.c.	וַיַּשְׁמֵר
Jussive + vav	וְיַשְׁמֵר

	***Participle* (*active*)**[1]			
	Singular	Plural	***Inf. Abs.***	הַשְׁמֵר
m	מַשְׁמִיר	מַשְׁמִירִים	***Inf. Const.***	הַשְׁמִיר
f	מַשְׁמִירָה מַשְׁמֶרֶת	מַשְׁמִירוֹת		

50.2 Characteristics of the Hiphil

50.2.1 **The Perfect, Imperative and Infinitives** all have a prefixed -ה.

50.2.2 **Prefixes** all have *pathah* (except the -הִ of the Perfect).

50.2.3 ***Hireq-yod* (ִי) or *tsere*** usually come after the second radical. An exception is the Perfect, where *pathah* is found in the second- and first-person.

50.2.4 **Parsing guide.** In parsing, we will abbreviate Hiphil as Hiph. You will see the following pattern in all parts except the Perfect:

50.2.5 **Stand-alone shortened form of Imperfect.** Note that, in the Hiphil, the *hireq-yod* can be replaced by a *tsere* (above), and this will make the verb shorter. This means that the Hiphil is the only form of the ▲**strong verb** (see box below) which has a shortened form of the Imperfect which can stand alone (that is, without having *vav* consecutive or being used as jussive or in a "normal prohibition"). Remember that, normally, the shortened form of the Imperfect is used only in three special situations:

- with *vav* consecutive[2] (§27.4.2, p. 81)
- for the jussive (§28.3.1, p. 85)
- with "normal prohibition" (אַל, §48, p. 144)

For instance, as we saw with the verb הָיָה (§27.4.2, p. 81), the Qal Impf with w.c. will usually appear as וַיְהִי not וַיִּהְיֶה. And normal prohibition will be אַל תְּהִי not the longer form of אַל תִּהְיֶה. And יְהִי by itself will be Jussive.

In the Hiphil Imperfect, however, we will see both the long form (יַשְׁמִיר) as well as the short form (יַשְׁמֵר) standing alone. Thus, the short form of the Hiphil Imperfect can indicate *either* Imperfect *or* Jussive. Example:

יַמְלִיךְ דָּוִד אֶת־שְׁלֹמֹה	means	*David will make Solomon (rule as) king*
	BUT	
יַמְלֵךְ דָּוִד אֶת־שְׁלֹמֹה	means either	*David will make Solomon (rule as) king* or *Let David make Solomon (rule as) king*

As usual, it is the context which will show the proper way to translate.

[1] The Hiphil is an active verb form, and so it has only an active participle.

[2] Remember the exception to this rule: The shortened form of the Imperfect will not be used with the first person singular (1cs) (See the footnote on §27.4.2, p. 81).

50.2.6 **This time the IA (not the IC) is the same as the Impv ms.** In Qal, Niphal and Piel, the Impv ms was the same as the IC. In the Hiphil, it is the IA that is the same as the Impv ms.

50.2.7 **Non-causative meanings.** We have already seen that some verbs come in Niphal but are not passive (§45.2.4, p. 134), or in Piel but are not intensive (§47.2.6, p. 141). Likewise, there are verbs which come only (or primarily) in Hiphil, but which have non-causative meanings. For instance, the verb בדל does not come in Qal. Its Hiphil is הִבְדִּיל and it means *to separate* (not *to cause to separate*). Likewise, the verbs שׁחת and שׁמד do not have Qal forms. Both come in the Hiphil. הִשְׁחִית means *to damage or destroy* and הִשְׁמִיד means *to exterminate* (*to completely destroy living things —people, insects, animals, etc. —so that none remain*).

50.2.8 **Similar appearance to Niphal Impv:** Be sure to study carefully the similarities and differences between the Niphal Impv and the Hiphil Impv (and IA). The Niph Impv ms is הִשָּׁמֵר, and looks very similar to the Hiph Impv ms and the Hiph IA (both are הַשְׁמֵר). But remember that the Niphal has *dagesh* and *qamets* in the first radical of the verb (§45.3, p. 134) and the Hiphil does not. Thus, הִשָּׁמֵר is Niphal, not Hiphil.

Strong and Weak Verbs

Strong verbs are verbs such as מלט, in which all three radicals are strong letters. The letters never disappear, and the verbs follow the noral verb patterns we have learned. **Weak verbs** have "weak" letters such as gutturals which reject *dagesh*, or they have נ ו י or ה which sometimes disappear, or cause other problems. Thus, they may also have shortened forms of the Imperfect. We shall study weak verbs later.

Things You Should Know

1. **The Hiphil is a "causative" form.** The subject causes the object to do something.
2. **The Hiphil Perfect** has a prefixed -הִ. **Other tenses/moods** have prefixes with *pathah*.
3. **A *hireq-yod* or *tsere*** is usually found between the second and third radical.
4. **Parsing:** In all parts except the Perfect, we shall see the following pattern:

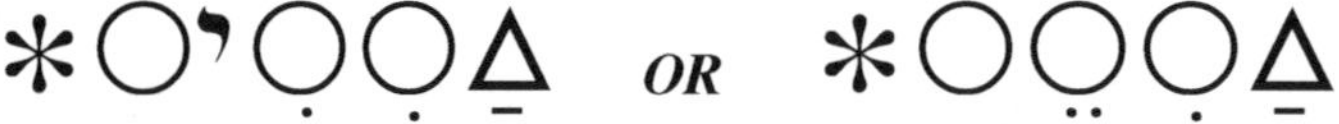

5. **Shortened form of Imperfect.** The shortened form of the Impf (*tsere* instead of *hireq-yod*) is used with *vav* consecutive, jussive, and normal prohibition (אַל). But in the Hiphil, it may also simply stand alone as an Impf.
6. **Non-causative Hiphils.** Some verbs come in the Hiphil but have non-causative meanings.
7. **Similar verb forms.** The Niphal Impv ms is הִשָּׁמֵר. It may at first look like Hiphil to you. But note the *dagesh* and *qamets*; they indicate Niphal, and are never found in Hiphil. Watch for this *dagesh* and *qamets* combination, since it will keep you from confusing the Niphal Impv with the Hiphil.

Exercise #33

אֱמֶת truth, faithfulness, reliability

בדל *Hi* הִבְדִּיל to separate, distinguish between

חָזַק to be(come) strong, have courage; *Piel* חִזַּק to make strong, strengthen; *Hi* הֶחֱזִיק to seize, take hold of (Note: *not* to make strong, etc.)

חָטָא to sin; to miss (a goal)

חֵטְא *m.* sin, fault, *pl.* חֲטָאִים, *pl. cs.* חֲטָאֵי; (*also f.* חַטָּאת, *cs.* חַטַּאת; *pl.* חַטָּאוֹת)

כִּסֵּא *m.* chair, throne; *pl.* כִּסְאוֹת

מָלַךְ to be king, to rule; *Hi* הִמְלִיךְ to make (someone) king

קָהָל assembly, gathering

קהל *Ni* נִקְהַל to assemble (*intr.*)[3]; *Hi* הִקְהִיל to assemble, call together (*tr.*)[3]

שְׁכֶם Shechem (person and place) (*lit.* both shoulders)

שמד *Ni.* נִשְׁמַד to be destroyed; *Hi* הִשְׁמִיד to destroy

[1] מֵת הַמֶּ֫לֶךְ וַיַּקְהֵל הָעָם לְהַמְלִיךְ אֶת־בְּנוֹ כִּי חָזָק הוּא וְחָכָם׃ [2] לֹא תֶחֶטְאוּ
בְּשִׂפְתֵיכֶם בַּקָּהָל הַקָּדוֹשׁ וְחִזְקוּ בְּיוֹם־הַצָּרָה׃ [3] הַלְלוּ[6] אֶת־יְהוָה[5] בַּאֲמִתּוֹ[4] כִּי פִזֵּר
אֶת־אֹיְבֵינוּ וַיְחַזֵּק אֶת־מַלְכֵּנוּ עַל כִּסְאוֹ׃ [4] וַיַּבְדֵּל[9] אֱלֹהִים בֵּין מַיִם לָמָיִם[8] וַיַּרְא[7]
אֱלֹהִים כִּי־טוֹב[10]׃ [5] נִמְלַט הַמְרַגֵּל בְּרַגְלָיו וַיִּסָּתֵר עַל עֵין־הַמָּיִם׃ [6] נִלְחֲמוּ
הַמְּלָכִים בָּעִיר וַתִּשָּׁמֵד וַיַּחֲזִקוּ אֶת־לוֹט וְגַם לָקְחוּ כָּל־אֶת־הַכֶּסֶף וְאֶת־הַזָּהָב׃
[7] שִׁבַּח הַמִּצְרִי הַהוּא אֶת־הַשֶּׁמֶשׁ וְלֹא יָדַע אֶת־אֱלֹהֵי[11]־הַמִּשְׁפָּט וְהַקֹּדֶשׁ׃ [8] הַקְהֵל
אֶת־הָעָם בִּשְׁכֶם וֶאֱמֹר[12] לָהֶם גְּדוֹלָה חַטָּאתֵנוּ וּפִזְּרוּ אֹיְבֵינוּ אֹתָנוּ׃ [9] מָלַךְ הַמֶּלֶךְ עַל
כִּסְאוֹ וַיַּבְדֵּל אֶת־אַנְשֵׁי־הַקָּהָל לֵאמֹר יֵשׁ לַאֲנָשִׁים הָאֵלֶּה חָכְמָה וְדַעַת וְרָעִים הָאֲנָשִׁים
הָהֵמָּה׃ [10] וַיֹּאמֶר לָבָן אֶל רָחֵל וְעַתָּה בִּתִּי אַל תִּשְׁכַּח אֶת־עֲצָתִי׃ [11] נִקְהֲלוּ
שְׁכֶם וְאַחְיוֹתָו עַל הֶעָרִים הָהֵנָּה וַתַּשְׁמִדוּ אֶתְהֶן מִן[14] חֶטְאָן׃ [12] עָבְרוּ הַמִּצְרַיִם[13]
אֶת־הַיַּרְדֵּן וַתִּמְצָא צָרָה גְּדוֹלָה אֹתָם כִּי לֹא הָיָה לֶחֶם לָהֶם׃ [13] לֹא נִקְדַּשׁ הָעָם

[3] Transitive (*tr.*) verbs have objects; intransitive (*intr.*) Verbs do not. See p. xix.

[4] Segholate noun with prefix and suffix. The pointing is unusual because of the guttural א.

[5] This phrase is usually written with a shortened form of יְהוָה as follows: הַלְלוּ יָהּ, that is *Halleluyah*!

[6] The dagesh in the first ל is missing. See page 146 note 4.

[7] Shortened Impf 3ms (√ראה) because of w.c.

[8] Translate this three-word phrase "waters from waters."

[9] Shortened form of Impf because of the w.c.

[10] "that (it was) good."

[11] Translate "God of" rather than "gods of."

[12] Qal Impv ms + w.c. The first two vowel points have been affected by the א.

[13] Should this word be translated *Egypt* or *Egyptians*? Why?

[14] Translate "because of."

וַיִּשְׁכְּחוּ[15] אֶת־אֱלֹהִים׃ [14] וַתֹּאמֶר הַנְּבִיאָה הַזְּקֵנָה הַזֹּאת לֵאמֹר חֲטָאתֶם כִּי הִשְׁמַדְתֶּם
אֶת־הָעִיר וְעַתָּה נִשָּׁמֵד כִּי לֹא הֲלַכְתֶּם בֶּאֱמֶת׃ [15] וַיְהִי הַשֶּׁמֶשׁ לָבוֹא[16] וַיַּקְהֵל הַכֹּהֵן
אֶת־הָעָם עַל שְׂפַת־הַנָּהָר לְמַעַן שַׁבַּח[17] אֶת־אֱלֹהִים׃ [16] לֹא מֵת דָּוִד וַיַּמְשִׁילוּ הָעָם
אֶת־שְׁלֹמֹה תַּחְתָּיו׃ [17] קִדְּשׁוּ הַכֹּהֲנִים אֶת־כְּלֵי־הַזָּהָב וְאֶת־כְּלֵי־הַכֶּסֶף [18]לַעֲבֹדַת־
בֵּית־יְהוָה׃ [18] הֲבָאתָ[19] עִם הָאִישׁ הַזֶּה וְהָאִשָּׁה הַהִיא׃

---

[15] Remember: the word עַם will sometimes take singular verbs, sometimes plural, and sometimes both even within one verse. Review p. 137, footnote 28. Concerning the parsing of this verb, see p. 147, footnote 19.

[16] Infinitive Construct (+ לְ) from בָּא (root בוא). Translate *And when the sun had set* or *And as the sun was setting*. The verb בָּא is used for the sun setting. Sometimes יָצָא is used for the sun rising.

[17] Piel IC. You have learned that this form usually has a *tsere* under the second radical (קַטֵּל, שַׁמֵּר), but in this case the final ח is a guttural and has attracted a *pathah*. **Question**: Why does this IC not have a prefixed -לְ? Answer: Because the preposition לְמַעַן (*in order to*) has taken the place of the (inseparable) preposition -לְ (*to*).

[18] How do you know that the *pathah* under the *lamed* does not represent a definite article? (See p. 60, §21.5) Translate the *lamed* "for (the purpose of)."

[19] The verb is Perf 2ms < בָּא. If you thought -תָ was a possessive suffix (*your*), see §23.3, p. 67.

51

THE VERB: HOPHAL

Hophal is a passive causative verb form. It pairs with Hiphil (active causative) the same way Pual pairs with Piel. The easiest way to understand Hophal is to look at some examples. We will begin with the examples we used for Hiphil and then add Hophal for comparison:

51.1 Examples of Hophal

Qal:	קָרַב שְׁמוּאֵל אֶל־דָּוִד	*Samuel came near to David*
Hiphil:	הִקְרִיב שְׁמוּאֵל אֶת־דָּוִד	*Samuel caused David to come near*, or better *Samuel brought David near*
Hophal:	הָקְרַב דָּוִד[1]	*David was caused to come near*, or better *David was brought near*

Remember that the ָ in הָקְרַב is *qamets-hatuph* (o). Here is another example:

Qal:	שָׁכַב הָאִישׁ	*The man lay down*
Hiphil:	הִשְׁכִּיב הָאִישׁ אֶת־הַיֶּלֶד	*The man caused the child to lie down*, or better *The man laid the child down*
Hophal:	הָשְׁכַּב הַיֶּלֶד	*The child was caused to lie down,* or better *The child was laid down*

51.2 The Hophal Verb Chart

	Perfect	*Imperfect*	*Imperative*
3ms	הָשְׁמַר	יָשְׁמַר	(does not occur)
3fs	הָשְׁמְרָה	תָּשְׁמַר	
2ms	הָשְׁמַרְתָּ	תָּשְׁמַר	
2fs	הָשְׁמַרְתְּ	תָּשְׁמְרִי	
1cs	הָשְׁמַרְתִּי	אָשְׁמַר	

---

[1] **Technical note:** The Hophal form of the verb קרב is not actually found in the Bible. But we use it here in order to compare to our example from the lesson on Hiphil.

	Perfect	Imperfect
3cp	הָשְׁמְרוּ	3mp יָשְׁמְרוּ 3fp תָּשְׁמַ֫רְנָה
2mp	הָשְׁמַרְתֶּם	תָּשְׁמְרוּ
2fp	הָשְׁמַרְתֶּן	תָּשְׁמַ֫רְנָה
1cp	הָשְׁמַ֫רְנוּ	נָשְׁמַר

Cohortative
(does not occur)

Jussive	יָשְׁמַר
Impf + w.c.	וַיָּשְׁמַר

Participle (passive)

	Singular	Plural
m	מָשְׁמָר	מָשְׁמָרִים
f	מָשְׁמֶ֫רֶת	מָשְׁמָרוֹת

Inf. Abs.	הָשְׁמֵר
Inf. Const.	הָשְׁמַר

51.3 Characteristics of Hophal

51.3.1 **All parts of the Hophal have a prefix with a *qamets-hatuph* under the prefix.** But there is one important exception:

51.3.2 **The *qamets-hatuph* under the prefix is sometimes replaced by a *qibbuts*** (ֻ). Thus, you may see:

הֻשְׁמַר instead of הָשְׁמַר
יֻשְׁמַר instead of יָשְׁמַר
etc.

This is especially true for the participles. For instance, we may see מֻשְׁמַר instead of מָשְׁמָר. In such cases, **there should be no confusion with Pual** since

- in the Hophal this *qibbuts* will come under the prefix (יֻשְׁמַר , מֻשְׁמָר), but
- in Pual, the *qibbuts* is always under the first radical (יְשֻׁמַּר, מְשֻׁמָּר), never under the prefix.

51.3.3 **Parsing Guide:** In all parts of the Hophal, there are

- a prefix,
- a *qamets-hatuph* (sometimes a *qibbuts*) under the prefix
- a *shewa* under the first radical.

Therefore, you will see:

51.3.4 **Non-causative meanings.** We saw in §50.2.7 that a few Hiphil verbs have meanings which are not causative. This is also true for a few Hophal verbs. We saw that שחת does not come in the Qal, and that in the Hiphil it simply means *to damage or destroy* (not *to cause to damage*). Likewise, the Hophal (הָשְׁחַת) means *to be damaged* (not *to be caused to be damaged*).

Another example is the verb שלך. It does not come in Qal, but the Hiphil means *to throw (down or away)*. The Hophal (הָשְׁלַךְ) means *to **be** thrown (down or away)*.

Things You Should Know

1. Hophal is a passive causative verb form. הָשְׁכַּב means "he was caused to lie down."
2. Some verbs have no Qal form, and their Hophal form then has only a passive (not a causative) meaning. For instance, הָשְׁחַת means *it was damaged*, not *it was **caused** to be damaged.*
3. All parts of Hophal have a prefix with a *qamets-hatuph* (sometimes a *qibbuts*), and there is a *shewa* under the first radical. The parsing guide is thus:

 and sometimes 

Exercise #34

בָּשָׂר	flesh, meat, humanity
חַיִּים	life (*pl.*[2])
נֶפֶשׁ	*f.* life, life force, person;[3] *pl.* נְפָשׁוֹת; נַפְשִׁי my life, *but often just* I *or* me
נָפַל	to fall
עִבְרִי	*adj.* and *n.* Hebrew; *pl.* עִבְרִים and עִבְרִיִּים
עֵדָה	*f.* gathering, group, congregation
עָזַב	to leave, abandon; *Impf* יַעֲזֹב
עוֹד	again, still, always
רָעֵב	*adj.* hungry (*also stative verb*, to be hungry)
רַק	only, but
רָשָׁע	*adj.* and *n.* guilty, wicked
שַׁבָּת	*c.* sabbath, day of rest; *pl.* שַׁבָּתוֹת

[1] בַּשַּׁבָּת נִקְהַל הָעָם בִּשְׁכֶם בְּעֵדָה גְּדוֹלָה וַיַּמְלֵךְ אֶת־שְׁלֹמֹה׃ [2] נָתַן אֱלֹהִים אֶת־
תּוֹרָתוֹ וְאֶת־מִצְוֹתָיו[4] לְמֹשֶׁה בְּהַר־סִינָי לְמַעַן יְסַפֵּר אֹתָהֶם לִקְהַל־הָעָם׃ [3] אִם
רְעֵבִים[5] אַתֶּם אָכוֹל תֹּאכְלוּ בָּשָׂר וְלֹא תֹאכְלוּ אֶת־דָּמוֹ׃ כִּי נֶפֶשׁ־כָּל־בָּשָׂר בְּדָמוֹ הִיא׃
[4] וַיִּקָּבְצוּ עוֹד הָעִבְרִיִּים לְמַעַן בַּקֵּשׁ[6] אֶת־אֹיְבֵיהֶם וַיַּשְׁמִדוּ אֹתָם׃ [5] בַּבֹּקֶר עָבַר

---

[2] The singular חַי is less common, and is used in oaths (for instance 1 Sam 1:26; 2 Sam 2:27; Num 14:21).

[3] Not *soul* (as in the more spiritual Greek idea). The Hebrew idea is more physical; life was believed to be "in the blood" (see, for instance, Gen 9:4; Lev 17:11,14; Deut 12:23; Ps 72:14).

[4] Is the ו in this word a consonant-plus-vowel (wō) or a vowel letter (ô)? How do you know? See the check box on p. 33 if you are unsure.

[5] Plural adjective.

[6] If you have trouble parsing this, see page 152 note 17 and read the "Question" in the middle of the note.

יַעֲקֹב אֶת־הַנָּהָר אֶת[9]־בְּקָרוֹ וַיְדַבֵּר אֶל עֵשָׂו אָחִיהוּ[8] לֵאמֹר יֶשׁ־לִי־כֹל[7]׃ [6] יָשַׁב
הַנָּבִיא הַזָּקֵן לְבַדּוֹ וַיֹּאמֶר נִשְׁמַד עַמִּי׃ הָשְׁבַּרְתִּי וַתֶּחֱזַק צָרָה אֹתִי׃ [7] בְּעֶרֶב נָשָׂא
מֹשֶׁה אֶת־לוּחוֹת־הָאֶבֶן אֶל רָאשֵׁי־הַקָּהָל וְזִקְנֵיהוּ׃ [8] בָּאוּ אֹיְבִים לְהַשְׁמִיד אֶת־הָעִיר
לְמַעַן חֶטְאָהּ וַיַּקְהֵל הַמֶּלֶךְ אֶת־הָעָם לְחַזֵּק אֹתְהֶם׃ [9] הָמְלַךְ שְׁלֹמֹה עַל כִּסְאוֹ
וַיְבֹרַךְ[11] כָּל־יְמֵי־חַיָּיו׃ [10] יֵשְׁבוּ הַשֹּׁפְטִים בְּתוֹךְ הַשַּׁעַר וַיִּשְׁמְעוּ הָעָם הַשָּׁפוּטִים[10]־בָּהֶם
אֶת־דִּבְרֵי־פִיהֶם׃ [11] יֶחֶזְקוּ[12] אַנְשֵׁי־אֱמֶת וְעָזְבוּ הָרְשָׁעִים וְנָפְלוּ׃ [12] קֻבְּצוּ הַנָּשִׁים
אֶת־כְּלֵי־הַמִּלְחָמָה וַתְּשַׁבֵּרְנָה אֹתְהֶם וַיְּשָׁמְדוּ׃ [13] צַוֵּה אֶת־הָעָם בְּשֵׁם־יְהוָה לֵאמֹר
זָכוֹר[14] אֶת־יוֹם־הַשַּׁבָּת וְלֹא תַעֲזֹב אֶת־בְּרִית־אֱלֹהֶיךָ׃ [14] סָפַר יַעֲקֹב אֶת־הַצֹּאן וַיַּבְדֵּל[13]
בֵּין צֹאנוֹ וּבֵין צֹאן־לָבָן׃ [15] הַחֲזֵק[15] אֶת־כִּסֵּא־אֲבוֹתֶיךָ רַק לֹא תֶחֱטָא כַּמְּלָכִים
הָרְשָׁעִים לְפָנֶיךָ׃ [16] וּבָא רוּחַ־אֱלֹהִים מֵהַיָּם[17] לְקַבֵּץ אֶת־עַמּוֹ וְרָאוּ[16] כָל־נֶפֶשׁ אֶת־
כְּבוֹדוֹ׃ [17] וַיְדַבֵּר עוֹד יְהוֹשֻׁעַ אֶל הָעִבְרִיִּים לֵאמֹר אַתֶּם יֹדְעִים בְּכָל־לְבַבְכֶם
וּבְכָל נַפְשְׁכֶם כִּי לֹא־נָפַל דָּבָר אֶחָד מִכֹּל הַדְּבָרִים הַטּוֹבִים אֲשֶׁר דִּבֶּר יְהוָה אֱלֹהֵיכֶם
עֲלֵיכֶם׃[18] [18] הִקְהִיל הַכֹּהֵן אֶת־הָעָם לֵאמֹר לָמָּה חֲטָאתֶם כָּל־יְמֵי־חַיֵּיכֶם׃ הִבְדִּילוּ
חַטֹּאתֵיכֶם אֶתְכֶם מִן אֱלֹהֵיכֶם וְעַתָּה רָעֵב אַתֶּם׃ [19] וַיְהִי קְהַל־זִקְנֵי־אֱמֶת בִּשְׁכֶם
וַיֶּחֶזְקוּ וַיְחַזְּקוּ אֶת־הָעָם׃

---

[7] **Technical note:** Translations often miss Jacob's boasting here (Genesis 33). After Esau says "I have much" (רָב), Jacob responds by saying, "*I* have *everything* (כֹּל)" (not "I have enough" [RSV], or "I have everything I want" [NRSV]) – because, indeed, he had taken Esau's birthright and both blessings.

[8] Alternate form of אָחִיו.

[9] Note that אֶת־ has two meanings in this sentence.

[10] This word is not a Niphal verb. What is the ה? Why is there a *dagesh* in the שׁ? If you do not know, see §14.1, p. 40, and §40, p. 118.

[11] Pual. **Technical note:** The *shewa* under the prefix tells you that this verb is either Piel or Pual. Both Piel and Pual have a *dagesh* in the second radical, but in this case the ר has rejected that *dagesh*. Thus, the *qibbuts* (ֻ) which originally appeared under the ב has lengthened to a *holem*.

[12] Qal Impf 3mp < חָזַק. The vowel pointing has changed because of the guttural.

[13] Short form of the Imperfect because of *vav* consecutive. Do not let the *dagesh* fool you; this is not Piel. The *dagesh* is there because the ד is a BEGADKEPAT letter. Again, your major parsing clue is the vowel under the prefix.

[14] Infinitive absolute, but translate as an imperative. Note that in the Hebrew Bible, as here, the third commandment uses an Infinitive Absolute at both Exod 20:8 (זָכוֹר) and Deut 5:12 (שָׁמוֹר).

[15] How do you parse this verb? **(1) Find its root:** you should recognize חזק. **(2) Look for prefixes and suffixes:** here we have only -הַ. **(3) Analyze:** It cannot be Hiphil Perf because that prefix is -הִ (with *hireq*). It can only be either a Hiphil Imperative or a Hiphil Infinitive. At this point, the context will help you decide. **Technical note:** Since ה is a guttural, the *shewa* which was originally under it has become a *hateph pathah*.

[16] The final ה of ראה has dropped out because it is a weak letter.

[17] Remember that יָם has two meanings.

[18] This is the preposition עַל with a 2mp suffix. We will study it in the next chapter.

52

POETIC PREPOSITIONS WITH SUFFIXES

The prepositions אֶל (*to*), עַל (*upon*) and אַחַר (*after, behind*) have longer forms which are often seen in poetry:[1]

אֱלֵי *to* עֲלֵי *upon* אַחֲרֵי *after, behind*

Personal suffixes (ִי - *me*, וֹ- *him*, etc.) may be attached to these longer forms. This is very similar to what we saw in §35, where inseparable prepositions -בְּ, -לְ and -כְּ took pronoun suffixes (בִּי, לוֹ, etc.). The poetic prepositions with suffixes will look very similar to plural nouns with suffixes (§34) because of the added *yod*.

אֵלַי *to me*	עָלַי *on me*	אַחֲרַי *after me*
אֵלֶיךָ *to you* (ms)	עָלֶיךָ *on you* (ms)	אַחֲרֶיךָ *after you* (ms)
אֵלַיִךְ *to you* (fs)	עָלַיִךְ *on you* (fs)	אַחֲרַיִךְ *after you* (fs)
אֵלָיו *to him*	עָלָיו *on him*	אַחֲרָיו *after him*
אֵלֶיהָ *to her*	עָלֶיהָ *on her*	אַחֲרֶיהָ *after her*
אֵלֵינוּ *to us*	עָלֵינוּ *on us*	אַחֲרֵינוּ *after us*
אֲלֵיכֶם *to you* (mp)	עֲלֵיכֶם *on you* (mp)	אַחֲרֵיכֶם *after you* (mp)
אֲלֵיכֶן *to you* (fp)	עֲלֵיכֶן *on you* (fp)	אַחֲרֵיכֶן *after you* (fp)
אֲלֵיהֶם *to them* (mp)	עֲלֵיהֶם *on them* (mp)	אַחֲרֵיהֶם *after them* (mp)
אֲלֵיהֶן *to them* (fp)	עֲלֵיהֶן *on them* (fp)	אַחֲרֵיהֶן *after them* (fp)

Notes:

1. The forms *without* suffixes (אֱלֵי, עֲלֵי, אַחֲרֵי) are usually found in poetry. But the forms *with* suffixes are found in both prose and poetry.

2. There are other prepositions which follow these patterns. For instance,

   עַד (*until, up to*) follows the pattern of עַל: עָדַי, עָדֶיךָ, עָדַיִךְ, etc.

   תַּחַת (*below, beneath, instead of*) generally follows the pattern of אַחַר, except for having simple *shewa* instead of composite: תַּחְתַּי, תַּחְתֶּיךָ, תַּחְתַּיִךְ, etc.

3. Do not confuse אֵלַי (*to me*) with אֵלִי (*my god/God*).[2]

---

[1] **Technical note:** These longer forms are actually the originals.

[2] **Technical note.** Advanced students may wonder about the plural construct of אֵל (*god/God*) with suffixes, and whether there is any danger of confusing it with אֵלַי (*to*) plus suffixes. This is not a problem. In the OT, the only suffixed form of אֵל (*god/God*) is the singular+1cs אֵלִי (found 12 times, 10 of which are in the Psalms). אֵלַי in Ps 7:7 (7:6 EVs) presents a translation challenge (compare NRSV and NASB). In all other cases, the OT uses the plural form אֱלֹהִים (construct אֱלֹהֵי). Thus אֱלֹהַי, אֱלֹהֶיךָ, אֱלֹהָיו, אֱלֹהֵיהֶם, etc.

53

THE VERB: HITHPAEL

Hithpael is a reflexive verb form. ▲"Reflexive" means that the action of the verb goes back to the subject. For instance, *He dressed himself* is a reflexive sentence. So are the sentences *I shall prepare myself* and *they are meeting at the school.* In English, we often using a helping word such as *myself, yourself, herself,* etc. Hebrew uses a special reflexive verb form: the Hithpael.

Consider the following examples:

Qal	גָּדַל	*he was great*
Hithpael	הִתְגַּדֵּל	*he made himself great, he boasted*

The next example uses the verb הלל. It also means *he boasted* in the Hithpael.[1]

Piel	הִלֵּל	*he praised*
Hithpael	הִתְהַלֵּל	*he boasted* (literally *he praised himself*)

53.1 The Hithpael Verb Chart[2]

	Perfect		*Imperfect*	
3ms	הִתְקַטֵּל		יִתְקַטֵּל	
3fs	הִתְקַטְּלָה		תִּתְקַטֵּל	
2ms	הִתְקַטַּ֫לְתָּ		תִּתְקַטֵּל	
2fs	הִתְקַטַּלְתְּ		תִּתְקַטְּלִי	
1cs	הִתְקַטַּ֫לְתִּי		אֶתְקַטֵּל	
		3mp	יִתְקַטְּלוּ	
3cp	הִתְקַטְּלוּ	3fp	תִּתְקַטֵּ֫לְנָה	(תִּתְקַטַּ֫לְנָה)
2mp	הִתְקַטַּלְתֶּם		תִּתְקַטְּלוּ	
2fp	הִתְקַטַּלְתֶּן		תִּתְקַטֵּ֫לְנָה	(תִּתְקַטַּ֫לְנָה)
1cp	הִתְקַטַּ֫לְנוּ		נִתְקַטֵּל	

	Imperative[3]
ms	הִתְקַטֵּל
fs	הִתְקַטְּלִי
mp	הִתְקַטְּלוּ
fp	הִתְקַטֵּ֫לְנָה

	Cohortative
1cs	אֶתְקַטְּלָה
1cp	נִתְקַטְּלָה

Jussive	יִתְקַטֵּל

[1] הלל is one of the verbs which does not come in the Qal. It has its basic meaning of *to praise* in the Piel.

[2] The chart uses the verb קטל instead of שׁמר because of problems which will be explained in §53.2.5.1.

[3] In this case, the Impv is formed when the Impf prefix drops away (see p. 76) but is then replaced by a ה.

	Participle			
	Singular	Plural	***Impf + w.c.***	וַיִּתְקַטֵּל
m	מִתְקַטֵּל	מִתְקַטְּלִים	***Inf. Abs.***	הִתְקַטֵּל[4]
f	מִתְקַטְּלָה (מִתְקַטֶּלֶת)	מִתְקַטְּלוֹת	***Inf. Const.***	הִתְקַטֵּל

53.2 Characteristics of Hithpael

53.2.1 **Perfect, Imperative and Infinitives** all have

- a -הִתְ prefix,
- a *pathah* under the first radical
- a *dagesh* in the second radical

As usual, the suffixes will follow the patterns we have already learned.

53.2.2 **Other parts of the Hithpael**, such as Imperfect, have additional prefixes. When these prefixes are added, they replace the -ה in the -הִתְ prefix, but the *hireq*, the ת and the *shewa* still remain (see the verb chart above). For instance, the Imperfect is יִתְקַטֵּל, תִּתְקַטֵּל, תִּתְקַטְּלִי, etc.

53.2.3 **Parsing Guide:** In general, the Hithpael is the easiest form to recognize because of the infixed -תְ-. Watch for the following pattern:

(The *hireq* appears under the prefix every time except in the Impf 1cs, *○⊙○תְאֶ

53.2.4 **Identical parts.** Some parts of the Hithpael will look the same; context will tell how to parse them. For instance:

הִתְקַטֵּל	can be Perf 3ms, Impv ms or an Infinitive
הִתְקַטְּלוּ	can be Perf 3cp or Impv mp

53.2.5 **Movement of the -תְ-.** Sometimes the -תְ- moves so that the word sounds better[5] and can be pronounced more easily. This happens when certain letters come right *after* the -תְ-: especially the "s" letters[6] (שׂ, שׁ, ס and צ) and letters which are similar to the -תְ- (ד, ט and, of course, ת). **This does not change the meaning of the word.**

53.2.5.1 The "s" letters. the -תְ- and "s" letters will sometimes reverse their positions in order to get a better sound. Thus:

from שָׁמַר	we first get הִתְשַׁמֵּר	which then becomes הִשְׁתַּמֵּר
from סָתַר	we first get הִתְסַתֵּר	which then becomes הִסְתַּתֵּר

---

[4] **Technical note:** The Infinitive Absolute occurs extremely infrequently if at all. The most likely possibility is at the end of Numbers 16:13 where the syntax is somewhat unusual: כִּי־תִשְׂתָּרֵר עָלֵינוּ גַּם־הִשְׂתָּרֵר׃

[5] **Technical note:** This is called ▲"euphony," which means "good sound" (from the Greek εὐ and φωνή).

[6] **Technical note:** "S" letters are called ▲"sibilants."

53.2.5.2 The letter צ. The -תְ- moves again, but this time it also changes to a ט:

from צָדַק we first get הִתְצַדֵּק which then becomes הִצְטַדֵּק

53.2.5.3 The letters ד, ט and ת. When these letters appear after the -תְ-, they sometimes swallow (assimilate) it:[7]

from טָהַר we first get הִתְטַהֵר which then becomes הִטַּהֵר

(Note the *dagesh* in the ט, which represents the assimilated ת.)

Again, none of these movements changes the meaning of the word.

In the above example, how can you tell that הִטַּהֵר

(1) is not Hiphil Perfect 3ms, and
(2) is not Niphal Impv ms?

✗ The word *cannot be Hiphil Perfect* because Hiphil never puts a *dagesh* in the first radical. (Hiphil Perf follows the pattern *○ִי○ְ○הִ or *○ִ○ְ○הִ) If טהר had a Hiphil Perfect ms, it would be הִטְהִיר.

✗ The word *cannot be Niphal* because, although Niphal does put a *dagesh* in the first radical, it also puts a *qamets* under it (*○○ָּ○∆). If טהר had a Niph Impv ms, it would be הִטָּהֵר.

Things You Should Know

1. **Hithpael is a reflexive verb form.** The action of the verb goes back to the subject.
2. **Hithpael Perfect, Imperative and Infinitives** have a -הִתְ prefix.
3. **Other parts of the Hithpael** will have different prefixes, and will follow the pattern:

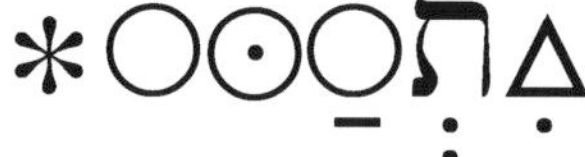

4. The -תְ- will often move if the first radical is an "s" letter (שׂ, שׁ, ס and צ) or a letter which is similar to the -תְ- (ד, ט and, of course, ת). It may switch position (הִשְׁתַּמֵּר), switch position and change to a ט (הִצְטַדֵּק), or be swallowed by the following letter (הִטַּהֵר)

---

[7] **Technical note:** This may also happen with the letter נ. Twice (Jer 23:13; Ezek 37:10) the Hitp of נבא (to prophesy) appears with an assimilation (הִנַּבְּאוּ and הִנַּבֵּאתִי). And the Hitp of נחם appears once (Ezra 5:13) as הִנֶּחָמְתִּי. This will occasionally happen with נשׂא, as well. But **in general the -תְ- will remain in verbs beginning with נ.**

Exercise #35

פלל *Hithp* הִתְפַּלֵּל to pray

פרד *Niph* נִפְרַד to be divided, separated; *Hiph* הִפְרִיד to separate (*tr.*)

צָבָא *m.* army, warfare, *pl.* צְבָאוֹת (sometimes translated "hosts;" יְהוָה צְבָאוֹת = "LORD of hosts," "LORD Almighty")

שׂים *Qal Perf* שָׂם to put, set, place (be sure not to confuse שָׂם with שָׁם or שֵׁם)

שָׁלֵם safe, complete, peaceful

תְּפִלָּה *f.* prayer (√פלל)

[1] גָּדוֹל צְבָא־מִצְרַ֫יִ וַיִּרְדֹּף אַחֲרֵי הָעִבְרִים בְּיוֹם־הַשַּׁבָּת׃ [2] הִתְפַּלְּלָה הָעֵדָה עוֹד
אֶל־יְהוָה־צְבָאוֹת וַיִּשְׁמַע אֶת־תְּפִלָּתָם׃ [3] אַל תַּעֲזֹב אֹתִי וְאַל תִּשְׁכַּח אֶת־נֶפֶשׁ־
עַבְדֶּ֫ךָ׃ [4] וַתִּמְצָא צָרָה אֶת־הָעָם וַיַּפְרִיד אֱלֹהִים אֹתָם מִכֹּל אֹיְבֵיהֶם וּשְׁלֵמִים הֵ֫מָּה׃
[5] יָכְלוּ הַנְּעָרִים הָרְשָׁעִים לִלְכֹּד אֶת־הָעִיר הַקְּטַנָּה וַיִּשְׂרְפוּ אֹתָהּ בָּאֵשׁ׃ [6] גְּדוֹלָה
מְאֹד הַמִּלְחָמָה וַיִּפָּרֵד הַמֶּ֫לֶךְ מִצְּבָאוֹ עַל־שְׂפַת־הַנָּהָר׃ [7] שָׁלֵם הָעָם רַק רָעֵב הוּא
כִּי לֹא הָיָה לָהֶם בָּשָׂר׃ [8] שָׂם אֱלֹהִים אֶת־עֵץ־הַחַ֫יִּים בַּגַּן וְגַם רָאָה הָאִישׁ אֹתוֹ
וְרָעֵב[9] הוּא׃ [9] זָקְנָה הַנְּבִיאָה וַתִּתְפַּלֵּל אֶל־יְהוָה וַיְהַלֵל[8] הָעָם אֶת־שְׁמָהּ׃ [10] שָׂם
אֱלֹהִים אֶת־הַשֶּׁ֫מֶשׁ בַּשָּׁמַ֫יִם וְכֹה הִפְרִיד אֶת־הַיּוֹם וְאֶת־הַלָּ֫יְלָה׃ [11] הֲיַעֲזֹב אֱלֹהִים
אֶת־נֶ֫פֶשׁ־הָרָשָׁע הֲיִשְׁמַע אֶת־תְּפִלּוֹת־שְׂפָתָיו׃ [12] קִדְּשָׁה הָעֵדָה אֶת־חַיֵּיהֶם בְּיוֹם־
הַשַּׁבָּת וַתְּשַׁבַּח אֶת־אֱלֹהֵי־הַצְּדָקָה׃ [13] אִם תַּעֲשִׂי[11] צֶ֫דֶק [10]וְכָבַדְתְּ וְשָׁכַבְתְּ וְיָשַׁנְתְּ
בְּשָׁלוֹם׃ [14] פִּזְּרָה יַד־יְהוָה אֶת־עַם־כְּנַעַן וְעוֹד נָפְלוּ לִפְנֵי הָעִבְרִיִּים׃ [15] מֵת
הַמֶּ֫לֶךְ וְלֹא יָדַע הָעָם וַתִּמְלֹךְ תַּחְתָּיו אַחַת מִבְּנוֹתָיו׃ [16] נָפַל אֶחָד מֵהַנְּבִיאִים עַל
פָּנָיו וַיֹּאמַר יְהַלֵּל[12] כָּל בָּשָׂר אֶת־שֵׁם־יְהוָה׃

---

[8] The *shewa* under the prefix is your clue for parsing this verb. Piel verbs also usually have a *dagesh* in their second root letter, but this *dagesh* is often missing in the Impf of הלל.

[9] Is this a verb plus *w.c.* or an adjective with simple *vav* ? How does the context help you answer this question?

[10] Translate the -וְ as *then*. (See page 143, footnote 18.)

[11] Qal Impf 2fs <עשׂה. **Technical note**: This verb is somewhat difficult to parse. Here are some hints which should help you: **Hint #1:** It is not Hiphil; the *pathah* is found under the prefix because of the guttural. **Hint #2:** The verb root is עשׂה. But ה is a "weak" letter, and has dropped out. Put the ה back in (between the שׂ and the י ; thus: תעשׂהי), and you should recognize the Impf 2fs form. We will study this kind of verb later.

[12] See note 8, above. Should this verb be translated Imperfect or Jussive?

54

THE VERB: A PARSING GUIDE

At the end of the last chapter, you were asked how you could know that הִטַּהֵר was not Hiphil or Niphal. The answer required knowing the patterns *○י○○△ and *○○○△ which were learned earlier. Knowing these patterns is important, and so the complete set of verb parsing guides is reproduced below.

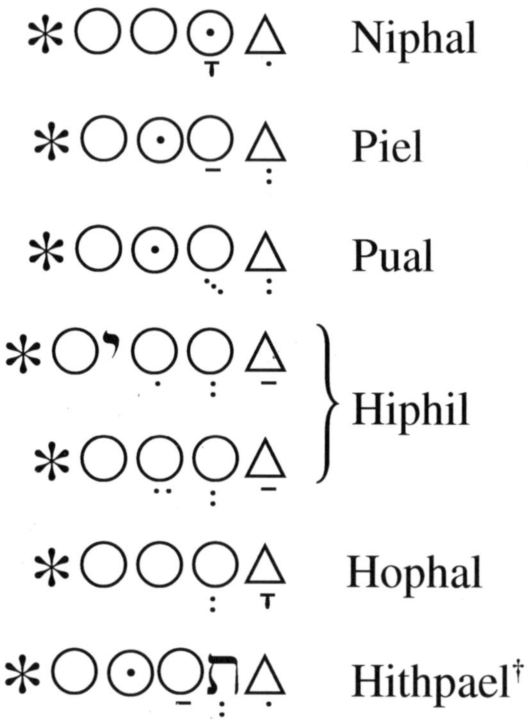

*○○⊙△	Niphal
*○⊙○△	Piel
*○⊙○△	Pual
*○י○○△ / *○○○△	Hiphil
*○○○△	Hophal
*○⊙○תְ△	Hithpael[†]

Participles and Infinitive Constructs:

These forms often have prefixes which will help you recognize them. For instance, all participles *except* Qal and Niphal have a prefixed מ (or מִתְ- in the case of Hithpael). And Infinitive constructs usually have a prefixed preposition: לְ, בְּ, or כְּ; or they may be preceded by another preposition such as לְמַעַן.

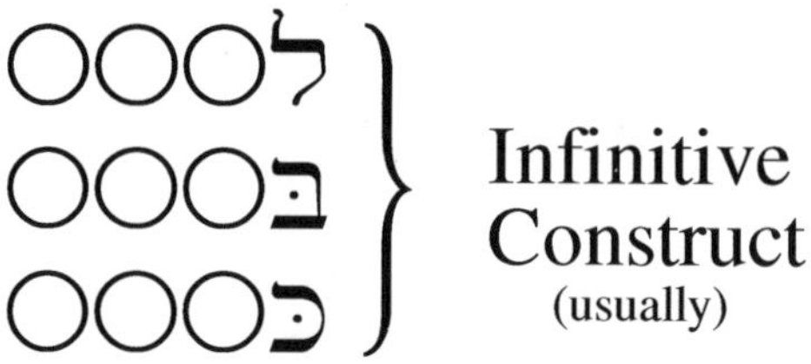

○○○מ Participle
(○○○מִתְ for Hithpael)

○○○לְ
○○○בְּ
○○○כְּ
Infinitive Construct (usually)

[†] Note on Hithpael: The *hireq* under the prefix appears in all forms except the Impf 1cs: *○○○אֶתְ

Above, on the left, are the guides which we have already discussed. Remember that they are for **parts other than the Perfect.** That is, they are for the Imperfect and most cases of the Imperative, Participle and Infinitives. The △ represents the prefix, and the * represents any suffix that might be present.

Learn these guides well. They will help you to parse accurately.

55

THE VERB: PERFECT WITH OBJECT SUFFIXES: QAL

In English, the subject, the verb and the object must each be a separate word: *He ruled them. He* is the subject, *ruled* is the verb, and *them* is the object. As we have seen, however, in Hebrew the subject and the verb are often contained in a single word. For instance, *He ruled them* in Hebrew is: מָלַךְ אֹתָם. The word מָלַךְ is Perf 3ms, and so this single word contains both the verb (*to rule*) and the subject (*he*).

In Hebrew it is also possible to put an *object* suffix on the verb. These suffixes look almost exactly like the possessive suffixes of the noun (review §23). For instance:

ָם + מָלַךְ ➜ מְלָכָם = *he ruled them*

The vowel pointing has changed because the word has become longer. In particular, the *qamets* under the מ has reduced to *shewa* because it has moved further away from the accent.

Study the following chart for the **singular Qal Perfect verb with suffixes**. (The *plural* Qal Perfect verb with suffixes is much simpler.) You already know most of the suffixes. Note, however, that

- the 3ms suffix often has two forms.
- the 1cs suffix is ־נִי not ִי .
- The Perf 1cp (שָׁמַ֫רְנוּ) and the Perf 3ms+1cp (שְׁמָרָ֫נוּ) are very similar in appearance.

55.1 The Qal Perfect Verb in the Singular with Suffixes

	Perf 3ms שָׁמַר	Perf 3fs שָֽׁמְרָה	Perf 2ms שָׁמַ֫רְתָּ	Perf 2fs שָׁמַרְתְּ	Perf 1cs שָׁמַ֫רְתִּי
Suffix 3ms	שְׁמָרוֹ שְׁמָרָ֫הוּ	שְׁמָרַ֫תּוּ שְׁמָרַ֫תְהוּ	שְׁמַרְתּוֹ שְׁמַרְתָּ֫הוּ	שְׁמַרְתִּ֫יהוּ	שְׁמַרְתִּיו שְׁמַרְתִּ֫יהוּ
3fs[1]	שְׁמָרָהּ	שְׁמָרַ֫תָּה	שְׁמַרְתָּהּ	שְׁמַרְתִּ֫יהָ	שְׁמַרְתִּ֫יהָ
2ms	שְׁמָֽרְךָ	שְׁמָרַ֫תְךָ	—	—	שְׁמַרְתִּ֫יךָ
2fs	שְׁמָרֵךְ	שְׁמָרָ֫תֶךְ	—	—	שְׁמַרְתִּיךְ
1cs	שְׁמָרַ֫נִי	שְׁמָרַ֫תְנִי	שְׁמַרְתַּ֫נִי	שְׁמַרְתִּ֫ינִי	—
3mp	שְׁמָרָם	שְׁמָרָ֫תַם	שְׁמַרְתָּם	שְׁמַרְתִּים	שְׁמַרְתִּים
3fp	—	—	—	—	שְׁמַרְתִּין
2mp	—	—	—	—	—
2fp	—	—	—	—	—
1cp	שְׁמָרָ֫נוּ[2]	שְׁמָרַ֫תְנוּ	שְׁמַרְתָּ֫נוּ	שְׁמַרְתִּ֫ינוּ	—

[1] The 3fs suffix loses its *mappiq* whenever the accent moves to the last but one syllable.

[2] *He kept us.* Do not confuse this form with Qal Perf 1cp (no suffix) שָׁמַ֫רְנוּ, *we kept.*

Notes:

1. **Learn the first column of the table**. Watch how suffixes join the verb. This pattern is followed in the other columns. In all cases, when suffixes are added, the first vowel of the word reduces to *shewa* because the word has become longer and the first syllable is further from the accent.

2. **Second person *object* suffixes are based on** כ **(**ךָ**).** But second person verb *subject* suffixes use ת. Thus:

   שָׁמַרְתָּ means *you kept* (תָּ- is the subject)

   שְׁמָרְךָ means *he kept you* (ךָ- is the object)

   This is very similar to the difference between *noun possessive* suffixes and *verb subject* suffixes which you saw in §23.3 (p. 67). Review the box found on p. 68. We can now revise it as follows:

> Nouns & Objects use כ, Verb subjects use ת.
>
> ---
>
> a b c d e f g h i j **K** l m **N O** p q r s **T** u **V** w x y z
> כ (K) → **N**oun   ת (T)→**V**erb subject
> →**O**bject

3. **Columns 2 and 3:** Perf 3fs and Perf 2ms are very similar because the הָ- of the 3fs (שָׁמְרָה) becomes ת when the verb takes suffixes. But the difference is easy to learn. **Listen to the *sound* of the words.** Remember, the letters are just symbols; the *reality* of a language is how it *sounds*:

   In the 3fs and all its suffixed forms, the third radical is at the *beginning* of a syllable (in our example, -רָ = rā-, or -רַ = ra-). Thus, שְׁמָרָה, שְׁמָרַתּוּ, שְׁמָרַתַן, etc. Even with the suffixes, we can hear the *sound* of the original רָה- verb ending.

   In the 2ms and all its suffixed forms, the third radical *closes* a syllable (in our example we find ַרְ- = -ar). Thus, שָׁמַרְתָּ, שְׁמַרְתּוֹ, שְׁמַרְתָּן, etc. Again, even with the suffixes, we can hear the sound of the original verb – in this case the -מַרְ-.

4. **Columns 4 and 5:** Perf 2fs and Perf 1cs are sometimes identical because the תְּ- of the 2fs becomes -תִּי- when the verb takes suffixes. This is only a problem with the third person suffixes, however.

5. **Some suffixed forms do not occur in Biblical Hebrew.** In these cases, there is a dash (—) in the table. This is because we do not say things like *you kept you,* or *I kept me.*

6. **Parsing.** Use a + sign to add the parsing of the object suffix after the rest of the parsing. Thus, parse שְׁמָרַנִי, *he kept me*, as: Qal Perf 3ms+1cs < שׁמר .

55.2 The Qal Perfect Verb in the Plural with Suffixes

As you can see on the next page, the Qal Perfect plural with suffixes has one unusual feature: the 2mp+suffix and 2fp+suffix are the same. Both become -שְׁמַרְתּוּ plus the suffix. Thus, all Perfect plural forms have ו before the suffix: -שְׁמָרוּ (3cp), -שְׁמַרְתּוּ (2m/fp), and -שְׁמַרְנוּ (1cp).

The chart below gives only a few representative examples.

Suffix	Perf 3cp שָֽׁמְרוּ	Perf 2mp or Perf 2fp שְׁמַרְתֶּם or שְׁמַרְתֶּן	Perf 1cp שָׁמַ֫רְנוּ
3ms	שְׁמָר֫וּהוּ	שְׁמַרְתּ֫וּהוּ	שְׁמַרְנ֫וּהוּ
3fs	שְׁמָר֫וּהָ	—	שְׁמַרְנ֫וּהָ
2fs	שְׁמָרוּךְ	—	שְׁמַרְנוּךְ
1cs	שְׁמָר֫וּנִי	שְׁמַרְתּ֫וּנִי	—
3mp	שְׁמָרוּם	שְׁמַרְתּוּם	שְׁמַרְנוּם

Things You Should Know

1. **Verbs can take object suffixes.** These suffixes very similar to the possessive suffixes of the noun. Both use כ (ךָ). The major difference is that the 1cs suffix is נִי- (not ִי-).
2. **The Perfect singular verb** never has a וּ before the suffix.
   a. The 3fs and 2ms with suffixes are similar, and need to be studied carefully. The key is to listen to their *sound*. (See note 3, page 164.)
   b. The 2fs and the 1cs with third person suffixes are identical. Both add suffixes to שְׁמַרְתִּי-. Context will tell you how to translate.
3. **The Perfect plural verb** always has a וּ before the suffix.
   a. 3cp and 1cp do not change their basic form when adding suffixes. They are easy to recognize.
   b. The 2mp and 2fp change to a single common form when they take suffixes: a -וּ- replaces the final ם- or ן-.
4. **Similar forms:** The Qal Perf 1cp (שָׁמַ֫רְנוּ) and the Qal Perf 3ms + 1cp (שְׁמָרָ֫נוּ) are very similar in appearance.

Exercise #36

The following exercises contain only verbs with object suffixes. There are no sentences. Just parse and translate the verbs. The verb קָטַל (*to kill*) is rare but is used at times because it has no weak letter.

[1] שְׁמָרוֹ שְׁמָרָם שְׁמַרְתָּ֫הוּ שְׁמָרַ֫תְהוּ שְׁמַרְתִּ֫יהוּ שְׁמַרְתִּיו שְׁמַרְתָּם שְׁמַרְתִּ֫ינוּ

[2] שְׁמָר֫וּהוּ שְׁמַרְנוּם שְׁמַרְתּ֫וּנִי שְׁמָרוּךְ שְׁמַרְנ֫וּהָ שְׁמָרוּכֶם[3] שְׁמַרְנוּן[3]

[3] קְטַלְתָּם קְטָל֫וּךְ שְׁמַרְנוּכֶן קְטַלְתוּם קְטָלַ֫תְנִי קְטַלְתִּים קְטַלְתּ֫וּהוּ

[4] מְלָכָ֫תַם עֲזַבְנ֫וּךְ שְׁכַחְתָּ֫הּ עֲבָד֫וּנִי בְּחַרְתּ֫וּנוּ רְדַפְתִּין שְׂרָפ֫וּהָ שְׁפָטָ֫נוּ

---

[3] The table in §55.2 gives only a few examples, not all. These two suffixes are not shown there, but you have seen them many times before and should recognize them. More examples are in Table 2 at the end of the book.

56

THE VERB: PERFECT WITH OBJECT SUFFIXES: PIEL AND HIPHIL

In general, only active verbs can have objects. There will not usually be object suffixes on Niphal, Pual, Hophal or Hithpael. Thus, only Qal, Piel and Hiphil verbs will have object suffixes.[1]

The **Piel** will continue to follow the *○ּ○ִ○ pattern[2] which we have already seen. Likewise, the **Hiphil** will continue to follow the *○י○ְ○הִ or *○ַ○ְ○הִ pattern (review the chart on p. 148). In both cases, object suffixes will attach just as they did in the Qal Perfect (§55). Again, we shall give only a few examples:

56.1 Piel

Suffix	Perf 3ms שִׁמֵּר		Perf 3fs שִׁמְּרָה	
3ms	שִׁמְּרוֹ	*he kept him*	שִׁמְּרַתּוּ	*she kept him*
2ms	שִׁמֶּרְךָ	*he kept you(ms)*	שִׁמְּרַתְךָ	*she kept you (ms)*
1cs	שִׁמְּרַנִי	*he kept me*	שִׁמְּרַתְנִי	*she kept me*

56.2 Hiphil

	Perf 3ms הִמְלִיךְ		Perf 3fs הִמְלִיכָה	
3ms	הִמְלִיכוֹ	*he caused him to rule*	הִמְלִיכַתּוּ	*she caused him to rule*
2ms	הִמְלִיכְךָ	*he caused you*(ms) *to rule*	הִמְלִיכַתְךָ	*she caused you*(ms) *to rule*
1cs	הִמְלִיכַנִי	*he caused me to rule*	הִמְלִיכַתְנִי	*she caused me to rule*

56.3 Appearance of *qibbuts*

Sometimes, when suffixes are added to verbs which end with וּ (such as שָׁמְרוּ), the final וּ will reduce to a *qibbuts* (ֻ). Thus, we may see שְׁמָרֻהוּ instead of שְׁמָרוּהוּ.

Thus, there are four places where *qibbuts* may appear in a verb:

*○○○ֻ△ = Hophal (§51.3.2, p. 154)

*○○ֻ○△ = Pual (§49, p. 145)

---

[1] There are some exceptions: for instance, Niphal verbs with active meanings such as לחם can have objects. וַיִּלָּחֲמוּנִי *and they fought me.*

[2] Remember, we are studying Perfect, not Imperfect, and so we will not be seeing the *○○○△ pattern.

*○○ֻ○	= Qal Pass Part (§40; note 3 on p. 118)	
suff + ○ֻ○○△	= suff + וּ○○○△	(often Perf 3cp + suff or Impf 3mp + suff)

56.4 Parsing Verbs with Object Suffixes

When you parse verbs with object suffixes, use a plus sign (+) between the verb and the object suffix:

שְׁמָרַנִי	*He kept me*	is parsed	Qal Perf 3ms + 1cs < שׁמר
הִמְלִיכַתְךָ	*She caused you* (ms) *to rule*	is parsed	Hiph Perf 3fs + 2ms < מלך

Things You Should Know

1. **Review the** Things You Should Know at the end of the last chapter.
2. **Only active verbs (Qal, Piel and Hiphil) will normally take object suffixes.** The Piel and Hiphil will take suffixes in a way very similar to the way the Qal does.
3. **Use a plus sign (+) when parsing** verbs with object suffixes:

   שְׁמָרַנִי = Qal Perf 3ms + 1cs < שׁמר
4. **Appearance of qibbuts.** Know the four places where you may see a *qibbuts* in a verb.

Exercise #37

אָבַד	to become lost; to die (people), to be ruined (things); ***Piel*** אִבַּד ***and Hiph*** הֶאֱבִיד ***both mean*** to destroy completely
אוֹ	or
בּוֹר	*m.* pit, cistern, underground prison cell; *pl.* בּוֹרוֹת
בְּלִי	without; no, no one, nothing
גְּבוּל	boundary, border
גִּבּוֹר	mighty man, hero (in battle), warrior
דּוֹר	*m.* generation, *pl.* דּוֹרוֹת
חוֹמָה	*f.* wall (around a city or building)
כֵּן	so, thus
לָכֵן	therefore
עַל־כֵּן	therefore
סוּס	horse
פְּלִשְׁתִּי	Philistine, *pl.* פְּלִשְׁתִּים

[1] וַיִּמָּלֵט עַד־הַגְּבוּל הַגִּבּוֹר אֲשֶׁר שָׁפַךְ דָּם כֵּן שָׂמוֹ[2] אִישׁ־צַדִּיק בְּבוֹר [1]עַל־חַטָּאתוֹ׃

[2] הָיְתָה הָעִיר בְּלִי חוֹמָה וַיְהִי לָהּ בּוֹר־גָּדוֹל־מָיִם׃ וַיִּהְיוּ[3] שָׁלֵם עִם־הָעִיר וַיֹּאמְרוּ

---

[1] Translate "because of."

[2] Look carefully at this word. It is not שְׁמוֹ, *his name*. Rather, it is the verb שָׂם plus object suffix.

[3] Impf 3mp +wc < היה. The final ה has dropped out from between the י and the וּ.

יְהִי[5] יְהוָה עִמָּנוּ[4] וְיִשְׁמַע אֶת־תְּפִלָּתֵנוּ׃ [3] וַיְמַלֵּט יִצְחָק שָׁלֵם מִן הָעִיר וַיִּפַּלֵּל אֶל־
יְהוָה לֵאמֹר מַלֵּט[6]־נָא אֶת־עַבְדְּךָ מִדּוֹר־הַדָּמִים הַזֶּה׃ [4] עַמִּי בְּלִי דַעַת עַל־כֵּן יִפָּרְדוּ
וְאִבְּדוּם אֹיְבֵיהֶם׃ [5] חָלְמָה הַנְּבִיאָה חֲלוֹם [8]לַיְלָה וַתִּרְאֶה[7] בַּחֲלוֹמָהּ גִּבּוֹרִים אֲשֶׁר
גֻּנְּבוּ סוּסִים וְגַם מְכָרוּם׃ [6] הִמְלִיךְ קְהַל־הָעָם אֶת־דָּוִד וַיֹּאמְרוּ נִתְפַּלְּלָה אֶל־אֱלֹהִים
לְמַעַן מַלְכֵּנוּ׃ וַיִּשְׁמַע אֱלֹהִים אֶת־תְּפִלָּתָם׃ [7] עָבְרוּ צִבְאוֹת־הַפְּלִשְׁתִּים וְסוּסֵיהֶם אֶת־
הַגְּבוּל וְהָעִירָה הָלְכוּ וַיַּשְׁמִדוּ אֶת־חוֹמָתָהּ׃ [8] יַקְהִיל דָּוִד אֶת־יֹשְׁבֵי־הָעִיר בְּשֶׁכֶם
וְחִזְּקָם׃ [9] לָמָּה תִהְיֶה יִרְאָתָם[9] עָלֵינוּ׃ יִהְיֶה כְּבוֹד־יְהוָה־צְבָאוֹת יְשׁוּעָתֵנוּ לָכֵן
נִבְטְחָה בּוֹ׃ [10] שָׁמַע הָעָם[11] אֶת־מוֹת־אֲבִי־שְׁלֹמֹה עַל־כֵּן נִקְהֲלוּ וּבְעֶרֶב קְבָרֻהוּ[10]
בְּקִבְרוֹ׃ [11] וַיִּקָּהֲלוּ אֵלָיו מַלְאָכִים לֵאמֹר מְלָכְנוּ[12] אָבִיךָ בֶּאֱמֶת׃ וְעַתָּה הַחֲזֵק אֶת־
כִּסְאֲךָ וְיֶחֱזַק[14] הַמֶּלֶךְ אוֹ אָבַדְנוּ[13]׃ [12] חָטְאוּ עַמִּי וְכֵן אַבְדִּיל בֵּין אֹתָם וּבֵין הַפְּלִשְׁתִּים
לְדֹרוֹת עוֹלָם׃ וְלֹא יַשְׁמִדוּ׃ [13] וַיֹּאמֶר הַנָּבִיא אֶל הַמֶּלֶךְ הֲלֹא בָטַחְתָּ בַּיהוָה׃ אוֹ
[16]הֲמִבְּלִי אֵין־אֱלֹהִים בְּיִשְׂרָאֵל[15] אַתָּה הֹלֵךְ אַחֲרֵי אֱלֹהִים אֲחֵרִים׃ לָכֵן חָטָאתָ וַאֲבַדְתֶּם
אַתָּה וּצְבָאֶךָ׃ [14] וַיהוָה אָמַר אֶל־אַבְרָם אַחֲרֵי הִפָּרֶד[18]־לוֹט מֵעִמּוֹ רְאֵה[17] נָא מִן־
הַמָּקוֹם אֲשֶׁר־אַתָּה שָׁם כִּי כָל־הָאָרֶץ אֲשֶׁר־אַתָּה רֹאֶה[19] לְךָ תִהְיֶה וּלְזַרְעֲךָ עַד־עוֹלָם׃
[15] אָמַרְתִּי אֶל־הָעָם לֵאמֹר גְּדוֹלָה מְאֹד הַמִּלְחָמָה וַאֲנַחְנוּ נִפְרָדִים עַל־הַחוֹמָה אִישׁ
מֵאָחִיו׃

---

[4] עִם plus suffix.

[5] Imperfect or jussive? How do you know? See also the next verb, וְיִשְׁמַע; does it have w.c. or just a *vav* ?

[6] This verb was learned as Niphal in Exercise 30, but it also comes in Piel. See the Vocabulary list at the end of the book.

[7] The verb is רָאָה. The vowel pointing under the א has changed because of the two weak letters: א and ה.

[8] Add the words "in the." You will often seen just לַיְלָה instead of בַּלַּיְלָה in the Hebrew Bible.

[9] Translate "fear of them" not "their fear."

[10] See §56.3, "Appearance of *kibbuts*," p. 166.

[11] Add *about* or *of* for smoother English translation.

[12] How can you tell that this word is a verb and not a noun? And how can you tell it is not Qal Perf 1cp? See p. 163 if you need help.

[13] Translate in the present tense.

[14] Is this verb Imperfect? Look at the vowel under the -וְ and then review §28.3.2, p. 85.

[15] Add the word *that*.

[16] Translate הֲמִבְּלִי אֵין־: "Is it because there is no...." The first word is בְּלִי plus מִן plus *He* interrogative.

[17] Qal Impv ms.

[18] IC with vowel shortening because the word is in construct. Note the preceding preposition instead of the inseparable preposition -לְ).

[19] Qal Act Part ms.

57

THE VERB: IMPERFECT AND IMPERATIVE WITH OBJECT SUFFIXES

This chapter is similar to the previous one. This time, we add object suffixes to the Imperfect and the Imperative.

57.1 The Qal Imperfect with Object Suffixes

The Imperfect uses the same object suffixes as the Perfect. For instance, the Imperfect 3ms with a 3fs suffix (that is, Impf 3ms + 3fs) is:

ה + יִשְׁמֹר ➜ יִשְׁמְרֶהָ   *He will keep her.*

57.1.1 In the singular: there is sometimes an extra נ[1]. Especially in pause, an extra -נ- is sometimes added between the verb and open suffixes (suffixes ending in vowels: וֹ-, ֶהָ-, ָה-, ךָ- and ֵנִי-):

ה + נ + יִשְׁמֹר ➜ יִשְׁמְרֶנָּה   *He will keep her.*

Thus, Hebrew has two ways to write *He will keep her*: יִשְׁמְרֶהָ and יִשְׁמְרֶנָּה.

Likewise, *He will keep me* (Impf 3ms + 1cs) can be either יִשְׁמְרֵנִי or יִשְׁמְרֶנִּי.

This occasional extra -נ- appears only in the singular.[2]

The 2ms suffix (ךָ-) sometimes swallows the extra נ. This will produce a *dagesh*[3], and so the Impf 3fs + 2ms may also appear as follows:

ךָ + נ + תִּשְׁמֹר ➜ תִּשְׁמְרֶנְךָ ➜ תִּשְׁמְרֶךָּ   *She will keep you* (ms).

Thus, Hebrew also has two ways to write *She will keep you*: תִּשְׁמָרְךָ (note *qamets-hatuph*) and תִּשְׁמְרֶךָּ. Both are parsed Impf 3fs + 2ms.

57.1.2 In the plural: The Impf 3/2fp (תִּשְׁמֹרְנָה) also does something very unusual. Its נָה- ending becomes -וּ- when it takes suffixes.[4] For instance, the Impf 3/2fp takes a 3ms suffix as follows:

הוּ + תִּשְׁמֹרְנָה ➜ הוּ + תִּשְׁמְרוּ ➜ תִּשְׁמְרוּהוּ

This means that Impf 3/2 fp (תִּשְׁמֹרְנָה) with suffixes will look exactly like Impf 2mp (תִּשְׁמְרוּ) with suffixes.

---

[1] **Technical note:** This extra *nun* is sometimes called *nun energic*.

[2] But it does not appear in the 2fs.

[3] A *dagesh* is often produced when a letter is "swallowed" (assimilated). We have already seen this when the word מִן joins the word after it, as in: מֶלֶךְ + מִן ➜ מִמֶּלֶךְ. We have also seen it in Niphal Imperfect.

[4] ָה endings cannot take suffixes. This is similar to what we saw in the Perfect with the 2mp/2fp (see p. 164).

Now, study the following table which shows the object suffixes (left column) which are then added to **Impf 3ms** (basic form and with -נ-), **Impf 3mp** and **Impf 2mp or Impf 3/2fp**.

	———Impf 3ms———		Impf 3mp	Impf 2mp or 3/2fp
	Basic form	with -נ-		
Suffix	יִשְׁמֹר	-יִשְׁמְרֶנּ	יִשְׁמְרוּ	תִּשְׁמֹ֫רְנָה, תִּשְׁמְרוּ
3ms	יִשְׁמְרֵ֫הוּ	יִשְׁמְרֶ֫נּוּ	יִשְׁמְר֫וּהוּ[5]	תִּשְׁמְר֫וּהוּ
3fs	יִשְׁמְרֶ֫הָ[6]	יִשְׁמְרֶ֫נָּה	יִשְׁמְר֫וּהָ	תִּשְׁמְר֫וּהָ
2ms	יִשְׁמָרְךָ[7]	יִשְׁמְרֶ֫ךָּ	יִשְׁמְר֫וּךָ	—
2fs	יִשְׁמְרֵךְ	—	יִשְׁמְרוּךְ	—
1cs	יִשְׁמְרֵ֫נִי	יִשְׁמְרֶ֫נִּי	יִשְׁמְר֫וּנִי	תִּשְׁמְר֫וּנִי
3mp	יִשְׁמְרֵם	—	יִשְׁמְרוּם	תִּשְׁמְרוּם
3fp	יִשְׁמְרֵן	—	יִשְׁמְרוּן	תִּשְׁמְרוּן
2mp	יִשְׁמָרְכֶם	—	יִשְׁמְרוּכֶם	—
2fp	יִשְׁמָרְכֶן	—	יִשְׁמְרוּכֶן	—
1cp	יִשְׁמְרֵ֫נוּ[8]	—	יִשְׁמְר֫וּנוּ	תִּשְׁמְר֫וּנוּ

57.2 The Piel and Hiphil Imperfect with Object Suffixes

Again, only active verbs can have objects.[9] Thus, in addition to the Qal, only the Piel and Hiphil will have object suffixes. However, neither the Piel nor the Hiphil will have the extra -נ-. This means that their paradigms are simpler than the Qal Impf. Again, we shall give only a few examples:

Suffix	**Piel Impf 3fs** תְּשַׁמֵּר		**Hiphil Impf 3ms** יַמְלִיךְ	
3ms	תְּשַׁמְּרֵ֫הוּ	*she will completely keep him*	יַמְלִיכֵ֫הוּ	*he will cause him to rule*
2ms	תְּשַׁמֶּרְךָ	*she will completely keep you(ms)*	יַמְלִיכְךָ	*he will cause you*(ms) *to rule*
3mp	תְּשַׁמְּרֵם	*she will completely keep them*	יַמְלִיכֵם	*he will cause them to rule*

5 The verbs in this column can also take the form יִשְׁמְרֻ֫הוּ, יִשְׁמְרֻ֫הָ, etc. Review §56.3, p. 166.

6 Also found as יִשְׁמְרָהּ .

7 In this column, every *qamets* under a מ is a *qamets-hatuph.*

8 Compare this form to Impf 3ms+3ms with -נ- (יִשְׁמְרֶ֫נּוּ).

9 Remember, though, that some Niphal verbs can have active meanings, and thus may have suffixes. Review footnote 1, p. 166.

57.3 The Imperative with Object Suffixes

The following chart shows the most common forms of the Imperative with object suffixes.

	Qal שְׁמֹר		**Piel** שַׁמֵּר		**Hiphil** הַשְׁמֵר	
Impv ms + 3ms	שָׁמְרֵהוּ	*keep him*	שַׁמְּרֵהוּ	*keep him*	הַשְׁמִירֵהוּ	*make him keep*
Impv ms + 3fs	שָׁמְרָהּ	*keep her*	שַׁמְּרָהּ	*keep her*	הַשְׁמִירָהּ	*make her keep*
Impv ms + 1cs	שָׁמְרֵנִי	*keep me*	שַׁמְּרֵנִי	*keep me*	הַשְׁמִירֵנִי	*make me keep*
Impv ms + 3mp	שָׁמְרֵם	*keep them*	שַׁמְּרֵם	*keep them*	הַשְׁמִירֵם	*make them keep*
Impv **mp** + 3ms	שִׁמְרוּהוּ	*keep him*	שַׁמְּרוּהוּ	*keep him*	הַשְׁמִירוּהוּ	*make him keep*
Impv **mp** + 3fs	שִׁמְרוּהָ	*keep her*	—		הַשְׁמִירוּהָ	*make her keep*
Impv **mp** + 1cs	שִׁמְרוּנִי	*keep me*	שַׁמְּרוּנִי	*keep me*	הַשְׁמִירוּנִי	*make me keep*
Impv **mp** + 3mp	שִׁמְרוּם	*keep them*	—		—[10]	

Notes:

1. The imperative with object suffixes is found only in Qal, Piel and Hiphil.
2. Note the *qamets-hatuph* in the Qal singular imperatives.
3. The Impv+1cp will look just like the Impv+1cs, except that נוּ- will replace נִי-.
4. There are no cases of Impv ms+3fp or Impv mp+3fp.
5. Feminine imperatives with suffixes are very rare in the OT.[11]
6. Adding suffixes makes verbs longer. Vowel shortening may occur (see the note on Vowel Reduction on p. 72). Vowels at the beginning of the word may reduce to *shewa*. You can see this in the Qal plural imperatives, where the following has occured: שָׁמְרוּהוּ → שְׁמְרוּהוּ → שִׁמְרוּהוּ. This may also occur occasionally in the Hiphil prefix (an example may be seen in footnote 11, below).

Things You Should Know

1. Like the Perfect, the Imperfect can also take object suffixes. Again, only the active verb forms (Qal, Piel and Hiphil) will take these suffixes.
2. The Qal Imperfect singular forms will sometimes have an extra *nun* between the verb and the object suffix.

---

[10] **Technical note:** The only example of Hiph Impv mp + 3ms in the OT is הַכּוּם < נכה (2 Kgs 10:25).

[11] **Technical note:** The only cases are the Hiph Impv fs + 1cs (הַשְׁמִיעִנִי < שׁמע, הַשְׁקִינִי < שׁקה, הַגְמִיאִינִי < גמא) and the Hiph Impv fs + 3ms (הֵינִקֵהוּ < ינק).

58

NUMBERS

Hebrew, like English, has both counting numbers (1, 2, 3, etc.) and ordering numbers (first, second, third, etc.).[1]

58.1 Counting numbers

Hebrew counting numbers are nouns (except for the number *one*, which is an adjective). Thus, they will be masculine or feminine, and will have absolute and construct states like other nouns. Perhaps the most unusual feature is that (for numbers greater than 2) feminine numbers are used with masculine nouns, and masculine numbers are used with feminine nouns.[2]

The number *two* itself is unusual. Rather than having a feminine and a masculine form, there is simply a difference in spelling: the letter נ changes to תּ when the number is used with feminine nouns.

Hebrew also uses individual letters of the alphabet to represent numbers. In the table below, the two center columns show western[3] numbers and the Hebrew letters which represent the numbers. They are printed here for your interest and later use; it is not necessary to learn them.

Used with masculine nouns				Used with feminine nouns	
Absolute	*Construct*			*Absolute*	*Construct*
אֶחָד, אַחַד	אַחַד	1	א	אַחַת	אַחַת
שְׁנַיִם	שְׁנֵי	2	ב	שְׁתַּיִם	שְׁתֵּי
שְׁלֹשָׁה	שְׁלֹשֶׁת	3	ג	שָׁלֹשׁ	שְׁלֹשׁ
אַרְבָּעָה	אַרְבַּעַת	4	ד	אַרְבַּע	אַרְבַּע
חֲמִשָּׁה	חֲמֵשֶׁת	5	ה	חָמֵשׁ	חֲמֵשׁ
שִׁשָּׁה	שֵׁשֶׁת	6	ו	שֵׁשׁ	שֵׁשׁ
שִׁבְעָה	שִׁבְעַת	7	ז	שֶׁבַע	שְׁבַע
שְׁמֹנָה	שְׁמֹנַת	8	ח	שְׁמֹנֶה	שְׁמֹנֶה
תִּשְׁעָה	תִּשְׁעַת	9	ט	תֵּשַׁע	תְּשַׁע
עֲשָׂרָה	עֲשֶׂרֶת	10	י	עֶשֶׂר	עֶשֶׂר

[1] **Technical note:** Counting numbers are called *cardinals*, and ordering numbers are called *ordinals*.

[2] **Technical note:** Actually, what is happening is this: the basic form of the numbers three through ten is feminine. This basic form is used with the masculine nouns. Another form was thus needed to use with feminine nouns. This other form (which appears in the two columns on the right) is not technically masculine. It is simply the original (feminine) form with its הָ removed (along with some resulting vowel changes) in order to have a different form for use with feminine nouns.

[3] **Technical note:** Actually, these "western" numbers (1, 2, 3, 4, etc.) were developed by the Arabs and are known as "Arabic numerals," as opposed to the Roman style of numbers I, II, III, IV, etc.

The number 2 will either be used

- as an *absolute* noun after another noun: בָּנוֹת שְׁתַּיִם = *daughters, two = two daughters* or
- in *construct* with the noun: שְׁתֵּי־בָנוֹת = *two-of-daughters = two daughters.*

The numbers 3-10 are used in the same way (בָּנוֹת שָׁלֹשׁ or שְׁלֹשׁ בָּנוֹת), although the absolute form can sometimes appear before the noun (שָׁלֹשׁ בָּנוֹת = *three, daughters = three daughters*).

The numbers 11-19 combine a slightly different form of the number ten (עָשָׂר masculine or עֶשְׂרֵה feminine) with one of the other numbers (again, using masculine or feminine). Note the alternative forms for the numbers 11 and 12.

Used with masculine nouns			Used with feminine nouns
אַחַד עָשָׂר / עַשְׁתֵּי עָשָׂר	11	יא	אַחַת עֶשְׂרֵה / עַשְׁתֵּי עֶשְׂרֵה
שְׁנֵים עָשָׂר / שְׁנֵי עָשָׂר	12	יב	שְׁתֵּים עֶשְׂרֵה / שְׁתֵּי עֶשְׂרֵה
שְׁלֹשָׁה עָשָׂר	13	יג	שְׁלֹשׁ עֶשְׂרֵה
אַרְבָּעָה עָשָׂר	14	יד	אַרְבַּע עֶשְׂרֵה
חֲמִשָּׁה עָשָׂר	15	יה	חֲמֵשׁ עֶשְׂרֵה
שִׁשָּׁה עָשָׂר	16	יו	שֵׁשׁ עֶשְׂרֵה
שִׁבְעָה עָשָׂר	17	יז	שְׁבַע עֶשְׂרֵה
שְׁמֹנָה עָשָׂר	18	יח	שְׁמֹנֶה עֶשְׂרֵה
תִּשְׁעָה עָשָׂר	19	יט	תְּשַׁע עֶשְׂרֵה

For 11-19, there is not an absolute and a construct form of each number. With masculine nouns, the masculine number עָשָׂר (ten) is used with an *absolute* form of one of the numbers from 1 to 9 (thus the number 13 is שְׁלֹשָׁה עָשָׂר). With feminine nouns, the feminine number עֶשְׂרֵה (ten) is used with a *construct* form of one of the numbers from 1 to 9 (thus 13 is שְׁלֹשׁ עֶשְׂרֵה).

The number 20 is the plural of the number 10. **The numbers 30, 40, 50, 60, etc.** are the plurals of the numbers 3, 4, 5, 6, etc. These numbers are joined to the units by the letter ו (עֶשְׂרִים וְאֶחָד, etc.).

Numbers such as 21 or 22 are sometimes written twenty-and-one, twenty-and-two, etc. At other times they are written one-and twenty, two-and-twenty, etc.[4] One example of each is given below. Thus:

עֶשְׂרִים	20	כ	חֲמִשִּׁים	50	נ
עֶשְׂרִים וְאֶחָד	21	כא	שִׁשִּׁים	60	ס
שְׁנַיִם וְעֶשְׂרִים	22	כב	שִׁבְעִים	70	ע
שְׁלֹשִׁים	30	ל	שְׁמֹנִים	80	פ
אַרְבָּעִים	40	מ	תִּשְׁעִים	90	צ

[4] **Technical note:** The earlier writings of the Old Testament will use the order twenty-and-one; the later writings reverse that order and use one-and-twenty. For details, see *Gesenius' Hebrew Grammar* §134*h*.

The **hundreds** and **thousands**: The numbers 200 and 2000 are duals based upon 100 and 1000. (Compare to the number 20, which is the plural of 10.) Larger numbers such as 300, 400, 3000, 4000, are written with a singular construct and a plural absolute: *three-of-hundreds, four-of-thousands,* etc.

With **large numbers** such as 2,345, the thousands will almost always come first, and the hundreds will usually come before the smaller numbers. Thus 7,337 will usually be written *seven-of-thousands three-of-hundreds thirty-and-seven*: שִׁבְעַת אֲלָפִים שְׁלֹשׁ מֵאוֹת שְׁלֹשִׁים וְשִׁבְעָה (Neh 7:67).[5]

מֵאָה	100	ק	אֶ֫לֶף	1,000
מָאתַ֫יִם	200	ר	אַלְפַּ֫יִם	2,000
שְׁלֹשׁ מֵאוֹת	300	ש	שְׁלֹ֫שֶׁת אֲלָפִים	3,000
אַרְבַּע מֵאוֹת	400	ת	אַרְבַּ֫עַת אֲלָפִים	4,000
חֲמֵשׁ מֵאוֹת	500		חֲמֵ֫שֶׁת אֲלָפִים	5,000
שֵׁשׁ מֵאוֹת	600		שֵׁ֫שֶׁת אֲלָפִים	6,000
שְׁבַע מֵאוֹת	700		שִׁבְעַת אֲלָפִים	7,000
שְׁמֹנֶה מֵאוֹת	800		שְׁמֹנַת אֲלָפִים	8,000
תְּשַׁע מֵאוֹת	900		תִּשְׁעַת אֲלָפִים	9,000
			עֲשֶׂ֫רֶת אֲלָפִים *or* רְבָבָה	10,000

Occasional use of singular nouns. Numbers are usually found with plural nouns. But there are some exceptions. The nouns אִישׁ (*man*), יוֹם (*day*), נֶ֫פֶשׁ (*life force, person*), שָׁנָה (*year*) and collective nouns[6] such as בָּקָר (*cows, cattle*) and צֹאן (*small cattle, sheep, goats*) may appear in the singular. For example, אַחַד עָשָׂר אִישׁ means *eleven men*. Another example:

חֲמִשָּׁה בָקָר ... תַּ֫חַת הַשּׁוֹר וְאַרְבַּע־צֹאן תַּ֫חַת הַשֶּׂה׃

"five oxen . . . in place of the ox and four sheep in place of the sheep"[7] (Exod 21:37 [22:1 in English versions[8]]).

Age. A person who is *X* years old is called "a son of *X* years." Thus, בֶּן־שִׁשִּׁים שָׁנָה הוּא means "He was sixty years old."

58.2 Ordering numbers

Hebrew ordering numbers (*first, second, third*, etc.) are adjectives, and thus are masculine or feminine. The word רִאשׁוֹן (*first*) comes from the word רֹאשׁ (*head*). The other ordering numbers are based upon the counting numbers. The most common characteristic is the double *hireq-yod* (ִי) found in all the ordering numbers except *first, second* and *sixth*. Thus, *five* is חֲמִשָּׁה, but *fifth* is חֲמִישִׁי. Note that the

---

[5] There are, of course, exceptions. In Numbers 3:50 we find the number 1,365 written in "backwards" order as חֲמִשָּׁה וְשִׁשִּׁים וּשְׁלֹשׁ מֵאוֹת וָאֶ֫לֶף.

[6] A collective noun is a word which is used in the singular, although it refers to a group (collection) of things. Examples in English would be: family, company, committee.

[7] **Technical note:** שׁוֹר means *ox*, but בָּקָר is often used for the collective noun *oxen*, as in this sentence. Likewise, שֶׂה means "(a single) sheep," and צֹאן is often used to mean the collective "(many) sheep."

[8] **Technical note:** Sometimes the verses in the Hebrew are different from the verses in the English translations. In this case, there are 37 verses in chapter 21 in the Hebrew, but only 26 verses in the English. Thus, 21:37 in the Hebrew is the same as 22:1 in the English.

words for *fourth* have lost their initial א (*four* = אַרְבָּעָה, but *fourth* = רְבִיעִי).

Masculine		*Feminine*
רִאשׁוֹן	**First**	רִאשׁוֹנָה
שֵׁנִי	**Second**	שֵׁנִית
שְׁלִישִׁי	**Third**	שְׁלִישִׁית
רְבִיעִי	**Fourth**	רְבִיעִית
חֲמִישִׁי	**Fifth**	חֲמִישִׁית
שִׁשִּׁי	**Sixth**	שִׁשִּׁית
שְׁבִיעִי	**Seventh**	שְׁבִיעִית
שְׁמִינִי	**Eighth**	שְׁמִינִית
תְּשִׁיעִי	**Ninth**	תְּשִׁיעִית
עֲשִׂירִי	**Tenth**	עֲשִׂירִית

There are only ten ordering numbers, *first* through *tenth*. Hebrew uses the counting numbers for numbers higher than *tenth*. Thus יוֹם רְבִיעִי *a fourth day* (Gen 1:19), but שִׁבְעָה־עָשָׂר יוֹם *seventeenth day* (literally *seventeen, day*) (Gen 7:11).

A common phrase such as *On the fifth month, on the seventh day of the month* is written in various ways. One common way is בַּחֹדֶשׁ הַחֲמִישִׁי בְּשִׁבְעָה לַחֹדֶשׁ. Note that, in this case, a counting number has been used for the day, rather than an ordering number. That is, literally *in-seven of* (לְ) *the month* rather than *in-seventh of the month*.

Things You Should Know

1. Hebrew has both counting numbers (one, two, three, etc.) and ordering numbers (first, second, third, etc.). These numbers are masculine or feminine, and the lower counting numbers are also absolute or construct.
2. The counting numbers are nouns. They will usually appear in absolute form after another noun (בָּנוֹת שָׁלֹשׁ), or in construct form before the noun (שְׁלֹשׁ בָּנוֹת).
3. The numbers 11-19 combine a form of the number 10 with one of the other numbers. שִׁשָּׁה עָשָׂר = 16. There are no construct forms for these numbers.
4. The number 20 is the plural of the number 10. The numbers 30-90 are the plurals of the numbers 3-9.
5. A person who is *X* years old is called "a son of *X* years." בֶּן־שִׁשִּׁים שָׁנָה הוּא
6. Ordering numbers are adjectives. There are ten ordering numbers, *first* through *tenth*. After *tenth*, the counting numbers are used. יוֹם רְבִיעִי *a fourth day*, but שִׁבְעָה־עָשָׂר יוֹם *seventeenth day*.

Exercise #38

Learn the numbers from the lesson. In addition, learn the words below, noting especially those which are very similar.

- אָמָה *f.* female slave (note *pl.* אֲמָהוֹת)
- אַמָּה *f.* cubit (50 cm) (*pl.* אַמּוֹת, *du.* אַמָּתַיִם)
- חָדָשׁ new, fresh
- חֹדֶשׁ month, new moon
- פַּעַם time (occurrence), footstep; פַּעֲמַיִם twice
- שָׁנָה *f.* year, *cs* שְׁנַת; *pl.* שָׁנִים, *cs.* שְׁנֵי

[1] שִׁבְעָה: שְׁמֹנֶה: חֲמִשָּׁה: שָׁלֹשׁ: עֶשְׂרִים וְתֵשַׁע: תִּשְׁעָה עָשָׂר: אַרְבָּעִים וְאַחַת:
שְׁלֹשׁ מֵאָה שִׁשִּׁים וּשְׁנַיִם: אֶלֶף וּמָאתַיִם: אַלְפַּיִם וּמֵאָה: שֵׁשׁ מֵאוֹת חֲמִשִּׁים וְאַרְבַּע:
שִׁבְעַת אֲלָפִים: אַרְבָּעָה וְשִׁשִּׁים אֶלֶף וּשְׁלֹשׁ מֵאוֹת: שֵׁשׁ־אַמּוֹת: חֲמֵשׁ עֶשְׂרֵה אַמָּה[9]:
שְׁלֹשִׁים וְאַחַת שָׁנִים: אַרְבָּעִים וּשְׁתַּיִם שָׁנָה[10]:

[2] קַיִן הַבְּכוֹר וְהוּא הָרַג אֶת־אָחִיהוּ אֲשֶׁר רֹעֵה־צֹאן הוּא: [3] כֵּן תַּעֲשֶׂה[12] אֹתָהּ[11]
שְׁלֹשׁ מֵאוֹת אַמָּה[17] אֹרֶךְ[16] הַתֵּבָה[15] חֲמִשִּׁים אַמָּה רָחְבָּהּ[14] וּשְׁלֹשִׁים אַמָּה קוֹמָתָהּ[13]:
[4] וַיִּהְיוּ[19] כָּל־מִסְפַּר[18] בְּנֵי־יִשְׂרָאֵל הַיֹּצְאִים מִמִּצְרַיִם שֵׁשׁ־מֵאוֹת אֶלֶף וּשְׁלֹשֶׁת
אֲלָפִים וַחֲמֵשׁ מֵאוֹת וַחֲמִשִּׁים: [5] עָבְרוּ אֶת־הַגְּבוּל בְּרַגְלֵיהֶם גִּבּוֹרֵי־הַפְּלִשְׁתִּים
שְׁתֵּי מֵאוֹת שִׁשִּׁים וַחֲמִשָּׁה וַיִּסָּתְרוּ בֶּהָרִים: [6] וּבְיוֹם הַשַּׁבָּת נִלְחֲמוּ בָעִבְרִים
וַיִּצְעֲקוּ הָעִבְרִים אֶל־יְהוָה לֵאמֹר לֹא תַעַזְבֵנוּ[21] לַדּוֹר הָרָע הַזֶּה: [7] בֶּן[20]־שְׁלֹשִׁים
שָׁנָה[22] דָּוִד כִּי הָמְלַךְ וְאַרְבָּעִים שָׁנָה מָלָךְ: מָלַךְ עַל־יְהוּדָה שֶׁבַע שָׁנִים וְשִׁשָּׁה
חֳדָשִׁים וּבִירוּשָׁלַם מָלַךְ שְׁלֹשִׁים וְשָׁלֹשׁ שָׁנָה עַל כָּל־יִשְׂרָאֵל וִיהוּדָה: [8] וְהַיָּמִים

---

[9] The singular אַמָּה is very often used when we would expect to see the plural אַמּוֹת. Here, translate as if it were in the plural.

[10] The singular form of שָׁנָה is usually used, even though we would expect to see the plural.

[11] Translate *it*, not *her*.

[12] Two changes have occurred in this weak verb. The final ה has brought in the *shewa*, and the ע has attracted *pathahs*. Thus, it is simply a Qal Imperfect (not Hiphil, in spite of the *pathah* under the prefix).

[13] קוֹמָה means *height*.

[14] רֹחַב means *width*.

[15] תֵּבָה means Noah's ark, as found in Genesis 6-9.

[16] אֹרֶךְ means *length*.

[17] See footnote 9, above.

[18] מִסְפָּר (√ספר) means *number*.

[19] Shortened imperfect of הָיָה.

[20] See the note on "Age" on p. 174.

[21] 2ms + suffix. (The guttural has attracted *pathahs*.)

[22] See footnote 10, above.

אֲשֶׁר מָלַךְ יָרָבְעָם[24] עֶשְׂרִים וּשְׁתַּיִם שָׁנָה וַיִּשְׁכַּב עִם־אֲבֹתָיו וַיִּמְלֹךְ נָדָב[23] בְּנוֹ
תַּחְתָּיו׃ וּרְחַבְעָם[25] בֶּן־שְׁלֹמֹה מָלַךְ בִּיהוּדָה בֶּן־אַרְבָּעִים וְאַחַת שָׁנָה רְחַבְעָם
[26]בְּמָלְכוֹ וּשְׁבַע עֶשְׂרֵה שָׁנָה מָלַךְ בִּירוּשָׁלָםִ׃ [9] בָּאוּ גִּבּוֹרֵי־הַפְּלִשְׁתִּים בְּלִי סוּסִים
וְכֵן לֹא יָכְלוּ לְהִמָּלֵט׃ וַיִּצְעֲקוּ לֵאמֹר וְעַתָּה אָבְדוּ חַיֵּינוּ[28] וְיָרְדוּ נַפְשֵׁנוּ [27] בּוֹר׃
[10] וַיִּהְיוּ[29] גַּנִּים אַרְבָּעָה לִשְׁתֵּים־עֶשְׂרֵה־אֲמָהוֹת וַיִּהְיוּ הַגַּנִּים אַמּוֹת עֶשְׂרִים מִן
חוֹמַת־הָעִיר׃ וְיוֹם בְּיוֹם עֲבָדוּם וַתִּשְׁמְרֻם[30]׃ [11] בָּא צְבָא־מִצְרַיִם עִם תִּשְׁעִים
אֲלָפִים תְּשַׁע מֵאוֹת וּשְׁמֹנִים אִישׁ[31] וְשָׁלֹשׁ פְּעָמִים נָפְלוּ הָעָם לִפְנֵיהֶם׃ [12] נָתַן
הַנָּבִיא עֵצָה אֶל־הָעָם לֵאמֹר שִׁלְחוּ מְרַגְּלִים לְמִצְרַיִם רַק שִׁלְחוּ אֹתָם עִם מִנְחוֹת׃
[13] וַיִּשְׁאָלוּם הַמִּצְרַיִם שָׁלֹשׁ פְּעָמִים לֵאמֹר מִי אַתֶּם וְאֵי עָרֵיכֶם[32]׃ [14] וַיֹּאמְרוּ
הַמְרַגְּלִים אָבְדָה חוֹמוֹת־עָרֵינוּ לָכֵן בָּאנוּ[34] אֲלֵיכֶם כִּי עַם־מִשְׁפָּט אַתֶּם׃ [33]וְנֹאכְלָה־
נָּא בָשָׂר אוֹ יֹרְדִים בּוֹר חַיֵּינוּ׃ [15] בָּאוּ הַמְרַגְּלִים עוֹד אֶל־עַמָּם וַיְסַפְּרוּ־לָהֶם
לֵאמֹר עוֹד הַמִּצְרַיִם עַל גְּבוּלֵנוּ׃ [16] אֱלֹהִים נָתַן לָנוּ אֶת־הָאָרֶץ הַזֹּאת עַל־כֵּן
אֵלֶּה גְּבוּלֵנוּ לְדוֹר וָדוֹר׃ [17] בָּחֹדֶשׁ הַשְּׁמִינִי בִּתְשְׁעָה לַחֹדֶשׁ בָּאוּ אֲמָהוֹת אַרְבַּע
פְּעָמִים[37] לִמְכֹּר פְּרִי חָדָשׁ׃ בְּחָרוּהוּ מֵעֲצֵי־גַנָּן[36] וַתִּמְכְּרֻהוּ[35] בָּעִיר כֵּן יֵשׁ לָהֶן כֶּסֶף
וְזָהָב׃ [18] רָעֵבָה עֲדַת־הָעָם מִבְּלִי[38] לָחֶם׃

---

[23] *Nadab* (a man's name).

[24] *Jeroboam.*

[25] *Rehoboam.*

[26] Translate "when he began to rule." We will study this form in the next chapter. (It is an IC with prefix and suffix. Note the *qamets-hatuph.*)

[27] Add the words "to the."

[28] חַיִּים: construct plus suffix.

[29] Impf 3mp < היה. Translate "and there were."

[30] Note the *qibbuts*. What does it represent? See §56.3, p. 166, if you are unsure.

[31] For the use of the singular here, see "Occasional Use of Singular Nouns" on p. 174.

[32] The root of this word is עִיר.

[33] This is a cohortative of the verb אָכַל (an Impf + w.c. would have a *pathah* under the ו and a *dagesh* in the נ). The א has caused the vowel pointing to change.

[34] Qal Perf 1cp < בָּא

[35] See footnote 30, above, and also the note on Impf 2/3p plus suffixes on p. 169.

[36] Noun plus plural suffix.

[37] Did the women return four times, or were there four women? How do you know?

[38] Translate "because they had no." Literally "from lack of."

59

THE INFINITIVE CONSTRUCT WITH SUFFIXES

The Infinitive Construct (IC) can also take suffixes (וֹ- + שְׁמֹר → שָׁמְרוֹ ; note the *qamets-hatuph*). In this case, however, the suffixes may mean either object *or subject*. That is, שָׁמְרוֹ can mean either *keeping him* (object, where *him* means the one who is kept) or *his keeping* (subject, where *he* is the one who keeps). In the 1cs, there are actually two separate suffix forms for these two meanings:

- the suffix נִי- : שָׁמְרֵנִי *keeping me* (do not confuse this with the Perf 3ms + 1cs שְׁמָרַנִי)
- the suffix ִי - : שָׁמְרִי *my keeping*

In all the other cases, the IC + suffix may mean *either subject or object*. This includes the 2ms and 2mp, where each of the two forms has both possible meanings.

59.1 The Infinitive Construct with suffixes

3ms	שָׁמְרוֹ	either *keeping him* or *his keeping*
3fs	שָׁמְרָהּ	either *keeping her* or *her keeping*
2ms	שְׁמָרְךָ *or* שָׁמְרְךָ	either *keeping you (ms)* or *your (ms) keeping*
2fs	שָׁמְרֵךְ	either *keeping you (fs)* or *your (fs) keeping*
1cs	שָׁמְרֵנִי	*keeping me*
	שָׁמְרִי	*my keeping*
3mp	שָׁמְרָם	either *keeping them (m)* or *their (m) keeping*
3fp	שָׁמְרָן	either *keeping them (f)* or *their (f) keeping*
2mp	שְׁמָרְכֶם *or* שָׁמְרְכֶם	either *keeping you (mp)* or *your (mp) keeping*
2fp	שָׁמְרְכֶן	either *keeping you (fp)* or *your (fp) keeping*
1cp	שָׁמְרֵנוּ	either *keeping us* or *our keeping*

Notes:

1. These are almost identical to the Qal Impv ms + suffix. (Remember that the IC usually looks the same as the Impv ms.) Again, the *qamets* in the first syllable is *qamets-hatuph*.
2. In the second person, the pattern is sometimes different. There may be a *shewa* under the first letter, and the *qamets-hatuph* then comes under the second letter.
3. In derived forms (Niphal, Piel, Pual, etc.), the IC+suffix will be the same as the Impv ms + suffix.

59.2 The Infinitive Construct plus prepositions and suffixes

Usually, the IC + suffix will also have a -בְּ or -כְּ or -לְ prefix. For instance, in §29.2, p. 90, we learned that the IC often combines with the inseparable preposition -לְ to give the sense of the English infinitive:

שְׁמֹר + לְ → לִשְׁמֹר = *to keep*

When the IC + suffix takes the inseparable prepositions -בְּ or -כְּ, these prepositions are translated *when*. For instance, the phrase *when he captured* can be written either:

	בְּ- + לְכֹד + וֹ	➔ בְּ- + לָכְדוֹ	➔ בְּלָכְדוֹ
or	כְּ- + לְכֹד + וֹ	➔ כְּ- + לָכְדוֹ	➔ כְּלָכְדוֹ

This construction may be used in several ways. The examples below use -בְּ, but -כְּ can also be used:

בְּלָכְדוֹ אֹתִי	*when-he-captured me . . . .*
וַיְהִי[1] בִלְכֹד הָאִישׁ אֹתָם	*and-it-happened-that, when the man captured them, . . .*
וְהָיָה בְּלָכְדְכֶן אֹתָנוּ	*and-it-will-happen-that, when you capture us, . . .*

Other prepositions may also be used with the IC. In this case, the IC and its suffix may stand alone.

לִפְנֵי לָכְדִי אֹתָךְ	*before I-captured you*(fs)

59.3 The negative of the Infinitive Construct

We have learned the negatives אַל and לֹא. A different word is used for the negative of the IC: בִּלְתִּי (which means *non-existence*). A prefixed -לְ is placed before בִּלְתִּי rather than before the IC, and we get לְבִלְתִּי = *so-as-not* (*to*) or *in-order-not* (*to*). Thus, לְבִלְתִּי שְׁמֹר מִצְוֹתָיו means *so-as-not to-keep his-commandments* (Deut 8:11).

Things You Should Know

1. The Infinitive Construct (IC) can take suffixes, just like the Perfect, Imperfect and Imperative. But with the IC these suffixes can represent either a subject or an object. (שָׁמְרוֹ can mean either *keeping him* or *his keeping*.)
2. The IC + suffix is almost identical to the Impv ms + suffix.
3. The IC + suffix will usually also have an inseparable preposition -בְּ or -כְּ prefix, which will mean *when*.
4. The IC + suffix may come after other prepositions (such as לִפְנֵי, *before*). These prepositions will stand alone. In this case, the IC will have no inseparable preposition.
5. The negative of the IC is formed by placing לְבִלְתִּי before the IC.

---

[1] **Technical note:** When -לְ is added before an IC, the *shewa* under the ל becomes *hireq* (§9.1.1). This means that the *shewa* under the first radical of the IC now closes the syllable and so becomes silent. A following BEGADKEPAT will thus gain a *dagesh*: לְכֹד + לְ ➔ לִלְכֹּד. But this is only true for -לְ. When -בְּ or -כְּ are added before an IC, the *shewa* of the IC remains vocal (as if the *hireq* had a *metheg*), and thus a following BEGADKEPAT will not take a *dagesh*: בִּלְכֹד, כִּלְכֹד.

60

INTRODUCTION TO THE WEAK VERB

A verb is considered "weak" if one or more of its radicals is:

(1) **guttural (or ר)** Gutturals (א ה ח and ע) and ר reject *dagesh* (§11.1.2, p. 31; §13.2, p. 38). For instance, one of the signs of Piel is a *dagesh* in the second radical: שִׁמֵּר. But the verb ברך has a ר for its middle radical. Its Piel is בֵּרַךְ. The ר has rejected the *dagesh* of the Piel, and so the original *hireq* under the ב has lengthened to *tsere* (§16.1.2, p. 46).

(2) **silent (quiescent)** The letter which most often becomes silent (quiescent) is א. But, as we have seen, ו and י may also change from consonants to vowel letters (§17, p. 49). א and י are often silent when they are the first radical of a verb. For instance, the Qal Impf 3ms of אָמַר is יֹאמַר, where the א is silent. Another example: The י of יָטַב becomes silent in the Impf 3ms: יִיטַב (from an original יִיְטַב).

(3) **the letter נ** The letter נ is often "swallowed" (assimilated), **especially if it stands over a silent *shewa*** (review footnote 2, p. 46). For instance, the נ of the verb נָצַר is assimilated by the צ when the verb takes a prefix. Thus the Qal Impf 3ms is formed as follows:

נצר + י → יִנְצֹר → יִצֹּר where the נ has been assimilated.

(4) **original ו** Some verbs such as יָלַד (*to bear children*) originally began with a ו (ולד). This original ו will return in certain situations such as the Hiphil (הוֹלִיד)

(5) **final ה** We have already seen that a final ה in a verb will often become a -ת- or וֹת-. For instance, the Perf 3fs of גָּלָה is גָּלְתָה (not גָּלְהָה), and its Infinitive Construct is גְּלוֹת (not גְּלֹה).

You do not yet need to learn these patterns. They are only a few examples of what can happen when one or more of the radicals in a verb is weak. We will use the rest of this book to study various kinds of weak verbs. You have now studied all of the basics of Hebrew. Now we must study the many changes which happen as a result of weak letters.

Classification of Weak Verbs

We have been calling the three letters of the verb the "first radical," the "second radical," and the "third radical." There is a short cut based upon the verb פָּעַל.[1] From now on, we shall call the first

---

[1] **Technical Note:** Although we have usually used the verb שָׁמַר for our model, old Hebrew grammars used the verb פָּעַל. You will remember that it is this verb which lies behind the words Niphal (נִפְעַל), Piel (פִּעֵל), Hiphil (הִפְעִיל), etc. This verb turned out not to be a good one to use, however, since its middle radical rejects *dagesh*.

radical of any verb its פ or *Pe* radical (since the first radical of the verb פָּעַל is פ). Likewise, we shall call the second radical of any verb its ע or *Ayin* radical; and we shall call the third radical the ל or *Lamed* radical. Thus, weak verbs can be described as follows:

עָבַד	has a guttural in its first radical	therefore it is called a *Pe* Guttural verb.
בָּחַר	has a guttural in its second radical	therefore it is called an *Ayin* Guttural verb.
בָּטַח	has a guttural in its third radical	therefore it is called a *Lamed* Guttural verb.

Likewise,

נָפַל has a נ in its first radical	therefore it is called a *Pe Nun* verb.
נָטַע has both a נ and an ע	therefore it is *Pe Nun* and *Lamed* Guttural, and is "doubly weak."

This system will be used to describe all the weak verbs in the chapters ahead.

Things You Should Know

1. Weak verbs are verbs which have one or more of the following letters:
   - a guttural (א ה ח or ע) or ר
   - a silent letter (א ו or י)
   - the letter נ
   - a final ה

   These letters will often disappear or cause rejection of *dagesh* or changes in vowel pointing.

2. The following system is used to identify the three radicals of the verb:
   - the first radical is called the *Pe* (פ) radical
   - the second radical is called the *Ayin* (ע) radical
   - the third radical is called the *Lamed* (ל) radical

Exercise #39

אָדוֹן	lord, master
אָתוֹן	*f.* female donkey; *pl.* אֲתֹנוֹת
בַּעֲבוּר	*prep.* for the sake of, so that, in order to (usually found before IC or Impf)
גָּמָל	camel
חֲמוֹר	male donkey
לְבִלְתִּי	so as not (to)
לָמַד	to learn, ***Pi*** לִמֵּד to teach
נָחָשׁ	snake
עֵדֶן	Eden
עָרוֹם	naked, *f.* עֲרֻמָּה, *m.pl.* עֲרֻמִּים
פֶּן־	lest, so that not
קָרַב	to come near

[1] הָלְכָה הָאִשָּׁה בְּתוֹךְ הַגָּן וּבְקָרְבָהּ אֶת־הָעֵץ וַיְדַבֵּר הַנָּחָשׁ אֵלֶיהָ׃ [2] הֲהָיָה
הַנָּחָשׁ עָרוֹם[3] מִן הָאָדָם׃ [3] שָׁלַח אֱלֹהִים אֶת־הָאִישׁ וְאֶת־הָאִשָּׁה[2] מִגַּן־עֵדֶן פֶּן־
יִקְרְבוּ אֶל עֵץ־הַחַיִּים׃ וְלֹא עֲרוּמִּים הֵמָּה כְּיָצְאָם מֵהַגָּן׃ [4] בַּעֲבוּר שָׂרָה נָתַן
פַּרְעֹה לְאַבְרָם צֹאן־וּבָקָר וַחֲמֹרִים[4] וַעֲבָדִים וַאֲמָהוֹת וַאֲתֹנוֹת וּגְמַלִּים׃ [5] וַיִּקְבֹּץ
יַעֲקֹב אֶת־הַצֹּאן וַיְסַפְּרֵם וַיַּפְרֵיד אֶת־צֹאנוֹ מִן אֶת־צֹאן־לָבָן׃ [6] וַיִּשְׁלַח יַעֲקֹב
מַלְאָכִים לְפָנָיו אֶל־עֵשָׂו אָחִיו לֵאמֹר יֶשׁ־לִי חֲמוֹר וְאָתוֹן וְעֶבֶד וְאָמָה וְגָמָל׃ וְעַתָּה
אֶמְצְאָה חֵן בְּעֵינֵי־אֲדֹנִי׃ [7] וַיֹּאמֶר יְהוָה אֶל־מֹשֶׁה וְאֶל־אַהֲרֹן בְּאֶרֶץ־מִצְרַיִם
לֵאמֹר׃[5] הַחֹדֶשׁ הַזֶּה לָכֶם רֹאשׁ חֳדָשִׁים רִאשׁוֹן הוּא לָכֶם לְחָדְשֵׁי־הַשָּׁנָה׃
[8] וּמֹשֶׁה בֶּן־שְׁמֹנִים שָׁנָה וְאַהֲרֹן בֶּן־שָׁלֹשׁ וּשְׁמֹנִים שָׁנָה בְּדַבְּרָם[6] אֶל־פַּרְעֹה׃
[9] וְעַתָּה לִמְדוּ אֶת־הַדְּבָרִים הָאֵלֶּה וְלַמְּדֵם[9] אֶת־בְּנֵי־יִשְׂרָאֵל בַּעֲבוּרָם[8] פֶּן־יֶחֶטְאוּ[7]
וְנִפְרְדוּ לִפְנֵי־אֹיְבֵיהֶם׃ [10] וַיִּקָּבְצוּ הָעָם בַּעֲבוּר הִתְפַּלֵּל[11] בְּאַרְבָּעָה עָשָׂר [10]לַחֹדֶשׁ

---

[2] Gen 3:24 actually mentions only the *man* being driven out of the garden – though both are then found together again in Gen 4.

[3] **Hebrew word play:** Hebrew writers had a sense of humor, and enjoyed playing with the sounds of words. Gen 3:1 says that the snake was more *clever* (עָרוּם) than any other creature, not more *naked* (עָרוֹם). However, these two words sound very similar, and the writer of Genesis uses them both. In the last verse of Genesis 2, he says that the man and the woman were *naked* (עֲרוּמִּים, the plural adjective, changes its וֹ to a וּ). Then in the very next verse (3:1) he introduces the snake, and says that it was more *clever* (עָרוּם) than any other creature. The writer is making a serious point in these chapters, of course. But perhaps the first readers of Genesis also laughed in hearing these words, knowing that the snake is also one of the most *naked* of all the creatures.

[4] *Holem vav* (וֹ) and *holem* (ֹ) are interchangeable. Thus words like חֲמוֹר and אָתוֹן (which also appears in this sentence) can also be written חֲמֹר and אָתֹן.

[5] In English, we would expect to see a comma here (and you should use one in your translation). But it is not unusual in Hebrew to find a *soph passuq* at this point, even though it may look strange to us.

[6] Piel verb form with prefix and suffix.

[7] Qal Impf 3mp. The guttural has changed the vowel pointing.

[8] Preposition plus suffix.

[9] This verse has two direct objects: (1) the verb suffix ם ֵ- and (2) the words after the -אֶת. Translate the second as an *in*direct object ("Grammar," p. xviii). That is, translate the -אֶת as *to*.

[10] Translate the preposition -לַ as "of the."

[11] Infinitive construct. It is preceded by the preposition בַּעֲבוּר instead of the inseparable preposition -לְ.

הַשִּׁשִּׁי׃ וּבְעָמְדָם לִפְנֵי־הַכֹּהֲנִים וַיְבָרְכוּם וַיְלַמֵּד וּם לְבִלְתִּי חֲטֹא לֵאלֹהִים׃ [11] שָׁמַע
אֱלֹהִים אֶת־תְּפִלּוֹת־עַמּוֹ וְכַאֲשֶׁר שָׁם שֹׁפְטִים עֲלֵיהֶם וַתְּהִי[12] עִירָם שְׁלֵמָה׃ [12] בִּקֵּשׁ
שָׁאוּל אֶת־בֶּן־יִשַׁי וַיֹּאמֶר אִם לֹא אֹיְבִי הוּא וְעָמַד לְפָנַי שָׁלֵם׃ [13] וַיְבַקְשׁוּ פַּעֲמַיִם
צְבָאוֹת־יִשְׂרָאֵל אֶת־צְבָא־פְלִשְׁתִּים וְאֶת־אֲדֹנֵיהֶם לְבִלְתִּי הִמָּלְטָם׃ [14] בָּא עַם מַיִם[13]
שָׁלֹשׁ פְּעָמִים בַּעֲבוּר שִׁבֵּר[14] אֶת־חוֹמַת־הָעִיר מִשַּׁעַר חָדָשׁ אֶל־שַׁעַר זָקֵן מֵאָה וַחֲמִשִּׁים
אַמָּה[16]׃ [15] וַיְסַפֵּר הַנָּבִיא אֶל הָעָם לֵאמֹר הִנֵּה רוּחַ גְּדוֹלָה בָּאָה[15] מַיִם וַתְּקַבֵּץ
רוּחַ־אֱלֹהִים אֶת־הַמַּיִם וּבִשְׁנֵי[18] מְקוֹמוֹת שָׁמָּה אֹתָם׃ [16] רָאֶה[17] יְהוָה אֶת־כָּל־הָעָם
מִגָּדוֹל וְעַד־קָטָן וּלְפָנָיו גַּם שָׁאוּל עָרוֹם׃ [17] מִי שָׁמַע כַּדָּבָר הַזֶּה[19] וּמַה־זֶּה בָּחֲרוּ
עַם אֱלֹהִים חֲדָשִׁים לָהֶם׃ אִם יֵשׁ אֱלֹהִים בְּיִשְׂרָאֵל מַדּוּעַ הֲלַכְתֶּם אַחֲרֵי אֱלֹהִים
אֲחֵרִים לְעָבְדָם׃

---

[12] Translate "(then) it was." Impf 3fs + w.c. < היה.

[13] Be careful here. This is not the word מַיִם

[14] See footnote 11, above.

[15] Qal Perf 3fs < בָּא.

[16] Remember that this word often appears in the singular even when it should be translated plural.

[17] Be careful here, too. This is not רֹעֶה. Rather, it comes from the verb רָאָה. The א and the ה have caused the original *tsere* to become a *seghol*.

[18] Does this mean *and in years of* or *and in two*? Context will tell you.

[19] מִי שָׁמַע כַּדָּבָר הַזֶּה. Translate: "Who has heard such a thing?"

61

THE VERB: *PE NUN*

The letter נ is weak, and when it comes at the end of a syllable within a word it often gets "swallowed" (assimilated) by the next letter.[1] We have already seen this when the word מִן joins a following word:

מִן+מֶלֶךְ ➜ מִנְמֶלֶךְ ➜ מִמֶּלֶךְ

↑ נ at the end of a syllable

61.1 *Pe Nun* Verbs and Assimilation

In Hebrew, *Pe Nun* verbs are verbs such as נָקַם[2] which have a נ for their first letter. When these verbs take prefixes, the נ becomes the last letter of a new syllable and is usually assimilated. For instance, the Qal Impf 3ms of נָקַם is formed as follows:

י+נקם ➜ יִנְקֹם ➜ יִקֹּם

The *dagesh* in the ק represents the assimilated נ.

If the second radical (the *Ayin* radical) of the verb is a guttural (for instance, נָעַם instead of נָקַם), then this *Ayin* guttural will reject the *dagesh* and the נ will not be assimilated. For this reason, the Qal Impf 3ms of נָעַם is regular (except for the attracted *pathah*): יִנְעַם. This means that:

Verbs which are *Pe Nun and Ayin Guttural* will be regular.

They are not technically considered to be *Pe Nun* verbs.

61.2 Qal: Two Types of *Pe Nun* Verb

Overview. The *Pe Nun* verb develops in two ways. Most verbs have an ***o* vowel in the Impf**: the Impf of נָפַל becomes יִפֹּל (as above). Other *Pe Nun* verbs (especially statives) have an ***a* vowel in the Impf**: the Impf of נָגַשׁ becomes יִגַּשׁ. There is very little difference between these two types of verbs until we get to Impv and IC:

(1) The **Imperative**. Here, the נ is assimilated by stative-type *a* vowel verbs (the imperative of נָגַשׁ is גַּשׁ), but not by regular *o* vowel verbs (the imperative of נָפַל is נְפֹל).

---

[1] See page 46, note 2. **Technical Note**: This also happens in English and Greek. The English word *illegal* was originally *in* + *legal* ➜ *inlegal*. But the weak *n* was then assimilated ("swallowed") by the *l* and the *l* was then doubled: *inlegal* ➜ *illegal*.

This also happens in Greek. The word ἐμμένω, *to remain in*, was originally ἐν + μένω ➜ ἐνμένω ➜ ἐμμένω. Again, we have an *n* (ν) being assimilated by a letter (μ) which is then doubled (μμ).

[2] **Technical note.** Many grammars begin with נפל or נגשׁ. The problem with using these verbs as the first example, however, is their *Ayin* BEGADKEPAT. In the development of the Imperfect of נָפַל, the *begadkepat* already takes a dagesh at the stage יִנְפֹּל and thus does not give a clear picture of the נ assimilation in the next step.

(2) The **Infinitive Construct** (IC). Again the נ is assimilated by *a* vowel verbs but not by *o* vowel verbs. In addition, the IC of *a* vowel verbs adds a ת at the end, as we shall see below.

The Perfect has no prefixes, and so is regular for *Pe Nun* verbs:

Qal Perfect

	נפל	נגשׁ
3ms	נָפַל	נָגַשׁ
3fs	נָפְלָה	נָגְשָׁה
2ms	נָפַלְתָּ	נָגַשְׁתָּ

etc.

The Imperfect and Imperative. Here, the "weakness" of *Pe Nun* verbs begins to appear:

Qal Imperfect

	o vowel	*a* vowel
3ms	יִפֹּל	יִגַּשׁ
3fs	תִּפֹּל	תִּגַּשׁ
2ms	תִּפֹּל	תִּגַּשׁ
2fs	תִּפְּלִי	תִּגְּשִׁי
1cs	אֶפֹּל	אֶגַּשׁ
3mp	יִפְּלוּ	יִגְּשׁוּ
3fp	תִּפֹּלְנָה	תִּגַּשְׁנָה
2mp	תִּפְּלוּ	תִּגְּשׁוּ
2fp	תִּפֹּלְנָה	תִּגַּשְׁנָה
1cp	נִפֹּל	נִגַּשׁ
Act. Part.	נֹפֵל	נֹגֵשׁ
Pass. Part.	—	נָגוּשׁ

Qal Imperative

	o vowel	*a* vowel
2ms	נְפֹל	גַּשׁ[3] *or* גְּשָׁה
2fs	נִפְלִי	גְּשִׁי
2mp	נִפְלוּ	גְּשׁוּ
2fp	נְפֹלְנָה	גַּשְׁנָה

Qal Cohortative

1cs	אֶפְּלָה	אֶגְּשָׁה
1cp	נִפְּלָה	נִגְּשָׁה

Qal Infinitive Construct

	נְפֹל	גֶּשֶׁת
with -לְ	לִנְפֹּל	לָגֶשֶׁת

Learn the strong letters

As you can see, letters start to disappear in the various forms of weak verbs. How will you learn all the various forms? Here are two answers:

- **Learn patterns, not charts.** It is almost impossible to memorize all of the charts. So when you study the charts, watch for general patterns and learn them instead.
- **Learn the strong letters.** Weak letters come and go; strong letter remain. When you learn verbs like נגשׁ and נפל, learn to recognize them as גשׁ and פל, since that is what you are going to be seeing in forms like תִּפֹּל, אֶגַּשׁ, etc.

---

[3] גְּשָׁה is more frequent (*Gesenius* §66*c*).

Notes:

1. **Perfect:** Regular.
2. **Imperfect:** The נ is always assimilated.
3. **Imperative:**
   - ***a* vowel verbs:** these follow the typical pattern of Impf minus prefix (יִגַּשׁ minus -יִ = גַּשׁ). Note the alternative form in 2ms.
   - ***o* vowel verbs:** the נ returns. The Impf is יִפֹּל, but the Impv ms is נְפֹל.
4. **Infinitive Construct:** *o* vowel verbs are regular, but *a* vowel verbs lose the -נ and gain a ת-. Thus, the IC will *not* be the same as the Impv ms for *a* vowel verbs.
5. **Not all Qal forms are shown above**. We show only those forms which have differences because of the *Pe Nun*. The Perfect, Participles, and Infinitive Absolute all follow regular patterns and therefore do not need to be studied. And the Jussive has no shortened form; it is simply the same as the Imperfect.

61.3 Niphal

The Niphal Perfect is irregular because it adds a -נ prefix before the *Pe Nun*:

נ+נצל → נִנְצַל → נִצַּל

In the Niphal, *o* vowel verbs and *a* vowel verbs do *not* behave two different ways. Rather, they follow a single pattern. Thus, we shall look at only one verb: נָצַל. Furthermore, only the **Perfect** and the (passive) **participle** are irregular in the Niphal. All other forms, including the Imperfect, are regular.

Niphal Perfect (the *dagesh* in the צ represents the swallowed נ)

Singular		*Plural*	
3ms	נִצַּל		
3fs	נִצְּלָה	3cp	נִצְּלוּ
2ms	נִצַּלְתָּ	2mp	נִצַּלְתֶּם
2fs	נִצַּלְתְּ	2fp	נִצַּלְתֶּן
1cs	נִצַּלְתִּי	1cp	נִצַּלְנוּ

Niphal Participle

נִצָּל (cf Perf 3ms)

Again, the difference between the Perf 3ms (נִצַּל) and the Participle (נִצָּל) is *pathah* vs. *qamets*, just as it was for the strong verb (נִשְׁמַר vs נִשְׁמָר)

Note on Piel: *Pe nun* verbs almost never have both a Niphal Perf and a Piel Perf (which is regular). On the rare occasions when they do, however, these forms will be the same. For instance, the Piel Perf 2mp of נצל is the same as the Niph Perf 2mp. Both are נִצַּלְתֶּם (compare above).

Hiphil and Hophal: The Hiphil and Hophal also add prefixes (-הִ and -הָ). This again puts the *Pe Nun* at the end of a syllable (-הִנְ and -הָנְ). Thus, there is assimilation in all parts of the Hiphil and the Hophal. Only a few examples are given below. See the verb table at the back of the book (p. 269) for the complete paradigm.

61.4 Hiphil

We learned earlier that the Hiphil has a *pathah* under its prefix (in all parts *except* the Perfect): ○ִי○ְ○△ַ. This *pathah* will remain, even when there is assimilation of the נ. Following are some examples:

○○נ + △ַ ➜ ○ִי○ְנ△ַ ➜ ○ִי⊙△ַ

Perfect	
3ms	הִצִּיל
3fs	הִצִּילָה
2ms	הִצַּלְתָּ
3cp	הִצִּילוּ
2mp	הִצַּלְתֶּם

Imperfect	
3ms	יַצִּיל
2fs	תַּצִּילִי
3mp	יַצִּילוּ
2/3fp	תַּצֵּלְנָה
1cp	נַצִּיל

(Active) Participle	
ms	מַצִּיל
fs	מַצִּילָה
mp	מַצִּילִים
fp	מַצִּילוֹת

Imperative	
2ms	הַצֵּל
2fs	הַצִּילִי
2mp	הַצִּילוּ
2fp	הַצֵּלְנָה

Infinitives	
absolute	הַצֵּל
construct	הַצִּיל

61.5 Hophal

Two things happen in the Hophal *Pe Nun* verb:

- There is assimilation of the נ, and
- the *qamets-hatuph* under the prefix changes to *qibbuts*:[4] ○○נ + הָ ➜ ○○ְנהָ ➜ ○⊙הֻ

Example: הֻצַּל. This verb may look like Pual because of the assimilation and the *qibbuts*. Here is where you need to know your vocabulary. On a test, how will you know if this is the Pual of הצל or the Hophal of נצל? (Remember: in Pual, the *qibbuts* comes under the *Pe* radical, not under the prefix. Review §56.4 "Appearance of *qibbuts*," p. 166.) If you know that there is a verb נצל, and that it comes in Hophal – and if you know that you have not learned הצל as a verb – then on a test you will know that it must be the Hophal of נצל. (And, for the record, there is no Hebrew verb הצל.) **Learn your vocabulary well.**

---

[4] **Technical note:** This change from *qamets-hatuph* to *qibbuts* is the result of a general pattern: **If a *dagesh* is added in a letter after an *o* vowel, the *o* vowel often becomes *qibbuts*.** Example: the word כֹּל (*all*) can take suffixes. When we add the 3ms suffix וֹ-, we first get כֹּלוֹ. But now the ל has a *dagesh*. Therefore, the *holem* which comes before this new *dagesh* becomes a *qibbuts* and we get כֻּלּוֹ. This also gives us a short vowel in what has become a closed unaccented syllable (-כָּל).

This same thing happens in the Hophal Pe Nun verb. At first, ○○נ + הָ ➜ ○○ְנהָ ➜ ○⊙הָ. However, *qamets-hatuph* is an *o* vowel. Now a *dagesh* has appeared after it. Thus it becomes *qibbuts*: ○⊙הָ ➜ ○⊙הֻ.

Following are some examples of *Pe Nun* Hophal:

Perfect

3ms	הֻצַּל
3fs	הֻצְּלָה
2ms	הֻצַּלְתָּ
3cp	הֻצְּלוּ
2mp	הֻצַּלְתֶּם

Imperfect

3ms	יֻצַּל
2fs	תֻּצְּלִי
3mp	יֻצְּלוּ
3fp	תֻּצַּלְנָה
1cp	נֻצַּל

(Passive) Participle

ms	מֻצָּל
fs	מֻצָּלָה
mp	מֻצָּלִים
fp	מֻצָּלוֹת

Infinitives

absolute	הֻצֵּל
construct	הֻצַּל

61.6 Parsing

Weak verbs are parsed just like other verbs. You do not need to mention the word "weak." יֻצַּל is parsed Hoph Impf 3ms < נצל.

Things You Should Know

1. **The נ of *Pe Nun* verbs** is usually assimilated when the verb takes a prefix.
2. On the other hand, **"*Pe Nun* and *Ayin* Guttural" verbs** will be regular.
3. **In the Qal**, some *Pe Nun* verbs have *a* vowel Imperfects, and others have *o* vowel Imperfects.
   - ***o* vowel Imperfect verbs:** Impv and IC do not assimilate the נ.
   - ***a* vowel Imperfect verbs:** the IC adds a ת- at the end.
4. **In the Niphal**, only the Perfect and the Participle are irregular (because they add a -נ prefix).
5. **The Hiphil and Hophal** also add prefixes which cause the *Pe Nun* to assimilate. The **Hiphil** is not difficult to recognize, since there continues to be a *pathah* under the prefix. In the **Hophal**, however, the *qamets-hatuph* under the prefix changes to *qibbuts*.
6. **Parsing:** It is not necessary to mention that a verb is weak when parsing it.

62

TWO COMMON VERBS: נָתַן AND לָקַח

The verbs נָתַן (*to give*) and לָקַח (*to take*) are very common in Hebrew, and so we need to study them closely. They occur mainly in Qal, and occasionally in Niphal.[1] Verb charts will be shown for Qal only.

- נָתַן is weak because it is *Pe Nun*. It also has a *Lamed Nun*, which is often assimilated when the verb has suffixes (especially in the Perfect).
- לָקַח is unusual because its ל acts just like the *nun* of a *Pe Nun* verb; that is, it is assimilated. (This is not true of other verbs which start with ל).

Therefore, we will often see -תּ- instead of -נת- (for instance, in the Impf), and -קּח- instead of -לקח-.

נָתַן (Qal)

Perfect

3ms	נָתַן	
3fs	נָתְנָה	
2ms	נָתַתָּ	*
2fs	נָתַתְּ	*
1cs	נָתַתִּי	*
3cp	נָתְנוּ	*cf. 1cp*
2mp	נְתַתֶּם	*
2fp	נְתַתֶּן	*
1cp	נָתַנּוּ	* *cf. 3cp*

Infinitive Absolute: נָתוֹן (regular)

Infinitive Construct: תֵּת
(with -לְ: לָתֵת)

Cohortative
1cs: אֶתְּנָה 1cp: נִתְּנָה

Imperfect

3ms	יִתֵּן
3fs/2ms	תִּתֵּן
2fs	תִּתְּנִי
1cs	אֶתֵּן
3mp	יִתְּנוּ
3fp/2fp	—
2mp	תִּתְּנוּ
1cp	נִתֵּן

Participles
נֹתֵן, נָתוּן, etc. (regular)

Imperative

2ms	תֵּן
2fs	תְּנִי
2mp	תְּנוּ
2fp	—

* The final *nun* (the *lamed nun*) has been assimilated by the suffix (נָתַנְנוּ ➜ נָתַנּוּ, etc.).

---

[1] **Technical note:** נָתַן occurs more than 1900 times in the Qal, and only 83 times in the Niphal. לָקַח is found more than 900 times in the Qal, and just 11 times in the Niphal. They are also found in an odd passive form which will be discussed below, at the end of the chapter.

Notes:

1. **Assimilation of *nun*:** We have already learned (§61.1, p. 184) that when a נ is found

    - in the middle of a word **and**
    - over a silent *shewa*

    then it will often be assimilated by the next letter:

    מִן+מֶּלֶךְ ➔ מִנְמֶּלֶךְ ➔ מִמֶּלֶךְ

    This will also happen with the verb נָתַן in the following cases:

    a. **When there are prefixes:** the first -נ will be assimilated. *Example:* Qal Impf 3fs/2ms:

    ת+נתן ➔ תִּנְתֵּן ➔ תִּתֵּן

    b. **In the Niphal Perfect and Participle:** Here, נָתַן behaves just like other *Pe Nun* verbs (review §61.3). Again, the first -נ is assimilated. The **Niphal Perfect** has a נ prefix, and thus we see

    נ+נתן ➔ נִנְתַּן ➔ נִתַּן

    The **Niphal Participle** becomes נִתָּן, which is the normal Pe Nun pattern (again, the *qamets* distinguishes it from the Niph Perf 3ms). Other parts of the Niphal of נָתַן are regular.

    c. **When there are suffixes:** The final ן- is assimilated in these cases. For instance, in the Qal Perf 2ms we see the following pattern:

    נתן+תָּ ➔ נָתַנְתָּ ➔ נָתַתָּ

    These verbs have a star (*) beside them in the chart on p. 189.

2. **Vowel point changes:** *Tsere* (ֵ) instead of *holem* (ֹ) is found in:

    - the Impf (יִתֵּן not יִנְתֹּן) and
    - the Impv (תֵּן not נְתֹן).

    Tsere also appears in the IC (תֵּת).

3. **Similar forms:** Be sure that you know the difference between

    - the Qal Perf 3cp (נָתְנוּ , which is regular) and
    - the Qal Perf 1cp (נָתַנּוּ, with assimilation from the original נָתַנְנוּ).

    Compare the sound and accent patterns of the above words with שָׁמְרוּ and שָׁמַרְנוּ.

לָקַח (Qal)

לָקַח acts just like a *Pe Nun* verb. That is, the ל will be assimilated when prefixes are added. (Again, this **does not happen with any other verb** beginning with ל.) This will usually produce a *dagesh* in the ק, although **sometimes the *dagesh* is missing**. For instance, the Qal Impf 1cs is אֶקַּח but the Qal Cohortative 1cs is אֶקְחָה (no *dagesh* in the ק). This will be discusses further in the Notes below.

לָקַח is also *Lamed Guttural*. Therefore, we shall also see attraction of *pathah* and furtive *pathah* (§13.3 and §13.4, p. 38).

Perfect (is regular)

3ms	לָקַח
3fs	לָקְחָה
2ms	לָקַחְתָּ
etc.	

Active Participle

ms	לֹקֵחַ
mp	לֹקְחִים
fs	—
fp	—

Passive Participle

ms	—
fs	—
mp	לְקֻחִים
fp	—

Cohortative

1cs	אֶקְחָה
1cp	נִקְחָה

Imperfect

3ms	יִקַּח
3fs/2ms	תִּקַּח
2fs	תִּקְחִי
1cs	אֶקַּח
3mp	יִקְחוּ
3fp/2fp	תִּקַּחְנָה
2mp	תִּקְחוּ
1cp	נִקַּח

Imperative

2ms	קַח (קְחָה)
2fs	קְחִי
2mp	קְחוּ
2fp	—

Infinitives

Absolute	לָקוֹחַ
Construct	קַחַת
	(with -לְ: לָקַחַת)

Notes:

1. **Missing *dageshes*.** Although the assimilated ל usually produces a *dagesh* in the ק, this *dagesh* disappears when the ח becomes the first letter of the last syllable (חִי- חוּ- or חָה-). This makes the word easier to pronounce. Thus:

   Qal Impf 2fs: תִּקְחִי (instead of תִּקְּחִי)

   Qal Impf 3mp: יִקְחוּ (instead of יִקְּחוּ)

   Qal Impf 2mp: תִּקְחוּ (instead of תִּקְּחוּ)

   Qal Cohortative 1cs: אֶקְחָה (instead of אֶקְּחָה; note that Impf 1cs = אֶקַּח)

2. **The Imperative** also lacks the *dageshes* which would show the assimilated ל.

3. **The Niphal of** לָקַח is regular (except for *pathahs* attracted by the guttural ח). The ל remains throughout, including in the Perfect: נִלְקַח נִלְקְחָה נִלְקַחְתָּ, etc.

4. **Odd Passive forms.** לָקַח has another passive form which is somewhat odd. In the Perfect, we will see לֻקַּח (*he has been taken*), לֻקְּחָה (*she has been taken*), etc. But in the Imperfect we will see יֻקַּח, תֻּקַּח, etc., with the *qibbuts* under the prefix, not under the Pe radical.[2]

Things You Should Know

1. **נָתַן is a *Pe Nun* verb which also has a *lamed nun*.** The *pe nun* will be assimilated when the verb has prefixes, and the final (*lamed*) *nun* will often be assimilated when the verb has suffixes.

2. **לָקַח *behaves* like a *Pe Nun* verb** because the ל is often assimilated. (This does not happen with other verbs which begin with -ל.) The guttural ח will also attract extra *pathahs*.

3. When the ל of לקח is assimilated, **a *dagesh* will usually appear** in the ק. However, it will be missing when the ח becomes the first letter of the last syllable of the verb.

4. In the **Niphal**, the first נ of נָתַן will be assimilated in the Perfect and the Participle, but the verb will otherwise be regular. לָקַח is regular in the Niphal, except for extra *pathahs* because of the guttural ח.

Exercise #40

בֶּטֶן	belly, womb
יְרִיחוֹ	Jericho
לָקַח	to take, receive
נגד	***Hi*** הִגִּיד to report, announce, tell; ***Ho*** הֻגַּד to be reported, announced, told
נָגִיד	chief, leader, prince
נָגַשׁ	to approach; ***Ni*** נִגַּשׁ to approach; ***Hi*** הִגִּישׁ to offer
קָצַף	to become angry
רַב	*adj.* many, great
רְכוּשׁ	property, goods, *cs.* רְכֻשׁ
רֵעַ	friend, companion; *pl.* רֵעִים, *cs.* רֵעֵי; רֵעֵהוּ or רֵעָיו his friends
שׁוּב	to return ***Qal Perf*** שָׁב
שׁוֹר	bull(s), ox(en), steer(s); (*pl.* שְׁוָרִים *is used only once in the Bible*)

[2] **Technical note:** What we may actually be seeing is a mixture of two forms, with the Perfect being Pual (*Pe* radical *qibbuts*, *ayin* radical *dagesh*), but the Imperfect being Hophal (*qibbuts* under the prefix). On the other hand, it has been suggested that these forms are not actually Pual and Hophal, but rather an unusual passive form of the Qal. (Remember, we have learned that Qal is active, except for its passive participle.) See *Gesenius* §52*e* and §53*u*.

נָתַן also has an Imperfect Passive (though not a Perfect Passive), which follows the same pattern: יֻתַּן.

[1] וַיְהִי הַנָּחָשׁ בְּעֵץ בְּעֵדֶן וַיֹּאמֶר־שָׁם אֶל־הָאִשָּׁה יֹדֵעַ אֱלֹהִים כִּי בְּיוֹם אֲכָלְכֶם[4] מִמֶּנּוּ[3]
וִהְיִיתֶם[9] כֵּאלֹהִים יֹדְעֵי[8]־טוֹב וָרָע׃ [2] וַתֵּרֶא[7] הָאִשָּׁה כִּי טוֹב הָעֵץ לְלֶחֶם[6] וַתִּקַּח[5]
מִפִּרְיוֹ וַתֹּאכַל[11] וַתִּתֵּן גַּם־לְאִישָׁהּ עִמָּהּ[10] וַיֹּאכַל׃ [3] וַיִּשְׁמְעוּ אֶת־קוֹל־יְהוָה אֱלֹהִים
מִתְהַלֵּךְ בַּגָּן לְרוּחַ־הַיּוֹם[13] וַיִּסְתַּתֵּר[12] הָאָדָם וְאִשְׁתּוֹ מִפְּנֵי־יְהוָה אֱלֹהִים בְּתוֹךְ עֵץ־הַגָּן׃
וַיִּקְרָא יְהוָה אֱלֹהִים אֶל־הָאָדָם וַיֹּאמֶר לוֹ אַיֶּכָּה[14]׃ וַיֹּאמֶר אֶת־קוֹלְךָ שָׁמַעְתִּי בַּגָּן
וָאִירָא[15] כִּי־עָרוֹם אָנֹכִי וָאֶסָּתֵר׃ וַיֹּאמֶר מִי הִגִּיד לְךָ כִּי עָרוֹם אַתָּה הֲמִן־הָעֵץ אֲשֶׁר
צִוִּיתִיךָ[17] לְבִלְתִּי[16] אֲכָל־מִמֶּנּוּ אָכָלְתָּ׃ [4] וַיִּשְׁמְעוּ הָאָדָם וְהָאִשָּׁה אֶת־קוֹל הַנָּחָשׁ עַל־
כֵּן אַל יָשׁוּבוּ[18] אֶל־גַּן־עֵדֶן׃ [5] הִגִּיד עֶבֶד־אַבְרָהָם אֶל־לָבָן לֵאמֹר יֵשׁ לַאדֹנִי רְכוּשׁ
רַב כִּי בֵרֲכוֹ אֱלֹהִים׃ וַיִּתֶּן לוֹ שׁוֹר[20] וַחֲמוֹרִים וַאֲתוֹנוֹת׃ וַתִּקְרַב רִבְקָה[19] לָתֵת מַיִם
לִגְמַלַּי וָאֶשְׁבַּח[21] אֶת־יְהוָה כִּי בֵרַךְ אֶת־בֶּן־אֲדֹנִי וַיִּתֶּן אִשָּׁה לוֹ׃ וַיֹּאמְרוּ לָבָן וְאָבִיהוּ
מֵיְהוָה יָצָא הַדָּבָר לֹא יָכֹלְנוּ[22] דַּבֵּר אֵלֶיךָ רַע אוֹ־טוֹב׃ [6] אָמַר יוֹסֵף גֻּנֹּב גֻּנַּבְתִּי
מֵאֶרֶץ־הָעִבְרִים וָאֶלָּקַח אֶל־מִצְרַיִם וְגַם־שָׂמוּ אֹתִי בַּבּוֹר׃ [7] וַיֹּאמֶר אֲבִיהֶם מֵת בְּנִי
הַקָּטֹן׃ וְעַתָּה אִם יֵרֵד אָחִיהוּ עִמָּכֶם מִצְרַיְמָה וּמָצְאָה צָרָה אֶת־נַפְשִׁי׃ [8] וַיֹּאמֶר
מֹשֶׁה אֲלֵיהֶם לֵאמֹר וּבָאוּ עָלֶיךָ[23] כָּל־הַבְּרָכוֹת הָאֵלֶּה כִּי תִשְׁמַע בְּקוֹל יְהוָה אֱלֹהֶיךָ

---

[3] This preposition with suffix has two sets of meanings. See §35.2, p. 108.

[4] This is not a Perf 2ms. That would be אֲכַלְתֶּם. So how should you parse this word? See p. 178.

[5] Remember that "Impf + w.c. . . . Impf + w.c. . . . ." can often be translated "When . . . then . . . ."

[6] לֶחֶם can mean *food* as well as *bread*. The word in Gen 3:6 is actually מַאֲכָל, which also means *food*.

[7] The verb רָאָה has lost its final ה in this shortened Imperfect form. Why is it shortened? (See the first note in the "Note the Following" section on p. 144.)

[8] See §32.3.3, p. 97 for this verb form. This is how the word appears in Genesis.

[9] Qal Perf 2mp + w.c. < היה. **Technical note:** The final ה of היה has become י because of the suffix.

[10] The Hebrew text of Gen 3:6 contains this word, which suggests that Adam was with the woman when the snake spoke to her. We might wonder why he was silent – and why some translations leave out the words "with her."

[11] Notice how this verb follows a pattern very similar to וַיֹּאמֶר. This is because both verbs begin with א.

[12] See §53.2.5.1, p. 159 for parsing. Note that the verb is singular, although the subject (which follows it) is plural. This is the pattern which is found in Gen 3:8.

[13] לְרוּחַ־הַיּוֹם. RSV translates this "in the cool of the day." NRSV: "at the time of the evening breeze."

[14] אֵי + 2ms suffix (long form כָה- instead of ךָ-).

[15] Impf 1cs + w.c. The vowel pointing has changed, but you should be able to recognize the verb.

[16] See §59.3, p. 179. This should also tell you how to parse the next word, אֲכָל.

[17] < צוה. The final ה has become י and there is a 2ms object suffix. We will study *Lamed He* verbs in §69.

[18] Qal Impf 3mp < שׁוּב.

[19] *Rebekah.*

[20] Translate plural. The actual plural שְׁוָרִים is found only in Hosea 12:12. In the rest of the Old Testament, the word שׁוֹר is used for both singular and plural.

[21] See note 5, above.

[22] Translate as present tense.

[23] אֲלֵיהֶם . . . עָלֶיךָ. This type of alternation between singular and plural is quite common in the book of Deuteronomy. For instance, it is not uncommon to find *you* singular and *you* plural in the same verse.

בָּרוּךְ פְּרִי־בִטְנְךָ[25] וּפְרִי־אַדְמָתְךָ וּפְרִי־צֹאנֶךָ׃ [9] וַיִּשְׁלַח יְהוֹשֻׁעַ מְרַגְּלִים מִשְּׂפַת[24]־
הַיַּרְדֵּן אֶל־יְרִיחוֹ׃ וַיֹּאמְרוּ נִקְחָה[26] פְּרִי־הָאָרֶץ וְנִתְּנָה אֹתוֹ לִיהוֹשֻׁעַ׃ [10] וַיִּגְּשׁוּ
הַמְרַגְּלִים אֶת־יְרִיחוֹ וַיִּקְצֹף הַמֶּלֶךְ׃ וַיֹּאמֶר מִצְאוּם[29] פֶּן־בָּא צְבָאָם וְהָיִינוּ[28] כַּמֵּתִים[27]׃
[11] וַיִּקְרְבוּ הָעָם אֶל־הַהֵיכָל בַּעֲבוּר לְמֹד אֶת־תּוֹרַת־יְהוָה וּלְהַגִּישׁ מִנְחוֹת לֵאלֹהִים׃
וַיְלַמְּדוּם הַכֹּהֲנִים וַיִּקְחוּ אֶת־מִנְחוֹתָם לִפְנֵי־יְהוָה׃ [12] וַיֹּאמְרוּ הַכֹּהֲנִים הִתְקַדְּשׁוּ
לַיהוָה וְהִקָּדְשׁוּ׃ לֹא תְהַלְלוּ אֶת־הַשֶּׁמֶשׁ כְּעַם־מִצְרָיִם׃ לֹא תַעֲשׂוּ[30] לָכֶם אֱלֹהִים כְּעַם־
כְּנָעַן׃ [13] וַיֹּאמֶר הָעָם נִלְמְדָה אֶת־דַּרְכֵי־יָהּ כִּי מְהֻלָּלִים הֵמָּה׃ אַל נִשְׁכָּחֵם פֶּן־
נֹאבֵד[32] בְּמָקוֹם בְּלִי דְבָרוֹ׃ [14] הַלְלוּ־יָהּ[31] כִּי קָדוֹשׁ הוּא וְלֹא־שָׁכַח אֶת־בְּרִיתוֹ עִמָּנוּ׃
יִהְיֶה כְּחוֹמָה בַּעֲבוּר עַמּוֹ לְדֹר וָדֹר לְבִלְתִּי אָבְדָם׃ [15] וּבָאוּ גוֹיִם רַבִּים לִירוּשָׁלִָם׃
כֵּן תְּלַמְּדוּם אֶת־דְּבַר־יָהּ פֶּן־יְפַזְּרוּם אֹיְבֵיהֶם כְּצֹאן׃ [16] וַיַּגֵּד נְגִיד־יְרִיחוֹ אֶל־
רֵעֵהוּ לֵאמֹר נֹגְשִׂים גִּבּוֹרִים רַבִּים׃ לָכֵן נְבַקְשָׁה סוּסִים מִמִּצְרַיִם לְהִלָּחֵם בָּהֶם לְבִלְתִּי
גְנָבָם אֶת־רְכֻשֵׁנוּ׃ [17] וַיַּקְרִיבוּ רֵעֵי־הַנָּגִיד שׁוֹר[33] וּגְמַלִּים וַחֲמֹרִים וַאֲתֹנוֹת לְמָכְרָם
לְמִצְרַיִם׃ עָבְרוּ אֶת־הַמִּדְבָּר שָׁלֵם וּבְעָבְרָם אֶת־הַגְּבוּל וַיִּקְצְפוּ אֲדֹנֵי־הַפְּלִשְׁתִּים׃
[18] וַיֹּאמֶר אִיּוֹב[36] עָרֹם[35] יָצָאתִי מִבֶּטֶן־אִמִּי וְעָרֹם אָשׁוּב שָׁמָּה יְהוָה נָתַן וַיהוָה[34] לָקָח
יְהִי שֵׁם יְהוָה מְבֹרָךְ׃

---

[24] Note, this is not the word מִשְׁפָּט.

[25] Translate "your(ms) body." This sentence is based upon a verse from Deuteronomy. Many times in Deuteronomy, the masculine singular is used when speaking to a group.

[26] Remember, the *dagesh* in the ק disappears when the ח after it starts a new syllable.

[27] The adjective מֵת is actually a participle of the verb מות, to die. Here, you may translate "like the-being-dead-ones," or "like dead men."

[28] Perf 1cp + w.c. < היה.

[29] Imperative with suffix.

[30] Impf 2mp < עשׂה. The final ה has dropped out again.

[31] יָהּ is a shortened form of יְהוָה. Especially in the Psalms, it is often used with the Piel Impv הַלְלוּ (note that the *dagesh* is usually missing in this word). This produces the well-known word *Halleluyah*!

[32] Impf 1cp. Again, the *Pe Aleph* gives this verb a pattern very much like the Impf of אמר (יֹאמַר). We will look at this in detail when we study *Pe Aleph* verbs.

[33] Translate *oxen*. The plural form שְׁוָרִים occurs only once in the OT (Hos 12:12). The singular is usually used even when the context is plural.

[34] Question: Why is there no vowel point under the *yod*? Answer: Remember that the unusual vowel pointing of יְהוָה is supposed to remind us to say אֲדֹנָי (see footnote 6, p. 21). Thus, וַיהוָה is using the vowel pointing of the word וַאדֹנָי, in which א has become quiescent (silent) and lost its vowel. Thus, no vowel is placed under the *yod*.

[35] Remember that *holem* and *holem-vav* are interchangeable. This word can also be spelled עָרוֹם.

[36] Job.

63

THE VERB: *PE YOD* : QAL

There are two types of *Pe Yod* verbs:

- those which have always begun with the letter י, and
- those which now begin with י but originally began with the letter ו.

The second type is sometimes called a *Pe Vav* verb, or an "original *Pe Vav* verb." In Qal Perfect, both types of verb look the same. But in the Imperfect they are slightly different, and in some of the derived forms (Niphal, Hiphil and Hophal), the original ו will come back

For instance, the verb יָנַק has always been a *Pe Yod* verb, and its Hiphil is הֵינִיק, as we would expect. The verb יָלַד, on the other hand, is "original *Pe Vav*." That is, in old Hebrew it was ולד. We do not see this form any more in the Qal, but in the Hiphil the original ו returns and we see the form הוֹלִיד.

True *Pe Yod* verbs are very few. Only three are common, and they are found only in Qal and Hiphil:

יָטַב	to be good or pleasing (***Hiph***. to *do* good)
יָנַק	to suck (***Hiph***. to nurse [a child])
ילל	***Hiph***. to cry loudly in sorrow, howl, wail

Original *Pe Vav* verbs are also few, and only eleven are common (occurring more than 200 times). In general, they are found only in Qal, Niphal, Hiphil and Hophal:

יָדַע	to know	יָסַף	to add	יָרַשׁ	to take possession
יָכֹל	to be able	יָצָא	to exit, to come or go out	יָשַׁב	to sit, to live or dwell
יָלַד	to bear [a child]	יָרֵא	to fear	ישׁע[2]	to save
יָלַךְ	to go[1]	יָרַד	to go down		

The verbs יָכֹל, יָצָא and יָרֵא will be discussed in more detail in later chapters.

Pe Yod and *Pe Vav* in Qal

In *Original Pe Vav* verbs, the original ו was a very weak letter. In the Qal, it always disappears. It may be replaced by a י but sometimes even the י disappears. Example: here is what happens to the verb יָשַׁב (originally ושׁב) in the Qal Impf 2ms:

וָשַׁב+תּ → תֵּישֵׁב → תֵּשֵׁב

The *vav* disappears completely.[3] The Impv is then formed by removing the prefix from the Impf:

---

[1] This verb is used in the Imperfect, but not in the Perfect. In the Perfect, הָלַךְ is used. These two verbs work like a team. We will learn about verb "teams" in §76.

[2] This verb does not come in the Qal, and so no vowel points are shown for its root form (p. 136 note 8).

[3] Note that in this case the *tsere* under the prefix does *not* represent a swallowed *nun* or rejected *dagesh*. Rather, it represents the first radical of the verb (the original ו which became a י and then disappeared).

תֵּשֵׁב minus תּ → שֵׁב

The IC also drops the original ו and then gains a final ת- (like the *Pe Nun* which loses its נ and gains a ת). Thus, the IC becomes שֶׁבֶת.

Following is a comparison of a true *Pe Yod* verb (יָנַק) and an original *Pe Vav* verb (יָשַׁב). They are both regular in the Qal Perfect, and so we only need to look at the Qal Imperfect and other Qal forms. In the Imperfect, the original *Pe Vav* verb has two forms:

- one in which the original *vav* is rejected completely: ושב + י → יֵשֵׁב
- a second in which it is replaced by a *yod*: ורשׁ + י → יִירַשׁ

Imperfect

	True Pe Yod	*Original Pe Vav*			*True Pe Yod*	*Original Pe Vav*	
3ms	יִינַק	יֵשֵׁב	יִירַשׁ	3mp	יִינְקוּ	יֵשְׁבוּ	יִירְשׁוּ
3fs	תִּינַק	תֵּשֵׁב	תִּירַשׁ	3fp	תִּינַקְנָה	תֵּשַׁבְנָה	תִּירַשְׁנָה
2ms	תִּינַק	תֵּשֵׁב	תִּירַשׁ	2mp	תִּינְקוּ	תֵּשְׁבוּ	תִּירְשׁוּ
2fs	תִּינְקִי	תֵּשְׁבִי	תִּירְשִׁי	2fp	תִּינַקְנָה	תֵּשַׁבְנָה	תִּירַשְׁנָה
1cs	אִינַק	אֵשֵׁב	אִירַשׁ	1cp	נִינַק	נֵשֵׁב	נִירַשׁ

Impf + w.c. (*note accent*)

	True Pe Yod	*Original Pe Vav*	
3ms	וַיִּינַק	וַיֵּשֶׁב	וַיִּירַשׁ

Act. Part.	יֹנֵק	יֹשֵׁב
Pass. Part.	יָנוּק	יָשׁוּב

Imperative

Original Pe Vav
(No examples are found in True Pe Yod)

2ms	שֵׁב	*(long form:* שְׁבָה*)*
2fs	שְׁבִי	
2mp	שְׁבוּ	
2fp	שֵׁבְנָה	

Infinitives

	True Pe Yod	*Original Pe Vav*
Absolute	יָנוֹק	יָשׁוֹב
Construct	יְנֹק	שֶׁבֶת

(*with* -לְ: לָשֶׁבֶת)
(*with* 1cs suff *and* -לְ: לְשִׁבְתִּי)

Things You Should Know

1. *Pe Yod* verbs are verbs which have a י for their first letter.
2. Some *Pe Yod* verbs were originally *Pe Vav*. This *vav* was a very weak letter, and it often disappears completely in the Qal. However, it returns in the Niphal, Hiphil and Hophal (next chapter).

64

THE VERB: *PE YOD* : NIPHAL, HIPHIL, HOPHAL

Original *Pe Vav* verbs are also found in Niphal, Hiphil and Hophal, and in all three cases the original ו returns. Original *Pe Yod* verbs are not found in Niphal or Hophal, but they are found in Hiphil where the י causes the *hireq* under the prefix to lengthen to a *tsere*.

64.1 *Pe Yod* and *Pe Vav* in Hiphil

Perfect

	True Pe Yod	*Original Pe Vav*
3ms	הֵינִיק	הוֹשִׁיב
3fs	הֵינִ֫יקָה	הוֹשִׁ֫יבָה
2ms	הֵינַ֫קְתָּ	הוֹשַׁ֫בְתָּ
2fs	הֵינַקְתְּ	הוֹשַׁבְתְּ
1cs	הֵינַ֫קְתִּי	הוֹשַׁ֫בְתִּי
3cp	הֵינִ֫יקוּ	הוֹשִׁ֫יבוּ
2mp	הֵינַקְתֶּם	הוֹשַׁבְתֶּם
2fp	הֵינַקְתֶּן	הוֹשַׁבְתֶּן
1cp	הֵינַ֫קְנוּ	הוֹשַׁ֫בְנוּ

Imperfect

	True Pe Yod	*Original Pe Vav*
3ms	יֵינִיק	יוֹשִׁיב
3fs	תֵּינִיק	תּוֹשִׁיב
2ms	תֵּינִיק	תּוֹשִׁיב
2fs	תֵּינִ֫יקִי	תּוֹשִׁ֫יבִי
1cs	אֵינִיק	אוֹשִׁיב
3mp	יֵינִ֫יקוּ	יוֹשִׁ֫יבוּ
3fp	תֵּינֵ֫קְנָה	תּוֹשֵׁ֫בְנָה
2mp	תֵּינִ֫יקוּ	תּוֹשִׁ֫יבוּ
2fp	תֵּינֵ֫קְנָה	תּוֹשֵׁ֫בְנָה
1cp	נֵינִיק	נוֹשִׁיב

Imperative

2ms	הֵינֵק	הוֹשֵׁב
2fs	הֵינִ֫יקִי	הוֹשִׁ֫יבִי
2mp	הֵינִ֫יקוּ	הוֹשִׁ֫יבוּ
2fp	הֵינֵ֫קְנָה	הוֹשֵׁ֫בְנָה

Participle (Active)	מֵינִיק	מוֹשִׁיב
Short Impf	יֵינֵק	יוֹשֵׁב
Impf + w.c.	וַיֵּ֫ינֶק	וַיּ֫וֹשֶׁב

(*Note accent shift, final short vowel*)

Infinitives

Absolute	הֵינֵק	הוֹשֵׁב
Construct	הֵינִיק	הוֹשִׁיב

Several of these forms are identical:

- Perf 3ms and Infinitive Construct
- Perf 3cp and Impv 2mp
- Impv 2ms and Infinitive Absolute

With most verb forms, the Impv 2ms is the same as the IC. This is not true for the Hiphil, however, as we have seen (§50.2.6, p. 150). Thus, with the *Pe Yod* Hiphil; the Impv 2ms = IA (not IC).

64.2 *Pe Vav* in Niphal and Hophal

As mentioned above, true *Pe Yod* verbs are found only in Qal and Hiphil. However, original *Pe Vav* verbs are also found in Niphal and Hophal (and, rarely, in a few other forms). Again, the original ו returns.

Perfect

	Niphal	Hophal
3ms	נוֹשַׁב	הוּשַׁב
3fs	נוֹשְׁבָה	הוּשְׁבָה
2ms	נוֹשַׁבְתָּ	הוּשַׁבְתָּ
2fs	נוֹשַׁבְתְּ	הוּשַׁבְתְּ
1cs	נוֹשַׁבְתִּי	הוּשַׁבְתִּי
3cp	נוֹשְׁבוּ	הוּשְׁבוּ
2mp	נוֹשַׁבְתֶּם	הוּשַׁבְתֶּם
2fp	נוֹשַׁבְתֶּן	הוּשַׁבְתֶּן
1cp	נוֹשַׁבְנוּ	הוּשַׁבְנוּ

Imperfect

	Niphal	Hophal
3ms	יִוָּשֵׁב	יוּשַׁב
3fs	תִּוָּשֵׁב	תּוּשַׁב
2ms	תִּוָּשֵׁב	תּוּשַׁב
2fs	תִּוָּשְׁבִי	תּוּשְׁבִי
1cs	אִוָּשֵׁב	אוּשַׁב
3mp	יִוָּשְׁבוּ	יוּשְׁבוּ
3fp	תִּוָּשַׁבְנָה	תּוּשַׁבְנָה
2mp	תִּוָּשְׁבוּ	תּוּשְׁבוּ
2fp	תִּוָּשַׁבְנָה	תּוּשַׁבְנָה
1cp	נִוָּשֵׁב	נוּשַׁב

Imperative

	Niphal	Hophal
2ms	הִוָּשֵׁב	—
2fs	הִוָּשְׁבִי	—
2mp	הִוָּשְׁבוּ	—
2fp	הִוָּשַׁבְנָה	—

Infinitives

	Niphal	Hophal
Absolute	—	—
Construct	הִוָּשֵׁב	הוּשַׁב
Participle (Passive)	נוֹשָׁב	מוּשָׁב

There are several things to note in the above chart.

1. The Hophal has *shureq* (וּ) rather than *qamets-hatuph*.
2. In the Niphal Impf, Impv and Inf, however, the ו is a consonant plus *dagesh forte* (וּ = ww), not *shureq* (û).[1] The verb is regular in these cases, and follows the normal Niphal pattern: ○○○̣△.

Things You Should Know

1. There are very few "true *Pe Yod* verbs," and they are found only in Qal and Hiphil.
2. "Original *Pe Vav* verbs" are also found in Qal and Hiphil. In addition, they are found in:
   - Niphal (where the ו often appears as a consonant with a *dagesh*: יִוָּשֵׁב) and
   - Hophal (where verbs use *shureq* rather than *qamets-hatuph*: יוּשַׁב).

[1] We know this because in these cases there are vowels before and under the וּ (review §5.2, p. 12).

Exercise #41

אֹהֶל	tent
חָזָק	*adj.* strong (*the verb is* חָזַק, *Ex. #33*)
יטב	***Qal** Impf*[2] יִיטַב to *be* good; **Hi** הֵיטִיב to *do* good
יָלַד	**Qal** to bear children (father or mother); **Ni** נוֹלַד to be born; **Hi** הוֹלִיד to become the father of
יֶ֫לֶד	male child (יַלְדָּה, female child, *occurs only 3 times*)
יָרַשׁ	**Qal** to take possession, inherit, displace someone; **Hi** הוֹרִישׁ to drive out
מְלָאכָה	*f.* work, craft, business; *cs.* מְלֶ֫אכֶת; *pl. cs.* מַלְאֲכוֹת (*do not confuse with* מַלְאָךְ, *which you learned in Ex. 28*)
מַלְכוּת	*f.* kingdom, power; *pl.* מַלְכֻיּוֹת
מַמְלָכָה	*f.* kingdom, power, *cs.* מַמְלֶ֫כֶת; *pl.* מַמְלָכוֹת, *cs.* מַמְלְכוֹת
נָגַף	**Qal** to hit, beat, injure; **Ni** נִגַּף[3] to be beaten
נצל	***Ni** Impf*[4] יִנָּצֵל to be rescued, saved; to escape; **Hi** הִצִּיל to take away, to rescue
שֵׁ֫בֶט	tribe; *pl.* שְׁבָטִים, *cs.* שִׁבְטֵי

[1] וַיֹּ֫אמֶר הַמֶּ֫לֶךְ חֲזָקָה מַלְכוּתִי מִן מַמְלָכוֹת אֲחֵרוֹת [6]וְאֵין־לִי בֵּן׃ וְעַתָּה יִיטַב[5]
בְּעֵינֵי־אֱלֹהִים לְהֵיטִיב לִי וּלְחַזֵּק אֶת־כִּסְאִי׃ [2] וּבַחֹ֫דֶשׁ הָרְבִיעִי בַּשָּׁנָה הָאַחֶ֫רֶת[7]
יָלְדָה הַמַּלְכָּה[9] בֵּן׃ וּמִן־הַבֶּ֫טֶן[8] בָּחַר הַיֶּ֫לֶד אֶת־דַּרְכֵי־יְהוָה לְשָׁמְרָם בְּכָל־לְבָבוֹ׃
וַיּוֹלִיד הַמֶּ֫לֶךְ בָּנִים אֲחֵרִים וּבָנוֹת אֲחֵרוֹת׃ [3] וַיְהִי זָקֵן הַמֶּ֫לֶךְ [10]וַיִּקָּהֵל הָעָם וַיַּמְלִ֫יכוּ
אֶת־בְּנוֹ׃ וַיִּמְלֹךְ בְּנוֹ בֶּאֱמֶת וְרָעִים רֵעָיו וַיֶּחֶטְאוּ[11] עַל־יְהוָה׃ [4] וַיַּגִּיד נְגִיד־הָעָם אֶת־
הַחֲטָאִים הָאֵ֫לֶּה אֶל־הַמֶּ֫לֶךְ־הֶחָדָשׁ וַיִּקְצֹף וַיִּקְרַב אֶל־רֵעָיו׃ וַיֹּ֫אמֶר אַתֶּם הַגְּדוֹלִים
[12]מֵרֵעַי וְלֹא אַתֶּם הַחֲכָמִים מֵהֶם׃ [5] שָׁלַח הַמֶּ֫לֶךְ מַלְאָכִים אֶל־כָּל־מַמְלַכְתּוֹ לִשְׁאֹל
[14]לִמְלֶ֫אכֶת־עֲבָדָיו[13]׃ וַיַּגִּידוּ לוֹ מַלְאָכָיו כַּאֲשֶׁר שָׁבוּ לֵאמֹר רַב רְכוּשְׁךָ וַחֲזָקָה
מַלְכוּתֶךָ׃ [6] הוֹי הַגּוֹיִם הָהֵם אֲשֶׁר כָּבְדָה אָזְנָם[15] וְלֹא שָׁמְעוּ אֶת־דִּבְרֵי־נְבִיאֵיהֶם׃
יִגְּפוּם וְהִשְׁמִידֻם[16] אֹיְבֵיהֶם וְלֹא יִהְיֶה לָהֶם לְהַצִּילָם׃ יוֹרִישׁוּם גּוֹיִם אֲחֵרִים וְלָקְחוּ אֶת־

---

[2] יטב has no Qal Perfect.

[3] Do not confuse נִגַּף with Piel. This verb does not have a Piel form. If it did, it would be נִגֵּף.

[4] The Niphal Perfect of נצל occurs only once in the OT: נִצַּלְנוּ.

[5] Should this word be treated as Imperfect or Jussive? Continue reading the sentence, and let the context help you answer this question.

[6] Translate the -וְ "but" or "and yet."

[7] Translate "the next."

[8] That is, from the time he was born.

[9] Translate "the queen" (wife of the king). The Hebrew word for *queen* occurs only 35 times in the OT and so it has not been included in the vocabulary above. The word מֶ֫לֶךְ occurs more than 2,700 times.

[10] Note the double use of w.c. in this sentence. See page 94, footnote 16 for help in translating.

[11] Qal Impf 3mp + w.c. This is a *Pe* Guttural verb, and will be studied in the next chapter.

[12] The מ is a prefixed מִן The *hireq* has lengthened to *ṣere* because of the rejected *dagesh*.

[13] עֶ֫בֶד plus suffix.

[14] Translate this ל prefix *about* or *concerning*.

[15] For the use of the singular here, see page 117, note 3. "Heavy ears" means unwillingness to listen.

[16] When the Perf 3cp takes object suffixes, the final וּ- of the 3cp often becomes *qibbuṣ* (ֻ); §56.3, p. 166.

אַרְצָם׃ [7] קָֽצְפוּ אֲחֵי־יוֹסֵף וַיֶּֽחֱזִיקוּ אֹתוֹ וְלֹא יָכֹל לְהִנָּצֵל׃ וַיִּמְכְּרוּהוּ מִצְרַיְמָה אֲשֶׁר
חָזַק שָׁם וְשָׁם שְׁמוֹ פַּרְעֹה עַל־כָּל־רְכֻשׁוֹ[18]׃ [8] וְחַכָמָה[17] הָאָמָה וַתֵּיטִב בְּעֵינֵי־נְגִיד־
יְרִיחוֹ׃ וַיִּתְּנֶהָ[19] שׁוֹר עֲשָׂרָה וּבָקָר רָב׃ [9] וַיַּקְהֵל יְהוֹשֻׁעַ אֶת־כָּל־שִׁבְטֵי־יִשְׂרָאֵל
שְׁכֶמָה וַיִּקְרָא לְזִקְנֵי־יִשְׂרָאֵל וּלְרָאשָׁיו וּלְשֹׁפְטָיו וּלְכָל־קְהַל־יִשְׂרָאֵל׃ וַיֹּאמֶר זִכְרוּ כִּי
הִבְדִּיל אֱלֹהִים אֹתְכֶם לוֹ לְעָם וַתִּנָּצְלוּ מִמִּצְרַיִם בְּיָדוֹ׃ וְעַתָּה הוֹרַשְׁתֶּם גּוֹיִם לִפְנֵיכֶם
וַתִּירְשׁוּ אֶת־אַרְצָתָם׃ [10] יְרוּשָׁלַם מְלֶאכֶת־יַד־יְהוָה הֻתְשָׁמֵד׃ הֲיִירָשׁוּהָ אֹיְבֶיהָ׃
הֲלֹא יַצִּילֶנָּה[21] יְהוָה׃ [11] שָׁב אִישׁ־יְרִיחוֹ אֶל־יְרוּשָׁלַם שֵׁנִית[20] וַיִּגַּשׁ אֶל־הַהֵיכָל לְמַעַן
הַגִּישׁ שׁוֹר׃ [12] וַיְהִי כִּי־יָשַׁב הַמֶּלֶךְ בְּבֵיתוֹ וַיהוָה[22] נָתַן־לוֹ שָׁלוֹם מִכָּל־אֹיְבָיו׃ וַיֹּאמֶר
הַמֶּלֶךְ אֶל־נָתָן[24] הַנָּבִיא רְאֵה[23] נָא אָנֹכִי יוֹשֵׁב בְּבֵית־עֵץ וַאֲרוֹן־הָאֱלֹהִים יֹשֵׁב בְּאֹהֶל׃
וַיֹּאמֶר נָתָן אֶל־הַמֶּלֶךְ כֹּל אֲשֶׁר בִּלְבָבְךָ לֵךְ[26] עֲשֵׂה[25] כִּי יְהוָה עִמָּךְ׃ [13] וַיְהִי בַּלַּיְלָה
הַהוּא וַיְהִי דְבַר־יְהוָה אֶל־נָתָן לֵאמֹר׃[27] לֵךְ וְאָמַרְתָּ אֶל־דָּוִד כֹּה אָמַר יְהוָה הַאַתָּה
תַּעֲשֶׂה־לִּי בַּיִת לְשִׁבְתִּי[29]׃ כִּי לֹא יָשַׁבְתִּי בְּבַיִת [28]לְמִיּוֹם הַצֲלֹתִי אֶת־בְּנֵי יִשְׂרָאֵל
מִמִּצְרַיִם וְעַד הַיּוֹם הַזֶּה וָאֶהְיֶה מִתְהַלֵּךְ בְּאֹהֶל׃ [14] וְעַתָּה כֹּה־תֹאמַר[30] לְעַבְדִּי לְדָוִד
כֹּה אָמַר יְהוָה־צְבָאוֹת אֲנִי לְקַחְתִּיךָ מֵאַחַר הַצֹּאן לִהְיוֹת[31] נָגִיד עַל־עַמִּי עַל־יִשְׂרָאֵל׃
[15] וָאֶהְיֶה עִמְּךָ בְּכֹל אֲשֶׁר הָלַכְתָּ וָאַכְרִתָה[33] אֶת־כָּל־אֹיְבֶיךָ מִפָּנֶיךָ וְעָשִׂתִי[32] לְךָ שֵׁם
גָּדוֹל כְּשֵׁם הַגְּדֹלִים אֲשֶׁר בָּאָרֶץ׃ וְהִגִּיד לְךָ יְהוָה כִּי־בַיִת יַעֲשֶׂה־לְּךָ יְהוָה׃

---

[17] Feminine adjective.

[18] This short form of רְכוּשׁ is found in Genesis. The long form is seen in the later Hebrew of Ezra and Chronicles.

[19] Impf of נָתַן plus w.c. and suffix.

[20] Add the word *time*. It is often missing in Hebrew. For the word שֵׁנִית, see §58.2, p. 174.

[21] Note the extra -נ- (§57.1, p. 169).

[22] For the vowel pointing, see p. 194, footnote 34.

[23] Qal Impv ms.

[24] Nathan (the prophet).

[25] Qal Impv ms.

[26] Qal Impv ms < הלך. **Technical note:** We will learn later that the impv of הלך actually comes from ילך.

[27] Remember that *soph passuq* sometimes appears where we would expect a comma (p. 182, note 5).

[28] This unusual construction, with two prefixed prepositions, is found this way in the Bible. Ignore the -לְ in your translation.

[29] Qal IC + suffix +ל < ישׁב. See the lesson, and note that the IC of an Original *Pe Vav* verb is a segholate. It will take suffixes in the same way as a segholate noun. Thus, the vowel pointing has changed.

[30] Qal Impf 3fs.

[31] IC + ל < היה.

[32] Qal Perf 1cs + w.c. < עָשָׂה.

[33] Hiph Cohortative. The word appears this way in the Bible. But here, it is best to translate it as an Impf+w.c.

65

THE VERB: *PE* GUTTURAL

Pe Guttural verbs have a guttural in the first radical. They have the following characteristics:

- **A simple *shewa* under the first radical may become a composite *shewa*.** Example: the Qal Perf 2mp of שָׁמַר is שְׁמַרְתֶּם, but for עָמַד it becomes עֲמַדְתֶּם.
- **The first radical will attract *pathahs* under it and near it**. Example: the Qal Impf 2fs of שָׁמַר is תִּשְׁמְרִי, but for עָמַד it becomes תַּעַמְדִי. (The *pathah* under the prefix may make you think this is Hiphil, but the Hiphil will also have either *hireq-yod* or *tsere*, as we shall see.)
- **The first radical will reject *dagesh*.** Example: the Niph Impf 3ms of שָׁמַר is יִשָּׁמֵר, but for עָמַד it becomes יֵעָמֵד. The *hireq* under the *yod* has lengthened to *tsere* because of the rejected *dagesh*.

Only the Qal, Niphal, Hiphil and Hophal are affected by the *Pe* guttural. (This is because the Piel, Pual and Hithpael never place a *shewa* under the *Pe* radical, and they never place a *dagesh* in it.)

65.1 Qal

In **Perfect, Infinitive Construct**, and **Imperatives**, a simple *shewa* will become composite *shewa* (עֲמַדְתֶּם ,עֲמֹד). In **Imperfect**, the guttural attracts *pathah* (יַעֲמֹד) – ***except for stative verbs***, where there are *e* vowels (יֶחֱזַק) instead of *a* vowels. The **Infinitive Absolute** and **Participles** are regular.

Perfect

3ms	עָמַד
3fs	עָמְדָה
2ms	עָמַדְתָּ
2fs	עָמַדְתְּ
1cs	עָמַדְתִּי
3cp	עָמְדוּ
2mp	עֲמַדְתֶּם
2fp	עֲמַדְתֶּן
1cp	עָמַדְנוּ

Infinitives

Absolute	עָמוֹד
Construct	עֲמֹד

Participles

Active	עֹמֵד
Passive	עָמוּד

Imperfect

	Non-Stative	Stative
3ms	יַעֲמֹד	יֶחֱזַק
3fs	תַּעֲמֹד	תֶּחֱזַק
2ms	תַּעֲמֹד	תֶּחֱזַק
2fs	תַּעַמְדִי	תֶּחֶזְקִי
1cs	אֶעֱמֹד	אֶחֱזַק
3mp	יַעַמְדוּ	יֶחֶזְקוּ
3fp	תַּעֲמֹדְנָה	תֶּחֱזַקְנָה
2mp	תַּעַמְדוּ	תֶּחֶזְקוּ
2fp	תַּעֲמֹדְנָה	תֶּחֱזַקְנָה
1cp	נַעֲמֹד	נֶחֱזַק

Imperative

2ms	עֲמֹד	חֲזַק
2fs	עִמְדִי	חִזְקִי
2mp	עִמְדוּ	חִזְקוּ
2fp	עֲמֹדְנָה	חֲזַקְנָה

A note on "Harsh Gutturals." The letters ח and ה are known as "harsh" (very sharp or strong) gutturals. They will sometimes behave differently than the other gutturals. At times, these harsh gutturals are able to take simple *shewa*. In the table above, the Impf 3ms of חָזַק is יֶחֱזַק, and the simple *shewa* has become a composite *shewa*. But the Impf 3ms of the verb חָמַד does not do this; it is יַחְמֹד. And the Impf 3ms of חָשַׁךְ is יֶחְשַׁךְ. In both of these cases, the ח has taken a simple *shewa*.

65.2 Niphal

In the **Perfect** and **Participle**, the guttural takes composite *shewa*, and we see ○○○ֱנֶ instead of ○○○ְנִ. In the **Imperfect, Imperative** and **Infinitives**, the guttural rejects the Niphal's *dagesh*, and the vowel under the prefix lengthens from *hireq* to *tsere*. Thus, we see ○○○ָ△ֵ instead of ○○○ּ△ִ. The rest of the vowel pointing remains unchanged.

Perfect		Imperfect		Imperative		Participle	
3ms	נֶעֱמַד	3ms	יֵעָמֵד	2ms	הֵעָמֵד	ms	נֶעֱמָד
3fs	נֶעֶמְדָה	3fs	תֵּעָמֵד	2fs	הֵעָמְדִי	**Infinitives**	
2ms	נֶעֱמַדְתָּ	2ms	תֵּעָמֵד	2mp	הֵעָמְדוּ	Con.	הֵעָמֵד[1]
2fs	נֶעֱמַדְתְּ	2fs	תֵּעָמְדִי	2fp	הֵעָמַדְנָה	Abs.	נַעֲמֹד,
etc.		etc.					הֵעָמֹד

Watch the similar forms: Qal Impf 1cp נַעֲמֹד, Niph Perf 3ms נֶעֱמַד and Niph Part ms נֶעֱמָד. Again, there is a *pathah/qamets* difference between the Perf 3ms and the Part ms.

65.3 Hiphil

Throughout the Hiphil, the guttural takes composite *shewa*. Thus, we see ○י○○ֱהֶ in Perfect, instead of ○י○○ְהִ; prefixed forms are ○י○○ֲ△ַ instead of ○י○○ְ△ַ. Other vowel pointing remains unchanged.

Perfect		Imperfect		Imperative		Participle	
3ms	הֶעֱמִיד	3ms	יַעֲמִיד	2ms	הַעֲמֵד	ms	מַעֲמִיד
3fs	הֶעֱמִידָה	3fs	תַּעֲמִיד	2fs	הַעֲמִידִי	**Infinitives**	
2ms	הֶעֱמַדְתָּ	2ms	תַּעֲמִיד	2mp	הַעֲמִידוּ	Con.	הַעֲמִיד
2fs	הֶעֱמַדְתְּ	2fs	תַּעֲמִידִי	2fp	הַעֲמֵדְנָה	Abs.	הַעֲמֵד
etc.		etc.					

65.4 Hophal

The guttural takes composite *shewa* throughout the Hophal, also. Thus, in Perfect we see ○○○ֳהָ and ○○○ֲהָ instead of ○○○ְהָ. And in prefixed forms we see ○○○ֳ△ָ and ○○○ֲ△ָ instead of ○○○ְ△ָ. But note:

The vowel point under the ה or the prefix is still *qamets-hatuph*, even though there is a *metheg*.

---

[1] With ל prefix, the ל replaces the ה just like it does with the definite article: לְ + הֵעָמֵד → לֵעָמֵד.

That is, הָֽעֳמַד is pronounced ho-ᶜᵒmad̲, in spite of the *metheg* which has opened the syllable. The rest of the vowel pointing remains unchanged.

Perfect		**Imperfect**		**Imperative**		**Participle**	
3ms	הָֽעֳמַד	3ms	יָֽעֳמַד	2ms	—	ms	מָֽעֳמָד
3fs	הָֽעֳמְדָה	3fs	תָּֽעֳמַד	2fs	—	fs	—
						Infinitives	
2ms	הָֽעֳמַדְתָּ	2ms	תָּֽעֳמַד	2mp	—	Con.	—
2fs	הָֽעֳמַדְתְּ	2fs	תָּֽעֳמְדִי	2fp	—	Abs.	הָֽעֳמֵד
	etc.		etc.				

Things You Should Know

1. The *Pe* Guttural verb has the following characteristics:
   - A simple *shewa* under the first radical may become a composite *shewa*
   - The first radical will often attract *pathahs* under it and near it
   - The first radical will reject *dagesh*
2. These characteristics will affect the Qal, Niphal, Hiphil and Hophal. Carefully study the charts in the lesson to note the particular changes which take place with the various forms.
3. The Qal Stative *Pe* guttural verb develops differently from the non-Stative verbs. It uses *e* vowels instead of *a* vowels.

66

THE VERB: *PE ALEPH*

Pe Aleph verbs have an א for their first radical. This א is a guttural, and so the *Pe Aleph* verbs will generally behave like the other *Pe Guttural* verbs. But there is one difference: the א often loses its vowel and becomes silent (quiescent; review §17, p. 49, if necessary). This especially affects the Qal Imperfect. The Qal Imperatives (2ms and 2fp) and Infinitive Construct are also slightly different from other *Pe Guttural* verbs.

Verbs are called *Pe Aleph* **only if the first-radical א sometimes becomes silent**. Other verbs with a first-radical א are simply called *Pe* Guttural. There are five *Pe Aleph* verbs:

אָבַד, to become lost; to die or to perish	אָמַר, to say
אָבָה, to be willing	אָפָה, to bake
אָכַל, to eat;	

Two of these verbs are also *Lamed He*, and so are doubly weak.

66.1 The Qal *Pe Aleph* verb

Perfect

(same as other *Pe Gutturals*)

Participles

(regular)

Imperative

2ms	אֱבֹד
2fs	אִבְדִי
2mp	אִבְדוּ
2fp	אֱבֹדְנָה

Infinitives

Abs. אָבוֹד

Const. אֱבֹד, אֲבֹד, with -לְ: לֶאֱבֹד

Imperfect

3ms	יֹאבַד	
3fs	תֹּאבַד	
2ms	תֹּאבַד	
2fs	תֹּאבְדִי	
1cs	אֹבַד	(see below)
3mp	יֹאבְדוּ	
3fp	תֹּאבַדְנָה	
2mp	תֹּאבְדוּ	
2fp	תֹּאבַדְנָה	
1cp	נֹאבַד	

66.1.1 **The Qal Impf 1cs** is especially unusual: אבד + א → אֹאבַד → אֹבַד

66.1.2 **In pause**, the Imperfect almost always becomes יֹאבַד (יֹאבֵד), תֹּאבַד (תֹּאבֵד), etc., with a *tsere* replacing the *pathah* under the second radical.

66.1.3 **Other forms** (Niphal, Piel, etc.) follow the patterns you have already studied for *Pe* Guttural verbs.

66.2 The verb אָמַר

The verb אָמַר is somewhat unusual. But it is so common that you will easily learn it as you read.

66.2.1 **The IC with** -לְ is pointed לֵאמֹר, and is usually translated *saying* or not translated at all. It often appears in sentences such as the following (Gen 8:15-16):

וַיְדַבֵּר אֱלֹהִים אֶל־נֹחַ לֵאמֹר׃ צֵא מִן־הַתֵּבָה....

"And God spoke to Noah saying, 'Go out of the ark . . .'" (Gen 8:15-16)

66.2.2 **In pause,** the Impf 3ms and Impf 1cs of אָמַר *do not* take *tsere* instead of *pathah* (cf. §66.1.2, above). Rather, the *pathah* remains: יֹאמַר (יֹאמַר) and אֹמַר (אֹמַר).

66.2.3 **With Impf + *vav* consecutive,** the accent moves forward (toward the prefix), and the second radical usually gains a *seghol*: וַיֹּאמֶר, וַתֹּאמֶר, etc. However,

- **in pause,** the *pathah* returns, and the accent returns to the last syllable: וַיֹּאמַר (וַיֹּאמַר), וַתֹּאמַר (וַתֹּאמַר), etc.
- In all cases, the **1cs** + w.c. will be וָאֹמַר (accent on last syllable)

Things You Should Know

1. ***Pe Aleph* verbs** act like other *Pe* Guttural verbs, except that the א often loses its vowel and becomes silent. This especially affects the Qal Imperfect.
2. **The Qal Impf 1cs** of *Pe Aleph* verbs follows the pattern אֹבַד (from אאבד).
3. **In pause**, the Imperfect will usually have a *tsere* under the second radical (יֹאבֵד) rather than a *pathah*. But the Impf 3ms and Impf 1cs of אָמַר will remain with *pathah* even in pause (יֹאמַר, אֹמַר).
4. **The verb** אָמַר is unusual in several ways.
   - The IC will be pointed לֵאמֹר and will be translated *saying*
   - With Impf + w.c., the accent moves forward and the vowel under the second radical becomes *seghol* (וַיֹּאמֶר) ***except*** for the 1cs (וָאֹמַר) and when in pause (וַיֹּאמַר).

Exercise #42

אָהַב to love, *Impf* יֶאֱהַב

אָסַף to gather, take away; ***Ni*** נֶאֱסַף to be gathered

חַיִל army, power, wealth

חֶסֶד faithfulness, loyalty

חֶרֶב *m.* sword, *pl.* חֲרָבוֹת

יָסַף to add, to do (something) again, to continue to do; ***Hi*** הוֹסִיף to add, increase, continue doing (something)

מִשְׁפָּחָה *f.* extended family, clan

נַחֲלָה *f.* inheritance, heritage

עָזַר to help

פָּקַד to appoint, number (count), punish

קֶרֶב middle of; בְּקֶרֶב[1] in the midst of, among (cf. קָרַב)

שַׂר prince, official, commander, leader

[1] לֹא יָסְפוּ הָאִישׁ וְהָאִשָּׁה לִהְיוֹת[3] עֲרֻמִּים עַל[2] הַנָּחָשׁ וְגַם לֹא יָסְפוּ לָשֶׁבֶת בְּעֵדֶן׃
[2] וַיֹּאמֶר יְהוָה לְאַבְרָם אֲבָרֲכֶךָּ[4] וְנִבְרְכוּ בְךָ כֹּל מִשְׁפְּחוֹת־הָאֲדָמָה׃ וְגַם בָּא לוֹט אֵת
אַבְרָם וַיַּעֲשֶׂה יְהוָה אֶת־חַסְדּוֹ לְאַבְרָם׃ וַיֵּשֶׁב בְּאֹהָלִים וַיִּהְיוּ לוֹ חֲמוֹרִים וַאֲתוֹנוֹת
וּגְמַלִּים וַיְהִי[5] אֲבִי־שְׁבָטִים רַבִּים׃ [3] אָהַב יַעֲקֹב אֶת־רָחֵל וַתֵּלֶד בֵּן וַתֹּאמֶר אָסַף
אֱלֹהִים אֶת־צָרָתִי׃ וַתִּקְרָא אֶת־שְׁמוֹ יוֹסֵף לֵאמֹר יוֹסֵף[7] יְהוָה לִי בֵּן אַחֵר׃ וַתִּהְיֶינָה[6]
הִיא וַאֲחוֹתָהּ אִמּוֹת־שִׁבְטֵי־יִשְׂרָאֵל׃ [4] וַתֹּאמַרְנָה נָשָׁיו לוֹ אֵין־לָנוּ נַחֲלָה מֵאָבִינוּ מִלָּבָן
לָכֵן נֵעַזְבָה[8] וְנֵשְׁבָה בְּקֶרֶב עַמֶּךָ׃ [5] וַיְהִי בַּיָּמִים הָהֵם וַיִּגְדַּל מֹשֶׁה וַיֵּצֵא בְּקֶרֶב־אֶחָיו
וַיַּרְא[10] אִישׁ־מִצְרִי נֹגֵף אִישׁ־עִבְרִי מֵאֶחָיו׃ וַיַּרְא כִּי אֵין אִישׁ וַיַּגֵּף אֶת־הַמִּצְרִי וַיַּהַרְגֵהוּ[9]
וַיַּצִּיל אֶת־חַיֵּי־אָחִיו׃ [6] וַיֵּצֵא בַּיּוֹם הַשֵּׁנִי וְהִנֵּה שְׁנֵי־[11]אֲנָשִׁים עִבְרִים נִלְחָמִים וַיֹּאמֶר
לָרָשָׁע לָמָּה תַגֹּף רֵעֶךָ׃ [7] וַיֹּאמֶר מִי שָׂמְךָ לְאִישׁ שַׂר וְשֹׁפֵט[13] עָלֵינוּ [12]הַלְהָרְגֵנִי אַתָּה
אֹמֵר[14] כַּאֲשֶׁר הָרַגְתָּ אֶת־הַמִּצְרִי׃ וַיִּירָא מֹשֶׁה וַיֹּאמֶר לָכֵן נוֹדַע הַדָּבָר׃ [8] לֹא

---

[1] קֶרֶב (and בְּקֶרֶב) can take noun suffixes. Note the small but important difference between בְּקִרְבָּהּ "in her/its midst" (Gen 18:12,24) and the IC with prefix and suffix בְּקָרְבָהּ "when she came near" (Ex. 39 #1, p. 182).

[2] Translate "because of."

[3] Qal IC + ל < היה.

[4] Originally אֲבָרֶכְךָ, but the vowel pointing has changed due to pause.

[5] Translate "And he (that is, Abram) became."

[6] The verb is היה. It is Impf with w.c. With this information, you should be able to parse it.

[7] Shortened imperfect (see p. 197). Why? How will this affect your translation? **Technical note:** In the Bible, the word is actually spelled with *holem*, not *holem vav*: יֹסֵף.

[8] This verb has an additional *qameṣ he* suffix. So does the next one. What does this tell you?

[9] The guttural has attracted a *pathah.*

[10] Shortened form of Imperfect (from רָאָה). Why is the short form used here? (Review the box on p. 144 if you don't know.)

[11] If you have trouble with this word, see p. 172.

[12] *He* interrogative. See §14.3, p. 41.

[13] לְאִישׁ שַׂר וְשֹׁפֵט. Translate "to (be) a (like a) prince judging."

[14] Translate "thinking" or "planning."

תְּעָבֵד[16] אֱלֹהִים אֲחֵרִים כִּי לֹא יַעַזְרוּךָ׃ [9] זָכוֹר[15] אֶת־יוֹם־הַשַּׁבָּת לְקַדְּשׁוֹ׃ שֵׁשֶׁת־
יָמִים תַּעֲבֹד וְכָל־מְלַאכְתֶּךָ תַּעֲשֶׂה׃ [10] וְיוֹם־הַשְּׁבִיעִי שַׁבָּת לַיהוָה אֱלֹהֶיךָ לֹא־תַעֲשֶׂה
כָל[17]־מְלָאכָה אַתָּה וּבִנְךָ־וּבִתֶּךָ וְעַבְדְּךָ וַאֲמָתְךָ וּבְקָרֶךָ׃ [11] כִּי שֵׁשֶׁת־יָמִים עָשָׂה יְהוָה
אֶת־הַשָּׁמַיִם וְאֶת־הָאָרֶץ אֶת־הַיָּם וְאֶת־כָּל־אֲשֶׁר־בָּם וַיָּנַח[18] בַּיּוֹם הַשְּׁבִיעִי עַל־כֵּן בֵּרַךְ
יְהוָה אֶת־יוֹם־הַשַּׁבָּת וַיְקַדְּשֵׁהוּ׃ [12] נִגַּף הָאִישׁ בְּאֹיְבֵי־אָבִיהוּ כַּאֲשֶׁר יֶלֶד הוּא וַיִּנָּצֵל
בְּרֵעָיו׃ וַיִּגְדַּל וַיְהִי מֶלֶךְ וַיִּירַשׁ אֶת־אָהֳלֵי־אֹיְבוֹ׃ וַיֵּיטִב אֶל־רֵעָיו וַתִּגְדַּל מַמְלַכְתּוֹ׃
[13] וַיִּפָּקְדוּ אֲדֹנֵי־פְלִשְׁתִּים שָׂרִים עַל צִבְאֹתָם בַּעֲבוּר הוֹרִישׁ אֶת־עִבְרִים׃ וּבְקִרְבָּם
אַתֶּם חֲזָקִים הָעִבְרִיִּים[20] וַיִּפְּלוּ הַפְּלִשְׁתִּים לְפִי־חָרֶב[19]׃ [14] וַיִּקָּבְצוּ עֲדַת־יִשְׂרָאֵל
בַּשַּׁבָּת וַיֹּאמְרוּ נִרְדְּפָה לָהֶם פֶּן יוֹסִיפוּ קְרֹב לָרֶשֶׁת אֶת־נַחֲלָתֵנוּ׃ [15] הַשָּׁמַיִם וְהָאָרֶץ
מְלֶאכֶת־יַד־אֱלֹהִים וּמַמְלַכְתּוֹ לְעוֹלָם׃ אֶלְמְדָה אֶת־תּוֹרַת־יְהוָה וְאֶת־חַסְדּוֹ לְבִלְתִּי
עֲבוֹר[22] תּוֹרָתוֹ כִּי אָהַב אֶת־עַמּוֹ וּפָקַד אֶת־חֶטְאָם׃ רַק אֲלַמְּדָה [21]הָרְשָׁעִים דְּרָכָיו כִּי
נֶעֶזְרוּ הָעֹבְדִים־אֹתוֹ׃ [16] רָעֵב הַיֶּלֶד וַתִּשְׁלַח אִמּוֹ אֶת־בִּתָּהּ לֶאֱסֹף פְּרִי לְמַעַן אָכְלוֹ׃
וּבַיּוֹם הַשֵּׁנִי שְׁלָחָהּ עוֹד אֶת־בִּתָּהּ וְאֶת־אֹהֶל־רֵעֶיהָ בָּאָה׃ וַתֹּאמֶר לָהֶם מִכְרוּ־נָא בָשָׂר
לָנוּ פֶּן יָרַד לְבוֹר נֶפֶשׁ־אָחִי׃ [17] וַיְדַבֵּר הַנָּבִיא אֶל־הַמֶּלֶךְ לֵאמֹר יִוָּלֵד בֵּן לְךָ
וְהֵיטִיב לְמִשְׁפְּחוֹת־יִשְׂרָאֵל׃ וְהָיוּ[23] חֵילוֹ וּמַלְכוּתוֹ חֲזָקִים וְלֹא יִמְלֹךְ בְּיַד־חָרֶב׃
וַיִּיטַב הַדָּבָר הַזֶּה בְּעֵינֵי־הַמֶּלֶךְ׃

---

[15] We would expect to see an imperative here (זְכֹר). But this is how the verse is written in Exodus 20.

[16] This is not Qal. What is it? Review the lesson on *Pe* Gutturals. This form is used in Ex 20:5; 23:24; Dt 5:9. Translate "be caused to serve."

[17] Translate "any."

[18] Impf 3ms + w.c. < נוח, "to rest." This verb, and other "middle vowel verbs," will be learned in §68-69.

[19] Literally "to the mouth of the sword." Translate "by the sword" or "by the edge of the sword."

[20] Note the two spellings of this word in this exercise. Both are found in the Bible.

[21] This phrase has two objects: רְשָׁעִים and דְּרָכָיו (compare to Ps 51.15). Poetry often skips the sign of the definite direct object אֶת־.

[22] This is the Infinitive Construct, in spite of the וֹ. The IA is עָבוֹר (with *qameṣ*).

[23] Perf 3cp + w.c. < היה.

67

THE VERB: *AYIN* GUTTURAL

The guttural in the middle of *Ayin* Guttural verbs such as בָּחַר (or the ר in בֵּרַךְ) will do several things:

- It will **reject *dagesh***. This will affect the Piel, Pual and Hithpael since they put a *dagesh* in the middle radical of the verb. For instance, the Piel Perf of בֵּרַךְ is בֵּרַךְ, not בִּרֵּךְ.
- It will take **composite *shewa* instead of simple *shewa***. For instance, the Qal Perf 3fs of בָּחַר is בָּחֲרָה, not בָּחְרָה. This will affect all forms except Hiphil (which never has simple *shewa* under the middle radical).[1]
- It will **attract *pathahs***. This will affect the Qal Imperfect, where a *pathah* will replace the normal *holem*. For instance, the Qal Impf 3ms of בָּחַר is יִבְחַר, not יִבְחֹר.

67.1 Qal

Throughout the Qal, there will be composite *shewa* instead of simple *shewa*. In addition, in the Imperfect we shall see attracted *pathahs* as noted above.

	Perfect		Imperfect		Imperative
3ms	בָּחַר	3ms	יִבְחַר	2ms	בְּחַר
3fs	בָּחֲרָה	3fs	תִּבְחַר	2fs	בַּחֲרִי
2ms	בָּחַרְתָּ	2ms	תִּבְחַר	2mp	בַּחֲרוּ
2fs	בָּחַרְתְּ	2fs	תִּבְחֲרִי	2fp	בְּחַרְנָה
1cs	בָּחַרְתִּי	1cs	אֶבְחַר		
3cp	בָּחֲרוּ	3mp	יִבְחֲרוּ		**Participle** (regular)
2mp	בְּחַרְתֶּם	3fp	תִּבְחַרְנָה		
2fp	בְּחַרְתֶּן	2mp	תִּבְחֲרוּ		**Infinitives** (regular)
1cp	בָּחַרְנוּ	2fp	תִּבְחַרְנָה		
		1cp	נִבְחַר		

67.2 Niphal

The Niphal is regular except that the *ayin* guttural will have composite *shewa* instead of simple *shewa*. Following are some comparisons of a strong verb[2] (שָׁמַר) and an *Ayin* Guttural verb (בָּחַר) in Niphal:

[1] **Technical note:** It will also not affect the Hophal since, in the Bible, it does not appear in forms such as Perf 3fs or Impf 2fs which have simple *shewa* under the middle radical.

[2] To review the definition of strong and weak verbs, see the box on p. 150.

	Strong	*Ayin Guttural*		*Strong*	*Ayin Guttural*
Perf 3fs	נִשְׁמְרָה	נִבְחֲרָה	Perf 3cp	נִשְׁמְרוּ	נִבְחֲרוּ
Impf 2fs	תִּשָּׁמְרִי	תִּבָּחֲרִי	Impf 3mp	יִשָּׁמְרוּ	יִבָּחֲרוּ
Impv 2fs	הִשָּׁמְרִי	הִבָּחֲרִי	Impv 2mp	הִשָּׁמְרוּ	הִבָּחֲרוּ

The Niphal Participles and Infinitives are regular. So are most of the other parts of the Niphal Perfect, Imperfect and Imperative. The only irregularities occur when there is a *shewa* under the middle radical.

67.3 Piel

The Piel normally puts a *dagesh* in the second radical. The *Ayin* Guttural verb – and also verbs with ר in the second radical – will reject this *dagesh*. The preceding vowel may then lengthen. This depends upon which letter is found in the second radical:

67.3.1 If the second radical is א or ר, then the preceding vowel will lengthen in compensation. (Example: The Piel Perf of ברך is not בִּרֵּךְ, but rather is בֵּרַךְ[3]. The *hireq* lenthens to *tsere*.

67.3.2 If the second radical is ה ח or ע, the preceding vowel will usually *not* lengthen. Example: the Piel Perf of בער is not בִּעֵּר or בֵּעֵר but rather is בִּעֵר. The *dagesh* is rejected, but the *hireq* does not lengthen to *tsere*. In this case, the verb is essentially regular, except that the *dagesh* is missing.

And of course, for both types of verb, if there is a simple *shewa* under the second radical, it will become composite *shewa* with the guttural (though usually not with ר). The following chart gives examples of both these types of *Ayin* Guttural verb: a verb with ר in the second radical (בֵּרֵךְ, to bless) and a verb with ע in the second radical (בִּעֵר, to burn).

> **Important Note:** Although we lose the middle consonant *dagesh*, we have not lost the *shewa* under the prefixes (○○○Δ̣). This *shewa* will continue to tell you that you are looking at either Piel or Pual.

	Perfect	
3ms	בֵּרַךְ	בִּעֵר
3fs	בֵּרְכָה	בִּעֲרָה
2ms	בֵּרַכְתָּ	בִּעַרְתָּ
2fs	בֵּרַכְתְּ	בִּעַרְתְּ
1cs	בֵּרַכְתִּי	בִּעַרְתִּי
3cp	בֵּרְכוּ	בִּעֲרוּ
2mp	בֵּרַכְתֶּם	בִּעַרְתֶּם
2fp	בֵּרַכְתֶּן	בִּעַרְתֶּן
1cp	בֵּרַכְנוּ	בִּעַרְנוּ

	Imperfect	
3ms	יְבָרֵךְ	יְבַעֵר
3fs	תְּבָרֵךְ	תְּבַעֵר
2ms	תְּבָרֵךְ	תְּבַעֵר
2fs	תְּבָרְכִי	תְּבַעֲרִי
1cs	אֲבָרֵךְ	אֲבַעֵר
3mp	יְבָרְכוּ	יְבַעֲרוּ
3fp	תְּבָרֵכְנָה	תְּבַעֵרְנָה
2mp	תְּבָרְכוּ	תְּבַעֲרוּ
2fp	תְּבָרֵכְנָה	תְּבַעֵרְנָה
1cp	נְבָרֵךְ	נְבַעֵר

[3] It is found twice in the Bible as בֵּרֵךְ.

Imperative

2ms	בָרֵךְ	בַעֵר
2fs	בָרֲכִי	בַעֲרִי
2mp	בָרֲכוּ	בַעֲרוּ
2fp	בָרֵכְנָה	בַעֵרְנָה

Participle	מְבָרֵךְ	מְבַעֵר
Inf. Abs.	בָרֵךְ	בַעֵר
Inf. Cons.	בָרֵךְ	בַעֵר

67.4 Pual

The Pual is very similar to the Piel. Again, the *dagesh* is rejected, and there is vowel lengthening (from *qibbuts* to *holem*) for verbs with א or ר. Thus, the Pual of ברך is בֹרַךְ instead of בֻרַךְ. Verbs with ה ח or ע will also reject the *dagesh*, but there will be no vowel lengthening with these verbs. Thus, the Pual Perf of בער will be בֻעַר (rejected *dagesh* but no vowel lengthening). The Pual Perf will be the same as the Piel Perf, except the first radical will be -בֹ or -בֻ rather than -בֵּ or -בִּ.

Again, note the *shewa* under the Imperfect and Participle prefixes (○○○△̣̇).

Perfect

3ms	בֹרַךְ	בֻעַר
3fs	בֹרְכָה	בֻעֲרָה
2ms	בֹרַכְתָּ	בֻעַרְתָּ
	etc.	etc.

Imperative
(none)

Participle	מְבֹרָךְ	מְבֻעָר
Inf. Abs.	—	—
Inf. Cons.	—	—

Imperfect

3ms	יְבֹרַךְ	יְבֻעַר
3fs	תְּבֹרַךְ	תְּבֻעַר
2ms	תְּבֹרַךְ	תְּבֻעַר
2fs	תְּבֹרְכִי	תְּבֻעֲרִי
1cs	אֲבֹרַךְ	אֲבֻעַר
3mp	יְבֹרְכוּ	יְבֻעֲרוּ
3fp	תְּבֹרַכְנָה	תְּבֻעַרְנָה
2mp	תְּבֹרְכוּ	תְּבֻעֲרוּ
2fp	תְּבֹרַכְנָה	תְּבֻעַרְנָה
1cp	נְבֹרַךְ	נְבֻעַר

67.5 Hithpael

The Hithpael behaves very much like the Piel. The only major differences are (1) the addition of the -הִתְ prefix, and (2) the lengthening of the first radical vowel to *qamets* rather than *tsere*. Again, verbs with ה ח or ע in their middle radical will not have this vowel lengthening (§67.3.2). Since the Hithpael is so similar to the Piel, we shall only give a few examples below.

Perfect

3ms	הִתְבָּרֵךְ	הִתְבַּעֵר
3fs	הִתְבָּרֲכָה	הִתְבַּעֲרָה
2ms	הִתְבָּרַכְתָּ	הִתְבַּעַרְתָּ

Imperfect

3ms	יִתְבָּרֵךְ	יִתְבַּעֵר
2fs	תִּתְבָּרֲכִי	תִּתְבַּעֲרִי
1cs	אֶתְבָּרֵךְ	אֶתְבַּעֵר
3fp	תִּתְבָּרֵכְנָה	תִּתְבַּעֵרְנָה

Inf. Abs.	——	——	**Imperative** (ms)	הִתְבָּרֵךְ	הִתְבַּעֵר
Inf. Cons.	הִתְבָּרֵךְ	הִתְבַּעֵר	**Participle**	מִתְבָּרֵךְ	מִתְבַּעֵר

Things You Should Know

1. The guttural in the middle of *Ayin* Guttural verbs such as בָּחַר will
   - **reject *dagesh***. This will affect the Piel, Pual and Hithpael.
   - **take composite *shewa* instead of simple *shewa***. This will affect all forms except Hiphil and Hophal.
   - **attract *pathahs***. This will affect the Qal Imperfect.
2. In the Piel, Pual and Hithpael, the *ayin* guttural (second radical) rejects *dagesh*. If the second radical is א or ר, the vowel under the first radical will lengthen. If the second radical is ה ח or ע, the vowel under the first radical will not lengthen.

Exercise #43

אַ֫יִל	male sheep (ram), *pl.* אֵילִים
בֶּ֫גֶד	clothes, piece of clothing; *pl.* בְּגָדִים
בְּהֵמָה	*f.* (wild) animal, beast, cattle; *pl.* בְּהֵמוֹת
חֻקָּה, חֹק	statute (law); *pl.* חֻקִּים and חֻקּוֹת
מַטֶּה	*m.* *usually* tribe, *but also* staff, rod, *cs.* מַטֵּה; *pl.* מַטּוֹת
מִסְפָּר	number, *cs.* מִסְפַּר (√ ספר)
מַעֲשֶׂה	*m.* work, deed(s), *pl.* מַעֲשִׂים (√ עשה)
נֶ֫גֶד	in front of, opposite (from)
שׁאר	***Ni*** נִשְׁאַר to be left, to remain, ***Hi*** הִשְׁאִיר to leave someone or something
עֵת	*c.* time
שׁחת	***Pi*** שִׁחֵת to destroy (*no Impf*); ***Hi*** הִשְׁחִית to destroy
שֶׁ֫מֶן	oil

[1] הֻגַּד לְלָבָן אֲשֶׁר לָקַח יַעֲקֹב אֶת־רְכֻשׁוֹ וְאֶת־בְּנוֹתָיו לְמַ֫עַן שׁוּב[4] אֶל־אֶרֶץ־
אֲבוֹתָיו וַיִּקְצֹף לָבָן מִן[6] מַעֲשָׂיו׃ [2] אָהַב יְהוָה אֶת־עַמּוֹ אֶת־יִשְׂרָאֵל[5] וְגַם עָשָׂה
אֶת־חַסְדּוֹ עִמָּם׃ וַיֶּאֱסֹף אֶת־מִשְׁפְּחֹתָם[7] מִבְּקֶ֫רֶב־מִצְרַיִם וַיַּפְרִיד אֶת־מֵי־הַיָּם נֶגְדָּם׃
וַיְדַבֵּר יְהוָה לָהֶם לֵאמֹר אֶתֵּן לָכֶם נַחֲלָה לְרִשְׁתָּהּ[8] וּבֵרַכְתִּיךָ׃ [3] הוּא מִסְפַּר

---

[4] Infinitive construct + לְמַ֫עַן. Therefore, there is no -לְ prefix.

[5] This double definite direct object, אֶת־עַמּוֹ אֶת־יִשְׂרָאֵל, is not uncommon. Simply translate the phrase "his people Israel."

[6] That is, "because of."

[7] You would expect this word to be מִשְׁפְּחוֹתֵיהֶם. Later Hebrew (Chronicles) does use the full *holem vav* (וֹ). But the word is usually found as shown – without the *yod* and with *holem* and not *holem-vav*.

[8] Infinitive Construct (IC) with suffix and -לְ prefix. The verb is an original *Pe Vav* verb like יָשַׁב, and so the IC follows the pattern of שֶׁ֫בֶת (see p. 196). The suffix has then caused the vowel pointing to change.

בְּנֵי־יִשְׂרָאֵל [11]לְבֵית־אֲבֹתָם כָּל־פְּקוּדֵי־הַמַּטּוֹת[10] לְצִבְאֹתָם[9] שֵׁשׁ־מֵאוֹת־אֶלֶף וּשְׁלֹשֶׁת
אֲלָפִים וַחֲמֵשׁ מֵאוֹת וַחֲמִשִּׁים׃ [4] בָּאוּ הָעָם אֶל־סִינַי וַיִּשְׁמְעוּ אֶת־מִצְוֹת[12]־אֱלֹהִים
מִפִּי־מֹשֶׁה כְּכָל־הַתּוֹרָה וּכְכָל־הַחֻקִּים אֲשֶׁר צִוָּה אֹתוֹ אֱלֹהִים׃ וַיִּכְתְּבוּ עַל־שְׁנֵי־
לֻחֹת־אֲבָנִים אֲשֶׁר נָשָׂא מֹשֶׁה׃ [5] עָשְׂתָה[13] הָאִשָּׁה בֶּגֶד וַיִּשְׁמֹר אִישָׁהּ צֹאן וַיִּמְכֹּר
שֶׁמֶן וַתִּמְכֹּר מַעֲשֵׂה־יָדֶיהָ׃ [6] וְאֵין־לָהּ בֵּן וּבַת׃ וַיְבָרֶךְ אֱלֹהִים אֶת־בִּטְנָהּ וְכַאֲשֶׁר
בָּאָה עִתָּהּ[15] וַתֵּלֶד בַּת׃ [7] וַיְהִי הַיּוֹם[14] בָּא אִישָׁהּ לְבַדּוֹ עִם מַטֵּהוּ בְּקֶרֶב צֹאנוֹ
וַיִּפְקֹד אֶת־אֵילֵיהוּ וַיְהִי מִסְפָּרָם עֶשְׂרִים וַחֲמִשָּׁה׃ [8] וַיִּקְרְבוּ אֹיְבָיו בַּחֲרָבוֹת
וַיֹּאמְרוּ נַשְׁחִתָה[17] אֶת־צֹאנוֹ וְלֹא נִשְׁאַר לוֹ צֹאן׃ וַיֹּאמֶר אָסַף[16] אֶת־צֹאנִי וְעָמַדְתִּי
נֶגְדָּם׃ וַיֹּאמֶר יַעַזְרֵנִי אֱלֹהַי[18] וְשָׁמַר אֶת־נַחֲלָתִי כִּי אֶקְרָא בִשְׁמוֹ וְאֶשְׁמֹר אֶת־חֻקּוֹתָיו׃
[9] וַיֶּאֱהָבֵהוּ אֱלֹהִים וְגַם עָשָׂה אֶת־חַסְדּוֹ עִמּוֹ וַיִּנָּצֵל[19] מֵאֹיְבָיו׃ [10] הוֹסִיפוּ שָׂרֵי־
חַיִל לָגֶשֶׁת אֶת־נְגִידֵי־יְרִיחוֹ וַיֹּאמְרוּ לָהֶם תְּנוּ־לָנוּ בְגָדִים וְאֵילִים וּבְהֵמוֹת פֶּן־קָרוֹב
נִקְרַב וְשִׁחַתְנוּ אֶת־עִירְכֶם׃ [11] וְכַאֲשֶׁר שָׁמְעוּ הָעָם אֶת־הַדָּבָר הַזֶּה וַיֹּאמֶר[20]
אִישׁ אֶל־רֵעוֹ נִתְפַּלְּלָה הִתְפַּלֵּל לֵאלֹהֵינוּ בַּעֲבוּר יַעַזְרֵנוּ[21] בְּעֵת־צָרָתֵנוּ׃ [12] וַיּוֹסִיפוּ
הָעָם בִּתְפִלּוֹתֵיהֶם[22] וַיֹּאמֶר מִשְׁפָּחָה אַחַת נִקְחָה חֲרָבוֹת פֶּן־לֹא יִשָּׁאֵר אֶחָד מִמֶּנּוּ׃
וַיִּפָּרְדוּ הָעָם עַל־הָעֵצָה הַזֹּאת׃ [13] וַיִּתְּנוּ הָעָם שׁוֹר וּבְהֵמוֹת רַבּוֹת וּכְלֵי־שֶׁמֶן
וַיָּשִׂימוּ[23] אֹתָם לִפְנֵי־נְגִידֵיהֶם׃ וַיִּתְּנוּ אֹתָם לְשָׂרֵי־חַיִל אֲשֶׁר נֶאֶסְפוּ עֲלֵיהֶם׃

The next section contains the names *Abiathar*, *Adonijah*, *Jonathan* and *Zadok*. Note that *Jo-* and *-jah* (*-yahu*) are short forms of יהוה.

---

[9] Note again how there is just a *holem* and not a *holem-vav*. This often happens in Hebrew.

[10] Translate this phrase "all the tribes being counted." Be sure you can parse both words and understand their relationship.

[11] Translate this -לְ "by" or "according to." Translate the next one the same way.

[12] Is the וֹ a vowel letter or a consonant plus vowel? If you are unsure, see p. 13, especially footnote 1.

[13] Perf 3fs < עָשָׂה. We will study verbs which end in ה- (*Lamed He* verbs) in §72. (In this case, the final ה has become a ת.)

[14] וַיְהִי הַיּוֹם. Translate "One day . . . ."

[15] עֵת with suffix.

[16] Study this form carefully. It is not a participle. What is it? See §66.1, p. 204, if you are unsure.

[17] Why is there an additional *qameṣ he* at the end of this verb?

[18] אֱלֹהִים plus possessive suffix.

[19] Note that God is not the subject of this verb, and it is not Qal.

[20] Add the word *each*.

[21] This is an Impf 3mp + suffix. The final וּ- of the 3mp has changed to *qibbuṣ* (ֻ). This often happens when suffixes are added. And now, since this verb is plural, how should you translate לֵאלֹהֵינוּ ?

[22] Noun with inseparable preposition and possessive suffix.

[23] Qal Impf 3mp + w.c. < שִׂים. "Middle vowel verbs" will be studied in §68-69.

[14] וַיֹּאמֶר יוֹנָתָן בֶּן־אֶבְיָתָר הַכֹּהֵן לַאֲדֹנִיָּהוּ אֲדֹנֵינוּ הַמֶּלֶךְ־דָּוִד הִמְלִיךְ אֶת־שְׁלֹמֹה׃
[15] וַיִּשְׁלַח אִתּוֹ־הַמֶּלֶךְ[25] אֶת־צָדוֹק הַכֹּהֵן וְאֶת־נָתָן הַנָּבִיא וַיָּשִׂמוּ[24] אֹתוֹ עַל חֲמֹר־
הַמֶּלֶךְ׃ [16] וַיִּמְלִיכוּ אֹתוֹ צָדוֹק הַכֹּהֵן וְנָתָן הַנָּבִיא לְמֶלֶךְ וְגַם יָשַׁב שְׁלֹמֹה עַל
כִּסֵּא־הַמַּמְלָכָה׃ [17] וְגַם־בָּאוּ עַבְדֵי־הַמֶּלֶךְ לְבָרֵךְ[26] אֶת־אֲדֹנֵינוּ הַמֶּלֶךְ דָּוִד לֵאמֹר
יֵיטֵב[28] אֱלֹהֶיךָ אֶת־שֵׁם־שְׁלֹמֹה מִשְּׁמֶךָ וְיַגַדֵּל[27] אֶת־כִּסְאוֹ מִכִּסְאֶךָ׃ [18] וְגַם אָמַר
הַמֶּלֶךְ בָּרוּךְ יְהוָה אֱלֹהֵי־יִשְׂרָאֵל אֲשֶׁר נָתַן הַיּוֹם[30] יֹשֵׁב[29] עַל־כִּסְאִי וְעֵינַי רֹאוֹת׃

---

[24] See note 23.

[25] "And the king has sent with him;" that is, "and the king has sent with Solomon."

[26] Translate "to congratulate."

[27] Study this form carefully. We would expect to see וַיְגַדֵּל. But the ו is *vav* conjunction not w.c. That is, we are ***not*** looking at יְגַדֵּל + וַ· ➜ וַיְגַדֵּל. Rather, we are looking at:

וְ + יְגַדֵּל ➜ וְיְגַדֵּל ➜ וִיגַדֵּל ➜ וִיגַדֵּל.

This affects the translation. How? See note 28 for another hint.

[28] Shortened form of Imperfect. Why? How does this affect your translation?

[29] Translate "a-sitting-one."

[30] Translate "today" or "this day."

68

THE VERB: MIDDLE-VOWEL (Ayin Vav and Ayin Yod)

Some verbs originally had ו or י in their middle (*Ayin*) radical. Examples are קוּם (*to stand up*) and שִׂים (*to put, set, place*). These weak letters drop out in the Qal Perfect. (That is, the Qal Perf 3ms of קוּם is קָם, and the Qal Perf 3ms of שִׂים is שָׂם). **But the ו and י return** in the Imperfect, Imperative and Infinitives. And in the dictionary you will look for the full form of these verbs (קוּם and שִׂים), not the Qal Perf 3ms קָם and שָׂם.

> **Note: Not all verbs with ו or י in their middle radical are *Ayin Vav* or *Ayin Yod* verbs.** If the ו or י do *not* drop out in the Perfect, but remain as consonants, the verb is not called *Ayin Vav* or *Ayin Yod*. For instance, verbs which are also *Lamed He* (such as צוה, היה and חיה) or *Lamed* Gutturals (such as גוע) will keep their middle letters as consonants in the Perfect 3ms (צִוָּה [Piel], הָיָה, חָיָה, גָּוַע). They are therefore not called *Ayin Vav* or *Ayin Yod* verbs.

Some verbs are at times *Ayin Yod* and at other times *Ayin Vav*. (For instance, שִׂים can sometimes be שׂוּם). But usually one form is more common than the other (שִׂים is more common than שׂוּם).

***Ayin Vav* verbs** are found in Qal (active and stative), Niphal, Hiphil and Hophal.[1] We learned that the strong stative verb (§42) usually comes with an *e* vowel (כָּבֵד) or an *o* vowel (קָטֹן). This is also true of *Ayin Vav* verbs. In addition to active verbs such as קָם, we will see stative verbs such as מֵת (*he died*, < מוּת) and בּוֹשׁ (*he was ashamed*).

***Ayin Yod* verbs** are found in Qal and Hiphil, and seldom in the other forms.

68.1 Qal

	Ayin Vav			*Ayin Yod*
	Active	Stative (*e*)	Stative (*o*)	
		Perfect		
3ms	קָם	מֵת	בּוֹשׁ (*or* בֹּשׁ)	שָׂם
3fs	קָמָה	מֵתָה	בּוֹשָׁה (*always with* וֹ)	שָׂמָה
2ms	קַמְתָּ	מַתָּה (*note the* ה)	בֹּשְׁתָּ	שַׂמְתָּ
2fs	קַמְתְּ	מַתְּ	בֹּשְׁתְּ	שַׂמְתְּ
1cs	קַמְתִּי	מַתִּי	בֹּשְׁתִּי	שַׂמְתִּי
3cp	קָמוּ	מֵתוּ	בּוֹשׁוּ	שָׂמוּ
2mp	קַמְתֶּם	מַתֶּם	בָּשְׁתֶּם (*qamets-hatuph*)	שַׂמְתֶּם
2fp	קַמְתֶּן	מַתֶּן	בָּשְׁתֶּן (*qamets-hatuph*)	שַׂמְתֶּן
1cp	קַמְנוּ	מַתְנוּ	בֹּשְׁנוּ	שַׂמְנוּ

---

[1] Piel, Pual and Hithpael occur in a somewhat different forms and will be studied in the next chapter.

	Ayin Vav			*Ayin Yod*
	Active	Stative (*e*)	Stative (*o*)	
Imperfect				
3ms	יָקוּם	יָמוּת	יֵבוֹשׁ	יָשִׂים
3fs	תָּקוּם	תָּמוּת	תֵּבוֹשׁ	תָּשִׂים
2ms	תָּקוּם	תָּמוּת	תֵּבוֹשׁ	תָּשִׂים
2fs	תָּק֫וּמִי	תָּמ֫וּתִי	תֵּב֫וֹשִׁי	תָּשִׂ֫ימִי
1cs	אָקוּם	אָמוּת	אֵבוֹשׁ	אָשִׂים
3mp	יָק֫וּמוּ	יָמ֫וּתוּ	יֵ֫בֹשׁוּ (*once* יֵבוֹשׁוּ)	יָשִׂ֫ימוּ
3fp	תְּקוּמֶ֫ינָה	תְּמוּתֶ֫ינָה	תֵּ֫בֹשְׁנָה	תְּשִׂימֶ֫ינָה
2mp	תָּק֫וּמוּ	תָּמ֫וּתוּ	תֵּב֫וֹשׁוּ	תָּשִׂ֫ימוּ
2fp	תְּקוּמֶ֫ינָה	תְּמוּתֶ֫ינָה	תֵּ֫בֹשְׁנָה	תְּשִׂימֶ֫ינָה
1cp	נָקוּם	נָמוּת	נֵבֹשׁ	נָשִׂים
Imperative				
2ms	קוּם	מוּת	בּוֹשׁ	שִׂים
2fs	ק֫וּמִי	מ֫וּתִי	בּ֫וֹשִׁי	שִׂ֫ימִי
2mp	קֻ֫מוּ, ק֫וּמוּ	מ֫וּתוּ	בּ֫וֹשׁוּ	שִׂ֫ימוּ
2fp	קֹ֫מְנָה	מֹ֫תְנָה	בֹּ֫שְׁנָה	—
Infinitives				
Absolute	קוֹם	מוֹת	בּוֹשׁ	שׂוֹם
Construct	קוּם	מוּת	בֹּשׁ (*once* בּוֹשׁ)	שִׂים
Participles				
Active ms	קָם	מֵת	בּוֹשׁ	שָׂם
fs	קָ֫מָה	מֵ֫תָה	בּוֹשָׁה	שָׂ֫מָה
Passive ms	קוּם	—	—	—

Remember: The *Ayin Vav* or *Ayin Yod* disappear in the Perfect (except in the 3rd person of בּוֹשׁ), but they appear again in most of the other forms. You do not need to memorize the above chart. Instead, try to see the patterns. Look for the radicals and see what changes happen when the middle vowel drops out. Over time, you will start to "see" and "feel" Hebrew just as you do your own first language.

68.2 Notes

68.2.1 Jussive. As usual, the Jussive will use a shortened form of the Imperfect:

יָקוּם (imperfect, *he will rise*) but יָקֹם (jussive, *let him rise*)

יָשִׂים (imperfect, *he will put*) but יָשֵׂם (jussive, *let him put*)

etc.

68.2.2 **Imperfect plus w.c.** will also use a shortened Imperfect, of course. Again, the accent moves and the final vowel will therefore reduce (become short)[2]:

יָקוּם *he will rise*	but	וַיָּ֫קָם *and he rose*	(Note *q.h.*: way-yā́-qom)
יָמוּת *he will die*	but	וַיָּ֫מָת *and he died*	(in pause: וַיָּמֹ֫ת)
יָשִׂים *he will put*	but	וַיָּ֫שֶׂם *and he put*	

68.2.3 ***Pe* radical accent.** Study the chart in §68.1, above, and note how often the accent moves onto the *Pe* radical. This is often the only thing which separates the Qal Perf 3fs from the Part fs:

קָ֫מָה	Qal Perf 3fs (*she rose*)	but	קָמָ֫ה[3]	Qal Part fs (*rising*)
מֵ֫תָה	Qal Perf 3fs (*she died*)	but	מֵתָ֫ה[3]	Qal Part fs (*dying*)
		etc.		

The masculine forms (Qal Perf 3ms and Qal Part ms) have only one syllable. There is therefore no difference in accent to separate them. Thus, קָם, מֵת, בּוֹשׁ, etc. can be either Perf 3ms or Part ms.

68.2.4 **The dictionary form** of these words is the three-radical form, not the Perf 3ms. In other words, in a dictionary or lexicon you will look for קוּם or שִׂים and not קָם or שָׂם.

Things You Should Know

1. **"Middle vowel verbs"** such as קוּם, מוּת, בּוֹשׁ and שִׂים are called *Ayin Vav* or *Ayin Yod* verbs. They will lose their middle vowel in the Perfect; however the *ayin vav* or *ayin yod* will return in the Imperfect and other forms.

2. **Lamed *He* or *Lamed* Guttural verbs** with second radical ו or י will not do this, and are not called Middle Vowel (*Ayin Vav* or *Ayin Yod*) verbs.

3. **Forms.** Middle vowel verbs are found in the Qal, Niphal and Hiphil. In addition, *Ayin Vav* verbs are found in Hophal.

4. **Jussive** will use a short form of the Imperfect (for instance, יָקֹם instead of יָקוּם, and יָשֵׂם instead of יָשִׂים).

5. **Imperfect plus *vav* consecutive** will also use a short form of the Imperfect. The accent will also move, and the final vowel will reduce (shorten): וַיָּ֫קָם (way-yā́-qom).

6. **Accent.** Especially in the Perfect, the accent will often move onto the *Pe* radical. This becomes important in separating the Perfect from Participles.

7. **The dictionary form** of these words will be the three-radical form, not the Perf 3ms.

---

[2] **Technical note:** When the accent moves forward, toward the w.c., the last syllable becomes closed and unaccented. This requires a short vowel (Syllable Rule 3, p. 18).

[3] It is not necessary to put an accent mark on the last syllable of a word, since this is where the accent is usually found. Here, however, it has been added in order to emphasize the difference between the words.

69

THE VERB: MIDDLE-VOWEL (Continued)

In the previous chapter, we studied the Qal form of Middle Vowel verbs. These verbs also come in Niphal and Hiphil (both *Ayin Vav* and *Ayin Yod* verbs), and in Hophal (*Ayin Vav* verbs only).[1] In the chart below, we use בִּין for our example of *Ayin Yod*, since it comes in both Niphal and Hiphil.

In addition, we will see that, for *Ayin Vav* verbs, the Piel, Pual and Hithpael will appear in slightly different forms called Polel, Polal and Hithpolel.

69.1 Niphal, Hiphil and Hophal

There are three things to notice in the chart below:

(1) **Niphal and Hiphil each have a single form** for both *Ayin Vav* and *Ayin Yod*. That is, the Niphal Perfect 3ms of קוּם[2] is נָקוֹם and for בִּין it is נָבוֹן; both use וֹ for a middle vowel. Likewise, the Hiphil of קוּם is הֵקִים and for בִּין it is הֵבִין; both use י for a middle vowel.

(2) **Niphal and Hiphil often have an extra וֹ before the suffix.** Example: Niph Perf 2ms = נְקוּמוֹתָ

(3) There is often **vowel lengthening in the Hiphil and Hophal.**[3] In **Hiphil**, there is often a *tsere* (instead of *hireq*) under the ה of the Perfect, and a *qamets* (instead of *pathah*) under the other prefixes (that is, ○○○△ָ). In **Hophal**, the prefix vowel, which is usually *qamets-hatuph*, lengthens to *šureq* (וּ) (that is, ○○○וּ△ instead of ○○○△ָ).

Perfect

	Niphal		**Hiphil**		**Hophal**
	Ayin Vav	*Ayin Yod*	*Ayin Vav*	*Ayin Yod*	*Ayin Vav*
3ms	נָקוֹם	נָבוֹן	הֵקִים	הֵבִין	הוּקַם
3fs	נָקוֹמָה	נָבוֹנָה	הֵקִימָה	הֵבִינָה	הוּקְמָה
2ms	נְקוּמוֹתָ	נְבוּנוֹתָ	הֲקִימוֹתָ	הֲבִינוֹתָ	הוּקַמְתָּ
2fs	נְקוּמוֹת	etc.	הֲקִימוֹת	etc.	הוּקַמְתְּ
1cs	נְקוּמוֹתִי		הֲקִימוֹתִי		הוּקַמְתִּי
3cp	נָקוֹמוּ		הֵקִימוּ		הוּקְמוּ
2mp	נְקֻמוֹתֶם		הֲקִימוֹתֶם		הוּקַמְתֶּם
2fp	נְקֻמוֹתֶן		הֲקִימוֹתֶן		הוּקַמְתֶּן
1cp	נְקוּמוֹנוּ		הֲקִימוֹנוּ		הוּקַמְנוּ

---

[1] **Technical note:** These verbs also come, rarely, in other forms, but they will not be considered here. The grammars give various treatments of *Ayin Yod* verbs. Some show Qal and Niphal forms, others show Qal and Hiphil forms. Since בִּין is found in both Niphal and Hiphil, we are including all three forms for *Ayin Yod*.

[2] **Technical note:** The verb קוּם does not actually have a Niphal form, but it is used here as a model.

[3] This happens because the first syllable of these verbs is now open. Normally, the first syllable of Hiphil and Hophal verbs is closed and unaccented, and thus has a short vowel (הִשְׁמִיר, הָשְׁמַר). But in *Ayin Vav* and *Ayin Yod* verbs, this syllable becomes open and the vowel then lengthens.

Imperfect

	Niphal		Hiphil		Hophal
	Ayin Vav	*Ayin Yod*	*Ayin Vav*	*Ayin Yod*	*Ayin Vav*
3ms	יִקּוֹם	יִבּוֹן	יָקִים	יָבִין	יוּקַם
3fs	תִּקּוֹם	תִּבּוֹן	תָּקִים	תָּבִין	תּוּקַם
2ms	תִּקּוֹם	תִּבּוֹן	תָּקִים	תָּבִין	תּוּקַם
2fs	תִּקּוֹמִי	etc.	תָּקִימִי	etc.	תּוּקְמִי
1cs	אֶקּוֹם		אָקִים		אוּקַם
3mp	יִקּוֹמוּ		יָקִימוּ		יוּקְמוּ
3fp	—		תְּקִימֶינָה[4], תַּקֵמְנָה		תּוּקַמְנָה
2mp	תִּקּוֹמוּ		תָּקִימוּ		תּוּקְמוּ
2fp	—		תָּקֵמְנָה		תּוּקַמְנָה
1cp	נִקּוֹם		נָקִים		נוּקַם

Imperative

2ms	הִקּוֹם	הִבּוֹן	הָקֵם	הָבֵן	—
2fs	הִקּוֹמִי	etc.	הָקִימִי	etc.	—
2mp	הִקּוֹמוּ		הָקִימוּ		—
2fp	—		—		—

Participles

ms	נָקוֹם	מֵקִים	מוּקָם

Infinitives

Const.	הִקּוֹם	הָקִים	הוּקַם
Abs.	הִקּוֹם, נָקוֹם	הָקֵם	—

69.2 Polel, Polal and Hithpolel

Piel, Pual and Hithpael normally have a *dagesh* in their middle (*Ayin*) radical. But the middle radical of *Ayin Vav* verbs (ו) is so weak that it cannot be doubled. Therefore, *Ayin Vav* verbs do not have a regular Piel, Pual or Hithpael.[5] Instead, these verbs will double their third (*Lamed*) radical. Study the following comparison of a strong verb (שָׁמַר) and an *Ayin Vav* verb (קוּם):

Root form	שָׁמַר	**Root form**	קוּם
Piel Perf 3ms	שִׁמֵּר	Polel Perf 3ms	קוֹמֵם
Pual Perf 3ms	שֻׁמַּר	Polal Perf 3ms	קוֹמַם
Hithpael Perf 3ms	הִתְשַׁמֵּר	Hithpolel Perf 3ms	הִתְקוֹמֵם

---

[4] The *shewa* under the prefix may cause you to think this is Piel or Pual. It is not. The *pathah* has shortened to *shewa* because the word is long (see box on p. 72). The first *hireq-yod* should show you that this is Hiphil.

[5] Remember, however, that not *all* verbs with a *vav* in the *Ayin* radical are true *Ayin Vav* verbs. Verbs such as צוה and גוע keep their second radical ו and it can be doubled. (Review the note at the beginning of §68, p. 214.) For instance, the verb צוה comes in the Piel (צִוָּה, ṣiv-vâ), and not in the Polel.

Notes:

1. **Polel has the same meaning as Piel:** it is an "intensive" (stronger) form of the verb. Likewise, **Polal has the same meaning as Pual**: it is a "passive intensive" form. And **Hithpolel has the same meaning as Hithpael**, since it is "reflexive." These three forms are not really new. They are just alternative forms of the Piel, Pual and Hithpael, and they exist because the ו is such a weak letter in *Ayin Vav* verbs.

2. **The Polel and Polal are identical in the Perfect** except for the 3ms, and they are **often the same in the Imperfect** as well. In these cases, only context will tell you whether to translate as active (Polel) or passive (Polal). Note the occasional *hateph pathah* (ֲ) under non-gutturals. We usually see them under gutturals, but sometimes they can appear under other consonants, too.

Perfect

	Polel	Polal	Hithpolel
3ms	קוֹמֵם	קוֹמַם	הִתְקוֹמֵם
3fs	קוֹמֲמָה	קוֹמֲמָה	הִתְקוֹמֲמָה
2ms	קוֹמַמְתָּ	קוֹמַמְתָּ	הִתְקוֹמַמְתָּ

Infinitives

Cons.	קוֹמֵם	—	הִתְקוֹמֵם
Abs.	—	—	הִתְקוֹמֵם

Participle

מְשׁוֹמֵם	מְקוֹמָם	מִתְקוֹמֵם

Imperfect

	Polel	Polal	Hithpolel
3ms	יְקוֹמֵם	יְקוֹמַם	יִתְקוֹמֵם
2fs	תְּקוֹמֲמִי	תְּקוֹמֲמִי	תִּתְקוֹמֲמִי
3mp	יְקוֹמֲמוּ	יְקוֹמֲמוּ	יִתְקוֹמֲמוּ
3/2fp	תְּקוֹמֵמְנָה	תְּקוֹמַמְנָה	תִּתְקוֹמֵמְנָה

Imperative

2ms	קוֹמֵם	—	הִתְקוֹמֵם
2fs	קוֹמֲמִי	—	הִתְקוֹמְמִי
2mp	קוֹמֲמוּ	—	הִתְקוֹמְמוּ
2fp	קוֹמֵמְנָה	—	הִתְקוֹמֵמְנָה

Things You Should Know

1. Middle Vowel verbs (*Ayin Vav* and *Ayin Yod*) come in the Qal (previous chapter), Niphal and Hiphil. *Ayin Vav* verbs also come in the Hophal.

2. *Ayin Vav* and *Ayin Yod* verbs have one common form for the Niphal. It is based upon the middle letter וֹ in both cases. Likewise, there is one common form for the Hiphil of these verbs. It is based upon the middle letter י in both cases.

3. There is vowel lengthening in the Hiphil and Hophal prefixes.

4. *Ayin vav* verbs have no Piel, Pual or Hithpael forms. Instead, they have Polel, Polal and Hithpolel forms. These have the same meaning as Piel, Pual and Hithpael.

Exercise #44

בּוֹשׁ	to be ashamed
בִּין	to understand, consider, ***Hi*** הֵבִין to understand, pay attention
כּוּן	***Ni*** נָכוֹן to be ready, stand firm; ***Polel*** כּוֹנֵן *and* ***Hi*** הֵכִין to prepare, make firm
מוּת	***Qal Perf*** מֵת to die; ***Hi*** הֵמִית to kill, to have someone killed
נְאֻם	says (*lit.* a saying of); נְאֻם־יְהוָה says the LORD
נוּס	*Perf* נָס to flee, escape
נוּחַ	***Qal Perf 3fs*** נָחָה[1] to rest, settle; ***Hi*** I. הֵנִיחַ to lower, to provide rest; II. הִנִּיחַ to set, leave, allow
סוּר	***Qal Perf*** סָר to turn aside, to leave; *Impf* יָסוּר; ***Hi*** הֵסִיר to remove, *Impf* יָסִיר
עָוֹן[2]	*m.* iniquity (sin), guilt, *pl.* עֲוֹנוֹת
קוּם	***Qal Perf*** קָם stand up, get up; ***Hi*** הֵקִים set up; provide
רוּם	***Qal Perf*** רָם to be high, exalted, to boast; ***Hi*** הֵרִים to raise
שָׂדֶה	*m.* field; *pl.* שָׂדוֹת (*w. suffix sometimes* -שְׂדֵי)

[1] וַיְדַבֵּר יְהוָה אֶל־מֹשֶׁה בְּמִדְבַּר־סִינַי בְּאֹהֶל־מוֹעֵד[4] בְּאֶחָד [3] לַחֹדֶשׁ הַשֵּׁנִי בַּשָּׁנָה
הַשֵּׁנִית[7] לְצֵאתָם[6] מֵאֶרֶץ־מִצְרַיִם לֵאמֹר׃ [2] שְׂאוּ אֶת־רֹאשׁ[5] כָּל־עֲדַת־בְּנֵי־יִשְׂרָאֵל
לְמִשְׁפְּחֹתָם לְבֵית־אֲבֹתָם בְּמִסְפַּר־שֵׁמוֹת [8]כָּל־זָכָר לְגֻלְגְּלֹתָם׃ [3] מִבֶּן־עֶשְׂרִים־
שָׁנָה וָמַעְלָה[10] כָּל־יֹצֵא צָבָא בְּיִשְׂרָאֵל תִּפְקְדוּ אֹתָם לְצִבְאֹתָם[9] אַתָּה וְאַהֲרֹן׃
[4] וְאִתְּכֶם יִהְיוּ אִישׁ אִישׁ לַמַּטֶּה[12] [11] אִישׁ רֹאשׁ לְבֵית־אֲבֹתָיו הוּא׃ [5] וַיִּקְרָא
יְהוֹשֻׁעַ אֶל־שְׁנֵים הֶעָשָׂר אִישׁ[14] אֲשֶׁר הֵכִין[13] מִבְּנֵי־יִשְׂרָאֵל אִישׁ־אֶחָד מִשָּׁבֶט׃
[6] וַיֹּאמֶר לָהֶם יְהוֹשֻׁעַ עִבְרוּ לִפְנֵי אֲרוֹן־יְהוָה אֱלֹהֵיכֶם אֶל־תּוֹךְ־הַיַּרְדֵּן וְהָרִימוּ

---

[1] When forms other than the 3ms are given, it means the 3ms does not appear in the Bible.

[2] Is the ו in this word ô or wō? If you are unsure, review §5.3, p. 13. Also study the plural, noting that vocal *shewa* or composite *shewa* are counted as vowels in this case.

[3] Add the word *day* (or *day of*).

[4] מוֹעֵד = *meeting.*

[5] שְׂאוּ אֶת־רֹאשׁ. Translate "Count the heads of" or "Take a census of." Be sure you can parse and literally translate the first word (imperative of a weak verb). (Normally, it does not mean "count" or "take.")

[6] The root of this word is יָצָא. How is it parsed?

[7] Add the word *after.*

[8] כָּל־זָכָר לְגֻלְגְּלֹתָם "every man/male (זָכָר) according to (the number of) their heads." **Technical note:** The last word actually means "skull," and is found in the New Testament as *Golgotha*, the "(place of the) skull."

[9] Translate "company by company."

[10] Translate "and upwards." That is, those twenty years old *and older.*

[11] Add the word *each.*

[12] אִישׁ אִישׁ לַמַּטֶּה. Translate "a man from each tribe."

[13] Translate "he appointed" or "he chose." Be sure you can parse the verb and give its more common definition.

[14] שְׁנֵים הֶעָשָׂר אִישׁ. Translate "the twelve men"

לָכֶם אִישׁ אֶבֶן אַחַת עַל־שִׁכְמוֹ לְמִסְפַּר[15] שִׁבְטֵי־בְנֵי־יִשְׂרָאֵל׃ [7] נִקְבְּצוּ הָעָם נֶגֶד
הַהֵיכָל וַיִּתְּנוּ אֵילִם וּבְהֵמוֹת וּבֶגֶד וְשֶׁמֶן אִישׁ כְּמַעֲשֵׂה־יָדוֹ׃ [8] זָקֵן דָּוִד וַיָּמֹת[16]
וַיָּמֶת שְׁלֹמֹה בְּנוֹ אֶת־אֹיְבֵי־אָבִיהוּ וַיִּמְלֹךְ תַּחְתָּיו׃ [9] וַיָּקָם שְׁלֹמֹה וַיִּתְפַּלֵּל
לֵאלֹהִים לֵאמֹר אָנֹכִי יֶלֶד קָטֹן׃ לָכֵן נָתַתָּ לְעַבְדְּךָ לֵב שֹׁמֵעַ לַעֲשֹׂה צְדָקָה וּלְהָבִין
בֵּין־טוֹב לְרָע כִּי מִי יוּכַל[17] לִשְׁפֹּט אֶת־עַמְּךָ הַכָּבֵד הַזֶּה׃ וַיִּיטְבוּ דְבָרָיו בְּעֵינֵי־
אֱלֹהִים׃ [10] וַיְהִי כְּשָׁכְבוֹ[20] לִישׁוֹן[19] וַיְדַבֵּר יְהוָה אֵלָיו בַּחֲלוֹם[18] לֵאמֹר שָׁאַלְתָּ
חָכְמָה וְצֶדֶק לָכֵן אֵיטִיב לְךָ וְהִגְדִּילְתִּיךָ׃ וְהָיְתָה[21] מַלְכוּתְךָ חֲזָקָה וּבֵרַכְתִּי אֶת־
מְלֶאכֶת־יָדֶךָ וְהוֹרַשְׁתִּי אֶת־אֹיְבֶיךָ וַהֲנִיחֹתִי[23] אֶת־מַטּוֹת־יִשְׂרָאֵל׃ [11] וַיָּכֶן[22] יְהוָה
מַמְלֶכֶת־שְׁלֹמֹה וּבָעֵת הַהִיא שְׁלֵמִים גְּבוּלֵי־יִשְׂרָאֵל וְחוֹמוֹת־עָרֶיהָ׃ [12] וְלֹא נָכוֹן
שְׁלֹמֹה וַיָּסַר מִן יְהוָה אֱלֹהָיו וַיְקַבֵּץ סוּסִים וְנָשִׁים רַבּוֹת וְגָדוֹל עֲוֹנוֹ׃ וַיֹּאמֶר יְהוָה
אַצִּיל מִן בֶּן־שְׁלֹמֹה עֲשֶׂרֶת שְׁבָטִים׃ וַיִּשְׁלַח יְהוָה נָבִיא אֲשֶׁר כָּרַת שְׁנֵים עָשָׂר
בְּגָדִים וַיִּתֵּן בְּגָדִים עֲשָׂרָה לְיָרָבְעָם[24]׃ [13] לָמָּה רָעֵב הָעָם וּמַדּוּעַ יֵשׁ מִלְחָמָה
לָמָּה יֹרְשִׁים הַפְּלִשְׁתִּים אֶת־שְׂדֹתֵינוּ׃ הֲלֹא כִּי סַרְתֶּם מֵחֻקֵּי־יְהוָה׃ [14] כֵּן כֹּה
אָמַר יְהוָה יֵבוֹשׁ הַדּוֹר הַזֶּה׃ יָנוּסוּ וְלֹא יִנָּצְלוּ כִּי לֹא הֵבִינוּ אֶת־עֲוֹנָם נְאֻם־יְהוָה׃
[15] מְבֹרֶכֶת[26] הָאִשָּׁה בְּלִי עָוֹן אֲשֶׁר הֵבִינָה[25] אֶת־חֻקּוֹת־אֱלֹהִים׃ תִּכּוֹן וְלֹא תֵבוֹשׁ יָרוּם
שְׁמָהּ וַהֲנִיחֹתִי לָהּ׃ [16] וְתֵלֶד אֵשֶׁת־הַנָּבִיא יֶלֶד וַיִּוָּלֵד הַיֶּלֶד וְלֹא הֵבִין טוֹב וָרָע׃
[17] קָם הַנָּבִיא נֶגֶד הָעָם וַיָּרֶם[27] אֶת־קוֹלוֹ וַיִּקְרָא כֹּה אָמַר יְהוָה׃ יֵאָסְפוּ גִבּוֹרִים

---

[15] Translate the -לְ "according to."

[16] This verb and the next one use shorted forms of the imperfect. Why? One of them is Hiphil. See §68.2.2, p. 216.

[17] Qal Impf 3ms < יָכֹל. **Technical note:** This *Original Pe Vav* verb does not follow the patterns you learned in §63 and has an unusual history (*Gesenius* §69*r*). See *Gesenius* §53*u* for other verbs which follow similar patterns.

[18] This can be translated either "in *a* dream" or "in *the* dream." Why? (If you are unsure, compare §16.2.3.3, p. 47, with §16.2.4.) How does the context help you decide?

[19] Another IC

[20] The subject of this IC is still Solomon.

[21] Perf 3fs + w.c. < היה.

[22] Shortened Imperfect.

[23] **Technical note:** This form is found in 2 Sam 7:11. But more often, it is written הֲנִחֹתִי (5 times) or, most strangely, הִנַּחְתִּי (3 times).

[24] Jeroboam.

[25] Translate as present tense. The Perfect is usually translated as a past tense, but sometimes as present.

[26] **Technical note:** When the phrase "Blessed is (the person who)" occurs in the Bible, it usually uses the word אַשְׁרֵי (not learned in this book). In a few cases, the rare Qal form בָּרוּךְ (passive participle) is used.

[27] Compare this word to the second word mentioned in footnote 16 above. **Technical note:** The phrase "to lift up one's voice" usually uses the verb נשׂא rather than רום.

רַבִּים עַל הָעִיר וְנִגַּפְתֶּם[28] לִפְנֵיהֶם׃ וְאָבְדוּ הַנִּשְׁאָרִים בָּעִיר וְנָפְלוּ בְּבוֹרוֹת הַנָּסִים׃
אַשְׁחִית אֶת־קָדְשִׁי[29] וְיָשְׁבוּ שָׁם בַּהֲמוֹת־הַשָּׂדֶה נְאֻם־יְהוָה׃ [18] שִׁחֲתוּ הַפְּלִשְׁתִּים
אֶת־בָּתֵּי־הָעָם וַיִּקְחוּ כָּל־רְכוּשָׁם עַד אֲשֶׁר־לֹא־הִשְׁאִירוּ שָׁם גַּם־כְּלִי־שָׁמֶן[30]׃ וַיֹּאמֶר
אִישׁ־הָאֱלֹהִים שׁוּב יָשׁוּב אֱלֹהִים אֵלֶיךָ כָּעֵת הַזֹּאת בַּשָּׁנָה הָאַחֶרֶת[32] וּבֵרַכְכֶם[31] וְנָתַן
לָכֶם אֵילִם וּבְהֵמָה אֵין מִסְפָּר[33]׃

---

[28] Niphal or Piel? This verb comes in one but not the other. Check the vocabulary list at the end of the book if you do not know. Also, the context should tell you which it is.

[29] Translate "my holy place," i.e., the Temple.

[30] The first *seghol* has lengthened to *qameṣ* in pause.

[31] וּבֵרַכְכֶם. Note: not וּבֵרַכְתֶּם. What is the difference between these two verbs.

[32] כָּעֵת הַזֹּאת בַּשָּׁנָה הָאַחֶרֶת "at this time next year."

[33] "Without number;" that is, so many that they cannot be counted.

70

THE VERB: *LAMED* GUTTURAL

Lamed Guttural verbs such as שָׁלַח are not difficult. We will see:

- attracted *pathahs* and
- furtive *pathahs*

(Review §13 on Gutturals if necessary.)

We will therefore look only at the Qal in detail. Other forms will be considered more briefly, since they develop in a very similar way.

70.1 Qal

Perfect

3ms	שָׁלַח
3fs	שָׁלְחָה
	etc. (regular)

Imperative

2ms	שְׁלַח
2fs	שִׁלְחִי
2mp	שִׁלְחוּ
2fp	שְׁלַחְנָה

Participles

Active	שֹׁלֵחַ, שֹׁלְחִים, שֹׁלַחַת, שֹׁלְחוֹת
Passive	שָׁלוּחַ, שְׁלוּחִים, שְׁלוּחָה, שְׁלוּחוֹת

Imperfect

3ms	יִשְׁלַח
3fs	תִּשְׁלַח
2ms	תִּשְׁלַח
2fs	תִּשְׁלְחִי
1cs	אֶשְׁלַח
3mp	יִשְׁלְחוּ
3fp	תִּשְׁלַחְנָה
2mp	תִּשְׁלְחוּ
2fp	תִּשְׁלַחְנָה
1cp	נִשְׁלַח

Infinitives

Construct	שְׁלֹחַ
Absolute	שָׁלוֹחַ

Notes:

1. **Imperfect and Imperative:** the guttural often attracts a *pathah* before it. Thus, in the Imperfect, we see יִשְׁלַח (instead of the vowel pattern of יִשְׁמֹר). And in the Imperative we see שְׁלַח and שְׁלַחְנָה (instead of the שְׁמֹר and שְׁמֹרְנָה patterns of the strong verb).
2. **Infinitives and Participles:** the guttural often takes a furtive *pathah*. Thus, in this case, the Impv ms (שְׁלַח) is *not* the same as the Infinitive Construct (שְׁלֹחַ).

70.2 Other Forms

The Niphal, Piel, Hiphil and Hithpael develop in similar ways. Again, we see attracted *pathahs* and furtive *pathahs*. (The Hophal and Pual are regular, and so are not included in the chart below.)

		Niphal	Piel	Hiphil	Hithpael[1]
Perfect	3ms	(regular)	שִׁלַּח	הִשְׁלִ֫יחַ	הִתְבַּקַּע
	3fs		שִׁלְּחָה	הִשְׁלִ֫יחָה	הִתְבַּקְּעָה
	2ms		שִׁלַּ֫חְתָּ	הִשְׁלַ֫חְתָּ	הִתְבַּקַּ֫עְתָּ
	2fs		שִׁלַּ֫חַתְּ	הִשְׁלַ֫חַתְּ	הִתְבַּקַּ֫עַתְּ
Imperfect	3ms	יִשָּׁלַח	יְשַׁלַּח	יַשְׁלִ֫יחַ	יִתְבַּקַּע
	3fp	תִּשָּׁלַ֫חְנָה	תְּשַׁלַּ֫חְנָה	תַּשְׁלַ֫חְנָה	תִּתְבַּקַּ֫עְנָה
Imperative	2ms	הִשָּׁלַח	שַׁלַּח	הַשְׁלַח	הִתְבַּקַּע
Infinitive	Construct	הִשָּׁלַח	שַׁלַּח	הַשְׁלִ֫יחַ	הִתְבַּקַּע
	Absolute	נִשְׁלוֹחַ	שַׁלֵּחַ	הַשְׁלֵחַ	הִתְבַּקַּע
Participle		נִשְׁלָח	מְשַׁלֵּחַ	מַשְׁלִ֫יחַ	מִתְבַּקֵּ֫עַ

Things You Should Know

1. *Lamed* Guttural verbs are almost regular. The only differences are:
   - occasional attracted *pathahs* and
   - occasional furtive *pathahs*
2. The Qal and Niphal Perfect are regular. Likewise, all parts of the Pual and Hophal are regular. Other forms have only minor irregularities.

---

[1] **Technical Note:** The verb בקע is used for the Hithpael to avoid the movement of the ת which occurs in Hithpael verbs when the first radical of the verb is an "s" or "t" letter. (For instance, the Hithpael of שָׁלַח is הִשְׁתַּלַּח.) See §53.2.5.1, p. 159, for details.

71

THE VERB: *LAMED ALEPH*

As we have already seen, the letter א often loses its vowel and becomes silent (quiescent, review §17 if necessary). When the א comes at the end of the verb, the verb is called a *Lamed Aleph* verb. The א does not disappear, but the verb often *acts* as if it has disappeared. In order to see this, let us compare the Qal Perf 2ms of a strong verb and a *Lamed Aleph* verb:

71.1 An Example: Qal Perf 2ms

שָׁמַרְתָּ **Strong verb.** The ר closes the syllable, and thus the syllable -מַרְ- has a short vowel (*pathah*). Likewise, the syllable is closed by a simple *shewa* and therefore the following תּ has a *dagesh*.

מָצָאתָ *Lamed Aleph* **verb.** The א does *not* close the syllable as the ר does above. Although the א is still present, the verb *acts* as if it is not there. Therefore, the syllable -צָא- is *open* (just as if the word were מָצָתָ). Two things have happened: (1) since the syllable is now open, its vowel has lengthened from *pathah* to *qamets*, and (2) the ת has lost its *dagesh* because it now comes after a vowel (see §11.1.4).

This will also affect **stative verbs**. Consider the following comparison of two Qal Perf 2ms *stative* verbs:

כָּבַדְתָּ **Strong stative verb.** As we learned in §42, stative verbs like כָּבֵד have a *tsere* in the Perf 3ms which reduces to the short vowel *pathah* in the rest of the Perfect. See the example at the left, where the ד closes the syllable.

מָלֵאתָ *Lamed Aleph* **stative verb.** The verb מָלֵא has a silent א instead of the ד we saw above. The word acts as if the א is not present, and the second syllable is therefore open. Thus, the *tsere* remains and does not reduce to *pathah*: -לֵא- . This again puts a vowel before the ת which then loses its *dagesh*.

As we did in the previous chapter, we will look at the Qal (both non-stative and stative verbs) in detail. After that, we will consider the other forms more briefly. Note that non-stative and stative verbs differ only in the Perfect. In the Imperfect and other moods, מָצָא and מָלֵא are pointed the same.

71.2 Qal

	Perfect			Imperfect	
	Non-stative	Stative		Non-stative	Stative
3ms	מָצָא	מָלֵא	3ms	יִמְצָא	יִמְלָא
3fs	מָצְאָה	מָלְאָה	3fs	תִּמְצָא	תִּמְלָא
2ms	מָצָאתָ	מָלֵאתָ	2ms	תִּמְצָא	etc.
2fs	מָצָאת	מָלֵאת	2fs	תִּמְצְאִי	
1cs	מָצָאתִי	מָלֵאתִי	1cs	אֶמְצָא	

3cp	מָֽצְאוּ	מָֽלְאוּ
2mp	מְצָאתֶם	מְלֵאתֶם
2fp	מְצָאתֶן	מְלֵאתֶן
1cp	מָצָאנוּ	מָלֵאנוּ

Infinitives

Construct	מְצֹא
Absolute	מָצוֹא

Participles

Active	מֹצֵא
Passive	מָצוּא

3mp	יִמְצְאוּ
3fp	תִּמְצֶאנָה
2mp	תִּמְצְאוּ
2fp	תִּמְצֶאנָה
1cp	נִמְצָא

Imperative

2ms	מְצָא
2fs	מִצְאִי
2mp	מִצְאוּ
2fp	מְצֶאנָה

Note the unexpected *seghol* in the Impf 3fp and 2fp, and also in the Impv 2fp. This will also be seen in the other forms, below.

71.3 Niphal, Hiphil and Hophal

Perfect

	Niphal	Hiphil	Hophal
3ms	נִמְצָא	הִמְצִיא	הֻמְצָא
3fs	נִמְצְאָה	הִמְצִיאָה	הֻמְצְאָה
2ms	נִמְצֵאתָ	הִמְצֵאתָ	הֻמְצֵאתָ

Infinitives

Cons.	הִמָּצֵא	הַמְצִיא	—
Abs.	נִמְצֹא	הַמְצֵא	—

Participle

נִמְצָא	מַמְצִיא	מֻמְצָא

Imperfect

	Niphal	Hiphil	Hophal
3ms	יִמָּצֵא	יַמְצִיא	יֻמְצָא
2fs	תִּמָּצְאִי	תַּמְצִיאִי	תֻּמְצְאִי
3mp	יִמָּצְאוּ	יַמְצִיאוּ	יֻמְצְאוּ
3fp	תִּמָּצֶאנָה	תַּמְצֶאנָה	תֻּמְצֶאנָה

Imperative

2ms	הִמָּצֵא	הַמְצֵא	—
2fs	הִמָּצְאִי	הַמְצִיאִי	—
2fp	הִמָּצֶאנָה	הַמְצֶאנָה	—

The Hophal (above) uses *qibbuts* (ֻ) instead of *qamets-hatuph* under its prefixes. This should not be confused with the Pual (below), which uses *qibbuts* under its first radical, not under its prefixes.

71.4 Piel, Pual and Hithpael

Piel, Pual and Hithpael are studied together because all three put a *dagesh* in their second radical.

Perfect

	Piel	**Pual**	**Hithpael**
3ms	מִצֵּא	מֻצָּא	הִתְמַצֵּא
3fs	מִצְּאָה	מֻצְּאָה	הִתְמַצְּאָה
2ms	מִצֵּאתָ	מֻצֵּאתָ	הִתְמַצֵּאתָ

Imperfect

	Piel	**Pual**	**Hithpael**
3ms	יְמַצֵּא	יְמֻצָּא	יִתְמַצֵּא
2fs	תְּמַצְּאִי	תְּמֻצְּאִי	תִּתְמַצְּאִי
3mp	יְמַצְּאוּ	יְמֻצְּאוּ	יִתְמַצְּאוּ
3fp	תְּמַצֶּאנָה	תְּמֻצֶּאנָה	תִּתְמַצֶּאנָה

Infinitives

Const.	מְצֹא	—	הִתְמַצֵּא
Abs.	מָצֹא	—	—

Participle

מְמַצֵּא	מְמֻצָּא	מִתְמַצֵּא

Imperative

2ms	מַצֵּא	—	הִתְמַצֵּא
2fs	מַצְּאִי	—	הִתְמַצְּאִי
2mp	מַצְּאוּ	—	הִתְמַצְּאוּ
2fp	מַצֶּאנָה	—	הִתְמַצֶּאנָה

Things You Should Know

1. In *Lamed Aleph* verbs, the א often loses its value as a letter, and the verb acts as if it is not present. The vowel which comes before the א usually lengthens. (And a ת which comes after it will lose its *dagesh*.) Example: Qal Perf 2ms of מצא is מָצָאתָ.
2. For all the forms (Qal, Niphal, Piel, etc.), a *seghol* will appear under the second radical of the Impf 3fp and 2fp, as well as under the second radical of the Impv fp.

Exercise #45

אַף (I) anger, nose (*du.* אַפַּיִם = nostrils)[1]
(II) also, indeed

זָבַח to sacrifice, slaughter; *Impf* יִזְבַּח; ***Pi*** זִבַּח to offer (a sacrifice)

זֶבַח a sacrifice

חוּץ the outside; a street; מִחוּץ לַבַּיִת outside the house (מִן + חוּץ. In this case, the *hireq* does not lengthen.)

חָצֵר a court(yard), unwalled village

טָמֵא to become (religiously) unclean;
Ni נִטְמָא to make oneself unclean;
Pi טִמֵּא to make/declare s.t. unclean;
also adj. unclean

מִזְבֵּחַ *m.* altar (√זבח), *cs.* מִזְבַּח; *pl.* מִזְבְּחוֹת

מָלֵא to fill, to be full (of); *also adj.* full;
Ni Impf יִמָּלֵא to be filled (with);
Pi מִלֵּא to fill, fulfill

פֶּתַח door, entrance; *pl.* פְּתָחִים, *cs.* פִּתְחֵי

שָׂמַח to rejoice, be glad; ***Pi*** שִׂמַּח to make someone glad

שָׂנֵא to hate

שבע ***Ni*** נִשְׁבַּע to swear, take an oath;
Hi הִשְׁבִּיעַ to make someone swear

[1] וַיִּקַּח יְהוָה אֱלֹהִים אֶת־הָאָדָם וַיַּנִּחֵהוּ[2] בְגַן־עֵדֶן לְעָבְדָהּ וּלְשָׁמְרָהּ׃ [2] שָׂנֵא קַיִן
אֶת־אָחִיו וְאַף בְּאַפּוֹ הֱמִיתוֹ בְּצֵאתָם[3] בְּקֶרֶב־הַשָּׂדֶה׃ [3] יְמַלֵּא אֱלֹהִים אֶת־דְּבָרוֹ וְנָתַן
לָכֶם הַנַּחֲלָה אֲשֶׁר נִשְׁבַּע לָתֵת לְאַבְרָהָם לְיִצְחָק וּלְיַעֲקֹב׃ וּמָלְאָה הָאָרֶץ מִשְׁפְּחוֹתֵיכֶם

[1] **Technical note:** The relationship between *anger* and *nose* is interesting. The Bible often says God is "slow to anger" (Exod. 34:6; Num. 14:18; etc.) Hebrew uses the dual אַפַּיִם (*nostrils*), and says that God is אֶרֶךְ־אַפַּיִם which means *long nostrils* (i.e., "God has a long nose"!). When people become angry, their noses sometimes become red or "hot." A long nose takes longer to get hot! Thus a person with a long nose is "slow to anger"!

[2] Hiphil plus suffix.

[3] Infinitive Construct with inseparable preposition and suffix.

וְרַמְתֶּם עַל חֵיל־אֹיְבֵיכֶם׃ [4] וַיְהִי שַׂר צַדִּיק אֲשֶׁר בֵּין תּוֹרַת־אֱלֹהִים וְלֹא־סָר מִמֶּנָּה׃
וַיִּבְטְחוּהוּ יֹשְׁבֵי־חֲצֵרוֹ כִּי עֲזָרָם וְיִרְאַת־יְהוָה עָלָיו׃ [5] בְּכָל־שָׁנָה וְשָׁנָה[4] בְּאֶחָד
לַחֹדֶשׁ הַשֵּׁנִי[5] הָלַךְ בֵּיתָה־יְהוָה לִזְבֹּחַ לַיהוָה׃ וַיִּקַּח הַכֹּהֵן אֲשֶׁר הָיָה בַחֲצַר־הַהֵיכָל
אֶת־זִבְחוֹ וַיִּזְבָּחֵהוּ עַל הַמִּזְבֵּחַ׃ [6] וַיָּסַר מֵהַהֵיכָל וַיִּשְׂמַח וַיָּשָׁב אֶל־חֲצֵרוֹ לֵאמֹר יְהִי
שֵׁם־יְהוָה מְבוֹרָךְ עַד־עוֹלָם [7] מֵת[6] הַמֶּלֶךְ וַיִּשְׁמְעוּ שָׂרֵי־הַמֶּלֶךְ אֶת־מוֹתוֹ וַיִּשְׁלְחוּ
מַלְאָכִים אֶל הָעָם לֵאמֹר יָרִים אֱלֹהִים מֶלֶךְ חָדָשׁ עָלֵינוּ׃ וַיַּשְׁבִּיעוּ אֶת־הָעָם לְהִכּוֹן
לֵאמֹר יְשׁוּעָתֵנוּ בְּשֵׁם־יְהוָה׃ [8] עָמַד הַנָּבִיא בְּפֶתַח־הַהֵיכָל וַיִּצְעַק אֶל־הָעָם לֵאמֹר
טְמָאתֶם כִּי טִמְּאוּ עֲוֺנֹתֵיכֶם אֶתְכֶם׃ לָכֵן תִּלְבְּשׁוּ כַּהֲסִירִי[7] אֶת־כְּבוֹדְכֶם נְאֻם־יְהוָה׃
[9] אַיֵּה מַלְכְּךָ עַתָּה וְיוֹשִׁיעֲךָ[8] בְּכָל־עָרֶיךָ׃ וְאַיֵּה שֹׁפְטֶיךָ אֲשֶׁר אָמַרְתָּ תְּנָה־לִּי מֶלֶךְ׃
אֶתֶּן־לְךָ מֶלֶךְ בְּאַפִּי וְאֶקַּח בְּעֶבְרָתִי[9]׃ [10] קָמוּ הָאֲמָהוֹת וַתַּעֲמֹדְנָה מִחוּץ לְבֵיתָן עַל
הַפֶּתַח אֲשֶׁר חֲמֵשׁ עֶשְׂרֵה אַמּוֹת מִן חוֹמַת־הָעִיר הוּא׃ וַתֹּאמַרְנָה לַזְּקֵנִים שִׁמְעוּנוּ עַתָּה
כִּי שָׁאַלְנוּכֶם שֶׁבַע פְּעָמִים׃ פִּקְדוּ שֹׁמְרִים לַחוֹמָה כִּי בָאִים[10] אֹיְבֵינוּ בַּחֲרָבוֹת וְלֹא
נוּכַל לָנוּס׃ [11] לֹא יָנוּחַ רוּחִי עֲלֵיהֶם אֲשֶׁר שֹׂנְאַי[11] נְאֻם־יְהוָה הָסֵר אָסִיר אֹתָהֶם
מִפָּנַי וּבוֹשׁוּ בֹּשׁ׃ [12] נִטְמֵאתֶם בַּעֲוֺנֹתֵיכֶם וַיִּמְצָאוּכֶם אֹיְבֵיכֶם׃ נֻסוּ מַלְּטוּ [12]נַפְשְׁכֶם
וְתִהְיֶינָה[15] כַּחֲמוֹר[14] בַּמִּדְבָּר׃ [13] לֹא תֵדַע[13] אֶת־בִּרְכוֹת־הָעִיר וְאֶת־בִּרְכוֹת־הַשָּׂדֶה
כִּי לֹא הֲבִינוֹתָ[16] דִּבְרֵי־נְבִיאַי אֲשֶׁר הֲקִימוֹתִי אֹתָם׃ לָמָּה סַרְתֶּם מִדְּבָרַי נְאֻם־יְהוָה׃
לָמָּה רַמֹּתֶם׃ וְלָמָּה תָּמְתוּ בֵּית יִשְׂרָאֵל׃ [14] הִנֵּה אָנֹכִי שֹׁלֵחַ מַלְאָךְ לְפָנֶיךָ לִשְׁמָרְךָ
בַּדֶּרֶךְ וְלַהֲבִיאֲךָ[20] אֶל־הַמָּקוֹם אֲשֶׁר הֲכִינֹתִי[19]׃ הִשָּׁמֶר מִפָּנָיו[18] וּשְׁמַע בְּקֹלוֹ אַל־תַּמֵּר[17] בּוֹ

---

[4] בְּכָל־שָׁנָה וְשָׁנָה. Translate: "Every year."

[5] בְּאֶחָד לַחֹדֶשׁ הַשֵּׁנִי. See the last paragraph (just above "Things You Should Know") on p. 175.

[6] This word can be either an adjective or a verb. Which fits best in this context?

[7] IC + prefix + suffix.

[8] This is not Impf + w.c. Note the vowel pointing on the first two letters of the word (§28.3.2, p. 85).

[9] The root of this word is עֶבְרָה = "wrath, fury, anger," a word which you have not learned.

[10] Qal Part ms < בוא. You have learned this verb as בָּא, but it is actually a middle vowel verb.

[11] Participle with suffix.

[12] We would normally expect to see an אֶת־ here. But this is from a poetic section of Jeremiah. The sign of the definite direct object is often left out in poetry. We will learn about Hebrew poetry in §77.

[13] Imperfect of original *Pe Vav* verb (§63, p. 196). The guttural has also attracted a *pathah*. Note also that Impf + לֹא is not always prohibition. It can simply mean "you will not."

[14] This last sentence (נֻסוּ . . . בַּמִּדְבָּר׃) comes from Jeremiah 48, where the Hebrew word is unclear but probably should be כְּעָרוֹד, "like a wild ass."

[15] From היה. *Lamed He* verbs will be studied in the next chapter. Note: -וְ not -וַ. Translate as Impv.

[16] See p. 217.

[17] From the verb מָרַר, "to rebel." We will learn about "Double *Ayin* verbs" in §73.

[18] הִשָּׁמֶר מִפָּנָיו. Translate "Obey him" or "Pay attention to him." But be sure you can also parse both words.

[19] Hiphil Perfect. As the word has gotten longer, the *pathah* under the ה has reduced to *hateph-pathah*.

[20] This Hiphil IC has two prefixes (ו and ל) and an object suffix. You should be able to recognize its root.

כִּי לֹא יִשָּׂא אֶת־חַטַּאתְכֶם כִּי שְׁמִי בְּקִרְבּוֹ׃ [15] הֵן[22] עַבְדִּי אֲשֶׁר בְּחַרְתִּיהוּ[21] וַיְשַׂמְּחֵנִי׃
נָתַתִּי [24]רוּחִי עָלָיו מִשְׁפָּט לַגּוֹיִם יוֹצִיא׃ לֹא יִצְעַק וְלֹא יִשָּׂא[23] וְלֹא־יַשְׁמִיעַ בַּחוּץ קוֹלוֹ׃
[16] חֶסֶד־יְהוָה מָלְאָה הָאָרֶץ[25] כִּי אָהֵב עַמּוֹ וְהֵנִיחַ אֶתְהֶם׃ שִׂמְחוּ וְזִבְחוּ זְבָחִים עַל
מִזְבְּחוֹ כִּי נִשְׁבַּע לֶאֱסֹף אֶת־עֲוֹנֹתֵינוּ׃

[21] Remember, this form can be either Perf 2fs + suffix or Perf 1cs + suffix. See p. 163.

[22] This is another form of הִנֵּה.

[23] Add "his voice."

[24] See footnote 12, above. This sentence is from a poetic section of Isaiah.

[25] Note carefully the structure of these four words. This is Hebrew poetry, and again the sign of the definite direct object (אֶת־) has not been written. Is the verb masculine or feminine? Which of the nouns has the same gender? That word must be the subject.

72

THE VERB: *LAMED HE*

Lamed He verbs are verbs such as גָּלָה. They originally ended with י- or ו-, but now they end with ה-. The ה- ending cannot take suffixes, and so one of several things happens. The following examples use the verb גָּלָה (originally גלי):

- The ה may be replaced by the original י or ו. Example: Qal Perf 2ms of גָּלָה is גָּלִ֫יתָ
- The ה may be replaced by a ת. Example: Qal Perf 3fs of גָּלָה is גָּלְתָה. Or it may even be replaced by *both* ו and ת. Example: Qal IC of גָּלָה is גְּלוֹת.
- The ה may simply disappear with no replacement. Example: Qal Perf 3cp of גָּלָה is גָּלוּ. And Qal Impf 3ms + w.c. of גָּלָה is וַ֫יִּגֶל.

As we have done in previous chapters, we will give a full development of the Qal (and, in this case, the Niphal) below. Then we will give summaries of the other forms.

72.1 Qal and Niphal

	Perfect			Imperfect	
	Qal	**Niphal**		**Qal**	**Niphal**
3ms	גָּלָה	נִגְלָה	3ms	יִגְלֶה	יִגָּלֶה
3fs	גָּלְתָה	נִגְלְתָה	3fs	תִּגְלֶה	תִּגָּלֶה
2ms	גָּלִיתָ	נִגְלִ֫יתָ, נִגְלֵ֫יתָ	2ms	תִּגְלֶה	תִּגָּלֶה
2fs	גָּלִית	נִגְלֵית	2fs	תִּגְלִי	תִּגָּלִי
1cs	גָּלִיתִי	נִגְלֵ֫יתִי	1cs	אֶגְלֶה	אֶגָּלֶה
			3mp	יִגְלוּ	יִגָּלוּ
3cp	גָּלוּ	נִגְלוּ	3fp	תִּגְלֶ֫ינָה	תִּגָּלֶ֫ינָה
2mp	גְּלִיתֶם	נִגְלֵיתֶם	2mp	תִּגְלוּ	תִּגָּלוּ
2fp	גְּלִיתֶן	נִגְלֵיתֶן	2fp	תִּגְלֶ֫ינָה	תִּגָּלֶ֫ינָה
1cp	גָּלִינוּ	נִגְלֵ֫ינוּ	1cp	נִגְלֶה	נִגָּלֶה

Infinitives

	Qal	Niphal
Construct	גְּלוֹת	הִגָּלוֹת
Absolute	גָּלֹה	נִגְלֹה

Impf + w.c.

Qal	Niphal
וַיִּגֶל	וַיִּגָּל

Imperative

	Qal	Niphal
2ms	גְּלֵה	הִגָּלֵה
2fs	גְּלִי	הִגָּלִי
2mp	גְּלוּ	הִגָּלוּ
2fp	גְּלֶינָה	הִגָּלֶינָה

Active Participles

	Qal	Niphal
m	גֹּלֶה, גֹּלִים	—
f	גֹּלָה, גֹּלוֹת	—

Passive Participles

Qal	Niphal
גָּלוּי, גְּלוּיִם	נִגְלֶה, נִגְלִים
גְּלוּיָה, גְּלוּיוֹת	נִגְלָה, נִגְלוֹת

Study the preceding chart. The *Lamed He* verb has a couple of important characteristics:

- There is a second-radical *seghol* in much of the Imperfect and in Imperative 2fp.
- There is an וֹת- ending on the Infinitive Construct and feminine plural participles.

You will see these characteristics in all the forms (Qal, Niphal, Piel, Pual, etc.).

> **Review: Learn the Strong Letters**
>
> Remember what was said in the box on p. 185 When you learn a weak verb, it is important to **learn the strong letters well**. That is, when you learn a verb such as גלה, learn to watch for -גל-, not גלה. Or, when you learn a verb such as ישׁב, learn to watch for -שׁב-. The *strong* letters will always be there to help you.

72.2 Hiphil and Hophal

Perfect

	Hiphil	Hophal
3ms	הִגְלָה	הָגְלָה
3fs	הִגְלְתָה	הָגְלְתָה
2ms	הִגְלֵיתָ, הִגְלִיתָ	הָגְלֵיתָ

The above -לִי- or -לֵי- variation in Hiph Perf 2ms is also found in Hiph Perf 2fs, 1cp and 2mp

Imperfect

	Hiphil	Hophal
3ms	יַגְלֶה	יָגְלֶה
2fs	תַּגְלִי	תָּגְלִי
3mp	יַגְלוּ	יָגְלוּ
3fp	תַּגְלֶינָה	תָּגְלֶינָה

Infinitives

	Hiphil	Hophal
Construct	הַגְלוֹת	—
Absolute	הַגְלֵה	הָגְלֵה

Participle

Hiphil	Hophal
מַגְלֶה	מָגְלֶה

Imperative

	Hiphil	Hophal
2ms	הַגְלֵה	—
2fs	הַגְלִי	—
2mp	הַגְלוּ	—
2fp	הַגְלֶינָה	—

72.3 Piel, Pual and Hithpael

Again, Piel, Pual and Hithpael are studied together because all three put a *dagesh* in their second radical.

Perfect

	Piel	Pual	Hithpael
3ms	גִּלָּה	גֻּלָּה	הִתְגַּלָּה
3fs	גִּלְּתָה	גֻּלְּתָה	הִתְגַּלְּתָה
2ms	גִּלִּיתָ	גֻּלֵּיתָ	הִתְגַּלִּיתָ

Imperfect

	Piel	Pual	Hithpael
3ms	יְגַלֶּה	יְגֻלֶּה	יִתְגַּלֶּה
2fs	תְּגַלִּי	תְּגֻלִּי	תִּתְגַּלִּי
3mp	יְגַלּוּ	יְגֻלּוּ	יִתְגַּלּוּ
3fp	תְּגַלֶּינָה	תְּגֻלֶּינָה	תִּתְגַּלֶּינָה

Infinitives

	Piel	Pual	Hithpael
Construct	גַּלּוֹת	גֻּלּוֹת	הִתְגַּלּוֹת
Absolute	גַּלֵּה, גַּלֹּה	—	—

Imperative

	Piel	Pual	Hithpael
2ms	גַּלֵּה	—	הִתְגַּלֵּה
2fs	גַּלִּי	—	הִתְגַּלִּי
2mp	גַּלּוּ	—	הִתְגַּלּוּ
2fp	גַּלֶּינָה	—	הִתְגַּלֶּינָה

Participles

Piel	Pual	Hithpael
מְגַלֶּה	מְגֻלֶּה	מִתְגַּלֶּה

Impf + w.c.

Piel	Pual	Hithpael
וַיְגַל	—	וַיִּתְגַּל

Things You Should Know

1. *Lamed He* verbs **originally** ended with י or ו, but now have a final ה- (for instance גָּלָה).
2. These verbs lose their final ה- when they take **suffixes**. This ה- may be replaced:
   (a) by the original י or ו. Example: Qal Perf 2ms גָּלִיתָ.
   (b) by the letter ת. Example: Qal Perf 3fs גָּלְתָה.
   (c) by *both* a ו and a ת. Example: Qal IC גְּלוֹת.
   (d) by nothing. The ה- may simply disappear. Example: Qal Perf 3cp גָּלוּ.
3. The **Imperfect** of all *Lamed He* forms (Qal, Niphal, Piel, Pual, etc.) often has a second radical *seghol*. The **Impv fp** also has a second radical *seghol*.
4. The **Infinitive Construct** of all *Lamed He* forms ends with וֹת- .

73

THE VERB: DOUBLE *AYIN*

W*hen the second and third* radicals of a verb are the same (for instance, סָבַב) we call the verb a Double *Ayin* verb. Double *Ayin* verb comes in all forms (Qal, Niphal, Piel, Pual, etc.). Because of the double *ayin*, however, the Piel, Pual and Hithpael are called Poel (סוֹבֵב), Poal (סוֹבַב) and Hithpoel (הִתְסוֹבֵב). These are just like the Polel, Polal and Hithpolel of the *Ayin Vav* verb (§69.2). We use these different names just to show that they come from Double *Ayin* verbs, not *Ayin Vav* verbs.

73.1 Qal

The **Qal Perfect** is not unusual, although there are long and short forms of the third person (singular and plural).[1] The **Imperfect**, however, not only has Active and Stative,[2] but the Active itself has two forms.[3] In the first form, the 3fp and 2fp are very tricky; they look like Pual because the word has lengthened and so the vowel under the prefix has reduced to *shewa* and the *holem* has reduced to *qibbuts*.

Perfect

3ms	סָבַב, סַב
3fs	סָבְבָה, סַבָּה
2ms	סַבּוֹתָ
2fs	סַבּוֹת
1cs	סַבּוֹתִי
3cp	סָבְבוּ, סַבּוּ
2mp	סַבּוֹתֶם
2fp	סַבּוֹתֶן
1cp	סַבּוֹנוּ

Imperative

2ms	סֹב
2fs	סֹבִּי
2mp	סֹבּוּ
2fp	סֻבֶּינָה

Imperfect

	Active	Active	Stative
3ms	יָסֹב	יִסֹּב	יֵקַל
3fs	תָּסֹב	תִּסֹּב	תֵּקַל
2ms	תָּסֹב	תִּסֹּב	תֵּקַל
2fs	תָּסֹבִּי	תִּסְּבִי	תֵּקַלִּי
1cp	אָסֹב	אֶסֹּב	אֵקַל
3mp	יָסֹבּוּ	יִסְּבוּ	יֵקַלּוּ
3fp	תְּסֻבֶּינָה	תִּסֹּבְנָה	תְּקַלֶּינָה
2mp	תָּסֹבּוּ	תִּסְּבוּ	תֵּקַלּוּ
2fp	תְּסֻבֶּינָה	תִּסֹּבְנָה	תְּקַלֶּינָה
1cp	נָסֹב	נִסֹּב	נֵקַל

Infinitives

Construct	סֹב	קֹל, קַל
Absolute	סָבוֹב	קָלוֹל

---

[1] The long form may be used for transitive and the shorter form for intransitive. (see Grammar, page xix.) For instance, צָרַר means "to tie or bind (something)," but צַר means "to be oppressed, in distress."

[2] **Technical note:** Not all Double *Ayin* stative verbs will follow the stative pattern. For instance, the verb תמם, "to be complete," follows the active pattern.

[3] **Technical note:** The Stative Imperfect actually has a second form, too, which is seen in the verb מלל. But this does not appear very often, and will not be covered.

Participles

	Active verb	Stative verb
Active participle	סוֹבֵב	קַל
Passive participle	סָבוּב	—

As you can see, sometimes the third radical disappears (-סבב- ➜ -סב-), and sometimes it combines with the second radical (-סבב- ➜ -סבּ-)

Other forms will now be shown in summary. They are less complex than the Qal. They have no statives and they have only a few alternative vowel pointings.

73.2 Niphal, Hiphil and Hophal

In the following chart, the vowels will often be different from what you expect. This is because when the verb reduces to two consonants (-סב-), two things happen:

(1) A **first syllable** which is usually closed will often **become open**. Its vowel therefore lengthens. Examples:

- Hiphil prefixes will become -הֵ instead of -הִ, and -יָ instead of -יַ
- Hophal prefixes will become -הוּ instead of -הָ, and -יוּ instead of -יָ.

Thus we get הֵסֵב and יָסֵב instead of the vowel patterns seen in הִשְׁמִיר and יַשְׁמִיר.

(2) A **second syllable** which is usually open will often **become closed**. Its vowel therefore shortens. Example: we will see *pathah* (-סַ-) in the first radical of the Niphal Imperfect instead of the *qamets* (-סָ-) which we usually expect. Thus יִסַּב instead of the pattern in יִשָּׁמֵר.

Perfect

	Niphal	Hiphil	Hophal
3ms	נָסַב, נָסֵב	הֵסַב, הֵסֵב	הוּסַב
3fs	נָסַבָּה	הֵסֵבָּה	הוּסַבָּה
2ms	נְסַבּוֹתָ	הֲסִבּוֹתָ	הוּסַבּוֹתָ

Imperfect

	Niphal	Hiphil	Hophal
3ms	יִסַּב	יָסֵב, יַסֵּב	יוּסַב, יֻסַּב
2fs	תִּסַּבִּי	תָּסֵבִּי	תּוּסַבִּי
3mp	יִסַּבּוּ	יָסֵבּוּ or יַסֵּבּוּ	יוּסַבּוּ
3fp	תִּסַּבֶּינָה	תְּסִבֶּינָה	תְּוּסַבֶּינָה

Infinitives

	Niphal	Hiphil	Hophal
Const.	הִסֵּב	הָסֵב	הוּסַב, הָסַבָּה
Abs.	הִסֵּב, הִסּוֹב	הָסֵב	—

Participle

Niphal	Hiphil	Hophal
נָסָב	מֵסֵב	מוּסָב

Imperative

	Niphal	Hiphil	Hophal
2ms	הִסֵּב	הָסֵב	—
2fs	הִסַּבִּי	הָסֵבִּי	—
2mp	הִסַּבּוּ	הָסֵבּוּ	—
2fp	הִסַּבֶּינָה	הֲסִבֶּינָה	—

73.3 Poel, Poal and Hithpoel

When we studied *Ayin Vav* verbs (§69), we learned that they had special forms of the Piel, Pual and Hithpael. These were called Polel, Polal and Hithpolel because they were based upon doubling the third radical of the verb (see §69.2, p. 218).

The situation is the same with Double *Ayin* verbs. In these verbs, the last two radicals are again the same. In this case, the special forms of Piel, Pual and Hithpael are called Poel, Poal and Hithpoel.[4]

Note that the Poel Perfect is exactly the same as the Poal Perfect, except in the 3ms.

Perfect

	Poel	Poal	Hithpoel
3ms	סוֹבֵב	סוֹבַב	הִתְסוֹבֵב
3fs	סֽוֹבֲבָה	סֽוֹבֲבָה	הִתְסוֹבֲבָה
2ms	סוֹבַבְתָּ	סוֹבַבְתָּ	הִתְסוֹבַבְתָּ

Infinitives

	Poel	Poal	Hithpoel
Cons.	סוֹבֵב	—	הִתְסוֹבֵב
Abs.	סוֹבֵב	סוֹבַב	הִתְסוֹבֵב

Participle

Poel	Poal	Hithpoel
מְסוֹבֵב	מְסוֹבָב	מִתְסוֹבֵב

Imperfect

	Poel	Poal	Hithpoel
3ms	יְסוֹבֵב	יְסוֹבַב	יִתְסוֹבֵב
2fs	תְּסוֹבֲבִי	תְּסוֹבֲבִי	תִּתְסֽוֹבֲבִי
3mp	יְסוֹבֲבוּ	יְסוֹבֲבוּ	יִתְסֽוֹבֲבוּ
3fp	תְּסוֹבֵבְנָה	תְּסוֹבַבְנָה	תִּתְסוֹבֵבְנָה

Imperative

	Poel	Poal	Hithpoel
2ms	סוֹבֵב	—	הִתְסוֹבֵב
2fs	סֽוֹבֲבִי	—	הִתְסֽוֹבְבִי
2fp	סוֹבֵבְנָה	—	הִתְסוֹבֵבְנָה

Things You Should Know

1. Double *Ayin* verbs have the same letter for the second and third radical (סָבַב). When the verb takes suffixes and prefixes, the third radical sometimes disappears (-סב-), and sometimes joins the second radical (-סבּ-). This makes the verb shorter.

2. When the verb becomes shorter, there will be vowel changes. This is because the first syllable of the verb (which is usually closed) may now be open and its vowel will lengthen. Likewise, the second syllable (which is usually open) may now be closed and its vowel will shorten.

3. The Double *Ayin* verb has special forms of the Piel, Pual and Hithpael. They are called Poel, Poal and Hithpoel. They are exactly the same as the Polel, Polal and Hithpolel forms you learned earlier when you studied *Ayin Vav* verbs.

---

[4] Not all double ayin verbs will use these special forms. The common verb פלל, for instance, follows the regular Hithpael pattern (הִתְפַּלֵּל). **Technical note.** The names of the special forms are actually Po^{c}el, Po^{c}al and Hithpo^{c}el, of course, just as Piel is technically Pi^{c}el. These forms are exactly the same as the Polel, Polal and Hithpolel which we learned earlier. As mentioned at the beginning of the chapter, the only reason we do not use the names Polel, Polal and Hithpolel again is so that we can distinguish between the two kinds of verbs which lie behind these forms: *Ayin Vav* and Double *Ayin*.

Exercise #46

בָּנָה	to build; *Ni* נִבְנָה to be built
גָּלָה	to uncover, go into exile; *Ni* נִגְלָה to be uncovered; *Pi* גִּלָּה to uncover; *Hi* הִגְלָה to take into exile
חָיָה	*Qal* (*Perf 3ms often* חַי) to live; *Pi* חִיָּה *and Hi* הֶחֱיָה to preserve, keep alive
חלל	(I) *Ni* נִחַל to be profaned (used in a common or otherwise improper way); *Pi* חִלֵּל to profane something; (II) *Hi* הֵחֵל to begin
חָנָה	to camp, set up a military camp; *Impf 2ms* תַּחֲנֶה; *3ms+wc* וַיִּחַן
כָּלָה	to be finished, consumed, destroyed; *Pi* כִּלָּה to finish, consume, destroy
כסה	*Pi* כִּסָּה to cover
מוֹעֵד	a meeting, an appointed time
מַחֲנֶה	*m.* a camp, army, company; *pl.* מַחֲנִים *and* מַחֲנוֹת; *dual* מַחֲנָיִם (√חָנָה)
סָבַב	*Qal* to turn, go around, surround; *Ni* נָסַב to turn, surround; *Polel Impf* תְּסוֹבֵב to turn, surround; *Hi* הֵסֵב to remove, cause to go around
סָבִיב	*adv.* around, all around, on every side
פָּנָה	to turn, to face
רָבָה	to become many or great; *Hi* הִרְבָּה to make many, to make great
שָׁתָה	to drink

[1] מֵהַנָּחָשׁ בְּעֵדֶן לָמְדוּ הָאִישׁ וְהָאִשָּׁה כִּי עֲרֻמִּים הֵם׃ כֵּן הוֹרִישָׁם יְהוָה פֶּן־יִקְרְבוּ
אֶת־עֵץ־הַחַיִּים וְחָיוּ[6] לְעֹלָם׃ [2] וַיְהִי כִּי־הֵחֵל הָאָדָם לָרֹבוֹת עַל־פְּנֵי־הָאֲדָמָה וּבָנוֹת[5]
יֻלְּדוּ[7] לָהֶם׃ וַיִּרְאוּ בְנֵי־הָאֱלֹהִים אֶת־בְּנוֹת־הָאָדָם כִּי טֹבֹת הֵנָּה וַיִּקְחוּ לָהֶם נָשִׁים
מִכֹּל אֲשֶׁר בָּחָרוּ׃ וַיֹּאמֶר יְהוָה לֹא־יִשָּׁאֵר רוּחִי בָאָדָם לְעֹלָם כִּי הוּא בָשָׂר וְחָיוּ מֵאָה
וְעֶשְׂרִים שָׁנָה׃ [3] וַיְהִי עֵת־הֵאָסֵף הַבְּהֵמָה בַּעֲבוּר יִשְׁתּוּ׃ וַיִּפֶן עֶבֶד־אַבְרָהָם וַיָּבֹא
הַמָּקוֹם׃ וַיֹּאמֶר לָהֶם הִשְׁבִּיעַנִי אֲדֹנִי לֵאמֹר לֹא־תִקַּח אִשָּׁה לִבְנִי מִבְּנוֹת־הַכְּנַעֲנִי׃ אִם־
לֹא[8] אֶל־בֵּית־אָבִי תֵּלֵךְ וְאֶל־מִשְׁפַּחְתִּי וְלָקַחְתָּ אִשָּׁה לִבְנִי׃ [4] וַיַּרְא הָעֶבֶד אֶת־
רִבְקָה[10] וַיְשַׂמְּחוּהוּ הַדְּבָרֶיהָ׃ וְאַחֲרֵי־כֵן[9] הָלְכוּ עַד־פֶּתַח־בֵּית־אָחִיהָ וַיָּבֹאוּ מִן הַחוּץ׃
וַיֹּאכְלוּ וַיִּשְׁתּוּ וַיֹּאמֶר אָחִיהָ יַרְבֶּה[11] אֱלֹהִים אֶת־זַרְעֵךְ׃ [5] וַיִּחֲנוּ הָעָם סָבִיב אֹהֶל־
מוֹעֵד וַיִּסְפְּרֵם אַהֲרוֹן לְמַחֲנֵיהֶם בְּמִסְפַּר־שְׁמוֹתָם׃ [6] נִשְׁבַּע אֱלֹהִים לֵאמֹר שָׂנֵאתִי
עָוֹן וְאַף לֹא אֲכַסֶּה אֶת־חֶטְאָם׃ כִּי נִטְמְאוּ נִטְמֹא לַעֲבֹד[12] אֶת־אֱלֹהֵי־הָעַמִּים אֲשֶׁר

---

5 This is a noun (with *vav*), not a verb form.

6 Qal Perf 3cp < חָיָה. Translate “and live” or “and should live.”

7 Original *Pe Vav* verbs do not normally come in Pual. But this form is found several places in the Old Testament, including in Gen 6, the source of this exercise sentence.

8 אִם־לֹא. Translate “But.”

9 וְאַחֲרֵי־כֵן. Translate "And afterwards."

10 Rebekah

11 Is this verb best translated Imperfect or Jussive?

12 Translate the -לְ as “by” or “by means of.”

סְבִיבֹתֵיהֶם[13]׃ [7] נִלְחֲמוּ מַטּוֹת־יִשְׂרָאֵל בַּכְּנַעֲנִי וַיִּמָּלֵט בְּרַגְלָיו אֶחָד מִן אֲדֹנֵי־הַכְּנַעֲנִי׃
וַיִּסָּתֵר וַיָּשֶׂם אֶת־כַּסְפּוֹ וְאֶת־זְהָבוֹ בְּאֹהֶל וַיְכַס[14] אֹתָם בְּבָגֶד׃ וַיָּסֹבּוּ אֹתוֹ מְרַגְּלִים מִן
יִשְׂרָאֵל וַיְגַלּוּ אֶת־כַּסְפּוֹ וְאֶת־זְהָבוֹ וַיָּבִיאוּ[16] אֶל־מַחֲנֵיהֶם[15]׃ [8] וַיִּבֶן שְׁלֹמֹה אֶת־הֵיכַל־
יְהוָה וַיְכַל מַעֲשֵׂהוּ וַיַּעֲמֹד נֶגֶד פֶּתַח־הַהֵיכָל וַיִּתְפַּלֵּל׃ וַיּוֹצִיאוּ אֶת־הַכֵּלִים מִן
אֹהֶל־מוֹעֵד וַיִּזְבְּחוּ זְבָחִים עַל־הַמִּזְבֵּחַ בֶּחָצֵר מִחוּץ לַהֵיכָל׃ וַיִּשְׂמְחוּ הָעָם וַיִּמְלָא
כְבוֹד־יְהוָה אֶת־הַבָּיִת[17]׃ [9] וַיְהִי אִישׁ מֹכֵר שֶׁמֶן וַיְהִי לוֹ רְכוּשׁ רָב׃ וַיִּהְיוּ לוֹ אֵילִים
וּגְמַלִּים וַאֲתֹנֹת[19] וַחֲמֹרִים׃ וַיֶּאֱהַב מִשְׁפָּט וַיִּשְׂנָא עָוֹן׃ וּבְכָל־חֹדֶשׁ וְחֹדֶשׁ[18] יָצָא מֵחֲצֵרוֹ
לִזְבֹּחַ בְּמִזְבַּח־יְהוָה׃ וַיְכַל[20] אֶת־זִבְחוֹ וַיִּפֶן מֵהַמִּזְבֵּחַ וַיָּשָׁב לִמְקוֹמוֹ׃ [10] וַיְהִי בִּשְׁנַת־
הַתְּשִׁיעִית לְמָלְכוֹ בַּחֹדֶשׁ הָעֲשִׂירִי בָּא נְבֻכַדְנֶאצַּר[22] מֶלֶךְ־בָּבֶל[21] הוּא וְכָל־חֵילוֹ עַל־
יְרוּשָׁלַםִ וַיִּחַן עָלֶיהָ וַיִּבְנוּ חוֹמָה סָבִיב׃ וַיַּעֲשׂוּ אֶת־הָעֲבֹדָה הַזֹּאת כַּעֲצַת־הַמֶּלֶךְ׃
בִּתְשְׁעָה לַחֹדֶשׁ לֹא־הָיָה לֶחֶם בָּעִיר לְעַם־הָאָרֶץ׃ [11] וַיְמַלֵּא אֱלֹהִים אֶת־דְּבָרוֹ[23]
לְאַבְרָהָם וַתְּמַלֵּא הָאָרֶץ[24] זַרְעוֹ וְלֹא שָׁמְרוּ עַמּוֹ אֶת־חֻקָּיו׃ וַיְחַלְּלוּ אֶת־הָאָרֶץ וַיְטַמְּאוּ
וּבְאַפּוֹ הֵסֵב אֱלֹהִים אֹתָם מֵהָאָרֶץ וַיִּגְלוּ עַמּוֹ׃ וֵאלֹהִים הֶחֱיָה אֹתָהֶם בַּעֲבוּר שְׁמוֹ
לְבִלְתִּי הַשְׁחִיתָם[26] וּמִקְּטֹן־הָאָרֶץ הִשְׁאִיר[25] לַעֲבֹד אֶת־הַשָּׂדוֹת׃

---

[13] The adverb סָבִיב is sometimes found with a plural ending (וֹת-) and a suffix (in this case, הֶם-). The plural ending refers to הָעַמִּים. The suffix refers to the *they* of the sentence, that is, God's people, Israel.

[14] Shortened form of the Imperfect. Why?

[15] Translate the noun as a singular, even though it is plural in form.

[16] Add *them* or *the things.*

[17] The word בַּיִת is often used for *temple* in the Old Testament.

[18] וּבְכָל־חֹדֶשׁ וְחֹדֶשׁ, that is, "And every month."

[19] *Holem* is often used instead of *holem vav*. This word can also be written אֲתֹנוֹת and אֲתוֹנוֹת.

[20] This is not the verb יָכֹל. Translate the w.c. "and when" and the next one "then."

[21] *Babylon.*

[22] *Nebuchadnezzar.*

[23] Translate "his promise." Hebrew does not have a specific word for *promise*, but uses the word דָּבָר.

[24] Add the word *with.*

[25] Add *some* or *some people.*

[26] Final vowel has lengthened due to being in pause.

74

VERBS WITH DOUBLE WEAKNESS (1)

Some verbs have more than one weak letter. For instance, the verb נָגַע is both *Pe Nun* and *Lamed Guttural*. Verbs with two weak letters are called "doubly weak" verbs, and usually the weaknesses will be in the first and last radical.[1]

74.1 *Pe Nun* and *Lamed* Guttural Verbs

Examples: נָגַע *to reach, touch;* נָסַע *to pull out, to start to travel;* נָטַע *to plant.*

Qal is regular in the Perfect. In the **Imperfect**, however the *pe nun* is assimilated and the *lamed guttural* attracts a *pathah*: יִגַּע (instead of יִנְגֹּע). The **Imperative** then becomes גַּע. The **Infinitive Construct** is found in two forms: one follows the *Pe Nun* pattern: גַּעַת[2], and the other follows the *Lamed Guttural* pattern: נְגֹעַ. The **Participle** has furtive *pathah*: נֹגֵעַ.

Niphal Perfect follows the *Pe Nun* pattern (assimilation): נ + נסע → נִנְסַע → נִסַּע

Piel has attracted *pathahs*. **Perf**: נִגַּע (instead of נִגֵּע); **Impf**: יְנַגַּע (instead of יְנַגֵּע)

Hiphil has both assimilation and furtive *pathah*. **Perf**: הִגִּיעַ; **Impf**: יַגִּיעַ.

74.2 *Pe Nun* and *Lamed Aleph* Verbs

The only important verb of this type is נָשָׂא, *to lift up, carry, forgive.* Again, there is assimilation of the נ. And the א often attracts a *qamets* instead of a *pathah.*[3]

Qal: Perf: נָשָׂא, נָשְׂאָה, נָשָׂאתָ, etc. **Impf:** יִשָּׂא. **Impv:** שָׂא. **IC:** שְׂאֵת (rarely נְשׂא).

Niphal: Perf: נִשָּׂא (same as Piel, below). **Impf:** יִנָּשֵׂא. **Impv** and **IC** are regular (הִנָּשֵׂא).

Piel: Perf: נִשָּׂא. **Impf:** regular (and always with object suffixes). Other forms seldom occur.

The **Hiphil** of נשׂא occurs only twice in the O.T. (Perf 3cp both times) and **Hithpael** is regular except for attracted *pathahs*.

---

[1] **Technical Note:** Gesenius lists six major groupings of doubly weak verbs (*Gesenius* §76.2). Five of them are considered in this chapter, but the remaining one (*Pe Yod*-and-*Lamed He* verbs) is concerned with verbs of low frequency (less than 55 occurrences in the Old Testament) and so are not included. There are, however, a few very common doubly weak verbs which are not discussed in Gesenius, and these have been added to the lesson under the headings *Pe Nun*-and-*Lamed Guttural*, *Pe Yod*-and-*Lamed Guttural* and *Pe Guttural*-and-*Lamed He*.

[2] The *Pe Nun* IC is usually of the form גֶּשֶׁת (from נָגַשׁ). But in the case of נָגַע, the guttural has attracted *pathahs*.

[3] **Technical Note:** Remember that א often becomes silent (quiescent) and loses its value as a letter. In effect, it disappears, and this opens up the syllable. Thus, we see a long vowel (the *qamets*). For instance, the Qal Perfect is נָשָׂא instead of נָשַׂא. Review *Lamed Aleph* Verbs, §71, if necessary.

74.3 *Pe Nun* and *Lamed He* Verbs

Examples: נָכָה, *to hit;* and נָטָה, *to turn, bend down, stretch out, set up a tent.*

In this type of verb, sometimes both the -נ and the ה- will disappear, leaving us with only -כ- or -ט- plus prefixes and/or suffixes. **Again, it is important to learn the strong letters of weak verbs.** And, as with other *Lamed He* verbs, the ה- ending cannot take suffixes; it will drop out or be replaced by י or ת or וֹת. There is also a shortened form of the Imperfect (used, for instance, with *vav* consecutive).

Qal:
Perf: נָטָה (3ms), נָטְתָה (3fs), נָטִיתָ (2ms), נָטִיתִי (1cs), etc.
Impf: יִטֶּה (3ms), וַיֵּט[4] (3ms+w.c.), יִטּוּ (3mp), etc.
Impv: נְטֵה **IC:** נְטוֹת [נְטֹת] **IA** נָטֹה **Part:** נֹטֶה

Hiphil:
Perf: הִטָּה (3ms), הִטְּתָה (3fs), הִטִּיתִי (1cs), etc.
Impf: יַטֶּה (3ms), וַיַּט[4] (3ms+w.c.), יַטּוּ (3mp), etc.
Impv: הַטֵּה **IC:** הַטּוֹת **IA:** הַטֵּה **Part:** מַטֶּה

Hophal:
Perf: הֻטָּה (3ms), הֻטְּתָה (3fs), etc.
Impf: only found as יֻטּוּ (3mp), תֻּטּוּ (2mp)
(No Impv or Infinitives) **Part:** מֻטֶּה

These verbs are also found, very infrequently, in Niphal and Pual. These will not be considered here.

74.4 *Pe* Guttural and *Lamed He* Verbs

Examples: the very common verbs עָלָה, *to go up*; עָנָה, *to answer*; and עָשָׂה, *to do, to make.* We will also consider רָאָה, *to see,* which acts as a *Pe Guttural-and-Lamed He* verb because the ר rejects *dagesh* just as a guttural does. רָאָה is actually "triple weak" because it has an א for its middle radical.

We will again see the characteristics of a *Lamed He* verb. In addition, the *pe* guttural will take composite *shewa* instead of simple *shewa*, and will attract *pathahs.*

Qal:
Perf: עָלָה (3ms), עָלְתָה (3fs), עָלִיתָ (2ms), etc.
Impf: יַעֲלֶה (3ms), וַיַּעַל[4] (3ms+w.c.), תַּעֲלִי (2fs), etc.
Impv: עֲלֵה **IC:** עֲלוֹת [עֲלֹת] **IA** עָלֹה **Part:** עֹלֶה

Niphal:
Perf: נַעֲלָה (3ms), נֶעֶלְתָ (3fs), נַעֲלֵיתָ (2ms), etc.
Impf: יֵעָלֶה (3ms), וַיֵּעַל[4] (3ms+w.c.), תֵּעָלִי (2fs), etc.
Impv: הֵעָלֵה **IC:** הֵעָלוֹת **IA:** נַעֲלֹה **Part:** נַעֲלֶה

Piel:
Perf: עִנָּה (3ms), עִנִּיתָ (2ms), עִנֵּיתִי (2ms), etc.
Impf: יְעַנֶּה (3ms), תְּעַנֶּה (2ms), יְעַנּוּ (3mp), etc.
Impv: עַנּוּ (mp) **IC:** עַנּוֹת **IA:** עַנֵּה **Part**(mp+2fs): מְעַנַּיִךְ

---

[4] *Vav* consecutive with shortened form of Imperfect.

Hiphil: **Perf:** הֶעֱלָה (3ms), הַעַלְתָה (3fs), הֶעֱלִיתָ (2ms), etc.
Impf: Same as Qal Impf (where guttural attracts a *pathah*)
Impv: הַעַל **IC:** הַעֲלוֹת [הַעֲלֹת] **IA:** הַעֲלֵה **Part:** מַעֲלֶה

The verb רָאָה appears primarily in Qal, Niphal and Hiphil. It has three weaknesses: the ר rejects *dagesh*; the א attracts *qamets*; and the ה drops out or is replaced by י or ת or וֹת when the verb takes suffixes.

Qal: **Perf:** רָאָה (3ms), רָאֲתָה (3fs), רָאִיתָ (2ms), etc.
Impf: יִרְאֶה (3ms), וַיַּרְא (3ms+w.c., same as Hiphil, below), תִּרְאֶינָה (3/2fp), etc.
Impv: רְאֵה **IC:** רְאוֹת or רְאֹו **IA:** רָאֹה or רָאוֹ **Part:** רֹאֶה

Niphal: **Perf:** נִרְאָה (3ms, cf. Participle), נִרְאֲתָה (3fs), נִרְאוּ (3cp), etc.
Impf: יֵרָאֶה (3ms), וַיֵּרָא (3ms+w.c.), etc.
Impv: הֵרָאֵה **IC:** הֵרָאוֹת **IA:** הֵרָאֹה **Part:** נִרְאֶה or נִרְאָה

Hiphil: **Perf:** הֶרְאָה (3ms), הִרְאִיתָ (2ms), הִרְאֵיתִי (1cs) (also הַרְאִיתִי and הֶרְאֵיתִי)
Impf: יַרְאֶה (3ms), וַיַּרְא (3ms+w.c., same as Qal), etc.
Impv with 1cs suff: הַרְאִנִי or הַרְאֵנִי **IC** (only): הַרְאוֹת **Part:** מַרְאֶה

ראה and ירא

It can be difficult to tell the difference between the Imperfects of these verbs. Both are common verbs, and both are weak. They each have the same strong letters: -רא-. In general, however, **the *yod* of ירא will remain in the Imperfect** This gives two *yods* in the 3ms or 3mp. Thus:

Qal Impf 3ms of ראה is יִרְאֶה or יֵרֶה (or, with w.c., וַיַּרְא), but
Qal Impf 3ms of ירא is יִירָא (or, with w.c., וַיִּירָא)

One form at first seems ambiguous (for example, see Ps 52:8):

יִרְאוּ is the Qal Impf 3mp of ראה, and
יִֽרְאוּ is the Qal Impf 3mp of ירא (though it is also found as יִירְאוּ)

But listen to their pronunciations. The *metheg* in יִֽרְאוּ gives almost the same *sound* as its other form יִירְאוּ. Think of the *metheg* as representing the original י of ירא.

Things You Should Know

1. **Doubly weak verbs** have two weak letters. Weaknesses are usually in first and last radicals.
2. **You do not need to memorize all the charts.** If you know the general rules for verbs with single weaknesses (*Pe Nun* verbs, *Lamed He* verbs, etc.) you will know what to expect from doubly weak verbs.
3. **Learn the strong letters** in weak verbs. They will remain, even when weak letters drop out.

75

VERBS WITH DOUBLE WEAKNESS (2)

In this chapter, we will study four more sets of doubly weak verb patterns. Again, if you understand the rules for verbs with a single weakness, you will be able to apply these rules to doubly weak verbs as well.

75.1 *Pe Yod* (original *Pe Vav*) and *Lamed Guttural* Verbs

Examples: יָדַע *to know;* ישׁע *to be victorious* (in Niphal), *to help, save* (in Hiphil). These verbs originally began with ו but now begin with י. The original ו returns in Niphal and Hiphil (§63, p.195).

Qal: **Perf:** (regular) **Impf:** יֵדַע (3ms), תֵּדְעִי (2fs), etc.

Impv: דַּע **IC:** דַּעַת **IA:** יָדוֹעַ [יָדֹעַ]

Act. Part.: יוֹדֵעַ [יֹדֵעַ] **Pass. Part.:** יָדוּעַ

Niphal: **Perf:** נוֹדַע (3ms), נוֹדְעָה (3fs), נוֹדַעְנוּ (1cp), etc.

Impf: יִוָּדַע (3ms), תִּוָּדְעִי (2fs), etc.

Impv: הִוָּשְׁעוּ (mp) **IC:** הִוָּדַע **Part:** נוֹדָע

Hiphil: **Perf:** הוֹדִיעַ (3ms), הוֹדַעְתָּ (2ms), הוֹדִיעוּ (3cp), etc.

Impf: יוֹדִיעַ (3ms), וַיֹּדַע (3ms+w.c.), יוֹדִיעוּ (3mp), etc.

Impv: הוֹדַע **IC:** הוֹדִיעַ **Part:** מוֹדִיעַ

יָדַע also appears infrequently in other forms (Piel, Pual, Hophal, Hithpael) which are not considered here.

75.2 *Pe Yod* (Original *Pe Vav*) and *Lamed Aleph* Verbs

Examples: יָרֵא *to fear, be in awe of,* and יָצָא *to go out or come out.* These two verbs also originally began with ו. They develop in different ways, since יָרֵא is a stative.

75.2.1 יָרֵא *to fear, be in awe of* (stative)

Qal: **Perf:** יָרֵא (3ms), יָרְאָה (3fs), יָרֵאתִי (1cs), etc.

Impf: יִירָא (3ms), וַיִּירָא or וַיִּרָא (3ms+w.c.), תִּירְאִי (2fs), etc.

Impv: יְרָא **IC:** יִרְאָה **Part:** יָרֵא

Niphal: Found only in **Imperfect** 2ms: תִּוָּרֵא, and **Participle**: נוֹרָא

75.2.2 יָצָא *to go or come out* (original *Pe Vav*)

Qal: **Perf:** יָצָא (3ms), יָצְאָה (3fs), יָצָ֫אתָ (2ms), etc.
Impf: יֵצֵא (3ms), תֵּצֵא (3fs), יֵצְאוּ (3mp), etc.
Impv: צֵא **IC:** צֵאת **IA:** יָצוֹא **Part:** יוֹצֵא [יֹצֵא]

Hiphil: **Perf:** הוֹצִיא (3ms), הוֹצֵ֫אתָ (2ms), הוֹצִיאוּ (3cp), etc.
Impf: יוֹצִיא or יֹצִא (3ms), תּוֹצִיא (3fs, 2ms), etc.
Impv: הוֹצֵא or הוֹצִיא (like Perf 3ms) **IC:** הוֹצִיא (like Perf 3ms) **Part:** מוֹצִא

75.3 *Pe Yod* (Original *Pe Vav*) and *Lamed He* Verbs

Examples: ידה *to praise, give thanks* (in Hiphil); יָרָה *to throw, shoot* (Qal and Hiphil); *to instruct, teach* (Hiphil only). (Both are actually original *Pe Vav* verbs.)

Qal: **Perf:** found only as יָרָה (3ms) and יָרִ֫יתִי (1cs)
Impf: only found as וַנִּירָם (1cp + 3mp suffix + w.c.)
Impv: יְרֵה **IC:** יְרוֹת **Part:** יֹרֶה

Hiphil: **Perf:** הוֹרֵ֫יתִי (1cs), etc. **Impf:** יוֹרֶה (3ms), וַיּוֹר (3ms+w.c.), יֹרוּ (3mp)
Impv: הוֹרֵה **IC:** הוֹרוֹת **Part:** מוֹרֶה

75.4 *Ayin Vav* and *Lamed Aleph* Verbs

Example: the very common verb בּוֹא *to enter, to come, to go.* Review §68 ("Middle Vowel Verbs (1)"), and compare to the patterns below. Watch the accents carefully. Again, only the accent separates Qal Perf 3fs and Part fs. Note also that ***holem*** **(ֹ)and *holem vav* (וֹ) are interchangeable**. That is, verbs like בּוֹא and יָבוֹא will also be found as בֹּא and יָבֹא. The **same is sometimes true of** בֵּי **and** בֵּ, בִּי **and** בִּ.

Qal: **Perf:** בָּא (3ms), בָּ֫אָה (3fs), וּבָאָ֫ה (3fs+w.c.), בָּאת (2fs), בָּ֫אתִי (1cs), etc.
Impf: יָבוֹא (3ms), תָּבֹ֫אִי (2fs), תָּבוֹאנָה (2/3fp), etc.
Impv: בּוֹא **IC:** בּוֹא **Part:** בָּא (ms), בָּאָה (fs)

Hiphil: **Perf:** הֵבִיא (3ms), הֵבִ֫יאָה (3fs), הֵבֵ֫יאתִי (1cs), הֵבִ֫יאוּ (3cp), etc.
Impf: יָבִיא (3ms), יָבִ֫יאוּ (3mp), תְּבִיאֶ֫ינָה (2/3fp), נָבִיא (1cp), etc.
Impv: הָבֵיא **IC:** הָבִיא **IA:** הָבֵא **Part:** מֵבִיא

Things You Should Know

1. Review the "Things You Should Know" section at the end of the previous chapter.
2. Some forms are identical (especially with the verb בּוֹא). Context will tell you how to parse.

Exercise #47

דָּרַשׁ	to seek, ask, demand; ***Ni*** נִדְרַשׁ to be sought
כַּף	*f.* palm of hand, sole of foot; *du.* כַּפַּיִם, *cs.* כַּפֵּי; *pl.* כַּפּוֹת, *cs.=* [1]
ישׁע	***Ni*** נוֹשַׁע to receive help, to be victorious, *Impf* יִוָּשַׁע; ***Hi*** הוֹשִׁיעַ to help, save, rescue
מַ֫עַל	*adv.* above, upward, high
נָגַע	to touch, reach, hit; ***Hi*** הִגִּיעַ to touch, reach, hit
נָטָה	to turn, bend down, stretch out, set up a tent; *Impf* יִטֶּה; ***Hi*** הִטָּה, *Impf* יַטֶּה to bend down, stretch out, to turn something. aside
נכה	***Hi*** הִכָּה to hit, strike; ***Ho*** הֻכָּה to be struck down, to be killed
עָלָה	to go up; ***Ni*** נַעֲלָה to be taken up, to go away; ***Hi*** הֶעֱלָה to bring up, to offer. Note: *Qal Impf = Hi Impf =* יַעֲלֶה
עָנָה	I. to answer; II. to bend down, to be in a miserable condition; ***Pi*** עִנָּה to oppress, humiliate
צָפוֹן	north
רֹב	*n.* abundance, greatness; *adj.* many
שׁחה	***Hitp*** *Perf. 3ms* הִשְׁתַּחֲוָה to bow down, worship, *Impf* יִשְׁתַּחֲוֶה, *IC* הִשְׁתַּחֲוֹת (sometimes listed as "hishtaphal" form of חוה)

[1] יָבִ֫יאוּ קַ֫יִן וְהֶ֫בֶל מִנְחוֹת לְהִשְׁתַּחֲוֹת לַיהוָה׃ וַיְהִי אַחֲרֵי־כֵן וַיַּךְ קַ֫יִן אֶת־אָחִ֫יהוּ
וְלֹא יָכֹל לְכַסּוֹת אֶת־דָּמוֹ׃ וַיְשַׁלְּחֵהוּ יְהוָה מֵהָאָ֫רֶץ אֲשֶׁר לָֽקְחָה2 אֶת־דַּם־אָחִיהוּ׃
[2] קָצַף עֵשָׂו כִּי בֵרַךְ אָבִיו אֶת־יַעֲקֹב וַיְסַפֵּר לְרִבְקָה3 הַדָּבָר׃ וַתָּ֫קָם וַתִּגַּשׁ אֶל־
יִצְחָק וַתְּדַבֵּר אֵלָיו לֵאמֹר אִם יִקַּח יַעֲקֹב אִשָּׁה מֵהָאָ֫רֶץ הַזֹּאת לֹא אוּכַל4 לִחְיוֹת׃
נִשְׁלְחָה אֹתוֹ אֶל־צָפוֹן אֶל־עִיר־אָחִי לְבַעֲבוּר5 מְצֹא אִשָּׁה׃ [3] וַיָּ֫שָׁב יַעֲקֹב מִפַּדַּן־
אֲרָם7 וַיִּרְאֵ֫הוּ6 עֵשָׂו וַיֹּ֫אמֶר מִי לְךָ כָּל־הַמַּחֲנֶה הַזֶּה׃ וַיֹּ֫אמֶר יַעֲקֹב קַח־נָא אֶת־
בִּרְכָתִי אֲשֶׁר הֵבֵאתִי לָךְ כִּי־בֵרְכַ֫נִי אֱלֹהִים וְכִי יֶשׁ־לִי־כֹל 8וַיְדַבֵּר־לוֹ וַיִּקָּח׃ וַיָּבֹא
יַעֲקֹב שָׁלֵם עִיר־שְׁכֶם וַיִּ֫חַן אֶת־פְּנֵי הָעִיר9׃ [4] וַיֹּ֫אמֶר יְהוָה אֶל־מֹשֶׁה לֵךְ אֶל־הָעָם
וְהָיוּ נְכֹנִים לַיּוֹם־הַשְּׁלִישִׁי כִּי בַּיּוֹם הַשְּׁלִישִׁי יֵרֵד יְהוָה לְעֵינֵי־כָל־הָעָם עַל־הַר־סִינָי׃
וְשַׂמְתָּ גְּבוּל לְהָעָם סָבִיב לֵאמֹר הִשָּׁמְרוּ לָכֶם10 עֲלוֹת בָּהָר וּנְגֹעַ בִּגְבֻלוֹ׃ כָּל־הַנֹּגֵעַ

[1] *cs.=* means that the construct is the same as the absolute. This abbreviation is also used in the vocabulary list at the end of the book.

[2] Who or what is the subject of this verb? It must be feminine, so it can't be Cain or God. What other noun appears in the sentence? Is it feminine?

[3] *Rebekah.*

[4] Qal Impf 1cs < יכל. We will study this verb in the next lesson (§76.4).

[5] Alternate form of בַּעֲבוּר.

[6] Did he *fear* him or did he *see* him? The root of this verb is ראה. If the root was ירא, the original *yod* would remain – either as a *yod* or as a *metheg* representing the yod. Thus, if the root were ירא we would see either the word וַיִּירָאֵהוּ or the word וַיִּֽרָאֵהוּ.

[7] *Paddan-Aram*, where Rebekah's brother Laban lived.

[8] Translate the ו "Thus."

[9] That is, "he camped before (in front of) the city."

[10] הִשָּׁמְרוּ לָכֶם. That is, "Do not," or "Keep yourself (so that you do not)."

בָּהָר מוֹת יוּמָת אִם־בְּהֵמָה אִם־אִישׁ לֹא יִחְיֶה׃ [5] [11]וּמֹשֶׁה יִקַּח אֶת־הָאֹהֶל וְנָטָה־
לוֹ[13] מִחוּץ לַמַּחֲנֶה וְקָרָא לוֹ אֹהֶל־מוֹעֵד וְהָיָה[12] כָּל־מְבַקֵּשׁ יְהוָה יֵצֵא אֶל־אֹהֶל־מוֹעֵד
אֲשֶׁר מִחוּץ לַמַּחֲנֶה׃ [6] וַיֹּאמֶר יְהוֹשֻׁעַ אֶל־בְּנֵי־יִשְׂרָאֵל הִנֵּה אֲרוֹן־הַבְּרִית־אֲדוֹן־
כָּל־הָאָרֶץ עֹבֵר לִפְנֵיכֶם בַּיַּרְדֵּן׃ וְעַתָּה קְחוּ לָכֶם שְׁנֵי עָשָׂר אִישׁ מִשִּׁבְטֵי־יִשְׂרָאֵל
אִישׁ־אֶחָד אִישׁ־אֶחָד לַשָּׁבֶט׃[14] וְהָיָה כְּנוֹחַ כַּפּוֹת־רַגְלֵי־הַכֹּהֲנִים נֹשְׂאֵי־אֲרוֹן־יְהוָה
אֲדוֹן כָּל־הָאָרֶץ[19] בְּמֵי[18]־הַיַּרְדֵּן מֵי־הַיַּרְדֵּן יִכָּרֵתוּן[17]׃ וְיַעַמְדוּ[16] הַמַּיִם הַיֹּרְדִים[15]
מִלְמָעְלָה[22] מָקוֹם אֶחָד׃ [7] וַיֹּאמֶר יְהוָה אֶל־יְהוֹשֻׁעַ הַיּוֹם הַזֶּה אָחֵל[21] גַּדֶּלְךָ[20] בְּעֵינֵי־
כָּל־יִשְׂרָאֵל אֲשֶׁר[25] יֵדְעוּן[24] כִּי כַּאֲשֶׁר הָיִיתִי עִם־מֹשֶׁה בְּאֹהֶל־מוֹעֵד אֶהְיֶה עִמָּךְ[23]׃
וַיֹּאמֶר יְהוֹשֻׁעַ אֶל־הָעָם בַּחֲרוּ לָכֶם הַיּוֹם אֶת־מִי תַּעַבְדוּן[26]׃ אִם תַּעַבְדוּן אֱלֹהִים
אֲחֵרִים [27]וְסָבַב יְהוָה וְעָשָׂה רַע לָכֶם וְכִלָּה אֶתְכֶם אַחֲרֵי אֲשֶׁר הֵיטִיב לָכֶם׃ וַיֹּאמֶר
הָעָם אֶל־יְהוֹשֻׁעַ לֹא כִּי[29] אֶת־יְהוָה נַעֲבֹד׃ [8] יָסְפוּ[28] הָעָם לָסוּר מִדֶּרֶךְ־יְהוָה וְלֹא

---

[11] **Technical note:** This sentence, adapted from the book of Exodus, uses imperfect verbs and perfect verbs with *vav* consecutive. Thus, you would normally translate using future tense. In this case, however, the context of the original story demands "habitual past" tense. That is, "And Moses *used to* take the tent ...."

[12] We might expect Impf + w.c. here, but this is the way it is in the Bible. Translate as past tense in this case.

[13] **Technical note:** Why is there a *metheg* under the נ in וְנָֽטָה־לוֹ? Remember, the *maqqeph* takes away the accent of נָטָה; the only accent is on לוֹ. Thus, we are seeing a *metheg* two syllables before the accent (see p. 30).

[14] אִישׁ־אֶחָד אִישׁ־אֶחָד לַשָּׁבֶט. That is, one man from each tribe.

[15] Read this word carefully. It is not "the Jordan."

[16] This is a rare Impf + vav (not wc), and it keeps its future meaning. If it were Impf + wc we would see וַיַּעַמְדוּ. It could also be a Jussive + vav, but the context does not allow for this.

[17] יִכָּרֵתוּן. Read this as יִכָּרֵתוּ. The extra *nun* at the end is from an older form of Hebrew. It is seen fairly often in the Old Testament, so it is good to get used to it. You will see it again in this set of exercises.

[18] See the vocabulary of Exercise #18 for this word. (It has a prefix here.)

[19] אֲדוֹן כָּל־הָאָרֶץ. Put this phrase in parentheses (like this) in your translation.

[20] Piel IC + suffix.

[21] From the verb חלל, second meaning (II).

[22] This word has two prefixed prepositions and a suffixed "*He* of direction toward." We would expect a *dagesh* in the first *lamed* (מִלְּמָעְלָה), but in this particular form of the word it does not appear.

[23] The suffix is 2ms. Remember that when a preposition with 2ms suffix (such as עִמְּךָ) is in pause, the accent moves and the *qamets* in the final ך shortens to *shewa*: עִמָּךְ (See §35.1 and footnote 1 on p. 107.). You will see this again, below.

[24] See footnote 17.

[25] Translate "so that."

[26] See footnote 17.

[27] Translate the *vav* "then."

[28] The first vowel is a *qamets* not a *qamets-hatuph*. We usually expect to see a *metheg* in this verb form: יָֽסְפוּ. But you will discover that in the Hebrew Bible this *metheg* is often missing in common verbs. We are just expected to know. Yes, it is sometimes confusing.

[29] Translate "for" or "because."

בּוֹשׁוּ מֵעֲוֺנוֹתֵיהֶם׃ וַיִּתְּנֵם[32] יְהוָה בְּיַד־אֹיְבֵיהֶם לְהַכּוֹתָם[31] וּלְעַנּוֹתָם׃ וְלֹא יָכְלוּ[30] לָנ וּס
וַיָּחֵלּוּ לִדְרשׁ אֶת־יְהוָה׃ וַיָּרִים שֹׁפְטִים[34] אֲשֶׁר רוּחוֹ עֲלֵיהֶם וַיּוֹשִׁעוּ מֵהֶם׃ וַיָּמָת[33]
הַשֹּׁפֵט וַיָּשֻׁבוּ הָעָם אֶל־דַּרְכֵיהֶם הָרָעִים׃ [9] וַיְהִי כְּכַלֹּתוֹ נָגִיד־יְרִיחוֹ לִבְנוֹת
הֵיכָלוֹ וַיִּקְרָא לְרֵעָיו לָבוֹא לֶאֱכֹל וְלִשְׁתּוֹת׃ וַיִּפֶן אֶל־רֵעֵהוּ וַיַּגֵּד אֵלָיו לֵאמֹר
רָבִּינוּ וְיָדוֹעַ יֵדְעוּ כָּל־הָעַמִּים מִצֵּאת־הַשֶּׁמֶשׁ[35] עַד־הַיָּם אֶת־רָב־שְׁמֵנוּ׃ [10] וַיַּגֵּד
נָתָן[38] לְדָוִד לֵאמֹר יִבְנֶה יְהוָה [37]אֲשֶׁר הוּא אֱלֹהִים בַּשָּׁמַיִם מִמַּעַל בַּיִת לְךָ[36] וְהֵכִין אֶת־
מַמְלַכְתְּךָ עַד־עוֹלָם׃ [11] הִרְבֵּיתִי אֶת־עַמִּי וְלֹא הֵבִינוּ כִּי אָנֹכִי נָתַתִּי לָהֶם בִּרְכוֹת־
שָׂדֶה וּבִרְכוֹת־בֶּטֶן וְשׁוֹר וּבְהֵמָה וְאֶת־כָּל־רְכוּשָׁם׃ לָכֵן לֹא אֲכַסֶּה אֶת־עֲוֺנָם וְגָלִּיתִי
אֶת־חֶטְאָם בְּעֵינֵי־אֹיְבֵיהֶם׃ וְגָלוּה יִגְלוּ נְאֻם־יְהוָה׃ [12] וַיָּבֹאוּ מַחֲנֵי־אַשּׁוּר[39]
הַגְּדוֹלִים מִצָּפוֹן וַיְסוֹבְבוּ אֶת־יְרוּשָׁלָםִ׃ וַיַּחֲנוּ עַל־הָעִיר סָבִיב וַיִּקָּבְצוּ[40] בַּעֲבוּר שַׁבֵּר
אֶת־שַׁעֲרֵי־הָעִיר׃ וְלֹא הָיָה לָעָם מַיִם לִשְׁתּוֹת׃ וַיְדַבֵּר יְשַׁעְיָהוּ[41] אֶל־הַמֶּלֶךְ וַיֹּאמַר
הִכּוֹן[45] כִּי יְהוָה בְּתוֹךְ־יְרוּשָׁלִָם׃ [13] יְהוָה[44] דְּרַשְׁתִּיךָ כִּי רָב[43]־חַסְדְּךָ הַט[42]־אָזְנְךָ לִי
שְׁמַע אֶת־דְּבָרָי׃ עֲנָנִי[46] יְהוָה וַיּוֹשִׁיעֵנִי מִכָּל־אֹיְבָי׃ לָכֵן אֶשְׁתַּחֲוֶה לַיהוָה וְהֶעֱלֵיתִי
זְבָחִים עַל־מִזְבְּחוֹ׃

---

[30] See footnote 28.

[31] I.C. with prefix and suffix. Only the -כּ- remains from the verb.

[32] The verb is נתן, and has both w.c. and an object suffix.

[33] Translate the ו "But when . . . ."

[34] שֹׁפְטִים is the object of וַיָּרִים, not its subject. (The verb is singular, not plural. Be sure you can parse it.)

[35] מִצֵּאת־הַשֶּׁמֶשׁ. Translate, "from the rising of the sun." How do you parse מִצֵּאת?

[36] The suffix is masculine, even though it looks feminine. See footnote 23, above.

[37] אֲשֶׁר הוּא אֱלֹהִים בַּשָּׁמַיִם מִמַּעַל. Put this phrase in parentheses (like this) in your translation.

[38] This is a name, not a verb.

[39] Assyria.

[40] We expect to see a *metheg* with the *qamets*, but again it is missing. See footnote 28.

[41] Isaiah.

[42] This is the Hiphil Impv of a weak verb. Remember that with weak verbs, you need to learn the strong letters. This verb has only one strong letter, ט. The other two letters have dropped out.

[43] Construct form. Therefore, the vowel has shortened to *qamets-hatuph.*

[44] You may translate "O Lord." Hebrew does not have a vocative case like Greek, but the idea is sometimes present. For instance, Ps 115:1: לֹא לָנוּ יְהוָה לֹא לָנוּ, *Not to us, O Lord, not to us.*

[45] Niph Impv

[46] Qal Perf 3ms + 1cs.

76

VERB "TEAMS" ("Defective" Verbs)

We have seen that a Hebrew verb comes in several moods (Perfect, Imperfect, Participle, etc.) and often in more than one form (Qal, Niphal, Piel, etc.). Sometimes, however, two weak verbs must work together as a "team" to provide a complete set of moods or forms. That is, each verb, by itself, is incomplete and is therefore called "defective." But when the two verbs are put together as a "team," the second verb provides moods or forms which the first one lacks.

For instance, the verb שָׁתָה means *to drink,* and comes in Qal but not in Hiphil. On the other hand, the verb שׁקה[1] also means *to drink*; but it comes in the Hiphil (meaning *to give a drink to*) and not in the Qal. These two verbs work together as a "team." When a Qal meaning is needed, the verb שָׁתָה is used, and when a Hiphil meaning is needed the verb שׁקה is used.

Each verb "team" is made up of two weak verbs which are spelled almost exactly the same. There will be only one letter difference in each case. Most of these verbs occur very seldom. Five of them are common, however, and will be mentioned here.[2]

76.1 בּוֹשׁ and יבשׁ, *to be ashamed*

In **Qal**, we find בּוֹשׁ, but in **Hiphil** we find not only הֵבִישׁ (from בּוֹשׁ), but also הוֹבִישׁ (and הֹבִישׁ), which seems to be based upon an original *Pe Vav* verb, יבשׁ < ובשׁ (§63).

76.2 הָלַךְ and ילךְ, *to go, to walk*

Qal: הָלַךְ is used for the Perfect, the Infinitive Absolute (הָלוֹךְ) and the Participle (הֹלֵךְ).
ילךְ is used for the Impf (יֵלֵךְ), the Impv (לֵךְ) and the Infinitive Construct (לֶכֶת).

Hiphil: ילךְ is used. It is an original *Pe Vav* verb, and thus will appear as הוֹלִיךְ.

76.3 טוֹב and יטב, *to be good* and *to do good*

The **Qal** means *to be good,* and the **Hiphil** means *to do good* (i.e., *to cause good*)

טוֹב is used for the **Qal Perf, the Infinitives and the Participle**. Note that *the Perf 3ms, the Infinitives and the participle all have the same form*: טוֹב.[3] The adjective *good* is also טוֹב, and it is often difficult to know if we are looking at a verb or an adjective.

יטב is used for the **Qal Imperfect** (יִיטַב) and the **Hiphil** (הֵיטִיב or יֵיטִיב, etc.).

---

[1] שׁקה is shows without vowel points because it does not have a Qal form. See p. 136, note 8.

[2] **Technical note:** Some rare verb "teams" are יָקַץ and קוּץ, both meaning "to awaken;" נָקַע and יקע, "to be alienated;" and נָפַץ and פּוּץ, "to shatter." Again, in each case the two verbs are weak, and they differ by only one letter.

[3] **Technical note:** Gesenius only lists the Perfect, and apparently does not acknowledge the other forms. The matter is complex.

76.4 יָכֹל and יוּכַל, *to be able*

This stative verb comes only in Qal, but it seems to have some type of mixed background:

The Perfect is יָכֹל, and the Infinitive Absolute is יָכוֹל.

But the Imperfect is יוּכַל, which seems to be Original *Pe Vav*. And the Infinitive Construct is most unusual: יְכֹלֶת.[4]

76.5 שָׁתָה and שקה *to drink*

Qal uses שָׁתָה (Perf שָׁתָה, Impf יִשְׁתֶּה, Impv שְׁתֵה, etc.).

Hiphil uses שקה (Perf הִשְׁקָה, Impf יַשְׁקֶה, Impv הַשְׁקוּ, IC הַשְׁקוֹת, etc.)

Parsing Two-Radical Verb Forms

Weak verbs often lose one or more of their radicals. This makes them difficult to parse. For instance, in Gen 2:8 we find the verbs וַיִּטַּע and וַיָּשֶׂם. And Gen 2:16 begins with וַיְצַו. Verbs have three radicals, and so when you see such patterns, you can assume that something has dropped out or has been assimilated. Thus, you should consider the following possibilities: The verb may originally have had

a. a first radical ה י or נ. Examples: הלך, ילד and נפל.
b. a second radical ו or י. Examples: קוּם and שׂים.
c. a third radical ה. Example: עלה

Thus, for the above three examples from Gen 2 (וַיִּטַּע, וַיָּשֶׂם and וַיְצַו), do the following:

For וַיִּטַּע, first take away the ו and י (they are clearly Impf+w.c. prefixes). You then get טַּע. The *dagesh* in the ט shows that the letter before it (the first radical) has been assimilated. This usually happens with נ. Look in the dictionary (lexicon) for נ+ טע and you find נטע, *to plant*.

For וַיָּשֶׂם, you again take away the ו and י to get שׂם. Begin by trying to add ה י or נ as *first* radicals (השׂם, ישׂם, נשׂם). You will fail to find these in the dictionary. Next try adding ו or י as a *middle* radical (שׂוּם or שׂים). This works. In the lexicon, you find שׂים, *to put, place, set.*

For וַיְצַו you again remove the prefixes to get צו. Adding ה י or נ as a first radical, or adding ו or י as middle radical, produces nothing. But when you add ה as a third radical, you will find the verb צוה, *to command.*

Summary: When you only have two radicals of the verb, try adding

- a first radical ה י or נ, or
- a second radical ו or י, or
- a third radical ה.

[4] **Technical Note:** The Infinitive Construct seems to be a mixture of *Pe Yod* (which would be כֹּלֶת) and original *Pe Vav* (which would be יְכֹל).

Things You Should Know

1. Sometimes two weak verbs work together as a "team" to provide a more complete set of forms or moods. Each verb, by itself, is thus considered incomplete or "defective."
2. The two "defective" verbs which make up a verb "team" will be weak and will have very similar spelling. Only one letter will be different (for instance, שׁתה and שׁקה).

Exercise #48

אָז	then
בַּ֫עַל	owner, lord, master, husband; Baal
יַחְדָּו, יַ֫חַד	together
יַ֫יִן	wine, *cs.* יֵין
ילך	***Qal*** *Impf* יֵלֵךְ to go, walk around; *Impv.* לֵךְ; ***Hi*** הוֹלִיךְ to bring, take, *Impf* יוֹלִיךְ
יָמִין	right (*opposite of* left), south
מִשְׁכָּן	*m.* tabernacle, home, *cs.* מִשְׁכַּן; *pl.* מִשְׁכָּנוֹת
נַ֫חַל	(dry) stream bed; valley
נְח֫שֶׁת	bronze (*do not confuse with* נָחָשׁ)
נָסַע	to pull something out, to travel, start to travel; ***Hi*** (no *Perf*) *Impf* יַסַּע to take something away, to make people start to travel
נָשִׂיא	leader, prince
רָעָה	to graze (*tr. & intr.*), to take care of sheep; *Pt.* רֹעֶה *is often used as noun*: shepherd

Be sure also to learn the verbs which are discussed in the lesson.

[1] וְגַם־לְלוֹט[5] הַנֹּסֵעַ אֶת־אַבְרָם הָיָה רַב־צֹאן־וּבָקָר וְאֹהָלִים׃ וְלֹא־נָשָׂא אֹתָם הָאָרֶץ
לִרְעוֹת־צֹאן יַחְדָּו כִּי־הָיָה רְכוּשָׁם רָב וְלֹא יָכְלוּ לָשֶׁבֶת יַחְדָּו׃ וַיֹּאמֶר אַבְרָם אֶל־לוֹט
הֲלֹא כָל־הָאָרֶץ לְפָנֶיךָ הִפָּרֶד נָא מֵעָלָי אִם־הַצָּפוֹן וְהָלַכְתִּי אֶל־הַיָּמִין׃ [2] וַיִּתְקַבְּצוּ
יַחְדָּו הַמְּלָכִים לְהִלָּחֵם עִם מֶלֶךְ־סְדֹם וְעִם נְשִׂיאִים אֲחֵרִים וַיִּסְעוּ אֶת־לוֹט׃ וַיִּרְדֹּף
אַבְרָם אַחֲרֵיהֶם וַיַּכֵּם[7] וַיּוֹשִׁיעַ אֶת־לוֹט׃ וּמַלְכִּי־צֶדֶק[6] מֶלֶךְ־שָׁלֵם הוֹצִיא לֶחֶם וָיַיִן
וַיְבָרֶךְ אֶת־אַבְרָם וַיְשַׁבַּח אֶת־אֵל־עֶלְיוֹן[9]׃ [3] וַיִּירָא[8] יַעֲקֹב מְאֹד וַתִּמְצָא צָרָה אֹתוֹ
וַיִּלָּחֶם בְּאִישׁ עַל־שְׂפַת־נַחַל׃ וַיִּפֶן הָאִישׁ וַיִּגַּע אֶת־כַּף־רֶגֶל[10]־יַעֲקֹב וְאָז אָמַר הָאִישׁ
שַׁלְּחֵנִי כִּי עָלָה הַשָּׁמֶשׁ׃ וַיַּעַן לֹא אֲשַׁלֵּחֲךָ כִּי אִם[11]־בֵּרַכְתָּנִי׃ [4] יָשְׁבוּ יִשְׂרָאֵל
בְּאֶרֶץ־גֹּשֶׁן[12] כִּי שָׂנְאוּ הַמִּצְרִים רֹעִים וַיִּרְעוּ אֶת־צֹאנָם וַיֵּלְדוּ יְלָדִים רַבִּים וַיִּהְיוּ חָזָק׃

---

[5] The ל prefix on this word works with the הָיָה in the second part of the sentence. See §46.2, p. 138.

[6] *Melchizedek*. What does his name mean?

[7] Hint: This verb has two prefixes and a suffix. Only one letter remains from the verb itself.

[8] Note how the Impf + w.c. of ירא preserves the original י along with the prefix (see p. 243, footnote 6).

[9] אֵל־עֶלְיוֹן, usually translated "God Most High." Note the relationship of the word עֶלְיוֹן to עַל and עָלָה.

[10] In the story in Genesis, the word is not רֶגֶל but rather the word יָרֵךְ, *thigh* (the upper leg).

[11] כִּי אִם־ often means *unless* or *except*.

[12] the land of Goshen.

[5] וְהָיָה מִשְׁכָּנִי בְּתוֹךְ־שִׁבְטֵיכֶ֑ן בַּעֲבוּר תְּזַבַּ֫חְנָה זְבָחִים מֵ֫עַל מִזְבַּח־נְחָשְׁתִּי וּלְהִשְׁתַּחֲוֺת
אֹתִי׃ יִקְרְבוּ הָעָם אֶת־פֶּתַח־חֲצֵרוֹ לְדָרְשֵׁ֫נִי וּלְהוּשַׁ֑ע וְלֹא יִגְּעוּ֫הוּ פֶּן יְטַמְּא֫וּהוּ וְהֻכּוּ׃
[6] וַיִּבְנוּ הָעָם אֶת־הַמִּשְׁכָּן כִּדְבַר־מֹשֶׁה׃ וַיָּבֹ֫אוּ כָּל־אִישׁ אֲשֶׁר־נְשָׂאוֹ לִבּ֑וֹ[13] וַיָּבִ֫יאוּ בְיָדָם
זָהָב וְכֶ֫סֶף לִמְלֶאכֶת־אֹהֶל־מוֹעֵד וּלְכָל־עֲבֹדָתוֹ וּלְבִגְדֵי־הַקֹּדֶשׁ׃ [7] וַיֶּחֶטְאוּ עוֹד הָעָם
וּבְאַף שָׁלַח יְהוָה נְחָשִׁים בְּתוֹכָ֑ם וַיָּבֹ֫אוּ אֶל־מֹשֶׁה וַיִּקְרְאוּ לֵאמֹר הִתְפַּלֵּל לֵאלֹהִים
בַּעֲבוּר יַט[14] אֶת־הַנְּחָשִׁים וְיוֹשִׁיעֵנוּ׃ וַ֫יַּעַשׂ מֹשֶׁה נְחַשׁ־נְחֹ֫שֶׁת וַיַּעֲלֵ֫הוּ מֵ֫עַל הָעָם וַיִּנָּצֵלוּ׃
וּמִשָּׁם נָסְעוּ צָפ֑וֹנָה וַיַּחֲנוּ בְּנַ֫חַל־זָרֶד[15]׃ [8] וְזֹאת הַבְּרָכָה אֲשֶׁר בֵּרַךְ מֹשֶׁה אִישׁ־
הָאֱלֹהִים אֶת־בְּנֵי־יִשְׂרָאֵ֑ל לִפְנֵי[18]־מוֹתוֹ׃ וּלְנַפְתָּלִי[17] אָמַר נַפְתָּלִי מָלֵא בִּרְכַּת־יְה֑ וָה[16] יָם
וְיָמִין[21] יְרָ֫שָׁה[20]׃ כֵּן שָׂמַח יִשְׂרָאֵל וַיֵּ֫שֶׁב בְּאֶרֶץ־יַ֫יִן־חָדָשׁ וְרֹב־לֶחֶם[19]׃ [9] וַיִּשְׁלַח יְהוֹשֻׁ֑עַ
שְׁנַיִם־אֲנָשִׁים מְרַגְּלִים לֵאמֹר לְכוּ רְאוּ אֶת־הָאָ֫רֶץ וְאֶת־יְרִיח֑וֹ וַיֵּלְכוּ וַיָּבֹ֫אוּ מֵהַחוּץ בֵּית־
אִשָּׁה וּשְׁמָהּ רָחָב[23] וַיִּשְׁכְּבוּ־שָׁ֫מָּה׃ וּבֵיתָהּ מֵ֫עַל חוֹמַת־הָעִיר׃ וַיֵּאָמֵר[22] לְנְשִׂיא־יְרִיחוֹ
לֵאמֹ֑ר הִנֵּה אֲנָשִׁים בָּ֫אוּ הַלַּיְלָה מִבְּנֵי־יִשְׂרָאֵל לִרְאוֹת אֶת־הָאָרֶץ׃ [10] וַתַּשְׁבֵּ֫עַ[24] רָחָב
אֶת־הָאֲנָשִׁים וַתֹּ֫אמֶר כִּי יָבֹ֫אוּ עִמְּכֶם לֹא תִגְּפוּ אֶת־אָבִי וְאֶת־אִמִּי וְאֶת־אַחַי וְאֶת־אַחְיוֹתַי
וְאֶת־כָּל־אֲשֶׁר לָהֶ֑ם וְהִצַּלְתֶּם אֶת־נַפְשֹׁתֵ֫ינוּ[25] מִמָּ֫וֶת׃ וַיִּיטַב בְּעֵינֵי־הָאֲנָשִׁ֑ים וַיֹּ֫אמְרוּ אֶל
נַעֲנֶה אֹתָךְ וְאֵת[27] כָּל־אֲשֶׁר לָ֑ךְ׃ [11] וַיָּ֫מָת דָּוִד מָלֵא[26] יָמִים וְכָב֑וֹד וַיִּמְלֹךְ שְׁלֹמֹה בְּנוֹ
תַּחְתָּיו׃ וְדִבְרֵי[32]־דָוִיד[31] הַמֶּ֫לֶךְ הָרִאשֹׁנִים וְהָאַחֲרֹנִים[30] הִנָּם[29] כְּתוּבִים עַל[28]־דִּבְרֵי־

---

[13] אֲשֶׁר־נְשָׂאוֹ לִבּ֑וֹ, *who it-lifted-him his-heart*. That is, everyone “whose heart led him.”

[14] Hiphil jussive (shortened Imperfect) < נָטָה. Translate: “so that he might . . . .”

[15] *Zered* (a location). The word is in pause, and so the first vowel has lengthened.

[16] “Naphtali, full of the blessing of the LORD.”

[17] *Naphtali* (the tribe).

[18] Remember that לִפְנֵי can refer to *time* as well as to *place*.

[19] Translate as “food.”

[20] The vowel pointing has changed because the word is in pause. See §28.2, p. 84, if you need help.

[21] יָם וְיָמִין. These two words are the *object* of the verb which comes after them.

[22] Look carefully at this vowel pointing. It is not וַיֹּ֫אמֶר. Hint: the *ṣere* under the י tells you that the א has rejected a *dagesh*. The subject of this verb does not appear in the sentence, but would probably be הַדָּבָר.

[23] *Rahab*.

[24] Hiphil. We might expect to see וַתַּשְׁבִּ֫יעַ, but this is the shortened form of the imperfect because of the w.c.

[25] Remember that נֶ֫פֶשׁ is feminine. You might find this word easier to parse if there was a וֹ between the שׁ and the ת, instead of just the *holem*. (Remember, *holem* and *holem-vav* are interchangeable.)

[26] Is this a verb or an adjective? How do you decide. Hint: the next word cannot be the subject since it is plural.

[27] Why is there a *tsere* instead of a *seghol* in the אֵת? Because, in this case, it is not joined to the following words with a *maqqeph* and therefore it has retained its accent and its original long vowel.

[28] Translate “in.”

[29] הִנֵּה plus suffix. “Behold, they . . . .”

[30] הָרִאשֹׁנִים וְהָאַחֲרֹנִים. These words describe דִּבְרֵי, not הַמֶּ֫לֶךְ. You know what the first word means. You should be able to figure out the second.

[31] This is a late spelling of the name דָּוִד. It is found in the latest books of the Old Testament.

[32] דָּבָר is used two ways in this sentence. Here, it means “acts.” Later: “records, chronicles, archives.”

שְׁמוּאֵל הָרֹאֶה[35] וְעַל־דִּבְרֵי־נָתָן הַנָּבִיא וְעַל־דִּבְרֵי־גָד[34] הַחֹזֶה[33]׃ עִם כָּל־מַלְכוּתוֹ
וּגְבוּרָתוֹ[37] וְהָעִתִּים אֲשֶׁר עָבְרוּ[36] עָלָיו וְעַל־יִשְׂרָאֵל וְעַל כָּל־מַמְלְכוֹת הָאֲרָצוֹת׃
[12] דְּבַר־יְהוָה אֲשֶׁר הָיָה אֶל־הוֹשֵׁעַ[38] בֶּן־בְּאֵרִי בִּימֵי־עֻזִּיָּה יוֹתָם אָחָז יְחִזְקִיָּה מַלְכֵי־
יְהוּדָה וּבִימֵי־יָרָבְעָם בֶּן־יוֹאָשׁ מֶלֶךְ־יִשְׂרָאֵל׃ אֶפְקֹד עַל־יִשְׂרָאֵל אֶת־הַזְּבָחִים[39]
לַבְּעָלִים׃ וְהִנֵּה אָז אָנֹכִי מְבַקְּשָׁהּ[41] וְהוֹלַכְתִּיהָ[40] הַמִּדְבָּר וְדִבַּרְתִּי עַל לִבָּהּ׃ וְהָיָה
בַיּוֹם־הַהוּא נְאֻם־יְהוָה תִּקְרְאִי[42] אִישִׁי וְלֹא־תִקְרְאִי־לִי עוֹד בַּעְלִי׃ וַהֲסִרוֹתִי אֶת־
שְׁמוֹת־הַבְּעָלִים מִפִּיהָ וְנִשְׁכְּחוּ שְׁמָם׃

[13] The final translation (below) is from the Psalms and is a fitting way to conclude this study of Biblical Hebrew. The words are printed exactly as found in *Biblia Hebraica Stuttgartensia* (the most popular version of the Hebrew Bible). The small raised circles (°) are not important, and will be mentioned in the next chapter. Other extra marks are accent marks. You do not need to know the specific meaning of each mark, but they are quite helpful in showing how to pronounce the word. You will also need the following additional vocabulary:

יָהּ	*a shortened form of* יְהוָה
רָקִיעַ	the dome of heaven, a firmament (one of the first things created by God (Gen 1:6))
עֹז	strength, power
גְּבוּרָה	mighty deed, mighty act
גֹּדֶל	greatness
נְשָׁמָה	blowing, breath; *thus*, כֹּל הַנְּשָׁמָה = everything that has breath, *or* everything that breathes.

הַֽלְלוּ °יָ֨הּ
הַֽלְלוּ־אֵ֥ל בְּקָדְשׁ֑וֹ הַ֝לְל֗וּהוּ בִּרְקִ֥יעַ עֻזּֽוֹ׃
הַֽלְל֥וּהוּ בִגְבוּרֹתָ֑יו הַ֝לְל֗וּהוּ כְּרֹ֣ב גֻּדְלֽוֹ׃
כֹּ֣ל °הַ֭נְּשָׁמָה תְּהַלֵּ֥ל יָ֗הּ
הַֽלְלוּ־°יָֽהּ׃

---

[33] This is the third word which means *prophet*. Like רֹאֶה, it can be translated *seer*. It comes from the verb חָזָה, *to see or perceive*. Note also that, although there is a *soph passuq*, the sentence does not end here. Treat this *soph passuq* as a second *athnah*.

[34] *Gad* (a name, like Samuel or Nathan).

[35] The sentence used three different words which mean *prophet*. This is the first; it means *seer* (one who sees). See 1 Sam 9:9.

[36] This looks like IC + 3ms suffix, but it is not. Again, it is Perf 3cp and should be pointed עָֽבְרוּ. But, as we have noticed several times already, in the Bible the *metheg* is often missing in verbs such as שָֽׁמְרָה and שָֽׁמְרוּ. The reader is just expected to know. And, of course, the context helps you.

[37] The root of this word is גְּבוּרָה, "mighty deeds" or "mighty acts."

[38] *Hosea*. This first sentence contains many names, including the name of Hosea's father (Beeri) and the names of several kings of Judah and the king of Israel.

[39] אֶפְקֹד עַל־יִשְׂרָאֵל אֶת־הַזְּבָחִים. Literally "I shall punish upon (or 'visit upon') Israel the sacrifices." In other words, "I shall punish Israel *for* (or *because of*) the sacrifices."

[40] Add the word *into*.

[41] The object refers to Israel, and is feminine because place names are feminine.

[42] Add the word לִי.

77

AN INTRODUCTION TO HEBREW POETRY

Much could be said about Hebrews poetry. In this chapter, we will briefly consider four characteristics, three of which distinguish Hebrew poetry from poetry in other languages.

77.1 Structure

Hebrew poetry has neither rhyme nor a simple meter.[1] Rather, its primary characteristic is structure. Several forms of structure are found; the most important are known as parallelism, chiasm, concentricity and acrostic. The first of these, parallelism, is the easiest to see.

77.1.1 Parallelism refers to the relationship between two parallel lines of poetry. (The second line is often indented in translation.) Parallelism can be *synonymous, synthetic* or *antithetic.*

77.1.1.1 With **synonymous parallelism**, one line of poetry has the same meaning as (or is *synonymous* with) the one which comes after it. We will use Psalm 24:1-3 as our example:

The earth is the Lord's and the fulness thereof,	*first line*
the world and those who dwell therein.	*second line repeats the thought of the first*
for he has founded it upon the seas,	*third line*
and established it upon the rivers.	*fourth line repeats the thought of the third*
Who shall ascend the hill of the Lord?	*fifth line*
And who shall stand in his holy place?	*sixth line repeats the thought of the fifth*

Note how the thought of the first line is repeated by the (indented) second line. Likewise, the thought of the third line is repeated by the fourth line, and the thought of the fifth line by the sixth. Each repeating line is thus *synonymous* with the line before it. This makes it simpler for the hearer, who gets two chances to catch what is being said. But it can make it more difficult for the translator, since poets must use words with similar meanings; thus, they sometimes choose uncommon words.

The second type of parallelism is called:

77.1.1.2 Synthetic parallelism. Here, the second part of the verse **extends** the thought rather than repeating it. We will consider Psalm 1. The first verse of Psalm 1 contains three lines of synonymous parallelism, and the second verse contains two. But verse three does something different; it extends or expands its thought as it develops:

He is like a tree
planted by streams of water
that yields its fruit in its season
and its leaf does not wither.
In all that he does he prospers.

---

[1] **Technical Note:** People disagree about whether Hebrew poetry has meter. For the purpose of this discussion, we will assume that it has none.

Note how each line adds more information. This time the lines do not repeat, but rather extend the thought further.

A third type of parallelism is called

77.1.1.3 Antithetic parallelism. In this case, the second part of the verse *opposes* the first. It is αντι or *against* its idea or *thesis*. Thus, it is *antithetic* to it, and so the second part of the verse will often begin with the word *but*. Look at the last verse of Psalm 1:6:

> the Lord knows the way of the righteous,
> but the way of the wicked will perish.

The first way is the way of the *righteous*, and the *LORD knows* it. The second way is the opposite of the first: it is the way of the *wicked*, and it will *perish*. Proverbs 14:20 brings another example, a rather wry observation everyone will acknowledge:

> The poor are disliked even by their neighbors,
> but the rich have many friends.

77.1.2 Chiasm is another structure, and it is often found with parallelism. The first line will contain two parts, A and B. The second line will repeat those two parts, but will reverse them. Thus, in the second line, we will see B first and A second. Another way of stating this is to say that the first part of the verse is A + B, and the second part is B' + A'. Psalm 7:16 gives an example:

> Their mischief returns (A) upon their own heads (B),
> and on their own heads (B') their violence descends (A').

B and B' are identical, and A and A' contain very similar ideas. Thus, we see:

> A + B
> B' + A'

If you draw a line from A to A', and then from B to B' you get an "X" or the Greek letter *chi* (χ). Thus, this pattern is called "*chi*asm." Even the example from Psalm 1:6 in §77.1.1.3, above, is chiastic – though the relationships are antithetic (opposite), not synonymous (same or similar):

> for the Lord knows (A) the way of the righteous (B),
> but the way of the wicked (B') will perish (A').

This example may not seem quite as clear as the first one, since A and A' at first seem rather different. But really they are not. The point is that A promises a good thing, and A' a bad thing.

77.1.3 Concentricity is similar to *chiasm*, but it has more parts and thus is diagramed differently. *Concentric circles* are circles which have the same center, such as circles A B and C in the first diagram on the right. In the second diagram, we follow a path through the three circles from left to right. When we do this, we first pass through A then B and then C. After passing through the center, we then pass through C again, then B and then A as we leave the circles. The path is thus ABC CBA.

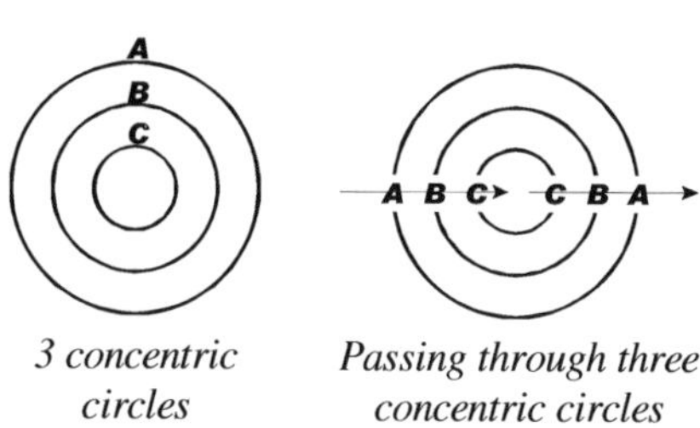

3 concentric circles *Passing through three concentric circles*

This ABC CBA pattern is also found in poetry; it is like an expanded chiasm. For instance, in Isaiah 6:10 we find:

Make the **mind** of this people dull,	A (mind)
and stop their **ears**,	B (ears)
and shut their **eyes**,	C (eyes)
so that they may not look with their **eyes**,	C' (eyes)
and listen with their **ears**,	B' (ears)
and comprehend with their **minds**,	A' (minds)

Concentric patterns may be larger than ABCCBA, and they may also have a single line at the center: ABC**D**CBA, etc. Here is an example of a larger concentric pattern with a center from Eccl 11:3-12:2b[2]:

A Clouds and Rain (11:3)
- **B** Light and Sun (11:7)
  - **C** Consider the days of darkness (11:8a)
    - **D** All that comes is breath (11:8b)
      - **E** Enjoy your Youth (11:9a)
        - **F** But know ... God will bring you to judgment (11:9b)
      - **E'** Enjoy your Youth (11:10a)
    - **D'** All of youth is breath (11:10b)
  - **C'** Consider God before the days of darkness (12:1)
- **B'** Sun and Light (12:2a)

A' Clouds and Rain (12:2b)

Concentric patterns may also be found in prose. In fact, it is possible that the entire book of Esther is built upon a concentric pattern.[3]

77.1.4 Acrostic. In a Hebrew acrostic, the first letter of the first word in each line (or group of lines) forms the alphabet. That is, the first word of the first line begins with א, the first word of the second line begins with ב, the next line begins with ג, and so on. This can be seen only in the original Hebrew, of course. For instance, Lamentations 1 begins as follows:

אֵיכָה יָשְׁבָה בָדָד הָעִיר רַבָּתִי ...	*verse 1 begins with* א
בָּכוֹ תִבְכֶּה בַּלַּיְלָה וְדִמְעָתָהּ ...	*verse 2 begins with* ב
גָּלְתָה יְהוּדָה מֵעֹנִי וּמֵרֹב עֲבֹדָה ...	*verse 3 begins with* ג
דַּרְכֵי צִיּוֹן אֲבֵלוֹת מִבְּלִי בָּאֵי ...	*verse 4 begins with* ד
הָיוּ צָרֶיהָ לְרֹאשׁ אֹיְבֶיהָ שָׁלוּ ...	*verse 5 begins with* ה
...	*and so on for 22 verses ...*

This also happens in Lamentations 2 and 4. Each of these chapters has 22 verses, corresponding to the 22 letters of the Hebrew alphabet (שׂ and שׁ were originally a single letter, ש). Lamentations 3 is different; it has 66 verses, because each letter of the alphabet appears three times, with verses 1-3 beginning with א, 4-6 with ב, 7-9 with ג, and so on.[4] The grandest acrostic in the Bible is Psalm 119, with its 22 groups of 8 verses (for a total of 176 verses). In each group of 8 verses, every verse begin with the same letter.

---

[2] Noted by Daniel C. Fredericks, "Life's Storms and Structural Unity in Qohelet 11:1-12:8," *Journal for the Study of the Old Testament* 52 (1991), 95-114.

[3] See James C. Bangsund, *You Can Understand the Old Testament*, 2nd edition (published through CreateSpace, 2014) 122. Available on Amazon.com.

[4] Lamentations 5 does not seem to follow the acrostic pattern, although it also has 22 verses.

77.2 Grammar

Hebrew poetry generally tries to **shorten the sentence** whenever possible. It does this by

- **shortening words** (for instance, using the shortened form of the imperfect even where normal prose would use the regular form), and by
- **dropping short (pieces of) words** such as the definite article (-הַ), the sign of the definite direct object (-אֶת), and אֲשֶׁר.

At other times, however, the **longer form of prepositions of place** will be used. For instance, you will often find עֲלֵי instead of עַל; אֱלֵי instead of אֶל; עֲדֵי instead of עַד.

The masculine plural suffixes may undergo some changes. For instance,

- the noun ending may change from ים.- to ין.- (similar to Arabic)
- the 3mp pronominal suffix ם- (for instance on the Infinitive Construct: שָׁמְרָם, *their keeping, keeping them*) may become מוֹ-. Thus: שָׁמְרָמוֹ

77.3 Vocabulary

Certain words appear more often in poetry than in prose. For instance:

Prose	Poetry	(English)
אָדָם	אֱנוֹשׁ	*man*
דֶּרֶךְ	אֹרַח	*way, path*
דָּבָר	מִלָּה	*word*
רָאָה	חָזָה	*to see*
בּוֹא	אָתָה	*to come, to enter*

77.4 Sound Patterns

Although Hebrew poetry does not have rhyme in the same way that we find in English poetry, it does use the sound of words to produce special effects. Here are some examples:

Repetition of consonant sounds. In Psalm 122:6, we read: "Pray for the peace of Jerusalem; may they prosper who love you." Listen to the sound of first four words in Hebrew, with its repetition of *sh* sounds:

שַׁאֲלוּ שְׁלוֹם יְרוּשָׁלָיִם יִשְׁלָיוּ ...

Repetition of vowel sounds. In the creation story of Genesis 1, the very unpoetic English phrase "without form and void" is, in the Hebrew, תֹהוּ וָבֹהוּ. In contrast to this image of chaos, animals and people are told to פְּרוּ וּרְבוּ, that is, "be fruitful and multiply."

Word play. Every language enjoys playing with words – especially words which sound alike but have different meanings. Jokes often depend upon word plays (and thus it is often impossible to translate a joke into another language). The Hebrew prophets often chose their words because of how they sounded. For instance, Amos 8:2 mentions a basket of *summer fruit*. Why *summer fruit*? Simply because the word sounds like another Hebrew word which means *end*:

> And [the Lord God] said, "Amos, what do you see?" And I said, "A basket of summer fruit (קָ֫יִץ)."
> Then the LORD said to me, "The end (קֵץ) has come upon my people Israel; I will never again pass by them."

In Isaiah 5:7, we find chiasm in the first four lines of the verse and then an interesting set of word pairs at the end. These word pairs were also chosen for the way they sounded together.

For the **vineyard** of the LORD of hosts
    is the house of **Israel**,
and the men of **Judah**
    are his pleasant **planting**;
and he looked for ***justice*** [מִשְׁפָּט]
    but behold, ***bloodshed*** [מִשְׂפָּח]
for ***righteousness*** [צְדָקָה]
    but behold, a ***cry*** [צְעָקָה]

chiasm at the left:	
vineyard (A) ...	Israel (B) ...
Judah (B') ...	planting (A') ...

Words which sound like what they describe. All languages have such words. In Judges 5:22, the sound of running horses can be heard not only in the Hebrew (מִדַּהֲרוֹת דַּהֲרוֹת) but also in the English translation (*galloping, galloping*):

אָז הָלְמוּ עִקְּבֵי־סוּס
מִדַּהֲרוֹת דַּהֲרוֹת אַבִּירָיו׃

Then loud beat the horses' hoofs,
    with the galloping, galloping of his steeds.

78

AN INTRODUCTION TO *BHS*

You have now studied all the basics of Hebrew. The purpose of this final chapter is to introduce you to *Biblia Hebraica Stuttgartensia*, the most widely used edition of the Hebrew Bible in the academic world.

78.1 The Order of the Books.

The Hebrew Bible and the Protestant Old Testament[5] contain the same books; however, the order of the books is different. In the Hebrew Bible: the books of Law (Torah) come first, then Prophets, then Writings. That is, תּוֹרָה נְבִיאִים וּכְתוּבִים, abbreviated תָּנַךְ.

And note that books are sometimes found in different sections in the Hebrew Bible. For instance, Ruth is found in the third section of the Hebrew Bible (the "Writings") just after Proverbs, not between Judges and 1 Samuel as in the Old Testament. And Daniel is not found in the Prophets section of the Hebrew Bible, but is also placed in the Writings.

Turn to p. lvii at the front of *BHS* and look at the Table of Contents. The names of the books are in Latin. Most of the Latin names are very similar to the English names, but several are quite different and need to be learned:

BHS name	*BHS* abbrev.	English
Judices	Jdc	Judges
Reges	R	Kings
Jesaia	Jes	Isaiah
Sacharia	Sach	Zechariah
Iob	Hi	Job
Canticum	Cant	Song of Solomon
Ecclesiastes	Qoh	Ecclesiastes
Threni	Thr	Lamentations

Be sure to learn these Latin names and abbreviations, along with their English equivalents.

78.2 The Introduction to *Biblia Hebraica Stuttgartensia*

Pages iii-xliii of *BHS* contain an Introduction, or Preface (Praefationes) in five languages: German, English, French, Spanish and Latin. You might want to read parts of the English Preface (Praefationes Anglicae, pp. xi-xviii). The first section describes some of the difficulties of producing *BHS*, including destruction of the printing plates in the bombing of Leipzig in World War II. Other parts describe the layout of the work, including the "Masorah" notations which you will see running down the margins of the Hebrew text. (The Masorah will be discussed below.)

---

[5] The Roman Catholic Old Testament contains additional books which were originally written in Greek (except for 2 Esdras, written in Latin), not Hebrew. The Jews do not accept these books as Scripture. See p. xiii for an explanation of why the phrase "Old Testament" is used in this grammar rather than "Hebrew Scriptures."

78.3 Page organization

Turn to any page of the Hebrew text in *BHS*. Note that the page is divided into four sections:

- the Hebrew text,
- a set of small Hebrew "Masoretic" notations in the side margin,
- some more Masoretic notations (Mm and Mp notes) just below the Hebrew text, and
- the "critical apparatus" just below these Masoretic notations.

We will not be concerned with the Masoretic notations (the Masorah). We will, however, study the critical apparatus.

78.4 Versions and Abbreviations

Pages xliv-l contain a detailed list of the versions mentioned in the "critical apparatus" (discussed below). The whole section is in Latin, and this may not seem helpful (unless you can read Latin). However, a list of some common abbreviations is found in §78.8 of this book (p. 261), and "An English Key" to the Latin may have come with your *BHS*.

This "Key" includes a list of symbols for *Manuscripts and Versions*. These manuscripts and versions are ancient copies of the Old Testament in many languages including Hebrew, Greek, Arabic and Syriac. Scholars have compared these texts with one another and with the Hebrew in order to produce the most accurate Hebrew text possible. This is important, since the original Hebrew text no longer exists, and we have only copies of copies of copies. Note in particular the following selection from the list in *BHS*:

α'	Aquila's Greek translation ...	ca. 130 AD. Very literal. The Greek is not smooth, because the translators were trying to stay close to the meaning of the Hebrew words. This may be bad for a Greek reader, but is helpful for scholars who want to know what the Hebrew original said.
𝔊	The Septuagint	A Greek translation (often abbreviated LXX) begun in the third century BC. Many copies of this text are available (see *BHS* p. xlv). It was the Bible of the early Church, and so it is often quoted in the New Testament.
K	The *Kethib*	*Kethib* (כְּתִיב < כָּתַב) means *what is actually written*. See *Qere*, below.
L	The Leningrad Codex	This is the primary text which was used for *BHS*. It is the oldest dated manuscript of the entire Old Testament: 1008 or 1009 AD.
𝔐	The Masoretic Text	The Hebrew text with vowel points and word counts. *BHS* is based on the Leningrad Codex of the Masoretic Text.
Q	The *Qere*	*Qere* (קְרֵי < קָרָא) means *what should be read*. Sometimes the Hebrew text contains errors. These errors were left unchanged, however, since the rabbis considered the text to be sacred. But when the text is read aloud in worship, the incorrectly written word (called the "Kethib," see above) is not spoken. Instead, the correct word is "read" aloud (thus "Qere"). This correct word will be found in the margin of the Hebrew Bible with a small ק̇ (note the dot) under it. If it is discussed in the critical apparatus, a Q will be used there. See, for example, 1 Sam 17:7 (p. 474 in *BHS*): כִּמְנוֹר אֹרְגִים וְחֵץ חֲנִיתוֹ, *and the arrow of his spear* (*was*) *like a weaver's beam*. This makes no sense. In the right margin, you will see

		a small קׄ under the word ועץ (vowel points are not given in the Qere). This means we should read ועץ (actually וְעֵץ) instead of וְחֵץ. Thus, *and the wood of his spear ....* This now makes sense. The misspelled word also has a footnote (a small [a]) in the Hebrew text, which points to the critical apparatus below. There, footnote 7[a] uses a Q as it discusses the problem.
𝔔	Qumran	These are manuscripts dating to a period approximately one century before and after the time of Christ, and discovered in 1947. Note that 𝔔 is not the same as Q (above).
𝔐	The Samaritan Pentateuch	This text was transliterated from the Hebrew alphabet into the Samaritan alphabet (though it is sometimes in closer agreement with the LXX). It was done perhaps as early as the fifth century BC, when the Jews and Samaritans separated. The oldest version today dates back to the early Christian centuries. The Samaritan Pentateuch is still used today in small Samaritan communities.
$𝔐^T$	The Samaritan Targum	This is a translation of the Hebrew text into a Samaritan-Aramaic idiom, done in the second or third century AD.
σ´	Symmachus' Greek translation	Late second century AD. Pure and smooth Greek (vs. Aquila, above).
𝔖	The Syriac version	Translation into the language of Syria around 200 AD. Also known as the Peshitta.
𝔗	The Targums	Aramaic comments upon the Hebrew text, dating from several centuries before and after the time of Christ. The Palestinian Targum is the oldest. Other important targums: the Jerusalem Targum (also known as Pseudo-Jonathan); and Onkelos Targum (the most literal).
θ´	Theodotian's Greek	Early 2nd century AD revision of the LXX.
𝔙	The Vulgate	Latin translation made by Jerome around 400 AD

Why study other versions? If the original text was Hebrew, why should we study other versions which were translated *from* the Hebrew? Is it not better to study the original than to study a copy or a translation? Yes, it is always better to study the original. But we do not have the original Hebrew text. We only have copies of copies of copies of copies.

Here is an example. The Septuagint (𝔊) was translated from the Hebrew around 250 BC. Later, both the Hebrew and the Septuagint were copied again and again. In this copying, both the Hebrew and the Septuagint picked up a number of errors. Let us say, for instance, that a copying mistake was made in the Hebrew text in the year 100 B.C., *after* the translation of the Septuagint. This error will then be *only in the 100 B.C. copy of the Hebrew* and not in the Septuagint, translated earlier. Later copies of the Hebrew will have the error, and later copies of the Septuagint will *not* have this error. In some places, therefore, the Septuagint is more accurate than the Hebrew. (Of course, in other places the Septuagint will have gained its own errors.) This is true of the other versions and translations as well. It is therefore important to compare the Hebrew with other ancient versions, since they may help us correct copying errors which later entered the Hebrew text.

78.5 The *Masorah*

In order to be sure that they copied the text precisely and accurately, a group called the Masoretes carefully counted the words of the text. They noted how many words were in each verse and chapter, and how often various words occurred.

Turn to the second page of Genesis. In the first line of Hebrew, at the top of the page, you will see that three words have little circles (°) over them. In the margin, there are three Hebrew letters with superscript number, separated by dots ([24]ג . ל . [24]ג). These refer to the three words with the circles.

This statistical information is not of much use to us today, and will not be discussed further here. This short explanation is included, however, because students always wonder what these notes mean.

78.6 The *Parashoth*

Today the Bible is divided into chapters and verses. This was not always true. There is a much older system of divisions in the Hebrew Bible: the Parashoth. Two letters are used as section markers:

ס	closed Parashah	indicates a minor division
פ	open Parashah	indicates a major division

You will find these markers throughout *BHS*. Sometimes they give a good division of the text. Other times, they seem illogical; for instance in Genesis 3, we find a "major" פ between 3:21 and 3:22 where we would expect a minor one. And there is a "minor" ס after 3:24 where we would expect a major break.

78.7 The Critical Apparatus

The *critical apparatus* is the material found at the very bottom of each page, and is the most important "extra" material in *BHS*. It comes *after* the Masorah (the fine-print paragraph of Mm and Mp entries), and always starts with either a boldface **Cp** (which means *chapter*) or a boldface verse number. The critical apparatus describes textual differences between the various versions and manuscripts (see §78.4 above). Sometimes it suggests possible changes to the Masoretic Text which would make it more clear or logical. As an example, let us look at the first page of the Bible, Genesis 1. A few examples will illustrate how these notes work.

a. On the first page of Genesis, the critical apparatus begins with **Cp 1,1**[a]. This means "Chapter 1, verse 1, note a." If you look above at the Hebrew of Gen 1:1, you will see a little [a] at the end of the first word ([a]בְּרֵאשִׁית). The critical apparatus discusses the Greek and Samaritan spellings of this word.

> **A note on numbers:** *BHS* is printed in Germany, and therefore uses the German numbering system. Germans use commas where the English language world uses decimal points, and they use decimal points (or periods or full stops) where the English language world uses commas. Thus, in *BHS*, a number such as one million is written 1.000.000 (not 1,000,000). And Genesis 1 verse 2 is written Gen 1,2 (not Gen 1.2 or Gen 1:2). This is why we see **Cp 1,1** and not **Cp 1.1** or **Cp 1:1**

b. Just after the above note, you will see a ‖. This separates the note on Gen 1:1 from the following note on Gen 1:6. After this ‖, there is a boldface **6** and a small [a] after the 6. This refers to the [a] in the Hebrew text which is found at the end of verse 6. The note in the critical apparatus says "huc tr 7[a-a] cf 𝔊 et 9.11.15.20.24.30." If we look up these Latin words and the symbol 𝔊 in the "Key," we will find that this note is telling us:

> "transpose (move) 7[a-a] to here; compare to the Septuagint and to verses 9, 11, 15, 20, 24 and 30."

(Again, note that *BHS* used decimal points where we would use commas.) What does this note tell us? The editors noticed that whenever God says *Let there be*, the verse then ends with *And it was so* – except in verse 6. That is, we see this *And let there be .... And it was so* pattern in verses 9, 11, 15, 20, 24 and 30. But the words *And it was so* are missing at the end of verse 6. At the same time, these words are present at the end of verse 7, where they do not seem to belong. In addition, the Septuagint (𝔊), which brings us a very old reading, does have *And it was so* at the end of verse 6 (and not at the end of verse 7).

Thus, the editors feel that the phrase got misplaced in the Hebrew. They suggest that it be moved (transposed) from the end of verse 7 to the end of verse 6. The critical apparatus note on verse 7 (after the ‖) also makes this suggestion.

c. In verse 9, we find the word מָקוֹם, *place,* in the Hebrew text. Note 9[a] tells us that the Septuagint has συναγωγήν = *gathering.* The editors suggest that perhaps the Hebrew was originally מִקְוֶה (which also means *gathering*), but that a scribe misread it as מָקוֹם. Ancient Hebrew had no vowel points, and without the vowel points the two words מקום and מקוה do appear rather similar, indeed. In addition, the editors of *BHS* point out that the phrase מקוה המים (*a gathering of water*) occurs in the next verse (verse 10). Perhaps there was some confusion in copying.

d. Verse 11 has three notes ([a], [b] and [c]). Note [a] begins with [a-a] because it refers to a phrase: the two words דֶּשֶׁא עֵשֶׂב (which have an [a] before and after them). The words mean *grass* and *plants,* and the question is: do we separate the two words (*put forth* ***grass, plants*** *producing seeds*) or connect them in a construct relationship (*put forth* ***grass-of-plants*** *producing seeds*). The Hebrew seems to favor the first interpretation (*put forth* ***grass, plants*** *producing seeds*), since a construct relationship would use a *maqqeph.*[6] But the note points out that the Septuagint and the Vulgate connect עשב with דשא ("cj" means *connect*, and "c" means *with*). This supports the second reading (*plants-of-grass,* βοτάνην χόρτου in the Septuagint). We therefore have several opinions and must decide how we are going to translate.

e. Note [b] on verse 11 says that the word *and* (וּ) is missing at the beginning of the word עֵץ. The editors suggest that we should add the וּ, thus getting וְעֵץ. Why? Because a few medieval Hebrew manuscripts (pc Mss) and some of the versions[7] all include the *and.* Thus, we are told to "Read with a few manuscripts" (l c pc Mss) and add the *and.* Furthermore, verse 12, which repeats the information contained in verse 11, also includes the *and* in its repetition.

Why does the note write וְעץ instead of וְעֵץ? This is because vowel points are shown only on that part of the word which is being looked at. Here we are discussing the addition of -וְ. The rest of the word is not in question.

Note also the conjunctive accent ֥ under the word in the Hebrew text: עֵ֥ץ . This shows that עֵץ is in construct to the next word, פְּרִי. It could have been written עֵץ־פְּרִי. It is this type of conjunctive accent (or a *maqqeph*) which we noted was missing when we discussed the words דֶּשֶׁא עֵשֶׂב, above (d).

f. Note [c] on verse 11 suggests that the word לְמִינוֹ should "probably be deleted" (prb dl), since it is not found in a similar location in the repetition of verse 12. However, the very similar expression לְמִינֵהוּ does occur twice in verse 12. Furthermore, the editors' suggestion is weakened by the fact that they cannot point to any manuscripts or texts which delete the word in verse 11. When there is no manuscript support for the editors' suggestion, the suggestion becomes weaker (for instance, see the unsupported suggestion in Amos 9:8[b-b] that words have been added). We therefore may not want to follow it.

None of the above notes changed the meaning of the text in an important way. But sometimes they will. Consider, for instance, Ezek 34:16. The RSV reads:

> I will seek the lost, and I will bring back the strayed, and I will bind up the crippled, and I will strengthen the weak, and the fat and the strong I will **watch over**; I will feed them **in** justice.

but the NRSV reads:

> I will seek the lost, and I will bring back the strayed, and I will bind up the injured, and I will strengthen the weak, but the fat and the strong I will **destroy**. I will feed them **with** justice.

---

[6] Or a conjunctive accent such as ֥ (discussed in the last paragraph of "e").

[7] The Samaritan Pentateuch, the Septuagint, the Syriac version of the OT, Targum Pseudo-Jonathan (see *BHS* p. xlviii for a list of the Targums) and the Vulgate.

I will watch over is quite different from *I will destroy*. The Hebrew of *BHS* has *destroy* (שָׁמַד), as found in the NRSV. But the RSV has chosen to follow the Septuagint, Syriac and Vulgate which have words like *guard* or *watch*. Remember how easy it is to confuse the letters ד and ר. It is possible that the word was originally שָׁמַר, and someone later miscopied it as שָׁמַד. Or it may have happened the other way (though early enough for it to get into the Septuagint). Or could the translators of Septuagint, Syriac and Vulgate have misread the ד as ר (as you have done many times!)? Important theological arguments are sometimes based upon information contained in the critical apparatus. You will want to keep your eyes open as you do your translations. Whenever you see a superscript letter ([a], [b], [c], etc.) in your reading, be sure to look at the bottom of the page to see what the issue is.

78.8 Some Important Abbreviations in *BHS*

We have suggested using the "English Key" to look up Latin abbreviations such as *huc, tr, cj,* and *c* which are used in the critical apparatus. There are many of these abbreviations – too many for most students to learn. But some of them are very common. The following symbols and abbreviations should be memorized, because you will see them often.

+	it adds, they add	leg	reads, it reads
>	it is missing in	mlt	many
||	comment separator	Ms(s)	Medieval OT manuscript(s)
*	the form of the word is a good guess by scholars	nonn	some, several
𝔊*	all versions of Septuagint	om	it omits, they omit
add	added	pc	a few
addit	it adds	pl	plural
c	with	post	after
cf	compare	pr	put before, to be put before, it puts before, etc.
cp, Cp	chapter	prb	probably
dl	delete	prp	it has been proposed (suggested)
dl?	possibly delete	Q	Qere (to be read)
et	and	sg	singular
ex, e	out of	sic	so, thus, as found in (sic L: as found in Leningrad codex)
frt	perhaps	tr	transpose (switch positions)
huc	to here	ut	as, so that
ins	insert, it inserts	vb	word(s)
K	Kethib (written)	vel	either, or
l	read	vers	version, translation.

Be sure also to learn the abbreviations for the versions (α', 𝔊, 𝔐, 𝔔, etc.) discussed in §78.4, above.

78.9 Using a lexicon[8]

There are more than 8,000 different Hebrew words in the Old Testament, and you have studied a little more than 700 of them. This means that you will always need to use a lexicon (as all Old Testament scholars

[8] A *lexicon* is a one-direction dictionary from one language to another. A large Hebrew lexicon will usually give the various forms of a verb and will show verbs and nouns with suffixes. It will also often list verses where examples of the word may be found.

must do). There are many Hebrew-English lexicons. Perhaps the best – though also the most expensive – is *The Hebrew & Aramaic Lexicon of the Old Testament* in five volumes by Ludwig Koehler and Walter Baumgartner (subsequently revised by Walter Baumgartner and Johann Jakob Stamm).

One of the largest and most complete single volume lexicons is the *Hebrew and English Lexicon of the Old Testament* (Oxford: University Press, 1972), edited by F. Brown, S. R. Driver and C. A. Briggs (often simply called Brown-Driver-Briggs or BDB). This lexicon can be difficult for the beginner because words are found not alphabetically but according to their roots. Even for the experienced user, the word indicators at the top of the pages are not well organized, although the edition produced by Hendrickson Publishers includes an index in the back.

A newer, and far more practical lexicon is *A Concise Hebrew and Aramaic Lexicon of the Old Testament* edited by William L. Holladay (Grand Rapids: Eerdmans, 1991). The author finds this to be the best lexicon for most students. If you use the Holladay lexicon, you should note the following:

a. **The verb.** As in other lexicons, Holladay lists definitions for the various forms of the verb (qal, niphal, piel, hiphil, etc.). Before giving the definition of the verb form, he gives examples of the various ways the verb form appears in the Old Testament. If you do not find the form you are seeking (or something *very* similar), it probably means you have not yet found the right word.

b. **Abbreviations.** Be sure you become familiar with the list of abbreviations found at the front of the lexicon (pp. xviii-xx). In this case, they are based upon English, not Latin. You do not need to memorize all of them, but you should know how to find this list quickly. In addition to the abbreviations for the verb forms (nif., hif., hitp., etc.), the meanings of some of the more familiar abbreviations should be memorized, such as:

n.pers.	personal name	inf.	infinitive	sg.	singular
n.gent.	name of tribe	juss.	jussive	s.one	someone
n.loc.	name of place	Kt	Kethib (written)	s.thg	something
n.peop.	name of people	LXX	Septuagint	v.	verse
		ms(s)	manuscript(s)	vb(s)	verb(s)
abs.	absolute	MT	Masoretic text	w.	with
adj.	adjective	OT	Old Testament	Y.	Yahweh
adv.	adverb	pass.	passive	†	all undisputed occurrences have been listed
coh.	cohortative	pf.	perfect		
conj.	conjunction	pl.	plural	F	see; refer to
cs.	construct	prep.	preposition	>	becomes
impf.	imperfect	pt.	participle	<	comes from
impv.	imperative	Qr	Qere (read)	√	verbal root

Finally, whatever lexicon you use, **be sure you know the order of the letters of the Hebrew alphabet** so that you can find words quickly.

78.10 Other Hebrew Helps

Several resources are particularly helpful for those who wish to do further work in Hebrew. Three of those listed below have already been mentioned in this book.

Grammars

Gesenius' Hebrew Grammar, edited by E. Kautzsch and revised by A. E. Cowley (Oxford: University Press, 1946). This extremely detailed grammar, usually just called *Gesenius*, contains a great deal of material, and covers almost every question a student might have. It is not for the beginning student, but will prove very helpful to those who are more advanced.

R. J. Williams, *Hebrew Syntax: An Outline*, second edition (Toronto: University of Toronto Press, 1976). This book is far smaller and less complex than *Gesenius*., and is an excellent resource for students who have finished a basic course in Hebrew. It explains in detail the structure of the Hebrew language (its syntax), that is, the particular ways Hebrew nouns, verbs, prepositions and other parts of the Hebrew language are used.

Lexicons and Theological Word Books

As noted above, a *lexicon* is a one-way dictionary, which gives short translations from one language to another. Sometimes you will want more discussion of a word. You will then turn to a *theological word book*, which is more like an encyclopedia. They usually have a number of volumes, and major words will be discussed for several pages.

Hebrew and Aramaic Lexicon of the Old Testament, edited by Ludwig Koehler and Walter Baumgartner (later revised by Walter Baumgartner and Johann Jakob Stamm), Leiden, The Netherlands: Brill, 2000. (Also available on CD.) Five volumes. Very complete, but also the most expensive.

Hebrew and English Lexicon of the Old Testament, edited by F. Brown, S. R. Driver and C. A. Briggs (Oxford: University Press, 1972). This lexicon, often simply called Brown-Driver-Briggs or BDB, is comprehensive, but somewhat difficult to use (see above).

A Concise Hebrew and Aramaic Lexicon of the Old Testament edited by William L. Holladay (Grand Rapids: Eerdmans, 1991). This lexicon is smaller and less expensive than the above works, and is much easier to use than BDB.

Theological Dictionary of the Old Testament, edited by G. Johannes Botterweck, Helmer Ringgren and (later volumes only) Heinz-Josef Fabry (Grand Rapids: Eerdmans, 1974-2006). This 15-volume set, often abbreviated *TDOT*, is a translation of the original German *Theologisches Wörterbuch zum Alten Testament*, and does for Biblical Hebrew what the well-known "Kittel" does for New Testament Greek.

Theological Wordbook of the Old Testament, edited by R. Laird Harris, Gleason L. Archer, Jr., and Bruce K. Waltke (Chicago: Moody Press, 1980). This book is not related to the German work mentioned above. It is far shorter and much less detailed than *TDOT*. But it covers all the words from אָב to תְּשַׁעִים (plus Biblical Aramaic) in a single volume (originally published in two volumes), and so is far less expensive than *TDOT*.

The Dictionary of Classical Hebrew, edited by David. J. A. Clines (Sheffield Academic Press). This large work is the most recent (completed in 2011) and is very detailed and complete. However, it is also very expensive with the eight large volumes costing approximately $1200.

Concordances

Concordances list all the verses in which a certain word is used. They are helpful when one wants to see how a word is used in context, which books use the word most often, or simply how often a word is used. There are several English-text-based concordances which allow the user to look up an English word and find the Hebrew word which lies behind it. Other places in the Old Testament where that Hebrew word is used may then be found. This is a long and tedious process, but it can be done using concordances such as:

The NIV Exhaustive Concordance, edited by Goodrick, Edward W., and John R. Kohlenberger III (Grand Rapids: Zondervan Publishing House, 1990).

Far more practical and useful, however, is the *magnum opus* by G. Lisowsky, *Konkordanz zum*

Hebräischen Alten Testament. The title is German, but the lexicon itself is entirely in Hebrew. Every word in the Hebrew Bible has been included, and all occurrences of that word are given, verse by verse, with part of the verse printed in Hebrew along with its reference. Verbs are listed by form (Qal, Niphal, etc.), and nouns are listed by usage (subject, object, other). The work was done by hand, and the publishers simply photographed Lisowsky's meticulous handwork rather than trying to typeset it and risk errors. It is available through the United Bible Societies:

G. Lisowsky, *Konkordanz zum Hebräischen Alten Testament* (Stuttgart: Deutsche Bibelgesellschaft, 1981)

Software

For computer users, many software programs are available which very quickly do the work of concordance and lexicon. Two of the best are:

"PocketBible," by Laridian Electronic Publishing, offers several English language versions of the Bible, along with a New American Standard (NASV) concordance. To do complex word searches, based on the Biblical languages (i.e., transliterated Hebrew, Aramaic or Greek) one must have both the NASV translation file as well as the concordance file. The program is very fast and efficient, and the price is very reasonable.
http://www.laridian.com.

"Bibloi" by Silver Mountain Software, provides the actual Hebrew (and Aramaic) and Greek fonts on the screen. The program comes with the complete text (though no critical apparatus) of *Biblica Hebraica Stuttgartensia* and the Greek New Testament, as well as the Septuagint, Vulgate, Luther's translation (German) and several English versions (AV, NRSV, RSV). In addition, this very complete utility comes with several lexicons (including BDB) and a collection of classical works including the Early Church Fathers, Josephus, and a collection of other works (Aristotle, Herodotus, Homer, Plato, Plutarch, Sophocles, Tacitus, Thucydides).
http://www.silvermountainsoftware.com.

Other software can be located by doing searches on the internet.

Things You Should Know

1. The pages of *Biblia Hebraica Stuttgartensia* are divided into four sections. Two of them are important: the Hebrew text, and the critical apparatus at the very bottom of the page.
2. The critical apparatus compares the Hebrew text to other ancient manuscripts which are written in several languages. They can help us when copying errors have entered the Hebrew text after these translations were made.
3. The critical apparatus also makes other suggestions concerning the spelling and arrangement of the Hebrew text.
4. The critical apparatus uses Latin abbreviations. Memorize the ones listed above. Also learn abbreviations which are used in the lexicon you use.

Suggestions and corrections

The author can be contacted at jim.bangsund@hotmail.com, and would be pleased to receive any suggestions for improvements or corrections of mistakes found in this text.

Verb Charts

1A. The Strong Verb

	Qal Active	Qal Stative (§42)		Niphal (§45)	Piel (§47)	Pual (§49)	Hiphil (§50)	Hophal (§51)	Hithpael (§53)
Perf. 3ms	קָטַל	כָּבֵד	קָטֹן	נִקְטַל	קִטֵּל	קֻטַּל	הִקְטִיל	הָקְטַל	הִתְקַטֵּל
3fs	קָטְלָה	כָּבְדָה	קָטְנָה	נִקְטְלָה	קִטְּלָה	קֻטְּלָה	הִקְטִילָה	הָקְטְלָה	הִתְקַטְּלָה
2ms	קָטַלְתָּ	כָּבַדְתָּ	קָטֹנְתָּ	נִקְטַלְתָּ	קִטַּלְתָּ	קֻטַּלְתָּ	הִקְטַלְתָּ	הָקְטַלְתָּ	הִתְקַטַּלְתָּ
2fs	קָטַלְתְּ	כָּבַדְתְּ	קָטֹנְתְּ	נִקְטַלְתְּ	קִטַּלְתְּ	קֻטַּלְתְּ	הִקְטַלְתְּ	הָקְטַלְתְּ	הִתְקַטַּלְתְּ
1cs	קָטַלְתִּי	כָּבַדְתִּי	קָטֹנְתִּי	נִקְטַלְתִּי	קִטַּלְתִּי	קֻטַּלְתִּי	הִקְטַלְתִּי	הָקְטַלְתִּי	הִתְקַטַּלְתִּי
3cp	קָטְלוּ	כָּבְדוּ	קָטְנוּ	נִקְטְלוּ	קִטְּלוּ	קֻטְּלוּ	הִקְטִילוּ	הָקְטְלוּ	הִתְקַטְּלוּ
2mp	קְטַלְתֶּם	כְּבַדְתֶּם	קְטָנְתֶּם	נִקְטַלְתֶּם	קִטַּלְתֶּם	קֻטַּלְתֶּם	הִקְטַלְתֶּם	הָקְטַלְתֶּם	הִתְקַטַּלְתֶּם
2fp	קְטַלְתֶּן	כְּבַדְתֶּן	קְטָנְתֶּן	נִקְטַלְתֶּן	קִטַּלְתֶּן	קֻטַּלְתֶּן	הִקְטַלְתֶּן	הָקְטַלְתֶּן	הִתְקַטַּלְתֶּן
1cp	קָטַלְנוּ	כָּבַדְנוּ	קָטֹנּוּ[1]	נִקְטַלְנוּ	קִטַּלְנוּ	קֻטַּלְנוּ	הִקְטַלְנוּ	הָקְטַלְנוּ	הִתְקַטַּלְנוּ
Impf. 3ms	יִקְטֹל	יִכְבַּד	יִקְטַן	יִקָּטֵל	יְקַטֵּל	יְקֻטַּל	יַקְטִיל	יָקְטַל	יִתְקַטֵּל
3fs	תִּקְטֹל	תִּכְבַּד	(These forms follow the pattern of יִכְבַּד)	תִּקָּטֵל	תְּקַטֵּל	תְּקֻטַּל	תַּקְטִיל	תָּקְטַל	תִּתְקַטֵּל
2ms	תִּקְטֹל	תִּכְבַּד		תִּקָּטֵל	תְּקַטֵּל	תְּקֻטַּל	תַּקְטִיל	תָּקְטַל	תִּתְקַטֵּל
2fs	תִּקְטְלִי	תִּכְבְּדִי		תִּקָּטְלִי	תְּקַטְּלִי	תְּקֻטְּלִי	תַּקְטִילִי	תָּקְטְלִי	תִּתְקַטְּלִי
1cs	אֶקְטֹל	אֶכְבַּד		אֶקָּטֵל[2]	אֲקַטֵּל	אֲקֻטַּל	אַקְטִיל	אָקְטַל	אֶתְקַטֵּל
3mp	יִקְטְלוּ	יִכְבְּדוּ		יִקָּטְלוּ	יְקַטְּלוּ	יְקֻטְּלוּ	יַקְטִילוּ	יָקְטְלוּ	יִתְקַטְּלוּ
3fp	תִּקְטֹלְנָה	תִּכְבַּדְנָה		תִּקָּטַלְנָה	תְּקַטֵּלְנָה	תְּקֻטַּלְנָה	תַּקְטֵלְנָה	תָּקְטַלְנָה	תִּתְקַטֵּלְנָה[3]
2mp	תִּקְטְלוּ	תִּכְבְּדוּ		תִּקָּטְלוּ	תְּקַטְּלוּ	תְּקֻטְּלוּ	תַּקְטִילוּ	תָּקְטְלוּ	תִּתְקַטְּלוּ
2fp	תִּקְטֹלְנָה	תִּכְבַּדְנָה		תִּקָּטַלְנָה	תְּקַטֵּלְנָה	תְּקֻטַּלְנָה	תַּקְטֵלְנָה	תָּקְטַלְנָה	תִּתְקַטֵּלְנָה[3]
1cp	נִקְטֹל	נִכְבַּד		נִקָּטֵל	נְקַטֵּל	נְקֻטַּל	נַקְטִיל	נָקְטַל	נִתְקַטֵּל

[1] from קָטֹנְנוּ.

[2] sometimes אִקָּטֵל.

[3] or תִּתְקַטַּלְנָה.

1b. The Strong Verb, continued

	Qal			Niphal	Piel	Pual	Hiphil	Hophal	Hithpael
	Active	Stative				*no dagesh in the yod*			
Impf.* + *w.c.	וַיִּקְטֹל	וַיִּכְבַּד	(These forms follow the pattern of כָּבֵד)	וַיִּקָּטֵל	וַיְקַטֵּל[1]	וַיְקֻטַּל	וַיַּקְטֵל	וַיָּקְטַל	וַיִּתְקַטֵּל
Juss.+vav	וְיִקְטֹל	וְיִכְבַּד		וְיִקָּטֵל	וִיקַטֵּל	וִיקֻטַּל	וְיַקְטֵל	וְיָקְטַל	וְיִתְקַטֵּל
Coh. 1cs	אֶקְטְלָה	אֶכְבְּדָה		אִקָּטְלָה	אֲקַטְּלָה	—	אַקְטִילָה	—	אֶתְקַטְּלָה
Impv. ms	קְטֹל	כְּבַד		הִקָּטֵל	קַטֵּל	—	הַקְטֵל	—	הִתְקַטֵּל
fs	קִטְלִי	כִּבְדִי		הִקָּטְלִי	קַטְּלִי	—	הַקְטִילִי	—	הִתְקַטְּלִי
mp	קִטְלוּ	כִּבְדוּ		הִקָּטְלוּ	קַטְּלוּ	—	הַקְטִילוּ	—	הִתְקַטְּלוּ
fp	קְטֹלְנָה	כְּבַדְנָה		הִקָּטַלְנָה	קַטֵּלְנָה	—	הַקְטֵלְנָה	—	הִתְקַטֵּלְנָה
Juss. 3ms	Same as Imperfect 3ms						יַקְטֵל	— Same as Impf 3ms —	
Act. Part. ms	קֹטֵל	כָּבֵד	קָטֹן	—	מְקַטֵּל	—	מַקְטִיל	—	מִתְקַטֵּל
fs	קֹטֶלֶת[2]	כְּבֵדָה	—	—	מְקַטֶּלֶת[3]	—	מַקְטִילָה	—	מִתְקַטֶּלֶת[4]
Pass. Part. ms	קָטוּל	—	—	נִקְטָל	—	מְקֻטָּל	—	מָקְטָל	—
fs	קְטוּלָה	—	—	נִקְטָלָה	—	מְקֻטֶּלֶת[5]	—	מָקְטֶלֶת	—
Inf. Abs.	קָטוֹל	כָּבוֹד	קָטוֹן	הִקָּטֵל[6]	קַטֹּל[7]	קֻטֹּל	הַקְטֵל	הָקְטֵל	הִתְקַטֵּל
Inf. Const.	קְטֹל	כְּבֹד[8]	קְטֹן[9]	הִקָּטֵל	קַטֵּל	—	הַקְטִיל	הָקְטַל	הִתְקַטֵּל

[1] No *dagesh* is found in the Piel Impf *yod* prefixes, that is, in the Piel Impf 3ms and 3mp. The *dagesh* does appear in the other prefixes such as -תְּ, etc. Thus, Piel Impf 3fs is וַתְּקַטֵּל.

[2] *or* קֹטְלָה [3] *or* מְקַטְּלָה [4] *or* מִתְקַטְּלָה [5] *or* מְקֻטָּלָה [6] *or* נִקְטֹל [7] *or* קַטֵּל [8] *or* כְּבַד [9] *or* קְטַן

2. The Qal Verb with Object Suffixes (§55, 56, 57, 59)

Suffix ↓	Perf 3ms קָטַל	Perf 3fs קָטְלָה	Perf 2ms קָטַ֫לְתָּ	Perf 2fs קָטַלְתְּ	Perf 1cs קָטַ֫לְתִּי	Perf 3cp קָטְלוּ	Perf 2mp or 2fp קְטַלְתֶּם or קְטַלְתֶּן	Perf 1cp קָטַ֫לְנוּ
3ms	{ קְטָלוֹ / קְטָלָ֫הוּ }	קְטָלַ֫תּוּ / קְטָלַ֫תְהוּ	{ קְטַלְתּוֹ / קְטַלְתָּ֫הוּ }	קְטַלְתִּ֫יהוּ	{ קְטַלְתִּיו / קְטַלְתִּ֫יהוּ }	קְטָלוּ֫הוּ[4]	קְטַלְתּוּ֫הוּ	קְטַלְנ֫וּהוּ
3fs	קְטָלָהּ	קְטָלַ֫תָּה	קְטַלְתָּהּ	קְטַלְתִּ֫יהָ	קְטַלְתִּ֫יהָ	קְטָלוּ֫הָ[4]	—	קְטַלְנ֫וּהָ
2ms	קְטָלְךָ	קְטָלַ֫תְךָ	—	—	קְטַלְתִּ֫יךָ	קְטָלוּ֫ךָ[4]	—	קְטַלְנ֫וּךָ
2fs	קְטָלֵךְ	קְטָלָ֫תֶךְ	—	—	קְטַלְתִּיךְ	קְטָלוּךְ[4]	—	קְטַלְנוּךְ
1cs	קְטָלַ֫נִי	קְטָלַ֫תְנִי	קְטַלְתַּ֫נִי	קְטַלְתִּ֫ינִי	—	קְטָלוּ֫נִי[4]	קְטַלְתּ֫וּנִי	—
3mp[1]	קְטָלָם	קְטָלָ֫תַם	קְטַלְתָּם	קְטַלְתִּים	קְטַלְתִּים	קְטָלוּם[4]	קְטַלְתּוּם	קְטַלְנוּם
2mp[2]	—	—	—	—	קְטַלְתִּיכֶם	—	—	קְטַלְנוּכֶם
1cp	קְטָלָ֫נוּ	קְטָלַ֫תְנוּ	קְטַלְתָּ֫נוּ	קְטַלְתִּ֫ינוּ	—	קְטָלוּ֫נוּ[4]	קְטַלְתּ֫וּנוּ	—

Suffix ↓	Impf 3ms יִקְטֹל	Impf 3ms + נ	Impf 3mp יִקְטְלוּ	Impf 2mp,2/3fp תִּקְטְלוּ , תִּקְטֹ֫לְנָה	Impv ms קְטֹל	Impv mp קִטְלוּ	Inf. Const.[3] קְטֹל
3ms	יִקְטְלֵ֫הוּ	יִקְטְלֶ֫נּוּ	יִקְטְלוּ֫הוּ[4]	תִּקְטְלוּ֫הוּ	קָטְלֵ֫הוּ[5]	קִטְלוּ֫הוּ	קָטְלוֹ[6]
3fs	[יִקְטְלָהּ] יִקְטְלֶ֫הָ	יִקְטְלֶ֫נָּה	יִקְטְלוּ֫הָ[4]	תִּקְטְלוּ֫הָ	קָטְלֶ֫הָ[5], קָטְלָהּ	קִטְלוּ֫הָ	קָטְלָהּ
2ms	יִקְטָלְךָ	יִקְטְלֶ֫ךָּ	יִקְטְלוּ֫ךָ[4]	—	—	—	קְטָלְךָ *or* קָטְלְךָ
2fs	יִקְטְלֵךְ	—	יִקְטְלוּךְ[4]	—	—	—	קָטְלֵךְ
1cs	יִקְטְלֵ֫נִי	יִקְטְלֶ֫נִּי	יִקְטְלוּ֫נִי[4]	תִּקְטְלוּ֫נִי	קָטְלֵ֫נִי[5]	קִטְלוּ֫נִי	קָטְלִי *or* קָטְלֵ֫נִי
3mp[1]	יִקְטְלֵם	—	יִקְטְלוּם[4]	תִּקְטְלוּם	קָטְלֵם[5]	קִטְלוּם	קָטְלָם
2mp[2]	יִקְטָלְכֶם	—	יִקְטְלוּכֶם[4]	—	—	—	קְטָלְכֶם *or* קָטְלְכֶם
1cp	יִקְטְלֵ֫נוּ	יִקְטְלֶ֫נּוּ	יִקְטְלוּ֫נוּ[4]	תִּקְטְלוּ֫נוּ	קָטְלֵ֫נוּ[5]	קִטְלוּ֫נוּ	קָטְלֵ֫נוּ

[1] 3fp is the same as 3mp, except ן- replaces ם- (for instance קְטָלָן instead of קְטָלָם). [2] 2fp follows 2mp except כֶן- replaces כֶם-. [3] See §57 for alternate forms.

[4] Forms such as קְטָלוּ֫הוּ and יִקְטְלוּ֫הוּ will also be found with *qibbuts*: קְטָלֻ֫הוּ and יִקְטְלֻ֫הוּ. [5] Note *qamets-hatuph*. [6] Note *qamets-hatuph* throughout.

3. The Pe Nun Verb (§61)

	Qal	Qal	Niphal	Hiphil	Hophal
Perf 3ms	נָפַל	נָגַשׁ	נִצַּל	הִצִּיל	הֻצַּל
3fs	(Follows pattern of the strong verb)		נִצְּלָה	הִצִּילָה	הֻצְּלָה
2ms			נִצַּלְתָּ	הִצַּלְתָּ	הֻצַּלְתָּ
2fs			נִצַּלְתְּ	הִצַּלְתְּ	הֻצַּלְתְּ
1cs			נִצַּלְתִּי	הִצַּלְתִּי	הֻצַּלְתִּי
3cp			נִצְּלוּ	הִצִּילוּ	הֻצְּלוּ
2mp			נִצַּלְתֶּם	הִצַּלְתֶּם	הֻצַּלְתֶּם
2fp			נִצַּלְתֶּן	הִצַּלְתֶּן	הֻצַּלְתֶּן
1cp			נִצַּלְנוּ	הִצַּלְנוּ	הֻצַּלְנוּ

	Qal	Qal	Niphal	Hiphil	Hophal
Impf 3ms	יִפֹּל	יִגַּשׁ	יִנָּצֵל	יַצִּיל	יֻצַּל
3fs	תִּפֹּל	תִּגַּשׁ	(Follows pattern of the strong verb)	תַּצִּיל	תֻּצַּל
2ms	תִּפֹּל	תִּגַּשׁ		תַּצִּיל	תֻּצַּל
2fs	תִּפְּלִי	תִּגְּשִׁי		תַּצִּילִי	תֻּצְּלִי
1cs	אֶפֹּל	אֶגַּשׁ		אַצִּיל	אֻצַּל
3mp	יִפְּלוּ	יִגְּשׁוּ		יַצִּילוּ	יֻצְּלוּ
3/2fp	תִּפֹּלְנָה	תִּגַּשְׁנָה		תַּצֵּלְנָה	תֻּצַּלְנָה
2mp	תִּפְּלוּ	תִּגְּשׁוּ		תַּצִּילוּ	תֻּצְּלוּ
1cp	נִפֹּל	נִגַּשׁ		נַצִּיל	נֻצַּל

	Qal	Qal	Niphal	Hiphil	Hophal
Coh. 1cs	אֶפְּלָה	אֶגְּשָׁה	(Follows strong verb pattern)	אַצִּילָה	—
					—
Impv. ms	נְפֹל	גַּשׁ		הַצֵּל	—
fs	נִפְלִי	גְּשִׁי		הַצִּילִי	—
mp	נִפְלוּ	גְּשׁוּ		הַצִּילוּ	—
fp	נְפֹלְנָה	גַּשְׁנָה		הַצֵּלְנָה	—
Juss. 3ms	(Same as Impf 3ms)				

	Qal	Qal	Niphal	Hiphil	Hophal
Impf.+w.c.	וַיִּפֹּל	וַיִּגַּשׁ	⟨Regular⟩	וַיַּצֵּל	וַיֻּצַּל
Juss.+vav	וְיִפֹּל	וְיִגַּשׁ		וְיַצֵּל	וְיֻצַּל
Act. Part. ms	נֹפֵל	נֹגֵשׁ	—	מַצִּיל	
Pass. Part. ms	—	נָגוּשׁ	נִצָּל	—	
Inf. Abs.	נָפוֹל	נָגוֹשׁ	הִנָּצֵל [נִצּוֹל]	הַצֵּל	הֻצֵּל
Inf. Const.	נְפֹל	גֶּשֶׁת	הִנָּצֵל	הַצִּיל	הֻצַּל

4. The Pe Yod (and Original Pe Vav) Verb (§63, 64)

	True Pe Yod		Original Pe Waw			
Perf.	Qal	Hiphil	Qal	Niphal	Hiphil	Hophal
3ms	(Follows pattern of the strong verb)	הֵינִיק	(Follows pattern of the strong verb)	נוֹשַׁב	הוֹשִׁיב	הוּשַׁב
3fs		הֵינִיקָה		נוֹשְׁבָה	הוֹשִׁיבָה	הוּשְׁבָה
2ms		הֵינַקְתָּ		נוֹשַׁבְתָּ	הוֹשַׁבְתָּ	הוּשַׁבְתָּ
2fs		הֵינַקְתְּ		נוֹשַׁבְתְּ	הוֹשַׁבְתְּ	הוּשַׁבְתְּ
1cs		הֵינַקְתִּי		נוֹשַׁבְתִּי	הוֹשַׁבְתִּי	הוּשַׁבְתִּי
3cp		הֵינִיקוּ		נוֹשְׁבוּ	הוֹשִׁיבוּ	הוּשְׁבוּ
2mp		הֵינַקְתֶּם		נוֹשַׁבְתֶּם	הוֹשַׁבְתֶּם	הוּשַׁבְתֶּם
2fp		הֵינַקְתֶּן		נוֹשַׁבְתֶּן	הוֹשַׁבְתֶּן	הוּשַׁבְתֶּן
1cp		הֵינַקְנוּ		נוֹשַׁבְנוּ	הוֹשַׁבְנוּ	הוּשַׁבְנוּ

	True Pe Yod		Original Pe Waw				
Impf.	Qal	Hiphil	Qal		Niphal	Hiphil	Hophal
3ms	יִינַק	יֵינִיק	יֵשֵׁב	יִירַשׁ	יִוָּשֵׁב	יוֹשִׁיב	יוּשַׁב
3fs	תִּינַק	תֵּינִיק	תֵּשֵׁב	תִּירַשׁ	(Follows pattern of the strong verb)	תּוֹשִׁיב	תּוּשַׁב
2ms	תִּינַק	תֵּינִיק	תֵּשֵׁב	תִּירַשׁ		תּוֹשִׁיב	תּוּשַׁב
2fs	תִּינְקִי	תֵּינִיקִי	תֵּשְׁבִי	תִּירְשִׁי		תּוֹשִׁיבִי	תּוּשְׁבִי
1cs	אִינַק	אֵינִיק	אֵשֵׁב	אִירַשׁ		אוֹשִׁיב	אוּשַׁב
3mp	יִינְקוּ	יֵינִיקוּ	יֵשְׁבוּ	יִירְשׁוּ		יוֹשִׁיבוּ	יוּשְׁבוּ
3/2fp	תִּינַקְנָה	תֵּינֵקְנָה	תֵּשַׁבְנָה	תִּירַשְׁנָה		תּוֹשֵׁבְנָה	תּוּשַׁבְנָה
2mp	תִּינְקוּ	תֵּינִיקוּ	תֵּשְׁבוּ	תִּירְשׁוּ		תּוֹשִׁיבוּ	תּוּשְׁבוּ
1cp	נִינַק	נֵינִיק	נֵשֵׁב	נִירַשׁ		נוֹשִׁיב	נוּשַׁב

	True Pe Yod		Original Pe Waw			
	Qal	Hiphil	Qal	Niphal	Hiphil	Hoph
Coh. 1cs	—	אֵינִיקָה	אֵשְׁבָה	—	—	—
Impv. ms	—	הֵינֵק	רַשׁ, שֵׁב	הִוָּשֵׁב	הוֹשֵׁב	—
fs	—	הֵינִיקִי	שְׁבִי	הִוָּשְׁבִי	הוֹשִׁיבִי	—
mp	—	הֵינִיקוּ	שְׁבוּ	הִוָּשְׁבוּ	הוֹשִׁיבוּ	—
fp	—	הֵינֵקְנָה	שֵׁבְנָה	הִוָּשַׁבְנָה	הוֹשֵׁבְנָה	—
Juss. 3ms	יִינַק	יֵינֵק	יֵשֵׁב	—	יוֹשֵׁב	—

	True Pe Yod		Original Pe Waw			
	Qal	Hiphil	Qal	Niphal	Hiphil	Hophal
Impf + w.c.	וַיִּינַק	וַיֵּינֶק	וַיֵּשֶׁב	—	וַיּוֹשֶׁב	—
Act. Part. ms	יֹנֵק	מֵינִיק	יֹשֵׁב		מוֹשִׁיב	
Pass.Part. ms	יָנוּק		יָשׁוּב	נוֹשָׁב		מוּשָׁב
Inf. Abs.	יָנוֹק	הֵינֵק	יָשׁוֹב	—	הוֹשֵׁב	—
Inf. Const.	יְנֹק	הֵינִיק	שֶׁבֶת	הִוָּשֵׁב	הוֹשִׁיב	הוּשַׁב

5. The Pe Guttural (and Pe Aleph) Verb (§65, 66)

Perf	Pe Guttural Qal	Pe Guttural Niphal	Pe Guttural Hiphil	Pe Guttural Hophal[2]	Pe Aleph Qal
3ms	עָמַד	נֶעֱמַד	הֶעֱמִיד	הָעֳמַד	(Follows pattern of other *Pe* Guttural verbs)
3fs	עָמְדָה	נֶעֶמְדָה	הֶעֱמִ֫ידָה	הָעָמְדָה	
2ms	עָמַ֫דְתָּ	נֶעֱמַ֫דְתָּ	הֶעֱמַ֫דְתָּ	הָעֳמַ֫דְתָּ	
2fs	עָמַדְתְּ	נֶעֱמַדְתְּ	הֶעֱמַדְתְּ	הָעֳמַדְתְּ	
1cs	עָמַ֫דְתִּי	נֶעֱמַ֫דְתִּי	הֶעֱמַ֫דְתִּי	הָעֳמַ֫דְתִּי	
3cp	עָמְדוּ	נֶעֶמְדוּ	הֶעֱמִ֫ידוּ	הָעָמְדוּ	
2mp	עֲמַדְתֶּם	נֶעֱמַדְתֶּם	הֶעֱמַדְתֶּם	הָעֳמַדְתֶּם	
2fp	עֲמַדְתֶּן	נֶעֱמַדְתֶּן	הֶעֱמַדְתֶּן	הָעֳמַדְתֶּן	
1cp	עָמַ֫דְנוּ	נֶעֱמַ֫דְנוּ	הֶעֱמַ֫דְנוּ	הָעֳמַ֫דְנוּ	

Impf	Pe Guttural Qal Active	Pe Guttural Qal Stative	Pe Guttural Niphal	Pe Guttural Hiphil	Pe Guttural Hophal[2]	Pe Aleph Qal
3ms	יַעֲמֹד	יֶחֱזַק	יֵעָמֵד	יַעֲמִיד	יָעֳמַד	יֹאבַד
3fs	תַּעֲמֹד	תֶּחֱזַק	תֵּעָמֵד	תַּעֲמִיד	תָּעֳמַד	תֹּאבַד
2ms	תַּעֲמֹד	תֶּחֱזַק	תֵּעָמֵד	תַּעֲמִיד	תָּעֳמַד	תֹּאבַד
2fs	תַּעַמְדִי	תֶּחֶזְקִי	תֵּעָמְדִי	תַּעֲמִ֫ידִי	תָּעָמְדִי	תֹּאבְדִי
1cs	אֶעֱמֹד	אֶחֱזַק	אֵעָמֵד	אַעֲמִיד	אָעֳמַד	אֹבַד
3mp	יַעַמְדוּ	יֶחֶזְקוּ	יֵעָמְדוּ	יַעֲמִ֫ידוּ	יָעָמְדוּ	יֹאבְדוּ
3/2fp	תַּעֲמֹ֫דְנָה	תֶּחֱזַ֫קְנָה	תֵּעָמַ֫דְנָה	תַּעֲמֵ֫דְנָה	תָּעֳמַ֫דְנָה	תֹּאבַ֫דְנָה
2mp	תַּעַמְדוּ	תֶּחֶזְקוּ	תֵּעָמְדוּ	תַּעֲמִ֫ידוּ	תָּעָמְדוּ	תֹּאבְדוּ
1cp	נַעֲמֹד	נֶחֱזַק	נֵעָמֵד	נַעֲמִיד	נָעֳמַד	נֹאבַד

	Pe Guttural Qal	Pe Guttural Niphal	Pe Guttural Hiphil	Pe Guttural Hophal[2]	Pe Aleph Qal
Act. Pt. ms	עֹמֵד	—	מַעֲמִיד	—	אֹבֵד
Pass. Pt. ms	עָמוּד	נֶעֱמָד	—	מָעֳמָד	אָבוּד
Inf. Abs.	עָמוֹד	נַעֲמוֹד, הֵעָמֵד	הַעֲמֵד	הָעֳמֵד	אָבוֹד
Inf. Const.	עֲמֹד	הֵעָמֵד[1]	הַעֲמִיד	הָעֳמַד	אֱבֹד
Juss.	Same as Impf 3ms except Hiphil: יַעֲמֵד				יֹאבַד

	Pe Guttural Qal Active	Pe Guttural Qal Stative	Pe Guttural Niphal	Pe Guttural Hiphil	Pe Guttural Hophal	Pe Aleph Qal
Coh 1cs	אֶעֶמְדָה	—	—	אַעֲמִ֫ידָה	—	אֹבְדָה
Impf+wc	וַיַּעֲמֹד	וַיֶּחֱזַק	וַיֵּעָמֵד	וַיַּעֲמֵד	—	וַיֹּאבַד
Impv ms	עֲמֹד	חֲזַק	הֵעָמֵד	הַעֲמֵד	—	אֱבֹד
fs	עִמְדִי	חִזְקִי	הֵעָמְדִי	הַעֲמִ֫ידִי	—	אִבְדִי
mp	עִמְדוּ	חִזְקוּ	הֵעָמְדוּ	הַעֲמִ֫ידוּ	—	אִבְדוּ
fp	עֲמֹ֫דְנָה	חֲזַ֫קְנָה	הֵעָמַ֫דְנָה	הַעֲמֵ֫דְנָה	—	אֱבֹ֫דְנָה

[1] With -לְ prefix, the ל replaces the ה just like it does with the definite article: הֵעָמֵד + לְ → לֵעָמֵד.

[2] Note *qamets-hatuph* with *metheg* under all Hophal prefixes.

6a. The Ayin Guttural Verb (except Ayin א or Ayin ר) (§67)

	Qal	Niphal	Piel	Pual	Hithp
Perf. 3ms	בָּחַר	נִבְחַר	בֵּעֵר	בֹּעַר	הִתְבָּעֵר
3fs	בָּחֲרָה	נִבְחֲרָה	בֵּעֲרָה	בֹּעֲרָה	הִתְבָּעֲרָה
2ms	בָּחַרְתָּ	נִבְחַרְתָּ	בֵּעַרְתָּ	בֹּעַרְתָּ	הִתְבָּעַרְתָּ
2fs	בָּחַרְתְּ	נִבְחַרְתְּ	בֵּעַרְתְּ	בֹּעַרְתְּ	הִתְבָּעַרְתְּ
1cs	בָּחַרְתִּי	נִבְחַרְתִּי	בֵּעַרְתִּי	בֹּעַרְתִּי	הִתְבָּעַרְתִּי
3cp	בָּחֲרוּ	נִבְחֲרוּ	בֵּעֲרוּ	בֹּעֲרוּ	הִתְבָּעֲרוּ
2mp	בְּחַרְתֶּם	נִבְחַרְתֶּם	בֵּעַרְתֶּם	בֹּעַרְתֶּם	הִתְבָּעַרְתֶּם
2fp	בְּחַרְתֶּן	נִבְחַרְתֶּן	בֵּעַרְתֶּן	בֹּעַרְתֶּן	הִתְבָּעַרְתֶּן
1cp	בָּחַרְנוּ	נִבְחַרְנוּ	בֵּעַרְנוּ	בֹּעַרְנוּ	הִתְבָּעַרְנוּ

	Qal	Niphal	Piel	Pual	Hithp
Coh. 1cs	אֶבְחֲרָה	אִבָּחֲרָה	אֲבָעֲרָה	—	אֶתְבָּעֲרָה
Impv. ms	בְּחַר	הִבָּחֵר	בָּעֵר	—	הִתְבָּעֵר
fs	בַּחֲרִי	הִבָּחֲרִי	בָּעֲרִי	—	הִתְבָּעֲרִי
mp	בַּחֲרוּ	הִבָּחֲרוּ	בָּעֲרוּ	—	הִתְבָּעֲרוּ
fp	בְּחַרְנָה	הִבָּחַרְנָה	בָּעֵרְנָה	—	הִתְבָּעֵרְנָה
Juss. 3ms	(Same form as Impf 3ms)				

	Qal	Niphal	Piel	Pual	Hithp
Impf. 3ms	יִבְחַר	יִבָּחֵר	יְבָעֵר	יְבֹעַר	יִתְבָּעֵר
3fs	תִּבְחַר	תִּבָּחֵר	תְּבָעֵר	תְּבֹעַר	תִּתְבָּעֵר
2ms	תִּבְחַר	תִּבָּחֵר	תְּבָעֵר	תְּבֹעַר	תִּתְבָּעֵר
2fs	תִּבְחֲרִי	תִּבָּחֲרִי	תְּבָעֲרִי	תְּבֹעֲרִי	תִּתְבָּעֲרִי
1cs	אֶבְחַר	אֶבָּחֵר	אֲבָעֵר	אֲבֹעַר	אֶתְבָּעֵר
3mp	יִבְחֲרוּ	יִבָּחֲרוּ	יְבָעֲרוּ	יְבֹעֲרוּ	יִתְבָּעֲרוּ
3/2fp	תִּבְחַרְנָה	תִּבָּחַרְנָה	תְּבָעֵרְנָה	תְּבֹעַרְנָה	תִּתְבָּעֵרְנָה
2mp	תִּבְחֲרוּ	תִּבָּחֲרוּ	תְּבָעֲרוּ	תְּבֹעֲרוּ	תִּתְבָּעֲרוּ
1cp	נִבְחַר	נִבָּחֵר	נְבָעֵר	נְבֹעַר	נִתְבָּעֵר

	Qal	Niphal	Piel	Pual	Hithp
Impf.+w.c.	וַיִּבְחַר	וַיִּבָּחֵר	וַיְבָעֵר	—	—
Act. Part. ms	Regular	Regular	מְבָעֵר		מִתְבָּעֵר
Pass. Part. ms	Regular	Regular		מְבֹעָר	
Inf. Abs.	Regular	Regular	בָּעֵר	—	—
Inf. Const.	Regular	Regular	בָּעֵר	—	הִתְבָּעֵר

6b. The Ayin Guttural (א or ר) Verb (§67)

	Qal	Niphal	Piel	Pual	Hithp
Perf 3ms	Qal and Niphal follow same pattern as other *Ayin* Guttural verbs		בֵּרַךְ	בֹּרַךְ	הִתְבָּרֵךְ
3fs			בֵּרְכָה	בֹּרְכָה	הִתְבָּרְכָה
2ms			בֵּרַכְתָּ	בֹּרַכְתָּ	הִתְבָּרַכְתָּ
2fs			בֵּרַכְתְּ	בֹּרַכְתְּ	הִתְבָּרַכְתְּ
1cs			בֵּרַכְתִּי	בֹּרַכְתִּי	הִתְבָּרַכְתִּי
3cp			בֵּרְכוּ	בֹּרְכוּ	הִתְבָּרְכוּ
2mp			בֵּרַכְתֶּם	בֹּרַכְתֶּם	הִתְבָּרַכְתֶּם
2fp			בֵּרַכְתֶּן	בֹּרַכְתֶּן	הִתְבָּרַכְתֶּן
1cp			בֵּרַכְנוּ	בֹּרַכְנוּ	הִתְבָּרַכְנוּ

	Qal	Niphal	Piel	Pual	Hithp
Impf. 3ms	Qal and Niphal follow same pattern as other *Ayin* Guttural verbs		יְבָרֵךְ	יְבֹרַךְ	יִתְבָּרֵךְ
3fs			תְּבָרֵךְ	תְּבֹרַךְ	תִּתְבָּרֵךְ
2ms			תְּבָרֵךְ	תְּבֹרַךְ	תִּתְבָּרֵךְ
2fs			תְּבָרְכִי	תְּבֹרְכִי	תִּתְבָּרְכִי
1cs			אֲבָרֵךְ	אֲבֹרַךְ	אֶתְבָּרֵךְ
3mp			יְבָרְכוּ	תְּבֹרְכוּ	יִתְבָּרְכוּ
3/2fp			תְּבָרֵכְנָה	תְּבֹרַכְנָה	תִּתְבָּרַכְנָה
2mp			תְּבָרְכוּ	תְּבֹרְכוּ	תִּתְבָּרְכוּ
1cp			נְבָרֵךְ	נְבֹרַךְ	נִתְבָּרֵךְ

	Qal	Niphal	Piel	Pual	Hithp
Coh. 1cs			אֲבָרְכָה	—	—
Impv. ms	Qal and Niphal follow same pattern as other *Ayin* Guttural verbs		בָּרֵךְ	—	הִתְבָּרֵךְ
fs			[1]בָּרְכִי	—	[1]הִתְבָּרְכִי
mp			[1]בָּרְכוּ	—	[1]הִתְבָּרְכוּ
fp			בָּרֵכְנָה	—	[1]הִתְבָּרֵכְנָה
Juss. 3ms	(Same form as Impf 3ms)				

	Qal	Niphal	Piel	Pual	Hithp
Impf.+w.c.	Qal and Niphal follow same pattern as other *Ayin* Guttural verbs		וַיְבָרֶךְ	—	—
Act. Part. ms			מְבָרֵךְ		מִתְבָּרֵךְ
Pass. Part. ms				מְבֹרָךְ	
Inf. Abs.			בָּרֵךְ	בֹּרַךְ	—
Inf. Const.			בָּרֵךְ	בֹּרַךְ	הִתְבָּרֵךְ

[1] Sometimes found with simple *shewa* under the *resh*: -רְ-.

7A. Middle-Vowel Verbs (Ayin Vav and Ayin Yod) (§68, 69)

	Qal									
	Ayin Yod	*Ayin Vav*								
		Active	(*e*) Stative	(*o*)	**Niphal**	(Piel) **Polel**	(Pual) **Polal**	**Hiphil**	**Hophal**	(Hithpael) **Hithpolel**
Perf. 3ms	שָׂם	קָם	מֵת	בּוֹשׁ	נָקוֹם	קוֹמֵם	קוֹמַם	הֵקִים	הוּקַם	הִתְקוֹמֵם
3fs	שָׂמָה	קָמָה	מֵתָה	בּוֹשָׁה	נָקוֹמָה	קוֹמֲמָה	(Same as Polel, except for the 3ms)	הֵקִימָה	הוּקְמָה	הִתְקוֹמֲמָה
2ms	שַׂמְתָּ	קַמְתָּ	מַתָּה[1]	בֹּשְׁתָּ	נְקוּמוֹתָ	קוֹמַמְתָּ		הֲקִימוֹתָ	הוּקַמְתָּ	הִתְקוֹמַמְתָּ
2fs	שַׂמְתְּ	קַמְתְּ	מַתְּ	בֹּשְׁתְּ	נְקוּמוֹת	קוֹמַמְתְּ		הֲקִימוֹת	הוּקַמְתְּ	הִתְקוֹמַמְתְּ
1cs	שַׂמְתִּי	קַמְתִּי	מַתִּי	בֹּשְׁתִּי	נְקוּמוֹתִי	קוֹמַמְתִּי		הֲקִימוֹתִי	הוּקַמְתִּי	הִתְקוֹמַמְתִּי
3cp	שָׂמוּ	קָמוּ	מֵתוּ	בּוֹשׁוּ	נָקוֹמוּ	קוֹמֲמוּ		הֵקִימוּ	הוּקְמוּ	הִתְקוֹמֲמוּ
2mp	שַׂמְתֶּם	קַמְתֶּם	מַתֶּם	בָּשְׁתֶּם	נְקוֹמוֹתֶם	קוֹמַמְתֶּם		הֲקִימוֹתֶם	הוּקַמְתֶּם	הִתְקוֹמַמְתֶּם
2fp	שַׂמְתֶּן	קַמְתֶּן	מַתֶּן	בָּשְׁתֶּן	נְקוֹמוֹתֶן	קוֹמַמְתֶּן		הֲקִימוֹתֶן	הוּקַמְתֶּן	הִתְקוֹמַמְתֶּן
1cp	שַׂמְנוּ	קַמְנוּ	מַתְנוּ	בֹּשְׁנוּ	נְקוּמוֹנוּ	קוֹמַמְנוּ		הֲקִימוֹנוּ	הוּקַמְנוּ	הִתְקוֹמַמְנוּ
Impf. 3ms	יָשִׂים	יָקוּם	(Follows same pattern as active verb)	יֵבוֹשׁ	יִקּוֹם	יְקוֹמֵם	יְקוֹמַם	יָקִים	יוּקַם	יִתְקוֹמֵם
3fs/2ms	תָּשִׂים	תָּקוּם		תֵּבוֹשׁ	תִּקּוֹם	תְּקוֹמֵם	תְּקוֹמַם	תָּקִים	תּוּקַם	תִּתְקוֹמֵם
2fs	תָּשִׂימִי	תָּקוּמִי		תֵּבוֹשִׁי	תִּקּוֹמִי	תְּקוֹמֲמִי	תְּקוֹמֲמִי	תָּקִימִי	תּוּקְמִי	תִּתְקוֹמֲמִי
1cs	אָשִׂים	אָקוּם		אֵבוֹשׁ	אֶקּוֹם	אֲקוֹמֵם	אֲקוֹמַם	אָקִים	אוּקַם	אֶתְקוֹמֵם
3mp	יָשִׂימוּ	יָקוּמוּ		יֵבֹשׁוּ	יִקּוֹמוּ	יְקוֹמֲמוּ	יְקוֹמֲמוּ	יָקִימוּ	יוּקְמוּ	יִתְקוֹמֲמוּ
3fp/2fp	תְּשִׂימֶינָה[2]	תְּקוּמֶינָה[3]		תֵּבוֹשְׁנָה	—	תְּקוֹמֵמְנָה	תְּקוֹמַמְנָה	תָּקֵמְנָה[4]	תּוּקַמְנָה	תִּתְקוֹמֵמְנָה
2mp	תָּשִׂימוּ	תָּקוּמוּ		תֵּבוֹשׁוּ	תִּקּוֹמוּ	תְּקוֹמֲמוּ	תְּקוֹמֲמוּ	תָּקִימוּ	תּוּקְמוּ	תִּתְקוֹמֲמוּ
1cp	נָשִׂים	נָקוּם		נֵבוֹשׁ	נִקּוֹם	נְקוֹמֵם	נְקוֹמַם	נָקִים	נוּקַם	נִתְקוֹמֵם

[1] Note the unusual final ה-.

[2] or תָּשֵׂמְנָה

[3] or תָּקֹמְנָה

[4] 3fp is also found as תְּקִימֶינָה (note unusual *shewa* under prefix)

7b. Middle-Vowel Verbs (Ayin Vav and Ayin Yod), continued

	Qal									
	Ayin Yod	*Ayin Vav*								
		Active	(*e*) Stative	(*o*)	Niphal	(Piel) Polel	(Pual) Polal	Hiphil	Hophal	(Hithpael) Hithpolel
Impf. + *w.c.*	וַיָּ֫שֶׂם	וַיָּ֫קָם	(Follows the same pattern as the active verb)	וַיֵּבוֹשׁ				וַיָּ֫קֶם		וַיִּתְקוֹמֵם
Coh. 1cs	אָשִׂ֫ימָה	אָקֿ֫וּמָה		אֵבֿ֫וֹשָׁה				אָקִ֫ימָה		
Impv. ms	שִׂים	קוּם		בּוֹשׁ	הִקּוֹם	קוֹמֵם		הָקֵם		הִתְקוֹמֵם
fs	שִׂ֫ימִי	ק֫וּמִי		בֹּ֫ושִׁי	הִקּ֫וֹמִי	קוֹמֲמִי		הָקִ֫ימִי		הִתְקוֹמְמִי
mp	שִׂ֫ימוּ	ק֫וּמוּ[1]		בֹּ֫ושׁוּ	הִקּ֫וֹמוּ	קוֹמֲמוּ		הָקִ֫ימוּ		הִתְקוֹמְמוּ
fp	—	קֹ֫מְנָה		בֹּ֫שְׁנָה	הִקּ֫וֹמְנָה	קוֹמֵ֫מְנָה		הָקֵ֫מְנָה		הִתְקוֹמֵ֫מְנָה
Juss. 3ms	יָשֵׂם	יָקוּם		יֵבוֹשׁ				יָקֵם		
Inf. Abs.	שׂוֹם	קוֹם		בּוֹשׁ	הִקּוֹם , נָקוֹם			הָקֵם	הוּקֵם	הִתְקוֹמֵם
Inf. Const.	שִׂים	קוּם		בּוֹשׁ	הִקּוֹם	קוֹמֵם		הָקִים	הוּקַם	הִתְקוֹמֵם
Act. Part. ms	שָׂם	קָם	מֵת	בּוֹשׁ		מְקוֹמֵם		מֵקִים		מִתְקוֹמֵם
fs	שָׂמָה	קָמָה								
Pass. Part. ms	שׂוּם , שִׂים	קוּם			נָקוֹם		מְקוֹמָם		מוּקָם	

[1] Also קֹ֫מוּ.

8a. Lamed Guttural Verbs (§70)

	Qal	Niphal	Piel	Pual	Hiphil	Hophal	Hithpael[1]
Perf. 3ms	(Follows pattern of strong verb)	(Follows pattern of strong verb)	שִׁלַּח	שֻׁלַּח	הִשְׁלִיחַ	הָשְׁלַח	הִתְבַּקַּע
3fs			שִׁלְּחוּ	שֻׁלְּחָה	הִשְׁלִיחָה	הָשְׁלְחָה	הִתְבַּקְּעָה
2ms			שִׁלַּחְתָּ	שֻׁלַּחְתָּ	הִשְׁלַחְתָּ	הָשְׁלַחְתָּ	הִתְבַּקַּעְתָּ
2fs			שִׁלַּחַתְּ	שֻׁלַּחַתְּ	הִשְׁלַחַתְּ	הָשְׁלַחַתְּ	הִתְבַּקַּעַתְּ
1cs			שִׁלַּחְתִּי	שֻׁלַּחְתִּי	הִשְׁלַחְתִּי	הָשְׁלַחְתִּי	הִתְבַּקַּעְתִּי
3cp			שִׁלְּחוּ	שֻׁלְּחוּ	הִשְׁלִיחוּ	הָשְׁלְחוּ	הִתְבַּקְּעוּ
2mp			שִׁלַּחְתֶּם	שֻׁלַּחְתֶּם	הִשְׁלַחְתֶּם	הָשְׁלַחְתֶּם	הִתְבַּקַּעְתֶּם
2fp			שִׁלַּחְתֶּן	שֻׁלַּחְתֶּן	הִשְׁלַחְתֶּן	הָשְׁלַחְתֶּן	הִתְבַּקַּעְתֶּן
1cp			שִׁלַּחְנוּ	שֻׁלַּחְנוּ	הִשְׁלַחְנוּ	הָשְׁלַחְנוּ	הִתְבַּקַּעְנוּ
Impf. 3ms	יִשְׁלַח	יִשָּׁלַח	יְשַׁלַּח	יְשֻׁלַּח	יַשְׁלִיחַ	יָשְׁלַח	יִתְבַּקַּע
3fs	תִּשְׁלַח	תִּשָּׁלַח	תְּשַׁלַּח	תְּשֻׁלַּח	תַּשְׁלִיחַ	תָּשְׁלַח	תִּתְבַּקַּע
2ms	תִּשְׁלַח	תִּשָּׁלַח	תְּשַׁלַּח	תְּשֻׁלַּח	תַּשְׁלִיחַ	תָּשְׁלַח	תִּתְבַּקַּע
2fs	תִּשְׁלְחִי	תִּשָּׁלְחִי	תְּשַׁלְּחִי	תְּשֻׁלְּחִי	תַּשְׁלִיחִי	תָּשְׁלְחִי	תִּתְבַּקְּעִי
1cs	אֶשְׁלַח	אֶשָּׁלַח	אֲשַׁלַּח	אֲשֻׁלַּח	אַשְׁלִיחַ	אָשְׁלַח	אֶתְבַּקַּע
3mp	יִשְׁלְחוּ	יִשָּׁלְחוּ	יְשַׁלְּחוּ	יְשֻׁלְּחוּ	יַשְׁלִיחוּ	יָשְׁלְחוּ	יִתְבַּקְּעוּ
3fp	תִּשְׁלַחְנָה	תִּשָּׁלַחְנָה	תְּשַׁלַּחְנָה	תְּשֻׁלַּחְנָה	תַּשְׁלַחְנָה	תָּשְׁלַחְנָה	תִּתְבַּקַּעְנָה
2mp	תִּשְׁלְחוּ	תִּשָּׁלְחוּ	תְּשַׁלְּחוּ	תְּשֻׁלְּחוּ	תַּשְׁלִיחוּ	תָּשְׁלְחוּ	תִּתְבַּקְּעוּ
2fp	תִּשְׁלַחְנָה	תִּשָּׁלַחְנָה	תְּשַׁלַּחְנָה	תְּשֻׁלַּחְנָה	תַּשְׁלַחְנָה	תָּשְׁלַחְנָה	תִּתְבַּקַּעְנָה
1cp	נִשְׁלַח	נִשָּׁלַח	נְשַׁלַּח	נְשֻׁלַּח	נַשְׁלִיחַ	נָשְׁלַח	נִתְבַּקַּע

[1] **Technical note:** The verb בקע is used for the Hithpael in order to avoid the transposition of letters. (The Hithpael of שׁלח is הִשְׁתַּלַּח, not הִתְשַׁלַּח; see §53.2.5.1.)

8b. Lamed Guttural Verbs, continued

	Qal	Niphal	Piel	Pual	Hiphil	Hophal	Hithpael[1]
Impf. + *w.c.*	וַיִּשְׁלַח	וַיִּשָּׁלַח	וַיְשַׁלַּח	וַיְשֻׁלַּח	וַיַּשְׁלַח	וַיָּשְׁלַח	וַיִּתְבַּקַּע
Coh. 1cs	אֶשְׁלְחָה	אִשָּׁלְחָה	אֲשַׁלְּחָה	—	אַשְׁלִיחָה	–	–
Impv. ms	שְׁלַח	הִשָּׁלַח	שַׁלַּח	—	הַשְׁלַח	–	הִתְבַּקַּע
fs	שִׁלְחִי	הִשָּׁלְחִי	שַׁלְּחִי	—	הַשְׁלִיחִי	–	הִתְבַּקְּעִי
mp	שִׁלְחוּ	הִשָּׁלְחוּ	שַׁלְּחוּ	—	הַשְׁלִיחוּ	–	הִתְבַּקְּעוּ
fp	שְׁלַחְנָה	הִשָּׁלַחְנָה	שַׁלַּחְנָה	—	הַשְׁלַחְנָה	–	הִתְבַּקַּעְנָה
Juss. 3ms	Same as Impf 3ms except for Hiphil which uses shortened form: יַשְׁלַח						
Inf. Abs.	שָׁלוֹחַ	נִשְׁלֹחַ	שַׁלֵּחַ	–	הַשְׁלֵחַ	הָשְׁלֵחַ	הִתְבַּקֵּעַ
Inf. Const.	שְׁלֹחַ	הִשָּׁלַח	שַׁלַּח	–	הַשְׁלִיחַ	–	הִתְבַּקַּע
Act. Part. ms	שֹׁלֵחַ		מְשַׁלֵּחַ		מַשְׁלִיחַ		מִתְבַּקֵּעַ
Pass. Part. ms	שָׁלוּחַ	נִשְׁלָח		מְשֻׁלָּח		מָשְׁלָח	

[1] **Technical note:** The verb בקע is used for the Hithpael in order to avoid the transposition of letters. (The Hithpael of שׁלח is הִשְׁתַּלַּח, not הִתְשַׁלַּח; see §53.2.5.1.)

9a. Lamed Aleph Verbs (§71)

	Qal Active	Qal Stative	Niphal	Piel	Pual	Hiphil	Hophal	Hithpael
Perf. 3ms	מָצָא	מָלֵא	נִמְצָא	מִצֵּא	מֻצָּא	הִמְצִיא	הֻמְצָא	הִתְמַצֵּא
3fs	מָצְאָה	מָלְאָה	נִמְצְאָה	מִצְּאָה	מֻצְּאָה	הִמְצִיאָה	הֻמְצְאָה	הִתְמַצְּאָה
2ms	מָצָאתָ	מָלֵאתָ	נִמְצֵאתָ	מִצֵּאתָ	מֻצֵּאתָ	הִמְצֵאתָ	הֻמְצֵאתָ	הִתְמַצֵּאתָ
2fs	מָצָאת	מָלֵאת	נִמְצֵאת	מִצֵּאת	מֻצֵּאת	הִמְצֵאת	הֻמְצֵאת	הִתְמַצֵּאת
1cs	מָצָאתִי	מָלֵאתִי	נִמְצֵאתִי	מִצֵּאתִי	מֻצֵּאתִי	הִמְצֵאתִי	הֻמְצֵאתִי	הִתְמַצֵּאתִי
3cp	מָצְאוּ	מָלְאוּ	נִמְצְאוּ	מִצְּאוּ	מֻצְּאוּ	הִמְצִיאוּ	הֻמְצְאוּ	הִתְמַצְּאוּ
2mp	מְצָאתֶם	מְלֵאתֶם	נִמְצֵאתֶם	מִצֵּאתֶם	מֻצֵּאתֶם	הִמְצֵאתֶם	הֻמְצֵאתֶם	הִתְמַצֵּאתֶם
3fp	מְצָאתֶן	מְלֵאתֶן	נִמְצֵאתֶן	מִצֵּאתֶן	מֻצֵּאתֶן	הִמְצֵאתֶן	הֻמְצֵאתֶן	הִתְמַצֵּאתֶן
1cp	מָצָאנוּ	מָלֵאנוּ	נִמְצֵאנוּ	מִצֵּאנוּ	מֻצֵּאנוּ	הִמְצֵאנוּ	הֻמְצֵאנוּ	הִתְמַצֵּאנוּ
Impf. 3ms	יִמְצָא		יִמָּצֵא	יְמַצֵּא	יְמֻצָּא	יַמְצִיא	יֻמְצָא	יִתְמַצֵּא
3fs	תִּמְצָא		תִּמָּצֵא	תְּמַצֵּא	תְּמֻצָּא	תַּמְצִיא	תֻּמְצָא	תִּתְמַצֵּא
2ms	תִּמְצָא		תִּמָּצֵא	תְּמַצֵּא	תְּמֻצָּא	תַּמְצִיא	תֻּמְצָא	תִּתְמַצֵּא
2fs	תִּמְצְאִי		תִּמָּצְאִי	תְּמַצְּאִי	תְּמֻצְּאִי	תַּמְצִיאִי	תֻּמְצְאִי	תִּתְמַצְּאִי
1cs	אֶמְצָא		אֶמָּצֵא	אֲמַצֵּא	אֲמֻצָּא	אַמְצִיא	אֻמְצָא	אֶתְמַצֵּא
3mp	יִמְצְאוּ		יִמָּצְאוּ	יְמַצְּאוּ	יְמֻצְּאוּ	יַמְצִיאוּ	יֻמְצְאוּ	יִתְמַצְּאוּ
3fp	תִּמְצֶאנָה		תִּמָּצֶאנָה	תְּמַצֶּאנָה	תְּמֻצֶּאנָה	תַּמְצֶאנָה	תֻּמְצֶאנָה	תִּתְמַצֶּאנָה
2mp	תִּמְצְאוּ		תִּמָּצְאוּ	תְּמַצְּאוּ	תְּמֻצְּאוּ	תַּמְצִיאוּ	תֻּמְצְאוּ	תִּתְמַצְּאוּ
2fp	תִּמְצֶאנָה		תִּמָּצֶאנָה	תְּמַצֶּאנָה	תְּמֻצֶּאנָה	תַּמְצֶאנָה	תֻּמְצֶאנָה	תִּתְמַצֶּאנָה
1cp	נִמְצָא		נִמָּצֵא	נְמַצֵּא	נְמֻצָּא	נַמְצִיא	נֻמְצָא	נִתְמַצֵּא

9b. Lamed Aleph Verbs, continued

	Qal	Niphal	Piel	Pual	Hiphil	Hophal	Hithpael
Impf. + *w.c.*	וַיִּמְצָא	וַיִּמָּצֵא	וַיְמַצֵּא	וַיְמֻצָּא	וַיַּמְצֵא	וַיֻּמְצָא	וַיִּתְמַצֵּא
Coh. 1cs	אֶמְצְאָה	אִמָּצְאָה	—	—	אַמְצִ֫יאָה	—	—
Impv. ms	מְצָא	הִמָּצֵא	מַצֵּא	—	הַמְצֵא	—	הִתְמַצֵּא
fs	מִצְאִי	הִמָּצְאִי	מַצְּאִי	—	הַמְצִ֫יאִי	—	הִתְמַצְּאִי
mp	מִצְאוּ	הִמָּצְאוּ	מַצְּאוּ	—	הַמְצִ֫יאוּ	—	הִתְמַצְּאוּ
fp	מְצֶ֫אנָה	הִמָּצֶ֫אנָה	מַצֶּ֫אנָה	—	הַמְצֶ֫אנָה	—	הִתְמַצֶּ֫אנָה
Juss. 3ms	Same as Impf 3ms except for Hiphil which uses shortened form: יַמְצֵא						
Inf. Abs.	מָצוֹא	נִמְצֹא	מַצֹּא	—	הַמְצֵא	—	
Inf. Const.	מְצֹא	הִמָּצֵא	מַצֵּא	—	הַמְצִיא	—	הִתְמַצֵּא
Act. Part. ms	מֹצֵא		מְמַצֵּא		מַמְצִיא		מִתְמַצֵּא
Pass. Part. ms	מָצוּא	נִמְצָא		מְמֻצָּא		מֻמְצָא	

10a. Lamed He Verbs (§72)

	Qal	Niphal	Piel	Pual	Hiphil	Hophal	Hithpael
Perf. 3ms	גָּלָה	נִגְלָה	גִּלָּה	גֻּלָּה	הִגְלָה	הָגְלָה	הִתְגַּלָּה
3fs	גָּלְתָה	נִגְלְתָה	גִּלְּתָה	גֻּלְּתָה	הִגְלְתָה	הָגְלְתָה	הִתְגַּלְּתָה
2ms	גָּלִיתָ	נִגְלֵיתָ [נִגְלִיתָ]	גִּלִּיתָה	גֻּלֵּיתָ	הִגְלִיתָ [הִגְלֵיתָ]	הָגְלֵיתָ	הִתְגַּלִּיתָ
2fs	גָּלִית	נִגְלֵית	גִּלִּית	גֻּלֵּית	הִגְלִית [הִגְלֵית]	הָגְלֵית	הִתְגַּלִּית
1cs	גָּלִיתִי	נִגְלֵיתִי	גִּלִּיתִי [גִּלֵּיתִי]	גֻּלֵּיתִי	הִגְלִיתִי [הִגְלֵיתִי]	הָגְלֵיתִי	הִתְגַּלִּיתִי
3cp	גָּלוּ	נִגְלוּ	גִּלּוּ	גֻּלּוּ	הִגְלוּ	הָגְלוּ	הִתְגַּלּוּ
2mp	גְּלִיתֶם	נִגְלֵיתֶם	גִּלִּיתֶם	גֻּלֵּיתֶם	הִגְלִיתֶם	הָגְלֵיתֶם	הִתְגַּלִּיתֶם
2fp	גְּלִיתֶן	נִגְלֵיתֶן	גִּלִּיתֶן	גֻּלֵּיתֶן	הִגְלִיתֶן	הָגְלֵיתֶן	הִתְגַּלִּיתֶן
1cp	גָּלִינוּ	נִגְלֵינוּ	גִּלִּינוּ	גֻּלֵּינוּ	הִגְלִינוּ	הָגְלֵינוּ	הִתְגַּלִּינוּ
Impf. 3ms	יִגְלֶה	יִגָּלֶה	יְגַלֶּה	יְגֻלֶּה	יַגְלֶה	יָגְלֶה	יִתְגַּלֶּה
3fs	תִּגְלֶה	תִּגָּלֶה	תְּגַלֶּה	תְּגֻלֶּה	תַּגְלֶה	תָּגְלֶה	תִּתְגַּלֶּה
2ms	תִּגְלֶה	תִּגָּלֶה	תְּגַלֶּה	תְּגֻלֶּה	תַּגְלֶה	תָּגְלֶה	תִּתְגַּלֶּה
2fs	תִּגְלִי	תִּגָּלִי	תְּגַלִּי	תְּגֻלִּי	תַּגְלִי	תָּגְלִי	תִּתְגַּלִּי
1cs	אֶגְלֶה	אֶגָּלֶה	אֲגַלֶּה	אֲגֻלֶּה	אַגְלֶה	אָגְלֶה	אֶתְגַּלֶּה
3mp	יִגְלוּ	יִגָּלוּ	יְגַלּוּ	יְגֻלּוּ	יַגְלוּ	יָגְלוּ	יִתְגַּלּוּ
3fp	תִּגְלֶינָה	תִּגָּלֶינָה	תְּגַלֶּינָה	תְּגֻלֶּינָה	תַּגְלֶינָה	תָּגְלֶינָה	תִּתְגַּלֶּינָה
2mp	תִּגְלוּ	תִּגָּלוּ	תְּגַלּוּ	תְּגֻלּוּ	תַּגְלוּ	תָּגְלוּ	תִּתְגַּלּוּ
2fp	תִּגְלֶינָה	תִּגָּלֶינָה	תְּגַלֶּינָה	תְּגֻלֶּינָה	תַּגְלֶינָה	תָּגְלֶינָה	תִּתְגַּלֶּינָה
1cp	נִגְלֶה	נִגָּלֶה	נְגַלֶּה	נְגֻלֶּה	נַגְלֶה	נָגְלֶה	נִתְגַּלֶּה

10b. Lamed He Verbs, continued

	Qal	Niphal	Piel	Pual	Hiphil	Hophal	Hithpael
Impf. + *w.c.*	וַיִּ֫גֶל	וַיִּגָּל	וַיְגַל	וַיְגֻלֶּה	וַיֶּ֫גֶל		וַיִּתְגַּל
Coh. 1cs	אֶגְלֶה						אֶתְגָּלֶה
Impv. ms	גְּלֵה	הִגָּלֵה	גַּלֵּה , גַּל		הַגְלֵה		הִתְגַּלֵּה , הִתְגַּל
fs	גְּלִי	הִגָּלִי	גַּלִּי		הַגְלִי		הִתְגַּלִּי
mp	גְּלוּ	הִגָּלוּ	גַּלּוּ		הַגְלוּ		הִתְגַּלּוּ
fp	גְּלֶ֫ינָה	הִגָּלֶ֫ינָה	גַּלֶּ֫ינָה		הַגְלֶ֫ינָה		הִתְגַּלֶּ֫ינָה
Juss. 3ms	יִ֫גֶל	יִגָּל	יְגַל		יֶ֫גֶל		יִתְגַּל
Inf. Abs.	גָּלֹה	נִגְלֹה , הִגָּלֵה	גַּלֹּה , גַּלֵּה		הַגְלֵה	הָגְלֵה	
Inf. Const.	גְּלוֹת	הִגָּלוֹת	גַּלּוֹת	גֻּלּוֹת	הַגְלוֹת		הִתְגַּלּוֹת
Act. Part. ms	גֹּלֶה		מְגַלֶּה		מַגְלֶה		מִתְגַּלֶּה
Pass. Part. ms	גָּלוּי	נִגְלֶה		מְגֻלֶּה		מָגְלֶה	

IIa. Double Ayin Verbs (§73)

	Qal (Active)	Qal (Active)	Qal (Stative)	Niphal	(Piel) Poel	(Pual) Poal	Hiphil	Hophal	(Hithpael) Hithpoel
Perf. 3ms	סָבַב, סַב			נָסַב, נָמֵס	סוֹבֵב	סוֹבַב	הֵסֵב, הֵסַב	הוּסַב	הִתְסוֹבֵב
3fs	סָבְבָה, סַבָּה			נָסַבָּה	סוֹבְבָה	(Same as Poel except in the 3ms)	הֵסַבָּה	הוּסַבָּה	הִתְסוֹבְבָה
2ms	סַבּוֹתָ			נְסַבּוֹתָ	סוֹבַבְתָּ		הֲסִבּוֹתָ	הוּסַבּוֹתָ	הִתְסוֹבַבְתָּ
2fs	סַבּוֹת			נְסַבּוֹת	סוֹבַבְתְּ		הֲסִבּוֹת	הוּסַבּוֹת	הִתְסוֹבַבְתְּ
1cs	סַבּוֹתִי			נְסַבּוֹתִי	סוֹבַבְתִּי		הֲסִבּוֹתִי	הוּסַבּוֹתִי	הִתְסוֹבַבְתִּי
3cp	סָבְבוּ, סַבּוּ			נָסַבּוּ	סוֹבְבוּ		הֵסַבּוּ, הֵסֵבּוּ	הוּסַבּוּ	הִתְסוֹבְבוּ
2mp	סַבּוֹתֶם			נְסַבּוֹתֶם	סוֹבַבְתֶּם		הֲסִבּוֹתֶם	הוּסַבּוֹתֶם	הִתְסוֹבַבְתֶּם
2fp	סַבּוֹתֶן			נְסַבּוֹתֶן	סוֹבַבְתֶּן		הֲסִבּוֹתֶן	הוּסַבּוֹתֶן	הִתְסוֹבַבְתֶּן
1cp	סַבּוֹנוּ			נְסַבּוֹנוּ	סוֹבַבְנוּ		הֲסִבּוֹנוּ	הוּסַבּוֹנוּ	הִתְסוֹבַבְנוּ
Impf. 3ms	יָסֹב	יִסֹּב	יֵקַל	יִסַּב	יְסוֹבֵב	יְסוֹבַב	יָסֵב, יַסֵּב	יוּסַב, יֻסַּב	יִתְסוֹבֵב
3fs	תָּסֹב	תִּסֹּב	תֵּקַל	תִּסַּב	תְּסוֹבֵב	תְּסוֹבַב	תָּסֵב	תּוּסַב	תִּתְסוֹבֵב
2ms	תָּסֹב	תִּסֹּב	תֵּקַל	תִּסַּב	תְּסוֹבֵב	תְּסוֹבַב	תָּסֵב	תּוּסַב	תִּתְסוֹבֵב
2fs	תָּסֹבִּי	תִּסְּבִי	תֵּקַלִּי	תִּסַּבִּי	תְּסוֹבְבִי	תְּסוֹבְבִי	תָּסֵבִּי	תּוּסַבִּי	תִּתְסוֹבְבִי
1cs	אָסֹב	אֶסֹּב	אֵקַל	אֶסַּב	אֲסוֹבֵב	אֲסוֹבַב	אָסֵב	אוּסַב	אֶתְסוֹבֵב
3mp	יָסֹבּוּ	יִסְּבוּ	יֵקַלּוּ	יִסַּבּוּ	יְסוֹבְבוּ	יְסוֹבְבוּ	יָסֵבּוּ, יַסֵּבּוּ	יוּסַבּוּ	יִתְסוֹבְבוּ
3fp	[1]תְּסֻבֶּינָה	תִּסֹּבְנָה	תְּקַלֶּינָה	תִּסַּבֶּינָה	תְּסוֹבֵבְנָה	תְּסוֹבַבְנָה	תְּסִבֶּינָה	תּוּסַבֶּינָה	תִּתְסוֹבֵבְנָה
2mp	תָּסֹבּוּ	תִּסְּבוּ	תֵּקַלּוּ	תִּסַּבּוּ	תְּסוֹבְבוּ	תְּסוֹבְבוּ	תָּסֵבּוּ	תּוּסַבּוּ	תִּתְסוֹבְבוּ
2fp	[1]תְּסֻבֶּינָה	תִּסֹּבְנָה	תְּקַלֶּינָה	תִּסַּבֶּינָה	תְּסוֹבֵבְנָה	תְּסוֹבַבְנָה	תְּסִבֶּינָה	תּוּסַבֶּינָה	תִּתְסוֹבֵבְנָה
1cp	נָסֹב	נִסֹּב	נֵקַל	נִסַּב	נְסוֹבֵב	נְסוֹבַב	נָסֵב	נוּסַב	נִתְסוֹבֵב

[1] Do not confuse with Piel/Poal. The vowel under the prefix has reduced to *shewa*, and the *holem* has reduced to *qibbuts*, because of the length of the verb.

IIb. Double Ayin Verbs, continued

	Qal			Niphal	(Piel) Poel	(Pual) Poal	Hiphil	Hophal	(Hithpael) Hithpoel
	Active		Stative						
Impf. + *w.c.*	וַיָּסָב	וַיִּסֹּב	וַיֵּ֫קַל	וַיִּ֫סַּב	וַיְסוֹבֵב	—	וַיָּ֫סֶב	—	וַיִּתְסֹבֵב
Coh. 1cs	אָסֹ֫בָּה	אֶסְּבָה	—	—	—	—	—	—	—
Impv. ms	סֹב			הִסַּב	סוֹבֵב	—	הָסֵב	—	הִתְסוֹבֵב
fs	סֹ֫בִּי			הִסַּ֫בִּי	סוֹבֲבִי	—	הָסֵ֫בִּי	—	הִתְסוֹבֲבִי
mp	סֹ֫בּוּ			הִסַּ֫בּוּ	סוֹבֲבוּ	—	הָסֵ֫בּוּ	—	הִתְסוֹבֲבוּ
fp	סֻבֶּ֫ינָה			הִסַּבֶּ֫ינָה	סוֹבֵ֫בְנָה	—	הֲסִבֶּ֫ינָה	—	הִתְסוֹבֵ֫בְנָה
Juss. 3ms	Same as Imperfect 3ms								
Inf. Abs.	סָבוֹב		—	הִסּוֹב, הִסֵּב	סוֹבֵב	סוֹבַב	הָסֵב	הוּסַב[1]	הִתְסוֹבֵב
Inf. Const.	סֹב		—	הִסֵּב	סוֹבֵב	—	הָסֵב	הוּסַב[1]	הִתְסוֹבֵב
Act. Part. ms	סוֹבֵב		קַל		מְסוֹבֵב		מֵסֵב		מִתְסוֹבֵב
Pass. Part. ms	סָבוּב			נָסָב		מְסוֹבָב		מוּסָב	

[1] Also הָסַבָּה.

12. Verbs with Double Weaknesses (Summary)

(Verbs and forms which rarely occur are omitted.) (§74, 75)

	Pe Nun & Lamed Guttural				*Pe Nun & Lamed Aleph*[1]			*Pe Nun & Lamed He*			*Pe Yod & Lamed Guttural*		
	Qal	Niph	Piel	Hiph	Qal	Niph	Piel	Qal	Hiph	Hoph	Qal	Niph	Hiph
Perf	נָגַע	נִגַּע	נִגַּע	הִגִּיעַ	נָשָׂא	נִשָּׂא	נִשֵּׂא	נָטָה	הִטָּה	הֻטָּה	יָדַע	נוֹדַע	הוֹדִיעַ
Impf	יִגַּע	יִנָּגַע	יְנַגַּע	יַגִּיעַ	יִשָּׂא	יִנָּשֵׂא	יְנַשֵּׂא	יִטֶּה	יַטֶּה	3mp יֻטּוּ	יֵדַע	יִוָּדַע	יוֹדִיעַ
Impv	גַּע	הִנָּגַע	נַגַּע	הַגַּע	שָׂא	הִנָּשֵׂא		נְטֵה	הַטֵּה		דַּע	הִוָּדַע	הוֹדַע
I.A.	נָגוֹעַ		נַגֵּעַ	הַגֵּעַ	נָשׂוֹא			נָטֹה	הַטֵּה		יָדוֹעַ, יָדֹעַ		הוֹדֵעַ
I.C.	גַּעַת, נְגֹעַ		נַגַּע	הַגִּיעַ	שְׂאֵת	הִנָּשֵׂא		נְטוֹת, נְטֹת	הַטּוֹת		דַּעַת	הִוָּדַע	הוֹדִיעַ
Part.	נֹגֵעַ		מְנַגֵּעַ	מַגִּיעַ	נֹשֵׂא			נֹטֶה	מַטֶּה	מֻטֶּה	Act. י[וֹ]דֵעַ Pass. יָדוּעַ	נוֹדָע	מוֹדִיעַ

	Pe Guttural & *Lamed He*			רָאָה			*Pe Yod* (original *Pe Vav*) & *Lamed Aleph*				*Pe Yod & Lamed He*		*Ayin Vav & Lamed Aleph*	
	Qal	Niph	Hiph	Qal	Niph	Hiph	Qal	Niph	Qal	Hiph	Qal	Hiph	Qal	Hiph
Perf	עָלָה	נַעֲלָה	הֶעֱלָה	רָאָה	נִרְאָה	הֶרְאָה	יָרֵא		יָצָא	הוֹצִיא	יָרָה	(1cs) הוֹרֵיתִי	[2]בָּא	הֵבִיא
Impf	יַעֲלֶה	יֵעָלֶה	יַעֲלֶה	יִרְאֶה	יֵרָאֶה	יַרְאֶה	יִירָא	(1cs) תִּוָּרֵא	יֵצֵא	יוֹצִיא		יוֹרֶה	יָב[וֹ]א	יָבִ[י]א
Impv	עֲלֵה	הֵעָלֵה	הַעַל	רְאֵה	הֵרָאֵה		יְרָא		צֵא	הוֹצֵא	יְרֵה	הוֹרֵה	בּ[וֹ]א	הָבֵ[י]א
I.A.	עָלֹה	נַעֲלֹה	הַעֲלֵה	רָא[וֹ]ה	הֵרָאֹה				יָצוֹא	הוֹצֵא			בּ[וֹ]א	הָבֵא
I.C.	עֲל[וֹ]ת	הֵעָלוֹת	הַעֲלוֹת	רְא[וֹ]ת	הֵרָאוֹת	הַרְאוֹת	יִרְאָה		צֵאת	הוֹצִיא	יְרוֹת	הוֹרוֹת	בּ[וֹ]א	הָבִיא
Part	עֹלֶה	נַעֲלֶה	מַעֲלֶה	רֹאֶה	נִרְאֶה נִרְאָה	מַרְאֶה	יָרֵא	נוֹרָא	י[וֹ]צֵא	מוֹצִ[י]א	יֹרֶה	מוֹרֶה	[2]בָּא	מֵבִיא

[1] נָשָׂא only. Other *Pe Nun* and *Lamed Aleph* verbs seldom occur.

[2] See §75.4 concerning the important accent pattern in the Perf 3fs and Part fs.

13. The Verb הָיָה

	Perf	Impf	Impf + w.c.	
3ms	הָיָה	יִהְיֶה	וַיְהִי	3ms
3fs	הָיְתָה	תִּהְיֶה	וַתְּהִי	3fs
2ms	הָיִיתָ	תִּהְיֶה	וַתְּהִי	2ms
2fs	הָיִית	תִּהְיִי[1]	וַתְּהִי[2]	2fs
1cs	הָיִיתִי	אֶהְיֶה	וָאֱהִי[3]	1cs
3cp	הָיוּ	יִהְיוּ	וַיִּהְיוּ	3mp
		תִּהְיֶינָה	וַתִּהְיֶינָה	3fp
2mp	הֱיִיתֶם	תִּהְיוּ	וַתִּהְיוּ	2mp
2fp	—	תִּהְיֶינָה	—	2fp
1cp	הָיִינוּ	נִהְיֶה	וַנְּהִי	1cp

Note on the verb הָיָה: Be sure to learn well the verb forms which have a white background. Verb forms with shaded background occur in scripture less than 50 times each.

14. Segholate Nouns with Possessive Suffixes

	Singular nouns			Plural nouns		
Absolute:	מֶ֫לֶךְ	סֵ֫פֶר	קֹ֫דֶשׁ	מְלָכִים	סְפָרִים	קֳדָשִׁים
Construct:	מֶ֫לֶךְ	סֵ֫פֶר	קֹ֫דֶשׁ	מַלְכֵי	סִפְרֵי	קָדְשֵׁי
1cs (my)	מַלְכִּי	סִפְרִי	קָדְשִׁי	מְלָכַי	סְפָרַי	קֳדָשַׁי
2ms (your)	מַלְכְּךָ	סִפְרְךָ	קָדְשְׁךָ	מְלָכֶיךָ	סְפָרֶיךָ	קֳדָשֶׁיךָ
2fs (your)	מַלְכֵּךְ	סִפְרֵךְ	קָדְשֵׁךְ	מְלָכַ֫יִךְ	סְפָרַ֫יִךְ	קֳדָשַׁ֫יִךְ
3ms (his)	מַלְכּוֹ	סִפְרוֹ	קָדְשׁוֹ	מְלָכָיו	סְפָרָיו	קֳדָשָׁיו
3fs (her)	מַלְכָּהּ	סִפְרָהּ	קָדְשָׁהּ	מְלָכֶיהָ	סְפָרֶיהָ	קֳדָשֶׁיהָ
1cp (our)	מַלְכֵּ֫נוּ	סִפְרֵ֫נוּ	קָדְשֵׁ֫נוּ	מְלָכֵ֫ינוּ	סְפָרֵ֫ינוּ	קֳדָשֵׁ֫ינוּ
2mp (your)	מַלְכְּכֶם	סִפְרְכֶם	קָדְשְׁכֶם	מַלְכֵיכֶם	סִפְרֵיכֶם	קָדְשֵׁיכֶם
2fp (your)	מַלְכְּכֶן	סִפְרְכֶן	קָדְשְׁכֶן	מַלְכֵיכֶן	סִפְרֵיכֶן	קָדְשֵׁיכֶן
3mp (their)	מַלְכָּם	סִפְרָם	קָדְשָׁם	מַלְכֵיהֶם	סִפְרֵיהֶם	קָדְשֵׁיהֶם
3fp (their)	מַלְכָּן	סִפְרָן	קָדְשָׁן	מַלְכֵיהֶן	סִפְרֵיהֶן	קָדְשֵׁיהֶן

[1] Twice. Also תִּהְיִי once. [2] Once. Also וַתְּהִיִי once. [3] Also וָאֶהְיֶה.

15. Nouns with Suffixes (§23, 34)

Singular Masculine Nouns with Possessive Suffixes					Singular Feminine Nouns with Possessive Suffixes			
Absolute	סוּס	נָבִיא	דָּבָר	ר֫וּחַ	תּוֹרָה	שָׁנָה	בְּרָכָה	Absolute
Construct	סוּס	נְבִיא	דְּבַר	רוּחַ	תּוֹרַת	שְׁנַת	בִּרְכַּת	Construct
Suffix: 3ms	סוּסוֹ	נְבִיאוֹ	דְּבָרוֹ	רוּחוֹ	תּוֹרָתוֹ	שְׁנָתוֹ	בִּרְכָתוֹ	3ms Suffix
3fs	סוּסָהּ	נְבִיאָהּ	דְּבָרָהּ	רוּחָהּ	תּוֹרָתָהּ	שְׁנָתָהּ	בִּרְכָתָהּ	3fs
2ms	סוּסְךָ	נְבִיאֲךָ	דְּבָרְךָ	רוּחֲךָ	תּוֹרָתְךָ	שְׁנָתְךָ	בִּרְכָתְךָ	2ms
2fs	סוּסֵךְ	נְבִיאֵךְ	דְּבָרֵךְ	רוּחֵךְ	תּוֹרָתֵךְ	שְׁנָתֵךְ	בִּרְכָתֵךְ	2fs
1cs	סוּסִי	נְבִיאִי	דְּבָרִי	רוּחִי	תּוֹרָתִי	שְׁנָתִי	בִּרְכָתִי	1cs
3mp	סוּסָם	נְבִיאָם	דְּבָרָם	רוּחָם	תּוֹרָתָם	שְׁנָתָם	בִּרְכָתָם	3mp
3fp	סוּסָן	נְבִיאָן	דְּבָרָן	רוּחָן	תּוֹרָתָן	שְׁנָתָן	בִּרְכָתָן	3fp
2mp	סוּסְכֶם	נְבִיאֲכֶם	דְּבַרְכֶם	רוּחֲכֶם	תּוֹרַתְכֶם	שְׁנַתְכֶם	בִּרְכַּתְכֶם	2mp
2fp	סוּסְכֶן	נְבִיאֲכֶן	דְּבַרְכֶן	רוּחֲכֶן	תּוֹרַתְכֶן	שְׁנַתְכֶן	בִּרְכַּתְכֶן	2fp
1cp	סוּסֵ֫נוּ	נְבִיאֵ֫נוּ	דְּבָרֵ֫נוּ	רוּחֵ֫נוּ	תּוֹרָתֵ֫נוּ	שְׁנָתֵ֫נוּ	בִּרְכָתֵ֫נוּ	1cp

Plural Masculine Nouns with Possessive Suffixes					Plural Feminine Nouns with Possessive Suffixes			
Absolute	סוּסִים	נְבִיאִים	דְּבָרִים	—	תּוֹרוֹת	שָׁנוֹת	בְּרָכוֹת	Absolute
Construct	סוּסֵי	נְבִיאֵי	דִּבְרֵי	—	תּוֹרוֹת	שְׁנוֹת	בִּרְכוֹת	Construct
Suffix: 3ms	סוּסָיו	נְבִיאָיו	דְּבָרָיו	—	תּוֹרוֹתָיו	שְׁנוֹתָיו	בִּרְכוֹתָיו	3ms suffix
3fs	סוּסֶ֫יהָ	נְבִיאֶ֫יהָ	דְּבָרֶ֫יהָ	—	תּוֹרוֹתֶ֫יהָ	שְׁנוֹתֶ֫יהָ	בִּרְכוֹתֶ֫יהָ	3fs
2ms	סוּסֶ֫יךָ	נְבִיאֶ֫יךָ	דְּבָרֶ֫יךָ	—	תּוֹרוֹתֶ֫יךָ	שְׁנוֹתֶ֫יךָ	בִּרְכוֹתֶ֫יךָ	2ms
2fs	סוּסַ֫יִךְ	נְבִיאַ֫יִךְ	דְּבָרַ֫יִךְ	—	תּוֹרוֹתַ֫יִךְ	שְׁנוֹתַ֫יִךְ	בִּרְכוֹתַ֫יִךְ	2fs
1cs	סוּסַי	נְבִיאַי	דְּבָרַי	—	תּוֹרוֹתַי	שְׁנוֹתַי	בִּרְכוֹתַי	1cs
3mp	סוּסֵיהֶם	נְבִיאֵיהֶם	דִּבְרֵיהֶם	—	תּוֹרוֹתֵיהֶם	שְׁנוֹתֵיהֶם	בִּרְכוֹתֵיהֶם	3mp
3fp	סוּסֵיהֶן	נְבִיאֵיהֶן	דִּבְרֵיהֶן	—	תּוֹרוֹתֵיהֶן	שְׁנוֹתֵיהֶן	בִּרְכוֹתֵיהֶן	3fp
2mp	סוּסֵיכֶם	נְבִיאֵיכֶם	דִּבְרֵיכֶם	—	תּוֹרוֹתֵיכֶם	שְׁנוֹתֵיכֶם	בִּרְכוֹתֵיכֶם	2mp
2fp	סוּסֵיכֶן	נְבִיאֵיכֶן	דִּבְרֵיכֶן	—	תּוֹרוֹתֵיכֶן	שְׁנוֹתֵיכֶן	בִּרְכוֹתֵיכֶן	2fp
1cp	סוּסֵ֫ינוּ	נְבִיאֵ֫ינוּ	דְּבָרֵ֫ינוּ	—	תּוֹרוֹתֵ֫ינוּ	שְׁנוֹתֵ֫ינוּ	בִּרְכוֹתֵ֫ינוּ	1cp

Lexicon (Dictionary)

NOUNS are masculine unless marked *f.* (feminine). If no construct (*cs.*) is given, it may be assumed that the construct form is the same as the absolute (*abs.*). In cases where this is unclear, *cs.*= will mean that the construct is the same as the absolute.

VERBS are first listed according to their ***Qal*** form (אָבַד). If a verb has no ***Qal*** form, its root will be shown without vowel points (בדל ***Ni*** to separate oneself ....). If an example is not given in the 3ms, it means that the 3ms is not found in the Bible.

Form abbreviations: *Ni* Niphal, ***Pi*** Piel, ***Pu*** Pual, ***Hi*** Hiphil, ***Ho*** Hophal, ***Hitp*** Hithpael.

Other abbreviations:

2x	form or word occurs only twice in scripture
=	"the same." For instance, *cs*= means "the construct is the same (as the absolute)."
√	root (base form of word)
<יְהִי>	shortened form of Imperfect
⟨י⟩	the letter (in this case, י) is sometimes missing in the word
&	and
act.	active
adj.	adjective
adv.	adverb
c.	common (that is, it can be *m.* or *f.*)
cf.	compare (to)
Coh.	cohortative
conj.	conjunction
d.a.	definite article
du.	dual
IA	Infinitive Absolute
IC	Infinitive Construct
Impf.	Imperfect
Impv.	Imperative
intr.	intransitive
Jus	Jussive
lit.	literally
obj	object
pass.	passive
Pt.	Participle
Perf.	Perfect
pl.	plural
prep.	preposition
insep. prep.	inseparable preposition
s.	singular
s.o.	someone
s.t.	something
subj.	subject
suff.	suffix
tr.	transitive
w.c.	vav consecutive

***Holem vav*:** words with *holem vav* (וֹ) often appear in the OT with just *holem*. For instance, the word גָּדוֹל is also found in scripture as גָּדֹל.

{ } at the end of an entry indicates the number of the exercise in which the word is introduced.

אאא

אָב *m.* father, *cs.* אֲבִי; *pl.* אָבוֹת, *cs.* אֲבוֹת {24}, *p. 112*

אָבַד ***Qal*** to become lost, to die (people) or be ruined (things); *Impf.* יֹאבַד. ***Pi*** אִבַּד to allow to be destroyed, to destroy completely. ***Hi*** הֶאֱבִיד to destroy completely {37}

אָבָה to be willing; *Impf.* יֹאבֶה

אֶבֶן *f.* a stone, stones; *pl.* אֲבָנִים, *cs.* אַבְנֵי {19}

אַבְרָהָם Abraham {11}

אַבְרָם Abram (Abraham's name before Gen 17:5) (see footnote in {16})

אֱדוֹם Edom

אָדוֹן lord, master, *cs.* אֲדוֹן; *pl.* אֲדֹנִים, *cs.* אֲדֹנֵי, *with 1cs suff.* אֲדֹנַי & אֲדֹנָי my lords. *But note that* אֲדֹנָי *is often used as substitute for the divine name* יהוה (LORD) *and is then translated* the Lord; *note also the phrase* אֲדֹנָי יְהוִה *which is translated* the Lord GOD (*not* the LORD GOD), *with* GOD *representing the word* יְהוִה) {39}

אָדָם man, humanity; Adam {14}

אֲדָמָה *f.* ground, soil, *cs.* אַדְמַת, *with d.a.* הָאֲדָמָה; *pl.* אֲדָמוֹת {14}

אָהַב to love, *Impf.* יֶאֱהַב, *Impv.* אֱהַב, *IC w lamed* לְאַהֲבָה {42}

אֹהֶל tent; *pl.* אֹהָלִים, *cs.* אָהֳלֵי {41}

אַהֲרֹן Aaron {13}

אוֹ or {37}

אוֹי Woe! Alas! (A cry of sorrow or warning) {25}

אוּלַי perhaps, suppose

אוֹר light, brightness; pl. אוֹרִים {14}

אֹת, אוֹת sign, mark, *pl.* אֹתוֹת

אָז then {48}

אֹ֫זֶן *f.* ear; *du.* אָזְנַ֫יִם, *cs.* אָזְנֵי {25}

אָח brother, blood relative, *cs.* אֲחִי; *pl.* אַחִים, *cs.* אֲחֵי {25}, *p. 112*

אֶחָד, אחד *adj. m.* one, *cs.* אַחַד; *f.* אַחַת, *cs.*= {20} *See also p. 172.*

אָחוֹת *f.* sister, *cs.* אֲחוֹת; *pl. found only in cs. form with suffixes* (*see p. 112*) {26}

אַחֲרֵי, אַחַר *prep.* after, behind, afterwards {20}

אַחֵר (an)other, different, *pl.* אֲחֵרִים; *f.* אַחֶ֫רֶת, *pl.* אֲחֵרוֹת {25}

אַיֵּה, אֵי Where? {22}

אֹיֵב enemy; *pl.* אֹיְבִים, *cs.* אֹיְבֵי {23}

אַ֫יִל male sheep (ram), *cs.* אֵיל; *pl.* אֵילִים, אֵלִים (cf. *pl.* of אֵל), *cs.* אֵילֵי, אֵלֵי {43}

אַ֫יִן there is not, *cs.* אֵין {25}

אִישׁ a man, husband; *pl.* אֲנָשִׁים, *cs.* אַנְשֵׁי {10}{15}, *p. 112*

אָכַל to eat; *Impf.* יֹאכַל (*but note 1cs* אֹכַל) {15}

אַל not, do not {32}

אֵל God, a god; *pl.* אֵלִים {10}

אֶל *prep.* to, toward {10}

אֵ֫לֶּה these (*c.pl.*) {26}

אֱלֹהִים *pl.* God, gods, *cs.* אֱלֹהֵי {12}

אֵלִיָּ֫הוּ Elijah

אֶ֫לֶף one thousand {38}

אַלְפַּ֫יִם two thousand {38}

אֵם *f.* mother; *pl.* אִמּוֹת {26}, *p. 112*

אִם if {16}

אָמָה *f.* female slave, *pl.* אֲמָהוֹת {38}

אַמָּה *f.* cubit (~50 cm), *pl.* אַמּוֹת, *du.* אַמָּתַ֫יִם {38}

אמן ***Ni*** נֶאֱמַן to be faithful, reliable, *Impf.* יֵאָמֵן; ***Hi*** הֶאֱמִין to believe, think, *Impf.* יַאֲמִין

אָמַר to say; *Impf.* יֹאמַר (*often with w.c.*: וַיֹּ֫אמֶר) {12}

אֱמֶת truth, faithfulness, reliability; *cs. found only with suffixes; no pl.* {33}

אֱנוֹשׁ man, men, people; *no pl.*

אֲנַ֫חְנוּ we (*subj.*) {22}

אֲנִי, אָנֹכִי I (*subj.*); *pause:* אָנִי, אָנֹכִי {12}

אֲנָשִׁים *see* אִישׁ

אָסַף ***Qal*** to gather, take away, *Impf.* יֶאֱסֹף; ***Ni*** נֶאֱסַף to be gathered, *Impf.* יֵאָסֵף {42}

אַף **(I)** anger, nose (*see p. 227, footnote 1*) **(II)** also, indeed {45}

אָפָה to bake

אֶ֫פֶס none, nothing, lack; end

אֵ֫צֶל beside, near

אַרְבַּע *see* אַרְבָּעָה

אַרְבָּעָה *m.* four, *cs.* אַרְבַּ֫עַת; *f.* אַרְבַּע, *cs.*= {38}

אַרְבָּעִים forty {38}

אֲרוֹן ark (*usually* of the covenant) (*with definite article*: הָאָרוֹן), *cs.*= {13}

אֲרִי lion, *pl.* אֲרָיוֹת

אֶ֫רֶץ *f.* land, earth (world) (*with d.a.* הָאָ֫רֶץ); *pl.* אֲרָצוֹת, *cs.* אַרְצוֹת. *See p. 50 footnote 10.* {13}

אָרַר to curse *Perf. 1cs* אָרוֹתִי; *Impf.* אָאֹר, תָּאוֹר; *Pass.Pt.* אָרוּר

אֵשׁ *f.* fire {20}

אִשָּׁה *f.* woman, wife, female, *cs.* אֵשֶׁת; *pl.* נָשִׁים, *cs.* נְשֵׁי {10}{15}, *p. 112*

אֲשֶׁר that, which, who {14}

אַתְּ you (*f.s., subj.*) {22}

אֵת, אֶת־ (1) with {24} (2) *sign of the definite direct obj.* {26}

אַתָּה you (*m.s., subj.*) {22}

אֹתָהּ her (*f.s. obj.*) {22}

אֶתְהֶם them (*m.p. obj.*) {22}

אֶתְהֶן them (*f.p. obj.*) {22}

אֹתוֹ him (*m.s. obj.*) {22}

אָתוֹן *f.* female donkey, *pl.* אֲתֹנוֹת {39}

אֹתִי me (*c.s., obj.*) {22}

אֹתְךָ you (*m.s., obj.*) {22}

אֹתָךְ you (*f.s., obj.*) {22}

אֶתְכֶם you (*m.p., obj.*) {22}

אֶתְכֶן you (*f.p., obj.*) {22}

אַתֶּם you (*m.p., subj.*) {22}

אֹתָם them (*m.p., obj.*) {22}

אֹתָן them (*f.p., obj.*) {22}

אַתֶּן you (*f.p., subj.*) {22}

אֹתָ֫נוּ us (*c.p., obj.*) {22}

בבב

-בְּ *insep. prep.* in, at, with, by {11}

בָּבֶל Babylon

בֶּ֫גֶד clothes, piece of clothing; *pl.* בְּגָדִים, *cs.* בִּגְדֵי {43}

בדל ***Ni*** נִבְדַּל to separate oneself, be excluded; *Impf.* יִבָּדֵל ***Hi*** הִבְדִּיל to set apart, separate, distinguish between; *Impf* יַבְדִּיל {33}

בְּהֵמָה *f.* (wild) animal, beast; cattle, *cs.* בֶּהֱמַת; *pl.* בְּהֵמוֹת, *cs.* בַּהֲמוֹת {43}

בוא ***Qal*** to enter, come, go; *Perf.* בָּא, *Impf.* יָבֹא, *Impv.* בֹּא; ***Hi*** הֵבִיא to bring, *Impf.* יָבִ[י]א {13}, *pp. 242, 284*

בּוֹר *m.* pit, cistern, underground prison cell; *pl.* בּוֹרוֹת {37}

בּוֹשׁ ***Qal*** to be ashamed; *Impf.* יֵבוֹשׁ, ***Hi*** הֵבִישׁ *and* הוֹבִישׁ to shame, behave shamefully, *Impf. 2mp* תָּבִישׁוּ {44}. *See p. 274.*

בָּזַז to loot, plunder, *Impf.* תָּבֹז (2ms)

בָּחַר to choose; *Impf.* יִבְחַר {25}, *p. 272*

בָּטַח ***Qal*** to trust, be confident, *Impf.* יִבְטַח, -בָּטַח בְּ *or* בָּטַח עַל to trust in; ***Hi*** הִבְטַ֫חְתָּ (2ms only) to cause s.o. to trust, *Impf.* יַבְטַח {29}

בֶּ֫טֶן belly, womb, *in pause* בָּטֶן {40}

בֵּין *prep.* between (בֵּין אִישׁ וּבֵין אִשָּׁה, between a man and a woman) {16}

בִּין ***Qal*** to understand, consider; *Impf.* יָבִין, יָבֵן (=***Hi***), וַיָּ֫בֶן(=***Hi***) ; ***Ni*** נְבֻנוֹתִי (1cs) to be perceptive, observant, *no Impf*; ***Hi*** הֵבִין to understand, pay attention; *Impf.* יָבִין (=***Qal***), וַיָּ֫בֶן(=***Qal***); ***Hitp*** הִתְבּוֹנֵן to be attentive, give attention to, יִתְבּוֹנָן {44}

בַּ֫יִת a house, family, *cs.* בֵּית; *pl.* בָּתִּים, *cs.* בָּתֵּי {10}, *p. 117*

בָּכָה to weep; *Impf.* וַיֵּבְךְּ, תִּבְכֶּה

בְּכוֹר first-born (both people & animals); *pl. cs.* בְּכוֹרֵי; *f.pl.cs.* בְּכוֹרוֹת {22}

בְּלִי without; no, no one, nothing; מִבְּלִי because {37}

בִּלְתִּי non-existence, not; לְבִלְתִּי *plus IC*: so as not (to) {39}

בָּמָה *f.* high place (that is, place of pagan worship), *pl.* בָּמוֹת

בֵּן son, *cs.* -בֶּן; *pl.* בָּנִים, *cs.* בְּנֵי {15}, *p. 112*

בָּנָה ***Qal*** to build, *Impf.* יִבְנֶה; ***Ni*** נִבְנָה, *Impf.* יִבָּנֶה to be built {46}

בַּעֲבוּר *prep.* for the sake of, so that, in order to, because of; *also* לְבַעֲבוּר {39}

בַּ֫עַד *prep.* behind, through, around, for

בַּ֫עַל owner, lord, master, husband; Baal; *pl.* בְּעָלִים {48}

בער ***Qal*** to burn *Perf.* בָּעֲרָה, בָּעֲרוּ, *Impf.* יִבְעַר; ***Pi*** בִּעֵר I. to start a fire, to burn down; II. to graze (a field), *Impf.* יְבַעֵר; *p. 272*

בָּקָר cows, (herd of) cattle, oxen, *cs.* בְּקַר {19}

בֹּ֫קֶר morning; *pl.* בְּקָרִים {19}

בְּקֶ֫רֶב *see* קֶ֫רֶב

בקשׁ ***Pi*** בִּקֵּשׁ to seek, look for; *Impf.* יְבַקֵּשׁ {31}

בָּרָא to create (*subj. almost always God*); *Impf.* יִבְרָא {11}

בָּרַח to run away, *Impf.* יִבְרַח

בְּרִית *f.* covenant, *cs.*= {16}

ברך ***Qal*** *pass. Pt.* בָּרוּךְ to be blessed; ***Pi*** בֵּרַךְ (בֵּרֵךְ 2x) to bless, *Impf.* יְבָרֵךְ; ***Pu*** *Impf.* יְבֹרַךְ, *Pt.* מְבֹרָךְ; ***Hitp*** הִתְבָּרֵךְ, *Impf.* יִתְבָּרֵךְ, *Pt.*

מִתְבָּרֵךְ {31}

בְּרָכָה *f.* blessing, *cs.* בִּרְכָּה; *pl.* בְּרָכוֹת, *cs.* בִּרְכוֹת {10}

בָּשָׂר flesh, meat; humanity {34}

בַּת *f.* daughter; *pl.* בָּנוֹת, *cs.* בְּנוֹת {26}, *p. 112*

בְּתוֹךְ see תָּוֶךְ

גגג

גָּאַל to buy back, redeem, rescue, *Impf.* יִגְאַל; *Pt.* גֹּאֵל *often* a male relative who has the duty to rescue one who has fallen into slavery or debt, provide a descendant for a widowed relative, or avenge a murder.

גָּבַהּ to be high, to be too proud, *Impf.* יִגְבַּהּ. *Note: mappiq will not appear when* ה *is not at end of the word:* גָּבְהוּ, גָּבַהְתָּ, etc.

גְּבוּל boundary, border, territory; *pl.* גְּבוּלֶיךָ & גְּבוּלָיִךְ *only* {37}

גִּבּוֹר mighty man, hero (in battle), warrior; *pl.* גִּבּוֹרִים {37}

גָּדוֹל *adj.* great, *cs.* גְּדוֹל *or* גְּדָל־; *pl.* גְּדוֹלִים, *cs.* גְּדֹלֵי; *f.* גְּדוֹלָה, *pl.* גְּדוֹלוֹת {18}

גָּדַל, גָּדֵל ***Qal*** to grow up; to be(come) great, wealthy, important, *Impf.* יִגְדַּל; ***Pi*** גִּדַּל to raise (a child), make great, honor; *Impf.* יְגַדֵּל; ***Hi*** הִגְדִּיל to make s.o. great; *Impf.* יַגְדִּיל {28}

גּוֹי nation; *pl.* גּוֹיִם nations, Gentiles, *cs.* גּוֹיֵי {25}

גוּר to live or travel in a foreign land, to seek shelter as a refugee *Perf.* גָּר, *Impf.* יָגוּר

גָּלָה ***Qal*** to uncover; to go away (into exile); *Impf.* יִגְלֶה; ***Ni*** נִגְלָה to be uncovered, exposed, revealed, *Impf.* יִגָּלֶה; ***Pi*** גִּלָּה to uncover, reveal, יְגַלֶּה; ***Hi*** הִגְלָה to take into exile, *Impf.* וַיֶּגֶל {46}, *p. 280*

גִּלְעָד Gilead

גַּם also, even, indeed {17}

גָּמָל camel, *pl.* גְּמַלִּים {39}

גַּן *m.* (occasionally *f.*) garden; *in pause* גָּן; *with d.a.* הַגָּן {11}

גָּנַב to steal, rob {21}

גֵּר foreign resident, refugee (√ גּוּר)

דדד

דִּבֵּר ***Pi*** דִּבֶּר to speak (to), talk (with, about); *Impf.* יְדַבֵּר {15} {31}

דָּבָר word, affair, thing, *cs.* דְּבַר; *pl.* דְּבָרִים, *cs.* דִּבְרֵי {17}

דָּוִד David {21}

דּוֹר *m.* generation; *pl.* דּוֹרוֹת {37}

דֶּלֶת *f.* door; *pl.* דְּלָתוֹת, *cs.* דַּלְתוֹת; *du.* דְּלָתַיִם, *cs.* דַּלְתֵי

דָּם blood; *pl.* דָּמִים = killing, murder, bloodshed {21}

דַּעַת *f.* knowledge (*IC* of יָדַע) (no *pl.*) {18}

דֶּרֶךְ way, path, behavior; *pl.* דְּרָכִים, *cs.* דַּרְכֵי {25}

דָּרַשׁ ***Qal*** seek, ask, demand, *Impf.* יִדְרֹשׁ; ***Ni*** *Perf. 1cs* נִדְרַשְׁתִּי to be sought, *Impf. 1cs* אִדָּרֵשׁ {47}

ההה

-הַ· the (definite article) {12}

-הֲ interrogative particle (Hebrew question mark). Found only at the beginning of the first word of a question. הֲיָדַע הַמֶּלֶךְ Did the king know? {12}

הֶבֶל Abel (son of Adam and Eve) {22}

הָגָר Hagar {16}

הוּא he, it {14}; that (*m.*) {22}{26}

הוֹי Woe! Alas! (A cry of sorrow or warning) {25}

הִיא she, it; that (*f.*) {22} {26}

הָיָה to be, become, happen; *Impf.* יִהְיֶה often with *w.c.*: וַיְהִי < יְהִי < יִהְיֶה (*short form of Impf*) {12}

הֵיכָל *m.* temple, palace, *cs.* הֵיכַל; *pl.* הֵיכָלוֹת {17}

הָלַךְ ***Qal*** to go, walk, *Impf.* (√ילך) יֵלֵךְ, וַיֵּלֶךְ, *Impv.* לֵךְ; ***Pi*** *1cp* הִלַּכְתִּי to go, walk around,

Impf. יְהַלֵּךְ; ***Hi*** (√ילך) הוֹלִיךְ to bring, take, *Impf.* יוֹלִיךְ; ***Hitp*** הִתְהַלֵּךְ to walk around, *Impf.* יִתְהַלֵּךְ {11, 48}

הלל ***Pi*** הִלֵּל to praise, *Impf.* יְהַלֵּל (*usually no dagesh*); ***Pu*** הֻלַּל to be praised, *Impf.* יְהֻלַּל; ***Hitp*** (*no Perf.*) *Impf.* יִתְהַלֵּל to boast, to be praised {32}

הֵם, הֵמָּה they (*m.*) {22}; those (*m.*) {26}

הֵן, הֵנָּה they (*f.*) {22}; those (*f.*) {26}

הִנֵּה, הֵן look, behold (emphasizes importance of the words which come next) {16}

הָפַךְ ***Qal*** turn, overthrow (destroy), change, *Impf.* יַהֲפֹךְ; ***Ni*** נֶהְפַּךְ be turned, be overthrown, *Impf.* יֵהָפֵךְ

הַר mountain (*with d.a.* הָהָר); *pl.* הָרִים (*with d.a.* הֶהָרִים), *cs.* הַרְרֵי & הָרֵי {19}

הָרַג to kill, murder; *Impf.* יַהֲרֹג {22}

וו

וְ- *conj.* and, but {11}

זזז

זֹאת this (*f.*) {26}

זָבַח to sacrifice, slaughter, *Impf.* יִזְבַּח; ***Pi*** זִבַּח to offer (a sacrifice), *Impf.* יְזַבֵּחַ {45}

זֶבַח a sacrifice, *pl.* זְבָחִים {45}

זֶה this (*m.*) {26}

זָהָב gold {30}

זָכַר ***Qal*** to remember, *Impf.* יִזְכֹּר; ***Hi*** הִזְכִּיר to mention, make known, *Impf.* יַזְכִּיר {16}

זָכָר a man, a male animal, *pl.* זְכָרִים

זָקֵן **(I)** *verb* to be old, *Impf.* יִזְקַן {28}; **(II)** *noun* an elder (see *adj.* for other forms) {19}; **(III)** *adj.* old, *cs.* זְקֵן; *pl.* זְקֵנִים, *cs.* זִקְנֵי {19}

זֶרַע seed, descendant(s), *cs.* זֶרַע & זְרַע; *pl.* (+*suff.*) זַרְעֵיכֶם (1x) {16}

חחח

חבא ***Ni*** נֶחְבָּא to hide, be hidden, *Impf. 2ms* תֵּחָבֵא; ***Hi*** *Perf. 3fs* הֶחְבִּיאָה to hide s.o. or s.t., to keep s.o. or s.t. hidden, *Impf. 3fs+w.c.* וַתַּחְבִּא

חַג (*also* חָג) festival, pilgrimage celebration

חגג *Perf. 2mp* חַגֹּתֶם to celebrate a pilgrimage festival, *Impf. 2ms* תָּחֹג

חָדָשׁ *adj.* new, fresh {38}

חֹדֶשׁ month, new moon; *pl.* חֳדָשִׁים {38}

חוֹמָה *f.* wall (around city or building), *cs.* חוֹמַת; *pl.* חוֹמוֹת, *cs.=* {37}

חוּץ outside, street; מִחוּץ לַבַּיִת outside the house {45}

חָזַק ***Qal*** to be or become strong, have courage; *Impf.* יֶחֱזַק; ***Pi*** חִזַּק to make strong, strengthen; *Impf.* יְחַזֵּק; ***Hi*** הֶחֱזִיק to seize, take hold of; *Impf.* יַחֲזִיק {33}, *p. 271*

חָזָק *adj.* strong; *f.* חֲזָקָה {41}

חָטָא to sin, to miss (a goal); *Impf.* יֶחֱטָא {33}

חֵטְא sin, fault; *pl.* חֲטָאִים, *cs.* חֲטָאֵי {33}

חַטָּאת *f.* sin, fault, *cs.* חַטַּאת; *pl.* חַטָּאוֹת, *cs.* חַטֹּאת {33}

חָיָה ***Qal*** to live (*Perf.* 3ms often חַי), *Impf.* יִחְיֶה; ***Pi*** חִיָּה to preserve, keep alive, *Impf.* יְחַיֶּה; ***Hi*** הֶחֱיָה to preserve, keep alive, *no Impf.* {46}

חַיִּים life (*pl.*) (*s.* חַי *is less common, and is used in oaths*) {34}

חַיָּה wild animal, beast, *cs.* חַיַּת; *pl.* חַיּוֹת

חַיִל army, power, wealth {42}

חָכַם to be or become wise, *Impf.* יֶחְכַּם, *Impv.* חֲכַם

חָכָם *adj.* wise, *cs.* חֲכַם; *pl.* חֲכָמִים; *cs.* חַכְמֵי; *f.* חֲכָמָה, *cs.* חַכְמַת; *pl.* חֲכָמוֹת, *cs.* חַכְמוֹת {18}

חָכְמָה *f.* wisdom, *cs.* חָכְמַת; (no *pl.*) {18}

חֲלוֹם *m.* a dream, *cs.=*; *pl.* חֲלוֹמוֹת {21}

חלל **(I)** ***Ni*** נִחַל to be profaned (i.e., to be used in a common or otherwise improper way), *Impf.* יֵחַ֫ל (1x); ***Pi*** חִלֵּל to profane or defile s.t., *Impf.* יְחַלֵּל

(II) ***Hi*** הֵחֵל to begin, *Impf.* יָחֵל {46}

חָלַם to dream; *Impf.* יַחֲלֹם {21}

חֵמָה *f.* anger, wrath (usually God's), *cs.* חֲמַת; *pl.* חֵמוֹת

חֲמוֹר male donkey, *cs.* חֲמֹר; *pl.* חֲמוֹרִים {39}

חֲמִישִׁי *m.* fifth; *f.* חֲמִישִׁית {38}

חָמֵשׁ *see* חֲמִשָּׁה

חֲמִשָּׁה *m.* five, *cs.* חֲמֵשֶׁת; *f.* חָמֵשׁ, *cs.* חֲמֵשׁ {38}

חֲמִשִּׁים fifty {38}

חֵן favor, attractiveness (√ חנן) {23}

חָנָה to camp, to set up a (military) camp, *Impf. 2ms* תַּחֲנֶה, *3ms+w.c.* וַיִּחַן {46}

חָנַן to be gracious, show favor, *Impf.* יָחֹן, וַיָּחָן; ***Hitp*** *3cp* הִתְחַנְּנוּ to plead for mercy, *Impf.* יִתְחַנֵּן

חֶסֶד faithfulness, loyalty, steadfast love {42}

חֲצִי half

חָצֵר a court or courtyard (enclosed area with no roof), village (without a wall), *cs.* חֲצַר; *pl.* חֲצֵרִים & חֲצֵרוֹת {45}

חֹק statute (law); *pl.* חֻקִּים, *cs.* חֻקֵּי {43}

חֻקָּה statute (law), *cs.* חֻקַּת; *pl.* חֻקּוֹת {43}

חֶרֶב sword, *in pause* חָרֶב; *pl.* חֲרָבוֹת, *cs.* חַרְבוֹת {42}

חָשַׁב ***Qal*** to plan, consider, think, *Impf.* יַחְשֹׁב; ***Ni*** נֶחְשַׁב to be considered as, *Impf.* יֵחָשֵׁב; ***Pi*** חִשֵּׁב to plan, consider, think, *Impf.* יְחַשֵּׁב

חֹשֶׁךְ darkness {14}

טטט

טוֹב **(I)** *verb* to be good *Impf.* (יִיטַב) is based on יטב. *See p. 246;* **(II)** *adj.* good; *pl.* טוֹבִים, *cs.* טוֹבֵי; *f.* טוֹבָה, *cs.* טוֹבַת; *pl.* טוֹבוֹת {18}. (*It is often not easy to tell the difference between the verb and the adj.*)

טָמֵא ***Qal*** to become (religiously) unclean, *Impf.* יִטְמָא; ***Ni*** נִטְמָא to make oneself unclean, *no Impf*; ***Pi*** טִמֵּא to make or declare s.t. unclean, *Impf. 2ms* תְּטַמֵּא {45}

טָמֵא *adj.* religiously unclean, *cs.* טְמֵא; *f.* טְמֵאָה, *cs.* טְמֵאַת {45}

ייי

יבשׁ *See p. 246.*

יָד *f.* hand, *cs.* יַד; *du.* יָדַיִם, *cs.* יְדֵי {20}

ידה ***Hi*** *3cp* הוֹדוּ to praise; *Impf.* יוֹדֶה, *p. 242*

יָדַע ***Qal*** to know; have sexual relations with; *Impf.* יֵדַע; *Impv.* דַּע; *IC* דַּעַת; ***Hi*** הוֹדִיעַ to make known, *Impf.* יוֹדִיעַ {18}. *See pp. 241, 284*

יְהוּדָה Judah {13}

יְהוָה the Lord (*see p. 21, footnote 6*) {12}

יְהוֹשֻׁעַ Joshua {13}

יוֹם day; *du.* יוֹמַיִם; *pl.* יָמִים, *cs.* יְמֵי {14}, *p. 117*

יוֹמָם during the day

יוֹסֵף Joseph {25}

יַחַד, יַחְדָּו together {48}

יטב ***Qal*** (no *Perf*) *Impf.* יִיטַב to be good; ***Hi*** הֵיטִיב to do good, *Impf.* יֵיטִיב {41}

יַיִן wine, *cs.* יֵין {48}

יָכֹל to be able, *Impf.* יוּכַל {28}, *p. 247.*

יָלַד ***Qal*** to bear children (father or mother), *Impf.* יֵלֵד; ***Ni*** נוֹלַד to be born, *Impf.* יִוָּלֵד; ***Hi*** הוֹלִיד to become the father of, *Impf.* יוֹלִיד {41}

יֶלֶד male child {41}

יַלְדָּה female child

ילך *see* הלך {48}

יָם sea, west; *pl.* יַמִּים {31}

יָמִין right (*opposite of* left), south {48}

יָנַק ***Qal*** to suck, *Impf.* יִינַק; ***Hi*** הֵינִיק to nurse (a child), *Impf.* יֵינִיק; *p. 270*

יָסַף ***Qal*** to add, to do (something) again, to continue, *no Impf*; ***Hi*** הוֹסִיף to add, increase, continue doing (something), *Impf.* יוֹסִיף {42}

יַעַן *prep.* because

יַעֲקֹב Jacob {19}

יָפֶה *adj.* handsome, beautiful; appropriate

יָצָא ***Qal*** to go or come out; *Impf.* יֵצֵא, IC צֵאת; ***Hi*** הוֹצִיא to bring or lead out; *Impf.* יוֹצִיא {15}, *pp. 242, 284*

יִצְחָק Isaac {29}

יָרֵא ***Qal*** to fear, be in awe of; *Impf.* יִירָא (*cf. Impf.* of ראה, *p. 240*); יָרֵא מִפְּנֵי or יָרֵא מִן to be afraid of; ***Ni*** (*no Perf*) *Impf.* (*1x*) *2ms* תִּוָּרֵא; *Pt.* נוֹרָא feared, terrifying (works of God) {15}, *pp. 240, 241, 284*

יִרְאָה *f.* fear, reverence {29}

יָרַד ***Qal*** to come or go down, *Impf.* יֵרֵד; ***Hi*** הוֹרִידוּ ,הוֹרִד to bring or thrown down, *Impf.* יוֹרֵד {24}

יַרְדֵּן Jordan (river) {26}

יָרָה ***Qal*** to throw, shoot; ***Hi*** הוֹרֵיתִי (*1cs*) to instruct, teach, *pp. 242, 284*

יְרוּשָׁלַםִ Jerusalem, *in pause* יְרוּשָׁלָםִ (*the proper original form* יְרוּשָׁלַיִם *is found only 4x in the O.T.*) {25}

יְרִיחוֹ Jericho {40}

יָרַשׁ ***Qal*** to take possession, inherit, displace s.o., *Impf.* יִ[י]רַשׁ; ***Hi*** הוֹרִישׁ to drive out, dispossess, *Impf.* יוֹרִישׁ {41}, *p. 270*

יִשַׁי Jesse (father of David) {23}

יִשְׂרָאֵל Israel {12}

יֵשׁ there is {31}

יָשַׁב to sit; to live or dwell; *Impf.* יֵשֵׁב *or* יֵשֵׁב; *Impv.* שֵׁב; *IC* שֶׁבֶת, *with* ל: לָשֶׁבֶת (*rarely* לְשֶׁבֶת); *IA* יָשֹׁב; *Pt.* יֹשֵׁב (*see next word*) {17}, *p. 270*

יֹשֵׁב (*pt. of* יָשַׁב) resident, inhabitant, dweller {28}

יְשׁוּעָה *f.* help, salvation {29}

יָשֵׁן to sleep, *Impf.* יִישַׁן {28}

ישׁע ***Ni*** נוֹשַׁע to receive help, to be victorious, *Impf.* יִוָּשֵׁעַ; ***Hi*** הוֹשִׁיעַ to help, save, rescue, *Impf.* יוֹשִׁיעַ {47}, *p. 241*

יָשָׁר *adj.* straight, right, correct, *cs.* יְשַׁר

יתר ***Ni*** נוֹתַר to be left over, *Impf.* יִוָּתֵר; ***Hi*** הוֹתִיר to leave over, *Impf.* יוֹתֵר

יֶתֶר remainder, that which is left over

ככך

-כְּ *insep. prep.* according to, as, like {13}

כַּאֲשֶׁר just as, when {27}

כָּבֵד **(I)** *verb* ***Qal*** to be heavy, dull, honored, *Impf.* יִכְבַּד; ***Ni*** נִכְבַּד to be honored, *Impf.* אֶכָּבֵד, אִכָּבְדָה; ***Pi*** כַּבְּדוּ to make dull, to honor, *Impf.* יְכַבֵּד; ***Hi*** הִכְבִּיד to make heavy, bring to honor, *Impf.* יַכְבֵּד {28}; **(II)** *adj.* heavy, severe

כָּבוֹד glory, weight, honor, *cs.* כְּבוֹד {29}

כבס ***Pi*** כִּבֵּס to wash, *Impf.* יְכַבֵּס

כֶּבֶשׂ lamb, young ram (male sheep), *pl.* כְּבָשִׂים

כֹּה so, thus, in this way {20}

כֹּהֵן priest; *pl.* כֹּהֲנִים, *cs.* כֹּהֲנֵי {17}

כּוֹכָב star, *cs.* כּוֹכַב; *pl.* כּוֹכָבִים, *cs.* כּוֹכְבֵי {16}

כּוּן ***Ni*** *Perf. 3fs* נָכוֹנָה to be ready, stand firm, be stable, *Impf.* יִכּוֹן; ***Polel*** כּוֹנֵן to prepare, establish, make firm, *Impf.* יְכוֹנֵן; ***Hi*** הֵכִין to prepare, install, make firm, *Impf.* יָכִין, וַיָּכֶן {44}

כֹּחַ strength, power, might; *also* כּוֹחַ; *no pl.*

כִּי *conj.* because, that, when; כִּי אִם־ (3x כִּי־אִם) for if, unless, nevertheless, except, but {12}

כֹּל all, each, every; *with maqqeph:* כָּל־ {17}

כָּלָה ***Qal*** to be finished, consumed, destroyed, *Impf.* יִכְלֶה; ***Pi*** כִּלָּה to finish, consume, destroy, *Impf.* וַיְכַל (*3ms+w.c.*), תְּכַלֶּה (*2ms*) {46}

כְּלִי thing, container, weapon; *pl.* כֵּלִים, *cs.* כְּלֵי {27}, *p. 117*

כֵּן so, thus, therefore {37}

כְּנַעַן Canaan {13}

כְּנַעֲנִי Canaanite(s)

כָּנָף *f.* wing, *cs.* כְּנַף; *pl. cs.* כַּנְפוֹת; *du.* כְּנָפַיִם, *cs.* כַּנְפֵי

כִּסֵּא *m.* chair, throne; *pl.* כִּסְאוֹת, *cs.=* {33}

כסה ***Pi*** כִּסָּה to cover, *Impf.* יְכַסֶּה, וַיְכַס {46}

כֶּסֶף silver, money {30}

כַּף *f.* hand, palm (of hand), sole (of foot), pan; *pl.* כַּפּוֹת, *cs.*=; *du.* כַּפַּיִם, *cs.* כַּפֵּי {47}

כפר ***Pi*** כִּפֶּר to cover or remove (sin, guilt), to reconcile, atone, *Impf.* יְכַפֵּר; ***Pu*** כֻּפַּר to be removed (sin, guilt), to be atoned for, *Impf.* יְכֻפַּר

כָּרַת ***Qal*** to cut, cut off, cut down; כָּרַת בְּרִית to make a covenant; ***Ni*** נִכְרַת to be cut off/down, eliminated, removed; ***Hi*** הִכְרִית to root out, eliminate, destroy {16}

כָּתַב ***Qal*** to write; ***Ni*** (*no Perf*), *Impf.* יִכָּתֵב to be written (down) {17}

ללל

-לְ *insep. prep.* to, for {11}

לֹא not {14}

לֵב heart; *pl.* לִבּוֹת {25}

לֵבָב heart; *pl.* לְבָבוֹת {25}

לְבַד alone; *with 1cs suff.* לְבַדִּי {27}

לָבָן *name* Laban; *adj.* white {26}

לָבַשׁ ***Qal*** to put on (clothing), to wear, *Impf.* יִלְבַּשׁ; ***Hi*** הִלְבִּישׁ to clothe, to put clothing on s.o. or s.t., *Impf.* + *w.c.* וַיַּלְבֵּשׁ, *1cs* אַלְבִּישׁ

לוּחַ *m.* flat piece of stone or wood (*also:* tablet, plank, slab); *pl.* לוּחוֹת; *du.* לוּחֹתַיִם (*pause*) {27}

לוֹט Lot {26}

לחם ***Ni*** נִלְחַם to fight, -נִלְחַם בְּ *or* נִלְחַם אֶת־ *or* נִלְחַם עִם to fight against, *Impf.* יִלָּחֵם {30}

לֶחֶם *c.* bread, food {30}

לַיְלָה *m.* night; at night *pl.* לֵילוֹת {14}

לָכַד to take, catch, capture {20}

לָכֵן therefore {37}

לָמַד ***Qal*** to learn, *Impf.* יִלְמַד; ***Pi*** לִמֵּד to teach, *Impf.* יְלַמֵּד {39}

לָמָּה why? (-לְ + מָה) {23}

לְמַעַן *prep.* in order to, for the sake of {27}

לִפְנֵי before (time or place) (*cs.* of פָּנִים + -לְ); *1cs suff.* לְפָנַי before me, in my presence {23}

לָקַח to take, receive, *Impf.* יִקַּח {13}{40}

לִקְרַאת to meet; toward, against, opposite. *See* קָרָא **(II)**

לָשׁוֹן *f.* tongue, language, *cs.* לְשׁוֹן; *pl.* לְשֹׁנוֹת

מממ

מְאֹד greatly, very {20}

מֵאָה one hundred {38}

מָאתַיִם two hundred {38}

מִבְּלִי because (מִן + בְּלִי)

מַגֵּפָה a plague (*often* disease), *cs.* מַגֵּפַת (*lit.* being struck or hit, *usually by God*; √ נגף)

מִדְבָּר uncultivated land (desert, pasture, wilderness) {24}

מַדּוּעַ Why? {23}

מָה What? How? Why? {23}

מוֹעֵד a meeting, an appointed time; *pl. cs.* מוֹעֲדֵי {46}

מוּת ***Qal*** מֵת to die, *Impf.* יָמוּת, וַיָּמָת; ***Hi*** הֵמִית to kill, to have s.o. put to death, *Impf.* יָמִית, וַיָּמֶת; ***Ho*** הוּמָת (*found in pause only*) to be killed, to be put to death, *Impf.* יוּמַת {44}, *p. 274*

מָוֶת *m.* death, dying, *cs.* מוֹת {29}

מִזְבֵּחַ *m.* altar, *cs.* מִזְבַּח; *pl.* מִזְבְּחוֹת, *cs.*= {45}

מַחֲנֶה *m.*(*f. 1x*) camp, army, company, *cs.* מַחֲנֵה; *pl.* מַחֲנִים & מַחֲנוֹת; *du.* מַחֲנָיִם (√ חנה) {46}

מָחָר tomorrow, the next day, in the future

מַטֶּה *m. usually* tribe, *but also* staff, rod, *cs.* מַטֵּה; *pl.* מַטּוֹת {43}

מִי Who? {23}

מַיִם water (*pl. only*), *cs.* מֵי & מֵימֵי {18}

מָכַר ***Qal*** to sell, *Impf.* יִמְכֹּר; ***Ni*** נִמְכַּר to be sold, to sell oneself, *Impf.* יִמָּכֵר {21}

מָלֵא ***Qal*** to fill, be full (of), *Impf. 3mp* יִמְלְאוּ; ***Ni*** נִמְלָא (*1x*) to be filled (with), *Impf.* יִמָּלֵא; ***Pi*** מִלֵּא to fill, fulfill, complete, install, *Impf.* יְמַלֵּא {45}, *p. 278*

מָלֵא *adj.* full {45}

מַלְאָךְ messenger, angel, *cs.* מַלְאַךְ; *pl.* מַלְאָכִים, *cs.* מַלְאֲכֵי {29}

מְלָאכָה *f.* work, craft, business, *cs.* מְלֶאכֶת; *pl.cs.* מַלְאֲכוֹת {41}

מִלְחָמָה *f.* fighting, war (√ לחם), *cs.* מִלְחֶמֶת; *pl.* מִלְחָמוֹת, *cs.* מִלְחֲמוֹת {28}

מלט ***Ni*** נִמְלַט to escape, *Impf.* יִמָּלֵט; ***Pi*** מִלֵּט to save, to leave alone, *Impf.* יְמַלֵּט {30}

מָלַךְ ***Qal*** to be king, to rule; *Impf.* יִמְלֹךְ; ***Hi*** הִמְלִיךְ to make (s.o.) king; *Impf.* יַמְלִיךְ {33}

מֶלֶךְ king; *pl.* מְלָכִים, *cs.* מַלְכֵי {10}

מַלְכָּה queen

מַלְכוּת *f.* kingdom, power, *cs.*=; *pl.* מַלְכֻיוֹת {41}

מַמְלָכָה *f.* kingdom, power, *cs.* מַמְלֶכֶת; *pl.* מַמְלָכוֹת, *cs.* מַמְלְכוֹת {41}

מִן *prep.* from, because of {10}

מִנְחָה *f.* offering, gift; *cs.* מִנְחַת; *pl.* מְנָחֹת {22}

מִסְפָּר number, *cs.* מִסְפַּר; *pl. cs.* מִסְפְּרֵי {43}

מַעַל *adv.* above, upward, high {47}

מַעֲשֶׂה *m.* work, deed(s), *cs.* מַעֲשֵׂה; *pl.* מַעֲשִׂים, *cs.* מַעֲשֵׂי {43}

מָצָא ***Qal*** to find; *Impf.* יִמְצָא; ***Ni*** נִמְצָא to be found, *Impf.* יִמָּצֵא ; {23}, *p. 278*

מִצְוָה *f.* command(ment), *cs.* מִצְוַת; *pl.* מִצְוֹת (√ צוה) {27}

מִצְרִי an Egyptian, *pl.* מִצְרִים; *adj.* Egyptian {32}

מִצְרַיִם Egypt; Egyptians (*see* מִצְרִי) {12, 31}

מָקוֹם *m.* place, space, *cs.* מְקוֹם; *pl.* מְקוֹמוֹת {24}

מִקְנֶה livestock, cattle (√ קנה), *cs.* מִקְנֵה; *no pl.*

מַרְאֶה appearance, vision, sight (√ ראה), *cs.* מַרְאֵה; *no pl.*

מְרַגֵּל a spy (√ רגל), *pl.* מְרַגְּלִים {30}

מֹשֶׁה Moses (*sometimes* מֹשֶׁה) {12}

מִשְׁכָּן *m.* tabernacle, home, *cs.* מִשְׁכַּן; *pl.* מִשְׁכָּנוֹת {48}

מָשַׁל to rule, govern, *Impf.* יִמְשֹׁל {21}

מִשְׁפָּחָה extended family, clan, *cs.* מִשְׁפַּחַת; *pl.* מִשְׁפָּחוֹת races, sub-groups, *cs.* מִשְׁפְּחוֹת {42}

מִשְׁפָּט justice, judgement, legal decision, lawsuit (√ שׁפט); *cs.* מִשְׁפַּט; *pl.* מִשְׁפָּטִים {30}

מִשְׁתֶּה banquet, feast, drinking (√ שׁתה), *cs.* מִשְׁתֵּה; *no pl.*

מֵת *adj.* dead (*Pt.* < מות) {32}. *For verb*: see מות

נ נ נ

נָא please, just, now {29}

נְאֻם says (*lit.* a declaration (of)); נְאֻם־יְהוָה says the LORD {44}

נבא ***Ni*** נִבָּא to prophesy, *Impf.* יִנָּבֵא; **Hitp** *Perf. 2ms* הִתְנַבִּיתָ to prophesy, *no Impf*

נבט ***Hi*** הִבִּיט to look, look out, look at, see, *Impf.* יַבִּיט

נָבִיא prophet; *pl.* נְבִיאִים, *cs.* נְבִיאֵי {17}

נְבִיאָה woman prophet, prophetess {17}

נֶגֶב south, Negeb *or* Negev (desert area south of Judah)

נגד ***Hi*** הִגִּיד to report, announce, tell; *Impf.* יַגִּיד, ***Ho*** הֻגַּד to be reported, announced, told; *Impf.* יֻגַּד {40}

נֶגֶד *prep.* in front of, opposite (from) {43}

נָגִיד chief, leader, prince, *cs.* נְגִ[י]ד, *pl.* נְגִידִים {40}

נָגַע ***Qal*** to touch, reach, hit, *Impf.* יִגַּע; ***Hi*** הִגִּיעַ to touch, reach, hit, *Impf.* יַגִּיעַ {47}, *pp. 238, 284*

נָגַף ***Qal*** to hit, beat, injure, *Impf.* יִגֹּף; ***Ni*** נִגַּף to be beaten; *Impf.* יִנָּגֵף {41}

נגשׁ ***Qal*** *Impf.* (*Ni used for Perf. & Pt.*) to step up, approach יִגַּשׁ, *Impv.* גַּשׁ; ***Ni*** *Perf.* נִגַּשׁ to step up, approach, *Pt.* נִגָּשִׁים (*1x*); ***Hi*** הִגִּישׁ to bring up or near, to offer, *Impf.* יַגִּישׁ, *Pt.* מַגִּישׁ {40}, *p. 269*

נָהָר *m.* river, *cs.* נְהַר; *pl.* נְהָרוֹת (*rarely* נְהָרִים), *cs.* נַהֲרֵי & נַהֲרוֹת {19}

נוח ***Qal*** *Perf. 3fs* נָחָה to rest, settle, *Impf.* יָנוּחַ, וַיָּנַח (=***Hi*** I.); ***Hi*** I. הֵנִיחַ to lower, to provide rest,

Impf. יָנִיחַ, וַיָּנַח(=***Qal***); II. הִנִּיחַ to set, leave, allow, *Impf.* יַנִּיחַ, וַיַּנַּח {44}

נוס *Perf.* נָס to flee, escape, *Impf.* יָנוּס, וַיָּנָס, וַיָּנֹס {44}

נַחַל stream bed (usually dry), valley; *pl.* נְחָלִים, *cs.* נַחֲלֵי; *du.* נַחֲלַיִם {48}

נָחַל ***Qal*** to get or receive (inherited) property, *Impf* יִנְחַל; ***Hi*** הִנְחַלְתִּי(*1cs*) to give (inherited) property, *Impf.* יַנְחִ[י]ל

נַחֲלָה *f.* inheritance, heritage (√ נחל), *cs.* נַחֲלַת; *no pl.* {42}

נָחָשׁ snake, serpent {39}

נְחֹשֶׁת bronze (a mixture of copper and tin, strong and very hard, used before people learned how to work with iron), *du.* נְחֻשְׁתַּיִם {48}

נָטָה ***Qal*** to turn, bend down, stretch out, set up a tent, *Impf.* יִטֶּה, *Impv.* נְטֵה, *IC* נְטוֹת, *act. Pt.* נוֹטֶה, *pass. Pt.* נָטוּי; ***Hi*** הִטָּה to bend down, stretch out, to turn s.t. aside, *Impf.* יַטֶּה, *Impv.* הַטֵּה, *IC* הַטּוֹת, *Pt.* מַטֶּה {47}, *pp. 239, 284*

נָטַע to plant, *Impf.* יִטַּע, *p. 238*

נכה ***Hi*** הִכָּה to hit, strike *Impf.* יַכֶּה, וַיַּךְ(*w.c.*); ***Ho*** הֻכָּה to be struck down, to be killed, *Impf.* יֻכּוּ(*3mp*) {47}, *p. 239*

נָסַע ***Qal*** to pull s.t. out, to travel, to start to travel, *Impf.* יִסַּע, *Impv.* סְעוּ, *IC* נְסֹעַ, *Pt.* נֹסֵעַ; ***Hi*** (*no Perf.*) to take s.t. away, to make people start to travel, *Impf.* יַסַּע, תַּסִּיעַ *Pt.* מַסִּיעַ {48}, *p. 238*

נַעַר boy, lad, young man; *pl.* נְעָרִים, *cs.* נַעֲרֵי {20}

נָפַל ***Qal*** to fall, *Impf.* יִפֹּל; ***Hi*** הִפִּיל to cause to fall, to let fall, *Impf.* יַפִּיל {34}, *p. 269*

נֶפֶשׁ *f.* life (force), person, "soul" (*but see note at Exercise 34*); נַפְשִׁי my life, *but often just* I *or* me; *pl.* נְפָשׁוֹת {34}

נצל ***Ni*** *Perf. 1cp* נִצַּלְנוּ (*1x*) to be rescued, saved; to escape, *Impf.* יִנָּצֵל; ***Hi*** הִצִּיל to take or snatch away, to rescue, *Impf.* יַצִּיל {41}, *p. 269*

נָשָׂא to lift up, carry, forgive; *Impf.* יִשָּׂא; *Impv.* שָׂא; *Inf.* שְׂאֵת {27}, *pp. 238, 284*

נָשִׂיא leader, prince, *cs.* נְשִׂיא; *pl.* נְשִׂ[י]אִים, *cs.* נְשִׂיאֵי {48}

נָשִׁים *see* אִשָּׁה

נָתַן ***Qal*** to give; *Impf.* יִתֵּן; *Impv.* תֵּן; *IA* נָתוֹן; *IC* תֵּת; *Pt.* נוֹתֵן, נֹתֵן; ***Ni*** נִתַּן; *Impf.* יִנָּתֵן {10}

ססס

סָבַב ***Qal*** to turn, go around, surround, *Impf.* יָסֹב, *Impv. & IC* סֹב, *Pt.* סוֹבֵב; ***Ni*** נָסַב to turn, go around, surround, *Impf.* (*3mp only*) יִסַּבּוּ; ***Pi (Polel)*** *no Perf.* to turn, surround *Impf.* תְּסוֹבֵב (*3fs/2ms*); ***Hi*** הֵסֵב to cause to go around, to remove, *Impf.* יָסֵב, *Impv. & IC* הָסֵב, *Pt.* מֵסֵב {46}, *p. 282*

סָבִיב *adv.* around, all around, on every side {46}

סוּס horse; *pl.* סוּסִים, *cs.* סוּסֵי {37}

סור ***Qal*** סָר to turn aside, to leave, *Impf.* יָסוּר, וַיָּסַר(***Hi***=), *Impv. & IC* סוּר, *Pt.* סָר; ***Hi*** הֵסִיר to remove, *Impf.* יָסִיר, וַיָּסַר(***Qal***=), *Impv. & IA* הָסֵר, *IC* הָסִיר, *Pt.* מֵסִיר {44}

סִינַי Sinai {27}

סָפַר ***Qal*** to count; *Impf.* יִסְפֹּר, *pausal* יִסְפּוֹר; *Pt.* סֹפֵר (*see also next word, below*); ***Pi*** סִפֵּר to count, report, tell; *Impf.* יְסַפֵּר; ***Pu*** סֻפַּר to be reported {31}

סֹפֵר writer, secretary, scribe; *pl.* סֹפְרִים

סֵפֶר scroll, "book" (*but see p. 70, footnote 5*); *pl.* סְפָרִים, *cs.* סִפְרֵי {17}

סתר ***Ni*** נִסְתַּר (*pause only*) to hide oneself, *Impf.* יִסָּתֵר; ***Hi*** הִסְתִּיר to hide s.t. or s.o., *Impf.* יַסְתִּיר; ***Hitp*** *Impf.* תִּסְתַּתָּר (1x); *Pt.* מִסְתַּתֵּר (4x) to hide oneself {30}

עעע

עָבַד to work, serve; cultivate (soil); worship (God); *Impf.* יַעֲבֹד {15}

עֶבֶד servant, slave; *pl.* עֲבָדִים, *cs.* עַבְדֵי {28}

עֲבֹדָה (עֲבוֹדָה *in 1&2 Chron only*) *f.* work, service, worship, *cs.* עֲבֹדַת; *no pl.* {30}

עָבַר ***Qal*** to cross, pass over, to go through; *Impf.* יַעֲבֹר; ***Hi*** הֶעֱבִיר to make pass over, pass by, pass through, *Impf.* יַעֲבִיר {26}

עֵבֶר side, other side, beyond

עִבְרִי *n. & adj.* Hebrew; *pl.* עִבְרִים & עִבְרִיִּים {34}

עַד *prep.* until, up to, near {29}

עֵדָה *f.* gathering, group, congregation, *cs.* עֲדַת (*no plural*) {34}

עֵדֶן Eden {39}

עוֹד again, still, always {34}

עוֹלָם eternity (עַד־עוֹלָם, לְעוֹלָם, forever) {29}

עָוֹן *m.* iniquity (sin), guilt, *cs.* עֲוֹן; *pl.* עֲוֹנוֹת {44}

עָזַב to leave, abandon; *Impf.* יַעֲזֹב {34}

עָזַר to help, *Impf.* יַעֲזֹר {42}

עַיִן *f.* **(I)** eye, **(II)** spring (of water); *cs.* עֵין; *du.* עֵינַיִם, *cs.* עֵינֵי; *pl.* (springs) עֲיָנוֹת, *cs.* עֵינוֹת {18}

עִיר *f.* city; *pl.* עָרִים, *cs.* עָרֵי {11}, *p. 117*

עַל *prep* above, over, against, near, concerning; עַל־דְּבַר־ because of, for the sake of; עַל־פְּנֵי־ in front of, before the face of {15}

עַל־כֵּן therefore {37}

עָלָה ***Qal*** to go up, *Impf.* (***Hi***=) יַעֲלֶה, וַיַּעַל(*w.c.*), *Impv.* עֲלֵה, *IA* עָלֹה, *IC* עֲלוֹת, *Pt.* עֹלֶה; ***Ni*** נַעֲלָה to be taken up, to go away, *Impf.* יֵעָלֶה, *Impv. mp* הֵעָלוּ, *IC* הֵעָלוֹת; ***Hi*** הֶעֱלָה to bring up, to offer, *Impf.* (***Qal***=) יַעֲלֶה, וַיַּעַל, *Impv.* הַעַל, *IC* הַעֲלוֹת, *Pt.* מַעֲלֶה {47}, *pp. 239, 284*

עֹלָה burnt offering, *cs.* עֹלַת; *pl.* עֹלוֹת

עִם *prep.* with {16}

עַם people (*with d.a.* הָעָם); *pl.* עַמִּים, *cs.* עַמֵּי {13}

עָמַד ***Qal*** to stand, *Impf.* יַעֲמֹד; ***Hi*** הֶעֱמִיד to set, station, appoint, *Impf.* יַעֲמִיד {23}, *p. 271*

עָנָה ***Qal*** **(I)** to answer, **(II)** to bend down, to be in a miserable condition, *Impf.* יַעֲנֶה, וַיַּעַן(*w.c.*), *Impv.* עֲנֵה, *IC* עֲנוֹת, *Pt.* עֹנֶה; ***Pi*** עִנָּה to oppress, humiliate, *Impf.* תְּעַנֶּה(*2ms*), *Impv.* עַנֵּה, *IA* עַנֵּה, *IC* עַנּוֹת {47}

עָפָר dust, *cs.* עֲפַר; *pl. cs.* עַפְרוֹת {14}

עֵץ tree, wood; *pl.* עֵצִים, *cs.* עֲצֵי {12}

עֵצָה *f.* counsel, advice, plan, scheme; *cs.* עֲצַת; *pl.* עֵצוֹת {30}

עֶצֶם *f.* bone(s), *pl.* עֲצָמִים & עֲצָמוֹת, *cs.* עַצְמוֹת

עֶרֶב evening; *du.* עַרְבַּיִם {19}

עָרוֹם *adj.* naked, *f.* עֲרֻמָּה; *m.pl.* עֲרֻמִּים {39}

עָשָׂה ***Qal*** to do, make; *Impf.* יַעֲשֶׂה; ***Ni*** נַעֲשָׂה to be done, made, *Impf.* יֵעָשֶׂה {24}, *p. 239*

עֵשָׂו Esau {19}

עֲשִׂירִי *m.* tenth; *f.* עֲשִׂירִית {38}

עֶשֶׂר *see* עֲשָׂרָה

עֲשָׂרָה *m.* ten, *cs.* עֲשֶׂרֶת; *f.* עֶשֶׂר, *cs.*= {38}

עֶשְׂרִים twenty {38}

עֵת *c.* time (*either* point of *or* period of), *cs.* עֵת־ & עֶת־; *pl.* עִתִּים {43}

עַתָּה now {22}

פפף

פֶּה *m.* mouth, *cs.* פִּי; *pl.* פִּיוֹת {27}, *p. 117*

פֹּה here, to here

פזר ***Pi*** פִּזַּר to scatter, disperse (*tr.*), *Impf.* יְפַזֵּר {32}

פלל ***Hitp*** הִתְפַּלֵּל to pray, *Impf.* יִתְפַּלֵּל {35}

פְּלִשְׁתִּי Philistine; *pl.* פְּלִשְׁתִּים {37}

פֶּן־ lest, otherwise, so that not {39}

פָּנָה to turn, to face, *Impf.* יִפְנֶה, וַיִּפֶן(*w.c.*), *Impv.* פְּנֵה, *IA* פָּנֹה, *IC* פְּנוֹת, *Pt.* פֹּנֶה; {46}

פָּנִים face (*pl. only*; √ פָּנָה *not found*); *cs.* פְּנֵי *cs.* with -ל (לִפְנֵי) before, in the presence of; לְפָנַי before me {22}

פֶּסַח Passover, *pl.* פְּסָחִים

פַּעַם time (occurrence), footstep; *pl.* פְּעָמִים; *cs.* פַּעֲמֵי; *du.* פַּעֲמַיִם *often means* twice {38}

פָּקַד ***Qal*** to appoint, to number, to punish; *Impf.* יִפְקֹד; ***Ni*** נִפְקַד to be missed or missing;

Impf. יִפָּקֵד; ***Hi*** הִפְקִיד to appoint, entrust; *Impf.* יַפְקִיד {42}

פַּר (young) bull, *pl.* פָּרִים

פרד ***Niph*** נִפְרַד to be divided, separated, *Impf.* יִפָּרֵד; ***Hiph*** הִפְרִיד to separate (*tr.*), *Impf.* יַפְרִיד {35}

פְּרִי fruit; *in pause* פֶּרִי {12}

פַּרְעֹה Pharaoh {12}

פָּתַח ***Qal*** to open, set free, *Impf.* יִפְתַּח, *Impv.* פְּתַח, *IA* פָּתוֹחַ, *IC* פְּתֹחַ, *act. Pt.* פֹּתֵחַ, *pass.Pt.* פָּתוּחַ; ***Ni*** נִפְתַּח to open (*intr.*), to be opened, *Impf.* יִפָּתַח; ***Pi*** פִּתַּח to loosen, take off, *Impf.* יְפַתַּח

פֶּתַח door, doorway, entrance, *pl.* פְּתָחִים, *cs.* פִּתְחֵי {45}

צצצ

צֹאן *c.* flock; small cattle, sheep, goats {22}

צָבָא army, warfare, *cs.* צְבָא; *pl.* צְבָאוֹת (*often translated* hosts, *as in* יְהוָה צְבָאוֹת Lord of Hosts) {35}

צַדִּיק righteous, just {29}

צֶדֶק *m.* what is right, just; rightness {28}

צְדָקָה *f.* blameless behavior, righteousness, *cs.* צִדְקַת; *pl.* צְדָקוֹת, *cs.* צִדְקֹת {28}

צוה ***Pi*** צִוָּה to command, *Impf.* יְצַוֶּה, *Impv.* צַוֵּה {27}

צָעַק to cry out, call for help; *Impf.* יִצְעַק {22}

צָפוֹן north {47}

צֹר Tyre

צָרָה *f.* trouble, distress, *cs.* צָרַת {32}

קקק

קָבַץ ***Qal*** to gather (*tr.*); ***Ni*** נִקְבַּץ to gather together (*intr.*), assemble; ***Pi*** קִבֵּץ to gather (*tr.*); *Impf.* יְקַבֵּץ {31}

קָבַר to bury {21}

קֶבֶר grave; *pl.* קְבָרִים, *cs.* קִבְרֵי {21}

קָדוֹשׁ *adj.* holy, *cs.* קְדוֹשׁ; *pl.* קְדוֹשִׁים {18}

קָדַשׁ ***Qal*** be holy, *Impf.* יִקְדַּשׁ; ***Ni*** נִקְדַּשׁ show oneself to be holy, *Impf.* יִקָּדֵשׁ; ***Pi*** קִדֵּשׁ make holy, consecrate, dedicate, *Impf.* יְקַדֵּשׁ; ***Pu*** *Pt. only* מְקֻדָּשׁ be made holy, consecrated; ***Hi*** הִקְדִּישׁ treat or declare holy, *Impf.* יַקְדִּישׁ; ***Hitp*** הִתְקַדְּשׁוּ (*3cp*) dedicate oneself, act as holy, *Impf.* יִתְקַדֵּשׁ {32}

קֹדֶשׁ, קוֹדֶשׁ holiness, holy place (*that is,* the sanctuary or temple), a holy thing; *pl.* קֳדָשִׁים & קָדָשִׁים, *cs.* קָדְשֵׁי {18}

קהל ***Ni*** נִקְהַל to assemble (*intr.*); *Impf.* יִקָּהֵל; ***Hi*** הִקְהִיל to assemble, call together (*tr.*); *Impf.* יַקְהֵל {33}

קָהָל assembly, gathering; *cs.* קְהַל; (*no pl.*) {33}

קוֹל *m.* sound, voice; *pl. abs. & cs.* קוֹלוֹת {15}

קוּם ***Qal*** *Perf.* קָם stand up, get up, *Impf.* יָקוּם, וַיָּקָם(*w.c.*), *Impv. & IC* קוּם, *IA* קוֹם, *Pt.* קָם; ***Hi*** הֵקִים set up, make stand, provide, *Impf.* יָקִים, וַיָּקֶם(*w.c.*), *Impv. & IA* הָקֵם, *IC* הָקִים, *Pt.* מֵקִים {44}, *p. 274*

קטל to kill (*although this word is used in the verb charts, it is very rare, found only 3x, all Qal Impf*)

קָטֹן, קָטָן small, young, insignificant {24}

קָטֹן to be small, *Impf.* תִּקְטַן {28}

קטר ***Pi*** קִטְּרוּ(*3cp*) to let (incense or a sacrifice) turn into smoke [*see Note below*], *Impf.* יְקַטֵּר; ***Hi*** הִקְטִיר to cause (incense or a sacrifice) to turn into smoke [*see Note below*], *Impf.* יַקְטִיר, וַיַּקְטֵר(*w.c.*)

Note: קטר *does not simply mean "burn," although the objects are indeed burned. The point is that they are not* destroyed (*as with* בער *or* שׂרף) *but rather are* changed *into another form – smoke – so that they can be sent up to God.*

קַיִן Cain (son of Adam and Eve) {22}

קלל ***Qal*** קַלּוֹתָ(*2ms*) to be small, to be quick, to be unimportant, *Impf.* וַתֵּקַל(*3fs + w.c.*); ***Ni*** נָקַל to be light or easy, to show oneself to be quick, to humble oneself, *Impf.* יִקַּלּוּ(*3mp*); ***Pi*** קִלֵּל to curse s.o., *Impf.* יְקַלֵּל, *Impv. & IC* קַלֵּל, *Pt.* מְקַלֵּל;

Hi הֵקַל to make s.t. lighter, to treat s.o. with contempt, *Impf.* יָקֵל, *Impv. & IC* הָקֵל, *p. 282*

קָנָה to get, buy, *Impf.* יִקְנֶה, *Impv.* קְנֵה, *IA* קָנֹה, *IC* קְנֹה

קָצַף to be or become angry, *Impf.* יִקְצֹף {40}

קָרָא **(I)** ***Qal*** to call; -קָרָא בְּ to read aloud (in); -קָרָא לְ to call, to name, to call to; *Impf.* יִקְרָא; ***Ni*** נִקְרָא to be called, read, named; *Impf.* יִקָּרֵא {14} **(II)** ***Qal*** to encounter, meet; *IC*+לְ: לִקְרַאת to meet; toward, against, opposite

קָרַב ***Qal*** to come or go near, approach, *Impf.* יִקְרַב; ***Hi*** הִקְרִיב to bring near, offer, *Impf.* יַקְרִיב {39}

קֶרֶב middle of, בְּקֶרֶב in the midst of, among {42}

קָרָה to happen to s.o. (used with d.o. or -לְ), *Impf.* יִקְרֶה, וַיִּקֶר(*w.c.*)

קָרַע to tear, *Impf.* יִקְרַע, *Impv. mp* קִרְעוּ, *IA* קָרֹעַ, *IC* קְרוֹעַ, *Pt.* קֹרֵעַ

ררר

רָאָה ***Qal*** to see; *Impf.* יִרְאֶה [יֵרֶה]; ***Ni*** נִרְאָה to appear; *Impf.* יֵרָאֶה; ***Hi*** הֶרְאָה to show; *Impf.* יַרְאֶה{10}, *pp. 240, 284*

רְאוּבֵן Reuben

רֹאשׁ head; *pl.* רָאשִׁים, *cs.* רָאשֵׁי {19}, *p. 117*

רִאשׁוֹן *m.* first; *f.* רִאשֹׁנָה {38}

רַב *m. adj.* much, many, great, *pl.* רַבִּים; *f.* רַבָּה, *pl.* רַבּוֹת {40}

רֹב abundance, greatness, many, *cs.* רֹב & -רָב, *pl. cs.* רֻבֵּי {47}

רְבָבָה very large group; ten thousand {38}

רָבָה to become many or great, *Impf.* יִרְבֶּה, וַיִּרֶב(*w.c.*), *Impv.* רְבֵה, *IC* רְבוֹת; ***Hi*** הִרְבָּה to make many, to make great, *Impf.* יַרְבֶּה, וַיֶּרֶב, *Impv.* הַרְבֵּה & הֶרֶב, *IA* הַרְבֵּה, *IC* הַרְבּוֹת {46}

רְבִיעִי *m.* fourth; *f.* רְבִיעִית {38}

רֶגֶל *f.* foot, *du.* רַגְלַיִם, *du. cs.* רַגְלֵי; *pl.* רְגָלִים {30}

רָדַף to pursue, persecute; *but with prepositions*: רָדַף אַחֲרֵי & רָדַף לְ- to pursue {20}

רוּחַ *c.* breath, wind, spirit; *pl.* רוּחוֹת {31}

רוּם ***Qal*** *Perf.* רָם to be high, exalted, to boast, *Impf.* יָרוּם, וַיָּרָם(*w.c.*), *Emphatic Impv.* רוּמָה, *IC* רוּם (*w prefix:* כְּרֻם), *Pt.* רָם; ***Polel*** to raise, to make grow *Perf. 1cs* רוֹמַמְתִּי, *Impf.* יְרוֹמֵם; ***Hi*** הֵרִים to raise, lift up, *Impf.* יָרִים, יָרֵם, וַיָּרֶם, *Impv. & IC* הָרִים and הָרֵם, *Pt.* מֵרִים {44}

רוע ***Hi*** *Perf. 3cp* הֵרִיעוּ to shout (in war, in joy, in triumph), *Impf.* יָרִיעַ, *Impv.* הָרִיעוּ(*mp*), *IC* הָרִיעַ, *Pt. (mp)* מְרִיעִים

רוּץ *Perf.* רָץ to run, *Impf.* יָרוּץ, *with w.c.* וַיָּרָץ, *Impv.* רוּץ, רֻץ, *IC* רוּץ, *Pt.* רָץ

רֹחַב width

רָחוֹק distance, far away

רָחֵל Rachel {26}

רָחַץ to wash or rinse s.t. (*tr.*); to bathe (*intr.*), *Impf.* יִרְחַץ, *Impv.* רְחַץ, *IC* רְחֹץ

רָחַק ***Qal*** to be far away, *Impf.* יִרְחַק; ***Hi*** הִרְחִיק to remove, to put something far away, *Impf.* אַרְחִיק (*1cs*)

רָכַב ***Qal*** to ride, *Impf.* יִרְכַּב, *Impv.* רְכַב; ***Hi*** הִרְכַּבְתָּ(*2ms*) to make s.o. ride, *Impf.* יַרְכִּיב, וַיַּרְכֵּב(*w.c.*)

רֶכֶב chariot(s), *pl. cs.* רִכְבֵי

רְכוּשׁ property, goods, wealth, *cs.* רְכֻשׁ {40}

רַע, רָע *adj.* bad, evil, inferior; *pl.* רָעִים, *cs.* רָעֵי; *f.* רָעָה, *pl.* רָעוֹת {18}

רֵעַ friend, companion; *pl.* רֵעִים, *cs.* רֵעֵי {40}

רָעֵב *verb* to be hungry, *Impf.* יִרְעַב {28}

רָעֵב *adj.* hungry {34}

רָעָב hunger, famine

רָעָה to graze (*tr. & intr.*), to take care of sheep, *Impf.* יִרְעֶה, *Impv.* רְעֵה, *IC* רְעוֹת, *Pt.* רֹעֶה (*often used as noun; see below*) {48}

רָעָה *f.* evil, trouble, harm, *cs.* רָעַת, *pl.* רָעוֹת

רֹעֶה shepherd (√רעה); *cs.* רֹעֵה; *pl.* רֹעִים (*sometimes used for* rulers, kings); *cs.* רֹעֵי {22}

רעע **Qal** *Perf.* רַע to be bad, displeasing, *Impf.* יֵרַע, *Impv. mp* רֹעוּ; **Hi** הֵרַע to do evil, behave badly, *Impf.* יָרֵעַ, *IC* הָרַע, *Pt.* מֵרַע

רָפָא to heal, *Impf.* יִרְפָּא, *Impv.* רְפָא, *IA* רָפוֹא, *IC*+לְ: לִרְפֹּא, *Pt.* רֹפֵא, רֹפֶה; **Ni** נִרְפָּא to be healed, *Impf.* אֵרָפֵא(*1cs*); **Pi** רִפֵּאתִי(*1cs*) to heal, to make healthy, *Impf.* יְרַפֵּא, *IA* רַפֹּא

רַק only, but {34}

רָשָׁע *adj. & n.* guilty, wicked {34}

שׂשׂשׂ

שָׂבַע **Qal** to have had enough (food, drink), to be full, *Impf.* יִשְׂבַּע, *Impv.* שְׂבַע, *IA* שָׂבוֹעַ, *IC* שְׂבֹעַ; **Hi** הִשְׂבִּיעַ to satisfy the hunger of s.o., to fill, *Impf.* תַּשְׂבִּיעַ(2ms)

שָׂדֶה field, open countryside, *cs.* שְׂדֵה; *pl.* שָׂדוֹת, *cs.* שְׂדוֹת {44}

שִׂים *Perf.* שָׂם to put, set, place, *Impf.* יָשִׂים, וַיָּשֶׂם, יָשֵׂם {35}, *p. 274*

שָׂמַח **Qal** to rejoice, be glad, *Impf.* יִשְׂמַח, *Impv.* שְׂמַח, *IC* שְׂמֹחַ, שְׂמוֹחַ; **Pi** שִׂמַּח to make s.o. glad, *Impf.* יְשַׂמַּח, *Impv.* שַׂמַּח, *IC* שַׂמֵּחַ {45}

שָׂנֵא to hate, *Impf.* יִשְׂנָא, *Impv.* שִׂנְאוּ(*mp*), *IA* שָׂנֹא, *IC* שְׂנֹא, *Pt.* שֹׂנֵא {45}

שָׂפָה lip, language; edge, shore or bank, *cs.* שְׂפַת; *du.* שְׂפָתַיִם; *pl.* שִׂפְתוֹת {32}

שַׂר prince, official, commander, leader; *pl.* שָׂרִים, *cs.* שָׂרֵי {42}

שָׂרָה Sarah {10}

שָׂרַף to burn {20}

שׁשׁשׁ

שָׁאוּל Saul {23}

שְׁאוֹל Sheol, place of the dead *(see p. 99, footnote 4)* {23}

שָׁאַל to ask; *Impf.* יִשְׁאַל {16}

שׁאר **Ni** נִשְׁאַר to remain, to be left, *Impf.* יִשָּׁאֵר; **Hi** הִשְׁאִיר, to leave s.t. or s.o., *Impf.* יַשְׁאִיר {43}

שׁבח **Pi** שִׁבַּח to praise, glorify; *Impf.* יְשַׁבַּח {32}

שֵׁבֶט *usually* tribe, *but also* stick, rod, staff; *pl.* שְׁבָטִים, *cs.* שִׁבְטֵי {41}

שׁבע **Ni** נִשְׁבַּע to swear, to take an oath, *Impf.* יִשָּׁבַע, *Emphatic Impv.* הִשָּׁבְעָה, *IA* הִשָּׁבֵעַ, *IC*+לְ: לְהִשָּׁבֵעַ, הִשָּׁבֵעַ, *Pt.* נִשְׁבָּע; **Hi** הִשְׁבִּיעַ to make s.o. swear, *Impf.* וַיַּשְׁבַּע(*w.c.*), תַּשְׁבִּיעוּ(*2mp*), *IA* הַשְׁבֵּעַ, *IC* הַשְׁבִּיעַ {45}

שֶׁבַע *see* שִׁבְעָה

שִׁבְעָה *m.* seven, *cs.* שִׁבְעַת; *f.* שֶׁבַע, *cs.* שְׁבַע {38}

שְׁבִיעִי *m.* seventh; *f.* שְׁבִיעִית {38}

שִׁבְעִים seventy {38}

שָׁבַר **Qal** to break; **Ni** נִשְׁבַּר to be broken; *Impf.* יִשָּׁבֵר; **Pi** שִׁבֵּר to break in pieces, shatter (*tr.*); *Impf.* יְשַׁבֵּר {31}

שַׁבָּת *c.* sabbath, day of rest; *pl.* שַׁבָּתוֹת {34}

שָׁוְא worthless, false, in vain

שׁוּב **Qal** *Perf.* שָׁב to return, *Impf.* יָשׁוּב, וַיָּשָׁב, *Impv.* שׁוּב; *IA* שׁוֹב; *IC* שׁוּב, שֹׁב; *Pt.* שָׁב; **Hi** הֵשִׁיב to bring back, *Impf.* יָשִׁיב; *Impv.* הָשֵׁב; *IA* הָשֵׁב; *IC* הָשִׁיב; *Pt.* מֵשִׁיב {40}

שׁוֹר bull, ox, steer (*used for singular and plural; the actual pl.* שְׁוָרִים *occurs only 1x*) {40}

שׁחה **Hitp** הִשְׁתַּחֲוָה to bow down, worship, *Impf.* יִשְׁתַּחֲוֶה, *Impv.* הִשְׁתַּחֲווּ(*mp*), *IC* הִשְׁתַּחֲוֹת, *Pt.* מִשְׁתַּחֲוֶה {47}

שָׁחַט to slaughter, *Impf.* יִשְׁחַט, *Impv.* שַׁחֲטוּ(*mp*), *IC* שְׁחֹט, *Pt.* שׁוֹחֵט

שַׁחַר dawn, morning

שׁחת **Ni** נִשְׁחַת to be corrupt, spoiled (*Impf. 1x only* תִּשָּׁחֵת); **Pi** שִׁחֵת to destroy (*tr.*), to cause trouble (*intr.*) (*no Impf*); **Hi** הִשְׁחִית to destroy, *Impf.* יַשְׁחִית {43}

שָׁכַב to lie down, sleep, *Impf.* יִשְׁכַּב. *Note also:* to have sex with = שָׁכַב עִם; *but compare* he was buried with his fathers = שָׁכַב עִם אֲבוֹתָיו {28}

שָׁכַח to forget; *Impf.* יִשְׁכַּח {32}

שׁכם **Hi** הִשְׁכִּים to get up (from sleep), to rise early, *Impf.* וַיַּשְׁכֵּם(*w.c.*), תַּשְׁכִּים(*3fs*)

שְׁכֶם Shechem (person and place) (*lit.* shoulders)

{33}

שָׁכַן to live (at a place), to stay or settle, *Impf.* יִשְׁכֹּן

שָׁלוֹם peace, well-being, wholeness {24}

שָׁלַח **Qal** to send, let go; *Impf.* יִשְׁלַח, *Impv.* שְׁלַח, *IA* שָׁלוֹחַ, *IC* שְׁלַח (*cf. Impv.*) & שְׁלֹחַ, *Pt.* שֹׁלֵחַ; **Pi** שִׁלַּח send, let go; *Impf.* יְשַׁלַּח, *Impv.* & *IC* שַׁלַּח, *IA* שַׁלֵּחַ, *Pt.* מְשַׁלֵּחַ {12}, *p. 276*

שלך **Hi** הִשְׁלִיךְ to throw down, to throw away, *Impf.* אַשְׁלִיךְ(*1cs*) וַיַּשְׁלֵךְ(*w.c.*), *Impv.* & *IA* הַשְׁלֵךְ, *IC* הַשְׁלִיךְ, *Pt.* מַשְׁלִיךְ; **Ho** הָשְׁלַךְ to be thrown down, *Impf.* תָּשְׁלְכִי(*2fs*)

שׁלם **Qal** שָׁלְמוּ(*3cp*) to be finished, to stay healthy, to be quiet, *Impf.* יִשְׁלַם; **Pi** שִׁלַּם to make complete, to repay, to reward, *Impf.* יְשַׁלֵּם, *Impv, IA & IC* שַׁלֵּם, *Pt.* מְשַׁלֵּם; **Hi** הִשְׁלִימָה(*3fs*) to finish, to surrender, to make peace, *Impf.* יַשְׁלִים

שָׁלֵם *adj.* safe, complete, peaceful {35}

שְׁלֹמֹה Solomon {21}

שָׁלֹשׁ *see* שְׁלֹשָׁה

שְׁלֹשָׁה *m.* three, *cs.* שְׁלֹשֶׁת; *f.* שָׁלֹשׁ, *cs.* שְׁלֹשׁ {38}

שְׁלִישִׁי *m.* third; *f.* שְׁלִישִׁית {38}

שְׁלֹשִׁים thirty {38}

שֵׁם *m.* name, *cs.* שֵׁם, שֵׁם־, שֶׁם־; *pl.* שֵׁמוֹת, *cs.* שְׁמוֹת {27}, *p. 117*

שָׁם there; שָׁמָּה to there {24}

שׁמד **Ni** נִשְׁמַד to be destroyed; *Impf.* יִשָּׁמֵד; **Hi** הִשְׁמִיד to destroy; *Impf.* יַשְׁמִיד {33}

שְׁמוּאֵל Samuel {17}

שָׁמַיִם (*pl.*) sky, the heavens, *cs.* שְׁמֵי {14}

שְׁמִינִי *m.* eighth; *f.* שְׁמִינִית {38}

שׁמם **Qal** *Perf. 3cp* שָׁמְמוּ to be deserted (place), removed (person), horrified, *Impf.* יֵשֹׁם, *Impv. mp* (*1x*) שֹׁמּוּ, *Pt.* שׁוֹמֵם, **Ni** נָשַׁמָּה(*3fs*) to be made deserted, be made horrified. *Pt.* נְשַׁמָּה (*fs*). *No Impf., Impv., IA, IC;* **Hi** הֲשִׁמּוֹתָ(*2ms*) הֵשַׁמּוּ (*3cp*) to make deserted, to make horrified, *Impf.* יַשִּׁים

שֶׁמֶן oil, *pl.* שְׁמָנִים {43}

שְׁמֹנָה *m.* eight, *cs.* שְׁמֹנַת; *f.* שְׁמֹנֶה, *cs.=* {38}

שְׁמֹנֶה *see* שְׁמֹנָה

שְׁמֹנִים eighty {38}

שָׁמַע **Qal** to hear, listen; *Impf.* יִשְׁמַע; שָׁמַע לְקוֹל *or* שָׁמַע בְּקוֹל to obey; **Ni** נִשְׁמַע to be heard; *Impf.* יִשָּׁמַע; **Hi** הִשְׁמִיעַ to announce, summon; *Impf.* יַשְׁמִיעַ {15}

שָׁמַר **Qal** to guard, watch, keep; *Impf.* יִשְׁמֹר; *Pt.* שֹׁמֵר (*pl.* שֹׁמְרִים= guards); **Ni** נִשְׁמַר to be careful; *Impf.* יִשָּׁמֵר {14}

שֶׁמֶשׁ the sun {32}

שָׁנָה *f.* year, *cs.* שְׁנַת; *pl.* שָׁנִים, *cs.* שְׁנֵי; *du.* שְׁנָתַיִם two years {38}

שֵׁנִי *m.* second; *f.* שֵׁנִית {38}

שְׁנַיִם *m.* two, *cs.* שְׁנֵי; *f.* שְׁתַּיִם, *cs.* שְׁתֵּי {38}

שַׁעַר a gate {31}

שָׁפַט **Qal** to judge, settle a dispute, punish, *Impf.* יִשְׁפֹּט; **Ni** נִשְׁפַּטְתִּי(*1cs*), *Impf.* אִשָּׁפֵט(*1cs*) {19}

שֹׁפֵט a judge (*Pt.* of שפט); *pl.* שֹׁפְטִים {31}

שָׁפַךְ to pour out, spill, shed {21}

שׁקה **Hi** הִשְׁקָה to give water to (person, plants or land), *Impf.* יַשְׁקֶה, *Impv.* הַשְׁקוּ(*mp*), *IC* הַשְׁקוֹת, *Pt.* מַשְׁקֶה. *p. 247.*

שֶׁקֶל shekel (unit of weight, approx. 12 grams)

שֶׁקֶר a lie, a deception, *pl.* שְׁקָרִים

שׁרת **Pi** שֵׁרֵת to serve, to minister, *Impf.* וַיְשָׁרֶת, *IC* שָׁרֵת, *Pt.* מְשָׁרֵת. *No Impv.. or IA.*

שֵׁשׁ *see* שִׁשָּׁה

שִׁשָּׁה *m.* six, *cs.* שֵׁשֶׁת; *f.* שֵׁשׁ, *cs.=* {38}

שִׁשִּׁי *m.* sixth; *f.* שִׁשִּׁית {38}

שִׁשִּׁים sixty {38}

שָׁתָה to drink, *Impf.* יִשְׁתֶּה, *Impv.* שְׁתֵה, *IA* שָׁתוֹ & שָׁתֹה, *IC* שְׁתוֹת, *Pt.* שֹׁתֶה {46}

שְׁתַּיִם *see* שְׁנַיִם

תתת

תְּהוֹם depths of the sea, mythological waters under

the earth, *pl.* תְּהוֹמוֹת

תְּהִלָּה praise, glory (√הלל), *cs.* תְּהִלַּת; *pl.* תְּהִלּוֹת

תָּוֶךְ middle, midst; *cs.* תּוֹךְ. בְּתוֹךְ in the midst of {31}

תּוֹלְדוֹת (*cs. only*) list of descendants, generations

תּוֹעֵבָה something which is awful or offensive, *cs.* תּוֹעֲבַת; *pl.* תּוֹעֵבוֹת

תּוֹרָה instruction, guidance, law (Torah) (√ירה, to teach), *cs.* תּוֹרַת; *pl.* תּוֹרוֹת {27}

תַּחַת *prep.* instead of, under {17}

תָּמִיד continual, continually

תמם ***Qal*** *Perf.* תַּם to be finished, complete, spent, *Impf.* יִתֹּם; ***Hi*** הֵתַמּוּ(*3cp*) to finish (doing s.t.), to make s.t. ready, *Impf.* יַתֵּם

תָּעָה ***Qal*** to go astray, wander; to stagger, *Impf.* יִתְעוּ(*3mp*), *no Impv., IC* תְּעוֹת, *Pt.* תֹּעֶה; ***Hi*** הִתְעָה to let or make s.o. go astray, wander, stagger, *Impf.* וַיֵּתַע(*w.c.*), *Pt.* מַתְעֶה. *No Impv., IA, IC.*

תְּפִלָּה *f.* prayer (√פלל) {35}

תְּשִׁיעִי *m.* ninth; *f.* תְּשִׁיעִית {38}

תִּשְׁעָה *m.* nine, *cs.* תִּשְׁעַת; *f.* תֵּשַׁע, *cs.* תְּשַׁע {38}

תִּשְׁעִים ninety {38}

Keys to Selected Exercises

Following are keys to selected lines of the exercises. They are provided primarily to assist the student who is studying alone, but they may also be used as progress checks for students who are studying in a class. Words which have been added for smoother translation are enclosed in **<pointed brackets>**. Words which are found in the Hebrew but which are best left untranslated are enclosed in **[square brackets]**. Literal meanings are enclosed in **{curly brackets}** and will include the abbreviation "lit." General comments and additional information will be in **(parentheses)**.

Exercise #2

1a. mʾḏ ngš spr rḏp ṣwh tḥṯ ʾrbʿ zbḥ hrḡ bṭḥ lmḏ

1c. ksʾ zrʿ šʾwl nṭḥ nṣl glʿḏ gzl nśʾ mṣwh yḏ ṣʿqh

2a. מלך עבד בּרך זבח יעקב צדּיק נבּיא מלחמה סתר שׁוב שׂרה

2c. נגשׁ דּגן קטל יוסף חכמה סוס נטע לחם בּרכה בּגד שׁחת

Exercise #3

1a. šāmaʿ mûṯ min mîn ḥeseḏ yayin ʾōṯ zāqēn hāraḡ bāṭaḥ buṣ zeraʿ hûʾ

1c. ʿōrep̄ ʾāšûḇ kaḥereś paṣû ʾāḥînû bēn nāḡaḏ sōrēr śāṭîṯ māṯay yāqum lēḵ

2a. נֶשֶׁךְ חֹרֶב טַף הַחַי כָּפַר יוּעַם לָקֵט בֵּנַיִם אֹמֶן עֶצֶב כָּתוּת

2c. נֹבַח שִׁיר חוּץ גָּדִישׁ זֵכֶר סֶסָתִי קֶשֶׁב נָתַן אוּלָם עֶוֶל חָטָאנוּ

Exercise #4

1a. yšʿyhw ben ʾāmôṣ ḥāzâ wîrûšālām bîmê yôṯām ʾāḥāz šāmayim ʾereṣ kî

1b. bānîm yāḏaʿ qōnēhû ʾēḇûs lōʾ ḥôy ḥōṭēʾ ʿam ʿāwōn zeraʿ nāzōrû ʾāḥôr

2a. חָיוּ עָלַי לָטֹרַח עֵינַי גַּם כִּי דָּמִים מָלֵאוּ הָסִירוּ הֵיטֵב חָמוֹץ

2b. יָתוֹם רִיבוּ יֹאמַר אִם תֹּאבוּ טוּב הָאָרֶץ תֹּאכֵלוּ חֶרֶב אֵיכָה

Exercise #5

2. *ah* = אָה אַה עָה or עַה *em* = אֶם or עֶם

4a. bā-rā[2] ✔ ʾēṯ ✔ hā-ʾā-reṣ ✔ tō-hû wā-ḇô-hû hā-ʾôr ✔ ha-ḥō-šeḵ ✔ ʿe-reḇ ✔ bō-qer ✔ ʾe-ḥaḏ ✔

4b. ma-yim ✔ lā-mā-yim ✔ mē-ʿal ✔ mā-qôm ✔ tē-rā-ʾeh ✔ tô-ṣēʾ ✔ ḇên ✔ hā-yû qā-ṭōn ✔ lay-lâ ✔

---

[2] **Technical note:** The matter of quiescent (silent) letters will be discussed later. For the purpose of the present exercise, the final **א** will be considered to be a consonant which closes the syllable.

Exercise #6

3. Pharaoh enslaved Is̭-rael but God had mercy on his pe̩o-ple: (Hyphens have been added to show the syllables, since the *athnah* and *silluq* must appear under **accented** syllables.)

5. a. ʾim lōʾ yā-šûḇ ḥar-bô yil-ṭôš, qaš-tô ḏā-raḵ way-kôn-ne-hā.

   b. kî ḏō-rēš dā-mîm ʾô-ṯām zā-ḵār, lōʾ šā-ḵaḥ ṣa-ʿa-qaṯ ʿa-nā-yîm.

Exercise #7

5. . . . bᵉrā-ḵâ mē-ʾēṯ YHWH, ṣᵉḏā-qâ mē-ʾᵉ̆lō-hê yiš-ʿô.

6. zeh dôr dōr-šāyw, mᵉḇaq-šê pā-ney-ḵā ya-ʿᵃ̆qōḇ se-lâ.

Exercise #8

2. v1. ʾîš ʾe-ḥaḏ min hā-rā-mā-ṯa-yim ṣô-pîm mē-har ʾep̄-rā-yim, û-šᵉmô ʾel-qā-nâ . . . ben ʾᵉ̆lî-hûʾ . . . .

   v3. wᵉʿā-lâ hā-ʾîš ha-hûʾ mē-ʿî-rô . . . lᵉhiš-ta-ḥᵃ̆wōṯ . . . ḇᵉši-lōh, wᵉšām šᵉnê ḇᵉnê ʿē-lî . . . kō-hᵃ̆nîm laYHWH.

Exercise #9

5. (1) There is a *dagesh forte* in the first letter (see §11.1.2)
   (2) There are two *shewas* at the beginning of the word (see §8.3)
   (3) There is a *mappiq* in middle of the word (see §11.2)
   (4) the last syllable is closed and unaccented, but it has a long vowel (see §7.2)

6. Verse 7: wa-tē-ṣēʾ min ham-mā-qôm ʾᵃ̆šer hā-yᵉṯâ šām-mâ šᵉtê ḵal-lō-ṯey-hā ʿim-māh, wat-tē-laḵ-nâ ḇad-de-reḵ lā-šûḇ ʾel ʾe-reṣ yᵉhû-ḏâ.

   Verse 10: wat-tōʾ-mar-nâ lāh, kî ʾit-tāḵ nā-šûḇ lᵉʿam-mēḵ.

Exercise #10

1a. qā-ṭal hoq-ṭal wᵉʾā-mᵉrû ʾaḇ-rā-hām mᵉlā-ḵîm hap-pā-lîṭ miṣ-rā-yᵉmâ ʾᵃ̆ḵā-lāṯ-hû lē-ḇāḇ

Exercise #11

[1] A woman went (or walked). [4] A man saw a house. [7] A man walked from a house to a city. [9] Sarah gave a house to Abraham. [11] God (or "a god") walked in a garden. [12] God (or "a god") created a man and a woman.

Exercise #12

[1] Israel was in Egypt. [2] God gave a blessing to Moses. [6] The LORD sent Moses to Pharaoh, because he saw Israel in Egypt. [9] Did a man give the fruit to a woman? [11] Was Pharaoh a king in Egypt? [13] In Egypt, did the LORD give Israel to Pharaoh?

Exercise #13

[1] God created a tree in the garden and the fruit in the tree. [3] The man said that the fruit <is or was> from God. [7] Did the king take a house from the woman? [9] Abraham sent fruit from the land to Canaan. [13] Aaron sent an ark to a city in Judah. [17] Moses said to Sarah, "Did Abraham see Joshua in the city?"

Exercise #14

[1] God called the light day, and the darkness he called night. [3] The LORD called the man Adam because he <was> from the ground. [5] The LORD said, "I <am> God who [he] created day and night." [7] Sarah said, "I entered a city, but I did not guard a house." [9] They gave (נָתְנוּ) a city, but we gave (נָתַ֫נּוּ) a land. [16] The man who walked in the dust did not see light because <it was> night and not day.

Exercise #15

[1] There was darkness upon the land in the night, but Adam saw the lights of the heavens (that is, the stars). [4] They were afraid because they heard the voice of the LORD when he walked in the garden [6] The LORD spoke to the man saying, "Did you eat the fruit from the tree?" [8] God sent Adam from the garden because he did not obey the voice of God. [10] The women spoke to the men saying the LORD gave a blessing to Israel. [13] There was darkness like night upon the land of Egypt but <there was> light in the houses of the people of Israel. [15] The sons of Israel went out from the land of Egypt.

Exercise #16

[1] God said to Hagar, "Behold, you (note: feminine singular) shall send Abram and Sarai to the land of Canaan." [2] The LORD spoke to Abram saying: "Abram, you will not (or "Abram, do not") fear." [3] Abram and Sarai went out from the house of Abram to the land of Canaan. [4] Did the LORD speak to Hagar saying, "I shall make {lit. 'cut'} a covenant with Abraham"? [5] Sarai asked the LORD [saying], "Will you remember Abram because there is no descendant {literally "seed"} in the house of Abram?" [6] Sarah feared Hagar because she said, "Behold, the son of Hagar took the covenant."

Exercise #17

[3] Samuel listened to the priest and also he wrote his every word all his words in a book. [4] The prophet and the prophetess went from their house in the night. [5] They said, "Behold, the stars of the heaven are like the dust of the ground." [6] They went from their house and they entered the palace of the king. [7] The priest sat in the temple of the LORD by day and also he read the book of the covenant to the people. [8] Adam ate the fruit but he did not eat its seed. [9] Hagar called to God and also she asked [saying], "Will you watch between my house and [between] the house of Sarah?"

Exercise #18

[1] Abraham and Sarah were in the land of Canaan but they feared the men of the land. [2] The word of Abraham was good in the eyes of Sarah, but <it was> bad in the eyes of God. [4] The people did not know the wisdom of a prophet, but Samuel knew. [5] Did the LORD give his blessing to all the sons of Samuel? [7] The wise women entered the holy city and in the palace they spoke to the king. [9] The priests served the god of Canaan instead of the LORD. [12] The man saw a spring of water in the garden which God created. [14] The priest <was/is> wise and his knowledge <was/is> great. [17] We walked in your(ms) garden and [we] ate fruit from your(ms) tree.

Exercise #19

[4] Moses said, "Remember(fs) the covenant which the LORD cut with Israel." [5] In the morning, Jacob walked to the mountain with his cattle and, behold, Esau came. [6] Pharaoh said to Sarah, "A king [he] <is> the head of his people, and I <am> the king of Egypt." [8] God cut the water of the river, and the thing/affair was bad in the eyes of Pharaoh. [9] The wise women will send the men, and also they will ask the prophetess. [12] Write(mp) the holy words upon the stone, and in the evening read(mp) the words to the people. [17] Behold, the LORD <is> with his people, and he <is> the head of the sons of Israel.

Exercise #20

[2] Esau saw that the herd of Jacob <was> very large, and he said, "God gave a blessing to Jacob." [5] And it happened <that> Jacob <was> very old (or just "And Jacob <was> very old"), and behold he went to Egypt. [6] And the holiness of the LORD <was> like a fire upon the head of the mountain in the eyes of the elders of Israel. [8] Joshua and the children {lit. "sons"} of Israel pursued the people, and the hand of the LORD was against the land of Canaan. [9] We captured the city in the morning, and in the evening we burned its temple with fire. [10] A certain prophetess who lived in Judah came (or went) to Samuel because he judged Israel.

Exercise #21

[1] And God called the light "day," and he called the darkness "night." And it was evening and it was morning, day one (that is, "the first day"). [2] The LORD took the man from the dust of the ground and he said, "Cultivate and keep the garden." [3] Pursue (emphatic imperative) the men who stole from the woman and sold her cattle. [6] Did Esau know that Jacob and his people were <coming> after the cattle? [7] The men of David said, "Let us not pursue the young men, but let us capture the city." [8] Will she (or "you(ms)") sell water from the spring to the men of David?

Exercise #22

The first sentences of this exercise are based upon Genesis 4. [1] [And] Abel was a shepherd of sheep but Cain tilled the soil. [2] And [it happened] in the morning, [and] Cain gave an offering to the LORD from the fruit of the ground. [3] And Abel gave, also he, an offering from the first-born of his flock. [9] He <is> our God, and we <are> his people and the flock of his hand (Ps 95:7). [11] And in the evening, the women cried out to the elder, and he indeed obeyed them {lit. "listened to their(fp) voice"}. [15] [And] Samuel was old and he indeed judged the people and he ruled them continually. [18] The man of bloodshed who steals {lit. "he stole"} cattle, <let> his blood <be> upon {lit. "in"} his head (or "his blood will be upon his <own> head"); and let them bury (jussive plus *vav*) him in a grave.

Exercise #23

[1] What did Cain say to Abel after they gave their offerings? [3] Why did Abram say to Sarai his wife, "Say before Pharaoh that you <are> not my wife." [4] One of the women asked, "Will the descendants of Hagar be like the stars of heaven?" [5] Thus says the LORD, I shall remember the-ones-cutting (f.pl.) a covenant with the first-born of Hagar. [7] Jacob said, "Behold, Esau shall see the gift going before me and afterwards I shall see his face." [8] Saul indeed asked, "Where is Sheol?" [10] And David asked, "Who <am> I, and what <is> my house, that I shall be in the house of the king?"

Exercise #24

[1] Jacob went with Esau to the place where they lived [there] to bury their father. [2] The father of the wife of Moses heard all that God had done for Moses and for Israel his people. [4] His father's enemies who [they] lived in the wilderness came to steal the cattle. [9] But God said to Samuel, "The youngest found favor in my eyes. instead of the firstborn." [12] The prophet stood in the presence of David and said, "Let my words find favor in your eyes." [14] Let the priest write the words of Solomon in a small scroll and let him bury the scroll in a grave. [16] Who is the prophetess [the-one-] dreaming dreams, and what did she dream?

Exercise #25

[1] Did Abel choose to keep sheep in the wilderness? [2] And Cain asked in his heart, "And now, where shall I kill my brother?" [5] The shepherds went down with their flock to a place where <the> water <was> good [there]. [10] And [it happened] after the shepherd gave his gift before the LORD, [3]then he went down from Jerusalem in peace. [11] Jerusalem <is the> great<est> of all the cities, and the holy house of God <is> in it. [13] The LORD spoke to us and said, "Woe to the nation which does evil in my eyes by serving {lit. "to serve"} other gods." [14] I said in my heart, "The place where we went [there] [it] <is> a holy place {lit. "a place-of-holiness"}."

Exercise #26

[1] Abram took Sarai his wife and Lot the son of his brother, and they went to the land of Canaan. [2] And also to Lot, the one going with Abram, there were sheep and cattle. (A smoother translation: "And Lot, who went with Abram, also had sheep and cattle.") [4] And Abraham said, "And also, she <is> my sister, the daughter of my father, but not the daughter of my mother, and she became my wife." [7] In the morning, Esau saw the men and women crossing the river before Jacob, and he asked, "Who are these with you?" [9] And Joseph said, "There is none greater than me in this house; and how shall I do this evil thing?"

Exercise #27

[3] Abraham asked, "Is God forgiving the city where Lot lives [there] for the sake of the good men in it?" [4] Rachel and Jacob went out from her father's house, and she stole his gods. [7] And Moses said to Pharaoh, "The sons of Israel are being sent into the wilderness in order to worship (or 'serve') God." [9] And the LORD said to Moses, "Come to me, you alone, on Mount Sinai." And there the LORD gave to Moses the stone tablets with the law and the commandment which he wrote [them] with his hand. [10] And Moses came down from the mountain, carrying the tablets of stone written by the hand of God.

Exercise #28

[1] Joseph was the wisest of his brothers, but they sold him to be a servant in the land of Egypt. [3] And Joseph became great in the eyes of Pharaoh, because he was able to tell the thing/affair (that is, "the content") of his dream [4] Pharaoh commanded Joseph saying, "You alone shall be over my house, and all my people shall do according to your command." [5] The LORD wrote his commandments on the tablets of the law, and Moses carried them from Sinai. [10] Solomon's older brother said, "Let me rule after my father, because I am the oldest of his sons;" but his words were unimportant {lit. "small"} in the ears of his father.

Exercise #29

[5] And Lot sent messengers to Abram saying, "Why should (or "will") there be fighting between the shepherds of your flock and [between] my shepherds?" [6] The shepherds of Lot indeed crossed the Jordan, and they watched his flock continuously. [9] [And it happened that] when Isaac was old and his eyes were weak {lit. "heavy"} from old age, [and/then] he was not able to see. And he called Esau, his firstborn son, and he said, "My son." And Esau said, "Here I am." [11] And Jacob came before his father and said, "I am Esau your first-born; I have indeed done as you told me." [12] Then Laban said to Jacob, "The daughters <are> my daughters, and the sons (or "children") <are> my sons (or "children"), and the flocks <are> my flocks, and all that you are seeing is mine {lit. "it <is> to me"]. But what can {lit. "will"} I do this day to these my daughters or to their children?"

Exercise #30

[1] God said, "I know {lit. "knew"} Abraham and he will command his sons and his daughters after him in order that they will do according to the command {lit. "mouth"} of the LORD." [2] The father of Isaac spoke to his servant [the-one-] standing before him saying, "I do not trust the inhabitants of this land." [6] And Moses said, "[And it shall be] when you [shall] serve God, [and] your children will say to you 'What <is> this service to you?' (that is, 'What does this service mean to you?')." [9] Moses sent spies toward the land, and they said to Moses,

---

[3] Translate the -ו as "then," or leave it untranslated (as here).

"Beware of the people of the land. We are not able to fight them."

Exercise #31

[1] And God spoke to Abraham, and he said, "Behold the heavens, and count the stars, if you are able to count them." And he said to him, "So shall your descendants be. And they shall have {lit. "it shall be to them"} all the land where your feet are walking [there]." [3] Jacob did all the work which Laban commanded him. And <when> he became great, [then] he gathered his wives and his children {lit. "sons"} and he went out from the house of Laban. [8] A great wind came from the sea (or "west"), and it broke in pieces every tree in the midst of the city. [14] The mother looked continually for her children {lit. "sons"} in the midst of the city; and when she found them she gathered them together and she blessed them.

Exercise #32

[1] Do not praise the sun as the Egyptians <do>, because you <are> my holy ones {lit. "my being-made-holy (ones)"}. [2] The prophetess reported to the priest saying, "The people <are> scattered and they shall choose the way of the nations." [3] Joseph was the wisest of his brothers; [and] why was he sent to Egypt (*he* of direction toward)? [4] The prophet said, "Woe to Jerusalem, for there is not fear of God in her, and all her residents have forgotten the LORD." [5] Isaac was dead, and messengers reported the news {lit. "the word" or "the affair"] to his sons. [6] Samuel said, "Do not write(2fs) the word/affair in a scroll in the temple, but write(fs) it in your heart."

Exercise #33

[1] The king was dead, and the people assembled to make his son king because he was strong and wise. [3] Praise the LORD because of {lit. "in"} his faithfulness, for he has scattered our enemies and he has strengthened our king upon his throne. [5] The spy escaped on foot {lit. "by his feet"}, and he hid himself by the spring of water. [6] The kings fought against the city, and it was destroyed; and they seized Lot and also they took all the silver and the gold. [10] And Laban said to Rachel, "And now, my daughter, do not forget my advice." [12] The Egyptians crossed the Jordan, and their distress was great {lit. "great distress found them"} because they had no bread.

Exercise #34

[1] On the Sabbath, the people assembled at Shechem in a large congregation, and they made Solomon king. [3] If you are hungry, you may {lit. "will"} indeed eat flesh; but do not eat its blood. For the life of all flesh [it] <is> in its blood. [5] In the morning, Jacob crossed the river with his herd of cattle; and he spoke to his brother Esau, saying "I have everything." [6] The old prophet sat by himself and said, "My people have been destroyed. I am shattered and distress has seized me." [10] The judges sat in the midst of the gate, and the people being judged by them listened to the words of their mouths {lit. "their mouth"}.

Exercise #35

[1] The Egyptian army was great and it pursued [after] the Hebrews on the day of the Sabbath. [2] The congregation prayed again to the LORD of hosts, and he heard their prayers. [3] "Do not abandon me, and do not forget [the person of] your servant". [6] The fighting/war <was> very great, and the king was separated from his army at the bank of the river. [10] God placed the sun in the heavens; thus he separated day and night. [11] Will God abandon the life of the wicked? Will he hear the prayers of his lips?

Exercise #36

[2] they kept him; we kept them(3mp); you(2mp or 2fp) kept me; they kept you(2fs); we kept her; they kept you(2mp); we kept them(3fp). [4] she ruled them(3mp); we left you(2ms); you(2ms) forgot her; they(3cp) served me; you(2mp or 2fp) chose us; I pursued them(3fp); they burned it(3fs) (or her); he judged us.

Exercise #37

[1] [And] the mighty warrior who had shed blood escaped to the border; therefore a righteous man put him in a prison (or "pit") because of his sin. [4] My people <are> without knowledge; therefore they will be divided and their enemies will destroy them. [6] The assembly of the people made David king, and they said, "Let us pray to God for the sake of our king." And God heard their prayer. [7] The armies of the Philistines and their horses crossed the border and went toward the city, and [they] destroyed its wall. [9] Why should the fear of them be upon us? The glory of the Lord of hosts will be our salvation; therefore, let us trust in him.

Exercise #38

[3] Thus you will make it: the length of the ark three hundred cubit<s>, its width fifty cubit<s>, and its height thirty cubit<s>. [5] 265 mighty warriors of the Philistines crossed over the border on foot, and they hid themselves in the mountains. [7] David was thirty years old when he was made king, and he reigned forty years. He reigned over Judah seven years and six months; and at Jerusalem he reigned over all Israel and Judah thirty-three years. [9] The Philistine warriors came without horses, and so they were not able to escape. And they cried out, saying "And now our lives are lost, and our lives (or simply "we") will go down <to the> pit." [10] Twelve female slaves had four new gardens, and the gardens were twenty cubits from the wall of the city. And day by day they tilled them them [obj suffix] and kept them [obj suffix].

Exercise #39

[1] The woman walked in the midst of the garden, and when she came near the tree the serpent spoke to her. [3] God sent the man and the woman from the garden of Eden lest they come near the tree of life. And they <were> not naked when they went out from the garden. [7] The Lord said to Moses and Aaron in the land of Egypt [saying], "This month <shall be> for you the beginning {lit. "head"} of months; it <shall be> the first month of the year for you." [9] And now, learn these words; and teach them to the children of Israel for their sake, lest they sin and be divided before their enemies. [16] The Lord sees all the people from great to small; and before him Sheol also <lies> naked.

Exercise #40

[1] The snake was in a tree in Eden, and there it said to the woman, God knows that in <the> day you eat from it you(2mp) will become like God knowing good and evil. [5] The servant of Abraham reported to Laban, saying, "My master has much property because God has blessed him. And he has given him bulls and male donkeys and female donkeys. And when Rebekah came near to give water to my camels I praised God that he had blessed the son of my master and gave him a wife." And Laban and his father said, "The thing is from God; we are not able to say good or evil to you." [6] [And] Joseph said, "I was indeed stolen from the land of the Hebrews, and I was brought to Egypt and also they put me in a dungeon."

Exercise #41

[1] The king said, my kingdom is stronger than other kingdoms, and <yet> I have no son. And now, may it be good in God's eyes to do good to me and to strengthen my throne. [2] And in the fourth month of the next year, the wife of the king bore a son. And from the womb the male-child chose the ways of the Lord, to keep them with all his heart. And the king fathered other sons and daughters. [5] The king sent messengers throughout his kingdom to ask about the work of his servants. And when they returned, they reported to him saying great <is> your property and strong <is> your kingdom. [12] And [it happened that] when the king lived in his house, and the Lord gave him peace from all his enemies, the king said to Nathan the prophet, "See now, I dwell in a house of wood, but the ark of God dwells in a tent." And Nathan said to the king, "Go, do all that is in your heart; for the Lord is with you."

Exercise #42

[1] The man and the woman were no longer naked, because of the snake. But they were also no longer living in Eden. [3] Jacob loved Rachel and she bore a son, and she said, God has taken away my distress. And she called

his name Joseph, saying, may God continue <to give> to me another son. And she and her sister became the mothers of the tribes of Israel. [4] And his wives said to him, we have no inheritance from our father, [from] Laban; therefore, let us leave and let us live in the midst of your own people. [5] And it happened in those days when Moses was grown up, he went out in the midst of his brothers, and [he] saw an Egyptian man beating a fellow Hebrew {lit. "a Hebrew man from his brothers"}. And he saw that there was no man and he hit the Egyptian and killed him, and he rescued the life of his brother.

Exercise #43

[1] It was reported to Laban that Jacob had taken his property and his daughters in order to return to the land of his fathers. And Laban became angry because of his deeds. [2] The LORD loved his people Israel and [also he] was faithful to them {lit. "and he did his faithfulness with them"}. He gathered their clans from the midst of Egypt, and divided the waters of the sea in front of them. And the LORD spoke to them and said, "I shall give you(2mp) a heritage to possess [it], and I shall bless you(2ms)." [4] The people came to Sinai, and they heard the commandments of God from the mouth of Moses, according to all the instruction and statutes which God had commanded him. And they were written on the two stone tablets which Moses carried. [12] And the people continued in their prayers. But one clan said "Let us take swords, otherwise not one of us will be left." And the people were divided concerning this advice.

Exercise #44

[1] The LORD spoke to Moses in the wilderness of Sinai, in the tent of meeting, on the first day of the second month, in the second year after they had come out of the land of Egypt, saying, [2] "Take a census {lit. "lift up the head"} of all the congregation of the people of Israel, by families, by fathers' houses, according to the number of names, every male, <according> to <the number of> their heads." [5] And Joshua called the twelve men whom he had appointed from the people of Israel, a man from <each> tribe. [6] And Joshua said to them, "Pass on before the ark of the LORD your God into the midst of the Jordan, and raise to you <each> man one stone upon his shoulder, according to the number of the tribes of the people of Israel." [15] Blessed is the woman without iniquity who understands the statues of God. She shall stand-firm and she shall not be ashamed. Her name shall be exalted, and I will give her rest.

Exercise #45

[2] Cain hated his brother, and also in his anger he killed him when they went out into the middle of the field. [3] God will fulfill his word, and will give you the inheritance which he swore to give to Abraham and Isaac and Jacob. And the land will be filled <with> your clans and you will be exalted above the power/armies of your enemies. [5] Every year, on the first day of the second month, he went to the house of the LORD to sacrifice to the LORD. And the priest who was in the courtyard of the temple took his sacrifice and offered it upon the altar. [8] The prophet stood at the door of the temple and cried out to the people [saying], You are unclean because your iniquities have made you unclean. Therefore, you shall be ashamed when I remove your glory/honor, says the LORD.

Exercise #46

[1] From the snake in Eden the man and the woman learned that they <were> naked. The LORD therefore drove them out lest they come near the tree of life and live forever. [2] When men {lit. "the man"} began to become many on the face of the ground, [and] daughters were born to them. And <when> the sons of God saw the daughters of men, that they <were> good (that is, "beautiful"), [and] they took to them<selves> wives from all whom they chose. And the LORD said, "My spirit shall not remain in man for ever, for he <is> flesh, but they shall live a hundred and twenty years {lit. "year"}." [7] The tribes of Israel fought against the Canaanites, and one of the lords of the Canaanites escaped on-foot{lit. "by his feet"}. [And] he hid himself, and he put his silver and gold in a tent and covered them with clothing. But spies from Israel surrounded him, and they uncovered his silver and gold and brought <them> to their camp.

Exercise #47

[2] Esau was angry because his father blessed Jacob, and the matter was reported to Rebekah. And she stood up and approached Isaac and spoke to him, saying, "If Jacob takes a wife from this land I will not be able to live. Let us send him north to the city of my brother to find a wife." [4] And the LORD said to Moses, "Go to the people, and they shall be ready by the third day; for on the third day the LORD will come down in the sight of all the people upon Mount Sinai. And you shall set a boundary for the people round about, saying, 'Do not go up into the mountain or touch its border. All the-ones-touching (that is, 'whoever touches') the mountain shall indeed be put to death; whether beast or man, he shall not live.'" [8] The people again turned aside from the ways of the LORD, and they were not ashamed of their iniquity. And the LORD gave them into the hands of their enemies, to strike them and to oppress them. And <when> they could not escape [and] they began to seek the LORD. And he raised up judges who<m> his spirit was upon [them], and they received help from them. But when the judge died the people returned to their wicked ways.

Exercise #48

[1] And Lot, who traveled with Abram, also had many flocks and herds and tents. And the land could not support<all of> them {lit. "did not lift them up"} to graze sheep together; for their wealth was great and they could not dwell together. Then Abram said to Lot, "Is not the whole land before you? Separate from me, now. If <you take> the north, then I will go to the south." [3] Jacob was greatly afraid and he was distressed {lit. "distress found him"}, and he fought with a man by the bank of the stream. And the man turned and touched the sole of Jacob's foot. [And] then the man set "Let me go, for the sun is rising;" and he answered "I will not let you go unless you bless me." [4] Israel (or "the Israelites") lived in the land of Goshen because the Egyptians hated shepherds. And they tended their flocks and they bore many children and they became strong. [11] Then David died, full of days and honor; and his son Solomon reigned in his place. And the acts {lit. "affairs"} of King David, <from> the first [and] <to> the last, behold-they are written in the records {lit. "affairs"} of Samuel the seer, in the records of Nathan the prophet, and in the records of Gad the seer, with all his reign, [and] his power, and the times (or "circumstances") which happened to {lit. "passed over") him, and to Israel, and to all the kingdoms of the lands.

Hebrew Words

The following is a list of Hebrew words which are discussed within the text.

Index of Subjects

42039065R00191

Made in the USA
Charleston, SC
17 May 2015